2 Samuel

CONCORDIA COMMENTARY

A Theological Exposition of Sacred Scripture

2 SAMUEL

Andrew E. Steinmann

Concordia Publishing House
Saint Louis

Copyright © 2017 Concordia Publishing House
3558 S. Jefferson Avenue, St. Louis, MO 63118-3968
1-800-325-3040 • www.cph.org

Unless otherwise indicated, translations of Scripture and other ancient literature are those of the author.

Scripture quotations marked ESV are from the ESV® Bible (The Holy Bible, English Standard Version®), copyright © 2001 by Crossway, a publishing ministry of Good News Publishers. Used by permission. All rights reserved.

Quotations from Scripture marked NRSV are from the New Revised Standard Version Bible, copyright © 1989, National Council of the Churches of Christ in the United States of America. Used by permission. All rights reserved worldwide.

Scripture quotations marked RSV are from the Revised Standard Version of the Bible, copyright © 1946, 1952, and 1971 National Council of the Churches of Christ in the United States of America. Used by permission. All rights reserved worldwide.

Scripture quotations marked GW are taken from GOD'S WORD®, © 1995 God's Word to the Nations. Used by permission of Baker Publishing Group.

Scripture quotations marked HCSB are taken from the Holman Christian Standard Bible®, Copyright © 1999, 2000, 2002, 2003, 2009 by Holman Bible Publishers. Used by permission. Holman Christian Standard Bible®, Holman CSB®, and HCSB® are federally registered trademarks of Holman Bible Publishers.

Scripture quotations taken from the New English Bible (NEB), copyright © Cambridge University Press and Oxford University Press 1961, 1970, are used by permission. All rights reserved.

Scripture quotations taken from the Revised English Bible (REB), copyright © Cambridge University Press and Oxford University Press 1989, are used by permission. All rights reserved.

Scripture quotations marked NASB are taken from the New American Standard Bible®. Copyright © 1960, 1962, 1963, 1968, 1971, 1972, 1973, 1975, 1977, 1995 by The Lockman Foundation. Used by permission. www.Lockman.org.

Scripture quotations marked NKJV™ are taken from the New King James Version®. Copyright © 1982 by Thomas Nelson, Inc. Used by permission. All rights reserved.

Quotations marked *NETS* are taken from *A New English Translation of the Septuagint*, © 2007 by the International Organization for Septuagint and Cognate Studies, Inc. Used by permission of Oxford University Press. All rights reserved.

Unless otherwise indicated, the quotations from the Lutheran Confessions in this publication are from THE BOOK OF CONCORD: THE CONFESSIONS OF THE EVANGELICAL LUTHERAN CHURCH, edited by Theodore G. Tappert, copyright © 1959 Fortress Press. Used by permission of Augsburg Fortress.

The SymbolGreekU, NewJerusalem, Jacobite, and TranslitLSU fonts used to print this work are available from Linguist's Software, Inc., PO Box 580, Edmonds, WA 98020-0580, USA; telephone (425) 775-1130; www.linguistsoftware.com.

Manufactured in the United States of America

Library of Congress Cataloging-in-Publication Data

Names: Steinmann, Andrew, author.

Title: 2 Samuel / Andrew E. Steinmann.

Other titles: Second Samuel

Description: St. Louis : Concordia Publishing House, 2017. | Series:
    Concordia commentary: a theological exposition of sacred scripture |
    Includes bibliographical references and index.

Identifiers: LCCN 2015049877 | ISBN 9780758650061 (alk. paper)

Subjects: LCSH: Bible. Samuel, 2nd—Commentaries.

Classification: LCC BS1325.53 .S74 2016 | DDC 222/.43077—dc23 LC record available at http://lccn.loc.gov/2015049877

1 2 3 4 5 6 7 8 9 10   26 25 24 23 22 21 20 19 18 17

To Grace Marie Steinmann,
who—like Stephen, on whose feast day she was born—is
of good reputation and full of faith and the Holy Spirit (Acts 6:5)

Contents

Editors' Preface

What may a reader expect from the Concordia Commentary: A Theological Exposition of Sacred Scripture?

The purpose of this series, simply put, is to assist pastors, missionaries, and teachers of the Scriptures to convey God's Word with greater clarity, understanding, and faithfulness to the divine intent of the original Hebrew, Aramaic, or Greek text.

Since every interpreter approaches the exegetical task from a certain perspective, honesty calls for an outline of the presuppositions held by those who have shaped this commentary series. This also serves, then, as a description of the characteristics of the commentaries.

First in importance is the conviction that the content of the scriptural testimony is Jesus Christ. The Lord himself enunciated this when he said, "The Scriptures … testify to me" (Jn 5:39), words that have been incorporated into the logo of this series. The message of the Scriptures is the Good News of God's work to reconcile the world to himself through the life, death, resurrection, ascension, and everlasting session of Jesus Christ at the right hand of God the Father. Under the guidance of the same Spirit who inspired the writing of the Scriptures, these commentaries seek to find in every passage of every canonical book "that which promotes Christ" (as Luther's hermeneutic is often described). They are *Trinitarian* and *Christological* commentaries.

As they unfold the scriptural testimony to Jesus Christ, these commentaries expound Law and Gospel. This approach arises from a second conviction— that Law and Gospel are the overarching doctrines of the Bible itself and that to understand them in their proper distinction and relationship to each other is a key for understanding the self-revelation of God and his plan of salvation in Jesus Christ.

Now, Law and Gospel do not always appear in Scripture labeled as such. The palette of language in Scripture is multicolored, with many and rich hues. The dialectic of a pericope may be fallen creation and new creation, darkness and light, death and life, wandering and promised land, exile and return, ignorance and wisdom, demon possession and the kingdom of God, sickness and healing, being lost and found, guilt and righteousness, flesh and Spirit, fear and joy, hunger and feast, or Babylon and the new Jerusalem. But the common element is God's gracious work of restoring fallen humanity through the Gospel of his Son. Since the predominant characteristic of these commentaries is the proclamation of that Gospel, they are, in the proper sense of the term, *evangelical*.

A third, related conviction is that the Scriptures are God's vehicle for communicating the Gospel. The editors and authors accept without reservation that the canonical books of the Old and New Testaments are, in their entirety, the inspired, infallible, and inerrant Word of God. The triune God is the ultimate author of the Bible, and every word in the original Hebrew, Aramaic, and Greek is inspired by the Holy Spirit. Yet rather than mechanical dictation, in the mysterious process by which the Scriptures were divinely inspired (e.g., 2 Tim 3:16; 2 Pet 1:21), God made use of the human faculties, knowledge, interests, and styles of the biblical writers, whose individual books surely are marked by distinctive features. At the same time, the canon of Scripture has its own inner unity, and each passage must be understood in harmony with the larger context of the whole. This commentary series pays heed to the smallest of textual details because of its acceptance of *plenary and verbal inspiration* and interprets the text in light of the whole of Scripture, in accord with the analogy of faith, following the principle that *Scripture interprets Scripture.* The entirety of the Bible is God's Word, *sacred* Scripture, calling for *theological* exposition.

A fourth conviction is that, even as the God of the Gospel came into this world in Jesus Christ (the Word Incarnate), the scriptural Gospel has been given to and through the people of God, for the benefit of all humanity. God did not intend his Scriptures to have a life separated from the church. He gave them through servants of his choosing: prophets, sages, evangelists, and apostles. He gave them to the church and through the church, to be cherished in the church for admonition and comfort and to be used by the church for proclamation and catechesis. The living context of Scripture is ever the church, where the Lord's ministry of preaching, baptizing, forgiving sins, teaching, and celebrating the Lord's Supper continues. Aware of the way in which the incarnation of the Son of God has as a consequence the close union of Scripture and church, of Word and Sacraments, this commentary series features expositions that are *ecclesiological* and *sacramental.*

This Gospel Word of God, moreover, creates a unity among all those in whom it works the obedience of faith and who confess the truth of God revealed in it. This is the unity of the one holy Christian and apostolic church, which extends through world history. The church is to be found wherever the marks of the church are present: the Gospel in the Word and the Sacraments. These have been proclaimed, confessed, and celebrated in many different cultures and are in no way limited nor especially attached to any single culture or people. As this commentary series seeks to articulate the universal truth of the Gospel, it acknowledges and affirms the confession of the scriptural truth in all the many times and places where the one true church has been found. Aiming to promote *concord* in the confession of the one scriptural Gospel, these commentaries seek to be, in the best sense of the terms, *confessional, ecumenical,* and *catholic.*

All of those convictions and characteristics describe the theological heritage of Martin Luther and of the confessors who subscribe to the Book of Concord (1580)—those who have come to be known as Lutherans. The editors and authors forthrightly confess their subscription to the doctrinal exposition of Scripture in the Book of Concord. As the publishing arm of The Lutheran Church—Missouri Synod, Concordia Publishing House is bound to doctrinal agreement with the Scriptures and the Lutheran Confessions and seeks to herald the true Christian doctrine to the ends of the earth. To that end, the series has enlisted confessional Lutheran authors from other church bodies around the world who share the evangelical mission of promoting theological concord.

The authors and editors stand in the exegetical tradition of Martin Luther and the other Lutheran reformers, who in turn (as their writings took pains to demonstrate) stood in continuity with faithful exegesis by theologians of the early and medieval church, rooted in the hermeneutics of the Scriptures themselves (evident, for example, by how the New Testament interprets the Old). This hermeneutical method, practiced also by many non-Lutherans, includes (1) interpreting Scripture with Scripture according to the analogy of faith, that is, in harmony with the whole of Christian doctrine revealed in the Word; (2) giving utmost attention to the grammar (lexicography, phonetics, morphology, syntax, pragmatics) of the original language of the Hebrew, Aramaic, or Greek text; (3) seeking to discern the intended meaning of the text, the "plain" or "literal" sense, aware that the language of Scripture ranges from narrative to discourse, from formal prose to evocative poetry, from archaic to acrostic to apocalyptic, and it uses metaphor, type, parable, and other figures; (4) drawing on philology, linguistics, archaeology, literature, philosophy, history, and other fields in the quest for a better understanding of the text; (5) considering the history of the church's interpretation; (6) applying the text as authoritative also in the present milieu of the interpreter; and (7) above all, seeing the fulfillment and present application of the text in terms of Jesus Christ and his corporate church; upholding the Word, Baptism, and the Supper as the means through which Christ imparts salvation today; and affirming the inauguration, already now, of the eternal benefits of that salvation that is yet to come in the resurrection on the Last Day.

To be sure, the authors and editors do not feel bound to agree with every detail of the exegesis of our Lutheran forefathers. Nor do we imagine that the interpretations presented here are the final word about every crux and enigmatic passage. But the work has been done in harmony with the exegetical tradition that reaches back through the Lutheran confessors all the way to the biblical writers themselves, and in harmony with the confession of the church: grace alone, faith alone, Scripture alone, Christ alone.

The editors wish to acknowledge their debt of gratitude for all who have helped make possible this series. It was conceived at CPH in 1990, and a couple of years of planning and prayer to the Lord of the church preceded its formal launch on July 2, 1992. During that time, Dr. J. A. O. Preus II volunteered his enthusiasm for the project because, in his view, it would nurture and advance the faithful proclamation of the Christian faith as understood by the Lutheran church. The financial support that has underwritten the series was provided by a gracious donor who wished to remain anonymous. Those two faithful servants of God were called to heavenly rest not long after the series was inaugurated.

During the early years, former CPH presidents Dr. John W. Gerber and Dr. Stephen J. Carter had the foresight to recognize the potential benefit of such a landmark work for the church at large. CPH allowed Dr. Christopher W. Mitchell to devote his time and energy to the conception and initial development of the project. Dr. Mitchell has remained the CPH editor and is also the Old Testament editor and the author of the commentary on the Song of Songs. Dr. Dean O. Wenthe served on the project since its official start in 1992 and was the general editor from 1999 until 2016; he is also the author of the commentaries on Jeremiah and Lamentations. Julene Gernant Dumit (M.A.R.) has been the CPH production editor for the entire series. Dr. Jeffrey A. Gibbs served on the editorial board as the New Testament editor from 1999 until 2012 and is the author of the commentaries on Matthew. Dr. Curtis P. Giese, author of the commentary on 2 Peter and Jude and the commentary on James, joined the board in 2011 and now serves as the New Testament editor.

CPH thanks all of the institutions that have enabled their faculty to serve as authors and editors. A particular debt of gratitude is owed to Concordia Theological Seminary, Fort Wayne, Indiana, for kindly allowing Dr. Dean O. Wenthe to serve on the editorial board and to dedicate a substantial portion of his time to the series for many years. CPH also thanks Concordia Seminary, St. Louis, Missouri, for the dedication of Dr. Jeffrey A. Gibbs during his tenure as the New Testament editor. Moreover, Concordia University Texas is granting Dr. Curtis P. Giese a reduced load to enable him to carry on as the New Testament editor of the series. These institutions have thereby extended their ministries in selfless service for the benefit of the greater church.

The editors pray that the beneficence of their institutions may be reflected in this series by an evangelical orientation, a steadfast Christological perspective, an eschatological view toward the ultimate good of Christ's bride, and a concern that the wedding feast of the King's Son may be filled with all manner of guests (Mt 22:1–14).

> Now to him who is able to establish you by my Gospel and the preaching of Jesus Christ, by the revelation of the mystery kept secret for ages past but now revealed also through the prophetic Scriptures, made known to all the nations by order of the eternal God unto the obedience of faith—to the only wise God, through Jesus Christ, be the glory forever. Amen! (Rom 16:25–27)

Author's Preface

When Dr. Christopher Mitchell of Concordia Publishing House first approached me about writing commentaries on the book of Samuel, I was quite reluctant to undertake this project. I had already written and published three volumes in the Concordia Commentary series (*Ezra and Nehemiah*, *Proverbs*, and *Daniel*) and was not convinced I ought to write others. However, eventually I agreed, and I am glad that I did. The book of Samuel is a rich trove of narratives of the late premonarchial period and early monarchy of Israel. But it is more than that—it is a record of God's love and mercy toward Israel and ultimately toward all humankind. The author of Samuel does not often place overt theological analysis of the narrative into his work. The challenge for readers is to understand the theological thrusts of his writings, his often subtle messages of God's Law and God's gracious Gospel. I have attempted to draw these out in this commentary.

Since our present 1 Samuel and 2 Samuel in English Bibles were originally one book, the commentary on 1 Samuel contains an introduction to the entire book of Samuel. This second volume contains commentary on 2 Samuel without an extensive introduction. For introductory matters, readers are invited to consult the 1 Samuel commentary. At times this volume repeats information found in the 1 Samuel commentary that is also relevant for 2 Samuel. Most of these repetitions are found in the textual notes and are repeated for the convenience of the reader who may not have the 1 Samuel commentary immediately at hand.

When seeking to understand historical narrative, it is most helpful to know when and where events took place. Throughout this commentary readers will find dates for the individual narratives. These are based on my published chronological work *From Abraham to Paul*. The identification of ancient sites with modern places is based in large part on the very helpful *Student Map Manual: Historical Geography of the Bible Lands* (J. Monson, general consultant; Jerusalem: Pictorial Archive [Near Eastern History] Est., 1979). In addition, I have included several maps as visual helps for understanding the events in 2 Samuel.

I would like to express my thanks to those who have made this work possible: Concordia University Chicago provided a sabbatical and Concordia Publishing House a grant, which allowed me leave from teaching for a year to complete this work. The very helpful librarians at the Klinck Memorial Library at Concordia University Chicago helped me obtain many of the articles and essays listed in the bibliography and provided workers to scan articles into PDF files for my use. The able editorial work by Dr. Christopher Mitchell and Julene Dumit is also appreciated. The opportunity to work with them again was another incentive for me to accept this assignment. Dr. Christopher Begg graciously sent me copies of some of his articles on Josephus' treatment of the book of Samuel that I could not obtain elsewhere. And, of course, I am grateful for the support of my wife, Rebecca, who followed my progress and at times, when I was a little too obsessed with the project, urged me to take a break and go for a walk with my binoculars and ornithology field guide. She even suggested that we take a one-week break in Costa Rica so that we could spend some time together. It helped reinvigorate me for the final push to complete this project.

May our gracious God continue to bless all who study his Word and trust his promises.

December 26, 2016
The Feast of Saint Stephen

Principal Abbreviations

Books of the Bible

Gen	2 Ki	Is	Nah	Rom	Titus
Ex	1 Chr	Jer	Hab	1 Cor	Philemon
Lev	2 Chr	Lam	Zeph	2 Cor	Heb
Num	Ezra	Ezek	Hag	Gal	James
Deut	Neh	Dan	Zech	Eph	1 Pet
Josh	Esth	Hos	Mal	Phil	2 Pet
Judg	Job	Joel	Mt	Col	1 Jn
Ruth	Ps (pl. Pss)	Amos	Mk	1 Thess	2 Jn
1 Sam	Prov	Obad	Lk	2 Thess	3 Jn
2 Sam	Eccl	Jonah	Jn	1 Tim	Jude
1 Ki	Song	Micah	Acts	2 Tim	Rev

Books of the Apocrypha and Other Noncanonical Books of the Septuagint

1–2 Esdras	1–2 Esdras
Tobit	Tobit
Judith	Judith
Add Esth	Additions to Esther
Wisdom	Wisdom of Solomon
Sirach	Sirach/Ecclesiasticus
Baruch	Baruch
Ep Jer	Epistle of Jeremiah
Azariah	Prayer of Azariah
Song of the Three	Song of the Three Young Men
Susanna	Susanna
Bel	Bel and the Dragon
Manasseh	Prayer of Manasseh
1–2 Macc	1–2 Maccabees
3–4 Macc	3–4 Maccabees
Ps 151	Psalm 151
Odes	Odes
Ps(s) Sol	Psalm(s) of Solomon

Reference Works and Scripture Versions

ANET   *Ancient Near Eastern Texts Relating to the Old Testament.* Edited by J. B. Pritchard. 3d ed. Princeton: Princeton University Press, 1969

ANF   *The Ante-Nicene Fathers.* Edited by A. Roberts and J. Donaldson. 10 vols. Repr., Peabody, Mass.: Hendrickson, 1994

Ap   Apology of the Augsburg Confession

BDB   Brown, F., S. R. Driver, and C. A. Briggs. *A Hebrew and English Lexicon of the Old Testament.* Oxford: Clarendon, 1979

CAL   *The Comprehensive Aramaic Lexicon.* Cincinnati: Hebrew Union College—Jewish Institute of Religion; http://cal1.cn.huc.edu

CDCH   *The Concise Dictionary of Classical Hebrew.* Edited by D. J. A. Clines. Sheffield: Sheffield Phoenix, 2009

DCH   *The Dictionary of Classical Hebrew.* Edited by D. J. A. Clines. 8 vols. Sheffield: Sheffield Academic Press, 1993–2011

DNWSI   Hoftijzer, J., and K. Jongeling. *Dictionary of the North-West Semitic Inscriptions.* 2 vols. Leiden: Brill, 1995

ESV   English Standard Version of the Bible

ET   English translation

FC SD   Formula of Concord, Solid Declaration

GKC   *Gesenius' Hebrew Grammar.* Edited by E. Kautzsch. Translated by A. E. Cowley. 2d ed. Oxford: Clarendon, 1910

GW   God's Word translation of the Bible

HALOT   Koehler, L., W. Baumgartner, and J. J. Stamm. *The Hebrew and Aramaic Lexicon of the Old Testament.* Translated and edited under the supervision of M. E. J. Richardson. 5 vols. Leiden: Brill, 1994–2000

HCSB   Holman Christian Standard Bible

IBH   Steinmann, A. E. *Intermediate Biblical Hebrew: A Reference Grammar with Charts and Exercises.* St. Louis: Concordia, 2007, 2009

Jastrow   Jastrow, M., comp. *A Dictionary of the Targumim, the Talmud Babli and Yerushalmi, and the Midrashic Literature.* 2 vols. Brooklyn: P. Shalom, 1967

Joüon   Joüon, P. *A Grammar of Biblical Hebrew.* Translated and revised by T. Muraoka. 2 vols. Subsidia biblica 14/1–2. Rome: Editrice Pontificio Istituto Biblico, 1991

KJV   King James Version of the Bible

LC   Large Catechism of M. Luther

LXX	*Septuaginta: Id est Vetus Testamentum graece iuxta LXX interpretes.* Edited by A. Rahlfs. 2 vols. Stuttgart: Deutsche Bibelgesellschaft, 1935, 1979
MT	Masoretic Text of the Hebrew Bible
Muraoka	Muraoka, T. *A Greek-English Lexicon of the Septuagint.* Louvain, Belgium: Peeters, 2009
n	Used after a year date to indicate that the year began in the spring month of Nisan (e.g., 969n began in the spring of 969 BC and ended after winter in early 968 BC)
NASB	New American Standard Bible
NEB	New English Bible
NET	NET Bible (New English Translation)
NETS	*A New English Translation of the Septuagint and the Other Greek Translations Traditionally Included under That Title.* Edited by A. Pietersma and B. G. Wright. Oxford: Oxford University Press, 2007
NIV	New International Version of the Bible
NKJV	New King James Version of the Bible
NPNF[1]	*The Nicene and Post-Nicene Fathers.* Series 1. Edited by P. Schaff. 14 vols. Repr., Peabody, Mass.: Hendrickson, 1994
NPNF[2]	*The Nicene and Post-Nicene Fathers.* Series 2. Edited by P. Schaff and H. Wace. 14 vols. Repr., Peabody, Mass.: Hendrickson, 1994
NRSV	New Revised Standard Version of the Bible
NT	New Testament
OT	Old Testament
REB	Revised English Bible
RSV	Revised Standard Version of the Bible
t	Used after a year date to indicate that the year began in the fall month of Tishri (e.g., 969t began in the fall of 969 BC and ended after summer in 968 BC)
Treatise	Treatise on the Power and Primacy of the Pope
TWOT	*Theological Wordbook of the Old Testament.* Edited by R. L. Harris, G. L. Archer Jr., and B. K. Waltke. 2 vols. Chicago: Moody, 1980
WA DB	*D. Martin Luthers Werke: Kritische Gesamtausgabe. Die Deutsche Bibel.* 12 vols. in 15. Weimar: Böhlau, 1906–1961 [Weimarer Ausgabe Deutsche Bibel]
Waltke-O'Connor	Waltke, B. K., and M. O'Connor. *An Introduction to Biblical Hebrew Syntax.* Winona Lake, Ind.: Eisenbrauns, 1990

Hebrew Verbal System

	G-Stem System[1] *Basic*	D-Stem System[2] *Doubling*	H-Stem System *H-Prefix*
Active	G (Qal)	D (Piel)	H (Hiphil)
Passive	Gp (Qal passive)	Dp (Pual)	Hp (Hophal)
Reflexive/Passive	N (Niphal)	HtD (Hithpael)	

---

[1] "G" is from the German *Grundstamm,* "basic stem."

[2] This also includes other doubling patterns such as Polel (D), Pilpel (D), Polal (Dp), Polpal (Dp), Hithpolel (HtD), and Hithpalpel (HtD).

Icons

These icons are used in the margins of this commentary to highlight the following themes:

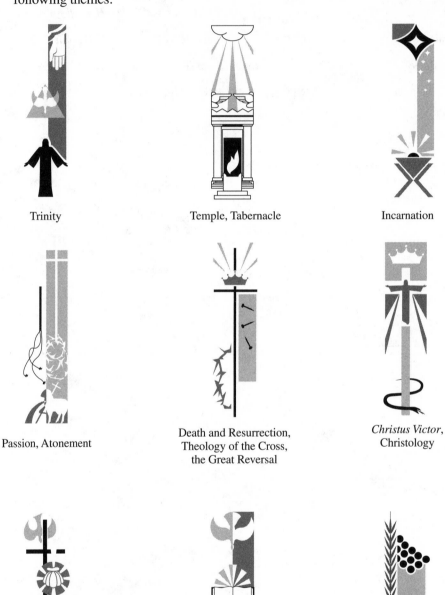

Trinity

Temple, Tabernacle

Incarnation

Passion, Atonement

Death and Resurrection,
Theology of the Cross,
the Great Reversal

Christus Victor,
Christology

Baptism

Catechesis,
Instruction, Revelation

Lord's Supper

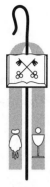

Ministry of Word and Sacrament,
Office of the Keys

The Church,
Christian Marriage

Worship

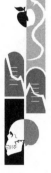

Sin, Law Breaking,
Death

Hope of Heaven,
Eschatology

Justification

Bibliography

Ababi, Ionel. "Quand les intrigues s'entrelacent: Une étude de l'organisation narrative de 2 S 11–12." *Ephemerides theologicae lovanienses* 87 (2011): 35–56.

Abadie, Philippe. "Pérennité dynastique ou éternité du temple? Deux lectures d'un même oracle (2 S 7 et 1 Ch 17)." Pages 117–30 in *Analyse Narrative et Bible*. Edited by Camille Focant and André Wénin. Leuven: Leuven University Press, 2005.

Abasili, Alexander Izuchukwu. "Was It Rape? The David and Bathsheba Pericope Re-Examined." *Vetus Testamentum* 61 (2011): 1–15.

Ackermann, Denise. "Ein neuer Blick auf einen alten Text: Die Geschichte von Tamar." *Zeitschrift für Mission* 29 (2003): 237–42.

Ackroyd, Peter R. *I and II Chronicles, Ezra, Nehemiah*. Torch Bible Commentaries. London: SCM, 1973.

———. *The Second Book of Samuel*. Cambridge Bible Commentary. Cambridge: Cambridge University Press, 1977.

Adler, Joshua J. "David's Last Sin: Was It the Census?" *Jewish Bible Quarterly* 23 (1995): 91–95.

———. "David's Census: Additional Reflection." *Jewish Bible Quarterly* 24 (1996): 255–57.

Ahlström, Gösta W. "Der Prophet Nathan und der Tempelbau." *Vetus Testamentum* 11 (1961): 113–27.

Alexander, T. Desmond. "Further Observations on the Term 'Seed' in Genesis." *Tyndale Bulletin* 48 (1997): 363–67.

Alster, Baruch. "Narrative Surprise in Biblical Parallels." *Biblical Interpretation* 14 (2006): 456–85.

Alter, Robert. "Harold Bloom's 'J.'" *Commentary* 90 (1990): 28–33.

———. *The David Story: A Translation with Commentary of 1 and 2 Samuel*. New York: Norton, 1999.

Althann, Robert. "The Meaning of ארבעים שנה in 2 Sam 15,7." *Biblica* 73 (1992): 248–52.

Amit, Yairah. "Araunah's Threshing Floor: A Lesson in Shaping Historical Memory." Pages 133–44 in *What Was Authoritative for Chronicles?* Edited by Ehud Ben Zvi and Diana Edelman. Winona Lake, Ind.: Eisenbrauns, 2011.

Amzallag, Gérard Nissim, and Mikhal Avriel. "Complex Antiphony in David's Lament and Its Literary Significance." *Vetus Testamentum* 60 (2010): 1–14.

Anderson, A. A. *2 Samuel*. Word Biblical Commentary 11. Dallas: Word, 1989.

Anderson, Roger W., Jr. "'And He Grasp Away Our Eye': A Note on II Sam 20,6." *Zeitschrift für die alttestamentliche Wissenschaft* 102 (1990): 392–96.

Arnold, Bill T. "The Amalekite's Report of Saul's Death: Political Intrigue or Incompatible Sources?" *Journal of the Evangelical Theological Society* 32 (1989): 289–98.

———. "Necromancy and Cleromancy in 1 and 2 Samuel." *Catholic Biblical Quarterly* 66 (2004): 199–213.

Auld, A. Graeme. "Tamar between David, Judah and Joseph." *Svensk exegetisk årsbok* 65 (2000): 93–106.

———. "A Factored Response to an Enigma." Pages 359–66 in *For and against David: Story and History in the Books of Samuel*. Edited by A. Graeme Auld and Erik Eynikel. Leuven: Peeters, 2010.

———. "Synoptic David: The View from Chronicles." Pages 117–28 in *Raising Up a Faithful Exegete: Essays in Honor of Richard D. Nelson*. Edited by K. L. Noll and Brooks Schramm. Winona Lake, Ind.: Eisenbrauns, 2010.

———. *I and II Samuel: A Commentary*. Old Testament Library. Louisville, Ky.: Westminster John Knox, 2011.

Avioz, Michael. "Nathan's Prophecy in II Sam 7 and in I Chr 17: Text, Context, and Meaning." *Zeitschrift für die alttestamentliche Wissenschaft* 116 (2004): 542–54.

———. *Nathan's Oracle (2 Samuel 7) and Its Interpreters*. New York: Peter Lang, 2005.

———. "Josephus' Retelling of Nathan's Oracle (2 Samuel 7)." *Scandinavian Journal of the Old Testament* 20 (2006): 9–17.

———. "The Story of Saul's Death in 1 Chronicles 10 and Its Sources." Pages 113–19 in *Thinking towards New Horizons*. Edited by Matthias Augustin and Hermann Michael Niemann. Frankfurt am Main: Peter Lang, 2008.

Bailey, Randall C. "Reading the Book of Samuel as a Message to the Exiles: A Hermeneutical Shift." *Journal of the Interdenominational Theological Center* 18 (1990–1991): 95–118.

———. "The Redemption of YHWH: A Literary Critical Function of the Songs of Hannah and David." *Biblical Interpretation* 3 (1995): 213–31.

Baird, James O. "Difficult Texts from Ruth, 1 and 2 Samuel." Pages 267–76 in *Difficult Texts of the Old Testament Explained*. Hurst, Tex.: Winkler, 1982.

Bakon, Shimon. "David's Sin: Counting the People." *Jewish Bible Quarterly* 41 (2013): 53–54.

Baldwin, Joyce G. *1 and 2 Samuel: An Introduction and Commentary*. Tyndale Old Testament Commentaries 8. Leicester, England: InterVarsity, 1988.

Bardtke, H. "Der Aufstand des Scheba (2 Samuelis 20)." Pages 15–27 in *Überlieferungsgeschichtliche Untersuchungen*. Edited by Franz Paschke. Berlin: Akademie, 1981.

Barnett, Richard D. "Six Fingers in Art and Archaeology." *Bulletin of the Anglo-Israel Archaeological Society* 6 (1986–1987): 5–12.

————. "Six Fingers and Toes: Polydactylism in the Ancient World." *Biblical Archaeology Review* 16/3 (May/June 1990): 46–51.

Barrick, W. Boyd. "Saul's Demise, David's Lament, and Custer's Last Stand." *Journal for the Study of the Old Testament* 73 (1997): 25–41.

Barton, John. "Dating the 'Succession Narrative.'" Pages 95–106 in *In Search of Pre-Exilic Israel*. Edited by John Day. London: T&T Clark, 2004.

Beck, Martin. "Messiaserwartung in den Geschichtsbüchern? Bemerkungen zur Funktion des Hannaliedes (1 Sam 2,1–10) in seinen diversen literarischen Kontexten (vgl Ex 15; Dtn 32; II Sam 22)." Pages 231–51 in *Auf dem Weg zur Endgestalt von Genesis bis II Regum: Festschrift Hans-Christoph Schmitt zum 65. Geburtstag*. Edited by Martin Beck and Ulrike Schorn. Berlin: De Gruyter, 2006.

Beckwith, Roger T. "The Courses of the Levites and the Eccentric Psalms Scrolls from Qumran." *Revue de Qumran* 11 (1984): 499–524.

Beecher, Willis Judson. "Three Notes." *Journal of the Society of Biblical Literature and Exegesis* 8 (1888): 137–42.

————. *The Prophets and the Promise*. New York: Thomas Y. Crowell, 1905. Repr., Grand Rapids: Baker, 1975.

Begg, Christopher T. "The Reading in 2 Sam 7:7: Some Remarks." *Revue biblique* 95 (1988): 551–58.

————. "The Rape of Tamar (2 Samuel 13) according to Josephus." *Estudios bíblicos* 54 (1996): 465–500.

————. "David's Transfer of the Ark according to Josephus." *Bulletin for Biblical Research* 7 (1997): 11–35.

————. "The Assassination of Ishbosheth according to Josephus." *Antonianum* 73 (1998): 241–53.

————. "David's Capture of Jebus and Its Sequels according to Josephus: *Ant.* 7,60b–70." *Ephemerides theologicae lovanienses* 74 (1998): 93–108.

————. "The Revolt of Sheba: According to Josephus." *Jian Dao* 9 (1998): 1–26.

————. "David's Initial Philistine Victories according to Josephus." *Skrif en kerk* 20 (1999): 1–14.

————. "David's Reaction to the Death of Saul: According to Josephus." *Jian Dao* 11 (1999): 1–13.

————. "The Dynastic Promise according to Josephus." *Sacris erudiri* 39 (2000): 5–19.

————. "David's Flight from Jerusalem according to Josephus." *Hervormde teologiese studies* 62 (2006): 1–22.

————. "David's Mourning for Absalom according to Josephus." *Jian Dao* 25 (2006): 29–52.

————. "David's Sin according to Josephus." *Ancient Near Eastern Studies* 43 (2006): 45–67.

———. "The Recall and Revolt of Absalom according to Josephus." *Svensk exegetisk årsbok* 71 (2006): 75–95.

Bellefontaine, Elizabeth. "Customary Law and Chieftainship: Judicial Aspects of 2 Samuel 14:4–21." *Journal for the Study of the Old Testament* 38 (1987): 47–72.

Bergen, Robert D. *1, 2 Samuel.* New American Commentary 7. Nashville: Broadman & Holman, 1996.

Berger, Yitzhak. "Ruth and the David-Bathsheba Story: Allusions and Contrasts." *Journal for the Study of the Old Testament* 33 (2009): 433–52.

Bewer, Julius A. "Notes on 1 Sam 13:21; 2 Sam 23:1; Psalm 48:8." *Journal of Biblical Literature* 61 (1942): 45–49.

Biberger, Bernd. " 'Du wirst nicht sterben': Vergebung und Vergeltung in 2 Sam 12,13–14." *Biblische Notizen* 151 (2011): 47–62.

Bietenhard, Sophia Katharina. *Des Königs General: Die Heerführertraditionen in der vorstaatlichen und frühen staatlichen Zeit und die Joabgestalt in 2 Sam 2–20; 1 Kön 1–2.* Göttingen: Vandenhoeck & Ruprecht, 1998.

Bledstein, Adrien J. "Was *Habbiryâ* a Healing Ritual Performed by a Woman in King David's House." *Biblical Research* 37 (1992): 15–31.

Blenkinsopp, Joseph. "Did Saul Make Gibeon His Capital?" *Vetus Testamentum* 24 (1974): 1–7.

Bloch, Yigal. "The Prefixed Perfective and the Dating of Early Hebrew Poetry—A Re-Evaluation." *Vetus Testamentum* 59 (2009): 34–70.

Blockman, Noga. "Bull-Leaping in Ancient Israel." *Ugarit-Forschungen* 37 (2005): 5–8.

Blum, Erhard. "Solomon and the United Monarchy: Some Textual Evidence." Pages 59–78 in *One God—One Cult—One Nation: Archaeological and Biblical Perspectives.* Edited by Reinhard G. Kratz and Hermann Spieckermann. Berlin: De Gruyter, 2010.

Bodi, Daniel. "Outraging the Resident-Alien: King David, Uriah the Hittite, and an El-Amarna Parallel." *Ugarit-Forschungen* 35 (2003): 29–56.

———. *The Demise of the Warlord: A New Look at the David Story.* Sheffield: Sheffield Phoenix, 2010.

Bodner, Keith. "Nathan: Prophet, Politician and Novelist?" *Journal for the Study of the Old Testament* 95 (2001): 43–54.

———. "Is Joab a Reader-Response Critic?" *Journal for the Study of the Old Testament* 27 (2002): 19–35.

———. "Motives for Defection: Ahithophel's Agenda in 2 Samuel 15–17." *Studies in Religion/Sciences religieuses* 31 (2002): 63–78.

———. "The Royal Conscience according to 4QSam[a]." *Dead Sea Discoveries* 11 (2004): 158–66.

———. *David Observed: A King in the Eyes of His Court.* Sheffield: Sheffield Phoenix, 2005.

————. "Crime Scene Investigation: A Text Critical Mystery and the Strange Death of Ishbosheth." *Journal of Hebrew Scriptures* 7, article 13 (2007). http://www .jhsonline.org/Articles/article_74.pdf.

Boer, Roland T. "National Allegory in the Hebrew Bible." *Journal for the Study of the Old Testament* 74 (1997): 95–116.

Borger, Rykle. "Die Waffenträger des Königs Darius: Ein Beitrag zur alttestament-lichen Exegese und zur semitischen Lexikographie." *Vetus Testamentum* 22 (1972): 385–98.

Borgman, Paul. *David, Saul, and God: Rediscovering an Ancient Story*. Oxford: Oxford University Press, 2008.

Bosworth, David A. "Faith and Resilience: Kings David's Reaction to the Death of Bathsheba's Firstborn." *Catholic Biblical Quarterly* 73 (2011): 691–707.

Branch, Robin Gallaher. "Women Who Win with Words: Deliverance via Persuasive Communication." *In die Skriflig* 37 (2003): 289–318.

Bratcher, Robert Galveston. "Where Was David? A Note on 2 Samuel 7.18 and 1 Chronicles 17.16." *Bible Translator* 52 (2001): 440–41.

Braun, Roddy. *1 Chronicles*. Word Biblical Commentary 14. Waco, Tex.: Word, 1986.

Brenner, Athalya. "Michal and David: Love between Enemies?" Pages 260–70 in *The Fate of King David: The Past and Present of a Biblical Icon*. Edited by Tod Linafelt, Claudia V. Camp, and Timothy Beal. New York: T&T Clark, 2010.

Bridge, Edward J. "Self-Abasement as an Expression of Thanks in the Hebrew Bible." *Biblica* 92 (2011): 255–73.

Britt, Brian. "Death, Social Conflict, and the Barley Harvest in the Hebrew Bible." *Journal of Hebrew Scriptures* 5, article 15 (2005). http://www.jhsonline.org/ Articles/article_45.pdf.

Brock, Sebastian P. "An Unrecognised Occurrence of the Month Name Ziw (2 Sam. xxi 9)." *Vetus Testamentum* 23 (1973): 100–103.

Brooke, Alan England, Norman McLean, and Henry St John Thackeray, eds. *The Old Testament in Greek*. Vol. 2: *The Later Historical Books*. Part 1: *1 and 2 Samuel*. Cambridge: Cambridge University Press, 1927.

Brooks, Simcha Shalom. "Was There a Concubine at Gibeah?" *Bulletin of the Anglo-Israel Archaeological Society* 15 (1996–1997): 31–40.

Brueggemann, Walter. "Life and Death in Tenth Century Israel." *Journal of the American Academy of Religion* 40 (1972): 96–109.

————. "On Coping with Curse: A Study of 2 Sam 16:5–14." *Catholic Biblical Quarterly* 36 (1974): 175–92.

————. "Prayer as an Act of Daring Dance: Four Biblical Examples." *Reformed Liturgy and Music* 20 (1986): 31–37.

————. "2 Samuel 21–24: An Appendix of Deconstruction?" *Catholic Biblical Quarterly* 50 (1988): 383–97.

———. *First and Second Samuel.* Interpretation: A Bible Commentary for Teaching and Preaching. Louisville, Ky.: Westminster/John Knox, 1990.

———. *David's Truth in Israel's Imagination and Memory.* 2d ed. Minneapolis: Fortress, 2002.

———. *Ichabod toward Home: The Journey of God's Glory.* Grand Rapids: Eerdmans, 2002.

Busto Saiz, José Ramón. "The Antiochene Text in 2 Samuel 22." Pages 131–43 in *VIII Congress of the International Organization for Septuagint and Cognate Studies, Paris 1992.* Edited by Leonard Greenspoon and Olivier Munnich. Atlanta: Scholars, 1995.

Camp, Phillip G. "David's Fall: Reading 2 Samuel 11–14 in Light of Genesis 2–4." *Restoration Quarterly* 53 (2011): 149–58.

Campbell, Antony F. "The Reported Story: Midway between Oral Performance and Literary Art." *Semeia* 46 (1989): 77–85.

———. *Joshua to Chronicles: An Introduction.* Louisville, Ky.: Westminster John Knox, 2004.

———. *2 Samuel.* Forms of the Old Testament Literature 8. Grand Rapids: Eerdmans, 2005.

———. "2 Samuel 21–24: The Enigma Factor." Pages 347–58 in *For and against David: Story and History in the Books of Samuel.* Edited by A. Graeme Auld and Erik Eynikel. Leuven: Peeters, 2010.

Caquot, André, and Philippe de Robert. *Les livres de Samuel.* Commentaire de l'Ancien Testament. Geneva: Labor et Fides, 1994.

Carlson, R. Agge. "David and the Ark in 2 Samuel 6." Pages 17–23 in *History and Traditions of Early Israel: Studies Presented to Eduard Nielsen.* Edited by André Lemaire and Benedikt Otzen. Leiden: Brill, 1993.

Cartledge, Tony W. "A House for God and a House for David." *Word and World* 23 (2003): 395–402.

Cazelles, Henri. "David's Monarchy and the Gibeonite Claim." *Palestine Exploration Quarterly* 87 (1955): 165–75.

Ceresko, Anthony R. "The Identity of 'the Blind and the Lame' (*'iwwēr ûpissēaḥ*) in 2 Samuel 5:8b." *Catholic Biblical Quarterly* 63 (2001): 23–30.

Chankin-Gould, J. D'ror, Derek Hutchinson, David Hilton Jackson, Tyler D. Mayfield, Leah Rediger Schulte, Tammi J. Schneider, and E. Winkelman. "The Sanctified 'Adulteress' and Her Circumstantial Clause: Bathsheba's Bath and Self-Consecration in 2 Samuel 11." *Journal for the Study of the Old Testament* 32 (2008): 339–52.

Chavel, Simeon. "Compositry and Creativity in 2 Samuel 21:1–14." *Journal of Biblical Literature* 122 (2003): 23–52.

Chinitz, Jacob. "Two Sinners." *Jewish Bible Quarterly* 25 (1997): 108–13.

Chisholm, Robert B., Jr. "Does God Deceive?" *Bibliotheca sacra* 155 (1998): 11–28.

Coats, George W. "2 Samuel 12:1–7a." *Interpretation* 40 (1986): 170–74.

Cody, Aelred. *A History of the Old Testament Priesthood*. Rome: Pontifical Biblical Institute, 1969.

Coggins, R. J. *The First and Second Books of the Chronicles*. Cambridge Bible Commentary. Cambridge: Cambridge University Press, 1976.

Cohen, Matty. "II Sam 24 ou l'histoire d'un décret royal avorté." *Zeitschrift für die alttestamentliche Wissenschaft* 113 (2001): 17–40.

Collins, C. John. "A Syntactical Note (Genesis 3:15): Is the Woman's Seed Singular or Plural?" *Tyndale Bulletin* 48 (1997): 139–48.

Cooley, Robert. "Gathered to His People: A Study of a Dothan Family Tomb." Pages 47–58 in *The Living and Active Word of God: Studies in Honor of Samuel J. Schultz*. Edited by Morris Inch and Ronald Youngblood. Winona Lake, Ind.: Eisenbrauns, 1983.

Couroyer, B. "Note sur 2 Sam 1:22 et Isa 55:10–11." *Revue biblique* 88 (1981): 505–14.

Craig, Kenneth M., Jr. "The Character(ization) of God in 2 Samuel 7:1–17." *Semeia* 63 (1993): 159–76.

Crenshaw, James L. "The Expression *mî yôdēaʿ* in the Hebrew Bible." *Vetus Testamentum* 36 (1986): 274–88.

Cross, Frank Moore. *Canaanite Myth and Hebrew Epic: Essays in the History of the Religion of Israel*. Cambridge, Mass.: Harvard University Press, 1973.

Cross, Frank Moore, and David Noel Freedman. "A Royal Song of Thanksgiving: II Samuel 22 = Psalm 18." *Journal of Biblical Literature* 72 (1953): 15–34.

Cross, Frank Moore, Donald W. Parry, Richard J. Saley, and Eugene Ulrich. *Qumran Cave 4.XII: 1–2 Samuel*. Discoveries in the Judaean Desert 17. Oxford: Clarendon, 2005.

Crouch, Carly L. "Funerary Rites for Infants and Children in the Hebrew Bible in Light of Ancient Near Eastern Practice." Pages 15–26 in *Feasts and Festivals*. Edited by Christopher Tuckett. Leuven: Peeters, 2009.

Curtis, Edward Lewis, and Albert Alonzo Madsen. *A Critical and Exegetical Commentary on the Books of Chronicles*. International Critical Commentary. Edinburgh: T&T Clark, 1910.

Dahood, Mitchell Joseph. "Philological Observations on Five Biblical Texts." *Biblica* 63 (1982): 390–94.

Darr, Katheryn Pfisterer. "Asking at Abel: A Wise Woman's Proverb Performance in 2 Samuel 20." Pages 102–21 in *From the Margins 1: Women of the Hebrew Bible and Their Afterlives*. Edited by Peter S. Hawkins and Lesleigh Cushing Stahlberg. Sheffield: Sheffield Phoenix, 2009.

Das, A. Andrew. *Galatians*. Concordia Commentary. St. Louis: Concordia, 2014.

Daube, David. "Absalom and the Ideal King." *Vetus Testamentum* 48 (1998): 315–25.

Davidson, Richard M. "Did King David Rape Bathsheba? A Case Study in Narrative Theology." *Journal of the Adventist Theological Society* 17 (2006): 81–95.

Day, John. "Gibeon and the Gibeonites in the Old Testament." Pages 113–37 in *Reflection and Refraction: Studies in Biblical Historiography in Honour of A. Graeme Auld.* Edited by Robert Rezetko, Timothy H. Lim, and W. Brian Aucker. Leiden: Brill, 2006.

Day, Peggy L. "Abishai the *śāṭān* in 2 Samuel 19:17–24." *Catholic Biblical Quarterly* 49 (1987): 543–47.

Delcor, M. "Les Kerethim et les Cretois." *Vetus Testamentum* 28 (1978): 409–22.

Derby, Josiah. "A Biblical Freudian Slip: II Samuel 12:6." *Jewish Bible Quarterly* 24 (1996): 107–11.

———. "David's Conquest of Jerusalem." *Jewish Bible Quarterly* 25 (1997): 35–39.

DeSilva, David Arthur. "'… And Not a Drop to Drink': The Story of David's Thirst in the Jewish Scriptures, Josephus, and 4 Maccabees." *Journal for the Study of the Pseudepigrapha* 16 (2006): 15–40.

Deterding, Paul E. *Colossians.* Concordia Commentary. St. Louis: Concordia, 2003.

Dick, Michael B. "The 'History of David's Rise to Power' and the Neo-Babylonian Succession Apologies." Pages 3–19 in *David and Zion: Biblical Studies in Honor of J. J. M. Roberts.* Edited by Bernard F. Batto and Kathryn L. Roberts. Winona Lake, Ind.: Eisenbrauns, 2004.

Dietrich, Walter. "Die Überführung der Lade nach Jerusalem (2 Sam 6): Geschichten und Geschichte." Pages 235–53 in *For and against David: Story and History in the Books of Samuel.* Edited by A. Graeme Auld and Erik Eynikel. Leuven: Peeters, 2010.

Dijk-Hemmes, Fokkelien van. "Tamar and the Limits of Patriarchy: Between Rape and Seduction (2 Samuel 13 and Genesis 38)." Pages 135–56 in *Anti-Covenant: Counter-Reading Women's Lives in the Hebrew Bible.* Edited by Mieke Bal. Sheffield: Almond, 1989.

Domeris, William. "The City of David: A Test Case for Biblical Archaeology." *Journal of Theology for Southern Africa* 48 (1984): 21–29.

Edelman, Diana. "The Authenticity of 2 Sam 1:26 in the Lament over Saul and Jonathan." *Scandinavian Journal of the Old Testament* 1 (1988): 66–75.

Edenburg, Cynthia. "David, the Great King, King of the Four Quarters: Structure and Signification in the Catalogue of David's Conquests (2 Samuel 8:1–14, 1 Chronicles 18:1–13)." Pages 159–75 in *Raising Up a Faithful Exegete: Essays in Honor of Richard D. Nelson.* Edited by K. L. Noll and Brooks Schramm. Winona Lake, Ind.: Eisenbrauns, 2010.

Eichenholtz, Eve. "The Nature of *Kinat David*: Public or Private?" *Jewish Bible Quarterly* 31 (2003): 130–33.

Eissfeldt, Otto. "Zwei verkannte militär-technische Termini im Alten Testament." *Vetus Testamentum* 5 (1955): 232–38.

Elitzur, Yehuda. "Ira ha-Yairi and the Sons of David." Pages 9–10 in the Hebrew section of the *Proceedings of the Tenth World Congress of Jewish Studies*. Division A: *The Bible and Its World*. Jerusalem: Magnes, 1990.

Emerton, John A. "Sheol and the Sons of Belial." *Vetus Testamentum* 37 (1987): 214–18.

Eschelbach, Michael A. *Has Joab Foiled David? A Literary Study of the Importance of Joab's Character in Relation to David*. New York: Peter Lang, 2005.

Esler, Philip Francis. "2 Samuel—David and the Ammonite War: A Narrative and Social-Scientific Interpretation of 2 Samuel 10–12." Pages 191–207 in *Ancient Israel: The Old Testament in Its Social Context*. Edited by Philip F. Esler. Minneapolis: Fortress, 2006.

Exum, J. Cheryl. "Bathsheba Plotted, Shot, and Painted." *Semeia* 74 (1996): 47–73.

———. "Rizpah." *Word and World* 17 (1997): 260–68.

Eynikel, Erik. "The Parable of Nathan (II Sam. 12,1–4) and the Theory of Semiosis." Pages 71–90 in *Rethinking the Foundations: Historiography in the Ancient World and in the Bible: Essays in Honour of John Van Seters*. Edited by Steven L. McKenzie and Thomas Römer. Berlin: De Gruyter, 2000.

———. "The Relation between the Eli Narratives (1 Sam. 1–4) and the Ark Narrative (1 Sam. 1–6; 2 Sam. 6:1–19)." Pages 88–106 in *Past, Present, Future: The Deuteronomistic History and the Prophets*. Edited by Johannes C. de Moor and Harry F. van Rooy. Leiden: Brill, 2000.

———. "Das Lied der Hanna (1 Sam 2,1–11) und das Lied Davids (2 Sam 22): Ein Vergleich." Pages 57–72 in *For and against David: Story and History in the Books of Samuel*. Edited by A. Graeme Auld and Erik Eynikel. Leuven: Peeters, 2010.

Faust, Avraham. "Warren's Shaft: Yes, It Really Was Used to Draw Water." *Biblical Archaeology Review* 29/5 (September/October 2003): 70–76.

Fensham, Frank Charles. "Battle between the Men of Joab and Abner as a Possible Ordeal by Battle." *Vetus Testamentum* 20 (1970): 356–57.

Fernández Marcos, Natalio. "On Double Readings, Pseudo-Variants and Ghost-Names in the Historical Books." Pages 591–604 in *Emanuel: Studies in Hebrew Bible, Septuagint, and Dead Sea Scrolls in Honor of Emanuel Tov*. Edited by Shalom M. Paul et al. Leiden: Brill, 2003.

Firth, David G. "Shining the Lamp: The Rhetoric of 2 Samuel 5–24." *Tyndale Bulletin* 52 (2001): 203–24.

———. "The Accession Narrative (1 Samuel 27–2 Samuel 1)." *Tyndale Bulletin* 58 (2007): 61–81.

Flanagan, James W. "Court History or Succession Document: A Study of 2 Samuel 9–20 and 1 Kings 1–2." *Journal of Biblical Literature* 91 (1972): 172–81.

Fokkelman, J. P. "שדי תרומת in II Sam 1:21a: A Non-Existent Crux." *Zeitschrift für die alttestamentliche Wissenschaft* 91 (1979): 290–92.

———. *Narrative Art and Poetry in the Books of Samuel: A Full Interpretation Based on Stylistic and Structural Analysis.* 4 vols. Vol. 1: *King David (II Sam 9–20 and I Kings 1–2).* Assen: Van Gorcum, 1981.

———. "A Lie, Born of Truth, Too Weak to Contain It: A Structural Reading of 2 Sam. i 1–16." Pages 39–55 in *Prophets, Worship and Theodicy: Studies in Prophetism, Biblical Theology, and Structural and Rhetorical Analysis and on the Place of Music in Worship.* Oudtestamentische Studiën 23. Leiden: Brill, 1984.

———. *Narrative Art and Poetry in the Books of Samuel: A Full Interpretation Based on Stylistic and Structural Analysis.* 4 vols. Vol. 2: *The Crossing Fates (I Sam 13–23 and II Sam 1).* Assen: Van Gorcum, 1986.

———. *Narrative Art and Poetry in the Books of Samuel: A Full Interpretation Based on Stylistic and Structural Analysis.* 4 vols. Vol. 3: *Throne and City (II Sam 2–8 and 21–24).* Assen: Van Gorcum, 1992.

Fontaine, Carole R. "The Bearing of Wisdom on the Shape of 2 Samuel 11–12 and 1 Kings 3." *Journal for the Study of the Old Testament* 34 (1986): 61–77.

Fouts, David M. "Who Really Killed Goliath? 2 Samuel 21:19 versus 1 Chronicles 20:5." *Journal of Translation and Textlinguistics* 13 (2000): 14–24.

Freedman, David Noel. "Patterns in the Early Poetry of Israel." *Journal of Biblical Literature* 83 (1964): 201–3.

———. "II Samuel 23:4." *Journal of Biblical Literature* 90 (1971): 329–30.

———. "The Refrain in David's Lament over Saul and Jonathan." Pages 263–74 in *Pottery, Poetry, and Prophecy: Studies in Early Hebrew Poetry.* Winona Lake, Ind.: Eisenbrauns, 1980.

———. "On the Death of Abiner." Pages 125–27 in *Love and Death in the Ancient Near East: Essays in Honor of Marvin H. Pope.* Edited by John H. Marks and Robert M. Good. Guilford, Conn: Four Quarters, 1987.

Frisch, Amos. " 'And David Perceived' (2 Samuel 5,2): A Direct Insight into David's Soul and Its Meaning in Context." *Scandinavian Journal of the Old Testament* 18 (2004): 77–92.

Frolov, Serge. "Succession Narrative: A 'Document' or a Phantom?" *Journal of Biblical Literature* 121 (2002): 81–104.

Frolov, Serge, and Vladimir E. Orel. "On the Meaning of 2 Sam 9,1." *Biblische Notizen* 73 (1994): 31–32.

———. "Rizpah on the Rock: Notes on 2 Sam 21:1–14." *Bibbia e oriente* 37 (1995): 145–54.

———. "David in Jerusalem." *Zeitschrift für die alttestamentliche Wissenschaft* 111 (1999): 609–15.

Fuss, Werner. "II Samuel 24." *Zeitschrift für die alttestamentliche Wissenschaft* 74 (1962): 145–64.

Gaiser, Frederick J. "The David of Psalm 51: Reading Psalm 51 in Light of Psalm 50." *Word and World* 23 (2003): 382–94.

Galpaz-Feller, Pnina. "David and the Messenger—Different Ends, Similar Means in 2 Samuel 1." *Vetus Testamentum* 59 (2009): 199–210.

Gard, Daniel L. "The Chronicler's David: Saint and Sinner." *Concordia Theological Quarterly* 70 (2006): 233–52.

Garfinkel, Yosef, Mitka R. Golub, Haggai Misgav, and Saar Ganor. "The ᵓIšbaʿal Inscription from Khirbet Qeiyafa." *Bulletin of the American Schools of Oriental Research* 373 (2015): 217–33.

Garsiel, Moshe. *The First Book of Samuel: A Literary Study of Comparative Structures, Analogies and Parallels.* Ramat-Gan, Israel: Revivim, 1983, 1985.

———. "The Story of David and Bathsheba: A Different Approach." *Catholic Biblical Quarterly* 55 (1993): 244–62.

———. "David's Warfare against the Philistines in the Vicinity of Jerusalem (2 Sam 5,17–25; 1 Chron 14,8–16)." Pages 150–64 in *Studies in Historical Geography and Biblical Historiography Presented to Zechariah Kallai.* Edited by Gershon Galil and Moshe Weinfeld. Leiden: Brill, 2000.

———. "David's Elite Warriors and Their Exploits in the Books of Samuel and Chronicles." *Journal of Hebrew Scriptures* 11, article 5 (2011). http://www.jhsonline.org/Articles/article_152.pdf.

Gelston, A. "A Note on II Samuel 7:10." *Zeitschrift für die alttestamentliche Wissenschaft* 84 (1972): 92–94.

Gentry, Peter John. "Rethinking the 'Sure Mercies of David' in Isaiah 55:3." *Westminster Theological Journal* 69 (2007): 279–304.

Geoghegan, Jeffrey C. "Israelite Sheepshearing and David's Rise to Power." *Biblica* 87 (2006): 55–63.

George, Mark K. "Fluid Stability in Second Samuel 7." *Catholic Biblical Quarterly* 64 (2002): 17–36.

Geyer, Marcia L. "Stopping the Juggernaut: A Close Reading of 2 Samuel 20:13–22." *Union Seminary Quarterly Review* 41 (1986): 33–42.

Gibbs, Jeffrey A. *Matthew 1:1–11:1.* Concordia Commentary. St. Louis: Concordia, 2006.

Gibson, John C. L. *Textbook of Syrian Semitic Inscriptions.* Vol. 1: *Hebrew and Moabite Inscriptions.* Oxford: Clarendon, 1971.

Gieschen, Charles A. *Angelomorphic Christology: Antecedents and Early Evidence.* Leiden: Brill, 1998.

Ginsberg, Harold Louis. "A Ugaritic Parallel to 2 Sam 1:21." *Journal of Biblical Literature* 57 (1938): 209–13.

Giveon, Raphael. " 'The Cities of Our God' (II Sam 10:12)." *Journal of Biblical Literature* 83 (1964): 415–16.

Glück, J. J. "Merab or Michal." *Zeitschrift für die alttestamentliche Wissenschaft* 77 (1965): 72–81.

Goldsmith, Dale. "Acts 13:33–37: A *Pesher* on II Samuel 7." *Journal of Biblical Literature* 87 (1968): 321–24.

Good, Robert M. "2 Samuel 8." *Tyndale Bulletin* 52 (2001): 129–38.

Gordon, Robert P. "The Variable Wisdom of Abel: The MT and Versions at 2 Samuel xx 18–19." *Vetus Testamentum* 43 (1993): 215–26.

Gray, Mark. "Amnon: A Chip off the Old Block? Rhetorical Strategy in 2 Samuel 13.7–15: The Rape of Tamar and the Humiliation of the Poor." *Journal for the Study of the Old Testament* 77 (1998): 39–54.

Greenwood, Kyle R. "Labor Pains: The Relationship between David's Census and Corvée Labor." *Bulletin for Biblical Research* 20 (2010): 467–77.

Grisanti, Michael A. "The Davidic Covenant." *Master's Seminary Journal* 10 (1999): 233–50.

Gunn, David M. "David and the Gift of the Kingdom (2 Sam 2–4, 9–20, 1 Kgs 1–2)." *Semeia* 3 (1975): 14–45.

———. *The Story of King David: Genre and Interpretation.* Sheffield: Dept. of Biblical Studies, University of Sheffield, 1978.

Haase, Ingrid M. "Uzzah's Rebellion." *Journal of Hebrew Scriptures* 5, article 3 (2004). http://www.jhsonline.org/Articles/article_33.pdf.

Haelewyck, Jean-Claude. "L'assassinat d'Ishbaal (2 Samuel iv 1–12)." *Vetus Testamentum* 47 (1997): 145–53.

Halberstam, Chaya. "The Art of Biblical Law." *Prooftexts* 27 (2007): 345–64.

Halpern, Baruch. *David's Secret Demons: Messiah, Murderer, Traitor, King.* Grand Rapids: Eerdmans, 2001.

Hamilton, Mark W. "At Whose Table? Stories of Elites and Social Climbers in 1–2 Samuel." *Vetus Testamentum* 59 (2009): 513–32.

Hauer, Christian E. "Jerusalem, the Stronghold and Rephaim." *Catholic Biblical Quarterly* 32 (1970): 571–78.

Haupt, Paul. "Deal Gently with the Young Man." *Journal of Biblical Literature* 45 (1926): 357.

Havea, Jione. "David W[e]aves." Pages 289–301 in *The Fate of King David: The Past and Present of a Biblical Icon.* Edited by Tod Linafelt, Claudia V. Camp, and Timothy Beal. New York: T&T Clark, 2010.

Heiser, Michael S. "Should אלהים (*ʾĕlōhîm*) with Plural Predication Be Translated 'Gods'?" *Bible Translator* 61 (2010): 123–36.

Hengel, Martin. *Crucifixion in the Ancient World and the Folly of the Message of the Cross.* Philadelphia: Fortress, 1977.

Herbert, Edward D. "2 Samuel v 6: An Interpretative Crux Reconsidered in the Light of 4QSamᵃ." *Vetus Testamentum* 44 (1994): 340–48.

Herrmann, Siegfried. "King David's State." Pages 261–75 in *In the Shelter of Elyon: Essays on Ancient Palestinian Life and Literature in Honor of G. W. Ahlström.* Edited by W. Boyd Barrick and John R. Spencer. Sheffield: JSOT, 1984.

Hertzberg, Hans Wilhelm. *I and II Samuel: A Commentary*. Translated by J. S. Bowden. Old Testament Library. Philadelphia: Westminster, 1964.

Heyler, Larry R. " 'Come What May, I Want to Run': Observations on Running in the Hebrew Bible." *Near East Archaeological Society Bulletin* 48 (2003): 1–12.

Hicks, Mitchell W., Earl Bland, and Lowell W. Hoffman. "Restoring the Voice of Tamar: Three Psychoanalytic Views on Rape in the Bible." *Journal of Psychology and Christianity* 29 (2010): 141–48.

Hill, Andrew E. "A Jonadab Connection in the Absalom Conspiracy." *Journal of the Evangelical Theological Society* 30 (1987): 387–90.

———. "On David's 'Taking' and 'Leaving' Concubines (2 Samuel 5:13; 15:16)." *Journal of Biblical Literature* 125 (2006): 129–50.

Hillers, Delbert R. "A Note on Some Treaty Terminology in the Old Testament." *Bulletin of the American Schools of Oriental Research* 176 (1964): 46–47.

Himbaza, Innocent. "4QSamᵃ (2 Sam 24:16–22): Its Reading, Where It Stands in the History of the Text and Its Use in Bible Translations." Pages 39–52 in *Archaeology of the Books of Samuel: The Entangling of the Textual and Literary History*. Edited by Philippe Hugo and Adrian Schenker. Leiden: Brill, 2010.

Hitzig, Ferdinand. *Die Psalmen*. 2 vols. Leipzig: Winter, 1863–1865.

Hoffmann, Georg. "Lexikalisches." *Zeitschrift für die alttestamentliche Wissenschaft* 2 (1882): 53–72.

Hoftijzer, J. "David and the Tekoite Woman." *Vetus Testamentum* 20 (1970): 419–44.

———. "A Peculiar Question: A Note on 2 Sam. xv 27." *Vetus Testamentum* 21 (1971): 606–9.

Hoglund, Kenneth G. "The Priest of Praise: The Chronicler's David." *Review and Expositor* 99 (2002): 185–91.

Holladay, William Lee. "Form and Word-Play in David's Lament over Saul and Jonathan." *Vetus Testamentum* 20 (1970): 153–89.

Holloway, Steven W. "Distaff, Crutch or Chain Gang: The Curse of the House of Joab in 2 Samuel III 29." *Vetus Testamentum* 37 (1987): 370–75.

Holm-Nielsen, Svend. "Did Joab Climb 'Warren's Shaft'?" Pages 38–49 in *History and Traditions of Early Israel: Studies Presented to Eduard Nielsen*. Edited by André Lemaire and Benedikt Otzen. Leiden: Brill, 1993.

Homan, Michael M. "Booths or Succoth? A Response to Yigael Yadin." *Journal of Biblical Literature* 118 (1999): 691–97.

Honeyman, Alexander Mackie. "The Evidence for Regnal Names among the Hebrews." *Journal of Biblical Literature* 67 (1948): 13–25.

Horn, Siegfried H. "The Crown of the King of the Ammonites." *Andrews University Seminary Studies* 11 (1973): 170–80.

Hubbard, Robert L. "The Hebrew Root *Pgᶜ* as a Legal Term." *Journal of the Evangelical Theological Society* 27 (1984): 129–33.

Huffmon, H. B. "A Tale of the Prophet and the Courtier: A Responsive Reading of the Nathan Texts." Pages 33–42 in *Sacred History, Sacred Literature: Essays on Ancient Israel, the Bible, and Religion in Honor of R. E. Friedman on His Sixtieth Birthday*. Edited by Shawna Dolansky. Winona Lake, Ind.: Eisenbrauns, 2008.

Hugo, Philippe. "L'archéologie textuelle du temple de Jérusalem: Étude textuelle et littéraire du motif théologique du temple en 2 Samuel." Pages 161–212 in *Archaeology of the Books of Samuel: The Entangling of the Textual and Literary History*. Edited by Philippe Hugo and Adrian Schenker. Leiden: Brill, 2010.

———. "The King's Return (2 Sam 19,10–16): Contrasting Characterizations of David, Israel and Juda in the *Old Editions*." Pages 95–118 in *After Qumran: Old and Modern Editions of the Biblical Texts: The Historical Books*. Edited by Hans Ausloos, Bénédicte Lemmelijn, and Julio Trebolle Barrera. Leuven: Peeters, 2012.

Hutton, Jeremy. "The Left Bank of the Jordan and the Rites of Passage: An Anthropological Interpretation of 2 Samuel xix." *Vetus Testamentum* 56 (2006): 470–84.

Hyman, Ronald T. "Power of Persuasion: Judah, Abigail, and Hushai." *Jewish Bible Quarterly* 23 (1995): 9–16.

Isbell, Charles D. "A Biblical Midrash on David and Goliath." *Scandinavian Journal of the Old Testament* 20 (2006): 259–63.

Ishida, Tomoo. "Solomon's Succession to the Throne of David: A Political Analysis." Pages 175–87 in *Studies in the Period of David and Solomon and Other Essays*. Edited by Tomoo Ishida. Winona Lake, Ind.: Eisenbrauns, 1982.

Janzen, David. "The Condemnation of David's 'Taking' in 2 Samuel 12:1–14." *Journal of Biblical Literature* 131 (2012): 209–20.

Japhet, Sara. *I and II Chronicles: A Commentary*. Old Testament Library. Louisville, Ky.: Westminster/John Knox, 1993.

Jensen, Hans Jørgen Lundager. "Desire, Rivalry and Collective Violence in the 'Succession Narrative.'" *Journal for the Study of the Old Testament* 55 (1992): 39–59.

Jobes, Karen H., and Moisés Silva. *Invitation to the Septuagint*. Grand Rapids: Baker Academic, 2000.

Jones, Ivor H. "Musical Instruments in the Bible, Pt 1." *Bible Translator* 37 (1986): 101–16.

Joo, Samantha. "שׁוּמָה (2 Sam. xiii 32): Lot (*šiāmu/šâmu/šīmtu*)?" *Vetus Testamentum* 58 (2008): 258–64.

Joüon, Paul. "Notes philologiques sur le texte hébreu de 2 Samuel 2, 13; 5, 23–24 (= 1 Chr. 14, 14–15); 6, 20–22; 7, 12–13; 9, 12; 10, 2; 11, 17; 12, 11; 12, 31; 13, 24; 13, 27; 13, 28; 14, 5; 14, 7; 14, 26; 14, 33; 16, 14; 16, 19; 17, 29; 18, 2; 18, 17; 18, 25; 19, 7; 19, 24; 19, 25; 20, 10; 21, 15–17." *Biblica* 9 (1928): 302–15.

Judisch, Douglas. "Propitiation in the Language and Typology of the Old Testament." *Concordia Theological Quarterly* 48 (1984): 221–43.

Kaiser, Walter C., Jr. "The Blessing of David: The Charter for Humanity." Pages 298–318 in *The Law and the Prophets: Old Testament Studies Prepared in Honor of Oswald Thompson Allis*. Edited by John H. Skilton, Milton C. Fisher, and Leslie W. Sloat. Nutley, N.J.: Presbyterian and Reformed, 1974.

Kasari, Petri. *Nathan's Promise in 2 Samuel 7 and Related Texts*. Helsinki: Finnish Exegetical Society, 2009.

Keefe, Alice A. "Rapes of Women/Wars of Men." *Semeia* 61 (1993): 79–97.

Keil, C. F. *Biblical Commentary on the Books of Samuel*. Translated by James Martin. Edinburgh: T&T Clark, 1866. Repr., Grand Rapids: Eerdmans, 1976.

Kelly, J. N. D. *Early Christian Creeds*. 3d ed. Harlow, England: Longman, 1972.

Kempinski, Aharon. "Hittites in the Bible: What Does Archaeology Say?" *Biblical Archaeology Review* 5/5 (September/October 1979): 20–45.

Kim, Eun Chul. "Cult of the Dead and the Old Testament Negation of Ancestor Worship." *Asia Journal of Theology* 17 (2003): 2–16.

Kim, Uriah (Yong-Hwan). "Uriah the Hittite: A Con(Text) of Struggle for Identity." *Semeia* 90–91 (2002): 69–85.

Kind, David A. "Polygamy and Its Contemporary Variations in Biblical Perspective." Pages 59–77 in *Ethics of Sex: From Taboo to Delight*. Edited by Gifford A. Grobien. St. Louis: Concordia, 2017.

Klein, Ralph W. "The Last Words of David." *Currents in Theology and Mission* 31 (2004): 15–23.

———. *1 Chronicles: A Commentary*. Hermeneia. Minneapolis: Fortress, 2006.

Kleinig, John W. *Leviticus*. Concordia Commentary. St. Louis: Concordia, 2003.

———. *Hebrews*. Concordia Commentary. St. Louis: Concordia, 2017.

Klement, Herbert H. "Structure, Context and Meaning in the Samuel Conclusion (2 Sa. 21–24)." *Tyndale Bulletin* 47 (1996): 367–70.

Kleven, Terence. "Rhetoric and Narrative Depiction in 2 Sam 1:1–16." *Proceedings of the Eastern Great Lakes and Midwest Biblical Societies* 9 (1989): 59–73.

———. "Reading Hebrew Poetry: David's Lament over Saul and Jonathan (2 Sam 1:17–27)." *Proceedings of the Eastern Great Lakes and Midwest Biblical Societies* 11 (1991): 51–65.

———. "Hebrew Style in 2 Samuel 6." *Journal of the Evangelical Theological Society* 35 (1992): 299–314.

———. "Up the Waterspout: How David's General Joab Got inside Jerusalem." *Biblical Archaeology Review* 20/4 (July/August 1994): 34–35.

———. "The Use of ṣnr in Ugaritic and 2 Samuel v 8: Hebrew Usage and Comparative Philology." *Vetus Testamentum* 44 (1994): 195–204.

———. "The Water System of Jerusalem and Its Implications for the Historicity of Joab's Conquest." *Near East Archaeological Society Bulletin* 47 (2002): 35–48.

Knoppers, Gary. *1 Chronicles 10–29: A New Translation with Introduction and Commentary*. Anchor Bible 12A. New York: Doubleday, 2004.

Krašovec, Jože. "Two Types of Unconditional Covenant." *Horizons in Biblical Theology* 18 (1996): 55–77.

Krinetzki, Günter. "Ein Beitrag zur Stilanalyse der Goliathperikope, 1 Sam 17,1–18,5." *Biblica* 54 (1973): 187–236.

Kruger, Paul A. "'Liminality' in 2 Samuel 19:1–9: A Short Note." *Journal of Northwest Semitic Languages* 24 (1998): 195–99.

Kruschwitz, Jonathan A. "2 Samuel 12:1–15: How (Not) to Read a Parable." *Review and Expositor* 109 (2012): 253–59.

Landy, Francis. "David and Ittai." Pages 19–37 in *The Fate of King David: The Past and Present of a Biblical Icon*. Edited by Tod Linafelt, Claudia V. Camp, and Timothy Beal. New York: T&T Clark, 2010.

Lasine, Stuart. "Judicial Narratives and the Ethics of Reading: The Reader as Judge of the Dispute between Mephibosheth and Ziba." *Hebrew Studies* 30 (1989): 49–69.

Latto, Antti. "Second Samuel 7 and Ancient Near Eastern Royal Ideology." *Catholic Biblical Quarterly* 59 (1997): 244–69.

Lawlor, John I. "Theology and Art in the Narrative of the Ammonite War (2 Samuel 10–12)." *Grace Theological Journal* 3 (1982): 193–205.

Layton, Scott C. "A Chain Gang in 2 Samuel 3:29: A Rejoinder." *Vetus Testamentum* 39 (1989): 81–86.

Lemos, T. M. "Shame and Mutilation of Enemies in the Hebrew Bible." *Journal of Biblical Literature* 125 (2006): 225–41.

Lessing, R. Reed, and Andrew E. Steinmann. *Prepare the Way of the Lord: An Introduction to the Old Testament*. St. Louis: Concordia, 2014.

Lewis, Theodore J. "The Ancestral Estate (נַחֲלַת אֱלֹהִים) in 2 Samuel 14:16." *Journal of Biblical Literature* 110 (1991): 597–612.

Linafelt, Tod. "Private Poetry and Public Eloquence in 2 Samuel 1,17–27: Hearing and Overhearing David's Lament for Jonathan and Saul." *Journal of Religion* 88 (2008): 497–526.

Loretz, Oswald. "The *Perfectum Copulativum* in 2 Sm 7,9–11." *Catholic Biblical Quarterly* 23 (1961): 294–96.

Louison-Lassablière, Marie-Joëlle. "La danse du roi David." Pages 127–37 in *Le recours à l'Écriture: Polémique et conciliation du XVe siècle au XVIIe siècle*. Saint-Étienne, France: Publications de l'Université de Saint-Étienne, 2000.

Luck, G. Coleman. "The First Meeting of Saul and Samuel." *Bibliotheca sacra* 124 (1967): 254–61.

Lunn, Nicholas P. "Patterns in the Old Testament Metanarrative: Human Attempts to Fulfill Divine Promises." *Westminster Theological Journal* 72 (2010): 237–49.

Lust, J. "The Story of David and Goliath in Hebrew and Greek." *Ephemerides theologicae lovanienses* 59 (1983): 5–25.

Lyke, Larry L. *King David with the Wise Woman of Tekoa: The Resonance of Tradition in Parabolic Narrative*. Sheffield: Sheffield Academic, 1997.

Mabee, Charles. "David's Judicial Exoneration." *Zeitschrift für die alttestamentliche Wissenschaft* 92 (1980): 89–107.

MacLaurin, E. C. B. "Qrt-ʾAblm." *Palestine Exploration Quarterly* 110 (1978): 113–14.

Magennis, Feidhlimidh T. *First and Second Samuel*. New Collegeville Bible Commentary 8. Collegeville, Minn.: Liturgical Press, 2012.

Malamat, Abraham. "The Danite Migration and the Pan-Israelite Exodus-Conquest: A Biblical Narrative Pattern." *Biblica* 51 (1970): 1–16.

Malone, Andrew S. "God the Illeist: Third-Person Self-References and Trinitarian Hints in the Old Testament." *Journal of the Evangelical Theological Society* 52 (2009): 499–518.

Malul, Meir. "*Lᵉdabbēr baššelî* (2 Sam. 3: 27) 'to Talk Peace.'" *Journal of Hebrew Scriptures* 4, article 8 (2003). http://www.jhsonline.org/Articles/article_30.pdf.

———. "Absalom's Chariot and Fifty Runners (II Sam 15,1) and Hittite Laws § 198: Legal Proceedings in the Ancient Near East." *Zeitschrift für die alttestamentliche Wissenschaft* 122 (2010): 44–52.

Mann, Steven T. "'You're Fired': An Application of Speech Act Theory to 2 Samuel 15.23–16.14." *Journal for the Study of the Old Testament* 33 (2009): 315–34.

Mastéy, Emmanuel. "A Linguistic Inquiry Solves an Ancient Crime: Re-examination of 2 Samuel 4:6." *Vetus Testamentum* 61 (2011): 82–103.

Matthews, Victor H., and Don C. Benjamin. "Amnon and Tamar: A Matter of Honor (2 Samuel 13:1–38)." Pages 339–66 in *Crossing Boundaries and Linking Horizons: Studies in Honor of Michael C. Astour on His 80th Birthday*. Edited by Gordon D. Young, Mark W. Chavalas, and Richard E. Averbeck. Bethesda, Md.: CDL, 1997.

Mattox, Mickey L. "From Faith to the Text and Back Again: Martin Luther on the Trinity in the Old Testament." *Pro ecclesia* 15 (2006): 281–303.

Matzal, Stefan C. "A Word Play in 2 Samuel 4." *Vetus Testamentum* 62 (2012): 462–64.

Mazar, Benjamin. "The Military Élite of King David." *Vetus Testamentum* 13 (1963): 310–20.

Mazar, Eilat. *The Palace of King David: Excavations at the Summit of the City of David: Preliminary Report of Seasons 2005–2007*. Translated by Ben Gordon. Jerusalem: Shoham, 2009.

McCarter, P. Kyle, Jr. *II Samuel: A New Translation with Introduction, Notes and Commentary*. Anchor Bible 9. Garden City, N.Y.: Doubleday, 1984.

———. "The Historical David." *Interpretation* 40 (1986): 117–29.

McCarthy, Dennis J. "2 Samuel 7 and the Structure of the Deuteronomic History." *Journal of Biblical Literature* 84 (1965): 131–38.

McConville, J. G. *God and Earthly Power: An Old Testament Political Theology, Genesis–Kings*. London: T&T Clark, 2006.

McDonough, Sean M. " 'And David Was Old, Advanced in Years': 2 Samuel xxiv 18–25, 1 Kings i 1, and Genesis xxiii–xxiv." *Vetus Testamentum* 49 (1999): 128–31.

McEvenue, Sean E. "The Basis of Empire: A Study of the Succession Narrative." *Ex auditu* 2 (1986): 34–45.

McKay, Heather A. "Lying and Deceit in Families: The Duping of Isaac and Tamar." Pages 28–41 in *The Family in Life and in Death: The Family in Ancient Israel: Sociological and Archaeological Perspectives*. Edited by Patricia Dutcher-Walls. New York: T&T Clark, 2009.

McKenzie, John L. "The Dynastic Oracle: II Samuel 7." *Theological Studies* 8 (1947): 187–218.

———. "Royal Messianism." *Catholic Biblical Quarterly* 19 (1957): 25–52.

McKenzie, Steven L. *King David: A Biography*. New York: Oxford University Press, 2000.

———. "The So-Called Succession Narrative in the Deuteronomistic History." Pages 123–35 in *Die sogenannte Thronfolgegeschichte Davids: Neue Einsichten und Anfragen*. Edited by Albert de Pury and Thomas Römer. Fribourg, Switzerland: Universitätsverlag, 2000.

———. "Why Did David Stay Home? An Exegetical Study of 2 Samuel 11:1." Pages 149–58 in *Raising Up a Faithful Exegete: Essays in Honor of Richard D. Nelson*. Edited by K. L. Noll and Brooks Schramm. Winona Lake, Ind.: Eisenbrauns, 2010.

McLean, Paul D. "The Kaige Text of Reigns: To the Reader." Pages 271–76 in *A New English Translation of the Septuagint and the Other Greek Translations Traditionally Included under That Title*. Edited by Albert Pietersma and Benjamin G. Wright. Oxford: Oxford University Press, 2007.

Merrill, Eugene H. "The 'Accession Year' and Davidic Chronology." *Journal of the Ancient Near Eastern Society* 19 (1989): 101–12.

Mettinger, Tryggve N. D. " 'The Last Words of David': A Study of Structure and Meaning in II Samuel 23:1–7." *Svensk exegetisk årsbok* 41–42 (1977): 147–56.

———. "Cui Bono? The Prophecy of Nathan (2 Sam. 7) as a Piece of Political Rhetoric." *Svensk exegetisk årsbok* 70 (2005): 193–214.

Middendorf, Michael P. *Romans 1–8*. Concordia Commentary. St. Louis: Concordia, 2013.

Milgrom, Jacob. *Leviticus 1–16: A New Translation with Introduction and Commentary*. Anchor Bible 3. New York: Doubleday, 1991.

Miscall, Peter D. "Texts, More Texts, a Textual Reader and a Textual Writer." *Semeia* 69–70 (1995): 247–60.

Mitchell, Christopher W. *The Song of Songs*. Concordia Commentary. St. Louis: Concordia, 2003.

Mohrmann, Christine. "Mulier: À propos de II Reg 1:26." *Vigiliae christianae* 2 (1948): 117–19.

Monson, J., general consultant. *Student Map Manual: Historical Geography of the Bible Lands*. Jerusalem: Pictorial Archive (Near Eastern History) Est., 1979.

Mulder, Martin Jan. "Un euphémisme dans 2 Sam. xii 14?" *Vetus Testamentum* 18 (1968): 108–14.

Muraoka, Takamitsu. *Hebrew/Aramaic Index to the Septuagint: Keyed to the Hatch-Redpath Concordance*. Grand Rapids, Baker, 1998.

Murray, Donald F. "Once Again ʾt ʾḥd šbṭy yśrʾl in II Samuel 7:7." *Revue biblique* 94 (1987): 389–96.

———. "*Mqwm* and the Future of Israel in 2 Samuel vii 10." *Vetus Testamentum* 40 (1990): 298–320.

———. "Under YHWH's Veto: David as Shedder of Blood in Chronicles." *Biblica* 82 (2001): 457–76.

Naʾaman, Nadav. "The List of David's Officers (*Šālîšîm*)." *Vetus Testamentum* 38 (1988): 71–79.

———. "The Kingdom of Ishbaal." *Biblische Notizen* 54 (1990): 33–37.

———. "Ittai the Gittite." *Biblische Notizen* 94 (1998): 22–25.

———. "Sources and Composition in the Biblical History of Edom." Pages 313–20 in *Sefer Moshe: The Moshe Weinfeld Jubilee Volume: Studies in the Bible and the Ancient Near East, Qumran, and Post-Biblical Judaism*. Edited by Chaim Cohen, Avi Hurvitz, and Shalom M. Paul. Winona Lake, Ind.: Eisenbrauns, 2004.

———. "In Search of the Ancient Name of Khirbet Qeiyafa." *Journal of Hebrew Scriptures* 8, article 21 (2008). http://www.jhsonline.org/Articles/article_98.pdf.

———. "The Sanctuary of the Gibeonites Revisited." *Journal of Ancient Near Eastern Religions* 9 (2009): 101–24.

———. "The Interchange between Bible and Archaeology: The Case of David's Palace and the Millo." *Biblical Archaeology Review* 40/1 (January/February 2014): 57–61, 68–69.

Naéh, Shlomo. "A New Suggestion regarding 2 Samuel xxiii 7." *Vetus Testamentum* 46 (1996): 260–65.

Nakarai, Toyozo W. "*Lmh* and *Mduʿ* in the TANAK." *Hebrew Studies* 23 (1982): 45–50.

Neiderhiser, Edward A. "2 Samuel 20:8–10: A Note for a Commentary." *Journal of the Evangelical Theological Society* 24 (1981): 209–10.

Nicol, George G. "Bathsheba, a Clever Woman." *Expository Times* 99 (1988): 360–63.

———. "The Alleged Rape of Bathsheba: Some Observations on Ambiguity in Biblical Narrative." *Journal for the Study of the Old Testament* 73 (1997): 43–54.

———. "David, Abigail and Bathsheba, Nabal and Uriah: Transformations within a Triangle." *Scandinavian Journal of the Old Testament* 12 (1998): 130–45.

Nielsen, Kirsten. "Metaphors and Biblical Theology." Pages 263–73 in *Metaphor in the Hebrew Bible*. Edited by P. van Hecke. Leuven: Leuven University Press, 2005.

Niu, Zhixiong. *"The King Lifted Up His Voice and Wept": David's Mourning in the Second Book of Samuel*. Rome: Pontificia Università Gregoriana, 2013.

Nordling, John G. *Philemon*. Concordia Commentary. St. Louis: Concordia, 2004.

Noth, Martin. *The Deuteronomistic History*. Sheffield: JSOT, 1981.

Nutkowicz, Hélène. "Propos autour de la mort d'un enfant: 2 Samuel xi, 2–xii, 24." *Vetus Testamentum* 54 (2004): 104–18.

O'Ceallaigh, G. C. "'And *So* David Did to *All the Cities* of Ammon.'" *Vetus Testamentum* 12 (1962): 179–89.

Ockinga, Boyo. "A Note on 2 Samuel 18:18." *Biblische Notizen* 31 (1986): 31–34.

———. "The Inviolability of Zion: A Pre-Israelite Tradition?" *Biblische Notizen* 44 (1988): 54–60.

O'Connor, M. "War and Rebel Chants in the Former Prophets." Pages 322–37 in *Fortunate the Eyes That See: Essays in Honor of David Noel Freedman in Celebration of His Seventieth Birthday*. Edited by Astrid B. Beck et al. Grand Rapids: Eerdmans, 1995.

Olmo Lete, G. del. "David's Farewell Oracle (2 Samuel xxiii 1–7): A Literary Analysis." *Vetus Testamentum* 34 (1984): 414–38.

Olyan, Saul M. "Honor, Shame, and Covenant Relations in Ancient Israel and Its Environment." *Journal of Biblical Literature* 115 (1996): 201–18.

———. "'Anyone Blind or Lame Shall Not Enter the House': On the Interpretation of Second Samuel 5:8b." *Catholic Biblical Quarterly* 60 (1998): 218–27.

———. "'Surpassing the Love of Women': Another Look at 2 Samuel 1:26 and the Relationship of David and Jonathan." Pages 7–16, 165–70 in *Authorizing Marriage? Canon, Tradition, and Critique in the Blessing of Same-Sex Unions*. Edited by Mark D. Jordan. Princeton: Princeton University Press, 2006.

Oosthuizen, Rudolph. "2 Sam 14:16: Stop the Wicked Man." *Scriptura* 68 (1999): 13–27.

Orel, Vladimir E. "The Deal of Machpelah." *Bibbia e oriente* 37 (1995): 3–11.

Orlinsky, Harry Meyer. "*Hā-rōqḏím* for *hā-rēqím* in II Samuel 6:20." *Journal of Biblical Literature* 65 (1946): 25–35.

Oswald, Wolfgang. "Is There a Prohibition to Build the Temple in 2 Samuel 7?" Pages 85–89 in *Thinking towards New Horizons*. Edited by Matthias Augustin and Hermann Michael Niemann. Frankfurt am Main: Peter Lang, 2008.

Ota, Michiko. "A Note on 2 Samuel 7." Pages 403–7 in *A Light unto My Path: Old Testament Studies in Honor of Jacob M. Myers*. Edited by Howard N. Bream, Ralph D. Heim, and Carey A. Moore. Philadelphia: Temple University Press, 1974.

O'Toole, Robert F. "Acts 2:30 and the Davidic Covenant of Pentecost." *Journal of Biblical Literature* 102 (1983): 245–58.

Pákozdy, Ladislas Martin. "ʾElḥånån—der frühere Name Davids." *Zeitschrift für die alttestamentliche Wissenschaft* 68 (1956): 257–59.

Park, Song-Mi Suzie. "The Frustration of Wisdom: Wisdom, Counsel, and Divine Will in 2 Samuel 17:1–23." *Journal of Biblical Literature* 128 (2009): 453–67.

Parry, Donald W. "4QSamᵃ (4Q51): A Preliminary Edition of 1 Samuel 25:3–31:4." Pages 58–71 in *The Provo International Conference on the Dead Sea Scrolls: Technological Innovations, New Texts, and Reformulated Issues*. Edited by Donald W. Parry and Eugene Ulrich. Leiden: Brill, 1999.

———. "4QSamᵃ and the Royal Song of Thanksgiving (2 Sam 22//Ps 18)." Pages 146–59 in *Sapiential, Liturgical and Poetical Texts from Qumran*. Edited by Daniel K. Falk, Florentino García Martínez, and Eileen M. Schuller. Leiden: Brill, 2000.

———. "The 'Word' or the 'Enemies' of the Lord? Revisiting the Euphemism in 2 Sam 12:14." Pages 367–78 in *Emanuel: Studies in Hebrew Bible, Septuagint, and Dead Sea Scrolls in Honor of Emanuel Tov*. Edited by Shalom M. Paul et al. Leiden: Brill, 2003.

Parsons, Michael. "Luther and Calvin on Rape: Is the Crime Lost in the Agenda?" *Evangelical Quarterly* 74 (2002): 123–42.

Payne, J. Barton. "1, 2 Chronicles." Pages 301–562 in vol. 4 of *The Expositor's Bible Commentary*. Grand Rapids: Zondervan, 1988.

Penchansky, David. "Four Vignettes from the Life of David: Recollections of the Royal Court." Pages 55–65 in *The Fate of King David: The Past and Present of a Biblical Icon*. Edited by Tod Linafelt, Claudia V. Camp, and Timothy Beal. New York: T&T Clark, 2010.

Perdue, Leo G. "'Is There Anyone Left of the House of Saul … ?': Ambiguity and the Characterization of David in the Succession Narrative." *Journal for the Study of the Old Testament* 30 (1984): 67–84.

Peters, John P. "Critical Notes." *Journal of Biblical Literature* 12 (1893): 47–60.

Peterson, Brian Neil. "The Gibeonite Revenge of 2 Sam 21:1–14: Another Example of David's Darker Side or a Picture of a Shrewd Monarch?" *Journal for the Evangelical Study of the Old Testament* 1 (2012): 201–22.

Petter, Donna. "Foregrounding of the Designation *ʾēšet ʾûriyyâ haḥittî* in II Samuel xi–xii." *Vetus Testamentum* 54 (2004): 403–7.

Phillips, Anthony. "Interpretation of 2 Samuel xii 5–6." *Vetus Testamentum* 16 (1966): 242–44.

Pick, Bernhard. "The Masoretic Piska in the Hebrew Bible." *Journal of the Society of Biblical Literature and Exegesis* 6 (1886): 135–39.

Pietsch, Michael. *"Dieser ist der Sproß Davids …": Studien zur Rezeptionsgeschichte der Nathanverheißung im alttestamentlichen, zwischentestamentlichen und neutestamentlichen Schrifttum.* Neukirchen-Vluyn: Neukirchener Verlag, 2003.

Pinker, Aron. "On the Meaning of קשת נחושה." *Journal of Hebrew Scriptures* 5, article 12 (2005). http://www.jhsonline.org/Articles/article_42.pdf.

Pisano, Stephen. "2 Samuel 5–8 and the Deuteronomist: Textual Criticism or Literary Criticism?" Pages 258–83 in *Israel Constructs Its History: Deuteronomistic Historiography and Recent Research.* Edited by Albert de Pury, Thomas Römer, and Jean-Daniel Macchi. Sheffield: Sheffield Academic, 2000.

Poirier, John C. "David's 'Hatred' for the Lame and the Blind (2 Sam 5.8a)." *Palestine Exploration Quarterly* 138 (2006): 27–33.

Polzin, Robert. "Curses and Kings: A Reading of 2 Samuel 15–16." Pages 201–26 in *The New Literary Criticism and the Hebrew Bible.* Edited by J. Cheryl Exum and David J. A. Clines. Sheffield: JSOT, 1993.

———. *David and the Deuteronomist: A Literary Study of the Deuteronomic History, Part Three: 2 Samuel.* Bloomington: Indiana University Press, 1993.

Porter, Joshua R. "The Interpretation of 2 Samuel 6 and Psalm 132." *Journal of Theological Studies* 5 (1954): 161–73.

Poulssen, N. R. M. "An Hour with Rispah: Some Reflections on 2 Sam 21:10." Pages 185–211 in *Von Kanaan bis Kerala: Festschrift für Prof. Mag. Dr. Dr. J. P. M. van der Ploeg zur Vollendung des siebzigsten Lebensjahres am 4. Juli 1979.* Kevelaer, Germany: Butzon & Bercker, 1982.

Propp, William H. "Kinship in 2 Samuel 13." *Catholic Biblical Quarterly* 55 (1993): 39–53.

Provan, Iain, V. Philips Long, and Tremper Longman III. *A Biblical History of Israel.* Louisville, Ky.: Westminster John Knox, 2003.

Pury, Albert de, Thomas Römer, and Jean-Daniel Macchi, eds. *Israel Constructs Its History: Deuteronomistic Historiography and Recent Research.* Sheffield: Sheffield Academic, 2000.

Pyper, Hugh S. *David as Reader: 2 Samuel 12:1–15 and the Poetics of Fatherhood.* Leiden: Brill, 1996.

———. "Reading David's Mind: Inference, Emotion and the Limits of Language." Pages 73–86 in *Sense and Sensitivity: Essays on Reading the Bible in Memory of Robert Carroll.* Edited by Alastair G. Hunter and Phillip R. Davies. London: Sheffield Academic, 2002.

Qimron, Elisha. "The Lament of David over Abner." Pages 143–47 in vol. 1 of *Birkat Shalom: Studies in the Bible, Ancient Near Eastern Literature, and Postbiblical Judaism Presented to Shalom M. Paul on the Occasion of His Seventieth Birthday.* Edited by Chaim Cohen et al. Winona Lake, Ind.: Eisenbrauns, 2008.

Rand, Herbert. "David and Ahab: A Study of Crime and Punishment." *Jewish Bible Quarterly* 24 (1996): 90–97.

Reich, Ronny, and Eli Shukron. "Light at the End of the Tunnel: Warren's Shaft Theory of David's Conquest Shattered." *Biblical Archaeology Review* 25/1 (January/February 1999): 22–33, 72.

Reinhartz, Adele. "Anonymity and Character in the Books of Samuel." *Semeia* 63 (1993): 117–41.

Reis, Pamela Tamarkin. "Cupidity and Stupidity: Woman's Agency and the 'Rape' of Tamar." *Journal of the Ancient Near Eastern Society* 25 (1997): 43–60.

———. "Killing the Messenger: David's Policy or Politics?" *Journal for the Study of the Old Testament* 31 (2006): 167–91.

Rendsburg, Gary A. "The Northern Origin of 'the Last Words of David' (2 Sam 23:1–7)." *Biblica* 69 (1988): 113–21.

———. "Additional Notes on 'the Last Words of David' (2 Sam 23:1–7)." *Biblica* 70 (1989): 403–8.

Rezetko, Robert. "David over Saul in MT 2 Samuel 6,1–5: An Exercise in Textual and Literary Criticism." Pages 255–71 in *For and against David: Story and History in the Books of Samuel*. Edited by A. Graeme Auld and Erik Eynikel. Leuven: Peeters, 2010.

Richardson, H. Neil. "The Last Words of David: Some Notes on II Samuel 23:1–7." *Journal of Biblical Literature* 90 (1971): 257–66.

Robert, Philippe de. "Juges ou tribus en 2 Samuel vii 7." *Vetus Testamentum* 21 (1971): 116–18.

Rofé, Alexander. "4QSamª in the Light of Historico-Literary Criticism: The Case of 2 Sam 24 and 1 Chr 21." Pages 109–19 in *Biblische und judaistische Studien: Festschrift für Paolo Sacchi*. Edited by Angelo Vivian. Frankfurt am Main: Peter Lang, 1990.

Rook, John. "Making Widows: The Patriarchal Guardian at Work." *Biblical Theology Bulletin* 27 (1997): 10–15.

———. "When Is a Widow Not a Widow? Guardianship Provides an Answer." *Biblical Theology Bulletin* 28 (1998): 4–6.

Rosén, Haiim B. "Arawna—Nom Hittite." *Vetus Testamentum* 5 (1955): 318–20.

Rosenberg, Joel. "The Institutional Matrix of Treachery in 2 Samuel 11." *Semeia* 46 (1989): 103–16.

Rosenblum, William I. "Tamar Times Three." *Jewish Bible Quarterly* 30 (2002): 127–30.

Rosenstock, Bruce. "David's Play: Fertility Rituals and the Glory of God in 2 Samuel 6." *Journal for the Study of the Old Testament* 31 (2006): 63–80.

Rost, Leonhard. *The Succession to the Throne of David.* Translated by Michael D. Rutter and David M. Gunn. Sheffield: Almond, 1982. Translation of *Die Überlieferung von der Thronnachfolge Davids*. Stuttgart: Kohlhammer, 1926.

Rudman, Dominic. "The Patriarchal Narratives in the Books of Samuel." *Vetus Testamentum* 54 (2004): 239–49.

Rudnig, Thilo A. *Davids Thron: Redaktionskritische Studien zur Geschichte von der Thronnachfolge Davids*. Berlin: De Gruyter, 2006.

Sachs, Gerardo G. "David Dances—Michal Scoffs." *Jewish Bible Quarterly* 34 (2006): 260–63.

Sacon, Kiyoshi K. "A Study of the Literary Structure of 'the Succession Narrative.' " Pages 27–54 in *Studies in the Period of David and Solomon and Other Essays*. Edited by Tomoo Ishida. Winona Lake, Ind.: Eisenbrauns, 1982.

Sailhamer, John H. "1 Chronicles 21:1—A Study in Inter-Biblical Interpretation." *Trinity Journal* 10 (1989): 33–48.

Salibi, Kamal S. "The 'Goliath' Problem." *Theological Review* 12 (1991): 3–13.

Sanders, Paul. "Ancient Colon Delimitations: 2 Samuel 22 and Psalm 18." Pages 277–311 in *Delimitation Criticism: A New Tool in Biblical Scholarship*. Edited by Marjo C. A. Korpel and Josef M. Oesch. Assen: Van Gorcum, 2000.

Särkiö, Pekka. " 'The Third Man'—David's Heroes in 2 Sam 23,8–39." *Scandinavian Journal of the Old Testament* 7 (1993): 108–24.

Sawyer, John F. A. "King David's Treatment of the Ammonites (2 Samuel 12:31)." Pages 165–78 in *Law, Morality, and Religion: Global Perspectives*. Edited by Alan Watson. Berkeley: University of California Press, 1996.

Schipper, Jeremy. "Reconsidering the Imagery of Disability in 2 Samuel 5:8b." *Catholic Biblical Quarterly* 67 (2005): 422–34.

———. "Did David Overinterpret Nathan's Parable in 2 Samuel 12:1–6?" *Journal of Biblical Literature* 126 (2007): 383–91.

———. "Disabling Israelite Leadership: 2 Samuel 6:23 and Other Images of Disability in the Deuteronomistic History." Pages 103–13 in *This Abled Body: Rethinking Disabilities in Biblical Studies*. Edited by Hector Avalos, Sarah J. Melcher, and Jeremy Schipper. Atlanta: Society of Biblical Literature, 2007.

Schreiner, David B. "The Election and Divine Choice of Zion/Jerusalem." *Journal for the Evangelical Study of the Old Testament* 1 (2012): 147–65.

Schulte, Leah Rediger, and Tammi J. Schneider. "The Absence of the Deity in Rape Scenes of the Hebrew Bible." Pages 21–33 in *The Presence and Absence of God*. Edited by Ingolf U. Dalferth. Tübingen: Mohr Siebeck, 2009.

Schwartz, Regina M. "Adultery in the House of David: The Metanarrative of Biblical Scholarship and the Narratives of the Bible." *Semeia* 54 (1991): 35–55.

Seebass, Horst. "Ephraim in 2 Sam xiii 23." *Vetus Testamentum* 14 (1964): 497–500.

Seiler, Stefan. *Die Geschichte von der Thronfolge Davids (2 Sam 9–20; 1 Kön 1–2): Untersuchungen zur Literarkritik und Tendenz*. Berlin: De Gruyter, 1998.

Sergi, Omer. "The Composition of Nathan's Oracle to David (2 Samuel 7:1–17) as a Reflection of Royal Judahite Ideology." *Journal of Biblical Literature* 129 (2010): 261–79.

Shalom-Guy, Hava. "Three-Way Intertextuality: Some Reflections of Abimelech's Death at Thebez in Biblical Narrative." *Journal for the Study of the Old Testament* 34 (2010): 419–32.

Shanks, Hershel. "The City of David after Five Years of Digging." *Biblical Archaeology Review* 11/6 (November/December 1985): 22–38.

Shanks, Hershel, ed. "Has Jerusalem's Millo Been Found?" *Biblical Archaeology Review* 8/4 (July/August 1982): 6–7.

Sharon, Diane M. "When Fathers Refuse to Eat: The Trope of Rejecting Food and Drink in Biblical Narrative." *Semeia* 86 (1999): 135–48.

Shea, William H. "Chiasmus and the Structure of David's Lament." *Journal of Biblical Literature* 105 (1986): 13–25.

Shedinger, Robert F. "Who Killed Goliath? History and Legend in Biblical Narrative." Pages 27–38 in *Who Killed Goliath? Reading the Bible with Heart and Mind*. Valley Forge, Pa.: Judson, 2001.

Shemesh, Yael. "Lies by Prophets and Other Lies in the Hebrew Bible." *Journal of the Ancient Near Eastern Society of Columbia University* 29 (2002): 81–95.

———. "Suicide in the Bible." *Jewish Bible Quarterly* 37 (2009): 157–68.

Shimron, Aryeh. "Warren's Shaft: No, It Really Was Not Used to Draw Water." *Biblical Archaeology Review* 30/4 (July/August 2004): 14–15.

Shimron, Aryeh, Avraham Faust, and Hershel Shanks. "Did Ancient Jerusalem Draw Water through Warren's Shaft?" *Biblical Archaeology Review* 33/2 (March/April 2007): 64–69, 77.

Simon, Uriel. "The Poor Man's Ewe-Lamb: An Example of a Juridical Parable." *Biblica* 48 (1967): 207–42.

Simpson, Timothy Frederick. "Paradigm Shift Happens: Intertextuality and a Reading of 2 Samuel 16:5–14." *Proceedings of the Eastern Great Lakes and Midwest Biblical Societies* 17 (1997): 55–69.

———. *Not "Who Is on the Lord's Side?" but "Whose Side Is the Lord On?" Contesting Claims and Divine Inscrutability in 2 Samuel 16:5–14*. New York: Peter Lang, 2014.

Singer, Itamar. "The Hittites and the Bible Revisited." Pages 723–56 in *"I Will Speak the Riddles of Ancient Times": Archaeological and Historical Studies in Honor of Amihai Mazar on the Occasion of His Sixtieth Birthday*. Edited by Aren M. Maeir and Pierre de Miroschedji. 2 vols. Winona Lake, Ind.: Eisenbrauns, 2006.

Skehan, Patrick William. "Joab's Census: How Far North (2 Sm 24,6)?" *Catholic Biblical Quarterly* 31 (1969): 42–49.

Slotki, I. W. *Chronicles: Hebrew Text and English Translation with an Introduction and Commentary*. Soncino Books of the Bible. London: Soncino, 1952.

Smelik, Klaas A. D. "The Ark Narrative Reconsidered." Pages 128–44 in *New Avenues in the Study of the Old Testament*. Edited by A. S. van der Woude. Leiden: Brill, 1989.

Smith, Henry Preserved. *A Critical and Exegetical Commentary on the Books of Samuel*. International Critical Commentary. Edinburgh: T&T Clark, 1899.

Smith, Jenny. "The Discourse Structure of the Rape of Tamar (2 Samuel 13:1–22)." *Vox evangelica* 20 (1990): 21–42.

Smith, Richard G. *The Fate of Justice and Righteousness during David's Reign: Rereading the Court History and Its Ethics according to 2 Samuel 8:15b–20:26*. New York: T&T Clark, 2009.

Soggin, J. Alberto. " 'Wacholderholz' 2 Sam vi 5a gleich 'Schlaghölzer,' 'Klappern'?" *Vetus Testamentum* 14 (1964): 374–77.

Sonnet, Jean-Pierre. "God's Repentance and 'False Starts' in Biblical History (Genesis 6–9; Exodus 32–34; 1 Samuel 15 and 2 Samuel 7)." Pages 469–94 in *Congress Volume Ljubljana 2007*. Edited by André Lemaire. Leiden: Brill, 2010.

Speiser, E. A. "An Analogue to 2 Sam 1:21: ʾAqht 1:44–45." *Journal of Biblical Literature* 69 (1950): 377–78.

Spielman, Larry W. "David's Abuse of Power." *Word and World* 19 (1999): 251–59.

Spina, Frank A. "Eli's Seat: The Transition from Priest to Prophet in 1 Samuel 1–4." *Journal for the Study of the Old Testament* 62 (1994): 67–75.

Stager, Lawrence E. "The Archaeology of the East Slope of Jerusalem and the Terraces of the Kidron." *Journal of Near Eastern Studies* 41 (1982): 111–21.

Standaert, Benôit. " 'N'avez-vous pas lu ce que fit David ... ?' (Mc 2,25): Étude biblique à partir de 2 Samuel 19,41–44." *Irénikon* 84 (2011): 244–62.

Steinmann, Andrew E. *Intermediate Biblical Hebrew: A Reference Grammar with Charts and Exercises*. St. Louis: Concordia, 2007, 2009.

———. *Daniel*. Concordia Commentary. St. Louis: Concordia, 2008.

———. *Proverbs*. Concordia Commentary. St. Louis: Concordia, 2009.

———. *Ezra and Nehemiah*. Concordia Commentary. St. Louis: Concordia, 2010.

———. *From Abraham to Paul: A Biblical Chronology*. St. Louis: Concordia, 2011.

———. "What Did David Understand about the Promises in the Davidic Covenant?" *Bibliotheca sacra* 171 (2014): 19–29.

———. *1 Samuel*. Concordia Commentary. St. Louis: Concordia, 2016.

Stoebe, Hans Joachim. "Die Einnahme Jerusalems und der Ṣinnôr." *Zeitschrift des deutschen Palästina-Vereins* 73 (1957): 73–99.

———. "David und Uria: Überlegungen zur Überlieferung von 2 Sam 11." *Biblica* 67 (1986): 388–96.

Stokes, Ryan E. "The Devil Made David Do It ... Or *Did* He? The Nature, Identity, and Literary Origins of the *Satan* in 1 Chronicles 21:1." *Journal of Biblical Literature* 128 (2009): 91–106.

Tan, Nancy. "The Chronicler's 'Obed-edom': A Foreigner and/or a Levite?" *Journal for the Study of the Old Testament* 32 (2007): 217–30.

Taylor, Bernard A. "The Old Greek Text of Reigns: To the Reader." Pages 244–48 in *A New English Translation of the Septuagint and the Other Greek Translations Traditionally Included under That Title.* Edited by Albert Pietersma and Benjamin G. Wright. Oxford: Oxford University Press, 2007.

Thiemann, Ronald F. "Radiance and Obscurity in Biblical Narrative." Pages 21–41 in *Scriptural Authority and Narrative Interpretation.* Edited by Garrett Green. Philadelphia: Fortress, 1987.

Thompson, J. A. *1, 2 Chronicles.* New American Commentary 9. Nashville: Broadman & Holman, 1994.

Thompson, Thomas L. "If David Had Not Climbed the Mount of Olives." *Biblical Interpretation* 8 (2000): 42–58.

Tidwell, N. L. "The Linen Ephod: 1 Sam. ii 18 and 2 Sam. vi 14." *Vetus Testamentum* 24 (1974): 505–7.

Tkacz, Catherine Brown. "A Biblical Woman's Paraphrase of King David: Susanna's Refusal of the Elders." *Downside Review* 128 (2010): 39–51.

Toeg, A. "A Textual Note on 1 Samuel xiv 41." *Vetus Testamentum* 19 (1969): 493–98.

Toorn, Karel van der, and Cees Houtman. "David and the Ark." *Journal of Biblical Literature* 113 (1994): 209–31.

Tov, Emanuel. *The Text-Critical Use of the Septuagint in Biblical Research.* Jerusalem: Simor, 1981.

———. *Textual Criticism of the Hebrew Bible.* 2d rev. ed. Minneapolis: Fortress, 2001.

Tsevat, Matitiahu. "Ishbosheth and Congeners: The Names and Their Study." *Hebrew Union College Annual* 46 (1975): 71–87.

Tsumura, David Toshio. "Tense and Aspect of Hebrew Verbs in 2 Samuel 7:8–16—from the Point of View of Discourse Grammar." *Vetus Testamentum* 60 (2010): 641–54.

Ulrich, Eugene Charles, Jr. *The Qumran Text of Samuel and Josephus.* Missoula, Mont.: Scholars, 1978.

———. "David, the Plague, and the Angel: 2 Samuel 24 Revisited." Pages 63–80 in *After Qumran: Old and Modern Editions of the Biblical Texts: The Historical Books.* Edited by Hans Ausloos, Bénédicte Lemmelijn, and Julio Trebolle Barrera. Leuven: Peeters, 2012.

Van Seters, John. "Love and Death in the Court History of David." Pages 121–24 in *Love and Death in the Ancient Near East: Essays in Honor of Marvin H. Pope.* Edited by John H. Marks and Robert M. Good. Guilford, Conn: Four Quarters, 1987.

———. "The Court History and DtrH: Conflicting Perspectives on the House of David." Pages 70–93 in *Die sogenannte Thronfolgegeschichte Davids: Neue Einsichten und Anfragen.* Edited by Albert de Pury and Thomas Römer. Fribourg, Switzerland: Universitätsverlag, 2000.

———. "The 'Shared Text' of Samuel–Kings and Chronicles Re-Examined." Pages 503–15 in *Reflection and Refraction: Studies in Biblical Historiography in Honour of A. Graeme Auld*. Edited by Robert Rezetko, Timothy H. Lim, and W. Brian Aucker. Leiden: Brill, 2006.

———. "David and the Gibeonites." *Zeitschrift für die alttestamentliche Wissenschaft* 123 (2011): 535–52.

Van Wijk-Bos, Johanna W. H. *Reading Samuel: A Literary and Theological Commentary*. Macon, Ga.: Smyth & Helwys, 2011.

Vanderhooft, David. "Dwelling beneath the Sacred Place: A Proposal for Reading 2 Samuel 7:10." *Journal of Biblical Literature* 118 (1999): 625–33.

VanGemeren, Willem A. "'Abbā' in the Old Testament?" *Journal of the Evangelical Theological Society* 31 (1988): 385–98.

Vermeylen, Jacques. " 'Comment sont tombés les héros?' Une lecture de 1 S 31 et 2 S 1,1–2,7." Pages 99–116 in *Analyse Narrative et Bible*. Edited by Camille Focant and André Wénin. Leuven: Leuven University Press, 2005.

Wahl, Otto. *Die Sacra-Parallela-Zitate aus den Büchern Josua, Richter, 1/2 Samuel, 3/4 Könige sowie 1/2 Chronik*. Göttingen: Vandenhoeck & Ruprecht, 2004.

Washburn, David L. "The King Is Weeping: A Textual/Grammatical Note on 2 Sam 19:2." *TC: A Journal of Biblical Textual Criticism* 1 (1996). http://purl.org/TC/vol01/Washburn1996.html.

Watson, Wilfred G. E. "David Ousts the City Ruler of Jebus." *Vetus Testamentum* 20 (1970): 501–2.

Wee, John Zhu-En. "Maacah and Ish-Tob." *Journal for the Study of the Old Testament* 30 (2005): 191–99.

Weingreen, Jacob. "The Rebellion of Absalom." *Vetus Testamentum* 19 (1969): 263–66.

Weir, J. Emmette. "The Poor Are Powerless: A Response to R. J. Coggins." *Expository Times* 100 (1988): 13–15.

Weiss-Rosmarin, Trude. "Note on II Sam. 14:27." *Journal of Biblical Literature* 52 (1933): 261–62.

Wellhausen, Julius. *Der Text der Bücher Samuelis untersucht*. Göttingen: Vandenhoeck and Ruprecht, 1871.

Wenham, Gordon J. "*Bᵉtûlāh* 'A Girl of Marriageable Age.' " *Vetus Testamentum* 22 (1972): 326–48.

———. "Were David's Sons Priests?" *Zeitschrift für die alttestamentliche Wissenschaft* 87 (1975): 79–82.

Wesselius, J. W. "Joab's Death and the Central Theme of the Succession Narrative (2 Samuel ix–1 Kings ii)." *Vetus Testamentum* 40 (1990): 336–51.

West, Gerald O. "Reading on the Boundaries: Reading 2 Samuel 21:1–14 with Rizpah." *Scriptura* 63 (1997): 527–37.

Wharton, James A. "A Plausible Tale: Story and Theology in II Samuel 9–20, I Kings 1–2." *Interpretation* 35 (1981): 341–54.

White, Ellen. "Michal the Misinterpreted." *Journal for the Study of the Old Testament* 31 (2007): 451–64.

Wiggins, Steve A. "Between Heaven and Earth: Absalom's Dilemma." *Journal of Northwest Semitic Languages* 23 (1997): 73–81.

Wilch, John R. *Ruth*. Concordia Commentary. St. Louis: Concordia, 2006.

Willey, Patricia Tull. "The Importunate Woman of Tekoa and How She Got Her Way." Pages 115–31 in *Reading between Texts: Intertextuality and the Hebrew Bible*. Edited by Danna Nolan Fewell. Louisville, Ky.: Westminster/John Knox, 1992.

Williamson, H. G. M. *1 and 2 Chronicles*. New Century Bible Commentary. Grand Rapids: Eerdmans, 1982.

Willi-Plein, Ina. "Keine Eroberung Jerusalems: Zu Stellung und Bedeutung von 2 Sam 5 in der Davidshausgeschichte der Samuelbücher." Pages 213–33 in *For and against David: Story and History in the Books of Samuel*. Edited by A. Graeme Auld and Erik Eynikel. Leuven: Peeters, 2010.

Willis, John T. "David and Zion in the Theology of the Deuteronomistic History: Theological Ideas in 2 Samuel 5–7." Pages 125–40 in *David and Zion: Biblical Studies in Honor of J. J. M. Roberts*. Edited by Bernard F. Batto and Kathryn L. Roberts. Winona Lake, Ind.: Eisenbrauns, 2004.

Willis, Timothy M. " 'Rest All Around from All His Enemies' (2 Samuel 7:1b): The Occasion for David's Offer to Build a Temple." Pages 129–47 in *Raising Up a Faithful Exegete: Essays in Honor of Richard D. Nelson*. Edited by K. L. Noll and Brooks Schramm. Winona Lake, Ind.: Eisenbrauns, 2010.

Winger, Thomas M. *Ephesians*. Concordia Commentary. St. Louis: Concordia, 2015.

Wolde, E. J. van. "In Words and Pictures: The Sun in 2 Samuel 12:7–12." *Biblical Interpretation* 11 (2003): 259–78.

Wong, Gregory. "Ehud and Joab: Separated at Birth?" *Vetus Testamentum* 56 (2006): 399–412.

Wood, Bryant G. "Hittites and Hethites: A Proposed Solution to an Etymological Conundrum." *Journal of the Evangelical Theological Society* 54 (2011): 239–50.

Wright, David P. "Music and Dance in 2 Samuel 6." *Journal of Biblical Literature* 121 (2002): 201–25.

Wyatt, Nicolas. " 'Araunah the Jebusite' and the Throne of David." *Studia theologica* 39 (1985): 39–53.

———. "David's Census and the Tripartite Theory." *Vetus Testamentum* 40 (1990): 352–60.

Yadin, Yigael. "Goliath's Javelin and the מנור ארגים." *Palestine Exploration Quarterly* 87 (1955): 58–69.

———. "Some Aspects of the Strategy of Ahab and David (I Kings 20; II Sam. 11)." *Biblica* 36 (1955): 332–51.

———. *The Art of Warfare in Biblical Lands in the Light of Archaeological Study.* Translated by M. Pearlman. 2 vols. New York: McGraw Hill, 1963.

Yaron, Reuven. "The Coptos Decree and 2 Sam xii 14." *Vetus Testamentum* 9 (1959): 89–91.

Yee, Gale A. "The Anatomy of Biblical Parody: The Dirge Form in 2 Samuel 1 and Isaiah 14." *Catholic Biblical Quarterly* 50 (1988): 565–86.

———. "'Fraught with Background': Literary Ambiguity in II Samuel 11." *Interpretation* 42 (1988): 240–53.

Yeivin, Israel. *Introduction to the Tiberian Masorah.* Translated and edited by E. J. Revell. Missoula, Mont.: Scholars, 1980.

Young, Theron. "Psalm 18 and 2 Samuel 22: Two Versions of the Same Song." Pages 53–69 in *Seeking Out the Wisdom of the Ancients: Essays Offered to Honor Michael V. Fox on the Occasion of His Sixty-Fifth Birthday.* Edited by Ronald L. Troxel, Kelvin G. Friebel, and Dennis R. Magary. Winona Lake, Ind.: Eisenbrauns, 2005.

Zahavi-Ely, Naama. "'Turn Right or Left': Literary Use of Dialect in 2 Samuel 14:19?" *Hebrew Studies* 53 (2012): 43–53.

Zapf, David L. "How Are the Mighty Fallen: A Study of 2 Samuel 1:17–27." *Grace Theological Journal* 5 (1984): 95–126.

Zehnder, Markus. "Observations on the Relationship between David and Jonathan and the Debate on Homosexuality." *Westminster Theological Journal* 69 (2007): 127–74.

Ziegler, Yael. "'As the Lord Lives and as Your Soul Lives': An Oath of Conscious Deference." *Vetus Testamentum* 58 (2008): 117–30.

Zipor, Moshe A., and L. J. Schramm. "Talebearers, Peddlers, Spies, and Converts: The Adventures of the Biblical and Post-Biblical Roots רגל and רכל." *Hebrew Studies* 46 (2005): 129–44.

Zorell, Franz. "Zu Ps. 18, 27 (= 2 Sm. 22, 27)." *Biblica* 9 (1928): 224.

Zwickel, Wolfgang. "Gibeat-Amma und Giach (2 Sam 2,24)." *Biblische Notizen* 69 (1993): 29–31.

David's Genealogy

(Men are in plain type; women are in *italics*; dotted lines indicate marriages.)

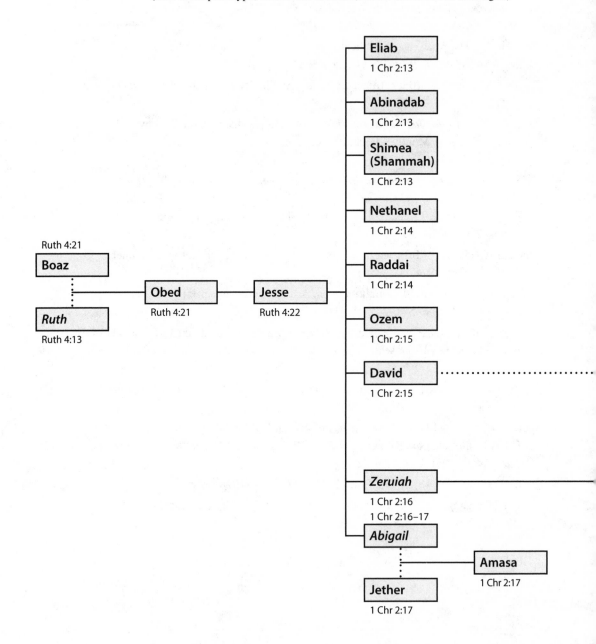

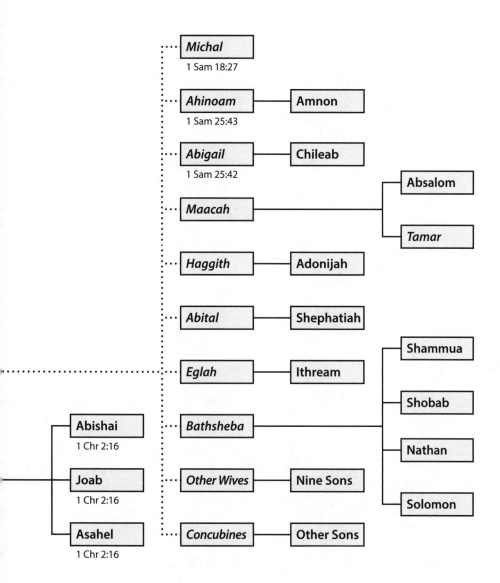

For David's seventh brother, see the commentary on 1 Sam 16:8–10.

For David's sons, see 2 Sam 3:2–5; 5:13–16; 1 Chr 3:1–9; 14:3–7.

The sons of David and Bathsheba are shown in the order given in 2 Sam 5:14;
1 Chr 3:5; 14:4, although Solomon was the oldest.

2 Samuel 1:1–4:12

Transition: David as King of Judah

David Learns of Saul's Death

Translation

1   ¹After the death of Saul, when David had returned from striking the Amalekites, David stayed in Ziklag for two days. ²On the third day, a man unexpectedly came from Saul's camp. His clothes were torn, and dirt was on his head. When he came to David, he fell to the ground and bowed. ³David said to him, "From where have you come?"

He said, "I escaped from the camp of Israel."

⁴David said to him, "What happened? Tell me."

He said, "The troops fled from the battle, and many of the troops also fell and died. In addition, Saul and his son Jonathan are dead."

⁵David said to the young man who had reported to him, "How do you know that Saul and his son Jonathan are dead?"

⁶The young man who had reported to him said, "I just happened to be on Mount Gilboa. There was Saul leaning on his spear. The chariots and chariot commanders were bearing down on him. ⁷He turned around, saw me, and called to me. I said, 'I'm here.'

⁸"He said to me, 'Who are you?'

"I said to him, 'I am an Amalekite.'

⁹"He said, 'Please stand over me and kill me, because I am in the throes of death, but I'm still alive.'

¹⁰"So I stood over him and killed him, because I knew that he could not live after he had fallen. Then I took the crown that was on his head and the bracelet on his arm and brought them here to my lord."

¹¹Then David took hold of his clothes and tore them, and all his men with him also [did this]. ¹²They mourned, wept, and fasted until evening for Saul, his son Jonathan, Yahweh's troops, and the house of Israel, because they had fallen in battle.

¹³David said to the young man who had reported to him, "Where are you from?"

He said, "I am the son of a resident alien, an Amalekite."

¹⁴David said to him, "Why weren't you afraid to raise your hand to destroy Yahweh's anointed one?" ¹⁵So David called one of the young men and said, "Come here, execute him." So he struck him, and he died. ¹⁶David said to him, "Your blood is on your head, because your mouth testified against you, 'I killed Yahweh's anointed one.'"

¹⁷Then David sang this lament concerning Saul and his son Jonathan ¹⁸and said to teach the Judahites "A Bow." It is written in the Book of the Upright:

[19]"Your beauty, O Israel, is slain on your heights!
How the mighty men have fallen!

[20]"Do not report [it] in Gath.
Do not proclaim news in streets of Ashkelon.
    Otherwise, the daughters of the Philistines will rejoice.
    Otherwise, the daughters of the uncircumcised will celebrate.

[21]"Mountains of Gilboa, may there be no dew and no rain on you,
nor fields producing grain offerings,
    because there the shield of mighty men was defiled,
    the shield of Saul, no longer anointed with oil.

[22]"From the blood of slain men,
from the fat of mighty men
    the bow of Jonathan did not turn away,
    and the sword of Saul did not come back empty.
[23]Saul and Jonathan were the beloved and the delightful in life,
and in their death they were not separated.
    They were swifter than eagles;
    they were mightier than lions.

[24]"Daughters of Israel, weep for Saul,
    who clothed you in scarlet with luxurious garments,
    who provided the gold jewelry on your clothes.

[25]"How the mighty men have fallen in the midst of the battle!
Jonathan is slain on your heights.
[26]I am in distress for you, Jonathan, my brother.
    You were quite delightful to me.
    Your love for me was more wonderful than women's love.

[27]"How the mighty men have fallen!
Weapons of war have perished!"

Textual Notes

1:1 וַיְהִי—The portion of the book of Samuel that we call 2 Samuel begins with the same verb as the book itself; see the first textual note on 1 Sam 1:1.[1]

מֵהַכּוֹת—This means "from striking." The Hiphil (H) of נָכָה is common throughout Samuel, with various nuances that include "attack," "defeat," and "slay." See the fourth textual note on 1 Sam 4:2 and the third textual note on 1 Sam 4:8.[2]

---

[1]   Steinmann, *1 Samuel*, 42.

[2]   Steinmann, *1 Samuel*, 120, 121.

הָעֲמָלֵק—The translation follows a few Masoretic manuscripts and the Syriac,[3] which have the gentilic form הָעֲמָלֵקִי, "the Amalekite(s)." The majority of Masoretic manuscripts read הָעֲמָלֵק, "the Amalek," in agreement with the LXX, τὸν Ἀμαληκ. But that reading is difficult and suspect because הָעֲמָלֵק occurs nowhere else in the OT.

יָמִים שְׁנָיִם:—Literally this means "days, two." The dual form of the numeral follows the plural form of the noun (Joüon, § 142 c). This unusual word order appears elsewhere only in 2 Chr 21:19.

1:2 וְהִנֵּה—This particle, traditionally rendered as "behold," is often used to introduce something new and unexpected (*HALOT*, 6). Here it is translated as "unexpectedly." See also 1 Sam 19:16; 30:3.

מִן־הַמַּחֲנֶה מֵעִם שָׁאוּל—These two prepositional phrases, literally "from the camp, from with Saul," form a hendiadys: "from Saul's camp." The LXX reads ἐκ τῆς παρεμβολῆς ἐκ τοῦ λαοῦ Σαουλ, reading the unpointed Hebrew מעם as מֵעָם, "from the people," instead of מֵעִם, "from with."

וַיִּשְׁתָּחוּ:—"And (he) bowed." For the Hishtaphel of חָוָה, "to bow down, worship," see the third textual note on 1 Sam 1:3.[4]

1:3 אֵי מִזֶּה—This means "from where?" This idiom, literally "where from this (place)?" (see Joüon, § 102 i), also appears in 1 Sam 25:11; 30:13; 2 Sam 1:13; 15:2.

1:4 הַגֶּד־נָא לִי—Literally "report, please, to me," this is translated as "tell me." הַגֶּד is the Hiphil (H) masculine singular imperative of נָגַד, "to declare, announce, make known." Subsequently the author will use the Hiphil participle of this verb with the definite article, הַמַּגִּיד, to refer to this man as הַנַּעַר הַמַּגִּיד לוֹ, "the young man who had reported to him [to David]" (1:5, 6, 13). This verb recurs as a negated Hiphil imperfect in the negative command אַל־תַּגִּידוּ, "do not report," in 1:20.

אֲשֶׁר־נָס הָעָם—"The troops fled." Direct speech may be introduced by אֲשֶׁר, as also in 1 Sam 15:20 (*HALOT*, B b; GKC, § 157 c). While הָעָם is often translated as "the people," in military contexts it denotes "the troops." See the first textual note on 1 Sam 4:3[5] and also 2 Sam 2:27–30.

הַרְבֵּה—The Hiphil (H) infinitive absolute of רָבָה can be used as a noun (Waltke-O'Connor, § 35.3.3a; BDB, Hiphil, 1 e (5)): "many."

1:5 הַנַּעַר—The noun, "young man," recurs in 1:6, 13, 15. The author engaged in skillful wordplay on it earlier in the book; see the commentary on 1 Sam 2:12–17 and the first textual note on 1 Sam 3:1.[6]

אֵיךְ—"How?" Here this interrogative is used for a true question (Waltke-O'Connor, § 18.4d, including example 18). Elsewhere it can be exclamatory; see the third textual note on 1:19.

מֵת שָׁאוּל וִיהוֹנָתָן בְּנוֹ:—"Saul and his son Jonathan are dead." Here the verb מֵת is first in the clause and is singular, in agreement with its nearest subject noun, שָׁאוּל, even

---

[3] See McCarter, *II Samuel*, 56.

[4] Steinmann, *1 Samuel*, 44.

[5] Steinmann, *1 Samuel*, 120.

[6] Steinmann, *1 Samuel*, 87, 109.

though it has a compound (plural) subject, שָׁאוּל וִיהוֹנָתָן. This construction emphasizes Saul more than Jonathan, suggesting that David was most concerned about the fallen king. Contrast 1:4, where, in the young man's speech (translated identically), the verb is last and is plural, in agreement with its compound subject, שָׁאוּל וִיהוֹנָתָן בְּנוֹ מֵתוּ, suggesting that, aside from Saul being first in the word order, the young man considered the king's importance to be more comparable to that of his son.

1:6 נִקְרֹא נִקְרֵ֫יתִי—"I just happened to be." This construction enables the Amalekite to claim that he had an encounter with Saul by random chance.[7] This was recognized early in the history of the interpretation of this text as shown by the LXX's περιπτώματι περιέπεσον, "by accident I encountered." The Niphal (N) infinitive absolute is followed by a Niphal perfect first person singular of the same verb, which can be spelled either קָרָא or קָרָה. Forms of final א verbs often interchange with forms of final ה verbs (see Joüon, § 79 l). The first form, with a final א, is most readily identified as the verb קָרָא II, "to happen; to meet," while the second form, with the vowel letter יִ-, fits the pattern of קָרָה.

בְּהַר הַגִּלְבֹּ֫עַ—"On Mount Gilboa." Mount Gilboa is modern Jebel Fuquʿah on the eastern edge of the Plain of Esdraelon.

וְהִנֵּה שָׁאוּל נִשְׁעָן עַל־חֲנִיתוֹ—"There was Saul leaning on his spear." The Amalekite's wording may be deliberately ambiguous to conceal what he actually did. The verb שָׁעַן, which is used only in the Niphal (N), can refer to "leaning" on something for support to keep oneself upright (e.g., Judg 16:26; 2 Ki 5:18; 7:2; Job 8:15), so this statement might mean that Saul remained standing, using his spear as support. However, in light of 1:9–10, the wording could indicate that, according to the Amalekite, Saul had pierced himself by falling on his own spear, a claim that would be inconsistent with 1 Sam 31:4–5. See further the commentary below as well as the commentary on 1 Sam 31:4–5.[8]

וּבַעֲלֵי הַפָּרָשִׁים—The plural of the noun פָּרָשׁ, with רֶכֶב, "chariot," denotes a team of horses for a chariot (*HALOT*, 1), so this literally means "and the masters of the teams of horses." It is translated as "and chariot commanders."

הִדְבִּקֻֽהוּ:—"They were bearing down on him." This is a Hiphil (H) perfect of דָּבַק, "to cling to," with a third masculine singular pronominal suffix. In the Hiphil דָּבַק denotes overtaking someone or something, as also in 1 Sam 14:22; 31:2 (*HALOT*, Hiphil, 1).

1:8 וָאֹמַר—"(And) I said" is the reading of the Qere, in agreement with the LXX (καὶ εἶπα). The Kethib is וַיֹּאמֶר, "and he said."

1:9 וּמֹתְתֵ֫נִי—"And kill me." This is the Polel (D) masculine singular imperative of מוּת, "to die." Its Polel has a causative meaning, "to kill," as does its Hiphil (H), but its Polel refers to finishing off someone who is already mortally wounded, as again in 2 Sam 1:10, 16 and previously in 1 Sam 14:13; 17:51. See the second textual note on 1 Sam 14:13.[9]

---

[7] Kleven, "Rhetoric and Narrative Deception," 63.

[8] Steinmann, *1 Samuel*, 569.

[9] Steinmann, *1 Samuel*, 249.

אֲחָזַנִי הַשָּׁבָץ—"I am in the throes of death." The subject noun, שָׁבָץ, is a hapax legomenon whose precise meaning is unknown, but it probably means something like "cramp" or "agony" (*DCH*). If so, this clause literally says "the death spasm [?] has seized me."

כִּי־כָל־עוֹד נַפְשִׁי בִּי:—"But I'm still alive" is literally "for all yet my life is in me." Cf. Job 27:3: כִּי־כָל־עוֹד נִשְׁמָתִי בִי, "for all yet [as long as] my breath is in me." Despite the intervening word עוֹד, the noun in construct, כָל, may go with נַפְשִׁי, "all of my life." Alternatively, כָל may function adverbially: "because my life is yet *wholly* in me" (GKC, § 128 e; emphasis added).

1:10 נְפָלוֹ—"He had fallen." Here the Qal (G) infinitive construct of נָפַל with a suffix is pointed with *hireq*, -נְ, whereas the identical word was pointed with *qamets*, נָפְלוֹ, in 1 Sam 29:3. See Joüon, § 65 b.

1:11 וַיַּחֲזֵק דָּוִד בִּבְגָדָיו וַיִּקְרָעֵם—"Then David took hold of his clothes and tore them." For the Hiphil (H) of חָזַק, which takes the preposition בְּ, "take hold of," see the first textual note on 1 Sam 15:27,[10] a verse that also includes קָרַע, "to tear." See also 2 Sam 2:16; 13:11. The Qere בִּבְגָדָיו, "his clothes/garments," is plural (with the preposition בְּ and a suffix), which agrees with the plural pronominal suffix on the verb וַיִּקְרָעֵם, "and he tore them," and with the LXX, τῶν ἱματίων αὐτοῦ. The Kethib is the singular בִּבְגָדוֹ, "his garment."

1:12 בֶּחָרֶב:—Literally "by the sword," this is translated as "in battle." The form of the noun חֶרֶב with the definite article and the preposition בְּ is pausal. The non-pausal form is בַּחֶרֶב, which appears in 3:29; 12:9; 20:10.

1:13 אִישׁ גֵּר—Literally "a man, a resident alien," this means "a resident alien." "When two or more nouns or nominal phrases are used in sequence and have the same referents and syntactic function, the trailing noun(s) are said to be *in apposition* to the first noun. ... The second noun may restrict the meaning of the first noun by further defining it as a group contained within the first noun."[11] Similar examples are אִישׁ כֹּהֵן, literally "a man, a priest," meaning "a priest" (Lev 21:9); אִשָּׁה־אַלְמָנָה, "a woman, a widow," meaning "a widow" (2 Sam 14:5; 1 Ki 7:14; 11:26; 17:9, 10); אִישׁ עֲמָלֵקִי, "a man, an Amalekite," meaning "an Amalekite" (1 Sam 30:13); and אִישׁ־נַעַר, "a man, a young man," meaning "a young man" (used collectively in 1 Sam 30:17).

1:15 פְּגַע־בּוֹ—"Execute him." The verb is the Qal (G) imperative of פָּגַע, "to meet," which can have the nuance of meeting someone in kindness (BDB, 2), or, oppositely, as here, to "fall upon" or "strike" someone (see BDB, 3). Hubbard has argued that this word is not simply a synonym for killing or slaying but is specifically used in legal contexts to denote execution.[12] See also the judicial idioms in the next two textual notes.

1:16 דָּמְךָ עַל־רֹאשֶׁךָ—"Your blood is on your head." This juridical idiom signifies the culpability of the slain person; the cause of his condemnation to death is his own sin (see Josh 2:19; 1 Ki 2:32–33, 37; Ezek 33:4). The Qere דָּמְךָ has the noun דָּם, "blood,"

---

[10] Steinmann, *1 Samuel*, 288.

[11] *IBH*, §§ 21 and 21 A. See also Waltke-O'Connor, § 12.3b; Joüon, § 131 b.

[12] Hubbard, "The Hebrew Root *Pgʿ* as a Legal Term."

in the singular (as in Josh 2:19; 1 Ki 2:32, 37; Ezek 33:4). The Kethib, דָּמֶיךָ, has the plural (as in 1 Ki 2:33). When the noun דָּם is plural, it signifies shed blood and is a plural of result.[13]

פִּיךָ עָנָה בְךָ—Literally "your mouth answered with you." The verb עָנָה with the preposition בְּ is a courtroom idiom, to "testify … against" someone in condemnation (BDB, s.v. עָנָה I, Qal, 3 a).

1:17 וַיְקֹנֵן דָּוִד אֶת־הַקִּינָה הַזֹּאת—"Then David sang this lament." The verb וַיְקֹנֵן is a Polel (D) preterite (imperfect with *waw* consecutive) of קִין. It is a denominative verb formed from the cognate noun used here, קִינָה, "a lament," and denotes the singing of a funeral dirge. The identical form recurs in 3:33.

1:18 קָשֶׁת—" 'A Bow.' " This is the pausal form of the feminine noun קֶשֶׁת, as in 1:22. Here it is often taken to be the title of the poem or a description of it.[14] Others believe that it is an extraneous word since the LXX omits it.[15] Still others argue that the use of this noun as the object of the Piel (D) of the verb לָמַד, "teach," in a military context denotes the training of someone for warfare (cf. 2 Sam 22:35; Ps 144:1). According to that interpretation, David commanded that the men of Judah be trained for war, presumably against the Philistines.[16]

הִנֵּה כְתוּבָה—Literally "look, it is written." The referent of the feminine Qal passive (Gp) participle כְתוּבָה, "written," could be the nearest feminine noun קֶשֶׁת, "Bow," or the earlier feminine noun קִינָה, "lament" (1:17).

סֵפֶר הַיָּשָׁר:—"The Book of the Upright" is also mentioned in Josh 10:13. This phrase is often translated as "the Book of Jashar." The adjective יָשָׁר literally means "straight" or, metaphorically, "upright, morally correct" as a synonym of "righteous" and an antonym of vocables for "crooked" and "twisted" (see *HALOT*, 5–6).

1:19 הַצְּבִי יִשְׂרָאֵל—"Your beauty, O Israel." Since this lament is being taught to the Judahites (1:18), יִשְׂרָאֵל is a vocative address to them, "O Israel."[17] There are two nouns spelled צְבִי. The first, צְבִי I, denotes "beauty," "glory," or "pride" (Is 4:2; Jer 3:19; Ezek 25:9; see *CDCH*, s.v. צְבִי I), and in context here it refers to Saul as the first king of Israel, the one Yahweh chose to be anointed by Samuel and to save his people Israel (see 1 Sam 9:15–10:1). This noun is used in Is 4:2 for the Messiah, "the Branch of Yahweh," who will be the "beauty" and "glory" of redeemed humanity (cf. Is 28:5; Ezek 7:20). The definite article on הַצְּבִי here probably functions as a possessive pronoun: in this address to Israel, "the glory" means "your glory."

---

[13] *IBH*, § 11 C; GKC, § 124 n; Waltke-O'Connor, § 7.4.1b; Joüon, § 136 b.

[14] Keil, *The Books of Samuel*, 288–89; Hertzberg, *I and II Samuel*, 238; Anderson, *2 Samuel*, 15; Bergen, *1, 2 Samuel*, 290; Baldwin, *I and 2 Samuel*, 178; HCSB; NET; NIV.

[15] McCarter, *II Samuel*, 67; Auld, *I and II Samuel*, 353; it is omitted by ESV.

[16] See the discussion in Kleven, "Reading Hebrew Poetry," 52. See also Eissfeldt, "Zwei verkannte militär-technische Termini im Alten Testament."

[17] See *IBH*, § 19 A. "Your beauty, O Israel" is also the NASB translation; see also "your glory, O Israel," in ESV. According to KJV, the words are a construct phrase, "the beauty of Israel," but it would defy the normal rules of Hebrew grammar for a noun in construct to have the definite article.

The second homographic noun, צְבִי II, means "gazelle" (2 Sam 2:18; 1 Chr 12:9 [ET 12:8]; see also, e.g., Deut 14:5; Song 2:9, 17). Freedman believes that צְבִי here is a reference to a "gazelle" as a characterization of either Saul or Jonathan as a swift warrior (2 Sam 2:18; 1 Chr 12:9 [ET 12:8]). The article, then, would be used as a vocative marker: "O Gazelle of Israel." Freedman notes the use of animal comparisons later in 1:23.[18]

חָלָל—This adjective, "slain," recurs in the plural in 1:22 and in the singular in 1:25. It is derived from the verb חָלַל, "to pierce," and so literally describes a person who has been pierced or fatally wounded by a sword, an arrow, or a spear. A homographic adjective חָלָל is derived from the verb חָלַל, "to defile," and so means "profaned, defiled" (Lev 21:7, 14; Ezek 21:34 [ET 21:29]). In light of "uncircumcised" in 2 Sam 1:20 and the Niphal (N) perfect נִגְעַל, "it was defiled," in 1:21, the idea of ritual defilement by death at the hands of the uncircumcised may be relevant here.

אֵיךְ נָפְלוּ גִבּוֹרִים:—"How the mighty men have fallen!" This exclamation as a lament is repeated in 1:25a and 1:27a. See GKC, § 148 b; Waltke-O'Connor, § 18.4e, example 21.

1:21 אַל־טַל וְאַל־מָטָר עֲלֵיכֶם—After each instance of the negative אַל, the jussive יְהִי is implied (GKC, § 152 g), "may there not be," i.e., *may there be no* dew and *no* rain on you."

וּשְׂדֵי תְרוּמֹת—Literally "and fields of offerings," this construct phrase means "nor fields producing grain offerings." Some seek to emend this phrase or find a different meaning for תְרוּמֹת other than "offerings."[19] However, the phrase is not difficult and is part of the curse on Mount Gilboa—without dew or rain, it would produce no grain for offerings.[20]

בְּלִי מָשִׁיחַ בַּשָּׁמֶן:—"No longer anointed with oil." While the rare poetic negative particle בְּלִי often simply means "no" or "not," it can also denote something that was true but is no longer true.[21] In this MT reading the noun מָשִׁיחַ refers to Saul as no longer the "anointed one." Many other Masoretic manuscripts read the Qal passive (Gp) participle מָשׁוּחַ, which could refer to Saul's "shield" as no longer "anointed with oil." The desacralization of his shield would be similar to the idea in 1:27b, although there is no well-attested custom of anointing shields or treating them with oil to improve their performance or appearance.

1:22 קֶשֶׁת יְהוֹנָתָן לֹא נָשׂוֹג אָחוֹר—"The bow of Jonathan did not turn away." The nuance of the perfect aspect of the Niphal (N) verb נָשׂוֹג may be that his bow *never* turned back" (Joüon, § 112 d; Waltke-O'Connor, § 30.5.1b, example 15). The subject noun קֶשֶׁת,

---

18 Freedman, "The Refrain in David's Lament," 267–68.

19 McCarter, *II Samuel*, 69; Anderson, *2 Samuel*, 12; Freedman, "The Refrain in David's Lament," 269–70; Fokkelman, "שדי תרומת in II Sam 1:21a"; Peters, "Critical Notes," 54–57; NIV.

20 Kleven, "Reading Hebrew Poetry," 59.

21 Deut 28:55; Jer 2:15; 9:9–11 (ET 9:10–12); Zeph 3:6; Mal 3:10; Ps 72:7; Job 4:11; 18:15. See also this same understanding in Linafelt's translation of 1:21 ("Private Poetry and Public Eloquence," 499).

"bow," is feminine, whereas the verb נָשׁוֹג, "(it) turned back," is masculine. In the parallel second clause of the verse, the feminine noun חֶרֶב, "sword," is the subject of the feminine verb תָשׁוּב, "(it) came back, returned." In this first clause, the verb נָשׁוֹג may be masculine due to attraction to the intervening masculine name יְהוֹנָתָן. This is the only instance in the OT where the verb is spelled with *sin*, שׁוֹג. Elsewhere it is always spelled with *samek*, סוּג.

1:23 שָׁאוּל וִיהוֹנָתָן הַנֶּאֱהָבִים וְהַנְּעִימִם —"Saul and Jonathan were the beloved and the delightful." הַנֶּאֱהָבִים is an articular Niphal (N) "gerundive" participle, meaning that it is used as adjective (Waltke-O'Connor, § 23.3d, including example 19), and וְהַנְּעִימִם is the plural of the adjective נָעִים (preceded by the article and the conjunction *waw*). These descriptors of Saul and Jonathan may mean that love and delight were the proper attitudes for the people to have toward their king and prince because of those men's divine offices as leaders under God, regardless of how imperfectly they carried out their vocations. Jonathan was "beloved" and "delightful" (1:23) to David, as is evident when cognate Hebrew vocabulary recurs in 1:26. Saul initially was desired by Israel (1 Sam 9:20), and the people showed their acceptance of God's choice of him by acclaiming him as their king (1 Sam 10:24; 12:13). At the end of King David's reign the same term for "delightful" (נָעִים) is applied to him (2 Sam 23:1).

מִנְּשָׁרִים קַלּוּ מֵאֲרָיוֹת גָּבֵרוּ׃ —"They were swifter than eagles; they were mightier than lions." In each of these two clauses the stative verb with the preposition מִן prefixed to the noun forms a comparative construction, "swift*er* ... mighti*er*" (*IBH*, § 30 E; Waltke-O'Connor, 14.4d, example 9; cf. *IBH*, § 22).

1:24 הַמַּלְבִּשְׁכֶם —"Who clothed you." It is the masculine singular Hiphil (H) participle of לָבֵשׁ, "to wear [clothing]," with the definite article and a second masculine plural pronominal suffix. The Hiphil of לָבֵשׁ takes a double accusative construction.[22] The first accusative is the pronominal suffix ("you"), which refers to the persons who are clothed, and the second accusative is שָׁנִי עִם־עֲדָנִים ("in scarlet with luxurious garments"), which denotes the material put on them as clothing. The antecedent of the suffix is "daughters of Israel," so one would instead expect the suffix to be feminine plural, כֶן־, as in some Masoretic manuscripts and rabbinic citations of this verse. However, the second feminine plural pronominal suffix is not well-attested on any verb in the OT, so the lack of concord, with the substitution of the common masculine form, is not unexpected.

עִם־עֲדָנִים —"With luxurious garments." The noun עֵדֶן denotes a "luxury." Most translations take its plural adverbially, "clothed you luxuriously," but it is best taken concretely as referring to garments that were "luxuries."

הַמַּעֲלֶה —"Who provided." The Hiphil (H) masculine singular participle of עָלָה with the definite article describes Saul literally as "the one who brought up" gold jewelry onto their clothes.

1:26 צַר־לִי עָלֶיךָ —"I am in distress for you." The literal meaning is "it is restricted for me on account of you." The verb צַר is the Qal (G) third masculine singular perfect of

---

[22] Cf. Waltke-O'Connor, § 37.3d, including example 37.

צָרַר, "to bind, constrict," used impersonally as a passive. See the first textual note on 1 Sam 13:6.[23]

נִפְלְאַתָה—"It was … wonderful." The verb is the Niphal (N) perfect third feminine singular of פָּלָא, "be wonderful, extraordinary, miraculous." The form here is anomalous; the expected form is נִפְלָאת (Ps 118:23). This has occasioned some attempts to emend the MT. However, most commentators prefer to retain the anomalous form and explain it as a result of the fact that forms of final *aleph* verbs (פלא) may exhibit forms more commonly associated with final *he* verbs (פלה).[24]

אַהֲבָתְךָ לִי מֵאַהֲבַת נָשִׁים:—"Your love for me … more than women's love." The noun אַהֲבָה, used twice here, is derived from the verb אָהֵב, "to love," which referred to Jonathan's love for David in 1 Sam 18:1, 3; 20:17.[25] The verb was also used for love toward David by Saul and his servants in 1 Sam 16:21; 18:22 and by Israel and Judah in 1 Sam 18:16. The verb refers to heterosexual love in 1 Sam 1:5; 18:20, 28; 2 Sam 13:1, 4, 15, as does the noun in 2 Sam 13:15. The book of Samuel does not warrant modern speculation about a homosexual relationship between Jonathan and David. See further the commentary.

Commentary

Nisan (March/April) 1009 BC[26]

David's reaction to Saul's death follows the trajectory started when David first refused to kill the king out of respect for Yahweh's anointed one (1 Samuel 24; see also 1 Samuel 26). David's respect for Saul did not stem from his admiration for Saul's character or actions. Instead, it was David's respect for Saul's divine office, God's choice and anointing of Saul,[27] that led him to honor the king in his death. David's grief, however, was genuine, not only because Israel had lost its first king but also because of his personal loss of his friend and brother-in-law Jonathan (1 Samuel 18–20).

During the nineteenth and early twentieth centuries, critical scholars often argued that 2 Sam 1:1–16 came from a different source than 1 Samuel 31, each with a distinct account of Saul's death.[28] This approach rejected the explanation that the report of Saul's death given to David by the Amalekite was a fabrication, whereas 1 Sam 31:2–6 is the factual account. However, more recent critical scholarship has agreed with more conservative scholars that the Amalekite was

---

[23] Steinmann, *1 Samuel*, 233.

[24] See the discussions in Zapf, "How Are the Mighty Fallen," 103–4; McCarter, *II Samuel*, 73; Anderson, *2 Samuel*, 13; GKC, § 75 oo; Joüon, § 78 g.

[25] See the second textual note on 1 Sam 18:3 (Steinmann, *1 Samuel*, 345).

[26] See "The Chronology of David's Reign" in the commentary on 5:1–5.

[27] 1 Sam 9:15–10:1; 24:7, 11 (ET 24:6, 10); 26:9, 11, 16, 23.

[28] See, e.g., Smith, *The Books of Samuel*, 254. See also the discussions of critical scholarship by the conservatives Kleven, "Rhetoric and Narrative Depiction," 59–60, and Arnold, "The Amalekite's Report of Saul's Death," 290–94.

contriving his version of Saul's death to ingratiate himself with David.[29] Reis notes:

> The Amalekite is lying, and (*contra* Fokkelman)[30] the author makes this fact abundantly clear. His most obvious means of providing clarity is by preceding the Amalekite's story with the narrator's account of Saul's suicide [1 Samuel 31]. By biblical convention, the narrator always tells the truth and knows everything; he even knows the mind of God ("And the Lord repented that he had made Saul king over Israel," 1 Sam. 15.35). The narrator's version must be believed, and readers, therefore, immediately understand that the Amalekite's version is a lie.[31]

There are several other indications that the Amalekite related a fictitious account of Saul's death to David (see immediately below), and it is obvious that 2 Sam 1:6–10 is not an accurate report of Saul's demise.[32]

An Amalekite Brings News of the Death of Saul and Jonathan (1:1–16)

The author begins with the setting of his account (1:1). It was after Saul's death (1 Samuel 31) and after David had returned from striking the Amalekites (1 Samuel 30). Originally Samuel was one book, but when it was split into two books,[33] the clause "(and it came to pass) after the death of Saul" may have suggested itself as the beginning of the second book in imitation of the beginnings of Joshua and Judges (Josh 1:1; Judg 1:1).

On the third day after David's return to Ziklag, a man from Saul's camp arrived. When characterizing this messenger as someone from Saul's camp, the author is allowing the man's own initial description of himself to introduce him to the reader in the same way the man introduced himself to David (1:3). The author subtly draws the reader into viewing this narrative through David's eyes. The messenger's arrival would have been four days after Saul's death. See figure 1.

---

[29] Hertzberg, *I and II Samuel*, 237; McCarter, *II Samuel*, 63–64; Anderson, *2 Samuel*, 5; Fokkelman, "A Lie, Born of Truth, Too Weak to Contain It." For the conservative view, see Baldwin, *1 and 2 Samuel*, 176, and Arnold, "The Amalekite's Report of Saul's Death."

[30] The reference is to Fokkelman, "A Lie, Born of Truth, Too Weak to Contain It," 40.

[31] Reis, "Killing the Messenger," 170–71.

[32] Arnold, "The Amalekite's Report of Saul's Death," argues that only 1:7–10 is a fabrication, but there is no reason to believe that 1:6 is not part of the Amalekite's lie.

[33] It is usually presumed that Samuel was divided into two books—two scrolls—when it was translated into Greek in antiquity. The entire book of Samuel in Hebrew could fit into one very capacious scroll. However the Greek text longer is longer, mainly due to that fact that Greek often requires more words to express a thought than does the Hebrew which it is translating. Thus, it is speculated that the book was split into two parts at a fairly logical location: 1 Samuel containing all the narrative through the death of King Saul and 2 Samuel containing the narrative of David's reign.

Figure 1

Chronology of Events in 1 Samuel 28–2 Samuel 1

Day	David	The Philistines and Saul
	David must accompany Achish (1 Sam 28:1).	The Philistines gather for war (1 Sam 28:1).
1	David arrives at Aphek (1 Sam 29:2).	The Philistines arrive at Aphek (1 Sam 29:1).
	[The Amalekites raid Ziklag (1 Sam 30:13–14).]	Saul camps at the spring in Jezreel (1 Sam 29:1).
2	David leaves for Ziklag (1 Sam 29:11).	The Philistines leave for Jezreel (1 Sam 29:11).
3	David travels to Ziklag.	The Philistines march to Jezreel.
		The Philistines arrive at Shunem (1 Sam 28:4).
4	David arrives at Ziklag (1 Sam 30:1).	Saul gathers forces on Gilboa for war (1 Sam 28:4).
		Saul goes to Endor at night (1 Sam 28:7–8).
	David raids the Amalekites at twilight (1 Sam 30:17).	Saul returns to Gilboa at night (1 Sam 28:25).
5	David strikes the Amalekites until evening (1 Sam 30:17).	The Philistines defeat Israel on Gilboa (1 Sam 31:1).
		Saul and his sons die (1 Sam 31:2–6).
6	David returns to Ziklag (1 Sam 30:26).	The Philistines capture Saul's corpse (1 Sam 31:8–10).
7	David is at Ziklag (1 Sam 30:26; 2 Sam 1:1).	
8	David is at Ziklag (2 Sam 1:1).	
9	An Amalekite informs David of Saul's death (2 Sam 1:2–16).	

The man exhibited signs of grief with his torn clothes and dirt-covered head (1:2). He also acknowledged David as the new king designate by bowing to him. This man sought from the beginning to identify himself with Israel. When David asked him from where he came, he replied that he was from "the camp of Israel" (1:3), leaving David to infer that he was serving among Saul's troops. This prompted David to ask about the battle (1:4). The young man's brief report is accurate, though simply a summary: the battle was lost, and Saul and Jonathan had died. No mention is made of Saul's two other sons who also died, the Philistine occupation of Israelite towns, or the abuse of Saul's body (1 Sam 31:6–10). This rather vague summary may also be an indication that this man may not have been an actual participant in these events and that he created his subsequent report of having killed Saul out of whole cloth to curry favor with David.

David's follow-up question then probed for confirmation of one specific statement by the informant: the deaths of Saul and Jonathan (1:5). Interestingly, for the first time the author calls him "the young man who had reported to him [to David]" (1:5, 6, 13).[34] This is a subtle clue that this man's account might not be true, but merely what he "reported" as true. This allows the author to identify him without revealing more about him until his own words do, once again placing readers into the same situation as David: they will discover this man's identity as David does.[35]

The reply to David's probe begins with a rather evasive circumstance, "I just happened to be" (1:6). This ought to raise the suspicions of the reader. How did he happen to be on Mount Gilboa? If he had been one of Saul's troops fighting the Philistines on Mount Gilboa, he *ought* to have been there, and it would not have been happenstance. He then provides a very specific account of Saul's death with details not found in 1 Samuel 31:

- Saul was leaning on his spear (2 Sam 1:6).
- Chariots were bearing down on Saul (1:6).
- Saul engaged a soldier whom he did not know in conversation (1:7).
- Saul asked to be killed because realized that he was in the throes of death (1:9).[36]
- The Amalekite killed Saul as a mercy killing (1:10).
- The Amalekite took Saul's crown and bracelet (1:10).

While David, who was not at the battle, would not have recognized these as contrary to the actual facts surrounding Saul's death, readers have already been told how Saul died. In 1 Sam 31:3–5 there was no mention of a spear. Archers, not chariots, were bearing down on Saul, whom they wounded. Saul engaged his armor bearer in conversation. Saul did not claim he was dying. Saul's request

---

[34] See the first textual note on 1:4.

[35] Kleven, "Rhetoric and Narrative Deception," 62.

[36] Note that in 1 Sam 31:4, Saul, out of fear of being tortured by the Philistines, requested his armor bearer to kill him.

to be killed by his armor bearer was denied, and Saul took his own life. All of these paint the picture of a prevaricating Amalekite whose identity is revealed in his own account of his conversation with Saul (2 Sam 1:8).

In addition, by describing the Amalekite as "the young man who had reported to him [to David]" (הַנַּעַר הַמַּגִּיד לוֹ, 1:5, 6, 13) both before and after his description of having dispatched Saul, the author is hinting that the man's words are false:

> As has been frequently noted, there are several correspondences in 2 Samuel 1 to the messenger scene in 1 Samuel 4. ... In both scenes a man with signs of mourning (dirt on his head and clothing rent) comes running from a battle-field on which the Philistines have routed the Israelites [1 Sam 4:12; 2 Sam 1:2]. In both scenes, and nowhere else in the Bible, the question "What has happened?" is asked [1 Sam 4:16; 2 Sam 1:4[37]]. It is obvious that there is, as Moshe Garsiel says, "a deliberate connection between the two stories in order to set up an analogy between the fates of Saul's house and of Eli's."[38] But, just as there is a deliberate connection, I submit that there is also a deliberate disconnection: the root בשר ["to bring news"], denoting reliable information, is used to denominate the messenger, המבשר, who brings an accurate report to Eli ["the one who brought the news," 1 Sam 4:17]. But the root for news is not used at all in the Amalekite's articulation. Instead of using המבשר ["the one who brought the news"], the bringer of true information, the author three times uses המגיד, literally translated as "the teller" ["the one who had reported," 2 Sam 1:5, 6, 13]. "The teller" can relay either information or mis-information. The absence of בשר ["to bring news"] connoting true news, and the insistent presence of the substitute phrase, flags the Amalekite's report as specious. ...
>
> In his eulogy for Saul and Jonathan, David's rhetoric includes the verse: "Tell it not in Gath, publish it (תבשרו [from the root "to bring news"]) not in the streets of Ashkelon; lest the daughters of the Philistines rejoice, lest the daughters of the uncircumcised triumph" (2 Sam. 1.20). While conforming to biblical poetry's convention of parallel clauses with variant terminology, David uses the root בשר ["to bring news," 1:20b]. I offer that he would not use a word signifying truth for a report he thought dubious, and so we apprehend that at this stage, the least David believes is that Saul is dead. We shall soon learn what else he believes. Ironically, although David does not know it, the actual news, the בשרה [from the root "to bring news"] of the death of Saul, has already been published by the Philistines: "And they cut off his head, and stripped off his armor, and sent into the land of the Philistines round about, to carry the news (לבשר [from the root "to bring news"]) unto the house of their idols, and to the people" (1 Sam. 31.9).[39]

---

[37] The Hebrew wording translated in this commentary as "what happened?" and by Reis as "what has happened?" is identical in 1 Sam 4:16 and 2 Sam 1:4, מֶה־הָיָה הַדָּבָר, and is not found elsewhere in the Bible, even though some English versions use the same translation for other Hebrew wordings in other verses, e.g., "what has happened?" in Jer 48:19 ESV.

[38] Garsiel, *The First Book of Samuel*, 106.

[39] Reis, "Killing the Messenger," 172–73.

The description of the chariots threatening Saul is also somewhat suspicious. Chariots were effective vehicles of war on plains and in valleys, but they were much less maneuverable on hilly terrain (see Judg 1:19).

Moreover, it appears as if the Amalekite is playing a dangerous game of attempting to appear loyal to Saul and yet an ally of David. He mourned Saul's death with his torn clothes and dirt-covered head (1:2) and claimed that he killed the king as an act of mercy (1:10). In his reported conversation with Saul, he responded with the respectful "I'm here" (הִנֵּנִי) when called by the king (1:7; cf. 1 Sam 3:4–8).[40] Yet, he bowed to David (2 Sam 1:2) and presented the symbols of kingship to the future king, whom he addressed as "my lord" (אֲדֹנִי, 1:10). Reis may be correct in stating:

> I do not think he assumes David will be happy to hear of Saul's death, for if he thought that Saul's death would gratify David, not only would mourning have been unnecessary, but the Amalekite would not have characterized the killing as compassionate euthanasia. He would have boasted of slaying Saul in fair combat. I believe he himself mourned Saul's death and thinks David will be grateful to him for following Saul's order and sparing his dying father-in-law torture and humiliation at the hands of the Philistines.[41]

What ought to be clear to the reader and what was clear to David—at least eventually if not at the time—is that the Amalekite was expecting a reward for bringing the emblems of the kingdom to David (1:10; cf. 4:10).

David's reaction as reported in 1:11–12 would not have been unexpected to the Amalekite. His show of mourning is matched by that of David and his men. The fasting lasted the rest of the day, that is, until evening, when the sun went down and a new day began by Israelite reckoning.

David's further conversation with the Amalekite then sought to identify him more precisely (1:13). He admitted to being the son of an Amalekite who was a "resident alien" (גֵּר, gēr, 1:13), and so he would have had the same status as his father. As a resident alien, he would have identified with the customs and laws of the people among whom he lived, as shown already by his outward signs of mourning over Israel's defeat on Mount Gilboa. In Israel, such persons were expected to identify with Israel's institutions:

> The gēr in Israel was largely regarded as a proselyte. He was to be present for the solemn reading of the Law (Deut 31:12) showing that he was exposed to its demands. The law concerning "unleavened bread" applied to him as well as the native (Exo 12:19), and a circumcised gēr could keep Passover (Exo 12:48[–49]; Num 9:14). He was also included in the festival of the Great Day of Atonement (Lev 16:29) and was expected to celebrate the Feast of Booths (Deut 16:14). With the native he was threatened with the death penalty if he offered a sacrifice to a foreign god (Lev 17:8[–9]) and was forbidden to eat blood (Lev 17:10, 12, 13). Though in contrast to the native he was allowed to

---

[40] Kleven, "Rhetoric and Narrative Deception," 63.

[41] Reis, "Killing the Messenger," 176.

eat what had died or was torn (Deut 14:21), like the native Israelite he under-
went special cleansing (Lev 17:15[–16]). He was also included in the rites
of cleansing with the ashes of the red heifer (Num 19:10). The laws of sexual chastity applied to him as well as the native (Lev 18:26) along with the
Sabbath laws (Exo 20:10; Exo 23:12). In a word he was to show the same
fidelity to the Lord (Lev 20:2).

He also enjoyed many of the same rights as the native and was not to be
oppressed (Exo 22:21 [MT 22:20]; Lev 19:33; Jer 7:6; Jer 22:3). He is mentioned in connection with the poor (Lev 19:10; cf. Lev 23:22) and with orphans
and widows (Deut 14:29; Deut 16:11, 14; Deut 24:17; Deut 26:13; Deut
27:19). With them he shared the sheaf left in the field (Deut 24:19) and the
gleanings in the olive trees and in the vineyards (Deut 24:20–21) along with
the tithe every three years (Deut 14:29; Deut 26:12). He was to be treated
righteously in judgment (Deut 1:16; Deut 24:17; Deut 27:19) and the six
asylum cities were also cities of refuge for him (Num 35:15). In a word the
Lord loves the *gēr* (Deut 10:18). Israel should not oppress him because they
themselves were oppressed and know his soul (Exo 22:21 [MT 22:20]; Deut
10:19). They were to love him as themselves (Lev 19:34).

David employed them as stonecutters (1 Chr 22:2) and they served in the
army (2 Sam 1:13). Solomon made them stonecutters and burden-bearers
(2 Chr 2:17[–18] [MT 2:16–17]).[42]

Upon learning of the young man's identity as not simply an Amalekite but
also a resident alien, David asked why he was not afraid to kill Saul (2 Sam
1:14). David himself twice refused to kill Saul, even when urged by his men
(1 Sam 24:4–8 [ET 24:3–7]; 26:7–11), who assumed that David, as the king
anointed by God to be Saul's replacement, could have legitimately killed his
apostate predecessor.[43] However, David in the second case appealed to a pre-
cept that silenced Abishai: no one who laid a hand on Yahweh's anointed would
remain guiltless (1 Sam 26:9). This general principle of honoring anyone who
had a God-given office was also respected by Saul's armor bearer (1 Sam
31:4).[44] David's verdict was that any Israelite or resident alien in Israel who
would attack God's anointed king would bear the punishment for his guilt.
Thus, David ordered the Amalekite's execution (1:15). David stated to him
that the shedding of his blood was his own fault and that his own words condemned him (1:16).

---

[42] *TWOT*, § 330.

[43] In 1 Sam 15:23, 26; 16:1, God declared that he had rejected Saul as king because of his apostasy. David was anointed as his replacement in 1 Sam 16:1–13. Yahweh's Spirit rested on
David (1 Sam 16:13) but departed from Saul and was replaced by an evil spirit (1 Sam 16:14).

[44] Contra Reis, "Killing the Messenger," 176–77, who states: "The problem … is that no one
other than David seems to promulgate this social norm, taboo, law." Reis appears to overlook
the refusal of Saul's armor bearer (1 Sam 31:4). However, both Fokkelman, "A Lie, Born of
Truth, Too Weak to Contain It," 47, and Mabee, "David's Judicial Exoneration," 95, argue
that the prohibition on killing Yahweh's anointed was generally acknowledged in Israel.

The execution of the Amalekite upheld David's high regard for Yahweh and his choice of king. David's action was a reflection of his deep trust in God.[45] It was also politically expedient. David could not expect that others would respect God's choice of him as anointed king if he countenanced violence against his predecessor. However, that does not mean that David ordered the execution of the Amalekite primarily for political reasons. David's genius was that, by the guidance of the Spirit,[46] he often took the godly and morally correct action in a way that was also politically advantageous.

That David was not pleased with the Amalekite's present of Saul's crown and bracelet is subtly signaled in that they are never again mentioned in 2 Samuel. David is never depicted as accepting these items that the Amalekite seemed to offer in order to ingratiate himself with David. Nor is David ever depicted as using them as tokens of his succession to the throne of Israel.

David's Lament for Saul and Jonathan (1:17–27)

David's lament over Saul and Jonathan is preceded by a two-verse super-scription (1:17–18). Here we are told that the poem was for both Saul and Jonathan (1:17) and that David apparently commanded all Judah to learn it and gave it the title "A Bow" (see the first textual note on 1:18). That it was an early composition by David may be indicated by the fact that only Judah, not all Israel, was commanded to learn it. This song was also recorded in "the Book of the Upright," where Joshua's appeal to God for the sun to stand still was also recorded (Josh 10:12–13).

The song has seven sections:

1. An opening lament (1:19)
2. Opposition to Philistine women celebrating the demise of Saul and Jonathan (1:20)
3. A curse on Mount Gilboa (1:21)
4. A remembrance of Jonathan and Saul (1:22–23)
5. A petition for Israelite women to weep for Saul (1:24)
6. David's grief over Jonathan (1:25–26)
7. A closing lament (1:27)

The positioning of the clause "how the mighty men have fallen!" (אֵיךְ נָפְלוּ גִבּוֹרִים) is significant. It closes the opening lament (1:19b) and opens the closing lament (1:27a). In the middle of the song, it prefaces David's grief over Jonathan (1:25a), emphasizing David's much closer relationship with Jonathan than with Saul.

David began his song by speaking of Saul as Israel's "beauty" who had been slain on its heights (1:19). Kings and their sons were often depicted as

---

[45] See "David and the Messianic Promise" in "Christ in Samuel" in the introduction (Steinmann, *1 Samuel*, 25–26).

[46] See 1 Sam 16:13 and "The Spirit of Yahweh" in Steinmann, *1 Samuel*, 30.

good looking.[47] The Messiah himself is the King who is more beautiful than all the children of men (Ps 45:3 [ET 45:2]; cf. Is 4:2), and those who serve on his behalf are imputed with his glorious pulchritude.[48]

The deaths of Israel's king and prince were certain to be celebrated among the Philistines (1 Sam 31:9–10), but David's poem implored that it not be so (2 Sam 1:20). The choice of Gath appears to be obvious, since this was the city of the Philistine Pentapolis (Josh 13:3; 1 Sam 6:17) with which David was most familiar (1 Sam 21:11, 13 [ET 21:10, 12]; 27:2–4, 11). Ashkelon may have been chosen for the sake of poetic parallelism (Ashkelon immediately precedes Gath in the lists in Josh 13:3; 1 Sam 6:17). To show his contempt for the Philistines, in the parallel line they are called "the uncircumcised" to indicate that they were excluded from the covenant of grace with Israel (Gen 17:14). This epithet for them is employed by Jonathan, David, and Saul (1 Sam 14:6; 17:26, 36; 31:4).

The curse on Gilboa for no moisture to water its fields with the result of no crops producing grain for offerings is connected with Saul, whose shield, along with those of the other mighty men, was "defiled" by death. Scholars have discussed the phrase (מָגֵן גִּבּוֹרִים מָגֵן שָׁאוּל בְּלִי מָשִׁיחַ בַּשָּׁמֶן, 1:21), which is often translated as "the shield of Saul, not anointed with oil." The question then arises whether "not anointed with oil" describes Saul or his shield.[49] Some argue that the shield was to be cast away and would not be oiled for battle (Is 21:5).[50] However, if that were the case, it is strange that there is no mention of Jonathan and his shield. Instead, the phrase depicts Saul as the one who is *no longer* anointed. God had taken the kingdom from apostate Saul, who rejected his Word (1 Sam 15:23–28; 28:16–19), and with the removal of God's Spirit from the king (1 Sam 16:14), the blessing of God's anointing had begun to be confiscated. This eventually ended in Saul's death as God abandoned him to the consequences of his idolatry and occultism (1 Sam 15:23; 28:7–20).

The central section of the poem centers on the military prowess of Jonathan and Saul, with David emphasizing the two as a team by the chiastic arrangement of their names: "Jonathan … Saul" (2 Sam 1:22) and "Saul and Jonathan" (1:23a). The two are characterized as bravely not turning from battle (1:22), "beloved" and "delightful" (1:23a),[51] and an inseparable team (1:23b). Clearly David's description is more apt for Jonathan than Saul: Jonathan attacked the Philistines when Saul was reluctant to do so (1 Sam 14:1–15). Jonathan remained loyal to his father, despite Saul's threats against him (1 Sam 14:43–45; 20:30–33). The comparison of their swiftness to eagles (2 Sam 1:23c) employs a

---

[47] See the description of Saul in 1 Sam 9:2; 10:23–24. See also the description of David in 1 Sam 16:12; 17:42 and of others in Judg 8:18; 2 Sam 14:25; 1 Ki 1:6; Ps 45:3 (ET 45:2); Is 33:17.

[48] See the hymn "Beautiful Savior" and Rom 10:15.

[49] See the discussion in Kleven, "Reading Hebrew Poetry," 59–60, as well as the third textual note on 1:21.

[50] Keil, *The Books of Samuel*, 290–91; McCarter, *II Samuel*, 76; Baldwin, *1 and 2 Samuel*, 180.

[51] See the first textual note on 1:23.

familiar OT metaphor (Deut 28:49; Prov 23:5; Lam 4:19; cf. Is 40:31). However, it ought to be noted that the Hebrew נֶשֶׁר is a broader term than the English "eagle" and can also denote other flesh-eating birds such as vultures. The comparison of Saul and Jonathan's strength to that of a lion (2 Sam 1:23d) is a less common metaphor, occurring elsewhere only in Judg 14:14, 18.

In imploring the Israelite women to weep over Saul (2 Sam 1:24), David notes that Saul's efforts to defend Israel's supremacy brought the women wealth—scarlet was the clothing of the rich, and gold denoted the most precious of jewelry. Perhaps this is a poetic reference to the spoils of Saul's wars (1 Sam 14:47–52).

The penultimate section of the song laments the death of Jonathan (2 Sam 1:25), repeating the opening verse (1:19) with variations. The mighty have fallen *in the midst of battle*, and it is now Jonathan who is "slain" (חָלָל) on the heights (compare 1:19a with 1:25b). Here David uses the intimate term "brother" for Jonathan (1:26), noting his delight in him and his love for his slain friend. The final line in 1:26 has been used to argue that David and Jonathan had a homoerotic relationship. This is clearly a misreading of David's words.[52] David is not necessarily comparing his love for Jonathan to his sexual attraction for women. The "love of women" David mentions may include the kind of godly, compassionate love he demonstrated toward his wives,[53] but it may also include the type of love shown to him by his mother or his sisters.[54] David's point is not focused on sexuality but on a broader and more general bond of kinship among the people of God that can be characterized as intimate love. David and Jonathan were faithful servants of Yahweh. They were united with each other by being joined to the God of Israel in a covenant of grace (1 Sam 18:3; 20:8, 16; 23:18). The NT uses the intimate language of love similarly.[55]

The ending refrain closes out the poem with "how the mighty men have fallen," which invites a comparison of 2 Sam 1:27 with 1:19 (as well as 1:25). In 1:19 Israel's "beauty" is characterized as "slain." Here in 1:27 the "weapons of war" are described as having "perished." Given the parallel nature of the opening and closing of this lament over Jonathan and Saul, the "weapons of war" refer to Saul and Jonathan as God's weapons wielded against Israel's enemies (1 Sam 8:20).[56]

---

[52] See the textual notes and the commentary on 1 Sam 18:1–5, including "Jonathan's Relationship with David," in Steinmann, *1 Samuel*, 344–49.

[53] See 1 Sam 18:20–27; 25:39–43; 27:3; 30:5–18.

[54] For David's sisters, see 1 Chr 2:16 and "David's Genealogy" before this pericope.

[55] E.g., Jn 13:35; Eph 5:25; 6:23–24; Col 1:4; 1 Pet 5:14; 1 Jn 3:1, 10, 18; 5:2; Jude 21.

[56] Already at the start of his reign Saul was called to wage war against the enemies of Israel, although he failed to carry out this vocation in the way God intended. See the commentary on 1 Sam 10:7–8 and figure 16, "Saul's Faltering Accession," in "Samuel Anoints Saul (9:26–10:8)" in the commentary on 1 Sam 9:26–10:16, as well as the beginning of the commentary on 1 Sam 10:17–27a (Steinmann, *1 Samuel*, 196–98, 203).

David Is Made King of Judah

Translation

2 ¹After this David inquired of Yahweh, "Should I go up to one of the cities of Judah?"

Yahweh said to him, "Go up."

David said to him, "Where should I go up?"

He said, "To Hebron."

²So David and also his two wives, Ahinoam the Jezreelitess and Abigail, the wife of Nabal the Carmelite, went up there. ³David brought up his men who were with him, each man and his household, and they dwelt in the cities of Hebron. ⁴Then the men of Judah came, and they anointed David there to be king over the house of Judah.

David was told, "[It was] the men of Jabesh-gilead who buried Saul." ⁵David sent messengers to the men of Jabesh-gilead and said to them, "May you be blessed by Yahweh because you have done this kindness for your lord, for Saul: you buried him. ⁶Now may Yahweh show you kindness and faithfulness. I also will show you this same benefit since you have done this thing. ⁷Now strengthen yourselves and be courageous because your lord Saul is dead, and in addition, the house of Judah has anointed me to be king over them."

Textual Notes

2:1 וַיִּשְׁאַל דָּוִד בַּיהוָה—"David inquired of Yahweh." See the first textual note and the commentary on 1 Sam 22:10, as well as the first textual note on 1 Sam 23:2.[1] In the book of Samuel, David always inquires of "Yahweh," the personal name of Israel's gracious God (1 Sam 23:2, 4; 30:8; 2 Sam 2:1; 5:19, 23). Presumably David inquires through the mediation of the high priest Abiathar, the successor of Ahimelech, whom Saul had put to death (1 Sam 22:16–23). Likewise, when Yahweh replies to David (e.g., 1 Sam 23:2; 2 Sam 2:1; 5:19, 23), he speaks through his high priest. For Saul inquiring of Yahweh or God, see 1 Sam 14:37; 28:6; see also the discussion of the contrast between Saul and David in the commentary on 2 Sam 5:19.

הַאֶעֱלֶה—"Should I go up?" The identical form recurs in 5:19. The interrogative *he* is prefixed to the Qal (G) first common singular imperfect of עָלָה, "go up." In this prayer the imperfect has a modal nuance, "shall/should I go up?" (cf. Joüon, § 113 l, m). When referring to military action the Qal of עָלָה may denote advancing against and attacking an enemy (e.g., 1 Sam 7:7; cf. *HALOT*, Qal, 3 d). Its Qal recurs twice more in 2 Sam 2:1 and also in 2:2 (see the next textual note), while its Hiphil (H), הֶעֱלָה, is in 2:3.

---

[1] Steinmann, *1 Samuel*, 426, 430, 435.

2:2 וַיַּ֤עַל שָׁם֙ דָּוִ֔ד—"So David ... went up there." The verb is masculine singular, in agreement with the first part of its compound subject, "David," even though the second part of its compound subject is feminine plural, וְגַם֙ שְׁתֵּ֣י נָשָׁ֔יו, "and also his two wives." The singular verb suggests that David is the primary actor and that his wives naturally accompany him.

הַכַּרְמְלִ֑י ... הַיִּזְרְעֵלִ֔ית—In Codex Leningradensis the first gentilic adjective is feminine, "the Jezreelitess," written defectively (with the omission of the א that appears elsewhere in the spelling הַיִּזְרְעֵאלִית, e.g., 3:2), and the second gentilic adjective is masculine, "the Carmelite," which then would describe the husband Nabal instead of his wife, Abigail. Many Masoretic manuscripts have the plene, or *male*, spelling of the first adjective, הַיִּזְרְעֵאלִית, and a few Masoretic manuscripts have the feminine form of the second, הַכַּרְמְלִית, which describes Abigail and is the preferred reading. The masculine form "the Carmelite" in Leningradensis is supported by the LXX, which reads Αβιγαια ἡ γυνὴ Ναβαλ τοῦ Καρμηλίου, "Abigaia, the wife of Nabal the Carmelite."[2] However, that is an impossible reading because Nabal was not from Carmel, but from Maon (1 Sam 25:2). Here "the Jezreelitess" refers to someone from the Jezreel in Judah in the vicinity of Maon, Ziph, and Carmel (Josh 15:55–56), not the more northerly city of Jezreel in Israel. "The Carmelitess" pertains to someone from the Judean city of Carmel, located at modern Khirbet al-Karmil, about eight miles (thirteen kilometers) southeast of Hebron (Josh 15:55; 1 Sam 15:12; 25:2–42; 27:3; 30:5; 2 Sam 3:3), not the more northerly mountain of Carmel on the Mediterranean coast.

וַאֲבִיגַ֕יִל אֵ֖שֶׁת נָבָֽל—"And Abigail, the wife of Nabal." The author of Samuel often refers to her in this way even after her marriage to David.[3]

2:4 לְמֶ֔לֶךְ—This prepositional phrase literally means "for/as a king." It is translated as "to be king." The LXX has the articular infinitive τοῦ βασιλεύειν, "to reign," which implies that the translator read the same consonants but understood them as לִמְלֹךְ, the Qal (G) infinitive construct of the verb מָלַךְ, "to reign," with לְ. When the identical Hebrew prepositional phrase לְמֶ֔לֶךְ recurs in 2:7, there the LXX translates it with the corresponding Greek prepositional phrase εἰς βασιλέα.

וַיַּגִּ֤דוּ לְדָוִד֙—Literally "and they reported to David." Such an impersonal verb with no stated subject can be rendered as a passive with its object as its subject: "David was told."

2:5 בְּרֻכִ֤ים אַתֶּם֙ לַֽיהוָ֔ה—"May you be blessed by Yahweh." The verb is the masculine plural Qal passive (Gp) participle of בָּרַךְ, "to bless." The preposition לְ is attached to the personal agent of the passive verb, "blessed by Yahweh" (GKC, § 121 f; Joüon, § 132 f). This expression is a benediction that confers a gracious blessing on the people now (cf. the blessing of the sacrifice in 1 Sam 9:13). It also serves as a prayer for them to be blessed in the future, in harmony with jussive יַ֣עַשׂ, literally "may Yahweh do,"

---

[2] See also the first paragraph of the textual note on 1 Sam 27:3, where the LXX has the same reading (Steinmann, *1 Samuel*, 506).

[3] See the second paragraph of the textual note on 1 Sam 27:3 and footnote 16 in the commentary on 1 Sam 30:1–6 (Steinmann, *1 Samuel*, 506–7, 558).

in 2:6. Similarly, benedictions that involve both present and future blessings appear in 1 Sam 2:20; 25:32–33; 2 Sam 6:18; 7:29; 8:10; 13:25; 21:3 (cf. 2 Sam 6:20).

אֲשֶׁר—The particle of relation has a causal meaning, "because, since," here and in 2:6 (Joüon, § 170 e).

עֲשִׂיתֶם הַחֶסֶד הַזֶּה עִם־אֲדֹנֵיכֶם עִם־שָׁאוּל—Literally "you did this kindness with your lord, with Saul." In place of the first preposition עִם, "with," the preposition עַל, "on, concerning," is read in 4QSamᵃ, [עַל אדניכ[ם,[4] "concerning yo[ur] lord," in harmony with the LXX, which reads ἐπὶ τὸν κύριον ὑμῶν ἐπὶ Σαουλ, "concerning your lord, concerning Saul." However, the standard Hebrew idiom for "showing mercy" or "kindness" to someone or "acting faithfully" toward someone is the Qal (G) of עָשָׂה, "do," plus the preposition עִם, "with," with the direct object noun חֶסֶד.[5] The only instance of this idiom with the preposition עַל instead of עִם is in 1 Sam 20:8. However, in that case, a few Masoretic manuscripts read עִם and the LXX agrees with μετά. Thus, most likely the MT is correct here and 4QSamᵃ and the LXX stem from a corrupt variant tradition.

2:7 תֶּחֱזַקְנָה יְדֵיכֶם—"Strengthen yourselves." Grammatically, the feminine dual of יָד with a suffix, יְדֵיכֶם, "your hands," is the subject of תֶּחֱזַקְנָה, the Qal (G) third feminine plural imperfect of חָזַק, "be strong," which has imperatival force, thus, "let your hands be strong" (see Joüon, §§ 113 l, m; 150 d).

וְהְיוּ לִבְנֵי־חַיִל—Literally "and become sons of valor," this is translated as "and be courageous." The identical command is in 2 Sam 13:28. The combination הָיָה לְ often means "to become." וְהְיוּ is the Qal (G) masculine plural imperative with a conjunctive *waw*. In the construct phrase בְּנֵי־חַיִל, the noun חַיִל serves as an attributive genitive. חַיִל denotes courageous military valor in, e.g., 1 Sam 2:4; 14:48; 16:18; 2 Sam 22:40. The men of Jabesh-gilead who retrieved the bodies of Saul and his sons were called אִישׁ חַיִל in 1 Sam 31:12 (a phrase used also in 2 Sam 24:9). See also אַנְשֵׁי־חַיִל in 2 Sam 11:16; בֶּן־חַיִל in 1 Sam 14:52; 18:17; 2 Sam 17:10; and בְּנֵי־חַיִל also in 2 Sam 17:10.

Commentary

Nisan (March/April) 1009 BC[6]

This account opens with the author's frequent transitional formula "after this" (וַיְהִי אַחֲרֵי־כֵן, 2:1).[7] While there is no indication of how much time transpired between the mourning for Saul and Jonathan (2 Samuel 1) and David's move to Hebron, it was probably not long.

In his characteristic reliance on God,[8] David did not leave Ziklag until he had inquired of God. When this verse speaks of "inquiring" (the verb שָׁאַל) of

---

[4] The part of the text with the next preposition is not extant.

[5] Gen 21:23; 24:12, 14; Josh 2:12, 14; Judg 1:24; 8:35; Ruth 1:8; 1 Sam 15:6; 2 Sam 3:8; 9:1, 3, 7; 10:2; 1 Ki 3:6; Ps 119:124; Ruth 1:8; 1 Chr 19:2; 2 Chr 1:8; 24:22.

[6] See "The Chronology of David's Reign" in the commentary on 5:1–5.

[7] See the formula also in 1 Sam 24:6 (ET 24:5); 2 Sam 8:1; 10:1; 13:1; 21:18 (cf. 2 Sam 15:1).

[8] See "David and the Messianic Promise" in "Christ in Samuel" in the introduction (Steinmann, *1 Samuel*, 25–26).

Yahweh, it employs a specialized expression relating to the use of Urim and Thummim. This idiom is drawn from Num 27:21:

וְלִפְנֵי אֶלְעָזָר הַכֹּהֵן יַעֲמֹד וְשָׁאַל לוֹ בְּמִשְׁפַּט הָאוּרִים לִפְנֵי יְהוָה
עַל־פִּיו יֵצְאוּ וְעַל־פִּיו יָבֹאוּ הוּא וְכָל־בְּנֵי־יִשְׂרָאֵל אִתּוֹ וְכָל־הָעֵדָה׃

And he [Joshua] will stand before Eleazar the high priest. He [the high priest] will inquire for him [Joshua] by a decision of the Urim in Yahweh's presence. He [Joshua] and all the Israelites with him—the entire community—will go out [to battle] according to his [the high priest's] authorization, and they will return [from battle] according to his authorization.

Thus, the author is implying that David consulted Yahweh by means of the Urim and Thummim.[9] Presumably the high priest handling them is Abiathar, the successor of Ahimelech, whom Saul had put to death (1 Sam 22:16–23).

"According to his authorization" in Num 27:21 is עַל־פִּיו, literally "according to his mouth." Moses is stating that when using the Urim, the message authorizing Joshua's military actions would come from the high priest's mouth. The high priest would act as an oracle of God. Here Yahweh replies with the words "go up" and "to Hebron" (2 Sam 2:1).

This inquiring of Yahweh is mentioned in numerous instances of consulting God in the OT historical books, but never after the reign of David:

- Josh 9:14: Israel did not inquire of Yahweh before making a treaty with the Gibeonites.
- Judg 1:1: Israel inquired as to which tribe should first conquer its allotted territory.
- Judg 20:18, 23, 27: Israel inquired *three* times concerning its attack on the Benjaminites.
- 1 Sam 10:22: Israel inquired as to Saul's whereabouts.
- 1 Sam 22:10, 13: Ahimelech inquired of Yahweh for David.
- 1 Sam 23:2, 4: David *twice* inquired as to whether to attack the Philistines, who were fighting against Keilah.
- 1 Sam 28:6: Saul inquired of Yahweh *by Urim*, but received no answer.
- 1 Sam 30:8: David inquired as to whether to pursue the Amalekites.
- 2 Sam 2:1: David inquired as to which city to make his base of operations.
- 2 Sam 5:19 ‖ 1 Chr 14:10: David inquired whether to wage war against the Philistines.
- 2 Sam 5:23 ‖ 1 Chr 14:14: David inquired about tactics for attacking the Philistines.

An additional incident of inquiring of Yahweh, but without the use of this idiom, is found in 1 Sam 23:9–12, when David summoned the high priest to bring the ephod (the high priestly vestment in which the Urim and Thummim were kept) and then asked God about the possible actions of Saul and the citizens of Keilah. Perhaps to this could be added the attempt to consult God that was aborted by Saul (1 Sam 14:18–19). In these verses Urim is mentioned only

---

[9] For a more complete discussion of these OT means of divine revelation, see the excursus "The Urim and Thummim" in Steinmann, *1 Samuel*, 272–75.

in 1 Sam 28:6 and LXX 1 Sam 14:41, and Thummim only in LXX 1 Sam 14:41. However, all of these verses that speak of inquiring of Yahweh most likely involved the high priest consulting the Urim and Thummim. After the time of David neither the Urim and Thummim nor the idiom "inquire [שָׁאַל] of Yahweh" are mentioned, except for Ezra 2:63 ‖ Neh 7:65, which notes that in postexilic Judah there was no priest with the Urim and Thummim who could be consulted.

David was directed to Hebron, formerly called Kiriath-arba (Judg 1:10), and that prior name probably meant "city of four quarters." Hebron lies nineteen miles (thirty-one kilometers) southwest of Jerusalem and is the highest city in Israel at about three thousand feet (nine hundred fourteen meters). David would reign here seven and a half years (2 Sam 2:11; 5:5).[10]

David followed God's instruction and went to Hebron, bringing his wives Ahinoam and Abigail (2:2).[11] David's men, who numbered six hundred,[12] also came with their families (2:3). Most ancient cities were rather small by modern standards, since they were confined within defensive walls. It would have been difficult for a single city to accommodate the additional two thousand persons who probably came with David. Thus, the author informs us that David's men settled in "the cities of Hebron" (2:3), probably indicating Hebron and nearby towns.

David's return to Judah led to immediate recognition of his right to the throne by his own tribe (2:4a). Their anointing of David simply confirmed that God had already made David king when Samuel had anointed him some years earlier (1 Sam 16:1–13; 1 Chr 11:3).

Immediately after reporting David's investiture at Hebron, the author moves to David receiving information about Saul's burial by the men of Jabesh (2 Sam 2:4b; cf. 1 Sam 31:11–13). This city in Gilead had a special connection with the house of Saul, since he had rescued it from the Ammonite king Nahash about forty years earlier (1 Sam 11:1–11). Thus, Jabesh's kindness to Saul was especially appropriate. David once again displayed his keen grasp of how to take the correct action and simultaneously advance his own political position for the good of the whole kingdom of God. Although the house of Saul was still a rival to David, he did not ignore the reverent gesture of the men of Jabesh or react in a hostile manner. Instead, he pronounced blessings from Yahweh because

---

[10]   This implies that David came to Hebron in Nisan (March/April) 1009, since the kings of Judah reckoned their regnal years as beginning in the month of Tishri (September/October). See the discussion in Steinmann, *From Abraham to Paul*, 18–21, 111–12.

[11]   For these women, who were David's second and third wives, respectively, see 1 Sam 25:39–43; 27:3; 30:5, 18. David's first marriage was to Saul's daughter Michal (1 Sam 18:20–27), but Saul later gave Michal to another man (1 Sam 25:44).

[12]   David initially gathered some four hundred men (1 Sam 22:2), but their ranks grew to six hundred (1 Sam 23:13; 25:13; 27:2; 30:9–10).

25

of their courageous rescue of Saul's body and their respectful treatment of his remains (2:5–6a). To not receive a decent burial was considered disgraceful.[13]

David's message was more than simply wishing them a blessing. He also offered to enter into a beneficial relationship with them, a relationship like the one they had had with Saul (2:6b).[14] He informed them that although Saul was dead, the house of Judah had acknowledged him as their new king (2:7). David thereby invited them as well to recognize him as Israel's king. Later God himself would designate David as the bearer of the messianic promise (2 Samuel 7), so fealty to him prefigured acceptance of the Messiah's royal reign in grace. Though the author does not comment on the success of David's effort to be accepted by the men of Jabesh as their king, later Abner would acknowledge that David had made inroads with the elders of Israel, who for some time had been seeking David as their king (3:17). David's diplomacy with Jabesh-gilead may simply be one example of how he courted the favor of the other tribes during his years in Hebron. In the fullness of time, the King of kings, Jesus Christ, would welcome all into God's kingdom of grace (e.g., Mt 6:33; Mk 9:1; Lk 4:43; 8:1; Jn 3:3–5).

---

[13] See, e.g., Gen 23:4; Deut 21:23; 1 Ki 14:10–11; 16:4; 21:24; 2 Ki 9:10, 34–35; Jer 14:16; 15:3; Ezek 39:13–14; Mt 8:21.

[14] Hillers, "A Note on Some Treaty Terminology in the Old Testament."

Conflict between David
and the House of Saul

Translation

2 ⁸Abner the son of Ner, commander of Saul's army, took Saul's son Ish-bosheth and brought him to Mahanaim. ⁹He made him king over Gilead, the Asherites, Jezreel, Ephraim, Benjamin, and Israel—all of it.

¹⁰Saul's son Ish-bosheth was forty years old when he became king over Israel, and he reigned two years. However, the house of Judah followed David. ¹¹The total time David was king in Hebron over the house of Judah was seven years and six months.

¹²Now Abner the son of Ner and the soldiers of Ish-bosheth the son of Saul marched from Mahanaim to Gibeon. ¹³So Joab the son of Zeruiah and David's soldiers marched out and met them at the pool of Gibeon, and they sat at the pool on opposite sides. ¹⁴Abner said to Joab, "Let the young men arise and hold a contest in front of us."

Joab said, "Let them arise."

¹⁵So they arose and crossed over by number: twelve for Benjamin and for Saul's son Ish-bosheth and twelve from David's soldiers. ¹⁶Each man grabbed his opponent by the head and [thrust] his dagger in his opponent's side. They fell down [dead] together. So that place in Gibeon is called the Flint Knives' Plot of Land.

¹⁷The battle was very fierce that day, and Abner and the men of Israel were defeated by David's soldiers. ¹⁸The three sons of Zeruiah were there: Joab, Abishai, and Asahel. (Now Asahel was a swift runner like one of the wild gazelles.) ¹⁹Asahel pursued Abner. He did not turn away to the right or to the left when pursuing Abner. ²⁰Abner turned around and said, "Are you really Asahel?"

He said, "I [am]."

²¹Abner said to him, "Turn away to the right or to the left. Seize one of the young men, and take for yourself what you can strip from him." But Asahel was not willing to turn away from pursuing him.

²²Abner again said to Asahel, "Turn away from pursuing me. Why should I strike you down to the ground? How could I look your brother Joab in the face?" ²³But he refused to turn away, so Abner struck him in the stomach with the butt end of his spear, and the spear came out his back. Asahel fell and died on the spot. When everyone who came to the place where Asahel fell and died—they stopped.

²⁴Joab and Abishai pursued Abner. By sunset they had come as far as the Hill of Ammah, which is opposite Giah on the road to the wilderness of Gibeon. ²⁵The Benjaminites gathered behind Abner, formed a single unit, and took their stand on the top of a hill. ²⁶Then Abner called to Joab, "Must the sword devour

forever? Don't you know that this will end in bitterness? How long? Won't you tell the troops to turn from pursing their brothers?"

²⁷Joab said, "As God lives, if you had not spoken, the troops certainly would not have stopped pursuing their brothers until morning." ²⁸So Joab blew a ram's horn, and all the troops stopped and no longer pursued Israel nor continued to fight. ²⁹Abner and his men marched through the Arabah all that night. They crossed the Jordan River. They marched all morning and came to Mahanaim.

³⁰Joab returned from pursuing Abner and gathered all the troops. His inspection revealed that nineteen of David's soldiers were missing, including Asah-el. ³¹David's soldiers had struck down [fighters] from Benjamin and among the men of Abner; three hundred sixty men had died. ³²They carried Asahel and interred him in the tomb of his father, which is in Bethlehem. Joab and his men marched all that night and reached Hebron at dawn.

3 ¹There was a protracted war between the house of Saul and the house of David. David kept growing stronger, and the house of Saul was growing weaker.

²Sons were born to David in Hebron. His firstborn was Amnon by Ahinoam the Jezreelitess. ³His second was Chileab by Abigail the Carmelitess. The third was Absalom the son of Maacah, the daughter of King Talmai of Geshur. ⁴The fourth was Adonijah the son of Haggith. The fifth was Shephatiah the son of Abital. ⁵The sixth was Ithream by David's wife Eglah. These [sons] were born to David in Hebron.

Textual Notes

2:8 שַׂר־צָבָא אֲשֶׁר לְשָׁאוּל—Literally "commander of (the) army which (belonged) to Saul," this is translated as "commander of Saul's army." This construction with the relative clause אֲשֶׁר לְשָׁאוּל (with a לְ of possession) is used instead of a three-word construct chain, שַׂר־צְבָא־שָׁאוּל, "commander of the army of Saul," probably to preserve the title שַׂר־צָבָא (see Joüon, § 130 c, e; Waltke-O'Connor, § 13.4b, example 23). For the construct phrase שַׂר־צָבָא or שַׂר־הַצָּבָא, "commander of (the) army," see also 1 Sam 12:9; 14:50; 17:55; 26:5; 2 Sam 10:16, 18; 19:14 (ET 19:13). Here 4QSamᵃ reads הצבא, "*the* army," supplying an article on צָבָא, probably in order to "correct" what may have been perceived as the grammatically inferior anarthrous reading of the MT. However, the trailing relative clause, "which (belonged) to Saul," makes the construct phrase שַׂר־צָבָא specific, eliminating the need for the article. Moreover, Hebrew commonly omits the article on a noun in a title such as this one (Joüon, § 137 r; cf. Waltke-O'Connor, § 13.4b, example 23).

אִישׁ בֹּשֶׁת—"Ish-bosheth." The names of some of the members of Saul's family were most likely purposely bowdlerized to avoid any royal association with the pagan god Baal.[1] This is evident when we compare the names of two men in Samuel with their

---

[1] However, it ought to be noted that it is possible that the names with בַּעַל, *ba'al*, might have intended that part of the name to mean "master" as a title for Yahweh. See בַּעַל in Hos 2:18 (ET 2:16), where Yahweh promises that in the future, Israel will call him "my husband" instead of

names in Chronicles. The first man in Samuel is named "Ish-bosheth,"[2] meaning "man of shame," instead of "Eshbaal," meaning "man of the master/Baal" (1 Chr 8:33; 9:39). Later in 2 Samuel we find "Mephibosheth,"[3] meaning "from the mouth of shame," instead of "Merib-baal," meaning "he contends with Baal" (1 Chr 8:34; 9:40). It ought to be noted that the name Ishbaal/Eshbaal has been found in an early inscription from Khirbet Qeiyafa that reads אשבעל בן בדע, "Ishbaal the son of Beda."[4] The inscription appears to date from the time of Saul and David, since radiocarbon dating of olive pits from the relevant excavation layer has yielded a date of ca. 1020–980 BC.[5] Since the MT and the LXX of Samuel consistently have the two names "Ish-bosheth" and "Mephibosheth" and never have the alternate names that are in Chronicles, "Eshbaal" and "Merib-baal," a scribe probably changed the names in Samuel to "Ish-bosheth" and "Mephibosheth" before the MT and the LXX became two distinct textual traditions. However, it appears unlikely that "Ish-bosheth" and "Mephibosheth" were part of the original text of the book of Samuel. Other examples of substituting בֹּשֶׁת for בַּעַל took place after the MT and the LXX arose as distinct traditions: Jerubbesheth (יְרֻבֶּשֶׁת, MT 2 Sam 11:21) occurs instead of Jerubbaal (Ιεροβααλ, LXX 2 Sam 11:21).[6] The MT of 1 Ki 18:19 and 1 Ki 18:25 reads הַבַּעַל, but the LXX has τῆς αἰσχύνης (=הַבֹּשֶׁת). In Jer 11:13 the MT reads מִזְבְּחוֹת לַבֹּשֶׁת מִזְבְּחוֹת לְקַטֵּר לַבָּעַל, "altars of shame, altars to burn incense to Baal," whereas the LXX simply reads βωμοὺς θυμιᾶν τῇ Βααλ, "altars to burn incense to Baal." Thus, it would appear that MT Jer 11:13 is a conflated reading that includes both the original "Baal" (as in the LXX) and the later substitution of "shame" for "Baal."[7]

The fact that Chronicles has the names "Eshbaal" and "Merib-baal" makes it virtually certain that the names were bowdlerized in Samuel by a later scribe, not by the original author. It is almost beyond contention that the Chronicler used portions

---

בַּעְלִי, "my *baʿal*," probably meaning "my master." See also the use of the cognate verb בָּעַל, *baʿal*, "to marry," for Yahweh marrying his people in Is 54:5; 62:4; Jer 3:14.

2   "Ish-bosheth" is named in 2 Sam 2:8, 10, 12, 15; 3:8, 14, 15; 4:5, 8, 12. His name probably is to be read also in 3:7; see the textual note there.

3   2 Sam 4:4; 9:6, 10, 11, 12, 13; 16:1, 4; 19:25, 26, 31 (ET 19:24, 25, 30); 21:7, 8.

4   Garfinkel et al., "The ʾIšbaʿal Inscription from Khirbet Qeiyafa," 223.

5   Garfinkel et al., "The ʾIšbaʿal Inscription from Khirbet Qeiyafa," 220.

6   See "Jerubbaal" in Judg 6:32; 7:1; 8:29, 35; 9:1, 2, 5, 16, 19, 24, 28, 57; 1 Sam 12:11.

7   Tsevat, "Ishbosheth and Congeners," argues that the "-bosheth" names are not bowdlerized but instead reflect names found in Akkadian that include the element *bāštu*, "strength." Thus, the name "Ish-bosheth" ought to be understood as "man of strength." However, Tsevat's argument suffers from several weaknesses: (1) There is no evidence for a Hebrew cognate of the Akkadian *bāštu*. (2) The hypothesis does not explain how "strength" consistently corresponds to בַּעַל, "baal," in the other two names with this phenomenon (Mephibosheth and Jerubbesheth) or *why this phenomenon with bowdlerized names is found only in 2 Samuel.* (3) It does not provide a convincing explanation for the lone change of "Jerubbaal" (e.g., Judg 6:32; 7:1; 1 Sam 12:11) to "Jerubbesheth" in MT 2 Sam 11:21 (see his discussion on p. 83). (4) It does not explain why MT 1 Ki 18:19 and 1 Ki 18:25 have הַבַּעַל, "(the) Baal," but the LXX in those verses has τῆς αἰσχύνης (=הַבֹּשֶׁת), "of shame." Neither does it explain why MT Jer 11:13 has the conflated reading מִזְבְּחוֹת לַבֹּשֶׁת מִזְבְּחוֹת לְקַטֵּר לַבָּעַל, "altars of shame, altars to burn incense to Baal," whereas the LXX simply reads βωμοὺς θυμιᾶν τῇ Βααλ, "altars to burn incense to Baal."

of Samuel and Kings as major sources, at times copying them almost verbatim. The Chronicler must have used portions of Samuel that, at the time of his borrowing, still had the names "Eshbaal" and "Merib-baal," before those names were bowdlerized in Samuel.

If the names had been bowdlerized by the original author of Samuel, one would have to posit one of these scenarios:

1. The names were originally the "baal" form.
2. The author of Samuel bowdlerized the names. However, he declined either to bowdlerize Jerubbaal in 1 Sam 12:11 or to change it to Gideon.
3a. A later scribe reverted the names to the "baal" form in Samuel, which the Chronicler then used as his source, but that reverted version of Samuel did not survive.

Or

3b. The Chronicler—who was working centuries later in the postexilic period—knew of the original names (perhaps by oral tradition?) and reverted them to the "baal" form despite the evidence from his source in the book of Samuel.

Or

3c. The Chronicler had another written source for the names of Saul's sons and Jonathan's son and chose the "baal" form used in it over the bowdlerized form he knew from his major source, the book of Samuel.

Each of those three scenarios is highly unlikely. The following explanation is more probable:

1. The names of the men were originally in the "baal" form, and they were included in that form by the author of Samuel.
2. During the Persian period, the Chronicler used Samuel as his source.
3. A later scribe in the Hellenistic period bowdlerized the names in Samuel, and the bowdlerized forms were carried into both the MT and the LXX. However, due to the influence of "Jerubbaal" in Judges 6–9, this scribe allowed the name "Jerubbaal" to stand in 1 Sam 12:11, for 1 Sam 12:11 is largely a reference to Judges.

Thus, it is highly unlikely that the original author of Samuel used bowdlerized names. Occam's razor suggests that the more simple scenario outlined immediately above is more probable.

מַחֲנָיִם:—The name "Mahanaim" was given to the place by Jacob (Gen 32:3 [ET 32:2]). This dual form of the noun מַחֲנֶה means "two camps." It was near the Jabbok River in the Transjordan on the border of Gad and (eastern) Manasseh. No modern location has been identified with it. The name recurs in 2:12, 29.[8]

2:9 וַיַּמְלִכֵהוּ אֶל־—"He made him king over …" Elsewhere in Samuel, the Hiphil (H) of מָלַךְ, "to make [someone] king," is used for the coronation of Saul (1 Sam 11:15; 12:1; 15:11, 35; cf. 1 Sam 8:22). The expected preposition for introducing territories or persons over whom the king reigns is עַל, "over," which is so used three times later in

---

[8] See "Mahanaim" also in Josh 13:26, 30; 21:38; 2 Sam 17:24, 27; 19:33 (ET 19:32); 1 Ki 2:8; 4:14; 1 Chr 6:65 (ET 6:80).

this verse. The Hiphil of מָלַךְ is regularly used with עַל elsewhere in the OT.[9] However, in this verse אֶל is used for the first three. Samuel is one of the OT books in which אֶל is often used in place of עַל (BDB, s.v. אֶל, note 2).

הָאֲשׁוּרִי—"The Asherites." This is the only instance of this orthography in the MT, which would literally be "the Ash*u*rite(s)." Its spelling is often thought to be a mistake for the name of the tribe אָשֵׁר, "Asher," but it is more likely a mistake for the more correct spelling הָאֲשֵׁרִי, "the Asherites" (Judg 1:32). The LXX incomprehensibly reads Θασιρι, "Thasiri," which appears to preserve the gentilic suffix ִי- and may be a corruption of ὁ Ἀσηρι, "the Asherites." The Syriac suggests גְּשׁוּר, "Geshur" (as in 2 Sam 3:3; 13:37–38; 14:23, 32; 15:8; 1 Chr 2:23; 3:2), and the Vulgate suggests הַגְּשׁוּרִי, "the Geshurites" (as in, e.g., 1 Sam 27:8). However, since Geshur is an independent kingdom in 2 Samuel, the readings of the Syriac and the Vulgate are most likely a corruption of הָאֲשׁוּרִי or אָשֵׁר. Targum Jonathan suggests בֵּית אָשֵׁר, "the house of Asher," but considering the somewhat periphrastic nature of that Targum, its reading gives little indication of what the underlying Hebrew text may have been.

2:10 וּשְׁתַּיִם שָׁנִים מָלָךְ—"And he reigned two years." The phrase שְׁתַּיִם שָׁנִים is an adverbial accusative expressing an extent of time (*IBH*, § 18 B). The verb form מָלָךְ is pausal for מָלַךְ.

הָיוּ אַחֲרֵי דָוִד:—Literally "they were after David," this is translated as "[the house of Judah] followed David." This idiom with the verb הָיָה, "be," and the preposition אַחֲרֵי, "after," indicates allegiance to a leader (here and in 1 Ki 12:20; 16:21) or giving in to peer pressure (Ex 23:2).

2:11 מִסְפַּר הַיָּמִים—This construct phrase, literally "the number of days," is translated as "the total time."

2:12 וַיֵּצֵא—Literally "and he went out," this is translated as "(he/they) marched." Qal (G) forms of the verb יָצָא often signify going out to battle, as again in 2:13. See the first textual note on 1 Sam 18:6.[10] For this use of the verb with "king" as the subject, see the second textual note on 11:1. Although the verb here has a compound subject, it agrees in number with its closest subject, Abner, indicating his importance in the view of the author (see also 2:17).

וְעַבְדֵי אִישׁ־בֹּשֶׁת—"And the soldiers of Ish-bosheth." The noun עֶבֶד can signify a king's official (*HALOT*, s.v. עֶבֶד I, 3). Here it probably refers to officers or soldiers in the army. See also David's officers/soldiers (עַבְדֵי דָוִד) in 2:13, 15, 17, 30, 31.

גִּבְעוֹנָה:—"To Gibeon." This is the place-name גִּבְעוֹן (as also in 2:13, 16, 24) with a suffixed *he* directive. "Gibeon" is mentioned thirty-seven times in the OT. It was attacked by Saul during his reign, and the Gibeonites eventually asked David for vengeance on Saul's house (21:1–9). It is located at modern el-Jib, about seven miles (eleven kilometers) northwest of Jerusalem.

---

9 Judg 9:18; 1 Sam 12:1; 15:35; 1 Ki 12:20; 16:16; 2 Ki 8:20; 1 Chr 12:39 (ET 12:38); 23:1; 28:4; 2 Chr 1:9, 11; 21:8; 36:4, 10.

10 Steinmann, *1 Samuel*, 350. See also, e.g., 1 Sam 4:1; 8:20; 18:13, 16, 30; 28:1; 29:6; 2 Sam 11:1; 21:17.

2:13 צְרוּיָה—"Zeruiah" (see also 2:18) was David's sister (1 Chr 2:16). Therefore, Joab, Abishai, and Asahel were David's nephews.

וַיִּפְגְּשׁוּם—"And they met them." The verb פָּגַשׁ, "to meet, encounter" (a synonym of the more common verb פָּגַע), occurs only fourteen times in the OT. Its Qal (G) often refers to a hostile or potentially hostile confrontation (e.g., Gen 32:18 [ET 32:17]; Ex 4:24; Hos 13:8; Prov 17:12; cf. 1 Sam 25:20).

יַחְדָּו—This adverb, "together," modifies the verb וַיִּפְגְּשׁוּם, "and they met them," and emphasizes the encounter of the two armed forces. It has a similar force in 2:16: "they fell down [dead] together [יַחְדָּו]." Here in 2:13 it is left untranslated since English idiom does not require it.

אֵלֶּה עַל־הַבְּרֵכָה מִזֶּה וְאֵלֶּה עַל־הַבְּרֵכָה מִזֶּה:—The typical Hebrew construction for a distributive idiom involves repetition (see Joüon, § 142 p; Waltke-O'Connor, §§ 7.2.3b; 15.6b). The expression here is repeated: "these on the pool from this [side] and these on the pool from this [side]." It is translated as "at the pool on opposite sides."

2:14 יָקוּמוּ נָא ... יָקֻמוּ—"Let them arise. ... Let them arise." The form of both instances of the Qal (G) of קוּם, "arise," could be either imperfect or jussive, and the context calls for the jussive meaning (cf. GKC, § 48 g; Joüon, § 114 g). In Biblical Hebrew, a standard way to answer a question in the affirmative is to repeat the key word (Joüon, § 161 l (1)), hence Joab repeats the verb in Abner's question. Cf. 2:20, where the question about identity is answered by the pronoun אָנֹכִי, "I [am]."

וִישַׂחֲקוּ—"And let them hold a contest." This is a Piel (D) imperfect jussive of the verb שָׂחַק, which in the Qal (G) means "to laugh" (as does its by-form צָחַק). In the Piel this verb means "to play" an instrument (2 Sam 6:5) or "amuse" someone or "make sport" of someone (see the Piel of צָחַק in Judg 16:25). Here it probably refers to holding a contest of gladiatorial skills.

2:15 לְבִנְיָמִן—Instead of the MT's "for Benjamin," 4QSamᵃ (לבני בנימין) and the LXX (τῶν παίδων Βενιαμιν) read "for the sons of Benjamin" (see 2:25). It is difficult to decide which is the better reading. The shorter MT could be defective due to haplography, or the longer reading in 4QSamᵃ and the LXX could be the result of dittography.

2:16 וַיַּחֲזִקוּ ... בְּרֹאשׁ—"And they grabbed ... by the head." For the Hiphil (H) of חָזַק with בְּ, "take hold of," see the first textual note on 1 Sam 15:27[11] and the textual note on 2 Sam 1:11.

אִישׁ ... רֵעֵהוּ—"Each man ... his opponent." Normally the noun רֵעַ denotes a "friend" or "neighbor." However, in this reciprocal idiom in this adversarial context, it is translated as "opponent." For its use in a reciprocal idiom, see BDB, s.v. רֵעַ II, 3, under the root רעה II.

וְחַרְבּוֹ—Usually חֶרֶב is translated as "sword," but here it must denote a weapon with a shorter blade, such as a "dagger," especially in light of הַצֻּרִים (see the fifth textual note on 2:16).

---

[11] Steinmann, *1 Samuel*, 288.

וַיִּקְרָא—"So it is called." Grammatically the Qal (G) verb is active, "and he called." However, an impersonal verb with no stated subject is often best translated as a passive (GKC, § 144 d (a); cf. Joüon, § 155 e).

חֶלְקַת הַצֻּרִים—"The Flint Knives' Plot of Land." This construct phrase is literally "the plot of the flints." As pointed by the Masoretes, הַצֻּרִים is the plural of צֹר (Ex 4:25; Ezek 3:9; Ps 89:44 [ET 89:43]) or צוּר, "flint (knife)," with the definite article. See צֻרִים, the plural of צוּר, in Josh 5:2–3. The LXX reading here, μερὶς τῶν ἐπιβούλων, the "Portion of the Conspirators," suggests a different pointing, חֶלְקַת הַצָּרִים, "the Enemies' Plot of Land," with the plural of the noun צַר, "adversary" (BDB, s.v. צַר III, under the root צרר II).

2:17 וַיִּנָּגֶף—Literally "and he was defeated." For the Niphal (N) of נָגַף with this military meaning, see the third textual note on 1 Sam 4:2.[12] It also appears in 1 Sam 4:10; 7:10; 2 Sam 10:15, 19; 18:7. Here, as in 2:12 (see the first textual note there), the singular verb agrees with its most important subject, Abner.

2:18 קַל בְּרַגְלָיו—The adjective קַל with the prepositional phrase בְּרַגְלָיו is literally "swift on his feet." The phrase is translated as "a swift runner." For the suffix on בְּרַגְלָיו, see Joüon, § 146 g.

כְּאַחַד הַצְּבָיִם אֲשֶׁר בַּשָּׂדֶה:—Literally "like one of the gazelles which are in the countryside," this phrase is translated as "like one of the wild gazelles." The numeral אֶחָד is in construct (אַחַד) with a plural noun (הַצְּבָיִם) to indicate indetermination (Joüon, § 137 v; Waltke-O'Connor, § 13.8a, including example 12), i.e., any gazelle, not a certain one. For the noun צְבִי II, "gazelle," see the second paragraph of the first textual note on 1:19. This form of the plural with the article, הַצְּבָיִם, is written defectively for הַצְּבָיִים, in which the first *yod* is a consonant and the second is a vowel letter (cf. GKC, § 93 x).

2:19 וְלֹא־נָטָה לָלֶכֶת עַל־הַיָּמִין וְעַל־הַשְּׂמֹאול מֵאַחֲרֵי אַבְנֵר:—"He did not turn away to the right or to the left when pursuing Abner" is literally "and he did not incline to go to the right or to the left from after Abner." The idiomatic vocabulary is repeated in 2:21. For מֵאַחֲרֵי, "from after" (the combination of the prepositions מִן and אַחֲרֵי), denoting pursuit, see also 2 Sam 2:22, 26, 27, 30. Here a *waw* suffices to introduce the second direction, וְעַל־הַשְּׂמֹאול, "and (or) to the left," but 2:21 will use the coordinating conjunction אוֹ, "or" (Joüon, § 175 a; Waltke-O'Connor, § 39.2.6b, example 2).

2:20 הַאַתָּה זֶה—"Are you really?" After the pronoun אַתָּה with an interrogative *he*, the demonstrative pronoun זֶה, "this," is used as an enclitic particle to add emphasis to the question, hence "really?"[13]

2:21 אֶת־חֲלִצָתוֹ—"What you can strip from him." The noun חֲלִיצָה denotes equipment stripped from the dead body of a soldier (its only other occurrence is in Judg 14:19). It is related to the verb חָלַץ, whose Qal (G) means "to pull off" clothing (Deut 25:9), but whose Qal passive (Gp) participle, חָלוּץ, is a frequent term for an "armed" or "equipped" soldier (e.g., Num 31:5; Deut 3:18; Josh 4:13).

---

[12] Steinmann, *1 Samuel*, 119–20.

[13] *IBH*, § 25 B; Waltke-O'Connor, § 17.4.3c; GKC, § 136 c; Joüon, § 143 g.

2:22 וַיֹּ֨סֶף ע֤וֹד אַבְנֵר֙ לֵאמֹ֣ר—"Abner again said." The Hiphil (H) of יָסַף, "to add; do again," functions adverbially, and the Qal (G) infinitive construct לֵאמֹר (with לְ), "to say," serves as the main verb, thus "said again." See Joüon, §§ 102 g, 124 c, 177 b, and the first textual note on 1 Sam 3:6.[14] See also the textual note on 2 Sam 2:28.

לָ֤מָּה אַכֶּ֨כָה֙ אַ֔רְצָה—"Why should I strike you down to the ground?" While phrased as a question, this clause provides the reason why Asahel should obey the preceding imperative to "turn away" (סוּר). It functions as a warning (GKC, § 150 e; cf. Joüon, § 161 h). The verb אַכֶּ֨כָה֙ is the first common singular Hiphil (H) imperfect of נָכָה, "strike down," with a second masculine singular suffix written in the fuller form כָה-, instead of the usual ךָ-, and the *daghesh* in -כָּ- may be due to an assimilated energic *nun* (GKC, § 58 i).

וְאֵיךְ֙ אֶשָּׂ֣א פָנַ֔י אֶל־יוֹאָ֖ב אָחִֽיךָ׃—"How could I look your brother Joab in the face?" is literally "how could I lift up my face to Joab your brother?" Here the use of the verb נָשָׂא for lifting up one's own face is a sign of having a good conscience (BDB, s.v. נָשָׂא, Qal, 1 b (3)).

2:23 בְּאַחֲרֵ֣י הַחֲנִ֗ית—"With the butt end of his spear." By using the blunt end, Abner showed his reluctance to kill Asahel. This is the only time in the OT that a form of אַחַר is used as a substantive, "back part." Elsewhere אַחֲרֵי (its plural form, always used in construct) is always used as a preposition, "behind, after."

אֶל־הַחֹ֗מֶשׁ—The noun חֹמֶשׁ II denotes the "stomach." Its only other occurrences in the OT are in 2 Sam 3:27; 4:6; 20:10, always in the context of stabbing someone. Bodner claims that חֹמֶשׁ means "fifth rib" (cf. חָמֵשׁ, "five"),[15] but it is unlikely that the author is locating all of these stabbings precisely in the fifth rib.

תַּחְתָּ֑יו—"On the spot" is literally "under himself" (Waltke-O'Connor, § 11.2.15b, including example 3). The Qere תַּחְתָּיו is the normal spelling of the plural form of the suffixed preposition תַּחַת. The Kethib is the singular suffixed form תַּחְתּוֹ. This Kethib occurs three other times, always as a Kethib (2 Sam 3:12; 16:8; Job 9:13).

וַיְהִ֡י כָּל־הַבָּ֣א ... וַֽיַּעֲמֹֽדוּ׃—"When everyone who came … they stopped." Here וַיְהִי expresses time, "when" (see GKC, § 111 g). The construct phrase כָּל־הַבָּא, "everyone who came," is a *casus pendens* (GKC, § 116 w; Joüon, § 156 e). The Qal (G) participle הַבָּא is masculine singular, but it represents any and all such individuals (Joüon, §§ 135 c, 139 i), so the Qal preterite (imperfect with *waw* consecutive) וַֽיַּעֲמֹדוּ is plural, literally "and they stood (still)." The Qal of עָמַד, "to stand," has a similar meaning, "to stop [an activity]," in 2:25, 28.

2:24 וְהַשֶּׁ֖מֶשׁ בָּ֑אָה—Literally "and the sun set," this is translated as "by sunset." When the noun שֶׁמֶשׁ is the subject of בּוֹא, "come," the idiom refers to the sun going down or setting.[16] שֶׁמֶשׁ can be construed either as feminine (as here) or as masculine. The verb form בָּ֑אָה with the accent on the first syllable is the third feminine singular Qal (G)

---

[14] Steinmann, *1 Samuel*, 110.

[15] Bodner, "Crime Scene Investigation."

[16] E.g., Gen 15:12; 28:11; Ex 22:25 (ET 22:26); Lev 22:7; Deut 16:6.

perfect of בּוֹא with an instantaneous meaning (Joüon, § 111 d). (If it were accented on the final syllable, בָּאָה, it would be the Qal feminine singular participle.)

גִּיחַ—This place-name, "Giah," is not mentioned elsewhere, and its location is unknown.

2:25 לַאֲגֻדָּה—Elsewhere the noun אֲגֻדָּה (four times in the OT) can refer to a "bunch" of hyssop (Ex 12:22), the "straps" of a yoke (Is 58:6), or the "vault" of heaven (Amos 9:6). Here alone it denotes a "band" of men as a military "unit."

רֹאשׁ־גִּבְעָה אֶחָת:—"(The) top of a hill." Occasionally the Hebrew number אֶחָד, "one," functions as an indefinite article (*HALOT*, 3). אַחַת is its feminine form, אֶחָת, in pause.

2:26 הֲלָנֶצַח תֹּאכַל חֶרֶב—"Must the sword devour forever?" The feminine noun חֶרֶב, "sword," is the subject of the Qal (G) imperfect of אָכַל, "to eat." The form תֹּאכַל is third feminine singular, not second masculine singular, and in this question the imperfect has the modal nuance of "should?" or "must?" (see Joüon, § 113 l, m).

הֲלוֹא יָדַעְתָּה—"Don't you know?" Occasionally the second masculine singular ending of a Qal (G) perfect verb is written תָה- instead of with the usual orthography, תָ- (GKC, § 44 g; Joüon, § 42 f).

מָרָה תִהְיֶה בָּאַחֲרוֹנָה—"This will end in bitterness" is literally "it will be bitter in the later/last (time)." Hebrew often uses the feminine for an abstract idea, and the implied subject of the feminine imperfect תִהְיֶה, "it will be," is the current situation. Its direct object, מָרָה, is the feminine form of the adjective מַר, "bitter," used as a substantive. The feminine adjective אַחֲרוֹנָה is often used adverbially, "afterward, later, at the last," either with (as here) or without a preposition (see BDB, s.v. אַחֲרוֹן, b (α), (β), (γ)).

לָעָם—"(To) the troops." For the definite noun הָעָם in the sense of "the troops," see the second textual note on 1:4. It recurs in this sense in 2:27, 28, 30.

2:27 חַי הָאֱלֹהִים כִּי—"As God lives …" This is the only instance of the oath formula חַי הָאֱלֹהִים in Samuel, but the corresponding חַי יהוה, "as Yahweh lives," is common.[17] For the use of these oath formulas with כִּי, see *IBH*, § 64 D; Joüon, § 165 e; Waltke-O'Connor, § 40.2.2b.

לוּלֵא דִבַּרְתָּ כִּי אָז—"If you had not spoken, then certainly …" The conjunction לוּלֵא with a perfect verb (דִּבַּרְתָּ) introduces a past unreal or contrary-to-fact condition in the negative ("if" something "had not" happened, when it fact it had happened). The adverb אָז, "then," introduces what the result would have been if the condition had been true (if Abner had not spoken). See *IBH*, § 58 B; Waltke-O'Connor, § 38.2e; GKC, § 159 x. Here כִּי emphasizes the absolute certainty (GKC, § 159 ee; cf. Joüon, § 167 s), hence "certainly."

מֵהַבֹּקֶר נַעֲלָה הָעָם—"The troops would not have stopped pursuing until morning" is literally "from the morning the troop took itself away." Here the preposition מִן has a temporal meaning (BDB, 4 b), so the prepositional phrase מֵהַבֹּקֶר does not refer to the terminus a quo ("from/starting in the morning") but to the terminus ad quem ("until the next morning"). The verb נַעֲלָה is the third masculine singular Niphal (N) perfect of עָלָה,

---

[17] E.g., 1 Sam 14:39, 45; 2 Sam 4:9; 12:5; 14:11; 15:21; 22:47.

"go up." Often its Niphal has a passive meaning, "be taken up, exalted." Here, however, it has a reflexive meaning, "take oneself away" (BDB, Niphal, 2; *DCH*, Niphal, 2), that is, "withdraw" or "stop the pursuit" (*HALOT*, Niphal, 3). In the context of the past contrary-to-fact conditional sentence in the negative, the meaning is, somewhat woodenly, "the troops would not have taken themselves away until morning." The various English versions represent different attempts to convey the thought adequately and smoothly (cf. KJV, RSV, ESV, NASB).

2:28 וְלֹא־יָסְפוּ עוֹד לְהִלָּחֵם:—Literally "and they did not add/do again to wage war," this is translated as "nor continued to fight." The Qal (G) of יָסַף is used adverbially ("continued") with the Niphal (N) infinitive construct (with לְ) לְהִלָּחֵם, "to fight." See the first textual note on 1 Sam 3:6.[18] For the same construction as used here (the Qal of יָסַף with an infinitive construct and the adverb עוֹד), see the first textual note on 1 Sam 7:13.[19]

2:29 בָּעֲרָבָה—"The Arabah" refers to the depression through which the Jordan River flows. It extends from Mount Hermon in the north to the Gulf of Aqaba in the south.

כָּל־הַבִּתְרוֹן—"All morning." The noun בִּתְרוֹן appears only here. It probably is cognate to the verb בָּתַר, "to cut in two" (Gen 15:10), and the noun בֶּתֶר, one "piece" of an animal cut in two (Gen 15:10; Jer 34:18–19). Since the first clause of 2 Sam 2:29 has כָּל הַלַּיְלָה, "all the night," the noun בִּתְרוֹן may refer to the morning as the remaining "piece" of the day. Alternatively, it could be a place-name, Bithron, possibly the name of a gorge, since in Song 2:17 בֶּתֶר denotes a "cleft" or "valley" between mountains. Cf. *HALOT*, s.v. בִּתְרוֹן, and *DCH*, s.v. בִּתְרוֹן.

וַיָּבֹאוּ מַחֲנָיִם:—The MT reads "and they came [to] Mahanaim" without a preposition or suffixed *he* directive. Movement to the place would be implied by the verb. However, בּוֹא is frequently used with a *he* directive suffixed on the noun that is the destination, and בּוֹא is used with מַחֲנָיְמָה, "to come to Mahanaim," in 2 Sam 17:24, 27.[20] The reading in 4QSamᵃ is [מחנ]ימה, "to [Maha]naim," with a *he* directive. That reading is supported by the preposition in the LXX, εἰς τὴν παρεμβολήν, "to the camp."[21]

2:30 וַיִּפְקְדוּ דָוִד מֵעַבְדֵי תִּשְׁעָה־עָשָׂר אִישׁ וַעֲשָׂה־אֵל:—"His inspection revealed that nineteen of David's soldiers were missing, including Asah-el" is literally "nineteen men and Asah-el were missing from the servants of David." The verb וַיִּפָּקְדוּ is the Niphal (N) preterite (imperfect with *waw* consecutive) third masculine plural of פָּקַד. In the Niphal, this verb can simply mean "to be missing" or "lacking, absent" (e.g., 1 Sam 20:18, 25, 27; see BDB, Niphal, 1, and *HALOT*, Niphal, 1). However, its Qal (G) often means "to make a careful inspection" (*HALOT*, Qal, 1), and in context it is evident that Joab had gathered the troops to inspect them. The Qal of פָּקַד is used for mustering or counting troops in 1 Sam 11:8; 13:15; 14:17; 15:4; 2 Sam 18:1.

---

[18] Steinmann, *1 Samuel*, 110.

[19] Steinmann, *1 Samuel*, 157.

[20] The verb בּוֹא is followed immediately by a noun with a *he* directive also in 1 Sam 22:9; 31:12; 2 Sam 10:17; 24:6.

[21] The LXX translates "Mahanaim" as παρεμβολή, "camp," also in 2:8.

In the compound subject תִּשְׁעָה־עָשָׂר אִישׁ וַעֲשָׂה־אֵל, the conjunction *waw* may mean "especially" or "in particular" (see *DCH*, 5; BDB, 1 a and 1 b), in which case "nineteen men" is the total number, "including Asah-el," who is singled out by name because of his importance (2 Sam 2:18–23, 32; cf. Mk 16:7). His name is spelled as two words here and in 2 Sam 3:27; 23:24; 1 Chr 2:16; 11:26; 27:7. It is a typical Hebrew compound theophoric name, a combination of the verb עָשָׂה and the noun אֵל, thus "God has acted" or "God does," probably referring to God's acts of salvation.

2:31 מִבִּנְיָמִן—The preposition מִן is used in a partitive sense: "[some of the fighters] from Benjamin." 4QSamᵃ (מבני] בנימן) and the LXX (τῶν υἱῶν Βενιαμιν) read "from/ of the sons of Benjamin." As in the textual note on 2:15, it is difficult to decide which is the superior reading.

וּבְאַנְשֵׁי אַבְנֵר—"And among the men of Abner." 4QSamᵃ reads [מאנשי] אבנר, "from the men of [Abner]," and that construct phrase is in apposition to the preceding one in 4QSamᵃ, [מבני] בנימן, implying that all of the men in Abner's force who were killed were Benjaminites.

2:32 בֵּית לָחֶם—This is an accusative of place (GKC, § 118 g; Joüon, § 126 h), so the translation adds the preposition "in": "in Bethlehem."

וַיֵּאֹר לָהֶם בְּחֶבְרוֹן:—"And they reached Hebron at dawn" is literally "and it became light to them at Hebron." The verb is a preterite (imperfect with *waw* consecutive) third masculine singular of אוֹר, "to become light; shine," used impersonally, with no subject.[22] BDB and *DCH* parse it as a Niphal (N), while *HALOT* and GKC, § 72 r, consider it to be a Qal (G).

3:1 וַתְּהִי הַמִּלְחָמָה אֲרֻכָּה—"There was a protracted war" is literally "and the war was lengthy." The definite feminine noun הַמִּלְחָמָה is the subject, and the predicate adjective, אֲרֻכָּה, is the feminine form of the adjective אָרֹךְ, "long," in a temporal sense.

וְדָוִד הֹלֵךְ וְחָזֵק—"David kept growing stronger." In this idiom, the Qal (G) participle of הָלַךְ, "go," is coordinated with the Qal participle of חָזַק, "be strong." The identical pair of participles is used in Ex 19:19 to describe the horn blast that kept getting louder. The more common way to express this idea of continual progression is the use of a pair of infinitive absolutes.[23]

וּבֵית שָׁאוּל הֹלְכִים וְדַלִּים:—"And the house of Saul was growing weaker." The plural participle הֹלְכִים and the plural of the adjective דַּל, "weak, low, poor," form an idiom equivalent to the participial idiom in the preceding textual note. The singular noun בֵּית, "house," refers to the many members of the family, and so it is construed with plurals as its predicate in this nominal sentence (GKC, § 145 c (*a*) (β)). However, the two words are singular in the readings of 4QSamᵃ (הולך ודנל]) and the LXX (ἐπορεύετο καὶ ἠσθένει).

---

[22] For the use of a masculine verb to express a neuter concept, see Joüon, § 152 e.

[23] For the participial idiom here, see Waltke-O'Connor, § 37.6d, including example 21, as well as GKC, § 113 u, and Joüon, § 123 s, which also cover the use of the infinitive absolute. Joüon parses חָזֵק here in 2 Sam 3:1 as a "verbal adjective," but BDB identifies it as the Qal (G) participle.

3:2 וַיִּוָּלְדוּ לְדָוִד בָּנִים—"Sons were born to David." The translation follows the Qere, וַיִּוָּלְדוּ, which is the Niphal (N) preterite (imperfect with *waw* consecutive) third masculine plural of יָלַד, "give birth," whose Niphal means "be born." Its subject is the masculine plural בָּנִים, "sons." Cf. the second textual note on 3:5. The Kethib, וַיֵּלְדוּ, is the Qal (G) preterite (imperfect with *waw* consecutive). Although the Kethib is masculine, its implied subject would have to be David's wives (named in 3:2–5), "they gave birth," and בָּנִים would be its direct object (which is the normal construction with the Qal). The plural aorist passive verb in the LXX supports the Qere: ἐτέχθησαν. The unpointed reading in 4QSam[a] appears to support the Niphal Qere but is singular: ויולד.

אַמְנוֹן לַאֲחִינֹעַם—"Amnon by Ahinoam." This expression with the preposition לְ prefixed to the name of one of David's wives, literally "to Ahinoam," serves as a circumlocution for a genitive dependent on an unexpressed nomen regens: "Amnon [son] *of Ahinoam*" (GKC, § 129 g). The translation uses "by" to conform to English idiom. The expression recurs in 3:3a and 3:5. Phrases with the express genitive occur in 3:3b–4.

3:3 כִלְאָב—"Chileab" is the reading of the MT. 4QSam[a] (דלי[ה]ן) and the LXX (Δαλουια) read "Daluiah." 1 Chr 3:1 (דָּנִיֵּאל) and Josephus (Δανίηλος)[24] read "Daniel."

לַאֲבִיגַיִל אֵשֶׁת נָבָל הַכַּרְמְלִי—The MT reads "by Abigail, the wife of Nabal, the Carmelite." The gentilic adjective הַכַּרְמְלִי is masculine, and so "the Carmelite" describes Nabal, rather than Abigail. However, Nabal was not from Carmel, but from Maon (1 Sam 25:2). The MT appears to have been assimilated to 1 Sam 27:3; 2 Sam 2:2. See the second and third textual notes on 2:2. The translation adopted above, "to Abigail the Carmelitess," is the reading of 4QSam[a] (לאביגיל ה[כ]כרמלית) and the LXX (τῆς Αβιγαιας τῆς Καρμηλίας).

3:4 בֶּן־אֲבִיטָל:—"The son of Abital" is the reading of the MT. 4QSam[a] reads לאב[ב]יטל, "by A[b]ital," and is supported by the LXX (τῆς Αβιταλ) and Josephus (τῆς Ἀβιτάλης).[25]

3:5 אֵשֶׁת דָּוִד—"David's wife." 1 Chr 3:3 reads אִשְׁתּוֹ, "his wife."

אֵלֶּה יֻלְּדוּ לְדָוִד בְּחֶבְרוֹן:—"These [sons] were born to David in Hebron." The two prepositional phrases, לְדָוִד בְּחֶבְרוֹן, are repeated from 3:2. The Pual (Dp) perfect יֻלְּדוּ is comparable in meaning to the Qere וַיִּוָּלְדוּ (see the first textual note on 3:2).

Commentary

David did not impose his reign on any of Israel's tribes. Instead, he was first recognized by Judah (2:4a) and had reached out to the tribes east of the Jordan River by his commendation of Jabesh-gilead (2:4b–7). Apparently, this effort to court the Transjordanian tribes met with some success, so after David had reigned for five years in Hebron, Abner decided to set up Saul's son Ish-bosheth as king over Israel. That this took place during the last years of David's reign in Hebron is suggested by the narrative in 2 Samuel 5, which implies that David was made king over all Israel shortly after Ish-bosheth's assassination. Confirmation of this can be found in Abner's comment to the elders of Israel that for some time they had been considering acknowledging David as king

---

[24] Josephus, *Antiquities*, 7.21.

[25] Josephus, *Antiquities*, 7.21.

(2 Sam 3:17). By placing Ish-bosheth on the throne, it would appear that Abner was attempting to stanch the erosion of the power he and his family had held during the previous four decades.

The Kingdom Is Divided (2:8–11)

Mid 1005 BC (2:8–9)[26]

Parallel: 2 Sam 2:11 ‖ 1 Chr 3:4

Abner, Saul's uncle, decided to check any inroads David had made with the tribes east of the Jordan River by installing Ish-bosheth as king in Mahanaim (2:8). The extent of the kingdom covered Gilead in the east, Asher in the northwest, and Benjamin in the south, as well as the central regions of Jezreel and Ephraim (2:9). The author calls this "Israel—all of it" (2:9), which may be a reference to the later Northern Kingdom of Israel. In 2 Samuel there are occasional glimpses of the cleft between Israel and Judah (e.g., 19:41–44 [ET 19:40–43]) that would later lead to the division of the kingdom after Solomon's death (1 Kings 12).

The author then summarizes the reigns of the kings of this divided Israel: Ish-bosheth's as two years (2:10) and David's as seven and a half years (2:11). Ish-bosheth's age of forty (2:10) implies that he was born shortly after Saul began to reign, and this may be why he was not listed among Saul's sons earlier, unless he is to be identified with Ishvi (יִשְׁוִי, 1 Sam 14:49).[27] David was a decade younger. This has led some commentators to puzzle over the age of Ish-bosheth, since they surmise that Jonathan, Saul's eldest son, must have been about the same age as David.[28] However, there is no reason to believe that Jonathan and David were about the same age simply because they had a strong bond of friendship (1 Samuel 19–20).[29] In fact, Jonathan led an attack on the Philistines as a senior commander in Saul's army (1 Samuel 14). Thus, Jonathan must have been at least thirty in c. 1021 BC, the latest date that can be assigned to that battle. On the other hand, in c. 1019 BC David killed Goliath, who despised Jesse's son because he was a young man (1 Sam 17:33, 42), probably barely twenty, the minimum age for military service. Therefore, there may have been a difference of a dozen or more years between the ages of Jonathan and David.

The Battle of Gibeon (2:12–3:1)

Early 1004 BC (2:12–32)[30]

After establishing Ish-bosheth as king, Abner appears to have moved westward to project the kingdom's power on its southern border with Judah at the

---

[26] See "The Chronology of David's Reign" in the commentary on 5:1–5.

[27] See the discussion of Saul's sons in the commentary on 1 Sam 14:47–52 (Steinmann, *1 Samuel*, 278–79).

[28] Anderson, *2 Samuel*, 34–35; Baldwin, *1 and 2 Samuel*, 185; Hertzberg, *I and II Samuel*, 250.

[29] See the third textual note on 2 Sam 1:26. See also the textual notes and the commentary on 1 Sam 18:1–5, including "Jonathan's Relationship with David," in Steinmann, *1 Samuel*, 344–49.

[30] See "The Chronology of David's Reign" in the commentary on 5:1–5.

strategic town of Gibeon (2:12). His maneuver was countered by Joab, who makes his first appearance in the book of Samuel (2 Sam 2:13; in 1 Sam 26:6 he is mentioned in passing as the brother of Abishai). The author is careful to identify Joab as the son of David's sister Zeruiah. In fact, he frequently introduces both Joab and his brother Abishai as sons of Zeruiah.[31]

Joab's army met Abner's at what must have been a well-known pool at Gibeon. Archaeological excavations in the mid-twentieth century found an Iron Age pool cut into the bedrock just inside the city walls of Gibeon. It has a spiral staircase of seventy-nine steps cut into the walls of the pool, continuing downward into a tunnel that provides access to a water chamber seventy-nine feet (twenty-four meters) below the level of the city. This may be the pool mentioned in 2:13.

Abner proposed a smaller confrontation between the two armies: a contest between a chosen few (2:14), somewhat reminiscent of Goliath's challenge to Israel to settle the battle by an individual match (1 Sam 17:8–9). While the reason for twelve warriors from each side (2 Sam 2:15) is not stated, it is tempting to speculate that this was to be a contest for dominance of all twelve tribes of Israel.

The author quickly relates the result of the tournament. In each pair of combatants, the men killed each other while holding their opponent by the head. The upshot is that the place was given a name that commemorated the weapons used: flint knives (2:16).

Since the contest ended in a draw, it proved nothing, and the armies joined in a battle that resulted in the defeat of Abner's forces (2:17). The author then introduces all three of Zeruiah's sons in order to explain their part in the pursuit of Abner (2:18).

In a parenthetical comment we are told that Asahel was swift like a gazelle. Gazelles are among the swiftest of animals and can dash in bursts of up to sixty miles (ninety-seven kilometers) per hour or run longer distances at a speed of thirty miles (forty-eight kilometers) per hour. Asahel, we are told, was single-minded in his pursuit of Abner (2:19). The conversation started by Abner during the chase revealed that Abner was seeking a way to avoid creating any personal animosity between himself and Joab (2:20–21). He even proposed that Asahel seek another soldier to engage, suggesting that he would be more likely to succeed and also to gain some spoil by stripping the dead body of an opponent. However, it appears as if Asahel was not looking for spoils but to remove the power behind Ish-bosheth's throne, thereby securing the kingdom for David.

Joab's second plea for Asahel to give up his pursuit clarifies Abner's concern: he was confident that he was a more skilled combatant than Asahel and could strike him down if necessary (2:22). However, he did not want to create a blood feud between the two commanders. Asahel's refusal led to a

---

[31] 1 Sam 26:6; 2 Sam 2:13; 8:16; 14:1; 16:9; 18:2; 19:22 (ET 19:21); 21:17; 23:18, 37.

demonstration that Abner's assessment was right on two scores: he was a more skilled warrior, who was able to kill Asahel in a decisive and gruesome manner (2:23), and he did create a blood feud that would lead to Joab's assassination of Abner (3:26–27). It appears as if Abner must have been at the forefront of his force's retreat, since we are told that others who followed—probably from both armies—stopped when they came to the place where Asahel's body lay (2:23), implying that they were trailing Abner and Asahel.

Joab and Abishai continued the pursuit until nightfall. They found themselves at a place called the Hill of Ammah (2:24), which probably was east of Gibeon. It was there that the Benjaminites regrouped around Abner (2:25), and Abner once again sought to halt more bloodshed, this time appealing to the bitterness that would ensue and engulf Israel should they continue the battle (2:26). Abner's appeal for a cessation of hostilities draws a contrast between his more conciliatory approach in this instance and the hardline attitude of Zeruiah's sons that David would later note (3:39; 16:10–11; 19:23 [ET 19:22]). This time, however, Joab was persuaded by Abner's call and called a halt to the battle (2:28). This allowed Abner's troops to return to the Transjordan (2:29).

The aftermath of the battle is related from the perspective of David's troops. They lost only nineteen men, including Asahel (2:30). This means that only six others fell during the battle, since twelve were killed in the opening contest (2:15–16). The loss from Abner's force was much more substantial. That three hundred sixty of his men died (2:31) implies that the two armies had mustered sizable contingents for the battle. Joab's men then traveled south to Bethlehem—the ancestral city of David's clan—where they interred Asahel in his father's tomb (2:32). Even with that detour, Joab's troops, who had a shorter journey than Abner's soldiers, reached David's capital at Hebron by dawn.

The author has related what apparently was the opening battle in a war between the two royal houses. He then simply summarizes the war by saying that David grew inexorably stronger (3:1), since, as his readers know, God was with him (1 Sam 18:12).[32]

David's House in Hebron (3:2–5)

1005–1003 BC (3:1–5)[33]

Parallel: 2 Sam 3:2–5 ‖ 1 Chr 3:1–4

David's advancement was not only in military might but also in the growth of his family. The house of Saul had been contracting: Saul and three of his sons died in battle with the Philistines (1 Sam 31:6). Both Abner and Ish-bosheth would soon be assassinated (2 Sam 3:26–27; 4:1–12). Even Saul's sons by his concubine would be executed (21:1–9). However, from the beginning of his reign, David's house expanded, and the author tells us about six sons who

---

[32] See also "Prosperity and Success Come Only from God" in Steinman, *1 Samuel*, 29.

[33] See "The Chronology of David's Reign" in the commentary on 5:1–5.

were born in Hebron, omitting any daughters.[34] Amnon, the firstborn, the son of Ahinoam the Jezreelitess (3:2), will figure prominently in 2 Samuel 13 in the account of his rape of his half sister Tamar and in the account of his death at the hand of David's third son, Absalom.

Nothing is known about David's second son, whose mother was Abigail the Carmelitess. He is called "Chileab" in the MT but by other names in various sources (see the first textual note on 3:3). He probably died early, since after the deaths of Amnon and Absalom, David's fourth son, Adonijah, assumed that he was next in line for the throne (1 Ki 1:5; 2:15).

Absalom, who figures prominently in 2 Samuel 13–18, was the son of Maacah, the daughter of the king of Geshur (3:3). Geshur was a small kingdom that bordered the Sea of Galilee on the northeast. David's marriage to its king's daughter is a clear sign that he had continued to pursue alliances in the Transjordan as part of his strategy to bring all of the tribes of Israel under his control.

Adonijah's mother, Haggith, is mentioned, but unlike David's three preceding wives, nothing is told of her origin or parentage (3:4). The same is true for Abital, the mother of David's fifth son, Shephatiah (3:4), and Eglah, the mother of Ithream, David's final son born in Hebron (3:5). Eglah, however, is called "David's wife" (אֵשֶׁת דָּוִד, 3:5), a phrase used elsewhere only to describe Michal, Saul's daughter (1 Sam 25:44), David's first wife.[35]

---

[34] The author does not mention daughters being born to David in Hebron, though he will later mention daughters born in Jerusalem (5:13). The only daughter of David he names is Tamar (2 Sam 13:1, 2, 4–8, 10, 15, 19–20, 22, 32; see also 1 Chr 3:9).

[35] After Michal's marriage to David (1 Sam 18:27), Saul had given her to another man (1 Sam 25:44), but she would later be returned to David (2 Sam 3:13–16).

Abner Defects and Joab Kills Him

Translation

3 ⁶While there was war between the house of Saul and the house of David, Abner was strengthening his position in the house of Saul. ⁷Now Saul had a concubine, and her name was Rizpah the daughter of Aiah.

Ish-bosheth the son of Saul said to Abner, "Why have you slept with my father's concubine?"

⁸Abner became very angry because of Ish-bosheth's words. He said, "Am I a dog's head that belongs to Judah? Until now I have been loyal to the house of Saul, your father, to his family, and to his friends, and I have not handed you over to David, yet you now accuse me of wrongdoing with this woman. ⁹Thus may God do to Abner and thus may he do even more to him if I don't do for him what Yahweh swore to David: ¹⁰to transfer the kingdom from the house of Saul and to establish the throne of David over Israel and Judah from Dan to Beersheba."

¹¹He was not able to respond to Abner because he was afraid of him.

¹²So Abner sent messengers to David on his behalf, saying, "To whom does the land belong?" [and] saying, "Make your treaty with me, and then I will support you by bringing all Israel around to you."

¹³He [David] said, "Good! I will make a treaty with you. I ask only one thing of you: you will not see my face unless you first bring Saul's daughter Michal to me when you come to see my face."

¹⁴David sent messengers to Ish-bosheth the son of Saul, saying, "Give [to me] my wife Michal for whom I paid a bride-price of a hundred Philistine foreskins." ¹⁵So Ish-bosheth sent and took her from [her] husband Paltiel the son of Laish. ¹⁶Her husband went with her, weeping all the way after her up to Bahurim.

Abner said to him, "Return home," so he returned.

¹⁷Abner sent word to the elders of Israel, "Previously you were seeking David to be king over you. ¹⁸Do [it] now, because Yahweh said to David, 'By my servant David I will save my people Israel from the power of the Philistines and the power of their enemies.'" ¹⁹Abner also spoke specifically to Benjamin. Abner also went to speak personally to David in Hebron about all that Israel and the entire house of Benjamin had approved.

²⁰So Abner came to David in Hebron, and twenty men were with him. David held a banquet for Abner and his men. ²¹Abner said to David, "Let me get up, go, and gather all Israel for my lord the king, so that they will make a treaty with you and you will rule over everything that you desire." David sent Abner away, and he left in peace.

²²Now David's servants and Joab were coming from a raid and brought a lot of plunder with them, but Abner was not with David in Hebron because he had

[already] sent him away and he went in peace. [23]When Joab and the entire army with him arrived, they told Joab, "Abner the son of Ner came to the king. He sent him away, and he went in peace."

[24]Joab came to the king and said, "What have you done? Abner came to you. Why in the world did you send him away so that he is already gone? [25]You know that Abner the son of Ner came to deceive you and to find out your operations and to know everything you are doing."

[26]Joab went out from David and sent messengers after Abner. They brought him back from the cistern at Sirah, but David was unaware [of this]. [27]When Abner returned to Hebron, Joab pulled him aside to the middle of the city gate to speak to him privately. There he stabbed him [in] the stomach. He died on account of the blood of Asah-el his [Joab's] brother.

[28]Later, David heard [about] this. He said, "I and my kingdom are forever innocent before Yahweh of shedding the blood of Abner the son of Ner. [29]May it [his shed blood] rage over the head of Joab and over the entire house of his father. May there never cease to be from the house of Joab a person with a bodily discharge or with a skin disease or a man who can work [only] a spindle or who falls by the sword or who lacks food." ([30]Joab and his brother Abishai killed Abner because he had killed their brother Asahel at Gibeon during the battle.)

[31]David said to Joab and to all the people with him [David], "Tear your clothes. Put on sackcloth, and mourn for Abner." King David was walking behind the funeral bier. [32]They buried Abner in Hebron. The king raised his voice and wept over Abner's tomb. All the people also wept.

[33]The king sang a funeral dirge over Abner. He said:

"Should the death of Abner be like the death of a godless fool?

[34]Your hands were not bound,

and your feet were not restrained with bronze shackles.

You fell like those who fall before malicious men."

All the people continued to weep over him. [35]All the people came to urge David to eat some food while it was still day. But David swore an oath, saying, "Thus may God do to me and thus may he add if I taste food or anything else before sunset." [36]All the people noticed [this], and it was pleasing to them. Everything that the king did pleased them. [37]All the people and all Israel knew that day that [the impulse] to kill Abner the son of Ner was not from David.

[38]The king said to his servants, "Don't you know that a great man and leader has fallen this day in Israel? [39]I am weak today, although I am anointed king. However, these men—the sons of Zeruiah—are more harsh than I am. May Yahweh repay the evildoer according to his evil deed."

Textual Notes

3:6 מִתְחַזֵּק—"Strengthening his position" is a Hithpael (HtD) masculine singular participle of חָזַק in a reflexive sense. For similar uses of the Hithpael of חָזַק, see 1 Chr 11:10; 2 Chr 12:13.

3:7 וּלְשָׁאוּל פִּלֶגֶשׁ—Literally "and (there was belonging) to Saul a concubine." This construction with the preposition לְ in the sense of possession is used to express indefiniteness: "now Saul had *a* concubine." If the noun were in construct with the proper name, פִּלֶגֶשׁ־שָׁאוּל, its meaning would be definite: "*the* concubine of Saul."

וּשְׁמָהּ—"And her name" is not present in 4QSam[a] or the LXX.

וַיֹּאמֶר אֶל־אַבְנֵר—Codex Leningradensis reads "and he said to Abner." After the verb וַיֹּאמֶר, a few Masoretic manuscripts include the name אִישׁ בֹּשֶׁת, "Ish-bosheth," as its subject. The LXX reads his name (although Mephibosheth rather than Ish-bosheth) plus his lineage as the subject, Μεμφιβοσθε υἱὸς Σαουλ, "Mephibosheth the son of Saul," which is adopted in the translation above. The LXX may be supported by 4QSam[a], which is fragmentary but does read שאול, "[of] Saul," and has room for the rest of the phrase. Many English versions follow the LXX (e.g., HCSB, ESV, GW, NET, NIV).

מַדּוּעַ בָּאתָה אֶל־פִּילֶגֶשׁ אָבִי׃—"Why have you slept with my father's concubine?" For the spelling בָּאתָה in place of בָּאתָ, see GKC, § 44 g; Joüon, § 42 f; and the second textual note on 2:26. Most often in Samuel and the rest of the OT the verb בּוֹא, "come," is used with the preposition אֶל, "to," to denote motion, "to come/travel to" or "to arrive at."[1] In some passages, the context indicates that this verb and preposition, literally "to go in to," are used idiomatically to refer to sexual intercourse (particularly when followed by the verb and preposition שָׁכַב עִם, "to lie with," as in 2 Sam 12:24; cf. 2 Sam 11:11; 13:11). Here it corresponds to the English idiom "to sleep with," which in English usage commonly covers sexual relations that are sinful. The context here indicates that the relations are unlawful, as also in 2 Sam 16:21, 22. Elsewhere, however, the Hebrew idiom often denotes the consummation of a marriage of a husband and wife (e.g., Gen 29:23, 30). For 2 Sam 12:24 and 2 Sam 17:25, see the commentary on those verses. The Hebrew idiom is also used for a man's intercourse with a concubine or maidservant given to him, as was permissible in ancient Near Eastern culture (e.g., Gen 16:2, 4; 30:3, 4). In 2 Sam 20:3, the negated idiom expresses that David had no sexual relations with his concubines after they had been violated by his son Absalom (2 Sam 16:21, 22). In the Hebrew sexual idiom, normally the verb בּוֹא is masculine and the preposition אֶל governs a feminine form denoting the woman. In a few passages a feminine form of בּוֹא is used in a sexual context, e.g., 2 Sam 11:4 וַתָּבוֹא אֵלָיו וַיִּשְׁכַּב עִמָּהּ, literally "and she came to him, and he lay with her"); 2 Sam 13:11 בּוֹאִי שִׁכְבִי עִמִּי אֲחוֹתִי, "come, lie with me, my sister"); see also Gen 19:33, 34.

3:8 וַיִּחַר לְאַבְנֵר מְאֹד—"Abner became very angry" is literally "and it became hot for Abner, very." The construction וַיִּחַר לְ- is also in 1 Sam 15:11; 18:8; 2 Sam 6:8; 13:21 (cf. 1 Sam 20:7). See also the construction with the perfect חָרָה לְ- in 2 Sam 19:43 (ET 19:42); 22:8.

הַיּוֹם אֶעֱשֶׂה־חֶסֶד עִם—"Until now I have been loyal to" is literally "(up to) this day I have done faithfulness with." Here the Qal (G) imperfect of עָשָׂה is used for durative past action. For עָשָׂה חֶסֶד עִם-, "to do faithfulness/kindness with," see the third textual note on 2:5.

---

[1] See, e.g., 2 Sam 1:2; 2:23; 3:20, 23, 24.

אֶל־אֶחָיו—"To his family" is literally "to his brothers."

מֵרֵעֵהוּ—The suffixed singular noun מֵרֵעַ, "friend" (from the root רעה II), is used as a collective: "his friends."

וְלֹא הִמְצִיתִךָ בְּיַד־דָּוִד—"And I have not handed you over to David." Usually the Hiphil (H) of מָצָא, "to find," means "to hand over." It is used with בְּיַד־, literally "into the hand of" someone, also in Zech 11:6. Its form here, הִמְצִיתִךָ, the first common singular perfect with a second masculine singular suffix, is written as if it were from the third-*he* verb מָצָה. Forms of third/final-*aleph* verbs (such as מָצָא) may exhibit forms more commonly associated with final-*he* verbs (GKC, § 75 oo; Joüon, § 78 g).

וַתִּפְקֹד עָלַי עֲוֺן הָאִשָּׁה הַיּוֹם:—"Yet you now accuse me of wrongdoing with this woman." Usually the Qal (G) of פָּקַד, "to visit," with the object noun עָוֺן, "iniquity," refers to punishing people because they are guilty of sin (e.g., Ex 20:5; Amos 3:2; see BDB, s.v. פָּקַד, Qal, A 3). However, the book of Samuel does not reveal whether or not Abner had committed the sin of which Ish-bosheth accused him in 2 Sam 3:7 (see further the commentary). Therefore instead of translating פָּקַד as "punish," which would imply Abner's guilt, the verb is rendered merely as "accuse" (cf. "charge" in ESV, NASB).[2]

3:9 כֹּה־יַעֲשֶׂה אֱלֹהִים לְאַבְנֵר וְכֹה יֹסִיף לוֹ—"Thus may God do to Abner and thus may he do even more to him." For this idiom, see the textual note on 1 Sam 3:17[3] and Joüon, § 165 a, including note 1. It recurs in 2 Sam 3:35; 19:14 (ET 19:13) and previously appeared also in 1 Sam 14:44; 20:13; 25:22.

כִּי כַּאֲשֶׁר נִשְׁבַּע יְהוָה לְדָוִד כִּי־כֵן אֶעֱשֶׂה־לּוֹ:—Literally "for just as Yahweh swore to David, so thus I will do for him." The word order in the translation has been adjusted to accommodate English style.

3:10 מִדָּן וְעַד־בְּאֵר שָׁבַע:—For "from Dan to Beersheba," see 1 Sam 3:20. The phrase recurs in 2 Sam 17:11; 24:2, 15.

3:11 וְלֹא־יָכֹל עוֹד לְהָשִׁיב אֶת־אַבְנֵר דָּבָר—Literally "and he was not able again to return to Abner a word."

מִיִּרְאָתוֹ אֹתוֹ:—"Because he was afraid of him." The verb יִרְאָה is a so-called feminine form (GKC, § 45 d) of the Qal (G) infinitive construct of יָרֵא, "to fear." It has the prefixed preposition מִן in a causative sense (Joüon, § 170 i) and a third masculine singular object suffix.

3:12 תַּחְתָּיו—"On his [Abner's] behalf." The preposition תַּחַת can mean "in the stead of, in place of." When it has a suffix it is normally spelled as a plural, which is the Qere here, תַּחְתָּיו. The Kethib תחתו is either the suffixed singular form, תַּחְתּוֹ, or a defective, or *haser*, spelling of the normal form, תַּחְתָּו.

לֵאמֹר ... לֵאמֹר—"Saying ... [and] saying." Typically לֵאמֹר (Qal [G] infinitive construct of אָמַר with לְ) introduces quoted speech (see also, e.g., 3:14, 17). The second לֵאמֹר here is unusual because it occurs between two quotes. The second לֵאמֹר is

---

[2]   BDB, *HALOT*, and *DCH* do not provide a special meaning for the verb here such as "accuse" or "charge, allege."

[3]   Steinmann, *1 Samuel*, 111–12.

missing in some Masoretic manuscripts, and some commentators believe it to be a textual corruption by dittography.[4] However, it serves to separate the preceding question
with the interrogative pronoun מִי, "who?" from the following imperatival request (see
the next textual note). See the similar use of לֵאמֹר in 3:13.

כָּרְתָה בְרִיתְךָ֣ אִתִּ֑י—Literally "cut your covenant with me." The verb כָּרְתָה is the
alternate form with paragogic ה of the Qal (G) masculine singular imperative of כָּרַת
(see GKC, § 48 i). The vowel in -כָּ is *qamets chatuph*, reduced from the *holem* in the
usual form of the imperative, which would be כְּרֹת. For the idiom כָּרַת בְּרִית, "to cut a
covenant" or "make a treaty," see the third textual note on 1 Sam 11:1.[5] It occurs also
in 1 Sam 18:3; 23:18; 2 Sam 3:13, 21; 5:3.

וְהִנֵּ֤ה יָדִ֣י עִמָּ֔ךְ—"And then I will support you" is literally "and behold, my hand is
with you." The suffix on עִמָּךְ appears to be feminine (second singular), but the form
with the *zaqeph qaton* accent (-֔מָּ) is pausal for עִמְּךָ with a masculine (second singular) suffix.

לְהָסֵב—"By bringing around." This is the Hiphil (H) infinitive construct of סָבַב,
"go around."

3:13 כִּ֣י | אִם־לִפְנֵ֤י הֲבִיאֲךָ֙—"Unless you first bring." The verb הֲבִיאֲךָ is the Hiphil (H)
infinitive construct of בּוֹא, "come," with a second masculine singular suffix. Normally
the combination כִּי אִם is used without לִפְנֵי ("first") to express the idea of "unless" or
"except" (see BDB, s.v. אִם־כִּי, 2 a). However, the reading here with לִפְנֵי is supported
by the parallel כִּי אִם־לְפָנֶ֖י בוֹא in 3:35, which uses the Qal (G) infinitive construct of
בּוֹא.

3:14 אֲשֶׁר֙ אֵרַ֣שְׂתִּי לִ֔י בְּמֵאָ֖ה עָרְל֥וֹת פְּלִשְׁתִּֽים׃—"For whom I paid a bride-price of a hundred Philistine foreskins." The first three Hebrew words are literally "whom I betrothed
to/for myself." The verb is the Piel (D) perfect first common singular of the verb אָרַשׂ,
which is used only in the Piel (D) and the Pual (Dp). Its Piel is used with the suffixed
preposition לִי similarly in Hos 2:21, 22 (ET 2:19, 20). In the Piel this verb is used in
the masculine to refer to a man who has claimed a woman as his betrothed as a preliminary action before consummating the marriage (Deut 20:7; cf. Deut 28:30). Here it is
followed by the preposition בְּ, which marks the price paid for the betrothal.[6] Its Pual is
used in the feminine to refer to a woman who is betrothed, but whose marriage has not
yet been consummated (Ex 22:15 [ET 22:16]; Deut 22:23–28).

3:15 פַּלְטִיאֵ֖ל—"Paltiel." This name may mean "God is my deliverer" or "God delivered me" if the first element is a derivative of the verb פָּלַט (2 Sam 22:2, 44). Here the
spelling of this name includes the theophoric ending אֵל־, "God," as in Num 34:26. The
shortened form without this ending, "Palti," was used in 1 Sam 25:44 (also attested in
Num 13:9). See further the commentary.

לָֽיִשׁ—This pausal form of לַיִשׁ, "Laish," is the Qere and the reading in many
Masoretic manuscripts. Most Masoretic manuscripts also have לָיִשׁ in 1 Sam 25:44,

---

4   McCarter, *II Samuel*, 107; Anderson, *2 Samuel*, 53.

5   Steinmann, *1 Samuel*, 209.

6   *IBH*, § 27 E; Waltke-O'Connor, § 11.2.5d.

although some read לוש, which is the Kethib here. לַיִשׁ is a place-name in Judg 18:7, 14, 27, 29 and a noun for "lion" in Is 30:6; Job 4:11; Prov 30:30. The verb לוּשׁ, "to knead," occurs in 1 Sam 28:24; 2 Sam 13:8 (also Gen 18:6; Jer 7:18; Hos 7:4).

3:16 הָלוֹךְ וּבָכֹה—"Weeping all the way." The Qal (G) infinitive absolute of הָלַךְ, "go," is used idiomatically with another infinitive absolute (here of בָּכֹה, "to weep") to express continuing action (as in 1 Sam 6:12) or increasing action (as in 2 Sam 5:10). See GKC, § 113 u; Joüon, § 123 m, s.

בַּחֻרִים—"Bahurim" is modern Ras eṭ-Ṭmim, just east of Mount Scopus in Jerusalem. It was in the territory of Benjamin (2 Sam 16:5; 19:17 [ET 19:16]; 1 Ki 2:8).

לֵךְ שׁוּב—"Go home" is an asyndetic pair of Qal (G) imperatives, from הָלַךְ and שׁוּב, respectively literally "go, return."

3:17 וּדְבַר־אַבְנֵר הָיָה עִם־זִקְנֵי יִשְׂרָאֵל—"Abner sent word to the elders of Israel" is literally "and the word of Abner was with the elders of Israel." The LXX reads καὶ εἶπεν Αβεννηρ πρὸς τοὺς πρεσβυτέρους Ισραηλ, "and Abner said to the elders of Israel." 4QSamᵃ appears to support the LXX, but only the word ויאמר[וּ] is extant.

גַּם־תְּמוֹל גַּם־שִׁלְשֹׁם—The Hebrew idiom with the combination of תְּמוֹל and שִׁלְשֹׁם, here literally "also yesterday, also the third day [i.e., the day before yesterday]," means "previously."[7] In 2 Sam 5:2 and in comparable phrases elsewhere in Samuel, תְּמוֹל is spelled with prosthetic *aleph*, אֶתְמוֹל. See the fifth textual note on 1 Sam 4:7,[8] as well as 1 Sam 10:11; 14:21; 19:7.

3:18 הוֹשִׁיעַ—Codex Leningradensis has this third masculine singular Hiphil (H) perfect of יָשַׁע, but that form does not fit the context here ("Yahweh said to David, 'By the hand of my servant David *he saved* …' "). Many Masoretic manuscripts have אוֹשִׁיעַ, "I will save," which is supported by the LXX (σώσω) and Vulgate (*salvabo*) and probably the Peshitta (ܐܦܪܘܩ, "I will do salvation") and is adopted in the translation above.

3:19 וַיְדַבֵּר גַּם־אַבְנֵר בְּאָזְנֵי בִנְיָמִין—"Abner also spoke specifically to Benjamin" is literally "and also Abner spoke in the ears of Benjamin." Later in the verse בְּאָזְנֵי דָוִד, "in the ears of David," is translated as "speak *personally* to David."

כָּל־אֲשֶׁר־טוֹב בְּעֵינֵי יִשְׂרָאֵל וּבְעֵינֵי כָּל־בֵּית בִּנְיָמִן:—"All that Israel and the entire house of Benjamin had approved" is literally "all that was good in the eyes of Israel and in the eyes of the entire house of Benjamin." טוֹב is the Qal (G) perfect verb, "be good/pleasing," rather than the homographic adjective. In 3:36 בְּעֵינֵי, literally "in the eyes of," recurs twice, once with the verb טוֹב, as here, and once with the cognate and synonymous verb יָטַב; there the expression is rendered as "it pleased" and "it was pleasing," respectively.

3:20 מִשְׁתֶּה:—This noun, rendered here as "a banquet," denoted Nabal's "feast" in 1 Sam 25:36 (twice).

---

[7]   See also Gen 31:2, 5; Ex 4:10; 5:7, 8, 14; 21:29, 36; Deut 4:42; 19:4, 6; Josh 3:4; 4:18; 20:5; 1 Sam 21:6 (ET 21:5); 2 Ki 13:5; Ruth 2:11; 1 Chr 11:2.

[8]   Steinmann, *1 Samuel*, 121.

3:21 אָקוּמָה ׀ וְאֵלְכָה וְאֶקְבְּצָה—"Let me get up, go, and gather." These three Qal (G) singular cohortatives (of קוּם, הָלַךְ, and קָבַץ, respectively) express Abner's desire and also constitute a request for the king to give him permission to act.

וְיִכְרְתוּ אִתְּךָ בְּרִית וּמָלַכְתָּ—After the cohortatives, these verbs express the desired result: *so that* they will make a treaty with you and you will rule" (cf. Joüon, § 119 e).

תְּאַוֶּה נַפְשֶׁךָ—"You desire" is literally "your soul desires." See the same clause in 1 Sam 2:16 and the equivalent construct phrase, אַוַּת נַפְשֶׁךָ, literally "the desire of your soul," in 1 Sam 23:20.

וַיְשַׁלַּח—The Piel (D) of שָׁלַח has the nuance "to send [someone] *away*" or "dismiss (amicably)." See the first textual note on 1 Sam 5:10.[9] In this chapter its Piel recurs in 3:22, 23, 24. Compare its Qal (G), "to send [someone]," i.e., messengers who are to return in 3:12, 14, 26 (cf. 3:15).

3:22 בָּא מֵהַגְּדוּד—Most Masoretic manuscripts have בָּא, which could be either the Qal (G) masculine singular participle of בּוֹא, "(he) was coming," or its third masculine singular perfect, "he came." Its grammatical subject is probably the immediately preceding noun, יוֹאָב, "Joab," even though the compound subject is plural and includes "David's servants." The singular verb may also have been influenced by the singular noun דָּוִד, as "David" is the controlling identifier of the group loyal to him. Such a construction (a singular verb with a plural subject) is often found (cf. Joüon, § 150 b, p). Two Masoretic manuscripts have the plural participle, בָּאִים, "(they) were coming," an easier reading which is supported by the LXX (παρεγίνοντο), the Syriac Peshitta, and the Vulgate. (The next clause refers to them with a plural pronominal suffix and a plural verb, עִמָּם הֵבִיאוּ, "and they brought with them," and the plural perfect בָּאוּ, "they came/arrived," is used for them in 3:23.) Some propose that the plural reading בָּאִים is original and that the plural ending מִי- may have been lost due to haplography, since the next word begins with a *mem* (the preposition מִן on מֵהַגְּדוּד). The noun גְּדוּד usually refers to a marauding band of troops or a division of an army. Only here does the context indicate that it refers to the soldiers' action of carrying out a "raid" or "foray."

וְאַבְנֵר אֵינֶנּוּ עִם־דָּוִד—Literally "and Abner—he was not with David." The construction is a *casus pendens*, which is common with the particle אַיִן (Joüon, § 156 m).

3:23 אֶל־הַמֶּלֶךְ—In place of this reading in the MT, "to the king," 4QSam[a] (אל דויד) and the LXX (πρὸς Δαυιδ) read "to David."

3:24 לָמָה־זֶּה—"Why in the world?" is literally "why this?" The demonstrative pronoun זֶה is used emphatically. This phrase recurs in 12:23; 18:22; 19:43 (ET 19:42). See *IBH*, § 25 B; Waltke-O'Connor, § 17.4.3c; GKC, § 136 c; Joüon, § 143 g.

וַיֵּלֶךְ הָלוֹךְ:—"So that he is already gone." The infinitive absolute הָלוֹךְ (from הָלַךְ) often means "going along" or "continuing" when it is coordinated with an infinitive absolute of another verb (see the first textual note on 3:16). Here, however, it is the only infinitive, and it follows a preterite (imperfect with *waw* consecutive) of הָלַךְ, literally "he went, going." Joab's emphasis here seems to be alarm that Abner "is already gone," so it is too late to rescind David's approval of Abner's plan in 3:21. Since each of the

---

9   Steinmann, *1 Samuel*, 137.

preceding three verses (3:21, 22, 23) concluded with the expression וַיֵּלֶךְ בְּשָׁלוֹם, "and he left/went in peace," this clause at the conclusion of 3:24 may also imply that Joab is distressed that David sent Abner away peacefully.

3:25 לְפַתֹּתְךָ—This is the Piel (D) infinitive construct of פָּתָה, with the preposition לְ and a second masculine singular pronominal suffix, expressing purpose: "to deceive you."

וְלָדַעַת ... וְלָדַעַת—This (occurring twice) is the Qal (G) infinitive construct of יָדַע, "to know." Such an infinitive with the preposition לְ and expressing purpose is regularly placed at the beginning of its clause (Joüon, § 155 r).

אֶת־מוֹצָאֲךָ וְאֶת־מִבוֹאֲךָ— "Your operations." These two suffixed nouns that form the direct objects (אֶת) of the preceding infinitive (וְלָדַעַת) are literally "your going out and your coming in," meaning David's military plans. The first singular noun with a second masculine singular suffix, מוֹצָא, is derived from the verb יָצָא, "go out," which is often used in Samuel for an army going forth to wage war (see the first textual notes on 1 Sam 18:6[10] and 2 Sam 2:12). Both forms (the Kethib and Qere) of the second noun are derived from the verb בוֹא, "to come," and refer to returning from war. The Qere is מוֹבָאֶךָ, which is the reading in many Masoretic manuscripts and is pausal for מוֹבָאֲךָ. This noun, מוֹבָא, appears elsewhere in the OT only in Ezek 43:11, where its plural denotes "entrances" into the eschatological temple, and the plural of מוֹצָא refers to its "exits." The Kethib is מְבוֹאֶךָ, pausal for מְבוֹאֲךָ. This suffixed noun, מָבוֹא, is common and can refer to an "entrance," e.g., into the temple (Jer 38:14; Ezek 44:5) or a city (Judg 1:24, 25), or the "setting" of the sun (e.g., Deut 11:30; Josh 1:4; see the Qal [G] infinitive construct בֹא in 3:35). 4QSam[a] does not help one decide between the Qere and the Kethib since its reading has been reconstructed at this point.

3:26 וַיָּשִׁבוּ אֹתוֹ—"They brought him back." The verb is a defective, or *ḥaser*, spelling of וַיָּשִׁיבוּ, the Hiphil (H) preterite (imperfect with *waw* consecutive) of שׁוּב, so its meaning is transitive: "they returned him."

3:27 חֶבְרוֹן—In the MT this noun is an accusative of place, indicating the destination of travel, and does not require a preposition or directive *he* suffix: "to Hebron." 4QSam[a] reads חבר[ונה], "to [Hebr]on," with a suffixed directive *he*. Such suffixed forms can be interchangeable with accusatives of place (Waltke-O'Connor, § 10.2.2b; cf. Joüon, § 125 n).

וַיַּטֵּהוּ יוֹאָב—"Joab pulled him aside." The verb is the Hiphil (H) preterite (imperfect with *waw* consecutive) of נָטָה, "turn aside," with a third masculine singular suffix. Its meaning is causative (see BDB, Hiphil, 3 a).

בַּשֶּׁלִי—"Privately." This vocalization is pausal for בַּשֶּׁלִי, literally "in the quietness." The noun שֶׁלִי with the preposition בְּ and the article functions adverbially. The noun occurs only here in the OT and is derived from the root שָׁלוּ or שָׁלָה.

הַחֹמֶשׁ—"[In] the stomach." See the second textual note on 2:23 for the same noun with the article. Here the MT lacks a preposition, so the noun is an accusative of specification or limitation (Joüon, § 126 g; see also GKC, § 117 ll), as it designates the specific part of the body that was affected by the verb וַיַּכֵּהוּ, literally "and he struck him." A

---

[10] Steinmann, *1 Samuel*, 350.

preposition is included in 4QSamᵃ, which reads עַד הַחֹמֶשׁ, "as far as (?) the stomach," and in the LXX, which reads ἐπὶ τὴν ψόαν, "on the loins."

בְּדַם עֲשָׂה־אֵל אָחִיו:—"On account of the blood of Asah-el his [Joab's] brother." The preposition בְּ can have causal force, "on account of," "because of" (BDB, III 5). For the name עֲשָׂה־אֵל, "Asah-el," see the textual note on 2:30. The third masculine singular pronominal suffix on אָחִיו, "his brother," is ambiguous, as it could refer to Abner or Joab. The same is true in 4QSamᵃ, אחיהו, where the suffix is spelled ־הו. The translation above includes "Joab's" to clarify that Asahel was Joab's brother, as does the LXX: τοῦ ἀδελφοῦ Ιωαβ.

3:28 מֵעִם יְהוָה—"Before Yahweh" is literally "from with Yahweh." This refers to Yahweh as the Judge; his verdict of guilt or innocence proceeds "from [מִן] with [עִם]" him. See BDB, s.v. מֵעִם, d, under עִם. The usage of מֵעִם in this sense is unique. In English translation "before Yahweh" conveys the idea of standing before him as the Judge. Compare the use of לִפְנֵי־ in passages such as 1 Sam 26:19. Elsewhere in the OT מֵעִם יהוה can refer to requesting something "from (with) Yahweh" (e.g., Deut 18:16; Is 7:11) or receiving something "from (with) Yahweh" (e.g., 1 Ki 2:33; Ps 121:2; Ruth 2:12).

מִדְּמֵי—"Of shedding the blood of" is literally "from the blood of." The prefixed preposition מִן indicates that the bloodshed is the cause of Yahweh's verdict, what elicits his judgment (see BDB, s.v. מִן, 2 e (*b*) and 2 f). דְּמֵי is the plural construct form of דָּם, "blood." It is a plural of result, indicating shed human blood (animal blood is always singular), as also in 1 Sam 25:26; 2 Sam 1:16 (Kethib).[11] In the MT the following verb of which "blood" is the implied subject is plural, יָחֻלוּ (see the first textual note on 3:29). 4QSamᵃ reads the singular ודם, "and the blood of," with the singular verb [י]חול, but that is probably a secondary reading.

3:29 יָחֻלוּ עַל—Literally "may they rage over." The verb יָחֻלוּ is a Qal (G) jussive third masculine plural of חוּל I. It is plural because its implied subject is the plural noun (in construct) דְּמֵי, "(shed) blood," in 3:28 (see the previous textual note). For the meaning of the verb here, some lexicons suggest "turn upon" (*HALOT*) or "fall" (*DCH*) because it is used with the preposition עַל; the LXX translates it as καταντησάτωσαν, "let it come" on Joab's head. For the Hebrew verb, however, that meaning would be attested in this passage only. Elsewhere it means either "to writhe in pain" or "to dance in a circle." Here, then, it probably means "whirl about" over Joab's head (BDB, Qal, 3). The translation uses "rage" since the image appears to be that the blood of Abner (3:28) is "writhing" or "raging" over Joab's head, looking for justice.

וְאֶל—"And over." Samuel is one of the OT books in which אֶל (usually meaning "to") is often used in place of עַל, "on, over," which was used in the preceding phrase with the verb that is also implied here (see the previous textual note). See the first textual note on 2:9 and BDB, s.v. אֶל, note 2. A number of Masoretic manuscripts read וְעַל,

---

[11] *IBH*, § 11 C; GKC, § 124 n; Waltke-O'Connor, § 7.4.1b; Joüon, § 136 b. See also the second textual note on 1 Sam 25:26 (Steinmann, *1 Samuel*, 477) and the first textual note on 2 Sam 1:16.

as does 4QSamª (ועל), which is supported by the LXX (ἐπί). Here וְאֶל may have been influenced by וְאֶל at the start of the next clause in this verse.

כָּל־בֵּית אָבִיו—"The entire house of his father" is the reading in the MT and the LXX (πάντα τὸν οἶκον τοῦ πατρὸς αὐτοῦ). 4QSamª apparently has a transposition of the letters of the last word: כ[ו]ל בית יואב, "the en[tire] house of Joab." This error probably occurred under the influence of בֵּית יוֹאָב, "house of Joab," later in the verse.

וְאַל־יִכָּרֵת—"May there never cease to be" is literally "may he never be cut off." The Niphal (N) jussive is singular. A singular verb is commonly used when it precedes a compound subject consisting of a number of (singular) individuals, as here.

זָב—"A person with a bodily discharge." This is the Qal (G) masculine singular participle of זוּב, "to flow," probably referring to a person with a running sore or hemorrhage (see BDB, 4).

וּמְצֹרָע—"Or (a person) with a skin disease." Older translations usually rendered this Pual (Dp) participle of צָרַע as "a leper" (KJV here and also in, e.g., Lev 14:2; 2 Ki 5:1), but scholars now recognize that the Hebrew terminology with צָרַע covers a broader range of skin diseases, not just the one we now call leprosy. This is likely true of λεπρός in the NT as well (e.g., Mt 8:2; 26:6).

וּמַחֲזִיק בַּפֶּלֶךְ—"Or a man who can work [only] a spindle." Such a man can do only women's work. The Hiphil (H) masculine singular participle of חָזַק with the preposition בְּ literally means "a man grasping/taking hold of." In Prov 31:19 a woman's hands grasp (תָּמְכוּ) the noun here, פֶּלֶךְ, referring to a "spindle" used in spinning wool into yarn. Some take this rare word, translated by the LXX here as σκυτάλη, "staff, pole," to mean a "crutch," supposedly based on the Phoenician cognate *plk*.[12] This is a questionable assertion, however, since the Phoenician noun generally refers to a spindle.[13] Holloway has proposed that this word denotes forced labor, the most humiliating type of labor for those deemed at the bottom of the social strata.[14] However, the evidence for that proposed meaning is meager and doubtful.[15]

3:30 הָרְגוּ לְאַבְנֵר—"They killed Abner." The Qal (G) verb הָרַג, "to kill," usually takes a direct object (e.g., 1 Sam 22:21; 24:12 [ET 24:11]; 2 Sam 4:10), but the preposition לְ can introduce a verb's object (see also Job 5:2). See GKC, § 117 n.[16]

עַל אֲשֶׁר—The preposition עַל commonly introduces the cause of an action, here in combination with אֲשֶׁר: "because." See Joüon, § 170 h; Waltke-O'Connor, § 38.4a, including example 8.

3:31 כָּל־הָעָם אֲשֶׁר־אִתּוֹ—"All the people with him." The pronominal suffix on אִתּוֹ, "with *him*," refers to David, not to Joab, as clarified in the translation. In this context

---

[12] Bergen, *1, 2 Samuel*, 313, including n. 20; McCarter, *II Samuel*, 118; NIV.

[13] Like the Hebrew noun פֶּלֶךְ, the two main meanings of the Phoenician noun *plk* are a "spindle" and a regional "district" or "province." See *DNWSI* 2:915–16.

[14] Holloway, "Distaff, Crutch or Chain Gang."

[15] Layton, "A Chain Gang in 2 Samuel 3:29: A Rejoinder."

[16] However, GKC, § 117 n, errs in calling this grammatical construction a "solecism of the later period" based on its frequency in Aramaic. Aramaisms can be found in early as well as in later Hebrew.

(also in 3:32, 34, 35, 36), the phrase "all the people" refers to all the people who were with David, not to all Israel. To include all Israel too, 3:37 will use the words כָּל־הָעָם וְכָל־יִשְׂרָאֵל, "all the people and all Israel."

קִרְעוּ בִגְדֵיכֶם וְחִגְרוּ שַׂקִּים—"Tear your clothes. Put on sackcloth." This Hebrew terminology designates two common customs for mourning and repentance. These two are combined also in Gen 37:34; 1 Ki 21:27; 2 Ki 6:30; 2 Ki 19:1 ‖ Is 37:1; Esth 4:1.

הַמִּטָּה:—Usually the noun מִטָּה denotes a "couch" or "bed." This is the only time it refers to a "funeral bier."

3:32 וַיִּשָּׂא הַמֶּלֶךְ אֶת־קוֹלוֹ וַיֵּבְךְּ—"The king raised his voice and wept." The Qal (G) of נָשָׂא, "lift up," with the object noun קוֹל, "voice," together with the Qal of בָּכָה, "weep," refers to weeping aloud. See the same vocabulary in 1 Sam 11:4; 24:17 (ET 24:16); 30:4; 2 Sam 13:36.

אֶל־קֶבֶר אַבְנֵר—"Over Abner's tomb." Here and in 3:33 (אֶל־אַבְנֵר), Codex Leningradensis reads the preposition אֶל, while a few Masoretic manuscripts have עַל and the LXX has ἐπί. See the second textual note on 3:29. The reading in 4QSamᵃ is reconstructed at this point in 3:32, but in 3:33 it reads עַל.

3:33 וַיְקֹנֵן הַמֶּלֶךְ—"The king sang a funeral dirge." For this Polel (D) preterite (imperfect with *waw* consecutive), see the textual note on 1:17.

הַכְמוֹת נָבָל יָמוּת אַבְנֵר:—"Should the death of Abner be like the death of a godless fool?" The word הַכְמוֹת consists of the interrogative *he* and the preposition כְּ, "as, like," prefixed to מוֹת, which could either be the Qal (G) infinitive construct of מוּת, "to die," or the noun מָוֶת, "death," in construct. Syntactically it is parallel to כִּנְפוֹל in the third clause of 3:34, which is an infinitive construct with כְּ (see the third textual note on 3:34). The second word following here, יָמוּת, clearly is the verb's imperfect, which has a modal sense, "*should* Abner *have died* like … ?" or "*did* Abner *have to die* like … ?" (Joüon, § 113 m). The substantival adjective נָבָל, *nabal*, denotes the most extreme kind of "fool." Such fools reject the very existence of God and mock him as if he were powerless (Pss 14:1; 53:2 [ET 53:1]; 74:22). When such people are given prosperity, they are insufferable (Prov 30:22).[17] The adjective נָבָל, *nabal*, recurs in 2 Sam 13:13 and matches the name of the churlish fool Nabal in 1 Samuel 25, whose contempt for Yahweh's anointed one (David) cost him his estate, life, and wife. David gained Nabal's sage widow, Abigail, as his own wife (1 Sam 25:39; 2 Sam 2:2; 3:3).

3:34 יָדֶךָ לֹא־אֲסֻרוֹת—"Your hands were not bound." Codex Leningradensis has the defective, or *ḥaser*, spelling of the suffixed feminine dual noun, יָדֶךָ, "your hands," whereas many Masoretic manuscripts have the plene, or *male'*, spelling יָדֶיךָ. (The LXX has the plural αἱ χεῖρές σου.) The dual (plural) noun exhibits concord with the following negated feminine plural Qal passive (Gp) participle אֲסֻרוֹת, "(were) not bound." The Qal passive participle of אָסַר often refers to prisoners bound in fetters (e.g., Gen 39:20;

---

17 See further "Fools in Proverbs" in Steinmann, *Proverbs*, 30–32.

40:3; Is 49:9; 61:1; Job 36:8). The negation of a participle by לֹא, as here, is unusual; see GKC, § 152 d. At the end of this clause, 4QSamᵃ adds בזקים, "in/with chains."[18]

וְרַגְלֶ֨יךָ֙ לֹא־לִנְחֻשְׁתַּ֖יִם הֻגָּ֑שׁוּ—"And your feet were not restrained with bronze shackles." The noun רַגְלֶיךָ, "your feet," is another suffixed feminine dual noun (see the previous textual note) and is the subject of the negated verb הֻגָּשׁוּ, "were not restrained," literally "were not brought near," the third common plural Hophal (Hp) of נָגַשׁ. Like the subject noun, נְחֻשְׁתַּיִם is in the dual number. It is related to the noun נְחֹשֶׁת, "bronze," and is used to signify bronze shackles or handcuffs.[19] Usually לֹא stands immediately before the verb it negates, but here the noun (with the preposition לְ) לִנְחֻשְׁתַּיִם intervenes, lending some emphasis to the noun, literally "and your feet *not in bronze shackles* were restrained" (see GKC, § 152 e; cf. Joüon, § 160 c).

כִּנְפֹ֧ול לִפְנֵֽי־בְנֵֽי־עַוְלָ֛ה נָפָ֑לְתָּ—"You fell like those who fall before malicious men." This clause begins and ends with a Qal (G) form of the verb נָפַל, "to fall." The initial word is its infinitive construct with the preposition כְּ, literally "like the falling." (It recurs, but written defectively, in 17:9: כִּנְפֹל. For the lack of a *daghesh* in the *pe*, see Joüon, § 49 f.) The concluding second masculine singular perfect, נָפָלְתָּ, is pausal for נָפַלְתָּ. The construct phrase בְנֵי־עַוְלָה is literally "sons of maliciousness." The noun עַוְלָה signifies maliciousness, injustice, or wickedness (see *HALOT*). See the same construct phrase with the plural בְּנֵי־ in 2 Sam 7:10; 1 Chr 17:9 and with the singular בֶּן־ in Ps 89:23 (ET 89:22).

וַיֹּסִ֥פוּ כָל־הָעָ֖ם לִבְכֹּ֥ות עָלָֽיו׃—"All the people continued to weep over him." For this construction, the Hiphil (H) preterite (imperfect with *waw* consecutive) of יָסַף, "to do again," followed by an infinitive construct (לִבְכֹּות, the Qal [G] of בָּכָה, "weep"), see the first textual note on 1 Sam 3:6[20] and Joüon, §§ 102 g, 124 c, 177 b.

3:35 לְהַבְרֹ֤ות אֶת־דָּוִד֙ לֶ֔חֶם—"To urge David to eat some food." The Hiphil (H) infinitive construct of בָּרָה, "eat," with the preposition לְ expresses purpose and signifies potential causation, literally "to cause David to eat bread." The Hiphil verb takes a double accusative construction: the first accusative is its direct object, אֶת־דָּוִד, "David," and the second accusative is what he would eat, לֶחֶם, "bread."

וַיִּשָּׁבַ֤ע דָּוִד֙ ... כִּ֣י אִם־—"But David swore an oath ... if." The combination כִּי אִם, "if," functions negatively to introduce the action David swears not to take (see BDB, s.v. כִּי אִם־, 1 a).

כֹּ֣ה יַעֲשֶׂה־לִּ֤י אֱלֹהִים֙ וְכֹ֣ה יֹסִ֔יף—"Thus may God do to me and thus may he add." For this oath formula, see the textual note on 1 Sam 3:17[21] and the first textual note on 2 Sam 3:9.

אֶטְעַם—The Qal (G) of טָעַם means "to taste" or "eat" a small quantity (also in, e.g., 1 Sam 14:24, 29; 2 Sam 19:36 [ET 19:35]).

---

[18] In the MT, see בַּזִּקִּים, "in the chains," in Is 45:14; Nah 3:10; Job 36:8 and בְזִקִּים, "in chains," in Ps 149:8.

[19] Judg 16:21; 2 Ki 25:7; Jer 39:7; 52:11; 2 Chr 33:11; 36:6.

[20] Steinmann, *1 Samuel*, 110.

[21] Steinmann, *1 Samuel*, 111–12.

3:36 הִכִּ֫ירוּ—"They noticed" is a Hiphil (H) perfect of נָכַר I. In the Hiphil this verb means "investigate, recognize, acknowledge, notice" (see *HALOT*, s.v. נכר I; *CDCH*, s.v. נכר I).

וַיִּיטַב בְּעֵינֵיהֶם—"And it was pleasing to them." For this idiom with the verb יָטַב, literally "and it was good/pleasing in their eyes," see the second textual note on 3:19.

כְּכֹל֙ אֲשֶׁ֤ר עָשָׂה֙ הַמֶּ֔לֶךְ בְּעֵינֵ֥י כָל־הָעָ֖ם טֽוֹב׃—This is literally "according to all that the king did, in the eyes of all the people it was good/pleasing." The syntax is difficult. For this idiom with the verb טוב, see the second textual note on 3:19. Elsewhere in the OT when the verb טוב, "be good," is used with בְּעֵינֵי, "in the eyes of," the verb is placed immediately before the prepositional phrase, as in the similar clause in 3:19 (כָּל־אֲשֶׁר־טוֹב֙ בְּעֵינֵ֣י יִשְׂרָאֵ֔ל; see also Num 24:1; 2 Sam 15:26; 19:38 [ET 19:37]). Here the translation of the LXX (πάντα ὅσα ἐποίησεν ὁ βασιλεύς) and most other ancient versions does not reflect the preposition כְּ before כֹל, leading some to propose that the preposition is a dittograph of the *kaph* on כֹל. However, omitting the כְּ does not alleviate the syntactical difficulty posed by the placement of the verb טוב at the end of the verse.

3:37 לֹ֤א הָיְתָה֙ מֵהַמֶּ֔לֶךְ—Literally "she/it was not from the king." The feminine gender (here the feminine verb הָיְתָה) is often used for abstractions. Here the abstraction is the impulse or idea "to kill Abner" (לְהָמִ֖ית אֶת־אַבְנֵ֑ר; see Waltke-O'Connor, § 36.2.3b, including example 4). For the preposition מִן denoting cause here, see Waltke-O'Connor, § 11.2.11d, including example 11.

3:38 שַׂ֧ר וְגָד֛וֹל—"A great man and leader" is literally "a leader and a great (man)." This reading with the conjunction is also attested in 4QSam^a (שר וגדול). The adjective גָּד֛וֹל is substantivized, "a great man," and it is in apposition to the first noun, שַׂ֧ר, "a prince, leader." Both words refer to the same person, Abner. The LXX translates the words without a conjunction, ἡγούμενος μέγας, "a great leader," and either followed a Hebrew text without the conjunction or considered the adjective to modify the noun.

3:39 רַךְ֙ וּמָשׁ֣וּחַ מֶ֔לֶךְ—Literally "weak although anointed king." The conjunction *waw* is disjunctive and concessive and signals a contrast with the preceding adjective, רַךְ, "weak, tender, soft."[22] מָשׁ֣וּחַ is a Qal passive (Gp) participle of מָשַׁח, "to anoint." This verb was used for Samuel anointing David in 1 Sam 16:3, 12, 13 and for the men of Judah anointing him in 2 Sam 2:4, 7. It recurs in reference to David again in 2 Sam 5:3, 17; 12:7. See also the discussion of the cognate noun מָשִׁ֫יחַ, "anointed one," in the commentary on 1 Sam 2:10, 35.[23]

Commentary

Late 1003 BC[24]

Previous to this, the author recounted the rift between Judah and the other tribes of Israel (2:1–3:5) with David ascendant and the house of Saul in decline (3:1). The account of the uniting of all Israel under David spans 3:6–5:5. Two

---

[22] GKC, § 141 e; Waltke-O'Connor, § 39.2.3b.

[23] Steinmann, *1 Samuel*, 80–81, 105–6.

[24] See "The Chronology of David's Reign" in the commentary on 5:1–5.

deaths in Saul's family—those of Abner and Ish-bosheth—are key to the rise of the united monarchy of Israel. Most of 2 Samuel 3 is devoted to the death of Abner and David's reaction to it, while in parallel fashion the shorter 2 Samuel 4 is given over to the death of Ish-bosheth and David's response. These accounts of two violent deaths set the words of Samuel to Saul in bold relief: "Yahweh has *torn* the kingdom of Israel from you today, and he has given it to your neighbor, who is better than you" (1 Sam 15:28). Neither the scheming of Abner nor the weak and ineffectual Ish-bosheth can survive in the face of God having awarded the kingdom to David.

The Rift between Abner and Ish-bosheth (3:6–11)

This account begins with a resumption of 3:1, echoing its words:

וַתְּהִי הַמִּלְחָמָה אֲרֻכָּה בֵּין בֵּית שָׁאוּל וּבֵין בֵּית דָּוִד

There was a protracted war between the house of Saul and the house of David. (3:1)

וַיְהִי בִּהְיוֹת הַמִּלְחָמָה בֵּין בֵּית שָׁאוּל וּבֵין בֵּית דָּוִד

While there was war between the house of Saul and the house of David ... (3:6)

While 3:1–5 depicts the growth of David's family in Hebron, 3:6–11 depicts the rift that had developed in Saul's house between Abner and Ish-bosheth during this time.

The author now introduces Rizpah for the first time (3:7). She will play an important role again in 21:1–14. She is characterized as Saul's concubine—that is, she was a wife for whom Saul probably did not pay a bride-price, and her children were not considered Saul's primary heirs.[25]

Ish-bosheth accused Abner of having slept with Rizpah, perhaps in an attempt to strengthen his claim over the northern tribes and eventually displace Ish-bosheth. Note the similarity to Adonijah's request to marry David's concubine Abishag, which Solomon understood to be an attempt to claim Israel's throne (1 Ki 2:13–25).

Ish-bosheth's accusation was rejected by Abner—who acknowledged it only as an allegation, not as a fact (2 Sam 3:8). Thus, the reader is left in the dark as to whether Abner was guilty as charged.[26] Abner's use of "a dog's head" as a pejorative term is not well-understood. It is clear that "dog" can be a negative

---

[25] Note that Jacob's "concubine" (פִּילֶגֶשׁ, Gen 35:22) Bilhah is also characterized as a "wife" (אִשָּׁה, Gen 30:4; plural, נָשִׁים, Gen 37:2). Yahweh's judgment that someone would sleep with David's "wives" (נָשִׁים, 2 Sam 12:11) was fulfilled when Absalom slept with ten of David's "concubines" (פִּלַגְשִׁים, 2 Sam 15:16; 16:21–22). Note that in 2 Sam 15:16 they are called "wives-concubines" (נָשִׁים פִּלַגְשִׁים), implying equal status.

[26] Although the text does not resolve the question of the truth of the accusation, some commentators assume that Abner was guilty (Smith, *The Books of Samuel*, 275; Hertzberg, *I and II Samuel*, 257; Auld, *I and II Samuel*, 378; Brueggemann, *First and Second Samuel*, 225–26; Eschelbach, *Has Joab Foiled David?* 68).

characterization of a person.[27] Yet, it is not clear what was meant by a dog's "head."[28] Perhaps Abner added "head" to indicate that Ish-bosheth was insinuating that Abner wanted to be "head" over the people, perhaps "head" over Israel as an ambassador/surrogate for David, making Israel a lowly dog to royal David's Judah. In any case, it is evident that the phrase is connected with Judah and implies that Abner believed that Ish-bosheth was accusing him of disloyalty to Saul's house in favor of David.

Abner's words also revealed a measure of contempt for Ish-bosheth. Abner positively affirmed his past loyalty to Saul's house, to Saul, and to his family and friends. However, Abner affirmed his loyalty to Ish-bosheth only negatively by claiming not to have handed Ish-bosheth over to David.

Then Abner brashly took a vow to do what Yahweh had promised to David: to establish his reign over all Israel (3:9–10).[29] Ish-bosheth, who was afraid of Abner, was unable to respond to him (3:11). This short statement demonstrates for the reader the power dynamic in Ish-bosheth's realm: Abner was the real power, and Ish-bosheth was simply a figurehead.

Abner Shifts His Support to David (3:12–21)

Confident that he wielded the actual authority and influence among the northern tribes of Israel, Abner boldly contacted David (3:12). His opening sentence was a rhetorical question, whose answer was obvious: Abner was affirming that David was the rightful king to whom the land belonged. His next sentence offered David his support by promising that he could bring all Israel under David's authority, but it came with a condition: David must make a "treaty" or "agreement" (בְּרִית, 3:12) with Abner. The author does not tell us what the terms of this treaty were to be. Was Abner to hold a high position in David's court? Would he displace Joab as the commander of the army? Or was Abner simply to be allowed to live out his life in Israel without threat of retaliation for his initial opposition to David's reign? This silence by the author helps build the tension of the story and also makes Joab's later action more ambiguous. Was Joab's murder of Abner simply revenge for Asahel's death (2:19–23; cf. 3:27)? Or was this also a chance for Joab to eliminate a potential rival in David's court? Or was Joab also acting in his own way to protect David from Abner's machinations (cf. 3:24–25)?

---

[27] 1 Sam 17:43; 24:15 (ET 24:14); 2 Sam 9:8; 16:9; 2 Ki 8:13.

[28] Some commentators (e.g., Ackroyd, *The Second Book of Samuel*, 42) take this to denote a "dog-faced baboon," based on the ancient Greek translation of 3:7 by Symmachus. However, this appears to be no more than a guess.

[29] There are no direct quotations of God's promise directly to David to make him king prior to this incident. However, there are several passages which imply that he did promise that: David's anointing (1 Sam 16:1–13, especially 1 Sam 16:1); the statement by David's men urging him to kill Saul (1 Sam 24:5 [ET 24:4]); and a similar statement by Abishai (1 Sam 26:8). Also see Nathan's statement concerning God's actions to make David king (2 Sam 12:7–8), which imply that this was promised when Samuel anointed him.

David's reply was positive, but cautious (3:13). He wanted a demonstration that Abner was able to wield the influence he claimed, so he demanded that his first wife, Michal, be returned to him. Saul had given her to David as a wife (1 Sam 18:20–27), but later he gave her to Palti (1 Sam 25:44). David tested Abner's influence in the royal court in Mahanaim by sending a demand for Michal directly to Ish-bosheth. David pressed his claim to her by referencing the bride-price demanded by Saul: a hundred Philistine foreskins (2 Sam 3:14; cf. 1 Sam 18:25). That David had paid twice that price (1 Sam 18:27) was immaterial to his demand, since he had satisfied the bride-price Michal's father, Saul, had originally required. We are told that Ish-bosheth complied with David's demand (2 Sam 3:15), confirming the weakness of this son of Saul and demonstrating to David that Abner was the actual authority that undergirded the throne in Israel. The author confirms this also in the following verse when Abner, not Ish-bosheth, commanded Paltiel to return to his home (3:16). In all of this Michal was treated like a pawn in the political jockeying for position between David and the house of Saul. David's reacquisition of Michal not only exhibited Abner's authority among the tribe of Benjamin,[30] but it also strengthened David's position as claimant to the throne over all Israel as a son-in-law of Saul, something Ish-bosheth was powerless to impede. Perhaps Michal's behavior in 2 Sam 6:16–23 can be attributed to her resentment at being treated as a trophy to be contested rather than as a beloved wife.

Michal's second husband is called by his full name, Paltiel, here (see the first textual note on 3:15). Earlier in 1 Sam 25:44 he was called by a hypocoristic form of that name, Palti. In 2 Sam 21:8 the MT states that "Michal" had five sons by her husband, Adriel the son of Barzillai. However, two Masoretic manuscripts, a number of LXX manuscripts, and the ancient Syriac version name the mother of the five sons of Adriel as "Merab," who was the older of Saul's two daughters (1 Sam 14:49; 18:17, 19). Most modern English versions adopt "Merab" as the correct name of Adriel's wife and the mother of the five sons in 2 Sam 21:8.[31]

Having proven to David that he was capable of influencing the northern Israelite tribes, Abner appealed to them to switch their allegiance from Saul's house to David (3:17–18). He mustered two arguments for this: they had been seeking to acknowledge David as king (probably after the death of Saul but before Abner proclaimed Ish-bosheth king in 2 Sam 2:8–10), and Yahweh had promised Israel deliverance from the Philistines and other enemies by David.[32]

---

[30] By reclaiming his Benjaminite wife, the daughter of the Benjaminite king whom God had placed over Israel, David was asserting his hegemony over the tribe of Benjamin in the place of his father-in-law. (Later the kingdom splits into two, but Benjamin remains with Judah, and the other ten tribes become a separate kingdom.)

[31] See "Merab" in, e.g., HCSB, ESV, GW, NET, NIV.

[32] This is implied in making David king, combined with the implication that the king was to deliver Israel from its enemies, especially the Philistines. Note that the request for a king in 1 Samuel 8 came after the ark (1 Samuel 6) and then the people (1 Samuel 7) were delivered

In both cases Abner was appealing to his audience's own self-interest. In addition, we are told that he spoke specifically to the tribe of Benjamin (3:19). Saul's tribe had the most to lose should the house of their kinsman Saul lose the throne altogether, so it appears that Abner, a fellow Benjaminite, took special precautions to persuade them. Abner then went personally to Hebron to tell David what the Israelite tribes had approved. The author emphasizes for a second time that "the entire house of Benjamin" also approved David's kingship over them.

Not much is told us of the initial conversation between David and Abner when he arrived in Hebron (3:19–21). However, the banquet David held for Abner and his retinue (3:20) appears to be a celebration of the completion of an agreement between the two men. Abner then requested leave to gather Israel for the purposes of making a treaty that would recognize David as king (3:21). The author tells us for the first time that David sent Abner away "in peace." This will be emphasized twice more in quick succession once Joab enters the narrative (3:22, 23). This triple acknowledgment of David's intention to honor his agreement with Abner presages Joab's unilateral abrogation of it. It emphasizes to readers that Joab acted without authorization from David and contrary to David's publicly demonstrated rapprochement with Abner.

Joab Murders Abner (3:22–27)

Joab has been conspicuously absent from the narrative of 2 Samuel 3 to this point. Joab, we are told, continued to raid and plunder (3:22) as David had done before he became king (e.g., 1 Sam 27:8–12). David was apparently occupied with establishing his kingdom and had delegated raiding to Joab as the leader of David's men. The notice of the raiding party's return is coupled with a note that by the time they returned, Abner had already left Hebron. However, Joab in short order received word of Abner's visit to Hebron and David's action: instead of apprehending and executing Abner, the king had sent him away on good terms (3:23).

Joab's boldness in confronting David is signaled by his direct confrontation and questioning of the wisdom of David's actions (3:24). This boldness was something that Joab would demonstrate repeatedly with David by verbally challenging his actions and orders (19:1–8 [ET 18:33–19:7]; 24:3), by manipulating his uncle (14:1–33), and by acting contrary to the king's explicit orders (18:5–14). In each case it could be argued that Joab acted in David's best interest when David could not or would not.[33] Here Joab's words signaled his suspicions of Abner, ostensibly because he suspected that Abner was simply spying on David and did not intend to bring all Israel under David's control

---

from the Philistines. The request for a king was at least partially for the purpose of fighting Israel's enemies (1 Sam 8:19–20). Also note that David's first great military successes were over the Philistines (1 Samuel 17 and 1 Sam 18:20–30, especially 1 Sam 18:30) and that his first victories after becoming king of all Israel were also over the Philistines (2 Sam 5:17–25).

[33] See, for example, the conclusions of Eschelbach, *Has Joab Foiled David?* 77–78.

(3:25). However, readers of the book of Samuel may suspect that Abner would have been a less-than-reliable ally of David. Abner had already manipulated his grandnephew Ish-bosheth and made himself more powerful to the point that Ish-bosheth was afraid to act independently of Abner's will. Had Abner lived, he may have attempted to maneuver himself into a similar position vis-à-vis David, something Joab, who viewed himself as David's loyal servant and nephew, would never allow.

Apparently, Joab did not miss Abner in Hebron by much. Joab's messengers caught up with Abner at the cistern in Sirah (3:26). According to Josephus, Sirah was a short distance from Hebron.[34] It is probably to be identified with modern ʿAin Sarah, about a mile and a half (two and a half kilometers) northwest of Hebron.

David was unaware that Joab had fetched Abner back to Hebron. It appears that Joab's messengers persuaded Abner to return to Hebron of his own accord. However, Abner did not complete his entry into the city. Instead, on the ruse of engaging Abner in a private conversation, Joab diverted him into the middle of the city gate and stabbed him in the stomach (3:27). The author of Samuel attributes Joab's action to revenge for Abner's killing of Joab's brother Asahel.[35] However, this statement does not preclude Joab from having had other motives which the author does not note.

David Mourns Abner (3:28–39)

David's reaction upon learning of Joab's action was immediately to foreswear any complicity in the death of Abner (3:28). Had Abner continued to be at war with David, this would not have been necessary. However, the writer has emphasized that David and Abner had established peaceful relations (3:21, 22, 23), so that David had bound himself to their mutual agreement. David made a public statement of his innocence (3:28), since he did not want to be perceived as duplicitous. David also pronounced a curse on Joab and his father's house (3:29). The curse involved five adversities. A bodily discharge would render a person unclean and unable to worship (Lev 15:2–3). A skin disease (traditionally translated as "leprosy") would also make a person unclean and would lead to banishment from society (Lev 13:44–46). Working a distaff and spindle to produce yarn was considered women's work, and the curse envisions a man who was unable to support his family by work deemed worthy of a man. Falling by the sword envisions a violent death in war, while lacking food evokes starvation.

The author then reiterates the reason for Joab's murder of Abner (3:30; cf. 3:27). However, this time he adds the circumstances surrounding Asahel's death (cf. 2:18–32).

---

[34] Josephus, *Antiquities*, 7.34.

[35] Some suggest that Joab saw himself acting as an avenger to defend innocent blood (Num 35:16–21). However, that is unlikely since Asahel was killed in battle (2 Sam 3:30).

David not only mourned Abner, but he also ordered mourning among the people who were with him (3:31). The author specifically notes that David ordered Joab to mourn, which constituted a rebuke of Joab for his actions. Abner's body was not returned to Benjamin for burial. Instead he was placed in a tomb in Hebron (3:32; cf. 4:12), and the mourning ritual continued with weeping at the tomb.

David's lament over Abner was short, but poignant (3:33–34). It opened with a rhetorical question. Abner certainly was not a "godless fool" (see the second textual note on 3:33) and did not deserve to die as he did. David then noted that Abner was not a prisoner; he was not a captive from battle, because he and David had agreed to end their hostilities. Instead, Abner was murdered like those who are killed by "malicious men" (בְּנֵי־עַוְלָה, 3:34). This is another rebuke of Joab and labels his behavior as malevolent and unjustified.

It was apparent to the people at the funeral that David had not eaten, and they urged him not to fast (3:35). However, in honor of Abner, David took an oath to fast until sunset, which pleased the people and, combined with all that David did, further convinced them that the king was not connected in any way to Abner's death (3:36–37).

Finally, David spoke to his courtiers about Abner and Joab (3:38–39). He not only acknowledged Abner as one of Israel's great leaders, but he also noted what he considered to be the weak position in which Joab had placed him. Even though he was the anointed king, he could neither prevent Abner's death nor punish Joab for it.[36] Instead, he noted that Zeruiah's sons—Joab and Abishai—were harsh men. David would use the phrase "Zeruiah's sons" (בְּנֵי צְרוּיָה, 3:39) twice more in rebuking Joab's brother Abishai (16:10; 19:23 [ET 19:22]).

The question these final statements of David raise is whether David had been placed in as weak a position as he claimed. In fact, it could be argued that Joab's execution of Abner actually strengthened David's position in Israel. Eschelbach notes:

> This was not a time of peace (3:1, 6, 22) and David had not made peace with the lawful heir of the northern tribes but with a traitorous general. Abner was not an innocent man but one who hoped to escape personal losses and the consequences of his killing of Asahel by making a deal with David. Joab remained true to his king and fallen brother, turning back from battle only for the sake of saving lives (2:27–28). Joab did not pursue the avenging of Asahel's blood until Abner presumed to play the traitor to his lord and presented himself in Joab's city to make a deal. For Joab there could be only one rightful king (or heir apparent) and one rightful kingdom. Abner's behavior demonstrated that he was a threat. David and Joab are similar because they

---

[36] David was in no position to punish Joab—he needed Joab's obvious skills to bolster his position as he sought to become king of all Israel. Moreover, to punish Joab would have risked David being seen as unsupportive of his subordinate, unsupportive of his clan (Asahel, Joab, and Abishai were his nephews), and less than careful in his dealing with a rival kingdom (the rest of Israel; see the quotation from Eschelbach). The best David could do was to protest and assert Abner's innocence (which the author of Samuel has left as an open question).

share an intense interest in a united, peaceful kingdom. David and Joab also have their differences. David ignored Abner's threat as he would ignore other threats that cost many lives and much bloodshed.[37] Joab saw the threat and took the opportunity to eliminate it at the cost of only one life, Abner's.[38]

Even so, observers of the present state of the Christian church might be led to conclude that Christ the anointed King is indeed a weak monarch (cf. 2 Sam 3:39). His crucifixion at the hands of malicious men was a public display of the foolishness and weakness of God (cf. 2 Sam 3:33–34; 1 Cor 1:18–25). The infighting and jockeying for power within his kingdom might suggest that his reign is ineffectual (1 Cor 1:10–11). Christians can commit atrocities against one another under the delusion that they are serving Christ and advancing his kingdom on earth. This passage of Samuel prompts us to reexamine our own actions and the motivations behind them, mindful that, in due time, we will be required to give an account to our exalted King and all will be brought fully under his reign (1 Cor 15:27–28; Heb 2:6–9).

---

[37] Eschelbach is referring to David's lack of decisive action in dealing with his sons Amnon (2 Samuel 13) and Absalom (2 Samuel 13–19).

[38] Eschelbach, *Has Joab Foiled David?* 68.

Ish-bosheth Is Murdered

Translation

4 ¹When Saul's son heard that Abner had died in Hebron, he was discouraged, and all Israel was dismayed. ²Now Saul's son had two men who were commanders of raiding parties. One was named Baanah; the second was named Rechab. [They were] the sons of Rimmon the Beerothite from the Benjaminites, since Beeroth is also considered part of Benjamin. ³The [original] Beerothites had fled to Gittaim. They are there as resident foreigners to this day.

(⁴Now Saul's son Jonathan had a son who was crippled. He was five years old when news of Saul and Jonathan came from Jezreel. His nurse picked him up and fled. She was in a hurry to flee, and he fell and became lame. His name was Mephibosheth.)

⁵The sons of Rimmon the Beerothite, Rechab and Baanah, left. During the heat of the day they came to Ish-bosheth's house when he was taking his midday nap. ⁶They entered the interior of the house under the pretense of getting some wheat and stabbed him in the stomach. Then Rechab and Baanah his brother escaped. (⁷They had entered the house while he was lying on his bed in his bedroom. They struck him and killed him. They beheaded him, and took his head [with them].) They traveled by way of the Arabah all night.

⁸They brought Ish-bosheth's head to David at Hebron. They said to the king, "Here is the head of Ish-bosheth, the son of your enemy Saul, who sought your life. Yahweh has given vengeance to my lord the king this day against Saul and his descendants."

⁹David replied to Rechab and Baanah his brother, the sons of Rimmon the Beerothite. He said to them, "As Yahweh lives, who has redeemed my life from all adversity, ¹⁰when someone told me, 'Look! Saul is dead,' he thought he was bringing good news. I seized him and killed him in Ziklag, which was the reward I gave him! ¹¹How much more when wicked men have killed an innocent man in his own home on his own bed! So now, should I not seek [vengeance for] his blood from your hand and remove you from the earth?" ¹²David ordered [his] young men, and they killed them, cut off their hands and their feet, and hung [them] at the pool in Hebron. They took Ish-bosheth's head and interred it in Abner's tomb in Hebron.

Textual Notes

4:1 בֶּן־שָׁאוּל—"Saul's son." The MT significantly does not include his name; see the commentary. However, the ancient versions supply a name in front of this construct phrase. 4QSamᵃ has מפיב[ש]ת, "Mephibo[she]th," in agreement with the LXX, Μεμφιβοσθε (the LXX also includes Μεμφιβοσθε in 4:2). For "Mephibosheth," see the third textual note on 4:4. The Syriac Peshitta gives ܐܫܒܫܘܠ, *ʾAshbashul*, which it uses for Ishbosheth elsewhere, e.g., 4:5, 8, 12. Some English versions add "Ish-bosheth" here (e.g., RSV, ESV, NASB). For his name, see the second textual note on 2:8.

וַיִּרְפּוּ יָדָיו—"He was discouraged" is literally "and his hands drooped," indicating a loss of power and motivation. The verb וַיִּרְפּוּ is a Qal (G) preterite (imperfect with *waw* consecutive) third masculine plural of רָפָה, "sink down, drop." Since the subject noun, יָד, "hand," is feminine (יָדָיו is the dual with a third masculine singular suffix in pause), one would expect the verb to be a third feminine plural form, וַתִּרְפֶּינָה (see Is 13:7; Ezek 7:17). The dual of the noun יָד is the subject of the Qal imperfect or preterite (imperfect with *waw* consecutive) of רָפָה six times in the OT. In four of those cases, however, the verb is masculine plural (2 Sam 4:1; Zeph 3:16; Neh 6:9; 2 Chr 15:7), whereas the expected feminine plural is used only twice (Is 13:7; Ezek 7:17; see also the feminine plural adjective רָפוֹת in Is 35:3; Job 4:3). See also GKC, § 145 p; Joüon, § 150 d.

וְכָל־יִשְׂרָאֵל נִבְהָלוּ:—"And all Israel was dismayed." The verb is a Niphal (N) perfect of בָּהַל, and in the Niphal it means "be disturbed, alarmed, terrified," as also in 1 Sam 28:21.

4:2 הָיוּ בֶן־שָׁאוּל—"Saul's son had." The MT literally says that the two men "*were* Saul's son." The sense must be that they belonged to and thus were under the authority of Saul's son. This normally would be conveyed by the preposition לְ in the sense of possession; see לִיהוֹנָתָן, "Jonathan had," in 4:4. Sometimes other prepositions are so used, as at the end of this verse, where עַל־בִּנְיָמִן means "belonging to (part of) Benjamin." The dative phrase in the LXX, τῷ Μεμφιβοσθε υἱῷ Σαουλ, suggests that such a preposition (along with his name, אִישׁ־בֹּשֶׁת in the MT) may have dropped out of the MT (so GKC, § 128 c).

4:3 גִּתָּיְמָה—The name גִּתַּיִם is a dual form of גַּת, "winepress." The form here has the directional *he* ending, thus "to Gittaim," and is in pause (-תָ- instead of -תַ-).

גָּרִים—This is the masculine plural Qal (G) participle of גּוּר, "to sojourn, live as a resident alien." It is a synonym of the noun גֵּר in 1:13. For the social status of "resident foreigners/aliens," see the commentary on 1:13.

4:4 בֶּן נְכֵה רַגְלָיִם—"A son who was crippled" is literally "a son, struck of feet." The adjective נָכֵה, "stricken, smitten," is derived from the verb נָכָה, whose common Hiphil (H) means "to strike down," as in 4:6, 7. This adjective is in construct with the dual noun רַגְלָיִם (pausal for רַגְלַיִם), "feet," which is a genitive that specifies the part of the body that is affected (GKC, § 128 y). See the same genitive with the same function in 9:3 and, with a suffix (רַגְלָיו), in 9:13. Compare the accusative of specification, הַחֹמֶשׁ, "the stomach," in the fourth textual note on 3:27.

בְּחָפְזָהּ לָנוּס—Literally "in her hurrying to flee." These are two Qal (G) infinitive constructs, of חָפַז and נוּס, respectively, each with a prefixed preposition. The third feminine singular suffix on the first (ـהָ-) serves as its subject: "she was in a hurry to flee."

מְפִיבֹשֶׁת:—"Mephibosheth" literally means "from [מִן] the mouth [פֶּה] of shame [בֹּשֶׁת]." Lucianic Greek manuscripts read Μεμφιβααλ, Memphibaal, meaning "from the mouth of the master" or "from the mouth of Baal," a reading also found in the Old Latin version. In Chronicles his name is מְרִי־בַעַל, Merib-baal, meaning "he contends with Baal" (1 Chr 8:34; 9:40). It appears as if Mephibosheth is a purposely bowdlerized name to avoid any association between the house of Saul and the pagan god Baal. See the second textual note on 2:8.

4:5 כְּחֹם הַיּוֹם—"During the heat of the day." In this phrase (also in Gen 18:1) the preposition כְּ has a temporal meaning. Cf. עַד־חֹם הַיּוֹם in 1 Sam 11:11. The lexica consider חֹם to be a noun, "heat," but it could also be the Qal (G) infinitive construct of the verb חָמַם, "be hot."

וְהוּא שֹׁכֵב אֵת מִשְׁכַּב הַצָּהֳרָיִם:—"When he was taking his midday nap" is literally "and he (was) sleeping the sleep of the noontime." The participle of the verb שָׁכַב, "lie down, sleep," takes as its direct object the cognate noun מִשְׁכָּב, which often denotes a "bed" (see the first textual note on 4:7), but here must refer to the act of sleeping. The noun is in construct with the dual noun צָהֳרַיִם, "noon." The construction of a verb with its cognate noun as its object is called an accusative of the internal object; see Joüon, § 125 r.

4:6 וְהֵנָּה—This adverb, הֵנָּה, is usually of place, "hither, to there," which fits the following prepositional phrase, עַד־תּוֹךְ הַבַּיִת, "unto the interior of the house," but it can also be an adverb of time, "hitherto, until then/now," which fits the preceding reference to הַצָּהֳרַיִם, "the noontime/midday," at the end of 4:5. The form הֵנָּה could also be the third feminine plural pronoun, "they [feminine]," but that does not fit the context.

לֹקְחֵי חִטִּים—"Under the pretense of getting some wheat." This construct phrase with the masculine plural Qal (G) participle of לָקַח is literally "takers of wheat." Grammatically it can be the subject of בָּאוּ, "they came," but its syntactical placement at the end of the clause, distant from the verb, is unusual, suggesting that it describes a pretense or ruse. The participle is in construct with its direct object; see GKC, § 128 h.

The LXX has a radically different text for this verse:

καὶ ἰδοὺ ἡ θυρωρὸς τοῦ οἴκου ἐκάθαιρεν πυροὺς καὶ ἐνύσταξεν καὶ ἐκάθευδεν, καὶ Ρεκχα καὶ Βαανα οἱ ἀδελφοὶ διέλαθον.

And behold, the porter of the house was cleaning wheat, and he slumbered and slept, and Rekcha and Baana, the brothers, escaped notice. (*NETS*)

A number of commentators argue that the LXX is a better text and that the MT seems somewhat laconic concerning Rechab and Baanah's entry into the house.[1] However, the LXX presents difficulties. First, LXX 2 Sam 4:6 is the only verse in the LXX with the two verbs νυστάζω and καθεύδω, both of which refer to sleeping.[2] Second, although Baanah is called "his [Rechab's] brother" in MT 2 Sam 4:6, 9, the two of them together are never called "brothers" (אַחִים, as implied by ἀδελφοί in LXX 2 Sam 4:6),

---

[1] For a summary of those who adopt the LXX reading, see Bodner, "Crime Scene Investigation," 8–16.

[2] Some other LXX verses pair νυστάζω with another verb for sleeping (LXX Is 5:27; 56:10; Nah 3:18; Ps 120:4 [MT/ET 121:4]; Prov 6:10; 24:33; Ps Sol 16:1; cf. LXX Jer 23:31) or use another pair of verbs for sleeping, such as κοιμάω with ὑπνόω (LXX 1 Ki 19:5; Pss 3:6 [ET 3:5]; 4:9 [ET 4:8]; Job 3:13; Prov 4:16). OT verses in which the MT has a pair of Hebrew verbs for sleeping include 1 Ki 19:5; Pss 3:6 (ET 3:5); 4:9 (ET 4:8); 121:4; Job 3:13 and perhaps also 1 Sam 26:7.

but rather "the sons of Rimmon" (2 Sam 4:2, 5, 9). Thus, it appears likely that the LXX represents a text written to remove the lacunae in thought that characterizes the MT.[3]

וַיַּכֵּהוּ אֶל־הַחֹמֶשׁ—Literally "they struck him into the stomach." The verb וַיַּכֵּהוּ is the Hiphil (H) third masculine plural preterite (imperfect with *waw* consecutive) of נָכָה with a third masculine singular pronominal suffix; the identical form recurs in 4:7. For the noun חֹמֶשׁ, see the second textual note on 2:23.

4:7 בַּחֲדַר מִשְׁכָּבוֹ—"In his bedroom" is literally "in the chamber of his bed."

וַיְמִתֻהוּ—This is the Hiphil (H) third masculine plural preterite (imperfect with *waw* consecutive) of מוּת, "to die," with a third masculine singular pronominal suffix: "and they killed him."

וַיָּסִירוּ אֶת־רֹאשׁוֹ—"They beheaded him" is literally "and they removed his head." וַיָּסִירוּ is a Hiphil (H) preterite (imperfect with *waw* consecutive) of סוּר.

דֶּרֶךְ הָעֲרָבָה—"The way of the Arabah" refers to a route through the Jordan Valley, and traveling along it would have been a convenient way to travel from north to south. This route is mentioned also in Deut 2:8; 2 Ki 25:4; Jer 39:4; 52:7. Rechab and Baanah were traveling southward along the Jordan and eventually would turn westward to travel to Hebron (4:8).

4:8 נְקָמֹת—This feminine plural of the noun נְקָמָה, "vengeance," may be an intensive plural, "(complete) vengeance," or a plural of a compound process, since the vengeance began with the death of Saul (1 Samuel 31) and continues with the later deaths of his sons and supporters (see the next textual note). Its plural recurs in 22:48 in a context that refers not only to the Saulides but to all the enemies of David (22:41), including foreigners (22:45–46) and those who will arise later in the book. Cf. מִכָּל־צָרָה, "from all adversity," at the end of 4:9.

מִשָּׁאוּל וּמִזַּרְעוֹ—"Against Saul and his descendants" is literally "from Saul and from his seed."

4:9 חַי־יְהוָה—For this oath formula, "as Yahweh lives," see the second textual note on 1 Sam 14:45.[4]

4:10 הַמַּגִּיד לִי—"Someone told me" is literally "the one who declared to me." הַמַּגִּיד is the masculine singular Hiphil (H) participle of נָגַד with the definite article. This participle is the referent of the third masculine singular pronominal suffix on the preposition בְּ later in the verse: וָאֹחֲזָה בוֹ, "I seized him." See Joüon, § 156 i.

וְהוּא־הָיָה כִמְבַשֵּׂר בְּעֵינָיו—"He thought he was bringing good news" is literally "and he was like a bearer of good news in his (own) eyes." כִמְבַשֵּׂר is the masculine singular Piel (D) participle of בָּשַׂר with the prefixed preposition כְּ. See the same participle in 1 Sam 4:17, "messenger," and 2 Sam 18:26, "(someone) bringing good news." For the cognate noun בְּשֹׂרָה, see the next textual note.

אֲשֶׁר לְתִתִּי־לוֹ בְּשֹׂרָה:—"Which was the reward I gave him!" is literally "which (was) for my giving to him a reward." The noun בְּשֹׂרָה usually refers to "good news"

---

[3]   See also the discussion of this verse in Mastéy, "A Linguistic Inquiry Solves an Ancient Crime."

[4]   Steinmann, *1 Samuel*, 265.

66

(18:25, 27), but it can also refer to a "reward" for a messenger (18:22). In this case the author intends an obvious double entendre with irony: David gave the Amalekite the "good news/reward" he deserved for thinking that "he was bringing good news" to David (see 1:1–16).

4:11 הָרְגוּ אֶת־אִישׁ־צַדִּיק—"They have killed an innocent man." The direct object is literally "a man, a righteous (one)." The object is indefinite but is marked with אֶת־ because it refers to a certain man, Ish-bosheth. See Joüon, § 125 h.

וּבִעַרְתִּי—"Should I [not] remove." This verb is the first common singular Piel (D) perfect with *waw* consecutive of בָּעַר II. It means "remove" when followed by מִן preceding a noun denoting the place from which someone or something is removed (*HALOT*, 4 and 4 a). David here engages in a second wordplay (for the first, see the last textual note on 4:10), since he will "purge" (בִעַרְתִּי, *bi'ertiy*) these two men, each of whom is a בְּאֵרֹתִי, "Beerothite" (4:2), from the land.[5]

4:12 וַיְקַצְּצוּ—"They cut off." In the Qal (G), the verb קָצַץ means "to cut off." In the Piel (D), as here, it can have a more forceful or violent meaning, "chop off" or "cut in pieces." Its Piel (D) and Pual (Dp) are used in Judg 1:6–7 for cutting off hands and feet. Cf. its Qal for cutting off a hand in Deut 25:12.

וַיִּתְלוּ—"And they hung." This Qal (G) third masculine plural preterite (imperfect with *waw* consecutive) of תָּלָה has no direct object. See the commentary for a discussion of what they hung. This verb is used in the Qal to mean "hang [something] up" for public display here and in 21:12,[6] which recalls how the Philistines had hung up the bodies of Saul and Jonathan. Its Qal passive (Gp) participle תָּלוּי in 18:10 refers to Absalom being suspended from a tree.

לָקְחוּ—"They took." This pointing of the third common plural Qal (G) perfect is pausal for לְקָחוּ. 4QSamª reads the third masculine singular, לקח, "he [David?] took." However, it is unlikely that David personally entombed Ish-bosheth's head.

בְּקֶבֶר־אַבְנֵר—"In Abner's tomb." This is the final mention of Abner in the book of Samuel. Here 4QSamª expands his name to אבנר בן נר, "Abner the son of Ner," which is probably based on this common formulaic version of Abner's name.[7]

Commentary

Early 1002 BC[8]

With the death of Abner (3:6–39), it was unlikely that Ish-bosheth could have maintained a separate kingdom in Israel, independent from David's dominion over Judah. The account of Ish-bosheth's assassination reinforces this impression, since it recounts how two of his own men turned against him in favor of David.

---

[5]   Matzal, "A Word Play in 2 Samuel 4."

[6]   See the second textual note on 21:12, which discusses the Qere, from תָּלָא or תָּלָה, and the Kethib, from תָּלָה.

[7]   1 Sam 14:50; 26:5, 14; 2 Sam 2:8, 12; 3:23, 25, 28, 37; 1 Ki 2:5, 32; 1 Chr 26:28.

[8]   See "The Chronology of David's Reign" in the commentary on 5:1–5.

Ish-bosheth's Men Baanah and Rechab (4:1–3)

The narrative begins with Ish-bosheth's reaction to the report of Abner's death and its consequences for "all Israel," that is, the eleven northern tribes that had not yet acknowledged David as king (4:1). Ish-bosheth is not mentioned by name here.[9] This deliberate exclusion emphasizes his rebellion against David and connection to the apostate house of Saul, as well as his connection to Jonathan (4:4). The author then immediately introduces the two sons of Rimmon who commanded Ish-bosheth's raiding parties. Rimmon was from the tribe of Benjamin, as was Saul, but he lived in Beeroth (4:2). The site of ancient Beeroth is not known, but some have identified it with modern Khirbet el-Burj, about four miles (six kilometers) northwest of Jerusalem.

The author then informs his readers how a Benjaminite came to be an inhabitant of Beeroth (4:3), which had been one of the four Gibeonite cities (Josh 9:16–18). The Beerothites had fled to Gittaim, and then apparently Beeroth was repopulated by Benjaminites and claimed as part of their territory. Gittaim is mentioned again in Neh 11:33, in a context where it appears to be located near or in Philistine territory.[10] The name probably means "double winepress"[11] and perhaps is the same as the Gath mentioned in 1 Chr 8:13 (which is probably not the Philistine Gath).

What caused the Gibeonites to flee from Beeroth? We cannot be certain. If Gittaim is the Gath mentioned in 1 Chr 8:13, then they were expelled by two Benjaminites named Beriah and Shema. However, another possibility is that their flight was in response to Saul's attack on the Gibeonites (see 2 Sam 21:1–2) and that they fled to Gittaim in Philistia to escape Saul. In that case, it is likely that Saul resettled Beeroth with members of his own tribe. This would explain Rimmon's connection with the house of Saul, which led to his sons Baanah and Rechab becoming part of Ish-bosheth's court.

Mephibosheth's Injury (4:4)

At first blush it might appear as if the notice about Mephibosheth's injury is out of place. However, the author probably wished to show that "Saul's son" (4:1–2) is not the last of the house of Saul. Mephibosheth's injury anticipates David's later provision for him (9:1–13). However, it also explains why the Israelite tribes that had not yet acknowledged David as king were not interested in transferring Ish-bosheth's throne to Mephibosheth. A lame king could hardly lead troops into battle (1 Sam 8:19–20).

---

[9] See the first textual note on 4:1.

[10] Of the cities mentioned in this context (Neh 11:33–35), the ones that can be confidently located (e.g., Hadid, Zeboim) are in the coastal plain north of Lydda, which would have been in or near Philistine territory.

[11] See the first textual note on 4:3.

Rechab and Baanah Murder Ish-bosheth (4:5–7)

Ish-bosheth's murder took place in the warmest part of the day. In warm climates it is not unusual for a naptime to be observed in the afternoon. Rechab and Baanah took advantage of this, posing as servants who came to get some wheat out of storage. They brutally murdered Ish-bosheth and took his head as proof that they had killed him. They traveled south through the Arabah, which afforded a relatively quick route to David at Hebron (see the fourth textual note on 4:7).

David Has Rechab and Baanah Executed (4:8–12)

Rechab and Baanah presented Ish-bosheth's head to David, seeking his approval because they had killed the son of Saul (4:8). Since Saul had sought David's life, they were expecting that David would be pleased. Moreover, they presented themselves as doing Yahweh's work when they claimed that he had granted David vengeance on his enemy's house.

David's reply may have been unexpected by Rimmon's sons, but it was consistent with his actions toward Saul's house. He began with an oath which affirmed that *Yahweh* had delivered his life from adversity (4:9)—*David* did not raise a hand against Saul, even when he had opportunities (1 Sam 24:2–23 [ET 24:1–22]; 26:1–25). Moreover, David had mourned the deaths of Saul and Jonathan (2 Sam 1:17–27) and even the death of Abner, Saul's uncle (3:31–37).

David continued by recounting his execution of the Amalekite who claimed to have killed Saul and thought he was bringing good news to David (4:10; cf. 1:1–16; his claim was probably fabricated). Saul was a guilty man who repeatedly attempted to kill David without just cause, but Ish-bosheth was an "innocent man" (see the first textual note on 4:11). He had not been part of his father's attempts on David's life. Thus, David condemned the two brothers to death for their act. This was also advantageous from a political viewpoint. David could not have been seen as having been responsible for the death of Ish-bosheth, which followed so closely upon the death of Abner (2 Sam 3:6–39). Had he welcomed the assassins and rewarded them, it may have appeared as if David's denial of complicity in Abner's death (3:28) was false and as if he had used Abner's assassination as a prelude to Ish-bosheth's.

It is interesting to note, however, that David did not call Ish-bosheth "king" or "my lord the king" or "Yahweh's anointed one," as he had called Saul.[12] He did not give anyone reason to believe that he recognized Ish-bosheth's reign as legitimate. At the same time, David was consistent throughout the book of Samuel in not seeking to obtain the kingdom of Israel by force. Instead, he patiently waited to receive it as Yahweh provided according to his promise (see the commentary on 3:9–10).

---

[12] David called Saul "king" in, e.g., 1 Sam 18:18; 20:5; "my lord the king" in 1 Sam 24:9 (ET 24:8); 26:17, 19; 29:8; and "Yahweh's anointed one" in 1 Sam 24:7, 11 (ET 24:6, 10); 26:9, 11, 16, 23.

David's order to execute Baanah and Rechab was carried out with frightening efficiency (4:12). Not only were they killed, but their hands and feet were also cut off as a sign of their utter impotence and a warning to anyone else who would threaten the kingdom of David. The Hebrew text does not state what was hung near the pool at Hebron—the brothers' hands and feet or their bodies.[13] It is most likely that the bodies were hung, as in other cases in the OT (Josh 8:29; 10:26–27; 2 Sam 21:9–10). However, it was forbidden to expose a dead body for more than a day (Deut 21:22–23). The placing of Ish-bosheth's head in Abner's tomb continued the respect that David had shown to all of the Saulides.

---

[13] See the second textual note on 4:12.

2 Samuel 5:1–8:18

David the Godly King

2 Samuel 5:1–5

David Is Made King over All Israel

Translation

5 **¹All of the tribes of Israel came to David at Hebron to say, "We are certainly your flesh and blood. ²Previously, when Saul was king over us, you were the one leading [Israel] out and the one leading Israel back [from battle]. Yahweh said to you, "You yourself will shepherd my people Israel, and you will become the designated ruler over Israel." ³So all the elders of Israel came to the king at Hebron, and King David made a covenant with them in Hebron before Yahweh. Then they anointed David to be king over Israel.**

⁴David was thirty years old when he became king, and he reigned forty years. ⁵In Hebron he reigned over Judah seven years and six months, and in Jerusalem he reigned thirty-three years over all Israel and Judah.

Textual Notes

5:1 וַיֹּאמְרוּ לֵאמֹר—The MT literally reads "and they said to say," with the infinitive construct לֵאמֹר introducing the quotation. Most manuscripts of the LXX read καὶ εἶπαν αὐτῷ, "and they said to him" (= וַיֹּאמְרוּ לוֹ). The translation above, "to say," omits וַיֹּאמְרוּ and retains לֵאמֹר. This follows the readings of 4QSamᵃ (לאמור), two LXX manuscripts (M [codex Coislinianus] and N [codex Basiliano-Vaticanus]), Old Latin manuscript 115 (the Napoli codex), and the Vulgate. See also the parallel 1 Chr 11:1, which has לֵאמֹר without וַיֹּאמְרוּ.

הִנְנוּ עַצְמְךָ וּבְשָׂרְךָ אֲנָחְנוּ:—Literally "look, we, your bone and your flesh [are] we." The two first common plural pronouns for "we," the pronominal suffix on הִנְנוּ and the independent pronoun אֲנָחְנוּ, form an emphatic identifying nominal sentence. The Hebrew wording is "your bone and your flesh," but "your flesh and blood" is the corresponding English idiom.

5:2 גַּם־אֶתְמוֹל גַּם־שִׁלְשׁוֹם—"Previously" is literally "also yesterday, also the third day [the day before yesterday]." See the second textual note on 3:17 and the fifth textual note on 1 Sam 4:7.[1]

אַתָּה הָיִיתָ הַמּוֹצִיא—"You were the one leading out." This is the Qere, which is supported by the LXX (σὺ ἦσθα ὁ ἐξάγων) and 1 Chr 11:2. The participle with the definite article, הַמּוֹצִיא, means "the one who was leading out" (see Joüon, § 137 I (1)). The Kethib has the same consonants but divides the second and third words differently, הָיִיתָה מוֹצִיא, "you were leading out," with the second masculine singular suffix of the perfect of הָיָה written as תָה- instead of the usual תָ- (see GKC, § 44 g; Joüon, § 42 f). Then מוֹצִיא, the Hiphil (H) participle of יָצָא, "go out," lacks the article. In either reading, the construction in which the perfect of הָיָה ("you were") takes a participle ("leading

---

out") as its object verb has a frequentative force, signifying repeated action (Joüon, § 155 m)—what David did each time there was a battle to be fought. See a similar construction with the same force in 1 Sam 18:16, but without הָיָה and with the participles of יָצָא and בּוֹא in the Qal (G). In the book of Samuel, יָצָא often refers to troops who "go out" for battle,[2] and its Hiphil form here refers to David "leading out" his troops for military campaigns. Conversely, בּוֹא, "to come," often refers to returning or coming home from battle,[3] and so its Hiphil participle can have the corresponding causative meaning, "to lead/bring [troops] back home" from battle; see the next textual note.

וְהַמֵּבִיא אֶת־יִשְׂרָאֵל—"And the one leading Israel back [from battle]." For the meaning of this Hiphil (H) masculine singular participle of בּוֹא (with the article and the conjunction *waw*), see the preceding textual note. The orthography of the Qere, וְהַמֵּבִיא, agrees with 1 Chr 11:2. The Kethib, וְהַמֵּבִי, is the same word but written without the final *aleph*, perhaps due to haplography caused by the initial *aleph* on the following word, אֶת־ (see GKC, § 74 k).

5:3 וַיִּכְרֹת לָהֶם ... בְּרִית ... לִפְנֵי יְהוָה—"And he made a covenant with them ... before Yahweh." For the idiom with this verb and noun, כָּרַת בְּרִית, "cut a covenant" or "make an agreement," see the third textual note on 1 Sam 11:1.[4] This idiom designates the making of the covenant between Jonathan and David in 1 Sam 18:3; 23:18, and the verb alone is used for it in 1 Sam 20:16; 22:8. Like the covenant here in 2 Sam 5:3, they made their covenant "before Yahweh" (1 Sam 23:18), and so their bond was called "a covenant of Yahweh" (1 Sam 20:8). See also בְּרִית for the "covenant/treaty" between David and Abner in 2 Sam 3:12, 13 and for Abner's hope in 3:21 that all Israel would make a "covenant/treaty" with David. In 23:5 David will refer to Yahweh's messianic promise to his house (2 Samuel 7) as the "eternal covenant" God established with him.

וַיִּמְשְׁחוּ אֶת־דָּוִד לְמֶלֶךְ—"Then they anointed David to be king." The same Qal (G) verb, מָשַׁח, and prepositional phrase, לְמֶלֶךְ, will recur in the reports of the anointing of David in 2 Sam 5:17 and also in 2 Sam 12:7, where Yahweh is said to be the one who anointed him. This combination was used for the Judahites anointing David to be king in 2 Sam 2:4, 7. Earlier the verb referred to Samuel's anointing of Saul "to be the designated ruler" (לְנָגִיד) in 1 Sam 9:16; 10:1 and "to be king" (לְמֶלֶךְ) in 1 Sam 15:1, 17 and for Samuel's anointing of David in 1 Sam 16:3, 12, 13 as "king" (מֶלֶךְ, 1 Sam 16:1). In 2 Sam 19:11 (ET 19:10) the verb refers to the anointing of Absalom. See also the discussion of the cognate noun מָשִׁיחַ, "anointed one," in the commentary on 1 Sam 2:10, 35.[5]

5:4 בֶּן־שְׁלֹשִׁים שָׁנָה דָּוִד בְּמָלְכוֹ—"David was thirty years old when he became king." The same formula, literally "a son of ___ years" with the Qal (G) infinitive construct of מָלַךְ, "to reign" (with בְּ and a third masculine singular suffix), designated how old

---

[2] For this meaning of יָצָא, "go out [to battle]," see the first textual note on 1 Sam 18:6 (Steinmann, *1 Samuel*, 350) and the first textual note on 2 Sam 2:12..

[3] For this meaning of בּוֹא, "come back [from battle]," see the first textual note on 1 Sam 18:6 (Steinmann, *1 Samuel*, 350). See also, e.g., 1 Sam 18:13, 16; 29:6; 2 Sam 1:2–3; 3:22.

[4] Steinmann, *1 Samuel*, 209.

[5] Steinmann, *1 Samuel*, 80–81, 105–6.

Saul was when he became king in the problematic verse 1 Sam 13:1 and likewise for Ish-bosheth in 2 Sam 2:10.

אַרְבָּעִים שָׁנָה מָלָךְ:—"And he reigned forty years." The translation reads a conjunction (וְ, "and") on the number, since וְאַרְבָּעִים is the reading of a number of MT manuscripts, supported by the LXX, the Syriac, some Targum manuscripts, and the Vulgate. Codex Leningradensis lacks the conjunction, which was probably omitted due to haplography, caused by the previous word ending with a *waw*, בְּמָלְכוֹ. The pointing of the verb here, מָלָךְ, with *qamets* and *silluq* (-לָ-) before *soph pasuq* (:), is pausal for מָלַךְ.

Commentary

The Chronology of David's Reign[6]

To the careful reader it quickly becomes obvious that the material about David's reign in 2 Samuel 5–24 (and its parallel, 1 Chronicles 11–21) is not arranged in strict chronological order.[7] First, it is clear that 2 Sam 5:9–16 is a summary of David's activity in Jerusalem throughout his reign there. 2 Sam 5:11–12 (∥ 1 Chr 14:1–2) notes that David's building activity was aided by Hiram of Tyre, whose reign began in 980t, some twenty years after David conquered Jerusalem. Clearly, this notice, plus the summary of the sons born to David in 2 Sam 5:13–16 (∥ 1 Chr 14:3–7), marks 2 Sam 5:9–16 as a summary of David's thirty-three years of reigning in Jerusalem.

Another indication that the events during David's reign in Jerusalem are not always narrated in chronological order is the Philistine war in 2 Sam 5:17–25 (∥ 1 Chr 14:8–17). This clearly was initiated before David conquered Jerusalem in mid 1002 BC. 2 Sam 5:17 notes that the Philistines threatened to attack shortly after David was anointed king over all Israel (1002t). In response, David went down to the "stronghold" (מְצָדָה, 2 Sam 5:17), a term used earlier to describe Jerusalem (2 Sam 5:7, 9).[8] Heretofore the Philistines probably considered David their ally, since both he and they opposed the house of Saul. However, as soon as David became king over a united Israel, the Philistines attacked him and he found a more secure capital in Jerusalem before retaliating and defeating the Philistines.

---

[6] This material is adapted from "The Reign of David" in "Chronological Issues in Samuel" in the introduction (Steinmann, *1 Samuel*, 18–22), which is drawn from Steinmann, *From Abraham to Paul*, 116–23.

[7] The following discussion uses notations for the two different ways in which a calendar year was reckoned. A year with a trailing lowercase "t" indicates a year that began in the fall month of Tishri, rather than the spring month of Nisan (designated with "n"). See Steinmann, *From Abraham to Paul*, 20–21. Much of the following discussion is dependent on the observations of Merrill, "The 'Accession Year' and Davidic Chronology." However, Merrill's chronology is not adopted because of two problems. First, Merrill incorrectly considers 977t as Hiram's first year instead of the correct 980t. Second, Merrill does not correctly reckon David's coregency with Solomon, so he counts 1004t as David's first year in Jerusalem instead of 1002t.

[8] That David "went down" (5:17) from Hebron to Jerusalem is geographically accurate, since Hebron is some five hundred feet higher in elevation than Jerusalem.

The very next event in the accounts of David's reign is David's bringing the ark to Jerusalem (2 Samuel 6; 1 Chronicles 13; 15–16). As 1 Chr 15:1 makes clear, the ark was brought to Jerusalem after David had built his palace—that is, after 980t, when Hiram became king of Tyre (2 Sam 5:11).

Later, the Ammonite war is related (2 Sam 10:1–11:1; 12:29–31; 1 Chr 19:1–20:3). There are two indications that this war took place before 980 BC. One is that the war was precipitated by the disrespect shown by the new Ammonite king Hanun to David's ambassadors (2 Sam 10:1–5; 1 Chr 19:1–5). This had to have taken place early in David's reign before he had become powerful. Later in David's reign Hanun would not have dared to insult him. In addition, Hanun was the son of Nahash (2 Sam 10:2; 1 Chr 19:2), who attacked Jabesh-gilead at the beginning of Saul's reign (1 Sam 11:1–11). If Hanun precipitated the Ammonite war sometime after 980t, as would be required if the material in 2 Samuel 5–24 were in strict chronological arrangement, then Nahash would have had to reign almost eighty years! If, however, the Ammonite war took place early in David's reign, Nahash would have had a very long—but not impossibly long—reign of forty-five or fifty years.

A second indication that the Ammonite war happened early in David's reign is the age of Solomon. Although we do not know exactly how old Solomon was when he became king, shortly after David's death he characterized himself as "a young child" (נַעַר קָטֹן, 1 Ki 3:7; cf. 1 Chr 22:5). While this is most certainly hyperbole on Solomon's part, it is probable that Solomon was in his early twenties when he took the throne. His eldest son, Rehoboam, was born in 973 BC,[9] two years before Solomon's first regnal year (971t).[10] This, in turn, requires Solomon to have been at least in his middle teens and more likely closer to twenty years old when his wife Naamah became pregnant (1 Ki 14:21). Since Solomon's birth followed David's adultery with Bathsheba during the Ammonite war (2 Sam 11:1–12:23), Solomon, Bathsheba's second child with David, was most likely born within two or three years after the siege of Rabbah. Thus, if we assume that Hanun ascended to the Ammonite throne in 998t, after a fifty-year reign by his father, the outbreak of the Ammonite war can also be placed in that year. The siege of Rabbah would then have been in the spring of 997 BC (2 Sam 11:1; 1 Chr 20:1) and the birth of Solomon about 994 BC (2 Sam 12:24). Solomon would have been twenty-one years old when Rehoboam was born and about twenty-three years old at the beginning of his own first regnal year (971t).

All this demonstrates that the material covering David's reign is not arranged in strict chronological order and that each incident in the narrative

---

[9] Steinmann, *From Abraham to Paul*, 147.

[10] Rehoboam ascended to the throne in 932 BC when he was forty-one years old (1 Ki 14:21; 2 Chr 12:13).

must be examined carefully to determine when it took place.[11] Sufficient clues exist, however, to estimate the dates of most major incidents in David's reign.

Key to determining the chronology of the remaining major events of David's reign is the narrative concerning Absalom (2 Samuel 13–19). The sequence of the events is related as follows:

1. Amnon raped Absalom's sister Tamar (2 Sam 13:1–22). At this time Absalom was old enough to have his own household (2 Sam 13:20)—at least twenty years old.

2. Two years later Absalom murdered Amnon (2 Sam 13:23–33; especially 2 Sam 13:23) and fled to Geshur (2 Sam 13:34–39). Absalom remained in exile in Geshur for three years (2 Sam 13:38).

3. Absalom's return from exile is facilitated by Joab (2 Sam 14:1–27).

4. Absalom is received by David two years after returning from exile (2 Sam 14:28–33).

5. Absalom spends four years preparing to overthrow David (2 Sam 15:1–11, especially 2 Sam 15:7).[12]

6. Absalom leads a rebellion, is defeated, and is killed by Joab (2 Sam 15:13–19:43).

There are two indications that Absalom's rebellion took place after David built his palace and moved the ark to Jerusalem. First, Absalom's defiling of David's concubines took place on the roof of David's palace (2 Sam 16:22). Second, when David fled Jerusalem, Zadok attempted to take the ark from the city, but David ordered him to return it (2 Sam 15:24–29). Thus, Absalom's rebellion took place several years after 980t, when Hiram became king of Tyre (2 Sam 5:11; 1 Chr 14:1). The most opportune time for Absalom to begin his political campaign to gain the support of the elders of Israel would have been while David was immersed in building his palace and moving the ark to Jerusalem. If we assume that Hiram made his first overture to David soon after assuming the throne of Tyre in 980t, then we can estimate that David began work on his palace in 979 BC.

About three years would have been a reasonable time to build a palace, placing the completion around 976 BC.[13] The ark would have been brought to Jerusalem the next year, 975 BC. Thus, a reasonable period for the four years

---

[11] A quick examination of 1 Chronicles in light of the discussion above will also reveal that its narrative for David's reign is also not arranged in chronological order. In both 2 Samuel and 1 Chronicles, it appears as if the account of David's reign is primarily arranged topically and chronological arrangement is a secondary concern.

[12] The Hebrew text of 2 Sam 15:7 reads "forty years," which is most certainly a scribal error. The Lucianic recension of the LXX, the Syriac, the Vulgate, and Josephus (*Antiquities*, 7.196) read "four years," a much more reasonable period and a reading that is adopted in most English translations. The suggestion of Althann, "The Meaning of ארבעים שנה in 2 Sam 15,7," that the text originally read "forty (days)" would leave an unreasonably short time for Absalom to have gathered the needed political support for his rebellion.

[13] Solomon spent thirteen years building his palace (1 Ki 7:1). However, Solomon's palace was a far more extravagant building, and Solomon certainly had more resources than David (1 Ki 4:20–5:14 [ET 4:20–34]). That David's palace was much smaller and less imposing is implied by Solomon's construction of another palace for himself.

Absalom spent undermining David's authority would have been from about 978 BC, when David was in the midst of palace construction, to about 974 BC, when Absalom rebelled.

Working backward yields 980 BC as the year when Absalom returned from exile, 983 BC as the date when Absalom murdered Amnon and went into exile, and 985 BC as the time when Amnon raped Tamar. It should be noted that Amnon was David's eldest son, the first of David's six sons born during the seven and a half years he ruled in Hebron (2 Sam 3:2–5; 1 Chr 3:1–4). Since David had been married to Ahinoam, Amnon's mother, sometime before coming to Hebron (1 Sam 25:43; 27:3), it is possible that Amnon was born as early as 1009 BC. Absalom's birth probably came a year or two later in 1008 or 1007 BC. This would have made Amnon about twenty-four years old when he raped Tamar. Absalom would have been twenty-two or twenty-three years old at the time.

Following Absalom's rebellion, Sheba incited Israel to revolt against David (2 Sam 20:1–2). This can be dated to about 973 BC. The census David ordered should probably be dated to most of 972 BC (2 Samuel 24; 1 Chronicles 21).[14] It may have been a reaction to these two rebellions and a result of David's desire to know how large an army he could raise in case of another revolt. This would explain God's anger, since David was relying on human might instead of God's power to retain his kingdom.[15]

The end of the narrative about the census tells of David buying the threshing floor of Araunah, which would become the site of the temple (2 Sam 24:16–25; 1 Chr 21:15–22:1).[16] The remaining two or three years of David's reign were primarily spent with a renewed dedication to build the temple. David made preparations for the construction of the temple as he reigned with his coregent son Solomon (1 Chr 22:2–29:25).

This leaves only two major events during David's reign undated: the avenging of the Gibeonites (2 Sam 21:1–14) and the later Philistine wars (2 Sam 21:15–22; 1 Chr 20:4–8). The avenging of the Gibeonites took place at the end of a three-year famine "during the days of David" (2 Sam 21:1). Since 2 Samuel 21 also relates the Philistine wars that took place after the capture of Rabbah (1 Chr 20:4), it is most likely that the famine and the avenging of the Gibeonites also should be placed after the conquest of Rabbah. The best that can be estimated chronologically is that both the famine and the Philistine wars are to be dated between the capture of Rabbah in about 997 BC and about 980 BC. A later date is not warranted, since by that time David had built his palace and God had granted him peace from his enemies (2 Sam 7:1, 9, 11; 1 Chr 17:8, 10).

---

[14] The census was conducted for nine months and twenty days (2 Sam 24:8).

[15] Taking a census per se was not sinful (Ex 30:11–16).

[16] Araunah is called Ornan in 1 Chronicles.

Therefore, the approximate chronology of the events of David's reign in Jerusalem can be summarized as shown in figure 2.

Figure 2
_____

Chronology of David's Reign[17]

Nisan 1009	David is made king of Judah in Hebron (2 Sam 2:1–7)
Mid 1005	Abner makes Eshbaal king (2 Sam 2:8–10)
Early 1004	Joab defeats Abner at Gibeon (2 Sam 2:11–32)
Late 1003	Joab murders Abner (2 Samuel 3)
Early 1002	Eshbaal/Ish-bosheth is assassinated (2 Samuel 4)
Mid 1002	David is made king of all Israel, conquers Jerusalem, and defeats the Philistines (2 Samuel 5; 1 Chr 11:4–9; 1 Chronicles 14)
998	The Ammonite war (2 Sam 10:1–11:1; 12:26–31; 1 Chr 19:1–20:3) begins
997	David commits adultery, and Rabbah is captured (2 Samuel 11–12)
994	Solomon is born (2 Sam 12:24–25)
985	Amnon rapes Tamar (2 Sam 13:1–22)
983	Absalom murders Amnon and goes into exile (2 Sam 13:23–39)
980	Absalom returns from exile (2 Sam 14:1–27)
979–976	David builds his palace (2 Sam 5:11; 1 Chr 14:1)
978	Absalom is received again by David (2 Sam 14:28–33)
975	The ark is moved to Jerusalem (2 Samuel 6; 1 Chronicles 13; 15–16); God's covenant with David (2 Samuel 7; 1 Chronicles 17)
974	Absalom rebels (2 Sam 15:13–19:43)
973	Sheba rebels (2 Samuel 20); Rehoboam is born (1 Ki 14:21; 2 Chr 12:13)
972	David orders a census taken (2 Samuel 24; 1 Chronicles 21)
972–969	David makes preparations for the construction of the temple (1 Chr 22:2–29:25)
971	Solomon is made coregent (1 Kings 1; 1 Chr 23:1)
969	David dies (1 Ki 2:10–12; 1 Chr 29:26–30)

This discussion points out that the material concerning David's reign over Israel is arranged topically in four sections:

1. David is made king of all Israel with a summary of David's reign in Jerusalem (5:1–16)
2. David enjoys God's blessings during his reign (5:17–8:18)
3. David's sin and its aftermath (9:1–20:26)
4. David's successes as a warrior-king (21:1–24:25)

_____

[17] For a discussion of the chronological issues in reconstructing David's reign, see Steinmann, *From Abraham to Paul*, 116–23.

David Is Anointed as Israel's King (5:1–3)

Mid 1002 BC

Parallel: 2 Sam 5:1–3 ‖ 1 Chr 11:1–3

It appears as if the northern tribes moved quickly after the death of Ish-bosheth to recognize David as king (5:1–2). They came to David and stated three reasons why they were now prepared to accept him as their monarch:

1. He was their flesh and blood.[18] The law concerning kings given by Moses required Israel to put over them only a king who was a fellow Israelite (Deut 17:15).

2. David already had shown himself to be a competent leader in battle,[19] and such prowess as a military commander was what Israel sought when they first asked for a king (1 Sam 8:19–20).

3. Yahweh had promised David the kingdom (2 Sam 5:2).[20]

They quoted Yahweh's promise to give the kingdom to David: "Yahweh said to you, 'You yourself will shepherd [רָעָה] my people Israel, and you will become the designated ruler [נָגִיד] over Israel' " (5:2). This is not found verbatim earlier in the book of Samuel. However, the prophet Samuel in 1 Sam 13:14 and Abigail in 1 Sam 25:30 state that Yahweh commanded that David would be the "designated ruler" (נָגִיד) over his people Israel, and 1 Sam 25:30 adds that this designation was according to what Yahweh had "said." Later, David's status as the one Yahweh chose to be Israel's "designated ruler" (נָגִיד) will be reaffirmed in 2 Sam 6:21; 7:8. "Shepherd" is a frequent characterization of kings in the ancient Near East. As Israel's ultimate King, Yahweh is often called by this title.[21] Interestingly, no ruling king is ever called "shepherd" in the OT,[22] though on a couple of occasions Jeremiah refers to future kings this way (Jer 3:15; 23:4). Ezekiel 34 condemns Israel's unfaithful and predatory "shepherds" (apostate kings and false prophets) and promises the Messiah as "one Shepherd, my servant David," who shall rescue and tend God's flock (Ezek 34:23; see also Ezek 37:24–25). Of course, readers will remember that David began as a shepherd over Jesse's sheep (1 Sam 16:11, 19; 17:15, 34) and now has become shepherd over Yahweh's flock Israel. Yahweh's choice of David to shepherd Israel and David's faithful service in that vocation are extolled in Ps 78:70–72.

The author of Samuel notes that the recognition of David as king involved a covenant (2 Sam 5:3). Though we are not told its contents, this probably spelled

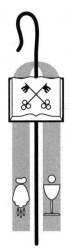

---

[18] See the second textual note on 5:1.

[19] See, e.g., 1 Sam 18:13, 16, which use forms of the same verbs that describe David's military leadership in 2 Sam 5:2 (see the second and third textual notes on 5:2). See also David's defeat of Goliath in 1 Samuel 17.

[20] See the commentary on 3:9–10.

[21] See רֹעֶה, "Shepherd," a Qal (G) participle of רָעָה, the verb used in 2 Sam 5:2, in Gen 48:15; 49:24; Is 40:11; Pss 23:1; 80:2 (ET 80:1).

[22] An exception would be Ps 78:70–72 if it was written during the reign of David. Psalm 78 is a psalm of Asaph, whom David appointed as a Levitical musician at the time the ark was moved to Jerusalem (1 Chr 15:16–17; 16:4–5, 7, 37; 25:6). But since that was only about six years before David's death, most probably Asaph wrote Psalm 78 during Solomon's reign.

out the king's responsibility to Israel and Israel's obligation to David. Then, for the third time, David was anointed as king (see previously 1 Sam 16:13; 2 Sam 2:4). As a predecessor and type of "the Son of David" (e.g., Mt 1:1; 9:27; 12:23) and Son of God (see Lk 20:40–44), his anointing prefigures the anointing of the Christ ("the Anointed One") with the Holy Spirit to empower his faithful completion of his earthly ministry (Lk 4:18; Acts 10:38). Thus, David portends the fulfillment of the prophetic promises of "the Messiah," "the Anointed One" (מָשִׁיחַ), including those by Hannah (1 Sam 2:10) and the unnamed man of God (1 Sam 2:35).[23]

A Summary of David's Reign (5:4–5)

1009–969 BC

Parallel: 2 Sam 5:5 ‖ 1 Chr 3:4

This notice is similar to other notices in the OT concerning the reigns of kings. Because of the round numbers thirty and forty, critical scholars often take this as an idealized summary of David's reign.[24] However, Baldwin notes that the breakdown of years in Hebron and Jerusalem demonstrates that the author intended this notice to be understood literally.[25]

David's time in Hebron is said to be seven and a half years (5:5). However, 1 Ki 2:11 reports it as seven years. The difference appears to be between the *actual* time in Hebron (2 Sam 5:5) and the *official* time in Hebron (1 Ki 2:11). This implies that the author of Kings was reckoning David's reign according to the accession-year system. Since it would be unlikely for a king to die on the exact day ending a particular year and for his successor take the throne on the first day of the following year, the last year of a king's reign usually was a partial year, and the rest of that year was served by the following king. Since both the old king and his successor served part of a year, to whom was that year assigned? In some systems used in the ancient world, the year was assigned to the end of the reign of the prior king. Therefore the partial year was not counted in the reign of his successor but was instead a sort of "year zero" for the new king, called his accession year. This *accession-year* system was typically used by the Assyrians and Babylonians and was apparently also used in the united monarchy for the reigns of David and Solomon. Therefore, the "six months" in 2 Sam 5:5 were not counted as part of his "seven years" in Hebron according

---

[23] See the commentary on 1 Sam 2:10 and 1 Sam 2:35 (Steinmann, *1 Samuel*, 80–81, 105–6). See further "David and the Messianic Promise" in "Christ in Samuel" in the introduction (Steinmann, *1 Samuel*, 25–26). As Jesus was anointed with the Spirit at his Baptism (Mt 3:16; Jn 1:32; cf. Acts 4:26–27; Heb 1:9), so he is also the one who baptizes with the Holy Spirit (Mt 3:11; Jn 1:33). The NT speaks of baptized believers in Christ as those whom God has "anointed" (2 Cor 1:21) and who have received "an anointing" (1 Jn 2:20).

[24] Ackroyd, *The Second Book of Samuel*, 53; Anderson, *2 Samuel*, 76–77; McCarter, *II Samuel*, 133.

[25] Baldwin, *1 and 2 Samuel*, 195; cf. Hertzberg, *I and II Samuel*, 267–68.

to 1 Ki 2:11 nor included in the "forty years" of David's official reign (2 Sam 5:4; 1 Ki 2:11).

David became king in Hebron shortly after the Philistine campaign that resulted in Saul's death. It appears as if David became Judah's king in the spring, when major campaigns were often initiated (see 2 Sam 11:1; 2 Ki 13:20; 1 Chr 20:1). Regnal years were generally reckoned from either the first month of spring (called Abib or Nisan; beginning in late March or early April) or the first month of autumn (called Ethanim or Tishri; beginning in late September or early October).[26] It appears, then, that during the united monarchy under David and Solomon, official regnal years were counted from the fall in the month of Tishri. This practice was continued in Judah after Solomon's death when the kingdom was divided.

David's "forty years" on the throne (2 Sam 5:4; 1 Ki 2:11) was a long reign, matched by Solomon (1 Ki 11:42; 2 Chr 9:30), Joash (2 Ki 12:2 [ET 12:1]; 2 Chr 24:1), and possibly Saul.[27] Only Judah's kings Asa (forty-one years; 1 Ki 15:9–10; 2 Chr 16:13), Azariah/Uzziah (fifty-two years; 2 Ki 15:1–2; 2 Chr 26:3), and Manasseh (fifty-five years; 2 Ki 21:1; 2 Chr 33:1), and Israel's king Jeroboam II (forty-one years; 2 Ki 14:23) are credited with longer reigns.

---

[26] Steinmann, *From Abraham to Paul*, 17–21.

[27] See the commentary on 1 Sam 13:1 (Steinmann, *1 Samuel*, 238–39).

A Summary of David's Reign over Israel

Translation

5 ⁶David and his men went to Jerusalem, to the Jebusites living in the land. They said to David, "You will never enter here. Instead, the blind and the lame can turn you away." (They thought, "David will never enter here.")

⁷David captured the stronghold of Zion (that is, the City of David). ⁸That day David said, "Anyone who strikes the Jebusites should attack both the lame and the blind—those who are hated by David—through the water tunnel." Therefore, they say, "A blind man and a lame man will never enter the palace."

⁹So David dwelt in the stronghold and called it the City of David. He built the city all around from the Millo and inward.

¹⁰David became increasingly more powerful, and Yahweh, the God of armies, was with him. ¹¹King Hiram of Tyre sent messengers to David as well as cedar logs, carpenters, and stonemasons. They built a palace for David. ¹²David knew that Yahweh had established him as king over Israel and exalted his kingdom for the sake of his people Israel.

¹³David married other concubines and wives from Jerusalem after he came from Hebron. Sons and daughters were again born to David. ¹⁴These are the names of those born to him in Jerusalem: Shammua, Shobab, Nathan, Solomon, ¹⁵Ibhar, Elishua, Nepheg, Japhia, ¹⁶Elishama, Eliada, and Eliphelet.

Textual Notes

5:6 הַיְבֻסִי—The Hebrew gentilic noun יְבֻסִי is singular but a collective and so is translated as a plural: "the Jebusites." The following verbs that have this Hebrew singular as their implied subject are also singular: יוֹשֵׁב, "living, inhabiting," a Qal (G) masculine singular participle, and וַיֹּאמֶר, "(and) they said," a Qal preterite (imperfect with *waw* consecutive) third masculine singular.

לֹא־תָבוֹא הֵנָּה ... לֹא־יָבוֹא דָוִד הֵנָּה:—"You will never enter here. ... David will never enter here." The Qal (G) of בּוֹא, "come," is used with the adverb הֵנָּה, "here, this far," also in 14:32 (see also the Hiphil [H] in 1:10). Both times here the translation of the negated verb includes "never," but each instance could have other nuances (Joüon, § 112 l, m, n). The imperfect aspect, negated by לֹא, could simply express a statement of fact about the future, "you/he will not enter," or it could be a prohibition, "you/he shall/must not enter" (see the injunction in 5:8: לֹא יָבוֹא). The imperfect can also have a variety of modal nuances, "you/he should not (try to) enter" (because the attempt will fail), or it can express a warning, "you/he had better not enter" (because you/he will be defeated), or a challenge or taunt (cf. 1 Sam 17:8–10). While any of these alternate nuances is possible, the present author considers them less likely given the context.

כִּי אִם־הֱסִירְךָ הַעִוְרִים וְהַפִּסְחִים—"Instead, the blind and the lame can turn you away." The combination of conjunctions in the MT, כִּי אִם־, means "instead" (cf. BDB, s.v. כִּי־אִם, 2 b). The readings כי in 4QSam[a] and ὅτι in the LXX mean "because" or "since." The MT verb הֱסִירְךָ is the Hiphil (H) of סוּר, "cause to turn aside," third masculine singular perfect with a second masculine singular suffix, literally "he turned you away." A perfect verb can express a future action (GKC, § 106 m), but it is unusual for such a perfect to express capability, "*can* turn you away." Despite the two plurals in its compound subject, הַעִוְרִים וְהַפִּסְחִים, "the blind men and the lame men," the verb is singular. Hebrew often uses a masculine singular verb form when it precedes a plural subject (Joüon, § 150 e, j).

The reading in 4QSam[a] is partially reconstructed as הסית[וך]. If this reconstruction (perhaps influenced by the LXX; see below) is correct, it would be vocalized הֱסִיתוּךָ (as in Jer 38:22), the third common plural Hiphil (H) perfect of סוּת with a second masculine singular object suffix, meaning that the blind and the lame "incited you." This, along with the rest of the verse, would mean that the disabled had incited David to attack by taunting him with "David will never enter here." This reading could explain why in 5:8 David commands his forces to attack "the lame and the blind" as those whom he hates: they were the instigators of the conflict. The LXX reads ἀντέστησαν οἱ τυφλοὶ καὶ οἱ χωλοί, "the blind and the lame incited/opposed" (with no direct object),[1] and the LXX indicates that the disabled are the ones who then say, "David will never enter here" (λέγοντες ὅτι οὐκ εἰσελεύσεται Δαυιδ ὧδε).

The translation follows the MT. For an explanation of its meaning, see the commentary.

לֵאמֹר—"They thought." The Qal (G) of אָמַר (this is the infinitive construct with לְ) can mean "to think" as well as "to speak." The following quote may be a thought or belief: the Jebusites considered the city impregnable. It could also be a quotation, possibly spoken by the Jebusites to one another to reassure themselves, or (as allowed by the LXX) a quotation of what the blind and the lame said to provoke David.

5:7 מְצֻדַת צִיּוֹן—"The stronghold of Zion." In the book of Samuel the feminine noun מְצוּדָה, "fortress, stronghold," always refers to a refuge for David. It recurs in reference to Zion in 2 Sam 5:9, 17. It designates other earthly strongholds used by David in 1 Sam 22:4–5; 24:23 (ET 24:22); 2 Sam 23:14, and it refers to Yahweh as his stronghold in 2 Sam 22:2.

5:8 וְיִגַּע—"He should attack." The MT has the conjunction וְ on the verb יִגַּע, the Qal (G) third masculine singular imperfect or jussive of נָגַע, "to touch, attack" (see *HALOT*, Qal, 2) or "reach, extend to" (BDB, Qal, 4; see also *HALOT*, Qal, 3). This *waw* apodosis

---

[1] The LXX lexicon of Muraoka (s.v. ἀνθίστημι, I b) defines this instance of ἀνθίστημι as "instigate, incite," and tentatively suggests that the implied direct object may be the Jebusite population. If correct, the blind and the lame could have incited the Jebusites to resist David by telling the population that David would not succeed against them. The Greek verb can also mean "*to rise* in rebellion or opposition" (s.v. ἀνθίστημι, II 2).

is normal Hebrew syntax after the preceding *casus pendens*, כָּל־מַכֵּה יְבֻסִי, literally "every striker of a Jebusite—and let him attack" (see GKC, § 116 w). Nevertheless, since no conjunction is found in the readings of 4QSam[a] (יגע) and the LXX (ἁπτέσθω), some propose that the *waw* in the MT may be the result of a graphic confusion between *yod* and *waw* combined with dittography. Note that the previous word (יְבֻסִי) ends in *yod*, while this verb (יִגַּע) begins with *yod*.

בַּצִּנּוֹר—"Through the water tunnel." The meaning of the noun צִנּוֹר is uncertain. Its only other appearance is in Ps 42:8 (ET 42:7), where it denotes a water channel of some sort, perhaps a downpour in a thunderstorm.[2] See also the related noun צַנְתְּרוֹת, "pipes," in Zech 4:12. In Rabbinic Hebrew צִנּוֹר may denote a pipe, spout, or duct.[3] The word, therefore, most probably denotes some type of conduit. The Ugaritic cognate *ṣnr* denotes "pipes" and therefore might support this understanding.[4] A shaft was discovered by Charles Warren in 1867. Initially scholars thought that water may have been drawn through this shaft from the Gihon Spring. However, this remains controversial, and it appears as if Warren's Shaft may not have been used to draw water. Instead, Jerusalem appears to have had a system of tunnels cut in the bedrock near the Gihon Spring though which water could be obtained by the inhabitants.[5] Perhaps צִנּוֹר refers to one of these tunnels. Some commentators prefer other suggestions, but most are far-fetched and speculative.[6] The LXX translated בַּצִּנּוֹר as ἐν παραξιφίδι, "with a dagger," apparently reading בצור, the preposition בְּ with the noun צוּר.[7] The LXX probably reflects a defective Hebrew Vorlage that suffered from haplography when the *nun* was omitted due to its similarity in shape to the following *waw*.

שֹׂנְאֵי נֶפֶשׁ דָּוִד—"Those who are hated by David." This construct chain is the Qere in Codex Leningradensis and the sole reading in many Masoretic manuscripts. The masculine plural Qal passive (Gp) participle of שָׂנֵא, "to hate," is in construct with "the soul of David" as a genitive of subject (Joüon, § 129 d), literally "hated of/by the soul of David." The Kethib in Codex Leningradensis is the (active) Qal (G) masculine plural perfect שָׂנְאוּ, "they hate(d) the soul/life of David," which agrees with the sense of the (active)

---

[2] It is translated as καταρράκτης, "waterfall," in LXX Ps 41:8 (MT 42:8; ET 42:7). Most modern English translations are similar.

[3] Jastrow, s.v. צִנּוֹר, צִינּוֹר.

[4] Kleven, "The Use of *ṣnr* in Ugaritic and 2 Samuel v 8"; Kleven, "Up the Waterspout." The similar meaning of a cognate in a related language is helpful but not decisive since cognates in related languages may have quite different meanings. Thus, the verbal root עבד in Hebrew means "serve," but in Aramaic it means "do, make" (usually expressed in Hebrew by the verb עָשָׂה). The German *bekommen* means "get, obtain," a meaning quite different from the English cognate "become."

[5] See the discussions in Domeris, "The City of David," 24–25; Reich and Shukron, "Light at the End of the Tunnel"; Kleven, "The Water System of Jerusalem and Its Implications for the Historicity of Joab's Conquest"; Faust, "Warren's Shaft: Yes, It Really Was Used to Draw Water"; Shimron, "Warren's Shaft: No, It Really Was Not Used to Draw Water"; Shimron, Faust, and Shanks, "Did Ancient Jerusalem Draw Water through Warren's Shaft?"

[6] E.g., McCarter translates it as "windpipe" and argues that David was calling on his men to strike at the throats of the Jebusites (*II Samuel*, 137). Yadin suggested that it means "trident" (*The Art of Warfare in Biblical Lands*, 268). NEB translates it as "grappling-iron."

[7] See חַרְבוֹת צֻרִים, "flint knives," in Josh 5:2–3.

participle in the LXX, τοὺς μισοῦντας τὴν ψυχὴν Δαυιδ, "the haters of the soul/life of David." The Kethib is the result of the rather common graphic confusion between *yod* and *waw*. 4QSamᵃ reads שנאה נפש דויד, "[those whom] David's soul hated." The feminine noun נֶפֶשׁ, "soul," is the subject and the verb שנאה, which has an active meaning, could be pointed either as a Qal third feminine singular perfect, שָׂנְאָה, or as a Qal feminine singular participle, שֹׂנְאָה (cf. the feminine participle in Ezek 16:27). The reading in 4QSamᵃ may have involved an earlier graphic confusion when the text was written in Paleo-Hebrew script, since *yod* (י) and *he* (ה) would have been quite similar.

הַבָּיִת:—Literally "the house." The translation "the palace" assumes that David's house is meant, since he expressed his contempt for the blind and the lame of the Jebusites. See also 5:11, where בַּיִת clearly refers to David's palace. Contrast its meaning in the third textual note on 5:9.

5:9 וַיִּבֶן דָּוִד—"And David built" (without a direct object) is the reading of the MT. But the translation follows the reading in the LXX, καὶ ᾠκοδόμησεν τὴν πόλιν, "(and) he built the city," which agrees with וַיִּבֶן הָעִיר in 1 Chr 11:8. 4QSamᵃ reads ויבנה עיר, "and he built it, a city." That probably represents the same reading as the LXX and 1 Chr 11:8, albeit with a misdivision of words: ה is joined to the preceding verb as its third feminine singular suffix (הָ-, "it") and direct object, rather than joined to the following noun as the article (הָעִיר, "the city").

הַמִּלּוֹא—"The Millo," which means "the fill" (from the verb מָלֵא, "be full"), was built by Solomon (1 Ki 9:15, 24; 11:27). Here the author uses the term proleptically, since it was a landmark that his readers would know as the northern extent of David's city.[8] The Millo is commonly assumed to be the Stepped Stone Structure uncovered by Kathleen Kenyon and demonstrated by Eilat Mazar to be connected to the adjacent Large Stone Structure. The Stepped Stone Structure is built over fill.[9] A recent excavation by Mazar directly above the Stepped Stone Structure indicates that it supports the Large Stone Structure. She found that the Stepped Stone Structure and the Large Stone Structure form a single, large royal palace. Mazar argues that the Large Stone Structure was an Israelite royal palace in continuous use from the tenth century until the fall of Jerusalem to the Babylonians in 587 BC, that is, from the time of David and Solomon onward.[10] It is probably the building called "the House of Millo" (בֵּית מִלֹּא) in 2 Ki 12:21 (ET 12:20).

---

[8] See "The Composition of Samuel" in "Authorship, Composition, and Date" in the introduction (Steinmann, *1 Samuel*, 1–3).

[9] Stager, "The Archaeology of the East Slope of Jerusalem and the Terraces of the Kidron"; Shanks, "Has Jerusalem's Millo Been Found?"; Shanks, "The City of David after Five Years of Digging," 26–29.

[10] Mazar, *The Palace of King David: Excavations at the Summit of the City of David*, 47–67, who argues that the Large Stone Structure was David's palace. Na'aman, "The Interchange between Bible and Archaeology," agrees with Mazar that the Large Stone Structure was David's palace. He argues that the Stepped Stoned Structure is the Millo, and he notes that the Bible attributes the Millo's construction to Solomon. There is no archaeological evidence that points to David rather than Solomon as the builder of the Stepped Stone Structure, and the biblical text is unambiguous about who built the Millo.

וּבֵיתָה:—"And inward." The noun בַּיִת, "house," can be used as a preposition, "within," or, as here, with the directional *he* as an adjective or adverb, "inward" (*HALOT*, s.v. בַּיִת I, A 3).

5:10 וַיֵּלֶךְ דָּוִד הָלוֹךְ וְגָדוֹל—"David became increasingly more powerful" is literally "and David walked/went, going and becoming great." הָלוֹךְ is the Qal (G) infinitive absolute of הָלַךְ, "walk." Its infinitive absolute is used idiomatically with another infinitive absolute to express continuing action (as in 1 Sam 6:12; 2 Sam 3:16) or increasing action (here in 2 Sam 5:10). See Joüon, § 123 m, s; Waltke-O'Connor, § 35.3.2c, including example 8. Most likely here גָדוֹל is the Qal (G) infinitive absolute of גָּדַל, "become great" (so Joüon, § 123 s), even though הָלוֹךְ is sometimes used with an adjective (Joüon, § 123 s) and in form גָּדוֹל could be the adjective, "big, great."

אֱלֹהֵי צְבָאוֹת—"(The) God of armies" is traditionally "(the) God of hosts." צָבָא denotes an army (as in 2:8; 3:23). The English word "host" denoting an army derives from the Latin *hostis*, "stranger, enemy."[11]

5:11 וְחָרָשֵׁי עֵץ—"(And) carpenters." This construct phrase (preceded by the conjunction *waw*, "and") is literally "craftsmen of wood" (see Joüon, § 129 g; Waltke-O'Connor, § 9.5.3g, including example 45). The noun חָרָשׁ denotes a skilled manual laborer of some kind, such as a craftsman, carpenter, mason, metal smith, or other artisan.

וְחָרָשֵׁי אֶבֶן קִיר—"And stonemasons" is literally "and craftsmen of a stone of a wall." The noun קִיר usually refers to the "wall" of a building but can designate a much larger city wall (more commonly called חוֹמָה) and other sorts of walls. Sizable stone walls were essential for ancient cities, buildings, and fortifications. 1 Chr 14:1 reads וְחָרָשֵׁי קִיר, "and craftsmen of a wall," and places it *before* וְחָרָשֵׁי עֵצִים, "and carpenters." 4QSam^a also reads וחרשי קיר, but places it *after* "and carpenters."

5:12 נִשֵּׂא מַמְלַכְתּוֹ—Yahweh "exalted his kingdom." The verb נָשָׂא, whose Qal (G) commonly has the physical meaning "lift up," can in the Piel (D) have the metaphorical meaning to "exalt" (*DCH*, Piel, 1 b). Instead of the Piel here with מַמְלַכְתּוֹ as its direct object, 1 Chr 14:2 has the feminine singular Niphal (N) participle נִשֵּׂאת with מַלְכוּתוֹ as its subject: "his kingdom was exalted."

5:13 מִירוּשָׁלַם—"From Jerusalem" is the reading of the MT. 1 Chr 14:3 reads בִּירוּשָׁלָם, "in Jerusalem." The reading in 4QSam^a is reconstructed at this point.

וַיִּוָּלְדוּ—"And they were born" is a Niphal (N) preterite (imperfect with *waw* consecutive) of יָלַד, "to give birth." The identical form recurs in 14:27 and was the Qere in 3:2 (see the first textual note on 3:2).

5:14 הַיִּלֹדִים—The adjective יִלּוֹד, "born," is clearly derived from יָלַד (see the preceding textual note). Here its plural is used as a substantive (preceded by the article) and is the *nomen rectum* of the construct chain שְׁמוֹת הַיִּלֹדִים: "the names *of those born*."

---

[11] The English word "host" denoting someone who entertains guests derives from the Latin stem *hospit-*, "host, guest, stranger," while the English word "host" denoting the bread in the Lord's Supper derives from the late Latin *hostia*, "eucharistic wafer" (from the Latin "victim, sacrifice").

Commentary

1002–969 BC[12]

This section summarizes David's reign over all the tribes of Israel and flows out of 5:4–5, which summarizes David's reign in both Hebron and Jerusalem. Here three items from David's time as king of all Israel are presented: David's conquest of Jerusalem at the beginning of this period, the height of David's power at the midpoint of his reign, and the children born to him during his thirty-three years in Jerusalem (5:5).

David's Conquest of Jerusalem (5:6–9)

1002 BC[13]

Parallel: 2 Sam 5:6–9 ‖ 1 Chr 11:4–8

David's choice of Jerusalem as his capital was a shrewd political move. Hebron, his former capital (5:5), was in central Judah and was quite a sensible choice as long as David ruled only that tribe. However, a location that signaled his commitment to all of Israel was needed.[14] Jerusalem was in the territory of Benjamin but was never claimed by that tribe and was still inhabited by Jebusites, one of the original Canaanite peoples.[15] It was an ideal option. David could conquer it and make it royal property. Moreover, by conquering Jerusalem, David could fulfill the divine mandate for Israel to defeat the Jebusites (Deut 7:1–2; 20:16–17), which was accompanied by the promise that Yahweh's Angel would go before them (Ex 23:23–24; 33:2). However, it appears that David did not completely fulfill that directive, since he did not extirpate the Jebusites.[16] Therefore, the author may be already hinting that while David had many successes, he also had his failings and flaws.

David and "his men" (5:6), that is, the standing army that was under the command of Joab in Hebron, came to Jerusalem, where the Jebusites taunted David, believing their city impregnable (see the second textual note on 5:6). They goaded David by claiming that even the blind and the lame among them could repel David's attack.[17] The author simply states that David captured the city (5:7) and then gives a further explanation of David's strategy of invading

---

[12] See "The Chronology of David's Reign" in the commentary on 5:1–5.

[13] See "The Chronology of David's Reign" in the commentary on 5:1–5.

[14] Note that David's attachment to all Israel would become an issue later. See 20:1–2.

[15] See, e.g., Gen 10:16; 15:21; Ex 3:8, 17; 13:5.

[16] See 2 Sam 24:16, 18; 1 Ki 9:20–21; 1 Chr 21:15, 18, 28; 2 Chr 3:1; 8:7–8.

[17] See the third and fourth textual notes on 5:6. Commentators have at times considered the reference to the blind and the lame difficult. Josephus claimed that the Jebusites placed lame and one-eyed defenders on the wall (*Antiquities*, 7.61). Taking this as a variant of a Hittite oath ceremony (*ANET*, 353–54), Yadin suggested that the Jebusites paraded blind and lame people on the walls while taking an oath that David would not enter the city (*The Art of Warfare in Biblical Lands*, 269–70). Stoebe argued that the Jebusites were mocking David's troops as blind and lame ("Die Einnahme Jerusalems"). None of these interpretations are likely, and the reference to the blind and the lame in 5:6 is clear enough without resorting to such explanations.

the city through its water system (see the second textual note on 5:8). Moreover, David here redefines "the lame and the blind" as his enemies ("those who are hated by David," 5:8), i.e., all of the Jebusites.[18] The author then connects this with the origin of a saying that barred "a blind man and a lame man," referring to the Jebusites, from "the house" (הַבַּיִת), that is, "the palace" (see the fourth textual note on 5:8). That this cannot have been a literal reference to blind and lame persons is clear from David hosting Mephibosheth at his table (9:1–13). Some have argued that the reference to the blind and the lame being banned from "the house" is actually a reference to a later practice of banning them from the temple.[19] This is unlikely, however, since David could not have banned anyone from the temple that was built only later by his son Solomon and since in a few short verses the "house" under discussion will be David's palace (בַּיִת, 5:11).

This section ends with David dwelling in the stronghold of Jerusalem and naming that portion "the City of David" (5:9). We are also told that David initiated building projects in his capital from the north, where the Millo would eventually be built by Solomon (1 Ki 9:15), and extending inward toward the stronghold.

David's Kingdom Prospers (5:10–12)

980–975 BC[20]

Parallels: 2 Sam 5:10 ‖ 1 Chr 11:9; 2 Sam 5:11–12 ‖ 1 Chr 14:1–2

This short section is set off by the mention of "Yahweh" at the beginning and the end. The rise of David in prominence was the consequence of Yahweh's gracious presence and support ("Yahweh … was with him," 5:10). God is called "Yahweh, the God of armies" (יהוה אֱלֹהֵי צְבָאוֹת), fourteen more times in the OT, but never again in 2 Samuel.[21] However, he is called by the shorter title "Yahweh of armies" (יהוה צְבָאוֹת) ten times in the book of Samuel.[22] Here the title is quite appropriate, since David's prominence came from Yahweh blessing David's armies with success.[23]

David's elevated international status brought him to the attention of a new king of Tyre, Hiram, who began his reign in 980 BC, when David was at the height of his power, some six years before Absalom's rebellion. The construction of David's palace is credited to Hiram's supply of cedar and skilled artisans (5:11). Cedar was especially prized for building, since this wood is hard,

---

[18] Bergen, *1, 2 Samuel*, 321.

[19] Olyan, "'Anyone Blind or Lame Shall Not Enter the House'"; McCarter, *II Samuel*, 140; Ackroyd, *The Second Book of Samuel*, 57.

[20] See "The Chronology of David's Reign" in the commentary on 5:1–5.

[21] 1 Ki 19:10, 14; Jer 5:14; 15:16; 35:17; 38:17; 44:7; Amos 4:13; 5:14, 15, 16, 27; 6:8; Ps 89:9 (ET 89:8).

[22] 1 Sam 1:3, 11; 4:4; 15:2; 17:45; 2 Sam 6:2, 18; 7:8, 26, 27.

[23] 2 Sam 5:17–25; 8:1–18; 10:1–19; 12:26–31; 21:15–22. See further "Prosperity and Success Come Only from God" in "Other Theological Themes in Samuel" in the introduction (Steinmann, *1 Samuel*, 29).

close-grained, and durable and takes a high polish. Cedar's resin preserves it from rot and from destructive insects.

David also grew in his knowledge that it was Yahweh who had established his throne (5:12). He recognized that this was not for his own personal gain, but for the sake of Yahweh's people. This is a reference to God's promises to David through Nathan (7:10–11 and David's response in 7:23–24). In Nathan's words and David's reply to Yahweh, Israel is mentioned six times as Yahweh's people (7:7, 8, 10, 11, 23, 24). Thus, the author is alerting us of the great messianic promise that came at the height of David's reign (7:4–16) as David completed his palace and sought to build a house for God (7:1–2).[24]

David's Children Born in Jerusalem (5:13–16)

1002–969 BC[25]

Parallels: 2 Sam 5:13–16 ‖ 1 Chr 3:5–8; 14:3–7

David's family grew in Jerusalem (5:13), and the children born to him were also a sign of Yahweh's blessing (Ps 127:3; cf. 2 Sam 12:18). We are told that David had concubines and wives.[26] Both were considered married to David, but a concubine was not acquired by the paying of a bride-price, as was a wife.[27] David's acquisition of many wives is also another subtle hint of David's flaws: he was disobeying the prohibition placed on Israel's kings in Deut 17:17. It has been suggested that David's concubines and wives *from Jerusalem* (מִירוּשָׁלַ֔ם, 2 Sam 5:13; LXX: ἐξ Ιερουσαλημ) were Jebusite women.[28] If this was the case, then David's reason for leaving the Jebusites in Jerusalem can be explained as his using the existing bureaucratic structure of the city to run everyday affairs,

---

[24] See further the commentary on 2 Samuel 7, as well as "The Promise to David (2 Samuel 7)" and "David and the Messianic Promise" in "Christ in Samuel" in the introduction (Steinmann, *1 Samuel*, 23–24, 25–26).

[25] See "The Chronology of David's Reign" in the commentary on 5:1–5.

[26] The OT records that David and Solomon (among others) practiced polygamy, but no passage of Scripture expresses approval for it. Instead, the narrative will reveal multiple family problems that stem from it in the reign of David (e.g., 2 Samuel 13–14) as also for Solomon (1 Kings 11). God's design for marriage in Genesis 1–2 was an exclusive relationship of one man with one woman for life. This is also affirmed in Eph 5:21–33, which extols the monogamous, exclusive, and sacrificial relationship of Jesus Christ to his bride, the church, as the archetype for human marriage (Eph 5:31–32). Polygamy was an innovation by Lamech, a murderer (Gen 4:19–24). See further the excursus "Polygamy in the Bible" in Steinmann, *1 Samuel*, 64–67; "Solomon's Polygamy (Song 6:8)" in Mitchell, *The Song of Songs*, 120–27; and Kind, "Polygamy and Its Contemporary Variations in Biblical Perspective."

[27] Note that Jacob's "concubine" (פִּילֶגֶשׁ, Gen 35:22) Bilhah is also characterized as a "wife" (אִשָּׁה, Gen 30:4; plural, נָשִׁים, Gen 37:2). Yahweh's judgment that someone would sleep with David's "wives" (נָשִׁים, 2 Sam 12:11) was fulfilled when Absalom slept with ten of David's "concubines" (פִּלַגְשִׁים, 2 Sam 15:16; 16:21–22). Note that in 2 Sam 15:16 they are called "wives-concubines" (נָשִׁים פִּלַגְשִׁים), implying equal status.

[28] Hill, "On David's 'Taking' and 'Leaving' Concubines." Hill argues that these concubines and wives were the ten left behind to take care of the palace when David fled Jerusalem during Absalom's rebellion (2 Sam 15:16). Their role as running the palace household would then have been a part of the function of the Jebusite bureaucracy. If so, Absalom's sleeping with them would have taken on a greater significance (see the commentary on 16:15–23).

and his marriages with Jebusite women would have been to secure the loyalty of key Jebusites. However, they would have exerted a pagan influence on him unless they were converted to faith in Yahweh. Again, the author may be hinting at flaws in David's character that would exhibit themselves more fully later in 2 Samuel.

This is heightened even more by listing the four children of Bathsheba first (2 Sam 5:14; see also 1 Chr 3:5), since she was the wife of Uriah before David seized her and murdered her husband (2 Samuel 11). Her sons are followed by seven other sons (5:15–16). Interestingly, though the author mentions David's "daughters" (5:13), he lists only the names of his sons. This is the shortest OT list of David's children born in Jerusalem. It omits David's sons Eliphelet/Elpelet and Nogah, born between Elishua and Nepheg, and does not mention his daughter Tamar. Eliada (2 Sam 5:16; 1 Chr 3:8) is called Beeliada in 1 Chr 14:7. Eliada means "God knows," whereas Beeliada means "the master [God] knows."[29]

Figure 3

___

David's Children Born in Jerusalem
(2 Sam 5:14–16; 1 Chr 3:5–9; 14:4–7)

2 Sam 5:14–16	1 Chr 3:5–9	1 Chr 14:4–7
Shammua	Shimea	Shammua
Shobab	Shobab	Shobab
Nathan	Nathan	Nathan
Solomon	Solomon	Solomon
Ibhar	Ibhar	Ibhar
Elishua	Elishama	Elishua
	Eliphelet	*Elpelet*
	Nogah	*Nogah*
Nepheg	Nepheg	Nepheg
Japhia	Japhia	Japhia
Elishama	Elishama	Elishama
Eliada	Eliada	Beeliada
Eliphelet	Eliphelet	Eliphelet
	Tamar (daughter)	

___

[29] In 1 Chr 3:6 "Elishama" is most likely a scribal mistake for "Elishua."

David Defeats the Philistines Twice

Translation

5   ¹⁷The Philistines heard that they [the elders] had anointed David to be king over Israel. So all the Philistines went up to seek David. When David heard [this], he went down to the stronghold. ¹⁸The Philistines came and spread out in the Valley of Rephaim.

¹⁹David inquired of Yahweh, "Should I go up to the Philistines? Will you hand them over to me?"

"Yahweh said, "Go up, for I will certainly hand the Philistines over to you."

²⁰David came to Baal-perazim. David attacked them there, and he said, "Yahweh has burst through my enemies in front of me like water bursts forth." Therefore, he called the name of that place Baal-perazim. ²¹The Philistines abandoned their idols there, and David and his men carried them away.

²²Once again, the Philistines came up and spread out in the Valley of Rephaim. ²³David inquired of Yahweh, and he [Yahweh] said, "Do not go up. Circle behind them and come to them opposite the trees. ²⁴When you hear the sound of the marching in the tops of the trees, act decisively, because that is when Yahweh has gone out [to battle] ahead of you to attack the Philistine camp."

²⁵David did this as Yahweh had commanded him, and he struck the Philistines from Gibeon to Gezer.

Textual Notes

5:17 מָשְׁחוּ אֶת־דָּוִד לְמֶלֶךְ עַל־יִשְׂרָאֵל—Literally "they anointed David to be king over Israel." The Hebrew wording is nearly identical to that in 5:3, where "the elders of Israel" are the ones who anoint David, so the translation here clarifies that "the elders" are the implied subject of the verb.

הַמְּצוּדָה:—For "the stronghold," see the textual note on 5:7.

5:18 וַיִּנָּטְשׁוּ בְּעֵמֶק רְפָאִים:—"And they spread out in the Valley of Rephaim." This clause is repeated in 5:22b. The verb וַיִּנָּטְשׁוּ is the third masculine plural Niphal (N) preterite (imperfect with *waw* consecutive) of נָטַשׁ, "to leave, abandon." In the Niphal, this verb can have the passive meaning "to be abandoned" (Amos 5:2), but here it has an intransitive meaning, "they spread out," as again in the identical clause in 5:22 (see also Judg 15:9; Is 16:8). 1 Chr 14:9 reads וַיִּפְשְׁטוּ, "and they raided," the Qal (G) of פָּשַׁט. That reading may have been the result of the graphic confusion of *nun* and *pe* and the transposition of *tet* and *shin*, since elsewhere in the book of Samuel the Qal of פָּשַׁט in the sense "to make a raid" is almost always followed by the preposition עַל or אֶל, introducing what was attacked.[1]

---

[1]   1 Sam 23:27; 27:8, 10; 30:1, 14. The mention of the first place attacked in 1 Sam 30:14 lacks any preposition, but then the preposition עַל is used twice to introduce the second and third places attacked.

5:19 וַיִּשְׁאַל דָּוִד בַּיהוָה—"David inquired of Yahweh." This clause recurs in 5:23a. See the first textual note on 2:1.

הַאֶעֱלֶה—"Should I go up?" See the second textual note on 2:1.

הֲתִתְּנֵם בְּיָדִי—"Will you hand them over to me?" is literally "will you give them into my hand?" The verb הֲתִתְּנֵם is the second masculine singular Qal (G) imperfect of נָתַן, "give," with a prefixed interrogative *he* and a third masculine plural pronominal suffix. The same idiom recurs later in the verse but with the infinitive construct before the imperfect: נָתֹן אֶתֵּן ... בְּיָדֶךָ, literally "most certainly I will give ... into your hand."

5:20 פָּרַץ יְהוָה אֶת־אֹיְבַי—"Yahweh has burst through my enemies." In the Qal (G) פָּרַץ means "break through" or "burst out." It is often used for God violently bursting forth in judgment (BDB, s.v. פָּרַץ I, Qal, 6), as also in 6:8, where it takes the preposition בְּ. Both here and in the parallel 1 Chr 14:11 it takes as its direct object אֶת־אֹיְבַי, "my enemies," denoting those who suffer divine judgment.

כְּפֶרֶץ מָיִם—"Like water bursts forth" is literally "like a bursting forth of water." The noun פֶּרֶץ, which recurs in 6:8, is cognate to the preceding verb (see the previous textual note). In this construct phrase the noun מַיִם (pausal: מָיִם), "water," is a subjective genitive: water bursting forth signifies a flood of divine judgment ("like a breaking flood," ESV). The OT often refers to raging waters of judgment (e.g., Genesis 6–9; Is 8:6–8; 10:22; 28:2, 17). The noun פֶּרֶץ can also refer to a "breach" in a city wall, leaving the city vulnerable to attack, either literally (1 Ki 11:27) or as a metaphor for impending divine judgment (e.g., Is 30:13; Ezek 13:5; 22:30). The plural of this noun פֶּרֶץ, *perets*, is the second element in the compound place-name Baal-perazim (twice in 5:20). See also its singular in the place-name Perez-uzzah (6:8).

5:21 עֲצַבֵּיהֶם—Instead of the MT's "their idols," the LXX (τοὺς θεοὺς αὐτῶν) and 1 Chr 14:12 (אֱלֹהֵיהֶם) read "their gods."

וַיִּשָּׂאֵם דָּוִד וַאֲנָשָׁיו:—"And David and his men carried them away." It is common in Hebrew for the verb, when it is placed first, to be singular (here וַיִּשָּׂאֵם, a third masculine singular Qal [G] preterite [imperfect with *waw* consecutive] of נָשָׂא with a third masculine plural object suffix), in agreement with the following singular subject noun (here דָּוִד, "David"), even though the verb has a compound (plural) subject (here it includes וַאֲנָשָׁיו, "and his men"). See GKC, § 146 f, and Joüon, § 150 q.

5:22 וַיֹּסִפוּ עוֹד פְּלִשְׁתִּים לַעֲלוֹת—"Once again, the Philistines came up." The Hiphil (H) of יָסַף, "add, do again," is used with an infinitive construct (לַעֲלוֹת, the Qal [G] of עָלָה, "go up," a military maneuver, with the preposition לְ) to denote a repetition of an action (Joüon, §§ 102 g, 124 c, 177 b).

5:23 הָסֵב—This is the Hiphil (H) masculine singular imperative of סָבַב, "go around, make a circuit." Here its meaning is intransitive: "circle."

מִמּוּל בְּכָאִים:—"Opposite the trees." The preposition מִן is prefixed to the preposition מוּל, "in front of." The MT lacks the article on the plural noun here, בְּכָאִים, but includes it in 5:24 (הַבְּכָאִים). It has the article in the parallel verse 1 Chr 14:14. Here the LXX includes the article, τοῦ κλαυθμῶνος, "the weeping place." The exact identification of this plant is unknown. Many translations read "balsam trees" (e.g., ESV, NRSV), although NEB has "aspens" and KJV has "mulberry trees." Josephus understood it as the name of a grove called the "groves of weeping" (from the verb בָּכָה, "weep").[2] McCarter argues that it is a place-name,[3] but this seems unlikely given what is said in 5:24.

5:24 וִיהִי—This is the Qal (G) jussive of הָיָה with a conjunctive *waw*, literally "*and let it be* when you hear." To express the next step in a series of actions, Hebrew more commonly uses וְהָיָה to begin a verse or clause (as in, e.g., 1 Sam 1:12; 3:9; 10:7; 2 Sam 6:16; 9:10; 11:20), but the jussive, וִיהִי, was so used also in 1 Sam 10:5. See GKC, §§ 109 k; 112 z; Waltke-O'Connor, § 34.3b, including example 7.

כְּשָׁמְעֲךָ—"When you hear." This Qere, which is the sole reading in many Masoretic manuscripts and in 1 Chr 14:15, prefixes the preposition כְּ in a temporal sense ("when") to the Qal (G) infinitive construct of שָׁמַע, "hear," with a subjective second masculine singular pronominal suffix. The Kethib בְּשָׁמְעֲךָ has the preposition בְּ in the same temporal sense and may be supported by the LXX (ἐν τῷ ἀκοῦσαί σε). Both prepositions can be used in temporal clauses, and attempts to distinguish their meanings may be tenuous (see Joüon, § 166 l, including note 1).

אֶת־קוֹל צְעָדָה—Literally "the sound of marching." Codex Leningradensis lacks the article on צְעָדָה. Many Masoretic manuscripts and 1 Chr 14:15 (הַצְּעָדָה) include the article, as does the LXX (τοῦ συγκλεισμοῦ). This noun is used only here and in 1 Chr 14:15 in this sense. It or a homograph also occurs in Is 3:20, but denoting an "ankle bracelet."

אָז תֶּחֱרָץ—Preceded by the adverb אָז, "then," the Qal (G) second masculine singular imperfect of חָרַץ, "decide," here has the nuance of acting decisively, that is, quickly, without hesitation, and with full determination, and is used in an imperatival sense: "act decisively."

יָצָא—"He has gone out [to battle]." In military contexts the Qal (G) of יָצָא often signifies going to battle. See the first textual note on 1 Sam 18:6[4] and the first textual note 2 Sam 2:12.

5:25 מִגֶּבַע—The MT reads "from Geba." "From Gibeon" is the reading in the LXX (ἀπὸ Γαβαων) and 1 Chr 14:16 (מִגִּבְעוֹן). Gibeon is the more likely location, since it would have been on the Philistines' route of retreat toward Gezer. If the Philistines had fled to Geba, they would have been going too far north and east; see figures 4 and 5 in the commentary. Moreover, Is 28:21, which appears to refer to this battle, mentions both "Mount Perazim" and "Gibeon," lending further weight to reading "Gibeon" here.

עַד־בֹּאֲךָ גָזֶר:—"To Gezer" is literally "until you come to Gezer." בֹּאֲךָ is the Qal (G) infinitive construct of בּוֹא, "come," with a subjective second masculine singular suffix. This form is used in this way, referring to a geographical direction and to the reader as "you," also in 1 Sam 15:7; 17:52; 27:8. See the textual note on 1 Sam 15:7.[5]

Commentary

Beginning with these accounts of David's victory over the Philistines, the author has grouped together a number of narratives with additional information

---

2   Josephus, *Antiquities*, 7.76; see the LXX.

3   McCarter, *II Samuel*, 156.

4   Steinmann, *1 Samuel*, 350.

5   Steinmann, *1 Samuel*, 285.

that demonstrates David's successes as king (5:17–10:19). These serve to expand on his statements that God was with David (5:10) and that David understood that God had blessed him for Israel's sake (5:12). These victories over the Philistines contrast the faithful David with his predecessor Saul, who failed to deliver Israel from these hostile neighbors on Israel's southwest flank.[6]

The First Philistine Invasion (5:17–21)

Mid 1002 BC[7]

Parallel: 1 Sam 5:17–21 ‖ 1 Chr 14:8–12

The Philistines heard of David's reign over all Israel and decided to attack him, hoping to defeat him as they had Saul (5:17). We are told that "all the Philistines"—probably forces from all five of the major cities in Philistia[8]—went to seek David. He reacted by going down (the verb יָרַד) to the stronghold, that is, to the City of David. This is clear from the context, since "stronghold" (מְצוּדָה) was used in 5:7, 9 as a designation of the old Jebusite city of Jerusalem. Some scholars argue that the stronghold mentioned here cannot be Jerusalem since one usually goes up (the verb עָלָה) to Jerusalem, as it is situated on the tallest mountain in the region.[9] However, the author had noted that David had built Jerusalem from the Millo "and inward" (5:9), that is, it appears that he began the expansion of the city to the north that Solomon continued. This area north of the old Jebusite city is higher in elevation. The notice that David "went down to the stronghold" (5:17) may simply mean that previously he was surveying the area north of the city for possible expansion. When he learned of the Philistine incursion, he left that area and entered the already fortified City of David as a precaution.

Sometimes scholars who assert that "the stronghold" mentioned in 5:17 cannot be Jerusalem claim that the incident discussed in 2 Sam 23:13–17 and 1 Chr 11:15–19, which also mentions "the Valley of Rephaim" (2 Sam 23:13; 1 Chr 11:15, as in 2 Sam 5:18), took place at this time.[10] In those other texts it is clear that David was not in Jerusalem, but at a "stronghold" near "Adullam" (2 Sam 23:13–14; 1 Chr 11:15–16). However, 2 Sam 23:13–17 (‖ 1 Chr 11:15–19) does not relate to David's time as king, but speaks of his men getting water for him when he was at the cave of Adullam (2 Sam 23:13; 1 Chr 11:15)[11]—a

---

6 See further "David and the Messianic Promise" in "Christ in Samuel" and "Prosperity and Success Come Only from God" in "Other Theological Themes in Samuel" in the introduction (Steinmann, *1 Samuel*, 25–26, 29).

7 See "The Chronology of David's Reign" in the commentary on 5:1–5.

8 The Philistine pentapolis consisted of Gaza, Ashdod, Ashkelon, Gath, and Ekron. These five cities are listed in Josh 13:3 and 1 Sam 6:17. See figures 4 and 5 below.

9 McCarter, *II Samuel*, 158; Ackroyd, *The Second Book of Samuel*, 60; Hertzberg, *I and II Samuel*, 273; Hauer, "Jerusalem, the Stronghold and Rephaim."

10 Hauer, "Jerusalem, the Stronghold and Rephaim," 575–76.

11 This cave was probably near or incorporated into the "stronghold" mentioned in 2 Sam 23:14; 1 Chr 11:16.

reference to the time when he was fleeing from Saul and was in "the cave of Adullam" (1 Sam 22:1).[12] Note that according to 2 Sam 23:14 and 1 Chr 11:16, the Philistines had a garrison at Bethlehem, a situation that speaks of the Philistine penetration into Israel before and during Saul's reign (see 1 Sam 10:5; 13:23; 14:1, 4, 6, 11, 15). Therefore, one cannot appeal to 2 Sam 23:13–17 and 1 Chr 11:15–19 to support the speculative notion that the stronghold mentioned in 2 Sam 5:17 is not Jerusalem.

We are told that when the Philistines came into Israel, they "spread out" (the verb נָטַשׁ) in the Valley of Rephaim (see the textual note on 5:18). This, combined with the note that they were searching for David (5:17), suggests that they knew that David had moved north from Hebron but did not know where he had gone. Note that the only other text (other than 5:22) that mentions the Philistines "spreading out" (the verb נָטַשׁ) is Judg 15:9, where they were searching for Samson.

The exact location of the Valley of Rephaim is unknown. However, many identify its probable site with modern el-Baqʻa southwest of Jerusalem. The northern extremity of this valley approaches the Hinnom Valley on the south end of Jerusalem.

David "inquired" (שָׁאַל) of Yahweh before engaging the Philistines in battle (5:19), showing his faith in God and his trust that Yahweh would save his people.[13] This is in clear contrast to Saul, who was terrified of the Philistines (1 Sam 17:11; 28:5; cf. 1 Sam 13:7, 12). Saul inquired of God twice about these enemies, but both times he received no answer and demonstrated his lack of faith by disobeying the Word of Yahweh.[14] In his overconfidence he believed that he could save Israel and himself by choosing his own course of action.

David's inquiry was through the high priest, who was authorized to ask and receive an answer from God by means of the Urim and Thummim.[15] "To inquire of Yahweh" appears to be a specialized expression relating to the high priest's use of the Urim and Thummim.[16] David's question was whether or not

---

[12] Note, however, that the "stronghold" mentioned in 1 Sam 22:4–5 was in Moab and was not the same stronghold as the one near Adullam mentioned in 2 Sam 23:14; 1 Chr 11:16. See the commentary on 1 Sam 22:4–5 (Steinmann, *1 Samuel*, 422).

[13] Another example of such saving faith in Yahweh is Hannah, who "inquired/asked" (שָׁאַל) Yahweh for a son, and he answered her prayer. See שָׁאַל in 1 Sam 1:17, 20, 27, 28; 2:20.

[14] Saul "inquired" (שָׁאַל) of God in 1 Sam 14:37 and of Yahweh in 1 Sam 28:6, both times regarding battle with the Philistines, but because of his lack of faith, God did not answer him either time. From the very start of his reign, Saul disobeyed Yahweh's Word regarding the Philistines. See the commentary on 1 Sam 10:7–8 and figure 16, "Saul's Faltering Accession," in "Samuel Anoints Saul (9:26–10:8)" in the commentary on 1 Sam 9:26–10:16, as well as the beginning of the commentary on 1 Sam 10:17–27a (Steinmann, *1 Samuel*, 196–98, 203). Before his first inquiry, Saul directly disobeyed the Word of Yahweh (1 Sam 13:8–14), and after his second failed inquiry, he resorted to the occult (thus violating the First Commandment and other commands in the Law of Moses) shortly before his death (1 Sam 28:7–20).

[15] See the commentary on 2:1–7, as well as the commentary on 5:23.

[16] For a more complete discussion of these priestly implements, see the excursus "The Urim and Thummim" in Steinmann, *1 Samuel*, 272–75.

to advance directly on the Philistine forces (5:19). God assured the king that he would hand the Philistines over to him in battle. David's attack was successful, an outcome he attributed to God, who burst forth like a flood against the Philistine forces (5:20). David named the site of the battle Baal-perazim, "the master who bursts forth."[17] David's words take on an ironic tone, since in the next chapter the reader will learn that Yahweh also burst forth against Uzzah, who touched the ark of the covenant (6:6–8).

The author also informs us that the Philistines were so panicked when David routed them that they abandoned their idols, and David and his men disposed of them (5:21). The Philistines most likely brought their idols in order to implore their gods to grant them victory over David. However, since the Israelites could not ensure that Yahweh would grant them victory simply if they carried the ark of the covenant into battle against the Philistines (1 Sam 4:1–11), the Philistines most certainly could not triumph by bringing their false and impotent gods against Yahweh, "the God of armies."[18] See figure 4.

The Second Philistine Invasion (5:22–25)

Late 1002 BC[19]

Parallel: 1 Sam 5:22–25 ‖ 1 Chr 14:13–16

The Philistines apparently were not decisively defeated, since they once again came to the Valley of the Rephaim to confront David (5:22). This time when David inquired of Yahweh, he was advised not to directly confront the Philistines but to circle behind them. God himself would go to battle against the Philistines, while David was to join the battle immediately upon God's signal (5:23–24).[20] God's reference to his leading the fight ties in well with the author's earlier characterization of him as "Yahweh, the God of armies" (5:10). David's victory is depicted as more complete this time, since he was able to pursue the fleeing Philistine armies all the way to Gezer as they fled back toward their own territory. See figure 5.

---

[17] Since this place-name contains the plural of the noun פֶּרֶץ, *perets*, a more literal translation would be "the master of the burstings-forth." For this noun, see the second textual note on 5:20.

[18] See the second textual note on 5:10. The reason for the Israelites' defeat was their idolatrous abuse of the ark; see the commentary on 1 Sam 4:1–11 (Steinmann, *1 Samuel*, 123–27).

[19] See "The Chronology of David's Reign" in the commentary on 5:1–5.

[20] This inquiry, like the one in 5:19, is a reference to the high priest's use of Urim and Thummim (see the commentary on 2:1; 5:19). Interestingly, Josephus attributes Yahweh's words to an oracle delivered through the high priest (*Antiquities*, 7.76). Urim and Thummim were placed in the high priest's breastplate for consulting Yahweh (Ex 28:30; Num 27:21).

Figure 4

**David's First Victory over the Philistines
in the Valley of Rephaim (2 Sam 5:17–21)**

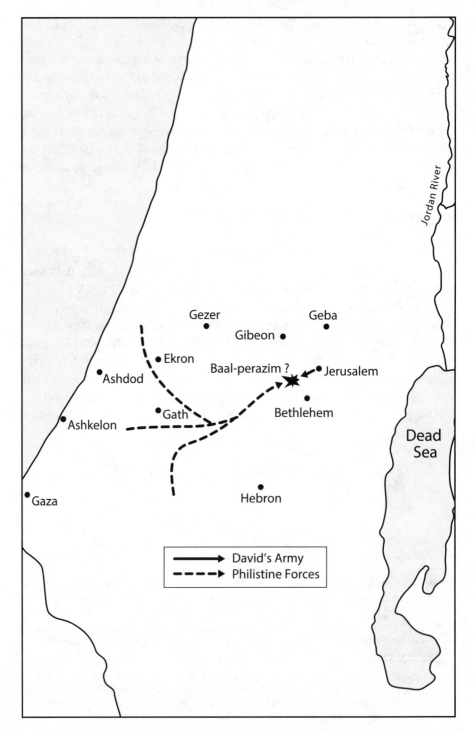

Figure 5

**David's Second Victory over the Philistines
in the Valley of Rephaim (2 Sam 5:22–25)**

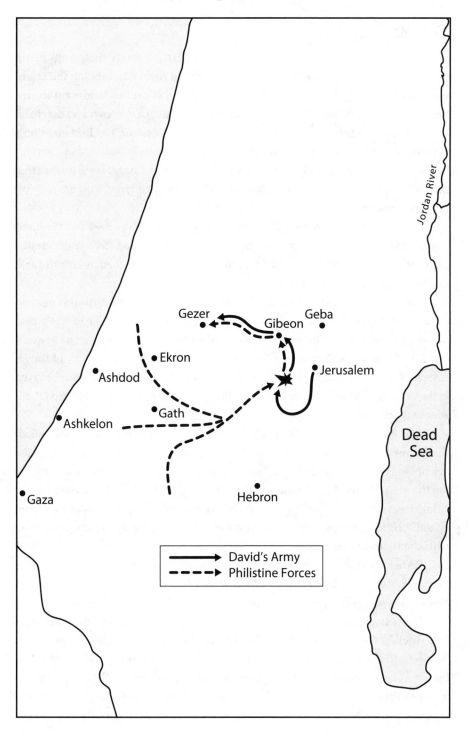

David Brings the Ark to Jerusalem

Translation

6 ¹David again assembled all the best men in Israel, thirty thousand [men]. ²David and all the troops with him went to bring up from Baale-judah the ark of God that is called by [the] name, the name of Yahweh of armies, who is enthroned [over] the cherubim on it. ³They placed the ark of God on a new cart and carried it from Abinadab's house, which was on the hill. Both Uzzah and Ahio, Abinadab's descendants, were leading the cart ⁴with the ark of Yahweh. Now Ahio was walking in front of the ark, ⁵and David and the entire house of Israel were celebrating before Yahweh with all [their] might and with songs, with lyres, with harps, with tambourines, with sistrums, and with cymbals.

⁶When they came to Nacon's threshing floor, Uzzah reached out his hand toward the ark of God and grabbed it, because the oxen stumbled. ⁷Yahweh was angry with Uzzah, and God struck him there because he reached out for the ark, and he died there with the ark of God.

⁸David became angry because Yahweh burst forth in an outburst against Uzzah. (That place is called Outburst against Uzzah to this day.) ⁹David was afraid of Yahweh that day and thought, "How can the ark of Yahweh ever come to me?" ¹⁰So David was not willing to take the ark of Yahweh with him to the City of David. Instead, David diverted it to the house of Obed-edom the Gittite. ¹¹The ark stayed in the house of Obed-edom the Gittite for three months, and Yahweh blessed Obed-edom and his entire household.

¹²King David was told, "Yahweh has blessed the house of Obed-edom and all that he owns because of the ark of God." So David went and joyfully brought the ark of God up from Obed-edom's house to the City of David. ¹³When those carrying the ark of Yahweh had gone six steps, he sacrificed bulls and fattened calves. ¹⁴David was dancing with all [his] might before Yahweh. David was wearing a linen ephod. ¹⁵David and the entire house of Israel were bringing up the ark of Yahweh with shouts and the sound of a ram's horn.

¹⁶When the ark of Yahweh was coming into the City of David, Saul's daughter Michal looked down from the window and saw King David leaping and dancing before Yahweh, and she despised him intensely.

¹⁷They brought the ark of Yahweh and set it in its place inside the tent David had pitched for it. David offered burnt offerings and peace offerings before Yahweh. ¹⁸When David had finished offering burnt offerings and peace offerings, he blessed the people in the name of Yahweh of armies. ¹⁹He apportioned a loaf of bread, a lump of dates, and a lump of raisins to all the people—to the entire crowd of Israelites, both men and women. Then all the people went home.

20When David returned to bless his household, Saul's daughter Michal came out to meet David. She said, "How the king of Israel has honored himself today! He exposed himself today in the sight of his servants' slave girls like one of the vulgar men exposes himself!"

21David said to Michal, "[I was celebrating] in the presence of Yahweh, who chose me rather than your father and his entire house, to appoint me designated ruler over Yahweh's people—over Israel—and I will celebrate in Yahweh's presence. 22I will be humbled more than this! I may be humiliated in your eyes, but with the slave girls whom you mentioned—with them I will be honored!" 23So Saul's daughter Michal had no child until the day she died.

Textual Notes

6:1 וַיֹּסֶף עוֹד דָּוִד—"David again assembled." The verb form וַיֹּסֶף appears eleven times elsewhere in Samuel, always as the Hiphil (H) third masculine singular preterite (imperfect with *waw* consecutive) of יָסַף, "add to; do again," which usually takes an infinitive construct as its verbal complement.[1] Here, however, the form is the Qal (G) third masculine singular preterite (imperfect with *waw* consecutive) of אָסַף, "to gather, assemble," normally spelled וַיֶּאֱסֹף (e.g., 2 Sam 10:17; 12:29). Forms of אָסַף commonly omit its first consonant as a quiescent *aleph* (GKC, § 68 h). The parsing of this verb as the Qal (G) of אָסַף, "assemble" (rather than the Hiphil [H] of יָסַף), is confirmed by its use with a direct object (see the next textual note), rather than an infinitive, and the use of the Qal of אָסַף elsewhere in Samuel for "gathering" troops as an army or for a battle (1 Sam 14:52; 17:1; 2 Sam 10:17; 12:28, 29). See also the Niphal of אָסַף for troops gathering (themselves) together for battle in, e.g., 1 Sam 13:5, 11; 17:1, 2; 2 Sam 10:15; 17:11; 23:9, 11.

אֶת־כָּל־בָּחוּר בְּיִשְׂרָאֵל—"All the best men in Israel" is literally "every choice man in Israel." בָּחוּר is a Qal passive (Gp) participle of בָּחַר, "to choose." This participle is often used to denote young men who are in the prime of their ability to render military service (e.g., 1 Sam 24:3 [ET 24:2]; 26:2; 2 Sam 10:9). A few Masoretic manuscripts, followed by the Syriac and the Targum, lack the preposition בְּ and read the construct phrase בָּחוּר יִשְׂרָאֵל, "the best men of Israel." The LXX reads πάντα νεανίαν ἐξ Ισραηλ, "every young man from Israel."

שְׁלֹשִׁים אָלֶף:—Instead of the MT's "thirty thousand," the LXX reads ὡς ἑβδομήκοντα χιλιάδας, "about seventy thousand."

6:2 וַיָּקָם ׀ וַיֵּלֶךְ דָּוִד וְכָל־הָעָם אֲשֶׁר אִתּוֹ—Literally "David arose and went, and all the people who (were) with him." The two verbs form a hendiadys and so are translated by the single English verb "went." The verbs are singular, in agreement with the nearer singular noun (דָּוִד) in the plural compound subject (GKC, § 146 f; Joüon, § 150 q). In military contexts the definite noun הָעָם often denotes "the troops" (see the second textual note on 2 Sam 1:4 and Waltke-O'Connor, § 11.4.3b).

---

[1] See וַיֹּסֶף in 1 Sam 3:6, 8, 21; 9:8; 18:29; 19:21; 20:17; 23:4; 2 Sam 2:22; 18:22; 24:1.

מִבַּעֲלֵי יְהוּדָה לְהַעֲלוֹת מִשָּׁם—The Hebrew syntax employs two prepositional phrases with מִן, "from." The first seems premature since it precedes the verb ("to bring up"), and the second has a retrospective adverb (שָׁם, "there") that seems redundant in English, literally "from Baale-judah, to bring up from there." In place of מִבַּעֲלֵי יְהוּדָה, "from Baale-judah," 4QSam[a] reads בעלה היא קרי[ת] יערים אשר ליהודה, "(to) Baalah, that is, Kiria[th-jearim, which] belongs to Judah." This is probably an expansion based on 1 Sam 6:21–7:2. Similarly, in the passage that is parallel to 2 Sam 6:1–2 the Chronicler first calls it "Kiriath-jearim" (1 Chr 13:5) and then explains its name for his readers: בַּעֲלָתָה אֶל־קִרְיַת יְעָרִים אֲשֶׁר לִיהוּדָה, "to Baalah, to Kiriath-jearim, which belongs to Judah" (1 Chr 13:6). This city is called Baalah in Josh 15:9–10, where it is also identified as Kiriath-jearim ("city of forests"). It is called Kiriath-baal ("city of Baal") in Josh 15:60; 18:14, and in each case it is identified as Kiriath-jearim. Earlier in the book of Samuel it was simply called Kiriath-jearim (1 Sam 6:21–7:2). The site is currently called Tell el-ʿAzhar, about fourteen miles (twenty-three kilometers) northwest of Jerusalem.

שֵׁם שֵׁם—In this construction, "[the] name, the name of … ," one might expect the first instance of the repeated noun שֵׁם, "name," to have the definite article because it refers to the proper name of Yahweh. This probably is an example of a rare Hebrew phenomenon of omitting the expected article to emphasize the noun, "indeterminateness for the sake of amplification" (GKC, § 125 c). The second instance of שֵׁם is definite because it is the head noun in a construct chain with the personal name יְהֹוָה (*"the* name of Yahweh"), and personal names are inherently definite.

יְהוָה צְבָאוֹת יֹשֵׁב הַכְּרֻבִים עָלָיו:—"Yahweh of armies, who is enthroned [over] the cherubim on it." This long title emphasizes Yahweh as a warrior (Ex 15:3) and a king at the head of his army. For the first four Hebrew words, see the second textual note on 1 Sam 4:4,[2] where they are identical. The title here includes the prepositional phrase עָלָיו, which clarifies that the cherubim are "on it," that is, attached to the top of the ark so that their touching wings overshadow the "mercy seat" (Ex 25:18–22). Sometimes the noun אָרוֹן, "ark," is construed as grammatically feminine (e.g., 1 Sam 4:17), but here the masculine (third singular) pronoun on עָלָיו ("on it") refers back to אָרוֹן earlier in this verse. The ark is referenced by a third masculine singular pronoun also in 6:10 (see the second textual note on 6:10).

6:3a וַיַּרְכִּבוּ—"They placed" is literally "and they caused [the ark] to ride" on a cart. In the Qal (G) the verb רָכַב means "to mount and ride" an animal or chariot. Its Hiphil (H), as here, often has the corresponding causative meaning.

אֶל־עֲגָלָה חֲדָשָׁה—"On a new cart." The adjectival phrase עֲגָלָה חֲדָשָׁה was also in 1 Sam 6:7. The noun עֲגָלָה, "cart," clearly is related to עֶגְלָה, "heifer" (e.g., 1 Sam 16:2). A "cart" was typically drawn by bovines. 2 Sam 6:6 refers to הַבָּקָר, "the oxen," as the animals drawing this cart; compare (הַ)פָּרוֹת, "(the) cows," drawing the cart with the ark in 1 Sam 6:7, 10. Here most Masoretic manuscripts have the preposition אֶל (often meaning "to"), but a few Masoretic manuscripts and 4QSam[a] have עַל (commonly meaning "on"), which is supported by the LXX: ἐφ᾽ ἅμαξαν καινήν. However, Samuel is

---

[2] Steinmann, *1 Samuel*, 120.

one of the OT books in which אֶל is often used in place of עַל and with its meaning. See the first textual note on 2 Sam 2:9 and the second textual note on 2 Sam 3:29.

6:3b   וְעֻזָּא—The name "Uzzah" recurs in 6:6, 7, 8 (twice) but with variant spellings. This name is spelled עֻזָּא in 2 Sam 6:3, 6; 1 Chr 13:7, 9, 10, 11 (twice) and in 4QSam[a] (עזא) in 2 Sam 6:3, 6, 8 (twice).[3] In addition, it is spelled עֻזָּא in many Masoretic manuscripts in 6:7, 8 (twice). However, in Codex Leningradensis it is spelled עֻזָּה in 6:7, 8 (twice). It appears as if the original spelling was עֻזָּא and a scribe introduced the variant עֻזָּה as a mistake in hearing after the two became homophones (pronounced identically). This name is shared by four other biblical men and is spelled עֻזָּא in 2 Ki 21:18, 26; עֻזָּא in Ezra 2:49; Neh 7:51; עֻזָּה in 1 Chr 6:14 (ET 6:29); and עֻזָּא in 1 Chr 8:7.

בְּנֵי אֲבִינָדָב—"Abinadab's descendants." While the Hebrew word בֵּן often denotes a "son," it may refer to any male descendant. The ark came to Abinadab's house in 1068 BC (1 Sam 7:1).[4] David moved the ark to Jerusalem about 975 BC. Therefore, nearly a century had passed since the ark came to Abinadab's house, making it highly unlikely that Uzzah and Ahio were Abinadab's sons. They were probably grandsons or even great-grandsons of Abinadab.

נֹהֲגִים—"Were leading." This is the Qal (G) masculine plural participle of נָהַג. In the Qal, it can mean to "drive" cattle or "lead" them.

6:3c–4a   At the end of 6:3 and the beginning of 6:4, the translation follows the shorter reading in 4QSam[a], [אֶ]ת] העגלה [עם ארון יהוה], "the cart [with the ark of Yahweh]," a reading largely supported by the LXX (τὴν ἅμαξαν σὺν τῇ κιβωτῷ). The MT reads as follows:

אֶת־הָעֲגָלָה חֲדָשָׁה׃ וַיִּשָּׂאֻהוּ מִבֵּית אֲבִינָדָב אֲשֶׁר בַּגִּבְעָה עִם אֲרוֹן הָאֱלֹהִים

… [were leading] the new cart. And they carried it from Abinadab's house, which was on the hill, with the ark of God.

However, the MT seems to include a long dittograph:

חֲדָשָׁה׃ וַיִּשָּׂאֻהוּ מִבֵּית אֲבִינָדָב אֲשֶׁר בַּגִּבְעָה

This dittograph repeats six Hebrew words from earlier in 6:3:

חֲדָשָׁה וַיִּשָּׂאֻהוּ מִבֵּית אֲבִינָדָב אֲשֶׁר בַּגִּבְעָה

… new. And they carried it from the house of Abinadab, which was on the hill.

Apparently a scribe, after copying the first occurrence of "cart" (עֲגָלָה) and the six words after it, came to the second occurrence of "cart" (הָעֲגָלָה, with the definite article) and then looked back up at the first occurrence of "cart" and recopied the six words after it. The suspicion of a textual corruption is supported by the lack of concord between the last two words of 6:3 in the MT, הָעֲגָלָה חֲדָשָׁה. The noun has the article, "the cart," whereas its modifying adjective, "new," does not, which defies explanation (cf. GKC, § 126 z).

---

[3]   In 6:7 the last two letters of the name are reconstructed in 4QSam[a].

[4]   Steinmann, *From Abraham to Paul*, 108.

6:4b–5　לִפְנֵי הָאָרוֹן׃ ... לִפְנֵי יְהוָה—Both prepositional phrases, "in front of the ark ... before Yahweh," use לִפְנֵי, implying that the ark is the actual location of the real, physical presence of Yahweh. To be in the presence of the ark is to be in the presence of Yahweh. This is confirmed by 6:6–8, where Yahweh demonstrates his presence there.

6:5　מְשַׂחֲקִים—"Were celebrating" is the masculine plural Piel (D) participle of שָׂחַק. This verb can refer to the playing of musical instruments (BDB, Piel, 3), as well as singing, dancing, and other forms of rejoicing. It recurs in 6:21.

בְּכֹל עֲצֵי בְרוֹשִׁים—The MT literally reads "with all timbers of junipers," which perhaps could be understood as "with all [kinds of] juniper-wood [instruments]." However, it seems to have been corrupted by an incorrectly vocalized or incorrectly heard phrase, with a confusion of the similar-sounding dental sibilants *zayin* and *tsade* (-עצ in place of -עז) and with a transposition of *resh* and *shin* (-רוש- in place of -שיר-). The noun בְּרוֹשׁ is the Phoenician juniper, *Juniperus phoenicea*, a conifer that grows to be a large shrub or small tree. It is native to the lands bordering the Mediterranean Sea, western Arabia, and the Canary Islands. It was unlikely that the Israelites were playing instruments made from juniper. The translation "with all [their] might and with songs" follows the reading of 4QSamᵃ (בכ]ול עז ו[ו]בשירים) and 1 Chr 13:8 (בְּכָל־עֹז וּבְשִׁירִים). The LXX appears to combine the two readings: ἐν ὀργάνοις ἡρμοσμένοις ἐν ἰσχύι καὶ ἐν ᾠδαῖς, "with harmonious instruments with might and with songs."

וּבְכִנֹּרוֹת—"And with lyres." See 1 Sam 10:5 and David's playing of a lyre (כִּנּוֹר) in 1 Sam 16:16, 23. In lists of nouns that share the same syntactical relationship, it is common for the preposition on the first noun (בְּ on בְּכֹל; see the preceding textual note) to be repeated on the subsequent nouns. Thus, "lyres" and the rest of the musical instruments are each introduced by בְּ, "with" (Joüon, § 132 g).

וּבִנְבָלִים—"And with harps." See נֶבֶל also in 1 Sam 10:5.

וּבְתֻפִּים—"And with tambourines." See תֹּף also in 1 Sam 10:5; 18:6 (and famously in Ex 15:20).

וּבִמְנַעַנְעִים—"And with sistrums." The Vulgate translates this with the plural of *sistrum*, denoting an Egyptian instrument that rattled when shaken. (The LXX reads καὶ ἐν κυμβάλοις, "and with cymbals.") This word (the plural of מְנַעֲנַע) is derived from the verb נוּעַ, "to wave, shake." In form it is a Piel (D) participle (hence the prefixed -מְ), but instead of a Piel, with doubling of the middle consonant, it is a Pilpel (D), and the originally biliteral root נע is reduplicated (מנענע). Its form is the same as the Pilpel participle מְכַרְכֵּר in 6:14, 16 (see the first textual note on 6:14; cf. the next textual note).

וּבְצֶלְצֶלִים׃—"And with cymbals." Like the preceding word, this noun is formed by reduplication of an originally biliteral root (צלצל), even though lexicons usually consider its root to be צלל. Its only other appearance is in Ps 150:5 (twice). More common is the cognate noun מְצִלְתַּיִם, whose dual form may denote a "pair of cymbals."

6:6　נָכוֹן—This name varies widely among the various textual traditions. Instead of the MT's "Nacon," 4QSamᵃ reads נודן, "Nodon." The LXX has Νωδαβ, "Nodab." The parallel verse 1 Chr 13:9 (כִּידֹן) and Josephus (Χειδῶνος)[5] read "Chidon," while the name is omitted in LXX 1 Chr 13:9. It may be impossible to decide which name is original.

וַיִּשְׁלַח עֻזָּא אֶל־אֲרוֹן הָאֱלֹהִים—Literally "and Uzzah sent to the ark of God." While the Qal (G) of שָׁלַח lacks a direct object here in the MT, it is commonly used with יָד, "hand," to mean "reach out with the hand" (e.g., 2 Sam 1:14; 15:5). Hebrew can omit the object noun in well-known formulae, resulting in an elliptical expression (GKC, § 117 g). The translation includes "his hand" based on 4QSamᵃ (אֶת [ידו]), the LXX (τὴν χεῖρα αὐτοῦ), the Syriac, some Targum manuscripts, and the Vulgate, as well as the parallel verse 1 Chr 13:9 (אֶת־יָדוֹ). One possibility is that these ancient versions added "his hand" to fill out the common idiom. Another possibility is that the MT omitted "his hand" by homoioarchton when the eye of a scribe reading אֶת־יָדוֹ אֶל־ skipped from the first *aleph*, the first consonant in אֶת, to the second *aleph*, the first consonant in אֶל.

וַיֹּאחֶז בּוֹ—"And he grabbed it." The verb is the Qal (G) third masculine singular preterite (imperfect with *waw* consecutive) of אָחַז, which takes the preposition בְּ. A translation with an infinitive of purpose, "to grab it," is supported by the LXX (κατασχεῖν αὐτήν) and the reconstructed reading in 4QSamᵃ (לֶאֱחֹז בּוֹ]), with the Qal infinitive construct of אָחַז. 1 Chr 13:9 also has the infinitive but reads לֶאֱחֹז אֶת־הָאָרוֹן, "to grab the ark." Apparently for the sake of clarity the Chronicler replaced the prepositional phrase with a pronominal suffix (בּוֹ) with the direct object noun (אֶת־הָאָרוֹן) to which the pronoun referred. Here in MT 2 Sam 6:6, the statement "and he grabbed it" likely is a clarification to ensure that the reader understands that Uzzah actually touched the ark and did not merely attempt to do so (as the infinitive could mean). This would protect readers from concluding that God struck Uzzah based on his intention rather than his accomplished action. The actual touching of the ark itself was prohibited by the Law of Moses (Ex 25:12–15; Num 4:15; see further the commentary on 2 Sam 6:1–5).

שָׁמְטוּ הַבָּקָר:—"The oxen stumbled." The singular noun בָּקָר is used as a collective with the plural verb, so it is best translated as an English plural, "oxen." The Qal (G) of שָׁמַט apparently has an intransitive meaning, "stumble," here and in the parallel verse 1 Chr 13:9. Elsewhere its Qal has a transitive meaning, "let [something] fall" (2 Ki 9:33), "remit [a debt]" (Deut 15:2), or "leave [land] fallow" (Ex 23:11). If the verb is transitive here, the cart or the ark is the implied direct object: "the oxen let [it] fall." See the discussion of possible meanings and the readings of the versions in *HALOT*, Qal, 3.

6:7 וַיִּחַר־אַף יְהוָה—Here the Qal (G) third masculine singular preterite (imperfect with *waw* consecutive) of חָרָה has a stated subject, literally "and the wrath of Yahweh burned." The construct phrase אַף יְהוָה serves as a circumlocution for Yahweh himself, and so the clause is translated as "Yahweh was angry." The verb is used in the same construction in 12:5 and similarly in 24:1. The identical verb form will be used at the beginning of 6:8, but in an impersonal construction (with no stated subject) and with the preposition לְ introducing the person who functions as the subject, וַיִּחַר לְדָוִד, "David became angry" (6:8). For that more common construction, see the second textual note

---

5   Josephus, *Antiquities*, 7.81.

on 1 Sam 20:7[6] and the first textual note on 2 Sam 3:8 (see also 13:21; 19:43 [ET 19:42]; 22:8).

עַל־הַשַּׁל—The noun שַׁל occurs nowhere else in ancient Hebrew, and all attempts at understanding it are only guesses from context. Most LXX manuscripts lack any translation of this phrase but some have ἐπὶ τῇ προπετείᾳ, "because of the indiscretion," and many English translations are similar. The translation "because he reached out for the ark" is based on the reading in 1 Chr 13:10 (עַל אֲשֶׁר־שָׁלַח יָדוֹ עַל־הָאָרוֹן) and apparently 4QSam[a] (עַל] אשׁר שׁלח ידו על [ה]ארון]). Josephus seems to support this.[7] The preceding verse in the MT states that he "reached out" and actually touched ("grabbed") the ark (see the third textual note on 6:6).

עִם אֲרוֹן הָאֱלֹהִים:—"With the ark of God" is the reading in the MT. 1 Chr 13:10 reads לִפְנֵי אֱלֹהִים, "before God," which may be supported by the fragmentary reading in 4QSam[a]: לִ]פני הא[ל]ו[הים. The LXX combines the two readings and changes the first instance of "God" to "the Lord": παρὰ τὴν κιβωτὸν τοῦ κυρίου ἐνώπιον τοῦ θεοῦ, "with the ark of the Lord before God."

6:8 עַל אֲשֶׁר פָּרַץ יְהוָה פֶּרֶץ בְּעֻזָּה—"Because Yahweh burst forth in an outburst against Uzzah" is literally "because Yahweh burst forth a bursting with Uzzah." פֶּרֶץ ... פָּרַץ forms a cognate accusative construction, where the verb and the direct object share the same root. Hebrew is fond of such constructions, but English avoids them. For the verb פָּרַץ, "break through" or "burst out," which takes the preposition בְּ here, see the first textual note on 5:20. For its cognate noun פֶּרֶץ, see the second textual note on 5:20.

6:9 וַיִּרָא דָוִד—"David was afraid." The verb is a defective spelling for וַיִּירָא, the Qal (G) third masculine singular preterite (imperfect with *waw* consecutive) of the stative verb יָרֵא, "be afraid."

אֵיךְ יָבוֹא —"How can it ever come?" The translation with "ever" reflects one of the many possible nuances of the imperfect. See the second textual note on 5:6, where this imperfect is negated and translated as "he will *never* enter."

6:10 לְהָסִיר אֵלָיו—"To take … with him." Usually the verb סוּר, "turn aside," in the Hiphil (this is the infinitive construct with לְ) means "to remove," but in the context here with the prepositional phrase אֵלָיו, "to himself," it must mean "to move" or "take."

וַיַּטֵּהוּ דָוִד—"Instead, David diverted it." The verb is the Hiphil (H) third masculine singular preterite (imperfect with *waw* consecutive) of נָטָה, "turn aside" (intransitive in the Qal [G]), with a third masculine singular object suffix, referring back to אֲרוֹן, the "ark," construed as masculine (see the fourth textual note on 6:2). The verb נָטָה in the Hiphil can have the transitive meaning "turn [something] aside" or "direct/lead [something] away" (see BDB, Hiphil, 3 a; *HALOT*, Hiphil, 6).

6:11–12 וַיְבָרֶךְ יְהוָה ... בֵּרַךְ יְהוָה—"And Yahweh blessed. … Yahweh has blessed." Here the Piel (D) of בָּרַךְ means that Yahweh has already conferred blessings solely out of his gracious love through his presence on the ark (see the textual note on 6:4b–5).

---

[6] Steinmann, *1 Samuel*, 390.

[7] Josephus, *Antiquities*, 7.81: ὅτι μὴ ὢν ἱερεὺς ἥψατο ταύτης, ἀποθανεῖν ἐποίησε, literally "because not being a priest, when he touched this, he [God] made [him] to die."

Based on passages such as Gen 39:5; Lev 25:21; Deut 7:14; 15:14; 28:3–8, Yahweh's blessing may have been manifested in prosperity, health, the gift of (the conception of) children, and the fecundity of livestock and crops (cf. "the house" and "all that he owns" in 2 Sam 6:12; see also Gen 24:35). The Piel is used for a benediction regarding children in 1 Sam 2:20 (also Gen 1:22) and for God's blessing of David and his descendants leading to the Messiah in 2 Sam 7:29 (along with the Pual [Dp]), while the Qal passive (Gp) participle is used regarding success in 1 Sam 26:25. Most often in Samuel the Piel refers to the pronouncement of a benediction that Yahweh would bless someone in the future or that Yahweh's favor now rests upon someone or something.[8] See the first textual note on 1 Sam 2:20 and the third textual note on 1 Sam 9:13.[9] See also the discussion of the Qal passive (Gp) participle בָּרוּךְ, "blessed," in the first textual note on 2 Sam 2:5 and in the textual notes on 1 Sam 15:13; 23:21.[10]

6:11 וְאֶת־כָּל־בֵּיתוֹ:—"And his entire household" is the reading of the MT. 1 Chr 13:14 reads וְאֶת־כָּל־אֲשֶׁר־לוֹ, "and all that he owned," which is supported by the LXX here (καὶ πάντα τὰ αὐτοῦ), but that is probably a secondary reading inserted in anticipation of the same phrase, וְאֶת־כָּל־אֲשֶׁר־לוֹ, in 6:12.

6:12 וַיַּעַל אֶת־אֲרוֹן הָאֱלֹהִים—The form of this verb of עָלָה (third masculine singular preterite [imperfect with *waw* consecutive]) could be either Qal (G), "went up" (as is וַיַּעַל in, e.g., 2 Sam 2:2; 15:24), or Hiphil (H), "brought up." Its use with a direct object here, "the ark of God," indicates that it is Hiphil. Likewise in 6:17 וַיַּעַל it has a direct object and so must be Hiphil. See also its other Hiphil forms in the context, e.g., the participle מַעֲלִים, "were bringing up," in 6:15 and the infinitive construct הַעֲלוֹת in 6:18.

בְּשִׂמְחָה:—"Joyfully." This prepositional phrase is literally "with joy." In the translation it has been moved from the end of the verse to earlier for the sake of English style.

6:13 כִּי צָעֲדוּ ... שִׁשָּׁה צְעָדִים—Literally "when they stepped ... six steps." The Qal (G) of צָעַד, "to step, march," is used with the cognate accusative noun צַעַד, "a step," in the plural.

שׁוֹר וּמְרִיא:—The translation understands these singular nouns as collectives: "bulls and fattened calves." The singular nouns in the MT agree with those in the LXX (μόσχος καὶ ἄρνα). 1 Chr 15:26 has plural nouns, שִׁבְעָה־פָרִים וְשִׁבְעָה אֵילִים, "seven bulls and seven rams," a reading supported by 4QSamᵃ: פרים ושבעה אילים] שבנ]עה.

6:14 מְכַרְכֵּר—"Was dancing" is a Pilpel (D) participle of כָּרַר. The same participle recurs in 6:16. The noun כִּכָּר, which refers to round objects ("loaf of bread" in 1 Sam 2:36; 10:3; "plain" in 2 Sam 18:23) is from the same root. For this reason, it is generally assumed that this verb refers to a dance that involved a circular whirling motion of some sort.[11]

---

[8] For the Piel (D) of בָּרַךְ, "to bless," in this sense, see 1 Sam 2:20; 9:13; 13:10; 25:14; 2 Sam 6:18, 20; 8:10; 13:25; 14:22; 19:40 (ET 19:39); 21:3.

[9] Steinmann, *1 Samuel*, 90, 179.

[10] Steinmann, *1 Samuel*, 286, 445. The Qal passive (Gp) participle בָּרוּךְ, "blessed," is in 1 Sam 15:13; 23:21; 25:32, 33 (twice), 39; 26:25; 2 Sam 2:5; 18:28; 22:47.

[11] *TWOT*, § 1046 (cf. § 1046c).

חָגוּר—"Was wearing" is a masculine singular Qal passive (Gp) participle of חָגַר. See the third textual note on 1 Sam 2:18.[12] This verb often refers specifically to wearing something around one's waist, e.g., a sword in 1 Sam 17:39; 25:13 (cf. 2 Sam 21:16). It can also refer more generally to the wearing of clothing, e.g., sackcloth in 2 Sam 3:31 (cf. 2 Sam 20:8) and a "linen ephod" here and in 1 Sam 2:18.

אֵפוֹד בָּד:—For "a linen ephod," see the fourth textual note on 1 Sam 2:18.[13] Although the participle חָגוּר, "wearing," is passive (see the preceding textual note), it takes the noun אֵפוֹד as its direct object (Joüon, § 121 o). David wears a "linen ephod" also in the parallel verse 1 Chr 15:27. Linen ephods were worn by priests (1 Sam 22:18), but they could also be worn by others who were leading or aiding in the worship of Yahweh. At the tabernacle the boy Samuel wore one, though he was a Levite, not a priest (1 Sam 2:18). An especially ornate linen ephod was crafted as one of the vestments for the high priest, who also wore linen undergarments (Ex 28:2–43). The high priest's ephod is referenced in 1 Sam 23:6, 9; 30:7. See further the commentary on 2 Sam 6:14.

6:15 בִּתְרוּעָה וּבְקוֹל שׁוֹפָר:—"With shouts and the sound of a ram's horn." These three Hebrew nouns, "shout" (תְּרוּעָה) and the "sound" (קוֹל) of a "ram's horn" (שׁוֹפָר, *shophar*) are used together in liturgical and military contexts. Liturgically, they are used for the covenant renewal ceremony in 2 Chr 15:14 and in a psalm of corporate worship (Ps 47:6 [ET 47:5]), and "shout" and "ram's horn" are paired for the formal proclamation of the Jubilee Year (Lev 25:9). Elsewhere in the OT the three nouns appear together in military contexts: Israel's siege of Jericho (Josh 6:5, 20) and prophecies of warfare as the result of divine judgment (Jer 4:19; Amos 2:2; see also the pairing of "shout" and "ram's horn" in Zeph 1:16; Job 39:25). Compare the use of "trumpet" in the NT for the announcement of the second coming of Christ, which brings judgment upon unbelievers but salvation for those in Christ (Mt 24:31; 1 Cor 15:52; 1 Thess 4:16; Rev 10:7; 11:15), as well as for other divine judgments (Rev 8:7, 8, 10, 12; 9:1, 13, 14) and the voice of the exalted Christ (Rev 1:10; 4:1).

6:16 וְהָיָה אֲרוֹן יְהוָה בָּא—"When the ark of Yahweh was coming." The MT has a perfect with a conjunctive *waw*, וְהָיָה, "and it happened," followed by a Qal (G) participle, בָּא, "was coming," forming a temporal circumstantial clause. The LXX appropriately translates וְהָיָה with an aorist verb and the Hebrew participle with a Greek participle in a genitive absolute construction (καὶ ἐγένετο τῆς κιβωτοῦ παραγινομένης). In form בָּא could also be the Qal (G) third masculine singular perfect, but that would not fit the syntax after וְהָיָה. 4QSamᵃ reads ויהי, as does the parallel verse 1 Chr 15:29 (וַיְהִי), which is the more common form of הָיָה at the beginning of clauses in historical narratives.[14]

נִשְׁקְפָה בְּעַד הַחַלּוֹן |—Literally "she looked down through the window." The verb שָׁקַף is used only in the Niphal (N) and the Hiphil (H), both of which refer to "looking

---

[12] Steinmann, *1 Samuel*, 89.

[13] Steinmann, *1 Samuel*, 89.

[14] GKC, § 112 uu, asserts that this is one of a number of verses in which וְהָיָה should be emended to וַיְהִי, and Joüon, § 119 z, asserts that the usage of וְהָיָה here and in some other verses is "abnormal." However, the fact that וְהָיָה is used in this way in a number of verses suggests that it represents a legitimate, intentional Hebrew usage.

down" from a higher vantage point. This verb is used with the same combination of prepositions (בְּ + עַד, "through") and noun חַלּוֹן, "window," also in Gen 26:8; Judg 5:28; 2 Ki 9:30; 1 Chr 15:29 (cf. 2 Ki 9:32; Prov 7:6). (See בְּעַד הַחַלּוֹן with a different verb in 1 Sam 19:12.) The form נִשְׁקְפָה is the Niphal third feminine singular perfect; the Niphal feminine singular participle would be pointed נִשְׁקָפָה (as in Song 6:10).

מְפַזֵּז—"Leaping" is the masculine singular Piel (D) participle of פָּזַז. Its only other occurrence in the OT is the Qal (G) in Gen 49:24, meaning "be agile" (see *HALOT*, s.v. פוז II).

וַתִּבֶז לוֹ בְּלִבָּהּ:—"And she despised him intensely" is literally "and she despised him in her heart." Usually the Qal (G) of בָּזָה, "to despise," takes a direct object. Here and in the parallel in 1 Chr 15:29, it takes the preposition לְ prefixed to its object (לוֹ, literally "to him").

6:17 וַיַּצִּגוּ אֹתוֹ—"And they set it up." The verb is the Hiphil (H) third masculine plural preterite (imperfect with *waw* consecutive) of יָצַג, a verb used only in the Hiphil and once in the Hophal (Hp). The first consonant, *yod*, assimilates into the sibilant *tsade* and is marked by the *daghesh* in it (-צִּ-), similar to the way in which the initial *nun* in a verb commonly assimilates into the following consonant, e.g., וַיִּפְּלוּ in 2 Sam 2:16.

לִפְנֵי יְהוָה—"Before Yahweh." Since Yahweh locates his real, personal presence on the ark (see the textual note on 6:4b–5), לִפְנֵי here is locative, "before," in a physical sense (*IBH*, § 34 A).

6:18 הָעוֹלָה—"Burnt offerings." This singular noun in the MT, here and in 1 Chr 16:2, ought to be understood as a collective in light of the plural (עֹלוֹת) in the previous verse (2 Sam 6:17 ‖ 1 Chr 16:1). 4QSamᵃ apparently adjusted this noun to the plural (העולות]) under the influence of 6:17. The LXX also reads the plural (τὰς ὁλοκαυτώσεις).

וַיְבָרֶךְ—For "he blessed," see the textual note on 6:11–12. The Piel (D) verb here has the same sense as does the Piel infinitive construct לְבָרֵךְ in 6:20.

6:19 וַיְחַלֵּק—"He apportioned." In both the Qal (G) and the Piel (D), as here, חָלַק can mean "to divide" or "to apportion, distribute."

הֲמוֹן יִשְׂרָאֵל—"Crowd of Israelites." The noun הָמוֹן can refer to "a whole people" (BDB, 3 b).

לְמֵאִישׁ וְעַד־אִשָּׁה לְאִישׁ—Literally "to from man and until woman, to (each) man." The first instance of אִישׁ, "man," refers specifically to males in contrast to females (אִשָּׁה), but the second אִישׁ has a distributive and inclusive meaning, referring to "each" person (Joüon, § 147 d), male and female alike. It has this latter meaning again toward the end of this verse; see the sixth textual note on 6:19.

חַלַּת לֶחֶם אַחַת—"A loaf of bread." The feminine noun חַלָּה, *challah*, is probably the term for a ring-shaped "loaf" and is usually used in the context of "unleavened bread" (מַצָּה) and/or "bread" (לֶחֶם).[15] It is the precursor of the modern Jewish challah.

וְאֶשְׁפָּר אֶחָד וַאֲשִׁישָׁה אֶחָת—"And a lump of dates and a lump of raisins." The first noun, אֶשְׁפָּר, appears elsewhere only in the parallel verse 1 Chr 16:3. It is traditionally

---

[15] See Ex 29:2, 23; Lev 2:4; 7:12, 13; 8:26; Num 6:15, 19. See also its use with "bake" (אָפָה, Lev 24:5).

translated as "a cake of dates." The second noun, אֲשִׁישָׁה, also occurs in 1 Chr 16:3, as well as Hos 3:1; Song 2:5, and is sometimes rendered as "a cake of raisins." However, these are not cakes in the usual English sense (i.e., a sweet, baked, breadlike food), but rather pressed lumps of dried fruit.

וַיֵּלֶךְ כָּל־הָעָם אִישׁ לְבֵיתוֹ׃—"Then all the people went home" is literally "and all the people went, each man to his house." Here the singular collective noun עַם, "people," is the subject of a singular verb, but elsewhere it can be used with a plural verb (Joüon, § 150 e). Here the noun אִישׁ ("man") is used in a distributive sense, "each" person (Joüon, § 147 d).

6:20 לִקְרַאת—For this Qal (G) infinitive construct of קָרָא II (with לְ), "to meet," see the second textual note on 1 Sam 4:1.[16]

מַה־נִּכְבַּד ... נִגְלָה—"How ... he has honored himself. ... He exposed himself." Here the interrogative מָה, "how?" is used "mockingly" (GKC, § 148 b). Each of the two Niphal (N) perfect verbs has a reflexive sense, referring to what one does to himself. The first, כָּבֵד, is often used in the Piel (D) to mean "to honor" or "glorify" someone, but Michal uses its Niphal (N) here sarcastically. The second, גָּלָה, means "to reveal" in the Qal (G), and both its Qal and its Niphal can be used for divine revelation (e.g., Niphal in 1 Sam 2:27; 3:7, 21; Qal in 1 Sam 9:15; 2 Sam 7:27), but Michal uses it in an obscene sense, "expose oneself," as again in the next clause (see the next textual note).

כְּהִגָּלוֹת נִגְלוֹת—"Like ... exposes himself." The Niphal (N) infinitive construct (with כְּ) of גָּלָה is followed by its Niphal infinitive absolute. This is the only instance in the OT where an infinitive absolute follows an infinitive construct of the same verb.[17] It most likely indicates a strong, assertive accusation by Michal against David.

אַחַד הָרֵקִים׃—"One of the vulgar men." The adjective רֵיק literally means "empty." When applied to people, it implies an absence of strong principles of right and wrong (Judg 9:4; 11:3; 2 Chr 13:7). The LXX reads εἷς τῶν ὀρχουμένων, "one of the dancers," probably rendering a Hebrew Vorlage that read a plural participle of רָקַד. See the Piel participle מְרַקֵּד, which describes David as "dancing," in 1 Chr 15:29.

6:21 מֵאָבִיךְ וּמִכָּל־בֵּיתוֹ—"Rather than your father and his entire house." The repeated preposition מִן, "from," connotes that God chose David (and subsequently his line [2 Samuel 7]) "rather than" and instead of Saul and his line, and, moreover, that God rejected Saul (and his line) and removed him from his office as king. See the second textual note on 1 Sam 8:7 and the fourth textual note on 1 Sam 15:23;[18] both of those verses use the verb מָאַס and the preposition מִן (prefixed to מִמֶּלֶךְ or מִמֶּלֶךְ): the people rejected Yahweh "from" being their king (1 Sam 8:7), and Yahweh rejected Saul "from" being king over Israel (1 Sam 15:23).

נָגִיד—For this noun, "designated ruler," see the first textual note on 1 Sam 9:16[19] and the commentary on 2 Sam 5:2.

---

[16] Steinmann, *1 Samuel*, 119.

[17] GKC, § 75 y, calls it "very extraordinary," but then unjustifiably attributes it to a scribal error.

[18] Steinmann, *1 Samuel*, 164, 288.

[19] Steinmann, *1 Samuel*, 180.

וְשִׂחַקְתִּי—"And I will celebrate." For the Piel (D) of שָׂחַק, see the first textual note on 6:5. A first common singular perfect verb is normally accented on the second syllable (שִׂחַקְתִּי). The shift of the accent to the final syllable (וְשִׂחַקְתִּי) indicates that this is a perfect with *waw* consecutive (see GKC, § 49 h). Its force could be a simple future tense, but more likely it designates continuing or repeated action and has a defiant, repudiating force: "I have been celebrating, (and despite your mockery) I will continue to celebrate (whenever I am moved to do so)."

6:22 וּנְקַלֹּתִי עוֹד מִזֹּאת—"I will be humbled more than this!" The Niphal (N) of קָלַל can mean to be "unimportant," "easy," or "lightly esteemed, contemptible" (see *DCH*, Niphal, 2) or "undignified, humbled." The accent is on the penultimate syllable (-לֹּ-), but that is not determinative for deciding whether the perfect has *waw* consecutive or *waw* conjunctive; see GKC, § 49 k, and the next textual note. David is speaking with irony about how he will be perceived, from Michal's perspective, when he will (continue to) celebrate.

וְהָיִיתִי שָׁפָל בְּעֵינָי—The MT reads "and I will be humiliated in my (own) eyes."[20] The adjective שָׁפָל can mean "low," "modest," or, as here, "humiliated" (BDB, 3). "In *your* eyes" is the reading in the LXX (ἐν ὀφθαλμοῖς σου) and two Old Latin manuscripts. That reading fits best in the context: the point is not that David considers himself humiliated, but that Michal does, and David is contrasting Michal's contempt for him with the servant girls' honoring of him. The verb is the perfect of הָיָה with *waw* consecutive, although, due to the form, the accent remains on the verb's second syllable (-יִי-); see GKC, § 49 k. Most English versions treat it as having the same future force as the preceding perfect with *waw* consecutive, "I will be … and I will be" (see, e.g., ESV, NASB). The translation "I may be …" interprets its force as concessive, in other words, "although I may be humiliated in *your* eyes, nevertheless, I will be honored" in the eyes of the slave girls. Cf. Prov 29:23.

אִכָּבֵדָה—"I will be honored." Here the meaning of the Niphal (N) of כָּבֵד is the passive of its usual Piel (D) meaning, "to honor" (see the first textual note on 10:3). Contrast the meaning of its Niphal in the second textual note on 6:20. This form (with the ending ה-) is cohortative, but Biblical Hebrew can use the cohortative form without a cohortative force and with the usual force of an imperfect. See Joüon, § 114 b, including note 1.

6:23 יֶלֶד—The noun יֶלֶד (in pause יָלֶד), "child," is derived from the verb יָלַד, which refers to the birthing of children to David by his wives in 2 Sam 3:2, 5; 5:13, thereby heightening the contrast to his barren wife Michal.[21]

Commentary

This chapter and the following one are bound together by the ark. While this chapter focuses on David moving the ark to Jerusalem, the next chapter mentions the ark residing in "a tent," that is, "a tabernacle" (7:6; see also 7:2).

---

[20] One Masoretic manuscript reads "in his eyes."

[21] Cf. the use of the noun יֶלֶד and/or the verb יָלַד for (the birth of) David's illegitimate child who dies in 2 Sam 11:27; 12:15, 18, 19, 21, 22, 24.

Though facilitated by David, the ark coming to Jerusalem was a consequence of God's choice of Jerusalem as his holy city.[22] This is followed in 2 Samuel 7 by God's choice of David to be the bearer of the promise of the Messiah and King who would save all people.[23] Thus, these two chapters depict God's blessing on all people through the Christ who would come through David and to Israel.

The connection of the events of these two chapters is explored in Psalm 132. It mentions the ark in Ephrathah and in Jaar (i.e., Kiriath-jearim) and implores God to come to his resting place (Ps 132:6, 8; cf. 2 Sam 6:2, 17). It then moves on to Yahweh's promise to David (Ps 132:11–12; see 2 Sam 7:12–16) and climaxes with his messianic promise to make sprout "a horn for David" (Ps 132:17). Therefore, the depiction of David as the godly king in 2 Samuel 6–7 is not done to glorify David for his own sake. Nor is it intended to overshadow David's faults that are exposed later in 2 Samuel. Instead, David's character is explored in these chapters as a means to illustrate God's grace and favor not only to the participants in these events—David and Israel—but also through David's descendant Jesus Christ for the benefit of all humankind.

It would be easy for the naïve reader to view this narrative as following shortly upon the events in 2 Samuel 5. However, as 1 Chr 15:1 makes clear, it took place *after* David had built his palace. The palace was constructed with materials supplied by Hiram of Tyre, who began to reign in 980 BC. Therefore the events of 1 Samuel 6 are separated by almost three decades from the events of 1 Samuel 5.

David's First Attempt to Bring the Ark to Jerusalem (6:1–5)

975 BC[24]

Parallel: 2 Sam 6:1–5 ‖ 1 Chr 13:1–8

The author begins with David assembling thirty thousand men from Israel "again" (6:1). This is a reference to the previous chapter where, at the beginning of his reign over all Israel, David apparently had twice assembled an army to defeat the Philistines (5:17–25). Now once again many years later David brought together an army, but this time it was to bring the ark of "Yahweh of armies" to Jerusalem (6:2). The ark is depicted as God's throne with the cherubim on its lid forming the seat upon which he sat.[25] With the assembled men of Israel, the procession of the ark represented a King at the head of his marching army (cf. Num 10:35).

---

[22] See Pss 78:68; 132:13. See also Yahweh's reiterated promise through Moses that he would choose a place for his "name" (שֵׁם) to "dwell" (שָׁכַן) in Deut 12:5, 11; 14:23; 16:2, 6, 11; 26:2.

[23] See the excursus "הָאָדָם as 'the Man' in 2 Samuel 7:19 and 1 Chronicles 17:17" following the commentary on 2 Sam 7:1–29, as well as "Christ in Samuel" in the introduction and the commentary on 1 Sam 2:10 and 1 Sam 2:35 (Steinmann, *1 Samuel*, 23–26, 80–81, 105–6).

[24] See "The Chronology of David's Reign" in the commentary on 5:1–5.

[25] See the fourth textual note on 6:2.

The author calls the city where the ark had been kept "Baale-judah," though previously he had called it by its more common name, Kiriath-jearim (see the second textual note on 6:2). Kiriath-jearim was within the territory given to the clans of Judah. It was eventually settled by the descendants of Shobal, a grandson of Caleb by his second wife, Ephrath (1 Chr 2:19, 50, 52). Upon the ark's return to Israel from Philistia, it was sent to Kiriath-jearim, to the Ephrathites who were distantly related to David (1 Sam 6:21–7:1). David was an Ephrathite, descended from Ephrath through Salma, another grandson of Caleb (1 Sam 17:12; 1 Chr 2:50–51; 4:4). Thus, the ark had been residing with distant relatives of David for almost a century.

To this point it appears as if David was seeking to return the ark to a place of honor. He may have assumed that since God had given him victory over his enemies and rest from the rigors of war (see 7:1), God had chosen him and his city Jerusalem (5:1–9; 6:21). However, honor for Yahweh and his ark seems to have been lacking when it was placed on a new cart. There was an attempt at respect—the cart was new, not one potentially defiled by prior use or contact with unclean things. Other objects associated with the tabernacle could be carried on carts (Num 7:6–9). However, the legislation in the Pentateuch clearly called for the ark to be carried by hand by the Kohathite Levites (Num 4:1–15; cf. Deut 10:8). However, not even they were permitted to touch the ark (Num 4:15).[26] Rather, poles were placed through the rings on the sides of the ark, and these Levites carried the ark by means of these poles (Ex 25:12–15). In placing the ark on a new cart, Israel was acting just like the Philistines (1 Sam 6:7–8)—the very people that David had defeated at the beginning of his reign in Jerusalem (2 Sam 5:17–25).

The cart was moved from Abinadab's house under the care of two of his descendants. Originally Abinadab's son Eleazar had been the ark's guardian (1 Sam 7:1). Now Uzzah and Ahio were in charge of the cart carrying the ark (6:3–4). The movement of the ark was a time of joyous celebration, and the author mentions songs and five different types of musical instruments as accompaniment for David and Israel (6:5). Two of them—"lyres" and "harps"—were stringed instruments, and the other three—"tambourines," "sistrums," and "cymbals"—were percussion instruments.[27]

The Death of Uzzah (6:6–11)

975 BC[28]

Parallel: 2 Sam 6:6–11 ‖ 1 Chr 13:9–14

The consequence of failing to respect God's instructions concerning transportation of the ark came at the threshing floor when the oxen stumbled.[29]

---

[26] See further the commentary on 6:7.

[27] See the textual notes on 6:5.

[28] See "The Chronology of David's Reign" in the commentary on 5:1–5.

[29] See the fourth textual note on 6:6.

Uzzah's reaction was probably not a conscious decision to touch the ark but simply an impulsive reaction to steady it.[30] Nevertheless, Yahweh was justified in striking down Uzzah, because he and his brother had disregarded the regulations regarding the holy objects of the tabernacle, including the ark (6:7). They had transgressed God's commands in the Torah in at least three ways:

1. They were transporting the ark on a cart instead of carrying it by hand on poles (Ex 25:12–15; Num 4:15; cf. Deut 10:8).
2. They were taking charge of the procession although they were Judahites, not Kohathite Levites, who had been given that privilege (Num 4:1–15; cf. Deut 10:8).
3. Uzzah touched the ark, although even the Kohathite Levites were not to touch it: "they must not touch the holy things, lest they die" (Num 4:15).

Interestingly, Josephus blames Uzzah's death on his contact with the ark, but then asserts that the priests alone *were allowed* to touch it.[31] However, there is no Pentateuchal approval for anyone, including priests, to touch the ark.

David's reaction to Uzzah's death was anger (6:8). While some readers might assume that David's anger was directed at God, the text does not say that.[32] Instead, the author states that David was angry *because of Yahweh's outburst* (עַל אֲשֶׁר פָּרַץ יְהוָה פֶּרֶץ), a circumstance that led to the place where Uzzah died receiving its infamous name (6:8). David's anger was probably directed at the human mistakes that were made in transporting the ark. He was infuriated by the lack of obedience to the instructions Moses had given. That ire indicted those, including Ahio and Uzzah, who took charge of the ark's passage and allowed such laxity. David's anger may have been especially directed at himself as the one who had the authority to prevent this malfeasance; after all, he was the thrice-anointed king over all Israel.[33] With the death of Uzzah he may have concluded that Yahweh would not choose David's city as his dwelling place on earth. As Saul had been rejected because of his unfaithfulness to the Word of Yahweh (1 Sam 15:23–16:1; 28:16–19), so also Jerusalem, and perhaps David himself, might be rejected because of the violations of the Torah. This also explains David's fear of Yahweh and his questioning of whether God's ark would come to him (2 Sam 6:9). While David had begun with confidence that God had chosen him and his city (5:12), he was now fearful because, despite his singing and rejoicing before the ark (6:5), he had not shown proper respect for Yahweh by demanding that the ark be handled properly.

Because David was not willing to have the ark brought to him in Jerusalem, he diverted it to the house of Obed-edom, who is twice called a "Gittite"

---

[30] See the second textual note on 6:6.

[31] Josephus, *Antiquities*, 7.81–82.

[32] Some commentators assume that David was angry with God: Ackroyd, *The Second Book of Samuel*, 66–67; Baldwin, *1 and 2 Samuel*, 208. Others, however, argue that he was not: Keil, *The Books of Samuel*, 333; Anderson, *2 Samuel*, 104; Bergen, *1, 2 Samuel*, 330.

[33] David was originally anointed in 1 Sam 16:12–13. He was then anointed a second time as king over Judah in 2 Sam 2:4 and a third time as king over Israel in 2 Sam 5:3.

(6:10–11). Surely there is irony in this. A "Gittite" was a resident of any city called Gath,[34] and the reader must recall that the ark had already been in the possession of Gittites after its capture by the Philistines and transport to the Gath (1 Sam 5:8–10) that was part of the Philistine pentapolis (1 Sam 6:17). David's deadly foe Goliath was from Gath (1 Sam 17:4, 23; cf. 1 Sam 17:52). However, Obed-edom was not from the Philistine Gath.[35] Instead, in 1 Chronicles we learn that he was a Kohathite who later would be appointed to be a singer, musician, and gatekeeper for the ark when it was brought to Jerusalem (1 Chr 15:18, 21, 24; 16:5, 38). Gath-rimmon, on the border of the territories of Ephraim and Manasseh, was a Kohathite city (Josh 21:25–26). Apparently Obed-edom had originally come from Gath-rimmon but had moved to somewhere in the vicinity of Jerusalem.[36] Thus, in an attempt to correct the problems encountered in moving the ark from Kiriath-jearim, David placed it in the care of a Kohathite, a member of the Levite clan designated in the Pentateuch as caretakers of the ark (Num 4:1–15; cf. Deut 10:8).

We are told that during the quarter of a year that the ark was in Obed-edom's house, Yahweh blessed his household (2 Sam 6:11). We are not told what form the blessing took,[37] though it is clear that it must have been obvious to everyone who observed Obed-edom's household. It would soon be reported to David (6:12).

David Brings the Ark to Jerusalem (6:12–19)

975 BC[38]

Parallels: 2 Sam 6:12–16 ‖ 1 Chr 15:25–29; 2 Sam 6:17–19 ‖ 1 Chr 16:1–3

When David was informed of the blessing experienced by Obed-edom, he reacted by bringing the ark to the City of David (6:12). Clearly, David interpreted God's favor on Obed-edom as a sign of God's forgiveness for Israel and for David himself after his repentance, which he had exhibited by entrusting the ark to a Kohathite. David, therefore, also concluded that God had chosen

---

[34] Since "gath" means "winepress," it was a common name for cities. Besides the Philistine Gath, there were several cities in Israel with this name, including Gath-hepher (גַּת הַחֵפֶר, "pit winepress," 2 Ki 14:25; see also Josh 19:13); Gittaim (גִּתַּיִם, "double winepress," 2 Sam 4:3; Neh 11:33); and two cities called Gath-rimmon (גַּת־רִמּוֹן, "pomegranate press"), one in Dan (Josh 19:45; 21:24; 1 Chr 6:54 [ET 6:69]) and one on the border of Ephraim and Manasseh (Josh 21:25). In addition, a place on the Mount of Olives is called Gethsemane (Γεθσημανί, "[olive] oil press," Mt 26:36; Mk 14:32).

[35] Some commentators assume that he was a Philistine: Hertzberg, *I and II Samuel*, 279; McCarter, *II Samuel*, 170.

[36] Since he would later serve as a musician and gatekeeper for the ark once it was brought to Jerusalem, it is reasonable to assume that he lived within walking distance of the city.

[37] See the textual note on 6:11–12. Bergen, *1, 2 Samuel*, 331, suggests that the blessing took the form of fertility, and he bases that on the sixty-two men from Obed-edom's household mentioned in 1 Chr 26:8. While an increase in conceptions and births may have taken place within the three-month period, it may have taken longer to observe the full effects of the divine blessing on Obed-edom's house.

[38] See "The Chronology of David's Reign" in the commentary on 5:1–5.

Jerusalem as his dwelling place (Pss 84:2 [ET 84:1]; 132:5, 7, 13; 2 Chr 36:15; Acts 7:45–46).

The author subtly signals that this time the ark was being moved correctly by mentioning "those carrying the ark" (2 Sam 6:13). The significance of offering sacrifices after six steps is not apparent, but clearly David was expressing his joy at receiving God's blessing. The bulls may have been sacrificed to atone for Uzzah's inadvertent sin of touching the ark (Leviticus 4). The fattened calves were probably offered in thanks for God's blessing (Lev 3:1–5; 7:11–21).

We are told that David danced before the ark as it entered Jerusalem and that he was wearing a linen ephod (2 Sam 6:14). Many have argued that the ephod signaled that David was acting as a priest.[39] Baldwin argues that as king of a kingdom of priests (Ex 19:6), David was entitled to wear the priestly ephod.[40] However, there is no explicit connection in the entire OT between a plain linen ephod and the priesthood. Most references in the OT to an ephod are to the specially made ephod for the high priest.[41] Judging from the description of the high priest's ephod (Ex 28:4–12; 39:1–8), it was some type of long robe undergarment[42] that was worn with an outer robe (מְעִיל) and secured around the waist with a belt (אַבְנֵט, Ex 28:4). Plain linen ephods (אֵפוֹד בָּד) are mentioned only in 1 Sam 2:18; 22:18; 2 Sam 6:14 ‖ 1 Chr 15:27.[43] In 1 Sam 2:18 the boy Samuel—a Levite, not a priest—wore a linen ephod when ministering in Yahweh's presence. The priests serving at the tabernacle in Nob who were slain by Saul also wore linen ephods (1 Sam 22:18). Here David wore an ephod. The common factor that unites Samuel, the priests at Nob, and David in wearing an ephod is that they were leaders in worship. *Plain linen ephods appear to be vesture that could be worn by anyone (other than the high priest) as he was leading or aiding in worship.* As king, David was not acting as a priest—that is, he was not doing any acts specifically reserved for priests according to the Pentateuch.[44] Instead, he was God's designated king of the holy people, the chief lay worshiper before Yahweh.

This time the celebration before the ark is described as more formal. Instead of songs with musical instruments, as in 6:5, there were shouts and the blasts

---

[39] Kleven, "Hebrew Style in 2 Samuel 6," 299; Tidwell, "The Linen Ephod"; Anderson, *2 Samuel*, 105; Hertzberg, *I and II Samuel*, 280. Ackroyd, *The Second Book of Samuel*, 69, notes that the ephod was not an exclusively priestly garment, but believes that wearing it implies that David was acting as a priest.

[40] Baldwin, *1 and 2 Samuel*, 209.

[41] Ex 25:7; 28:4, 6, 12, 15, 25, 26, 27, 28, 31; 29:5; 35:9, 27; 39:2, 7, 8, 18, 19, 20, 21, 22; Lev 8:7; 1 Sam 2:28; 14:3; 21:10 (ET 21:9); 23:6, 9; 30:7.

[42] According to Ex 28:12; 39:7, the high priest's ephod had shoulder pieces.

[43] Other references to an "ephod" (אֵפוֹד) include Gideon's fabrication of a gold ephod that led to Israel's idolatry (Judg 8:26–27) and an ephod made by a certain Micah and associated with idolatrous worship (Judg 17:5; 18:14, 17, 18, 20; see also Hos 3:4). None of these ephods are described as being a "*linen* ephod" (אֵפוֹד בָּד).

[44] Contrast, for instance, King Uzziah's usurping of the priestly office in 2 Chr 26:16–21 (cf. 2 Ki 15:5).

of a ram's horn (6:15). These have liturgical and military overtones as befits the church militant.[45]

In a foreshadowing of 6:20–23, we are told of Michal's viewing of David's leaping and dancing, which led to her despising him (6:16). The text does not reveal *why* she despised David, though her words later are an indication that she did not think David's manner of celebration was appropriate.

The ark was placed in a "tent" prepared by David (6:17; see also 7:2, 6). We are not told whether this was a replacement for the tabernacle, which had been in Shiloh (1 Sam 1:3, 9, 24; 2:22), or simply a temporary shelter. After the offerings, we are told that David blessed the people (2 Sam 6:18). Like the "linen ephod" in 6:14, this benediction cannot be forced to indicate that David was acting as a priest. While the priests were authorized to bless Israel with the Aaronic benediction (Num 6:23–27), and while the high priest Eli had blessed the parents of Samuel (1 Sam 2:20), many blessings by laypersons are also mentioned, some of which are recorded, in Samuel and the rest of the OT.[46]

David also distributed rations to everyone who came to celebrate the ark's presence in Jerusalem (2 Sam 6:19). The author notes that David gave these rations to both men and women. This is an indication that while there were some stark differences in gender roles in ancient Israelite society, God deems all the faithful as Abraham's offspring without distinction. The seal of the old covenant, circumcision, could be received only by males,[47] but the seal of the new covenant is Baptism into Christ, which can be received by males and females alike of any age, ethnicity, or social status, making them sons of Abraham and heirs of the promise (Gal 3:26–29; Col 2:11–14).[48] The outpouring of God's grace upon all in Christ does not nullify, but rather enables and enhances God-pleasing life according to the natural distinctions of gender and family relationships that are built into God's creation[49] and that remain in place among Christians and within the church.[50]

---

[45] See the textual note on 6:15.

[46] For "bless" (בָּרַךְ), see the textual note on 2 Sam 6:11–12, as well as the first textual note on 1 Sam 2:20 and the third textual note on 1 Sam 9:13 (Steinmann, *1 Samuel*, 90, 179). For blessings by laypeople in Samuel, see also 1 Sam 13:10; 15:13; 23:21; 25:14, 32, 33, 39; 26:25; 2 Sam 2:5; 8:10; 13:25; 14:22; 18:28; 19:40 (ET 19:39). For lay blessings elsewhere in the OT see, e.g., Josh 14:13; 22:6–7; Ruth 2:20; 3:10; Neh 11:2.

[47] See, e.g., Gen 17:10–14, which specifies that circumcision was to be performed on the eighth day (one week after birth), although adults could and needed to be circumcised too (Gen 17:23–27; Ex 12:44, 48; Josh 5:3–7).

[48] For expositions of Gal 3:26–29, see Das, *Galatians*, 376–90, and Nordling, *Philemon*, 60–68. For Col 2:11–14, see Deterding, *Colossians*, 102–11.

[49] All humanity, including the reprobate, are governed by the natural law of God, which is evident in the order of creation. See the exposition of Rom 1:18–32 in Middendorf, *Romans 1–8*, 115–50.

[50] These relationships include, for example, the marriage of a husband and wife (Eph 5:21–33) and relationships between parents and children (Eph 6:1–4). See Winger, *Ephesians*, 598–653 and 654–63, 671–82, respectively. For the office of the ministry in the church (Eph 4:7–16), see Winger, *Ephesians*, 490–501.

Michal Resents David's Celebration before the Ark (6:20–23)

975 BC[51]

Since all the people went to their homes, David also went home, intending to bless his household. However, the narrative takes a different turn when Michal purposely came out to criticize her husband (6:20). Her denunciation focused on what she perceived as David's lack of decorum. According to her, his dancing had exposed his genitals to everyone observing him, including the slave girls of his servants.[52]

David turned her accusation against her father (6:21): David was chosen to replace Saul *and his entire house*, which would include his daughter Michal,[53] and David declared that he would again celebrate that he was Yahweh's choice— and, by implication, that the City of David was also God's choice as his dwelling place. David may not have been honored by Michal, but he knew that he would be honored by the "slave girls" (6:22). Earlier Hannah and Abigail, women of great faith, had used this same term of humility (אָמָה) for themselves when speaking to God (1 Sam 1:11; cf. 1 Sam 1:16) or to David (1 Sam 25:24–41), and two wise women will employ it for themselves later (2 Sam 14:15–16; 20:17).

The final note about Michal in the Scriptures tells us that she died without bearing any children (6:23).[54] Some have sought to explain this as Michal having estranged herself from David so that they had no conjugal relations from that time onward.[55] However, David's words in 6:21 hint that her childlessness was part of the judgment of God on *Saul's entire house*—and this verdict of God was so thorough that Saul's house would not continue even through his daughters (cf. 21:8–9). Thus, it is likely that God made Michal barren.[56] Note that Michal had no children by either David or Paltiel (1 Sam 25:44; 2 Sam 3:15), indicating that her lack of fertility was not due to David's neglect of his role as her husband.

---

[51] See "The Chronology of David's Reign" in the commentary on 5:1–5.

[52] This is the force of the verbs נִגְלָה and כְּהִגָּלוֹת נִגְלוֹת, translated with "expose himself" (2 Sam 6:20).

[53] David had originally married Saul's daughter Michal with her father's approval (1 Sam 18:20–27). Later, Saul gave Michal to another man, Paltiel (1 Sam 25:44; 2 Sam 3:15). She was returned to David in 2 Sam 3:13–16.

[54] In 2 Sam 21:8 most Masoretic manuscripts credit "Saul's daughter Michal" with five sons. However, two Masoretic manuscripts, some LXX manuscripts, the Syriac, and the Targum credit these to her sister Merab. Most scholars and translations agree that the correct reading in 21:8 is "Merab." See further the textual note and the commentary on 21:8.

[55] Baldwin, *1 and 2 Samuel*, 211; McCarter, *II Samuel*, 187.

[56] Ackroyd, *The Second Book of Samuel*, 71; Hertzberg, *I and II Samuel*, 281.

God's Covenant with David

Translation

7 ¹When the king was dwelling in his palace and Yahweh had given him rest from his enemies on all sides, ²the king said to the prophet Nathan, "Look! I am dwelling in a cedar palace, but God's ark is dwelling inside the tent curtain."

³Nathan said to the king, "Go do everything that is in your heart, because Yahweh is with you."

⁴During that night Yahweh spoke to Nathan, ⁵"Go say to my servant, to David, 'Thus says Yahweh: "Will you build me a house for me to dwell in? ⁶I have not dwelt in a house from the day I brought the Israelites up from Egypt until this day. I have been moving about in a tent, that is, in a tabernacle. ⁷In all [the places] where I have moved about with all the Israelites, have I ever asked one of the tribes of Israel whom I commanded to shepherd my people Israel, 'Why haven't you built me a cedar house?'"'"

⁸"Now thus you will say to my servant, to David: 'Thus says Yahweh of armies: "I took you from the pasture, from following the flock to be designated ruler over my people, over Israel. ⁹I was with you in every place you went, and I cut off all your enemies in front of you. I will make a great name for you, like the name of the greatest ones on earth. ¹⁰I will appoint a place for my people, for Israel, and I will plant them. They will live on it and not be apprehensive anymore. Malicious men will not oppress them again as they did previously ¹¹from the time that I appointed judges over my people Israel. Now I will give you rest from all of your enemies. Moreover, Yahweh declares to you that Yahweh will build a house for you. ¹²When your days end and you lie down with your fathers, I will raise up your descendant after you who will come from your own body. I will establish his kingdom. ¹³He will build a house for my name, and I will secure the throne of his kingdom forever. ¹⁴I will be his Father, and he will be my son. When he does wrong, I will discipline him with a human rod and with blows inflicted by people. ¹⁵However, my favor will not be removed from him as I removed it from Saul whom I removed before you. ¹⁶Your house and your kingdom will endure forever before me. Your throne will be established forever."'"

¹⁷Nathan spoke all these words and this entire vision to David exactly.

¹⁸King David came and sat before Yahweh and said, "Who am I, my Lord Yahweh, and what is my house that you have brought me this far? ¹⁹And yet this was a small thing in your eyes, my Lord Yahweh, and you have also spoken about your servant's house for a long while to come: this is the teaching about the man, my Lord Yahweh. ²⁰What more is David able to say to you? You know your servant, my Lord Yahweh. ²¹Because of your Word and according to your desire, you have done all these great things in order to make your servant know [them].

²²"Therefore, you are great, my Lord Yahweh, because there is no one like you. There is no god other than you, in all we have heard with our own ears. ²³Who is like your people Israel: one nation on the earth that God came to redeem [as] a people for himself, to establish a name for himself, to do great and awesome deeds, and to drive out nations and their gods before your people whom you redeemed from Egypt? ²⁴You have secured for yourself your people Israel for your own people forever. You, Yahweh, have become their God.

²⁵"Now, Yahweh God, the Word that you spoke concerning your servant and concerning his house—fulfill it forever. Do as you have said, ²⁶and your name will be great forever: 'Yahweh of armies, God over Israel,' and the house of your servant David will be established before you. ²⁷For you, Yahweh of armies, God of Israel, have revealed this to your servant: 'I will build a house for you.' Therefore your servant has found the courage to pray this prayer to you.

²⁸"Now, my Lord Yahweh, you are the one who is God, and your words are truth. You have spoken this good [promise] to your servant. ²⁹Now, be willing to bless your servant's house so that it continues before you forever, for you, my Lord Yahweh, have spoken, and because of your blessing your servant's house will be blessed forever.'"

Textual Notes

7:1 הֵנִֽיחַ־לֹו—"He had given him rest." In the Hiphil (H), the verb נוּחַ has two paradigms with distinct meanings. This form is from the first paradigm, which has the expected forms of נוּחַ as a second-*waw* verb. It is usually used with the preposition לְ, meaning "to give rest to" someone (BDB, s.v. נוּחַ, Hiphil, A 1 b). See also וַהֲנִיחֹתִי לְךָ in 7:11. In the second paradigm (BDB, s.v. נוּחַ, Hiphil, B), the forms double the first root letter, *nun* (-נּ-), and therefore appear as if from a root נגנ. They mean "set, place" (1 Sam 6:18; 10:25), "leave behind" (2 Sam 16:21; 20:3), or "leave alone" (2 Sam 16:11).

7:2 הַיְרִיעָה:—"The tent curtain." This noun, יְרִיעָה, usually denotes the curtains in the tabernacle (Ex 26:1–10, 12–13; 36:8–17; Num 4:25). It can be used together with אֹהֶל, "tent," in reference to the tabernacle (e.g., Ex 26:7, 9, 12, 13), or in parallel to אֹהֶל, "tent," as a near synonym (Is 54:2; Jer 4:20; 10:20; 49:29; Hab 3:7; Song 1:5).

7:3 יְהוָה עִמָּךְ:—"Yahweh is with you." עִמָּךְ is pausal for עִמְּךָ. This expression means that Yahweh is gracious toward a person and will bless his endeavors with success.[1] It recurs in 2 Sam 5:10; 14:17. See the second textual note on 1 Sam 3:19.[2] Contrast Yahweh's departure from being "with" Saul because of his apostasy (1 Sam 16:14; 18:12), resulting in Saul's demise and the failure of his dynasty.

7:4 וַיְהִי דְּבַר־יְהוָה אֶל־נָתָן—"Yahweh spoke to Nathan" is literally "and the Word of Yahweh was to Nathan." This same formula (including with slight variations) is used for divine revelation to the prophet Samuel in 1 Sam 15:10 and to the prophet Gad in

---

[1] See "Prosperity and Success Come Only from God" in "Other Theological Themes in Samuel" in the introduction (Steinmann, *1 Samuel*, 29).

[2] Steinmann, *1 Samuel*, 112. See also 1 Sam 16:18; 17:37; 18:12, 14, 28; 20:13.

2 Sam 24:11. It is frequent in the writing prophets (about eighty-seven times), especially Jeremiah (e.g., Jer 1:2, 4) and Ezekiel (e.g., Ezek 1:3; 3:16).

7:5 אֶל־עַבְדִּי אֶל־דָּוִד—"To my servant, to David." This could have been expressed more concisely in a more common construction, אֶל־דָּוִד עַבְדִּי, "to David my servant," as in the parallel verse 1 Chr 17:4. The LXX simplifies this with only one preposition, πρὸς τὸν δοῦλόν μου Δαυιδ, "to my servant David." The author of Samuel intentionally repeats the preposition אֶל and delays דָּוִד to be the final word to emphasize his name, "David." Similar repetitions occur in 2 Sam 7:7 (אֶת־עַמִּי אֶת־יִשְׂרָאֵל, "[direct object marker] my people, [direct object marker] Israel"); 7:8 (לְעַבְדִּי לְדָוִד, "to my servant, to David"; מִן־הַנָּוֶה מֵאַחַר הַצֹּאן, "from the pasture, from [following] after the flock"; and עַל־עַמִּי עַל־יִשְׂרָאֵל, "over my people, over Israel"); and 7:10 (לְעַמִּי לְיִשְׂרָאֵל, "for my people, for Israel").

כֹּה אָמַר יְהוָה—"Thus says Yahweh." This is another prophetic formula for divine revelation (see also the textual note on 7:4) that is frequent in the latter prophets (around two hundred twenty-seven times) and appears occasionally in Samuel.[3]

הַאַתָּה תִּבְנֶה־לִּי בַיִת לְשִׁבְתִּי:—Literally "will *you* build for me a house for me to dwell (in)?" The redundant pronoun אַתָּה, "you," is emphatic. The context indicates that this rhetorical question expects a negative answer (GKC, § 150 d). It is correctly interpreted by both the LXX (οὐ σὺ οἰκοδομήσεις μοι οἶκον τοῦ κατοικῆσαί με) and 1 Chr 17:4 (לֹא אַתָּה תִּבְנֶה־לִּי הַבַּיִת לָשָׁבֶת) as a negative statement: "*you* will *not* build for me a house (for me) to dwell (in)." In form לְשִׁבְתִּי here could be the noun שֶׁבֶת with the preposition לְ and a pronominal suffix, "for my dwelling place," but the syntax and the context suggest that it is the Qal (G) infinitive construct of יָשַׁב, "for me to dwell (in)." See the Qal of יָשַׁב in the following clause, לֹא יָשַׁבְתִּי, "I have not dwelt" (7:6).

7:6 הֶעֱלֹתִי—"I brought up." The Hiphil (H) of עָלָה (this is the suffixed infinitive construct) is part of the classic terminology for God saving his people through the exodus redemption. See the textual note on 1 Sam 10:18–19;[4] see also 1 Sam 12:6.

מִמִּצְרַיִם—"From Egypt" is missing from the parallel verse 1 Chr 17:5. It varies in its position in the ancient versions; for example, the LXX has ἀνήγαγον ἐξ Αἰγύπτου τοὺς υἱοὺς Ισραηλ, "I brought up out of Egypt the sons of Israel." It appears to have accidentally dropped out of the Chronicler's Vorlage and the Vorlage of the versions. Some supplied it, but in a different position.

מִתְהַלֵּךְ—"Moving about" is the Hithpael (HtD) masculine singular participle of הָלַךְ, "walk." Its Hithpael perfect, הִתְהַלַּכְתִּי, appears in 7:7. For this verb and a small number of others, the Hithpael denotes an action that is repeated, habitual, or regular.[5]

בְּאֹהֶל וּבְמִשְׁכָּן:—Literally "in a tent and in a tabernacle." The conjunction *waw* is epexegetical, "in a tent, *that is*, in a tabernacle." The two nouns are overlapping synonyms that here refer to the same thing. Technically, אֹהֶל is used for the "tent" that is the outer covering pitched "over the tabernacle" (אֹהֶל עַל־הַמִּשְׁכָּן, Ex 26:7; 36:14; 40:19;

---

[3] Also 1 Sam 2:27; 10:18; 15:2; 2 Sam 7:8; 12:7, 11; 24:12.

[4] Steinmann, *1 Samuel*, 200–201.

[5] *IBH*, § 42 A.

see also Ex 35:11). By etymology מִשְׁכָּן, "tabernacle," refers to the place where God "dwells" (the verb שָׁכַן).[6] However, מִשְׁכָּן, "tabernacle," is often used together with and as a synonym for אֹהֶל מוֹעֵד, the "tent of meeting" (e.g., Ex 39:32, 40; 40:2, 22, 29; Num 3:25, 38). This is the only instance of מִשְׁכָּן, "tabernacle," in Samuel. The construct phrase אֹהֶל מוֹעֵד, "tent of meeting," was used for the tabernacle in 1 Sam 2:22.

7:7 הֲדָבָר דִּבַּרְתִּי אֶת־אַחַד שִׁבְטֵי יִשְׂרָאֵל—"Have I ever asked one of the tribes of Israel?" is literally "have I spoken a word with one of the tribes of Israel?" The particle אֶת is the preposition "with" rather than the direct object marker. The Piel (D) verb דִּבֶּר takes the preposition אֶת, "to speak with," about thirty times in the OT (BDB, s.v. דָּבַר, Piel, 3 d). In place of שִׁבְטֵי, "the tribes of," 1 Chr 17:6 reads שֹׁפְטֵי, "the judges of," the Qal (G) masculine plural participle of שָׁפַט in construct, although LXX 1 Chr 17:6 reads φυλὴν Ισραηλ, "tribe of Israel." 1 Chr 17:6 may be a scribal mistake in anticipation of 1 Chr 17:10 (‖ 2 Sam 7:11), which has שֹׁפְטִים, "judges," in the absolute state. While the noun here, שֵׁבֶט, commonly refers to a "tribe" of Israel (BDB, 2), it can also refer to a ruler's "scepter" (see BDB, 1 d; e.g., messianically in Gen 49:10). By metonymy, then, it may refer to a "ruler," as possibly in Deut 29:9 (ET 29:10). "Rulers" would fit well with the rest of the verse as those whom Yahweh "commanded to shepherd" (צִוִּיתִי לִרְעוֹת) his people Israel. However, the royal and messianic promise to the tribe of Judah (e.g., Gen 49:10), and specifically to David, could be considered a divine designation of his "tribe" to govern the other tribes. Liturgically, the tribe of Levi may be said to "shepherd" the other tribes since the priests were Levites (sons of Aaron) and the other Levites were given charge of the administration of the sanctuary and the transportation of the ark (see the commentary on 6:1–5 and 6:6–11).

7:8 הַנָּוֶה—This masculine noun, נָוֶה, has its literal meaning, "pasture," here, but it can also be used metaphorically for the peaceful dwelling place of God's redeemed people as his flock (Jer 23:3; Ezek 34:14). It recurs in 2 Sam 15:25, where it refers to the ark's "resting place." Cf. Ex 15:13, where it refers to Yahweh's holy "abode." The feminine form of the noun, נָוָה, appears mainly in the latter prophets and the psalms (e.g., Ps 23:2).

נָגִיד—For "designated ruler," see the first textual note on 1 Sam 9:16[7] and the commentary on 2 Sam 5:2.

7:9 וָאֶהְיֶה עִמְּךָ—"I was with you." This clause with a verb is equivalent in meaning to the nominal clause in 7:3. See the textual note on 7:3.

וָאַכְרִתָה—"And I cut off." This is the Hiphil (H) preterite (imperfect with *waw* consecutive) of כָּרַת, although the form of the verb itself, אַכְרִתָה (written defectively for אַכְרִיתָה), with the unaccented ending הָ‍-, is that of a cohortative (cf. Joüon, § 114 b). Compare וָאַכְרִית in 1 Chr 17:8.

וְעָשִׂתִי—"(And) I will make." This is translated as a Gospel promise, parsing the verb as the first common singular Qal (G) perfect with *waw* consecutive of עָשָׂה. This form is written defectively for וְעָשִׂיתִי. It is accented with *mehuppak* on the penultimate

---

6   See this verb in Ex 25:8; 29:45, 46; 40:35; Deut 12:5, 11; 14:23.

7   Steinmann, *1 Samuel*, 180.

syllable (-ֶשׂ-), with the secondary accent *metheg* on the final syllable (-תִי-). The penultimate accent is not decisive for determining whether the perfect has *waw* consecutive or *waw* conjunctive; see GKC, § 49 k, and the first and second textual notes on 6:22. The form could also be read as a Qal perfect with conjunctive *waw*, "and I made" (KJV: "and have made"). However, since the previous two first person verbs were preterites (imperfects with *waw* consecutive), one would expect a preterite (imperfect with *waw* consecutive) if past action were in view here. Note the following string of promises expressed with perfect verbs with *waw* consecutive (וְשָׂמְתִּי ... וּנְטַעְתִּיו וְשָׁכַן, 7:10) and two negated imperfects (וְלֹא־יֹסִיפוּ ... וְלֹא יִרְגַּז, 7:10).

שֵׁם גָּדוֹל—"A great name." The LXX and 1 Chr 17:8 omit the adjective "great." Given the tendency of both the LXX and the Chronicler to simplify the language throughout this oracle, the adjective ought to be retained here.

הַגְּדֹלִים—"The greatest ones." An adjective with an article can form a superlative (Joüon, § 141 j; Waltke-O'Connor, § 14.5c, including example 38).

7:10 וְשָׁכַן תַּחְתָּיו—"They will live on it" is literally "and he [Israel] will dwell under himself." The sense of the suffixed preposition תַּחַת is that Israel will dwell "on the spot" or "in place," without being forced to move, with no threat of captivity or exile. See the similar uses of תַּחַת with a suffix in 1 Sam 14:9; 2 Sam 2:23. This is the only instance of the verb שָׁכַן in Samuel, and here Israel is the one who is dwelling. See the discussion of the verb's use in connection with the tabernacle in the fourth textual note on 7:6.

וְלֹא יִרְגַּז—"And they will not be apprehensive." The verb is the third masculine singular Qal (G) imperfect of רָגַז, "to tremble, quake, be anxious."

וְלֹא־יֹסִיפוּ ... לְעַנּוֹתוֹ—"They will not oppress them again." For this construction, the Hiphil (H) imperfect of יָסַף, "to do again," followed by an infinitive construct, see the first textual note on 2 Sam 2:22 and the first textual note on 1 Sam 3:6.[8] Here the infinitive is the Piel (D) of עָנָה III, "to afflict, oppress, abuse." This Piel verb recurs in 2 Sam 13:12, 14, 22, 32, referring to Amnon's rape of Tamar.

בְּנֵי־עַוְלָה—For "malicious men," see the third textual note on 3:34.

7:11 וּלְמִן־הַיּוֹם—"From the time" is literally "and to from the day." The preposition לְ can be used temporally to mean "at" a certain time or "on" a particular occasion. Here, with the following preposition מִן, "from," לְ indicates the starting point for a period of time. 1 Chr 17:10 reads וּלְמִיָּמִים, "and to from the days." LXX 2 Sam 7:11 is similar: ἀπὸ τῶν ἡμερῶν, "from the days." The force of all three readings is identical. Cf. the first textual note on 7:19.

וַהֲנִיחֹתִי לְךָ—For "now I will give you rest," see the textual note on 7:1.

בַּיִת יַעֲשֶׂה־לְּךָ יְהוָה:—In Hebrew word order, the direct object noun בַּיִת is placed first for emphasis, literally "*a house* Yahweh will make for you."

7:12a כִּי ׀ יִמְלְאוּ יָמֶיךָ—"When your days end" is literally "when your days are full." Cf. וְלֹא מָלְאוּ הַיָּמִים in 1 Sam 18:26, literally "and the days were not full/fulfilled," translated as "so before the time expired."

---

8 Steinmann, *1 Samuel*, 110.

וְשָׁכַבְתָּ֙ אֶת־אֲבֹתֶ֔יךָ—"And you lie down with your fathers." אֶת is the preposition "with," not the direct object marker (as in the next clause; see the next textual note). This idiom appears only here in Samuel, but it (with the preposition עִם rather than אֶת) is frequent in Kings, e.g., in reference to David in 1 Ki 1:21; 2:10; 11:21 and regularly for the deaths of later kings. It literally signifies that the body will lie in a family tomb beside the remains of one's ancestors. Especially when used for faithful kings, it may suggest the possibility of awakening from sleep at the resurrection. Cf. the NT use of κοιμάω, "to sleep," for David "sleeping" in death (Acts 13:36) in the context of Christ's resurrection (Acts 13:37) and for other believers "sleeping" in death in connection with being raised to life again in this world (Mt 27:52; Jn 11:11–12) or in connection with being raised to everlasting life on the Last Day (e.g., 1 Cor 15:20, 51; 1 Thess 4:13–15).

אֶת־זַרְעֲךָ֙—Literally "your seed." The singular Hebrew noun זֶרַע, as with the English word "seed," can either denote a single seed or serve as a collective noun for many seeds (e.g., "a bag of grass seed"). However, when זֶרַע is the subject or implied subject of a singular verb and/or when זֶרַע is the antecedent of a singular pronoun, a single seed is intended. Here זֶרַע is the implied subject of these singular verbs: יֵצֵא, "[who] will come out," 7:12; יִבְנֶה, "he will build," 7:13; and יִהְיֶה, "he will be," 7:14. זֶרַע is also the antecedent of these singular pronominal suffixes and independent pronouns: מַמְלַכְתּוֹ, *his* kingdom," 7:12, 13; הוּא, "he," 7:13, 14; לּוֹ לְאָב, "*his* Father," 7:14; בְּהַעֲוֹתוֹ, "when *he* does wrong," 7:14; וְהֹכַחְתִּיו, "I will discipline *him*," 7:14; and מִמֶּנּוּ, "from *him*," 7:15.[9]

אֲשֶׁר יֵצֵא מִמֵּעֶיךָ—"Who will come from your own body" is literally "who will come out from your internal organs." The noun מֵעֶה is used only in the plural and can denote internal organs such as intestines, as in 20:10, but here it denotes the source of male procreation, as also in 16:11, where David refers to his son Absalom. See further the commentary on 7:12.

7:12b–13 וַהֲכִינֹתִי אֶת־מַמְלַכְתּוֹ ... וְכֹנַנְתִּי אֶת־כִּסֵּא מַמְלַכְתּוֹ—"I will establish his kingdom. … And I will secure the throne of his kingdom." Each of the two verbs is a perfect form of כּוּן with *waw* consecutive. The first is Hiphil (H), and the second is Polel (D). In each of these stems, this verb is often used for God "establishing," "setting up," or "making secure" a kingdom, a king, or his royal throne (see BDB, Hiphil, 1 a, and Polel, 1 b). This verb has the same contextual meaning in the Hiphil in 1 Sam 13:13; 2 Sam 5:12 and in the Polel in 2 Sam 7:24. The Niphal (N) participle נָכוֹן has the corresponding passive meaning, "be established," in reference to David's throne in 7:16 and his house in 7:26; see the second textual note on 7:16.[10]

7:14 אֲנִי אֶהְיֶה־לּוֹ לְאָב וְהוּא יִהְיֶה־לִּי לְבֵן—"I will be his Father, and he will be my son" is literally "I myself will be(come) in relation to him a Father, and he himself will be(come) in relation to me a son." The pronouns (אֲנִי ... הוּא) are emphatic ("myself … himself"). In each of these clauses, the verb הָיָה takes two prepositional phrases with לְ

---

[9] See Collins, "A Syntactical Note (Genesis 3:15)"; Alexander, "Further Observations on the Term 'Seed' in Genesis."

[10] See Waltke-O'Connor, § 23.6.3a, example 6. For the Piel (D) or Polel (D) as resultative, see *IBH*, § 41 B; Waltke-O'Connor, § 24.3.

(see BDB, s.v. הָיָה, Qal, II 2 f). In the first prepositional phrase in each clause (לִי ... לוֹ), the לְ indicates relation (BDB, s.v. לְ, 5 a (*d*)), "in relation to him" = "his," and "in relation to me" = "my." In each clause, the second prepositional phrase (לְבֵן ... לְאָב) represents the use of הָיָה with a predicate object introduced by לְ with the meaning "to become," indicating a new relationship (see BDB, s.v. הָיָה, Qal, II 2 e), thus "I will be(come) ... a Father ... he will be(come) ... a son." This construction (הָיָה plus the object marked with לְ) is often used to signal that the verb in the Qal is being used in the sense of "become" (*HALOT*, Qal, 7 c).

These two clauses appear verbatim also in the parallel verse 1 Chr 17:13. David recites them, but in reverse order (and without אֶהְיֶה), when speaking to his son Solomon in 1 Chr 22:10. When speaking about Solomon in 1 Chr 28:6, David again reverses the order of the clauses in Yahweh's words: he paraphrases the second clause (בָּחַרְתִּי בוֹ לִי לְבֵן, "I chose him for myself to [be my] son") before quoting the first clause.

In reference to David's son Solomon, who will not be conceived and born until later, these clauses indicate the creation of a new filial relationship (of Solomon to God the Father) that did not exist previously. In contrast to this, note that the Messiah/Christ has an eternal relationship with God the Father, not one that was brought into being at some point in time. He is the coeternal Son of God; his Sonship to his Father is nothing new, for this relationship has existed from eternity past and will endure forever (Jn 1:1–2, 18; Col 1:15–20; 2:9). What will be new in time is the Son's incarnation and perfect life, when he will experience Sonship in terms of suffering in obedience to the Father, and his resurrection, by which he is declared to be the Son in power (e.g., Mt 26:39; Jn 18:11; Rom 1:4; Heb 5:8–9; 7:28). However, instead of using the phraseology of "becoming," Jesus is declared *to be* the Son (already and eternally) at his Baptism and transfiguration (Mt 3:16–17; 17:5 and parallels). Similarly in Psalm 2 the Messiah and Son (Ps 2:12), as the anointed King in Zion (Ps 2:6), declares, "Yahweh said to me, 'You are my Son; today I myself have begotten you' " (יְהוָה אָמַר אֵלַי בְּנִי אַתָּה אֲנִי הַיּוֹם יְלִדְתִּיךָ, Ps 2:7). See further the commentary on 2 Sam 7:12–15.

אֲשֶׁר בְּהַעֲוֹתוֹ וְהֹכַחְתִּיו—The first two words form a *casus pendens* about the son, literally "who, when he commits iniquity, and I will discipline him." See GKC, § 112 mm. בְּהַעֲוֹתוֹ is the Hiphil (H) infinitive construct with a prefixed preposition בְּ in a temporal sense: "when he commits iniquity." The verb עָוָה is denominative from the noun עָוֹן, "iniquity." Its Hiphil means "commit iniquity," as also in 2 Sam 19:20 (ET 19:19); 24:17. It always denotes actual sinning,[11] not simply being considered sinful or being accused of sin. For its Niphal (N), "be perverted," see the second textual note on 1 Sam 20:30.[12] This verb applies literally to Solomon, who will commit iniquity (see 1 Kings 11). In contrast to the son mentioned in Nathan's prophecy, the Messiah, the divine Son of the Father, did nothing wrong (Lk 23:41), as he is sinless (2 Cor 5:21). If this verb were to be applied to him, it would by necessity have to refer to the imputation of the

---

[11] 2 Sam 19:20b (ET 19:19b); 24:17; 1 Ki 8:47; Jer 3:21; 9:4 (ET 9:5); Ps 106:6; Job 33:27; 2 Chr 6:37.

[12] Steinmann, *1 Samuel*, 395.

iniquities of sinful humanity on him and the next verb ("I will discipline") would have to refer to his vicarious suffering for them (Isaiah 53; Jn 1:29; 2 Cor 5:21; 1 Pet 2:24). However, there is no example in the OT where this verb means "sin is imputed [to the verb's subject]." See further the commentary on 2 Sam 7:12–15.

וְהֹכַחְתִּיו—"I will discipline him." The Hiphil (H) of יָכַח is used for Yahweh or his Messiah executing divine judgment in, e.g., Is 2:4; 11:3–4; Micah 4:3. Believers petition Yahweh not to discipline them as they deserve (Pss 6:2 [ET 6:1]; 38:2 [ET 38:1]; cf. Job 5:17; Heb 12:6).

בְּשֵׁבֶט אֲנָשִׁים וּבְנִגְעֵי בְּנֵי אָדָם:—The wording "with a human rod and with blows inflicted by people" finds fulfillment in Solomon's discipline by God for his sin of idolatry (1 Kings 11). However, read in light of the work of Christ, Christians will call to mind a greater, efficacious suffering: the passion of Christ, as he is beaten with fists and struck with a reed (e.g., Mt 26:67; 27:30; Jn 18:22; 19:3), although not for any sin of his own. See further the commentary on 2 Sam 7:12–15.

7:15 וְחַסְדִּי—"However, my favor." David speaks of this messianic promise (Yahweh's favor) in 2 Sam 22:51. The noun חֶסֶד preeminently refers to God's grace, favor, and love, which are deserved by no one except his sinless Son, but which he delights in bestowing on his penitent people. Exercising this divine attribute is a part of God's character (2 Sam 2:6; 15:20).[13] The word then often refers to an action by God's people as they show his kindness, faithfulness, and love even when under no human obligation to do so (2 Sam 9:3). See the third textual note on 2 Sam 2:5 and also, e.g., 1 Sam 15:6; 20:8; 2 Sam 3:8; 9:7; 10:2.

לֹא־יָסוּר ... כַּאֲשֶׁר הֲסִרֹתִי ... אֲשֶׁר הֲסִרֹתִי—"It will not be removed ... as I removed [it] ... whom I removed." The threefold translation "removed" reflects that all three verbs are forms of סוּר. The first is Qal (G), which has an active but intransitive meaning, "to depart, turn away," but for the sake of consistency in English, it is translated as a passive, "be removed." The second and third are Hiphil. The Qal of סוּר was used in 1 Sam 16:14; 18:12 when Yahweh and his Spirit "departed" from the apostate Saul and in 1 Sam 28:15, where Saul, shortly before his death, admits that God had "departed" from him (see also 1 Sam 28:16).

7:16 לְפָנֶיךָ—Most Masoretic manuscripts, including Codex Leningradensis, have this reading: "before you." However, a few Masoretic manuscripts read לְפָנַי, "before me," which is supported by the LXX (ἐνώπιον ἐμοῦ), Old Latin Codex Cyprianus, and the Syriac Peshitta. The reading לְפָנֶיךָ, "before you," may be the result of dittography triggered by the following *kaph*, the first consonant of כִּסְאֲךָ, "your throne." Cf. לְפָנֶיךָ in a similar context at the end of 7:26 and also in 7:29.

יִהְיֶה נָכוֹן—"It will be established." This is the Qal (G) imperfect of הָיָה with the Niphal (N) participle of כּוּן. For כּוּן, see the textual note on 7:12b–13. This periphrastic construction (הָיָה + a participle) emphasizes durative action, "will continue to be/remain established" (see Joüon, §§ 121 c and 154 m). The identical words recur in 7:26. The

---

[13] See also, e.g., Ex 34:6–7; Num 14:18–19; Is 54:8; Joel 2:13; Jonah 4:2; Micah 7:18; Pss 25:6–7; 51:3 (ET 51:1); Lam 3:32.

durative force is clearer than it would be if expressed by an imperfect alone. However, Niphal imperfects of כּוּן have a durative meaning in reference to a king's throne in Prov 25:5; 29:14. Its Niphal imperfect is negated regarding the continuation of Saul's kingdom in 1 Sam 20:31.

7:17 כֵּן ... וּכְכֹל ... כְּכֹל—Literally "according to all ... and according to all ... thus." In such a context כֹּל is practically equivalent to "exactly" (Joüon, § 139 e, note 1).

הֶחָזְיוֹן—The noun חִזָּיוֹן, "vision," is derived from the verb חָזָה, "to see." Divine revelations to prophets are often described in visual terms even when the revelation is verbal; they "see" the Word of God because it/he is real and personal. This uncommon noun refers to prophetic visions also in Joel 3:1 (ET 2:28) and to false ones in Zech 13:4. The cognate noun חָזוֹן, which is the reading in 1 Chr 17:15, is much more common in the OT for a prophetic "vision." See the fourth textual note on 1 Sam 3:1.[14] The participle of חָזָה refers to the prophet Gad as David's "seer" in 2 Sam 24:11. For the participle of רָאָה denoting a prophetic "seer" (1 Sam 9:9, 11, 18, 19; 2 Sam 15:27), see the commentary on 1 Sam 9:9.[15]

7:18 אֲדֹנָי יְהוִה—"My Lord Yahweh." In this title the Masoretes pointed the Tetragrammaton with *shewa* and *hireq* (יְהוִה), the first and third vowels of אֱלֹהִים, "God," and intended for it to be read aloud as that word so that this title would be pronounced *'adonai 'elohim*, "(my) Lord God." (The usual Masoretic convention was to point the Tetragrammaton as יְהוָה, with the vowels from אֲדֹנָי, so that יְהוָה would be pronounced as *'adonai*, but pronouncing the title here as *'adonai 'adonai* would imply that one Hebrew word is repeated, which is not the case.) This formulaic title for God appears some three hundred times in the OT, but in the book of Samuel it occurs only in this prayer of David (7:18, 19 [twice], 20, 22, 28, 29). Therefore David uses it as an intimate address to God, expressing the boldly confident relationship he enjoys with Yahweh because of the messianic promise. Before David, this address for God was used only by Abraham (Gen 15:2, 8), Moses (Deut 3:24; 9:26; see also Ex 23:17; 34:23), Joshua (Josh 7:7), Gideon (Judg 6:22), and Samson (Judg 16:28). Its first uses in Scripture were by Abraham (Gen 15:2, 8) in response to Yahweh's gracious blessing promises (Gen 12:1–3, 7; 13:14–17; 15:4–7). Solomon will use it in his prayer at the consecration of the temple as he recalls the exodus redemption (1 Ki 8:53). God had disclosed his personal name, "Yahweh" (יהוה), to identify himself as the God of the patriarchs as he began to fulfill his patriarchal promises through the exodus redemption (Ex 3:14–15). The title "(my) Lord Yahweh" (אֲדֹנָי יְהוִה) was commonly used by the prophets, especially by the priest-prophet Ezekiel (two hundred and seventeen times), and appears sporadically elsewhere in the OT.

וּמִי בֵיתִי—"And what is my house?" This is a rare example where the interrogative מִי, "who?" is used for a thing rather than a person (Joüon, § 144 b).

7:19 לְמֵרָחוֹק—"For a long while to come." This is the adjective רָחֹק, "far away" (in space or time), with the prefixed prepositions לְ and מִן in a temporal sense. See לְמִן in

---

14 Steinmann, *1 Samuel*, 109.

15 Steinmann, *1 Samuel*, 184–85.

the first textual note on 7:11, which referred to a starting point in past time. The same wording as here, לְמֵרָחוֹק refers to the past, "long ago," in 2 Ki 19:25 ‖ Is 37:26. Here, however, as in the parallel verse 1 Chr 17:17, it refers to future time.

וְזֹאת תּוֹרַת הָאָדָם—"This is the teaching about the man." See the commentary on 7:19, as well as the excursus "הָאָדָם as 'the Man' in 2 Samuel 7:19 and 1 Chronicles 17:17" following this pericope.

7:20 וּמַה־יּוֹסִיף דָּוִד עוֹד לְדַבֵּר—"What more is David able to say?" For the construction with the Hiphil (H) of יָסַף (יּוֹסִיף) and an infinitive construct (לְדַבֵּר), see the first textual note on 1 Sam 3:6.[16]

7:21 וּכְלִבְּךָ—"And according to your desire" is literally "and according to your heart." See the same prepositional phrase (כְּ but with the longer form of the noun "heart," לֵבָב instead of the shorter form לֵב, as here) in 1 Sam 13:14, where Samuel announces that Yahweh has sought אִישׁ כִּלְבָבוֹ, "a man according to his own heart." In 1 Sam 13:14 that man would be David, and here in 2 Samuel 7, "the man" (הָאָדָם, 2 Sam 7:19) will be the Son of David, the Messiah.

עָשִׂיתָ—"You have done." This form of עָשָׂה is perfect, which ordinarily would refer to the past. However, in context it refers not only to the things God has already done for David but especially to his Gospel promises for the future. It can, therefore, be considered a prophetic perfect (Joüon, § 112 h). God's Word is so certain that one can trust its fulfillment as if God has already performed the action.

כָּל־הַגְּדוּלָה הַזֹּאת—The Hebrew noun גְּדוּלָה is singular, so the phrase literally means "all this greatness." It is translated with a plural, "all these great things," because it refers to the multiple Gospel promises in this chapter. See הַגְּדוּלָה again in the third textual note on 7:23. In this context, note the cognate adjective גָּדוֹל, "great," twice in 7:9 and the cognate verb גָּדַל, "be great," in 7:22, 26.

7:22 וְאֵין אֱלֹהִים זוּלָתֶךָ—"There is no god other than you." Monotheism is expressed with almost the same wording in Is 45:5 and similarly (including זוּלָה, "other, besides, except") in Is 45:21; 64:3 (ET 64:4); Hos 13:4; Ps 18:32 (ET 18:31). See also the first two of these words, אֵין אֱלֹהִים, in Deut 32:39; 2 Ki 5:15; Is 44:6.

7:23 הָלְכוּ־אֱלֹהִים—"God came." The plural noun אֱלֹהִים is usually considered a plural of majesty when it refers to the one true "God." Usually it is construed as a singular, but occasionally it is grammatically plural, as here, where it is the subject of a plural verb (הָלְכוּ). See Joüon, §§ 136 d; 148 a; 150 f (citing this verse). The parallel verse 1 Chr 17:21 has the singular form of the same verb, הָלַךְ.

לִפְדּוֹת—"To redeem." This is the Qal (G) infinitive construct of פָּדָה. Its Qal perfect is used later in this verse (פָּדִיתָ, "you redeemed"). It refers to God's redemptive action also in 2 Sam 4:9. In Deuteronomy this verb denotes the exodus redemption of Israel from Egypt (Deut 7:8; 9:26; 13:6 [ET 13:5]; 15:15; 21:8; 24:18). For other verbs in Samuel with exodus associations, see the textual note on 1 Sam 10:18–19.[17]

---

[16] Steinmann, *1 Samuel*, 110.

[17] Steinmann, *1 Samuel*, 200–201.

וְלַעֲשׂוֹת לָכֶם הַגְּדוּלָּה וְנִרְאֹות—Literally the MT reads "and to do for yourselves the greatness and fearsome things." The awkward prepositional phrase לָכֶם, "for yourselves," is omitted in 4QSam^a (ולע[שׂ]ות נדולה ונוראות]) and is not reflected in the LXX (τοῦ ποιῆσαι μεγαλωσύνην καὶ ἐπιφάνειαν). A few Masoretic manuscripts correct לָכֶם to לָהֶם, "for them." The definite noun הַגְּדוּלָּה, "the greatness," is feminine singular, but, as in 7:21, it refers to a plurality (see the third textual note on 7:21). Despite the lack of concord in definiteness (נִרְאֹות lacks an article) and number, it combines with the feminine plural Niphal (N) participle נִרְאֹות (written defectively for נוֹרָאֹות, from יָרֵא, "to fear") to mean "great and awesome deeds." This Niphal participle is combined with the adjective גָּדֹול, "great," to refer to God's salvific miracles in Deut 10:21, and a masculine singular Niphal participle of יָרֵא and the adjective גָּדֹול, "great," describe God himself in Deut 10:17. נוֹרָאֹות refers to divine miracles also in Is 64:2 (ET 64:3); Pss 65:6 (ET 65:5); 106:22; 145:6.

לְאַרְצֶךָ—The MT reads "to your land," which is difficult syntactically and semantically. The translation "to drive out" follows the reading לְגָרֵשׁ in 1 Chr 17:21, which is supported by LXX 2 Sam 7:23 (τοῦ ἐκβαλεῖν σε). This is the reading followed by most modern translations. In this reading, six Hebrew words intervene between the Piel (D) infinitive construct and its compound direct object, which consists of the last two words of the verse, גֹּויִם וַאֱלֹהָיו, "nations and its [their] gods."

7:24 וַתְּכֹונֵן—"You have secured." For this Polel (D) verb, see the textual note on 7:12b–13.

לְךָ ... לְךָ לְעָם—"For yourself ... for your own people." In the first instance of the repeated phrase לְךָ, the preposition לְ has a reflexive meaning (BDB, s.v. לְ, 5 h). In the second instance, the לְ indicates possession (BDB, s.v. לְ, 5 a, 5 b).

7:25 הַדָּבָר ... הָקֵם—"The Word ... fulfill." The verb is the masculine singular Hiphil (H) imperative of קוּם, "arise." In the Hiphil, this verb can refer to carrying out or fulfilling a word, oath, or covenant promise (see BDB, Hiphil, 6 f).

7:26 וְיִגְדַּל שִׁמְךָ—"And your name will be great." The Qal (G) imperfect of גָּדַל (cf. the third textual note on 7:21) with a conjunctive *waw* is translated as a result clause: because Yahweh will fulfill his spoken Word, his name "will be" great (cf. ESV). This fits best with the verbal construction at the end of the verse (see the next textual note). It could also be taken as a purpose clause, "fulfill ... so that your name may/will be great" (cf. NASB). Since it follows two imperatives in 7:25 (הָקֵם ... וַעֲשֵׂה), it could also be a jussive, which is an indirect imperative, "may/let your name be great" (cf. KJV, NKJV).

יִהְיֶה נָכֹון—"It will be established." For this periphrastic construction, see the second textual note on 7:16.

7:27 גָּלִיתָה אֶת־אֹזֶן עַבְדְּךָ—"You have revealed this to your servant." The Qal (G) of גָּלָה, "uncover," is used idiomatically with the direct object אֹזֶן, "ear," literally "you have uncovered the ear of your servant." See the textual note on 1 Sam 9:15.[18]

מָצָא עַבְדְּךָ אֶת־לִבֹּו—"Your servant has found the courage" is literally "your servant found his heart."

---

[18] Steinmann, *1 Samuel*, 180. See also 1 Sam 20:2, 12, 13; 22:8, 17.

לְהִתְפַּלֵּל ... אֶת־הַתְּפִלָּה הַזֹּאת:—"To pray this prayer." In this cognate accusative construction, the Hithpael (HtD) of פָּלַל is used with its cognate noun תְּפִלָּה. This Hithpael verb was used for Hannah's praying, which God answered, in 1 Sam 1:10, 12, 26, 27; 2:1. It is used for intercessory prayer in 1 Sam 2:25; 7:5; 8:6; 12:19, 23.

7:28 אַתָּה־הוּא הָאֱלֹהִים—"You are the one who is God" is literally "you (are) he (who is) God." The force of the syntax is "it is you who are the (true) God" (Joüon, § 154 j). See a similar confession in 1 Ki 8:60.

וּדְבָרֶיךָ יִהְיוּ אֱמֶת—"And your words are truth." Most English versions translate the second noun adjectivally, "are *true*." However, the object of the plural copulative verb is the singular noun אֱמֶת, "truth," which God displays in his actions toward his people (2 Sam 2:6; 15:20; cf. 1 Sam 12:24). See רֹאשׁ־דְּבָרְךָ אֱמֶת in Ps 119:160 and especially Jesus' affirmation in his prayer to the Father: ὁ λόγος ὁ σὸς ἀλήθειά ἐστιν, "your Word is truth" (Jn 17:17).

7:29 הוֹאֵל וּבָרֵךְ—"Be willing to bless" is literally "be willing and bless." Both of these verbs are masculine singular imperatives, the Hiphil (H) of יָאַל and the Piel (D) of בָּרַךְ, respectively. The verbs are coordinated, and the second serves as the verbal complement of the first; "bless" specifies what action Yahweh would "be willing" to do. See GKC, § 120 d; Joüon, § 177 d. For בָּרַךְ, "bless," see the first textual note on 1 Sam 2:20;[19] the third textual note on 1 Sam 9:13;[20] and the textual note on 2 Sam 6:11–12. "Bless" could refer to Yahweh's speaking of his benediction, but since he has already articulated his Gospel promises in the preceding part of the chapter, the emphasis here is more on the conferral of the gracious benefits of which he has spoken.

וּמִבִּרְכָתְךָ יְבֹרַךְ—"And because of your blessing ... it will be blessed." The preposition מִן has a causal force, "because." The divine Word is efficacious (Is 55:10–11). Therefore the noun בְּרָכָה, "blessing," can refer both to God's prior spoken Gospel promises and also to the blessings he confers in fulfillment of his speaking. The verb יְבֹרַךְ is the Pual (Dp) imperfect of בָּרַךְ, "bless," whose meaning is the passive of the Piel (D) in the first part of the verse; see the preceding textual note.

Commentary[21]

975 BC[22]

In the NT one certainty about the identity of the Messiah is that he is a royal descendant of David.[23] Matthew's genealogy of Jesus acclaims him "the Son of David" even before his lineage is given (Mt 1:1; see also Mt 1:6, 17, 20; Lk 1:27; 3:31). In the Synoptic Gospels, those who appeal to Jesus as the

---

[19] Steinmann, *1 Samuel*, 90.

[20] Steinmann, *1 Samuel*, 179.

[21] Much of the discussion in the section is drawn from Steinmann, "What Did David Understand about the Promises in the Davidic Covenant?"

[22] See "The Chronology of David's Reign" in the commentary on 5:1–5.

[23] See further "The Promise to David (2 Samuel 7)" and "David and the Messianic Promise" in "Christ in Samuel" in the introduction (Steinmann, *1 Samuel*, 23–24, 25–26).

Christ often refer to him as "Son of David."[24] Jesus compares himself to David in the narrative of Samuel (1 Sam 21:2–7 [ET 21:1–6]) to justify his actions (Mt 12:3–4; Mk 2:25–26; Lk 6:3–4). Moreover, in a well-known conversation about the Messiah, even Jesus' opponents acknowledge that the Christ is "the Son of David," and none of them can contest Jesus' assertion, based on Psalm 110, that the Christ is also David's "Lord" (Mt 22:41–46; cf. Mk 12:35–37; Lk 20:41–44).[25]

Luke's narratives leading to Jesus' birth emphasize his Davidic connection: Gabriel announces that Mary's child will occupy "the throne of his father David" (Lk 1:32); John the Baptist's father, Zechariah, prophesies the salvation to come from "the house" of God's "servant David" and that his own son will go before "the Lord" to prepare his ways (Lk 1:69, 76); the angel of the Lord announces Jesus' birth "in the city of David" (Lk 2:11; cf. Jn 7:42). Paul also emphasizes Jesus' descent from David (Rom 1:3; 2 Tim 2:8), and this was no doubt part of his "proving that Jesus was the Christ" (Acts 9:22; cf. Acts 17:2–3). In the Apocalypse, Jesus is identified three times as the scion of David's house (Rev 3:7; 5:5; 22:16).

Of course, this emphasis on the Messiah as the descendant of David follows the trajectory set forth in the prophets.[26] The identity of the Messiah is so closely bound up with David that at times the prophets simply call the promised Savior "David" (Jer 30:9; Ezek 34:23–24; 37:24–25; Hos 3:5). The NT affirmation of the Davidic identity of the Messiah certainly draws on the prophets' depiction of a specific descendant of David as the coming Savior, King, and Shepherd (Is 9:5–6 [ET 9:6–7]; 16:5; Jer 23:5; 30:9; 33:15; Ezek 34:23–24; 37:24–25).

This flowering of messianic prophecy connected to David first buds from Nathan's prophecy to David and David's reaction to it as related in 2 Samuel 7. In addition to identifying the Messiah as the descendant of David, this chapter also teaches that he will have an eternal house, throne, and kingdom.

Nathan Delivers God's Promise to David (2 Sam 7:1–17)

Parallel: 2 Sam 7:1–17 ‖ 1 Chr 17:1–15

Having brought the ark to Jerusalem, David returned to his palace (7:1). The author also informs us that Yahweh had given David rest from his enemies on all sides. The author is referring to God's protection of David from the enemies who previously had taken hostile action against him: the Philistines (2 Sam 5:17–25) and the Ammonites (2 Samuel 10). David had been given rest in the sense that he no longer had to fear that foes might attack his kingdom. This is not stating that David would fight no more wars. After this prophecy

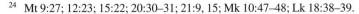

24 Mt 9:27; 12:23; 15:22; 20:30–31; 21:9, 15; Mk 10:47–48; Lk 18:38–39.

25 See also Acts 2:33–35; Eph 1:20; Col 3:1; Heb 1:3, 13; 8:1; 10:12–13; 12:2; 1 Pet 3:22.

26 Is 7:13–14; 9:5–6 (ET 9:6–7); 11:1–10; 16:3–5; 22:22; 37:35; 55:3; Jer 17:25; 23:5; 33:15; Amos 9:11; Zech 12:8, 10; 13:1.

was delivered, King David fought wars that expanded his rule from Israel to encompass several neighboring territories: Philistia (8:1), Moab (8:2), Edom (8:13–14), Zobah (8:3–8), and Aram (8:5).

With no fear of attack, David was ready to take on a new royal endeavor, and he noticed a stark difference between his house and the housing of God's ark, which he had recently placed in a tent in Jerusalem (7:2; cf. 6:17). Since David no longer had to fear incursions by his enemies, such a peacetime project appeared to be feasible not only to David but also to the prophet Nathan (7:3). Nathan's first reaction was that David should do what he desired, since God was with him. This probably was a conclusion based on God's recent blessing that confirmed David's choice of Jerusalem for the ark's resting place (see 2 Samuel 6).

Nathan appears here for the first time in the narrative of Samuel. He has no introduction other than his name and his title: "Nathan the prophet" (נָתָן הַנָּבִיא, 7:2).[27] Nathan played key roles at three important junctures in David's reign: he delivered the prophecy here in 2 Samuel 7; he conveyed God's rebuke of David for his adultery (2 Samuel 12); and he prompted the aged David to place Solomon on the throne (1 Kings 1). Nathan also appears to have served along with Gad as a prophetic advisor to David in appointing Levites for service in the temple (2 Chr 29:25). Like several other prophets in his era, Nathan recorded events that took place during the years of Israel's united monarchy (1 Chr 29:29; 2 Chr 9:29).

However, God's plan for a temple differed from David's. That evening Nathan received an oracle from Yahweh (2 Sam 7:4). Revelations from God at night—including dreams—are common in the OT.[28] This oracle instructed Nathan to speak to David a revelation that would build on David's observation of the difference between God's house and David's house (7:2). The noun "house" (בַּיִת) forms a key word in this chapter. It appears six times in the divine disclosure to David (2 Sam 7:5, 6, 7, 11, 13, 16), and he mirrors this in his response with seven more uses of the word (2 Sam 7:18, 19, 25, 26, 27, 29 [twice]).

The rhetorical question that opens the oracle (7:5) expresses another question to David below the surface: why were you thinking that you ought to build Yahweh a house? This is reinforced by the short historical review of God's presence with Israel (7:6–7). The review mentions "the tribes of Israel" whom Yahweh commanded to shepherd his people.[29] From Moses through Saul, God

---

[27] 1 Ki 4:5 mentions a Nathan who was the father of Azariah and Zabud, two of Solomon's officials. This Nathan would have been a contemporary of David, and perhaps he was the prophet who served during David's reign. In a list of the descendants of Judah, 1 Chr 2:36 mentions a Nathan who was the father of Zabad. If this Zabad was the same man as Zabud (1 Ki 4:5), then he and his father, Nathan, were from the tribe of Judah.

[28] Gen 15:12–21; 20:3–7; 26:24; 31:10–13, 24; 37:5–10; 40:5; 41:1–7; 46:2–4; Judg 7:13; 1 Ki 3:5; Zech 1:8; Dan 2:1, 19; 4:2 (ET 4:5); 7:2–14; 2 Chr 7:12.

[29] See the textual note on 7:7.

had chosen leaders for his people from every tribe except Reuben, Simeon, and Asher.[30] The review ends with another rhetorical question that also anticipates a negative answer (7:7): did Yahweh ever request a cedar house?

The oracle next moves to God's history with David (7:8–9a). God states that he did three things for David in the past: (1) he promoted the shepherd boy to become Israel's "designated ruler" (נָגִיד);[31] (2) he was with David everywhere he went; and (3) he cut off all of David's enemies. A comparison of the history of Israel with Yahweh's statements about David in 7:5, 8–9a demonstrates how David's life mirrors the history of God's people and how David embodies them as their ruler:

Israel	**David**
God brought them up from Egypt (7:6)	God took David from the pasture (7:8)
God moved about with the Israelites (7:7)	God was with David wherever he went (7:9a)
God commanded tribes to shepherd Israel (7:7)	God ordained David as designated ruler over Israel (7:8)
God never asked Israel to build him a cedar house (7:7)	God calls into question David's plan to build him a house (7:5)

---

[30] Note the ancestral tribes of the following leaders:

- From the tribe of *Levi*: Moses and Aaron (Ex 6:18–20), Eli (1 Sam 1:9), and Samuel (1 Sam 1:1–2, 20; 1 Chr 6:7–12 [ET 6:22–27]).
- From the tribe of *Ephraim*: Joshua (Ex 33:11; Num 13:8), Deborah (Judg 4:5), and Abdon (Judg 12:15).
- From the tribe of *Judah*: Othniel (Judg 3:9; see also Num 13:6) and Ibzan (Judg 12:8), as well as possibly Jair (see the note on Jair in the entry for the tribe of Manasseh).
- From the tribe of *Benjamin*: Ehud (Judg 3:15) and Saul (1 Sam 9:21).
- From the tribe of *Naphtali*: Barak (Judg 4:6).
- From the tribe of *Manasseh*: Gideon and possibly Jair. In Judg 8:2, Gideon connects himself with the descendants of Abiezer, and Abiezer is one of the clans of Manasseh (Josh 17:2). Jair was from Gilead (Judg 10:3–5), part of which was assigned to Manasseh, and he may have been a descendant of the Jair mentioned in Num 32:41; Deut 3:14; 1 Ki 4:13 (cf. Josh 13:30), who was from the tribe of Manasseh. A fuller genealogy for that earlier Jair is given in 1 Chr 2:21–23, which shows that he was from the tribe of Manasseh on his paternal grandmother's side and from the tribe of Judah on his paternal grandfather's side.
- From the tribe of *Issachar*: Tola (Judg 10:1).
- From the tribe of *Gad*: Jephthah, who was from Mizpah (Judg 11:34) in the center of the territory of Gad.
- From the tribe of *Zebulun*: Elon (Judg 12:11).
- From the tribe of *Dan*: Samson (Judg 13:2–3, 24).

[31] For this Hebrew term, see the first textual note on 1 Sam 9:16 (Steinmann, *1 Samuel*, 180) and the commentary on 2 Sam 5:2.

There is one point Yahweh made about his work in David's life that is not explicit in his recapitulation of Israel's history: God cut off David's enemies.[32] The unstated parallel is that in cutting off David's enemies, God was also delivering Israel from oppressors (see 7:10b–11a).

Yahweh then moved on to four promises to David (7:9b–16):

1. He would give David "a great name" (7:9b).
2. Yahweh would "appoint a place" for Israel, where his people and David would have no fear of enemies (7:10–11a).
3. Yahweh would "build a house" for David (7:11b) and raise up one of David's progeny, "your descendant" (7:12–15).

   a. The descendant would come from David's "own body" (7:12a).

   b. Yahweh would "establish his kingdom" (7:12b).

   c. The descendant would "build a house" for Yahweh's "name" (7:13a).

   d. Yahweh would "secure … his kingdom forever" (7:13b).

   e. The descendant would be Yahweh's son, and Yahweh would be his Father—and would discipline him as a father would (7:14).

   f. Yahweh would not remove his "favor" from the descendant as he had from Saul (7:15).

4. David's "house," "kingdom," and "throne" would last forever (7:16).

The first of these promises is that David would have "a great name" (שֵׁם גָּדוֹל, 7:9b). There are only three great names in the OT: Yahweh, Abraham, and David.[33] At his call from Haran, Abram was promised a great name (Gen 12:2). The promise to David of an everlasting kingdom is similar to the promise to Abram that he would be a father of kings (Gen 17:6). This promise was associated with the changing of Abram's name to Abraham (Gen 17:5), the name by which he would be known henceforth. The great patriarch of Israel was also promised a descendant who would do the royal work of conquering the gates of his enemies and through whom all the nations of the earth would be blessed.[34]

In addition, the promise to Abraham included the land of Canaan for the people of Israel (Gen 12:7; 15:7, 18), a promise reiterated to David (2 Sam

---

[32] The fact that David in the tenth century BC still faced enemies of Israel shows that God had not completely cut off the nation's foes. The history of Israel since its conquest (ca. 1400 BC) and settlement in the land included conflicts with the native Canaanite inhabitants, whom Israel had not completely extirpated (e.g., the Jebusites mentioned in 5:6), as well as attacks from surrounding peoples. See the books of Joshua and Judges.

[33] For Yahweh's great name, see Josh 7:9; 1 Sam 12:22; 2 Sam 7:26; 1 Ki 8:42; Jer 10:6; 44:26; Ezek 36:23; Mal 1:11; Pss 76:2 (ET 76:1); 99:3; 138:2; 1 Chr 17:24; 2 Chr 6:32. These passages connect the noun "name" (שֵׁם) with either the verb גָּדַל, "become great," or its cognate adjective גָּדוֹל, "great."

[34] Gen 22:17b–18; see also Gen 12:2–3; 18:18; 26:3–4; 28:14. While many understand the noun זֶרַע, "seed, descendant," to be a collective that refers to Abraham's descendants in general, the grammar of Gen 22:17b–18 indicates that in that part of the passage it is to be understood as referring to a specific descendant. See Alexander, "Further Observations on the Term 'Seed' in Genesis." Alexander's work builds upon Collins, "A Syntactical Note (Genesis 3:15)."

7:10). It is impossible to escape the conclusion that David had been designated Abraham's heir and had received the promises first given to the patriarch.[35]

Genesis traces the promise made to Abraham as it was transmitted first to Isaac and then to Jacob. In Jacob's deathbed prophecy to his sons (Gen 49:1–28), the royal promise was granted to Judah, David's ancestor (Gen 49:8–12). Thus, David was being granted a "great name" (2 Sam 7:9b) as well as an everlasting "house," "throne," and "kingdom" (7:16). This entailed the messianic promise.

The next promise was that Yahweh would "appoint a place" for Israel and "plant" them there (7:10–11a). This also was part of God's promise to Abraham: to give him the land of Canaan.[36] This had already been partially fulfilled since the days of Israel's conquest of the land under Joshua. However, it would not be completely fulfilled until God chose a place to put his name and to dwell there (Deut 12:4–7). Yahweh would fulfill this promise by delivering Israel and David from oppressors and enemies and by the construction of a house for his name by David's descendant (cf. 2 Sam 7:12–13). With the coming of the ark to Jerusalem, God had already begun the final steps in keeping the promise concerning the land of Canaan, and it was logical that David wanted to complete it by building a temple for the ark that bore God's name (cf. 6:2; 7:1–2). Eschatologically, the prophets looked even farther ahead to the permanent home of all God's people in the new Jerusalem in the new heavens and new earth.[37]

The third promise is the longest (7:11b–15). It concerns God making a "house" for David. The multivalent Hebrew word בַּיִת, "house," can refer to an extended family or household (7:18; see also, e.g., 1 Sam 1:21; 2 Sam 6:11–12), a family domicile (e.g., 1 Sam 1:19), the tabernacle (1 Sam 1:7) or a temple (2 Sam 7:5, 6, 7, 13; 1 Ki 6:1–38) as God's house, or a royal palace (2 Sam 7:1–2; see also 1 Sam 18:10), but the contextual emphasis here is on another of its meanings, a royal dynasty (7:11, 16, 19, 25, 26, 27, 29; see also, e.g., 1 Sam 20:15–16; 2 Sam 3:1; 23:5; so used by Solomon in 1 Ki 2:24). The play on it is also evident in the English word "house." David wanted to build God a house—a building in which to dwell—but instead God would build David a house—a dynasty (7:11b).

The following words about a descendant of David who would come from David's body (7:12–15) have often been understood by Christians as a direct prophecy that is fulfilled in Jesus and only by him, with no earlier, partial,

---

[35] David was a biological descendant of Abraham and, through God's prophetic Word, he became the heir of the Abrahamic promises. According to the NT, baptized believers in Jesus Christ (who is the Seed and the Son of David) are the heirs of the Abrahamic promises. See Gal 3:26–29; Titus 3:5–7; see also Romans 4; 8:17; Gal 3:6–18, 22; Eph 3:6.

[36] Gen 12:7; 13:14–17; 15:7, 18–21; 17:8; cf. Gen 26:3–4; 28:13; 35:12.

[37] See, e.g., Is 2:2–4; 65:17–25; Ezekiel 40–48 ("and the name of the city henceforth will be "Yahweh Is There," Ezek 48:35); Amos 9:11–15 ("I will plant them on their land," Amos 9:15). See also Gal 4:26; Heb 12:22; Rev 3:12; 21:1–22:21. In fulfillment of the prophecy of Jeremiah (Jer 3:16), this city has no need for the ark or for a temple (Rev 21:22).

typological fulfillment.[38] There are several problems with this interpretation however. First of all, 7:12–15 does not, on its surface, speak of a messianic king who would arise only centuries later. The prophecy is about someone who would come from David's "body" or "internal organs" (מֵעִים; see the fourth textual note on 7:12a). Elsewhere, when this term is used for procreation, the descendant who comes from or is already in someone's "body" is always an immediate descendant in the next generation.[39] Second, the promise that this descendant would "build a house" for God's "name" (7:13) is a clear reference to the temple David wished to build (7:1–3) and which Solomon actually built.[40] Third and most important, this descendant of David would sin and be disciplined, though God promised never to take his favor from him (2 Sam 7:14b–15).[41] This can hardly be a straightforward description of the Messiah, who commits no sin (e.g., Is 53:9b).[42] In the parallel verse 1 Chr 17:13 the Chronicler omits the material concerning the descendant's sin and God's disciplining of him. This may indicate that the Chronicler understood this prophecy to be a reference to Solomon, since he omits any reference to Solomon's sin of idolatry and its

---

[38] The following early church fathers speak of the fulfillment of this prophecy only in Christ: Justin Martyr (c. AD 100–165), *Dialogue with Trypho, a Jew*, 118 (*ANF* 1:258); Tertullian (c. AD 160–c. 225), *The Five Books against Marcion*, 3.20 (*ANF* 3:339); Lactantius (c. AD 250–c. 325), *The Divine Institutes*, 4.13 (*ANF* 7:113); Augustine of Hippo (AD 354–430), *The City of God*, 17.8 (*NPNF*[1] 2:348–49). However, elsewhere Augustine appears to take these prophecies as pertaining to Solomon as a type of Christ (*On Christian Doctrine*, 3.34 [*NPNF*[1] 2:570]). For a contemporary Christian interpretation that applies these words directly to Jesus, see Bergen, *1, 2, Samuel*, 337–38, 340–41.

[39] Gen 15:4; 25:23; 2 Sam 16:11; Is 49:1; Ps 71:6; Ruth 1:11; 2 Chr 32:21. The only possible exception is Is 48:19, which speaks of the descendants of Israel through Judah who would be captives in Babylon (Is 48:20). However, this may be understood in one of two ways. First, it may be speaking about the loss of a potential blessing in a large generation that theoretically could have followed the one that was instead taken into captivity. Or, second, it may be hyperbolic and apply an expression to multiple future generations even though the expression ordinarily applies to the next generation. Whichever interpretation one chooses, it is instructive to note that shortly after this statement, the prophet returns in Is 49:1 to normal usage of this idiom: the Suffering Servant declares that when he was still in his mother's "womb" (בֶּטֶן) and "body" (מֵעִים, as in 2 Sam 7:12), Yahweh had already called him to his mission.

[40] 1 Kings 5–8 records how Solomon built the temple and consecrated it. The first eight chapters of 1 Kings include many allusions to 2 Samuel 7. For example, in 1 Ki 5:17–19 (ET 5:3–5), Solomon refers to 2 Sam 7:1–13. Compare 2 Sam 7:12 to 1 Ki 2:10. See also Acts 7:47.

[41] Augustine, who earlier applied this passage (7:8–16) to Jesus (*The City of God*, 17.8 [*NPNF*[1] 2:348–49]), noted that this statement (7:14b–15) is more readily taken as applying to Solomon (*The City of God*, 17.9 [*NPNF*[1] 2:349]).

[42] One might argue that 2 Sam 7:14 depicts the Messiah in that Jesus would be accounted sinful and bear the sin of others (Is 53:4–6; Mt 8:17; 2 Cor 5:21; Heb 9:28; 1 Pet 2:21, 24; 3:18). However, if Nathan's prophecy did refer to the vicarious atonement of Christ unambiguously, and not to Solomon's iniquity, one might expect forensic wording such as the expression "to impute/reckon iniquity to" him (e.g., חָשַׁב עָוֹן לְ, 2 Sam 19:20a [ET 19:19a]), that is, to deem or consider him to be sinful, instead of the verb "when he commits iniquity" or "does wrong" (בְּהַעֲוֺתוֹ); see the second textual note on 7:14. While some NT passages depict Solomon as a type of Christ (Mt 12:42; Lk 11:31; cf. Mt 6:29; Lk 12:27), it is difficult to construe 2 Sam 7:12–14 as having been understood by David as a description of the Messiah alone.

consequences.[43] Moreover, the Chronicler quotes David as identifying Solomon as this promised descendant: "He [Yahweh] said to me [David], 'Your son *Solomon* will build my house and my courtyards, because I have chosen him *to be my son, and I will be his Father*' " (1 Chr 28:6; cf. 2 Sam 7:14; 1 Chr 17:13).

God would establish Solomon's kingdom, ensuring David a dynasty (2 Sam 7:12; 1 Ki 2:12, 46). That this prophecy of Solomon looks beyond that son of David to Jesus is evident from the statement "I will secure the throne of his kingdom forever" (2 Sam 7:13; see Dan 7:13–14). The language in 2 Sam 7:14, "I will be(come) his Father, and he will be(come) my son,"[44] can be understood as a promise that God would adopt David's future son Solomon as God's own son and chosen king (1 Kings 1–2), but his reign would end (1 Ki 11:11, 42–43). However, the Messiah was not adopted and did not "become" the Son of God at some point in history. Rather, he is and has always been God's begotten Son, from eternity past and for eternity to come, and his reign has no end (Is 9:6 [ET 9:7]; Lk 1:32–33; Rev 11:15). See the quotations of Ps 2:7 in Acts 13:33; Heb 1:5; 5:5, and the language of the Niceno-Constantinopolitan Creed, "the only-begotten Son of God, begotten from the Father before all ages."[45]

David's son Solomon would be disciplined when he sinned (2 Sam 7:14; see 1 Ki 11:1–40). However, Yahweh also promised that the sin of David's descendant would not cause him to lose divine favor as Saul had lost it by his apostasy with the result that his dynasty was terminated (2 Sam 7:15).[46] This promise looks beyond Solomon to the Messiah, the sinless Son of God upon whom God's favor rested in perpetuity and who would by his vicarious atonement enable that gracious favor to rest upon all baptized believers in him.[47] In Ps 132:17–18 the psalmist notes that God, as he had promised, would always remember his messianic pledge to David (despite Solomon's sin). This is emphasized in 1 Ki 11:36 in Ahijah's prophecy to Jeroboam: "But I will give one tribe to his son [i.e., Solomon's son Rehoboam], *so that there will always be a lamp for my servant David in my presence in Jerusalem*, the city I chose for myself in order to put my name there." This promise of a lamp is messianic and is referenced two more times at junctures where either the writer of Kings or the Chronicler notes that, despite the sins of the kings of Judah, God maintained David's house so

---

43 The Chronicler concludes his account of Solomon with a note that further material about him can be found in other sources, including the record written by the prophet Nathan (2 Chr 9:29–31). The Chronicler never mentions Solomon's marriages to pagan wives and his resultant lapse into gross idolatry as recorded in 1 Kings 11.

44 See the first textual note on 7:14.

45 For the Niceno-Constantinopolitan Creed, see Kelly, *Early Christian Creeds*, 296–305.

46 See 1 Sam 13:13; 15:23–16:1; 16:14; 18:12; 26:21; 28:15–16. Saul's disobedience to the prophetic Word of God began as soon as he was anointed king. See the commentary on 1 Sam 10:7–8 and figure 16, "Saul's Faltering Accession," in "Samuel Anoints Saul (9:26–10:8)" in the commentary on 1 Sam 9:26–10:16, as well as the beginning of the commentary on 1 Sam 10:17–27a (Steinmann, *1 Samuel*, 196–98, 203).

47 See, e.g., Jn 1:14–17; Rom 3:21–26; Eph 1:2–14; Titus 3:5–7; Heb 2:9; 4:16.

that David would have a lamp (1 Ki 15:4; 2 Ki 8:19 ‖ 2 Chr 21:7). The psalmist connects this lamp with the Messiah, God's Anointed One, who would be the King to come from David's line.

The fourth and final promise to David (7:16) flows out of the steadfastness of God's promise of favor that would not depart from David's dynasty, which starts with Solomon. David would have an enduring, eternal house, kingdom, and throne. This is a prophecy about the nature of the Messiah's kingdom.[48] The messianic significance of Nathan's prophecy is expounded by Ethan the Ezrahite in Psalm 89 (especially Ps 89:5, 30, 37–38 [ET 89:4, 29, 36–37]). The permanence of the Davidic kingdom signifies the eternal reign of the Son of David, Jesus Christ, on his throne.[49] As such, 2 Sam 7:16 is explicitly connected to the Messiah via earlier promises of his royal reign such as Gen 49:8–12 and Num 24:17.[50]

Following Yahweh's oracle to Nathan, the author quickly notes that Nathan did as he was instructed: he told David what Yahweh had said (2 Sam 7:17). Interestingly, the words of Yahweh to Nathan are said to have come in a "vision" (see the second textual note on 7:17).

David's Prayer of Thanksgiving (2 Sam 7:18–29)

Parallel: 2 Sam 7:18–27 ‖ 1 Chr 17:16–27

David's immediate reaction to God's promises was to respond with a prayer of thanks and praise to Yahweh (7:18). We are told that he "sat before Yahweh," apparently approaching, if not entering, the tent where the ark was housed. Just as Yahweh had begun his oracle to David with a rhetorical question (7:5), so David began his prayer to Yahweh with one: who was he and what was his house to deserve this favor from God? (7:18). Like God's questions, this one also anticipated a negative answer: David and his house did not deserve such lavish grace. His humble gratitude is comparable to that expressed by Elizabeth in a similar rhetorical question when she was visited by her cousin Mary, pregnant with Jesus in her womb: "whence is it given to me that the mother of my Lord should come to me?" (Lk 1:43). No one deserves a family connection to

---

[48] The Messiah's kingdom is eternal (see, e.g., Lk 1:32–33; Heb 1:8). See the abundant teaching about the kingdom of God/heaven in the Gospels.

[49] Is 9:5–6 (ET 9:6–7); 16:5; Lk 1:32–33; cf. the quotation of Ps 45:7 (ET 45:6) in Heb 1:8.

[50] This is especially possible if "Shiloh" in Gen 49:10 (either the Qere שִׁילוֹ or the Kethib שִׁילֹה) is understood as meaning "the one to whom it [the kingdom] belongs" (see HCSB, NET; cf. the LXX: ἕως ἂν ἔλθῃ τὰ ἀποκείμενα αὐτῷ, "until there comes the things stored up for him"). The Hebrew for "Shiloh" may be a combination of the relative pronoun (אֲשֶׁר or שֶׁ-), "who," and preposition לְ in the sense of possession, "belonging to," with a third masculine singular pronominal suffix (וֹ- or הֹ-), thus "who possesses it [the kingdom]" or "to whom it belongs." See the Hebrew wording אֲשֶׁר־לוֹ, "to whom it belongs," in Ezek 21:32 (ET 21:27), where God speaks of a coming one to whom the kingdom belongs and to whom he will give "justice" or "the right" to reign: "until he comes to whom the right belongs, and I [God] will give it [to him]" or "… give [it] to him" (עַד־בֹּא אֲשֶׁר־לוֹ הַמִּשְׁפָּט וּנְתַתִּיו).

Christ, yet all are invited to receive him as their King and thereby become children of God.

David then stated that it was a small thing for Yahweh to bring him to this point (7:19). His title for God is "my Lord Yahweh" (אֲדֹנָי יְהוִה), which, in the book of Samuel, appears only in this prayer (7:18–20, 22, 28–29). This is the first hint that David understood that he had become the heir of the messianic promise first given to Abraham, because this title was first used by Israel's great patriarch as he appealed to God to keep his promise to him (Gen 15:2, 8).[51]

David then expanded on the messianic promise in two ways: he noted that Yahweh had spoken about the royal house of the Judean king for a long time to come—that is, until its culmination in the Messiah—and he noted that this was "the teaching about the man" (2 Sam 7:19). "Teaching" translates the noun תּוֹרָה, *torah*, which is often translated as "law," but has its derivation in the verb יָרָה, which in the Hiphil (H) can mean "teach, instruct."[52] Here David acknowledged that God was teaching him about the Messiah, "the man" (הָאָדָם), and the Messiah's eternal kingdom. Some have proposed that "the man" (הָאָדָם) ought to be understood as a collective here, "mankind." However, besides the technical exegetical difficulties this presents, it ought also to be noted that even though the promised Messiah would procure salvation for all humanity, in context David was not stressing the promise's universal benefits. David, instead, focused on the benefits for Israel (7:23–24) and for David's house (7:25–29). He also connected God's name, "Yahweh," and his title, "my Lord Yahweh," with Israel by calling him "the God over/of Israel" (7:26, 27; see also "their God" in 7:24). Therefore, David was not speaking generally about God's teaching for הָאָדָם in the sense of "humanity," but specifically regarding God's teaching about הָאָדָם in the sense of "the man," the Messiah, who would come to save all humanity.[53] See further the excursus "הָאָדָם as 'the Man' in 2 Samuel 7:19 and 1 Chronicles 17:17" following this pericope.

Next David noted that he could not say anything in reply that would praise and thank Yahweh adequately or make Yahweh more favorable to him (7:20). Instead, Yahweh had acted according to his Word and desire in order to reveal his truth to David (7:21). The author of Samuel has then recorded this truth to be proclaimed to and for all.

David then affirmed God's greatness and uniqueness—there is no God like him; indeed, there is no other god at all (see the textual note on 7:22). David exclaimed on behalf of his fellow Israelites, "We have heard [this] with our

---

[51] See further the textual note on 7:18.

[52] See *DCH*, s.v. ירה III, Hiphil; *HALOT*, s.v. ירה III, Hiphil.

[53] The patriarchal promises emphasized that God's blessing would come through the Seed of Abraham to benefit all peoples on the earth, that is, all humanity (Gen 12:3; 18:18; 22:18; 26:4; 28:14). See also the first Gospel promise, in Gen 3:15, that the Seed of Eve would crush the serpent's head (for the sake of all the descendants of Adam and Eve), and, after the universal flood, the covenant with Noah that encompasses all his descendants, that is, all surviving humanity (Gen 9:9–17).

own ears" as they had listened to the words of Moses repeated to them (cf. Deut 7:7–8; 9:26; 13:6 [ET 13:5]; 15:15; 24:18). Like their God, Israel was also unique in that God had redeemed them from Egypt and had driven out nations before them (2 Sam 7:23). Thus, Israel became God's people, and he was their God (7:23).

David continued by making the first of two requests of Yahweh (7:25–27), both of them based on the promises given through Nathan. First, David asked God to fulfill his Word by establishing David's house forever (7:25). He made this request not so that he would be glorified but so that God would have a great name (7:26). Although Yahweh had promised David a great name (7:9), the response of faith is to ascribe all glory to God for the sake of his name. The specific name that David used for Yahweh, "Yahweh of armies, God over/of Israel" (7:26–27), emphasizes God's awesome deeds of judgment and salvation, especially his victory over Egypt and his driving out of the pagan Canaanite nations (see 7:23). David also confessed that his courage to ask this was based on God's promise (7:27).

David's second request built on the first: because God's "words are truth" (see the second textual note on 7:28)—and because he had spoken that truth to David in "this good [promise]" (7:28)—David asked for a general blessing on his house, a blessing that would be forever (7:29). This was a less specific request but encompassed all that had been promised.[54]

David, like the faithful of all eras, prayed for the fulfillment of Yahweh's promises. This is proper, for it fixes the hopes of the petitioner on the trustworthiness, faithfulness, and grace of God according to his Word. In a similar way, Jesus taught his disciples to pray for God to continue to be true to his nature and to fulfill his promises—for God's name to be holy, for his kingdom to come, for his will to be done, for daily bread, and for deliverance from temptation and from the evil one (Mt 6:9–13; Lk 11:2–4). As David confidently anticipated the advent of his greater Son and Lord (Ps 110:1), even so the constant prayer of the church is for his return: "maranatha" (1 Cor 16:22); "amen; come, Lord Jesus" (Rev 22:20).

---

[54] See the first and second textual notes on 7:29.

הָאָדָם as "the Man" in 2 Samuel 7:19 and 1 Chronicles 17:17[1]

That the definite noun הָאָדָם (and also without the article, אָדָם) is often used as a collective, "mankind," is beyond dispute.[2] However, הָאָדָם can at times also refer to a specific individual, "the man."[3] The difference is critical here. If וְזֹאת תּוֹרַת הָאָדָם in 2 Sam 7:19 is to be understood as "(and) this is the teaching for humankind,"[4] then David's response to God would be less directly messianic. However, if this clause is to be understood as "(and) this is the teaching about *the* man," then David was telling God that he understood that Nathan's prophecy entailed the promise that David would be the ancestor of the Messiah. This would make a strong case that 2 Sam 7:19 is the source of subsequent identifications in the prophets and in the NT of the Messiah as the Son of David. Even if uncertainties remain about the exact meaning of this clause and the more challenging clause in the parallel verse 1 Chr 17:17, the chapter as a whole is a clear prophecy that the eternal kingdom of God will be established and ruled by a King from the line of David.

1 Chronicles 17:17

What can arbitrate between the two possible uses of הָאָדָם? A close look at the Chronicler's parallel to 2 Sam 7:19 in 1 Chr 17:17 is in order. David's words in 1 Chr 17:17 are below. The underlined Hebrew words are also in 2 Sam 7:19. The translation includes two ellipses, marking the words כְּתוֹר and הַמַּעֲלָה, respectively, each of which will be discussed below:[5]

---

[1] This excursus is adapted from Steinmann, "What Did David Understand about the Promises in the Davidic Covenant?" 23–27.

[2] The most common use of הָאָדָם is for "mankind" or "humanity." This includes its frequent use in the construct phrase בְּנֵי הָאָדָם, "the sons of men." See הָאָדָם by itself in, for example, Gen 6:1, 2, 4, 5, 6, 7; 7:21; 8:21; 9:5, 6; 11:5; Ex 9:9, 19, 22; 33:20; Lev 5:4; 5:22 (ET 6:3); 27:29; Num 12:3; 18:15; 31:28, 30, 47; Deut 5:24; 8:3; 20:19; Josh 11:14; Judg 16:7, 11, 17; 1 Sam 16:7; 26:19; 1 Ki 5:11 (ET 4:31); 8:38, 39; Is 2:17, 20, 22; 6:12; 17:7; Jer 4:25; 7:20; 9:21 (ET 9:22); 21:6; 27:5; 47:2; Ezek 4:12, 15; 38:20; Jonah 3:7–8; Zeph 1:3; Hag 1:11; Zech 8:10; 11:6; Pss 104:14; 116:11; Job 7:20; Prov 27:20; Eccl 3:11, 13; 5:18; 7:2, 29; 8:6, 17; 9:1; 2 Chr 6:18, 29; 32:19. See בְּנֵי הָאָדָם, "the sons of men," in, for example, Ps 33:13; Eccl 1:13; 2:3, 8; 3:10, 18, 19, 21; 8:11; 9:3, 12; 2 Chr 6:30.

[3] Lev 18:5; Num 19:13; Josh 14:15; Jer 31:30; Ezek 20:11, 13, 21; Prov 27:19; Eccl 2:12; 3:22; 6:7; 7:14; 8:9; 10:14; 11:8. To these could be added the first occurrence in Eccl 9:12, as well as the places where it refers to Adam (Gen 1:27; 2:7, 8, 15, 16, 18, 19, 20, 21, 22, 23, 25; 3:8, 9, 12, 20, 22, 24).

[4] E.g., Beecher, *The Prophets and the Promise*, 237, translates 2 Sam 7:19 as "this being the *torah* of mankind."

[5] See "Proposals for the Meaning of כְּתוֹר and הַמַּעֲלָה" below.

וַתִּקְטַ֤ן זֹאת֙ בְּעֵינֶ֣יךָ֙ אֱלֹהִ֔ים וַתְּדַבֵּ֗ר עַל־בֵּית־עַבְדְּךָ֖ לְמֵרָח֑וֹק
וּרְאִיתַ֛נִי כְּת֥וֹר הָאָדָ֖ם הַֽמַּעֲלָ֑ה יְהוָ֥ה אֱלֹהִֽים׃

And this was a small thing in your eyes, O God, and you have spoken about
your servant's house for a long while to come. So you have seen me according to the … of mankind/the man … , O Yahweh God.

This makes 1 Chr 17:17 somewhat different from 2 Sam 7:19. However, a
number of the differences are minor:

- The Chronicler omits עוֹד, "yet," and גַם, "also."
- The Chronicler's first vocative is אֱלֹהִים , "O God," as compared to אֲדֹנָי יְהוִה, "my
  Lord Yahweh," in 2 Sam 7:19.
- The preposition עַל, "about," is substituted for אֶל, "about," as is common in cer-
  tain biblical books.[6]
- The Chronicler's second vocative is יְהוָה אֱלֹהִים, "O Yahweh God," as compared
  to אֲדֹנָי יְהוִה, "my Lord Yahweh," in 2 Sam 7:19.[7]

The major difference is found in the second half of the verse, which has
proved notoriously difficult—so much so that some interpreters have simply
labeled the passage corrupt or impossible to understand.[8] Only one word in
1 Chr 17:17b is identical to a word in 2 Sam 7:19: הָאָדָם, "the man." Yet, while
1 Chr 17:17b is difficult, it is not beyond comprehension.

In place of וְזֹאת, "(and) this," in 2 Sam 7:19, the Chronicler has וּרְאִיתַנִי, literally "and you saw me" (the second masculine singular Qal [G] perfect of רָאָה
with a first common singular pronominal suffix). This is not difficult, though
some have sought to emend it to וַתִּרְאֵנִי, the second masculine singular Hiphil
(H) preterite (imperfect with *waw* consecutive) of רָאָה with a first common
singular object suffix, meaning "and you have shown me."[9] This emendation, however, is based on conjecture alone and ought, therefore, to be rejected.

Proposals for the Meaning of כְּתוֹר and הַמַּעֲלָה in 1 Chr 17:17

At least five interpretive options are possible for the phrase in 1 Chr 17:17
with the two difficult words: כְּתוֹר הָאָדָם הַמַּעֲלָה. First, the initial word כְּתוֹר

---

[6] The substitution of עַל for אֶל is common in Samuel, Kings, Jeremiah, and Ezekiel and can
be found in other books. See the first textual note on 2:9 and the second textual note on 3:29,
as well as BDB, s.v. אֶל, note 2.

[7] Throughout the OT, the Masoretes pointed the title that is in 2 Sam 7:19, אֲדֹנָי יְהוִה ("my Lord
Yahweh"), so that it is to be pronounced *ʾadonai ʾelohim*, "my Lord God." The Masoretes
pointed the title that is in 1 Chr 17:17 as יְהוָה אֱלֹהִים, which also is to be pronounced *ʾadonai
ʾelohim*, "my Lord God," the same as the pronunciation of the title in 2 Sam 7:19. See the first
textual note on 7:18.

[8] Curtis and Madsen, *The Books of Chronicles*, 229; Ackroyd, *I and II Chronicles, Ezra,
Nehemiah*, 68; Williamson, *1 and 2 Chronicles*, 137; Braun, *1 Chronicles*, 197; Thompson,
1, 2 Chronicles, 149.

[9] Wellhausen, *Der Text der Bücher Samuelis untersucht*, 172; see also Knoppers, *1 Chronicles
10–29*, 678; Klein, *1 Chronicles*, 371, 373; ESV.

never appears elsewhere in the OT.[10] Some take it to be the preposition כְּ, "as, like," plus the masculine noun תּוֹר, meaning "a turn." The noun תּוֹר is used in Song 1:10–11, apparently for a turning or braiding of hair, or perhaps for jewelry.[11] It also occurs in Esth 2:12, 15, where it has the sense of an opportunity, when the "turn" came for each young woman (one per evening), including Esther, to visit the king.[12] In 1 Chr 17:17 the phrase כְּתוֹר הָאָדָם הַמַּעֲלָה is often interpreted to mean "the turn of mankind to come," that is, "the generation to come."[13] This interpretation suffers from at least three weaknesses. First, for this to make sense in the context, proponents of this interpretation often advocate the emendation of the preceding verb.[14] Second, while the noun תּוֹר can refer to a "turn" for an individual to do something in the near future, in no other passage is it used with "mankind" or for a generation to be born later. Third, the second difficult word, מַעֲלָה, is not used elsewhere for an upcoming event or era, and it is feminine, whereas תּוֹר is masculine.[15]

A second option is to understand תּוֹר as a postexilic form of the masculine noun תֹּאַר, "form, appearance, stature," which is used elsewhere in Samuel.[16] If so, the א in תֹּאַר became quiescent, leaving only the vowel *holem* (-תֹ), for which the *waw* was supplied as a vowel letter (-תּוֹ).[17] In this case David would

---

[10] The feminine noun תּוֹר or תֹּר, "turtledove," is common in the OT, but it is never used with the preposition כְּ and would make little sense in the context here. The word כְּתוֹרִין appears in the Aramaic portion of Daniel (Dan 4:22, 29, 30 [ET 4:25, 32, 33]; 5:21). It is the preposition כְּ with the plural of the noun תּוֹר, "bull, ox" (cognate to the Hebrew שׁוֹר), meaning "like oxen," but that too would be nonsensical here. The Qal (G) infinitive construct of the verb תּוּר, "to spy," is vocalized תּוּר and is never used with the preposition כְּ.

[11] See the discussion of the possible meanings of the noun תּוֹר in Song 1:10–11 in Mitchell, *The Song of Songs*, 627.

[12] See also תּוֹר in Rabbinic Hebrew, meaning a "turn, order" in which words of the Law are read or a "string, twist" (Jastrow, s.v. תּוֹר I).

[13] McCarter, *II Samuel*, 233. Payne, "1, 2 Chronicles," 396–97, allows that McCarter "may be correct." Wellhausen (*Der Text der Bücher Samuelis untersucht*, 172–73) famously proposed emending the noun כְּתוֹר to דֹּרֹת (the plural of the noun דּוֹר), "generations." He also emended the preceding verb to make the clause וַתַּרְאֵנִי דֹּרֹת, "and you showed me generations," and compared that clause to לְמֵרָחוֹק in 2 Sam 7:19, which this commentary renders "for a long while to come." Wellhausen's emendations are the basis for the RSV translation: "thou … has shown me future generations." McCarter, *II Samuel*, 233, concurs with Wellhausen's emendation of the verb but not with his emendation of the noun. Both emendations are rightly rejected by Japhet, *I and II Chronicles*, 339, as "substantially and orthographically weak."

[14] See the preceding footnote.

[15] The word מַעֲלָה appears as a feminine noun forty-nine times in the OT. It can denote a "stair," with its plural referring to "steps" or a staircase (e.g., Ex 20:26), or an "ascent" (Ezra 7:9). It can be parsed as the feminine singular Hiphil (H) participle of עָלָה, but that would have the causative meaning "to bring [something] up," and it would require a direct object (supplied or implied), for example, "the generation that is bringing [something or someone] up." This would also require תּוֹר, as its subject noun, to be feminine in gender. See further the discussion of הַמַּעֲלָה in the fourth and fifth options below.

[16] In 1 Sam 16:18 תֹּאַר is used in a description of David and is translated as "handsome." In the depiction of Abigail in 1 Sam 25:3, it is translated as "beautiful." Saul used it in his question about the overall "appearance" of the apparition in 1 Sam 28:14.

[17] See Knoppers, *1 Chronicles 10–29*, 677–78.

be describing himself as "like someone of human appearance/stature." This understanding may be supported by LXX 1 Chr 17:17, καὶ ἐπεῖδές με ὡς ὅρασις ἀνθρώπου, "and you have looked at me as (the) sight/visage of a man." However, if תּוֹר in 1 Chr 17:17 is to be understood as a form of תֹּאַר, this would be the only place where the LXX translates תֹּאַר with the Greek noun ὅρασις, "sight, vision, appearance"; elsewhere the LXX translates תֹּאַר with other Greek words.[18] This suggestion for the Hebrew founders for lack of evidence that the א was ever omitted in the noun תֹּאַר in the OT era.[19] This second option, like the first one, also suffers from the lack of concord between the masculine gender of the noun (תּוֹר or תֹּאַר) and the feminine form of מַעֲלָה.

A third option is to take כְּתוֹר הָאָדָם הַמַּעֲלָה as a three-word construct chain and to translate 1 Chr 17:17b as something like "and you have regarded me as a man of high degree"[20] or "and you have looked upon me as a man embarked on a high career."[21] This is grammatically suspect, however, because of the definite article on הָאָדָם. Those translations ignore the article, and, moreover, normally a noun in the construct state cannot have the definite article.[22]

A fourth option is to follow the reading found in 1 Chr 17:17 in a few Masoretic manuscripts, בְּתוֹךְ, "in the midst of," in place of כְּתוֹר. This reading is a common phrase, the preposition בְּ prefixed to the noun תָּוֶךְ in construct. If the original reading was בְּתוֹךְ, then כְּתוֹר may have arisen due to a double graphic confusion: כ for ב and ר for ך. In this case, the original reading in 1 Chr 17:17 might have been וּרְאִיתַנִי בְּתוֹךְ הָאָדָם, "and you have seen me in the midst of mankind" or perhaps "and you have seen my humanity." However, this reading has little else to commend it, since the following difficult word, הַמַּעֲלָה, becomes inexplicable. The LXX translator of 1 Chr 17:17 apparently read the unpointed word המעלה as הַמַּעֲלֶה, the masculine singular Hiphil (H) participle of עָלָה with the definite article,[23] and rendered it as καὶ ὕψωσάς με, "and you exalted me." The pointing of this word as הַמַּעֲלֶה, supported by the LXX, is attractive and is adopted in this commentary (see further below). However, the Greek pronoun με, "me," which is the direct object in LXX 1 Chr 17:17, lacks any Hebrew counterpart. There is, therefore, little to recommend this option,

---

[18] See the various Greek expressions used by the LXX to translate תֹּאַר in Muraoka, *Hebrew/ Aramaic Index to the Septuagint*, 156. Muraoka notes that 1 Chr 17:17 is the only place where the LXX uses ὅρασις.

[19] In the OT תֹּאַר occurs fifteen times, always with this same spelling.

[20] See Slotki, *Chronicles*, 100. See also the Jewish Publication Society Tanakh translation, quoted with general approval by Japhet, *I and II Chronicles*, 339.

[21] See Coggins, *The First and Second Books of the Chronicles*, 95. Similar is NEB, "and now thou lookest upon me as a man already embarked on a high career," which is cited favorably by Japhet, *I and II Chronicles*, 339.

[22] See Joüon, §§ 129 a, 140 c.

[23] The word as pointed in the MT, הַמַּעֲלֶה, could be the corresponding feminine form of that Hiphil (H) participle.

and even the reading בְּתוֹךְ is suspicious, since it appears to substitute this common prepositional phrase[24] for a unique one.

A fifth option is to understand כְּתוֹר as כְּתוֹרַת־, "according to the teaching of," the preposition כְּ prefixed to the feminine noun תּוֹרָה, *torah*, in construct. 2 Sam 7:19 has that word in construct (תּוֹרַת), but without a preposition. Thus, כְּתוֹר would be either an apocopated form of כְּתוֹרַת־ or simply a scribal error where the final ת was accidently omitted. While this option relies either on an unattested apocopation or an unsubstantiated scribal mistake, it has one important advantage over the other options: it aligns nicely with the reading in 2 Sam 7:19, making 1 Chr 17:17 an interpretive paraphrase of David's words there. This option is endorsed by several evangelical commentators, following the lead of Kaiser, who appealed to Beecher's translation of כְּתוֹר הָאָדָם הַמַּעֲלָה as "according to the upbringing law [*torah*] of mankind"[25] or "elevating *torah* of mankind."[26] Kaiser elaborates on this, suggesting that it means something like "according to the elevating charter of mankind."[27] This option is superior to the first two options regarding grammatical gender: if the word כְּתוֹר stands for כְּתוֹרַת־, then the noun is feminine in gender, which agrees with the feminine form of הַמַּעֲלָה. This option also explains the definite article on הַמַּעֲלָה: the noun is definite ("the law/charter") because it is in construct with a definite noun (הָאָדָם, "the man/mankind"), and so הַמַּעֲלָה, as its modifier, has the definite article.

Yet some questions remain. The interpretations of Beecher and Kaiser understand הַמַּעֲלָה as a Hiphil (H) feminine singular participle, used adjectivally and modifying תוֹר or תוֹרַת־, thus, 1 Chr 17:17 refers to "the upbringing *torah* of mankind."[28] The verb עָלָה is transitive in the Hiphil (H), and they apparently understand its direct object to be an implied repetition of the preceding *nomen rectum* in the construct phrase, הָאָדָם, "mankind." Elsewhere in the OT, Hiphil (H) participles of עָלָה usually have an explicit direct object

---

[24] The phrase בְּתוֹךְ appears over three hundred times in the OT.

[25] Beecher, "Three Notes," 138. He considers תוֹר to be a form of תּוֹרָה, *torah*. He explains that throughout the OT תּוֹרָה regularly refers to "divine law" and that " 'the upbringing law of mankind' naturally means (by a usage of עלה familiar to the later Old Testament writings) Jehovah's law for the uplifting or the exalting of mankind." Beecher, *The Prophets and the Promise*, 229–40, interprets the promise in 2 Samuel 7 as a continuation of God's promises to the patriarchs that through Abraham and his seed all the nations of the earth would be blessed. He maintains that the promise to David was mainly a "religious teaching" rather than "a foretelling of the future. Here was a great fact concerning God's relations to men—a truth for the prophets to teach and for the people to feed upon; a truth suitable for purifying and stimulating their loyalty, for controlling their conduct, for the building of character" (240).

[26] Beecher, *The Prophets and the Promise*, 238.

[27] See Kaiser, "The Blessing of David," 314–16.

[28] This is the translation of 1 Chr 17:17 by Beecher, *The Prophets and the Promise*, 237, quoted by Kaiser, "The Blessing of David," 315.

rather than an implied one.[29] Beecher and Kaiser only cryptically explain in what sense the *torah*/charter uplifts, brings up, or elevates.[30] Kaiser appeals to the use of the Hiphil of עָלָה in Ezek 19:3 (וַתַּעַל), where it signifies that a lioness "brought up," "raised," or "trained" one of her cubs.[31] Yet Kaiser does not explore or substantiate how God's Torah accomplishes this action. In what way and through what means does it do this? How does the promise to David about his seed benefit all mankind? Or does one need faith in the promised seed to receive the benefits of the promise? The proposal relies on a denotation of the verb עָלָה that is uncommon.[32] Nevertheless, it is true that its Hiphil can be used for God's salvific actions, such as bringing his people Israel up from Egypt through the exodus redemption (cf. 2 Sam 7:23), and it commonly means "to cause to ascend," so "uplift" or "elevate" are plausible nuances.[33] The evangelical interpretation that 2 Sam 7:19 and 1 Chr 17:17 are ultimately fulfilled in Jesus Christ is certainly to be commended.

Another way to explain this phrase also takes המעלה adjectivally, but repoints it as הַמַּעֲלֶה, following the LXX.[34] The noun הָאָדָם should be understood as denoting a specific man, and וּרְאִיתַנִי כְּתוֹר הָאָדָם הַמַּעֲלֶה should be translated as "and you have viewed me according to the teaching about the ascending man." This would then be a statement by David declaring his understanding that, in making the promise of an everlasting house, kingdom, and

---

[29] Hiphil (H) participles of the verb עָלָה occur in Lev 11:3–6, 26, 45; Deut 4:6–7; 20:1; Josh 24:17; 1 Sam 7:10; 2 Sam 1:24; 6:15; 2 Ki 17:7; Is 8:7; 63:11; 66:3; Jer 2:6; 33:6, 18; 48:35; 50:9; Nah 3:3; Pss 81:11 (ET 81:10); 135:7; Ezra 4:2; 1 Chr 15:28; 2 Chr 24:14. The direct object is explicitly given in the text in all of these passages, with the exception of Jer 48:35 and possibly also Nah 3:3. In Jer 48:35 the context clearly implies that the direct object is the cognate noun עֹלָה, "sacrifice" ("he who offers up sacrifice"). In Nah 3:3 the direct objects could be the following two construct phrases (KJV: "the horseman lifteth up both the bright sword and the glittering spear").

[30] For Beecher, see the beginning of the discussion of the fifth option.

[31] Kaiser, "The Blessing of David," 316. Ezek 19:3 goes on to say that the lioness taught her cub to hunt so that he became a man-eating lion.

[32] BDB, s.v. עָלָה, Hiphil, 3, gives the meaning "train" for the Hiphil of עָלָה in Ezek 19:3, but it is the only verse cited that attests this meaning. The word could also be parsed as the noun מַעֲלָה, but it normally denotes a "step" (plural: "a staircase") or someone's ascent (Ex 20:26; 1 Ki 10:19–20; 2 Ki 9:13; 20:9–11; Is 38:8; Ezek 11:5; 40:6, 22, 26, 31, 34, 37, 49; 43:17; Amos 9:6; Pss 120:1; 121:1; 122:1; 123:1; 124:1; 125:1; 126:1; 127:1; 128:1; 129:1; 130:1; 131:1; 132:1; 133:1; 134:1; Ezra 7:9; Neh 3:15; 12:37; 2 Chr 9:18–19).

[33] For the exodus redemption, see BDB, s.v. עָלָה, Hiphil, 1 a. For "cause to ascend," see BDB, s.v. עָלָה, Hiphil, 1 d, 4, 8. The meaning "exalt" is also attested (BDB, s.v. עָלָה, Hiphil, 7).

[34] This assumes that the Masoretic pointing הַמַּעֲלָה (as a feminine singular noun or participle) is in error and that the pointing should be that of a masculine singular participle, הַמַּעֲלֶה, following LXX 1 Chr 17:17. See the discussion of this in the fourth option above. The lone remaining grammatical issue would be the lack of a direct object for this Hiphil (H) masculine singular participle. Either the Chronicler is assuming an unstated direct object ("the man who is bringing up [something]") or, as assumed here, he is simply blurring the distinction between the Hiphil (H) and the Qal (G) participles of this verbal root, i.e., "the ascending man." In the Qal, עָלָה commonly has a person as its subject and means "go up, ascend ... from low place to high" (BDB, Qal, 1 and 1 a). It can also mean "excel" or "be superior" (BDB, Qal, 10).

throne to David (2 Sam 7:16), God viewed him in light of a future ascending Man—the Messiah, who was crucified and buried, then rose from the dead and ascended into heaven (see Prov 30:4; Jn 3:13; Eph 4:10; see also Luke 23–24; Acts 1). Therefore, since 2 Sam 7:19 is clearly parallel to 1 Chr 17:17, the Chronicler's parallel is his expanded version of David's understanding of the implication of God's words delivered through Nathan.

This leads to the conclusion that both passages are speaking about "*the* man" (both passages include הָאָדָם), the one who would be the fulfillment of the messianic promise. This man, then, is the means through which God accomplishes salvation for all humanity. By his faithful ministry, vicarious death, and glorious resurrection, he procures the forgiveness of sins for mankind. In this way the promise to David benefits all people, not only Israelites, but also Gentiles. To be sure, this does not mean universalism. As David believed this "teaching" (2 Sam 7:19) and rejoiced that God's "words are truth" (2 Sam 7:28), the benefits of this redemption accomplished by his Seed are received by grace alone and through faith alone (see Gen 15:6; Romans 4; Galatians 3). All who believe in the promised Seed are gathered into God's one people, whom he has redeemed for himself (2 Sam 7:23).

Conclusion

While a number of exegetical difficulties surround David's words as recorded in 2 Sam 7:19 and 1 Chr 17:17, on close examination it ought to be concluded that David knew that God had made him the promise that he would be the ancestor of the promised Man to come, the Messiah. As an Israelite who was chosen to be king and whose heart was aligned with God's own heart (compare 1 Sam 13:14 to 2 Sam 7:21), David understood this upon receiving Nathan's words. This, then, is the source that gives rise to the wealth of messianic passages in both the OT and the NT that emphasize that the Messiah/Christ is a descendant of David, the promised Son of David, the King who reigns for eternity.

David's Victories

Translation

8 ¹After this David defeated the Philistines, humbled them, and took Metheg-ammah from Philistine control.

²He defeated Moab. He divided them into portions with a rope, making them lie down on the ground. He measured off two rope lengths to be put to death and one full rope length to be allowed to live. So Moab became David's servants who brought [him] tribute.

³David defeated Hadadezer the son of Rehob, the king of Zobah, when he went to restore his control at the Euphrates River. ⁴David captured a thousand chariots, seven thousand charioteers, and twenty thousand foot soldiers from him. David disabled all except a hundred of the chariot horses. ⁵When the Arameans from Damascus came to assist King Hadadezer of Zobah, David struck down twenty-two thousand Aramean men. ⁶David placed garrisons in the Aramean kingdom of Damascus. So Aram became David's servants who brought [him] tribute.

So Yahweh gave David victory wherever he went.

⁷David took the gold quivers that belonged to Hadadezer's officers and brought them to Jerusalem. ⁸King David took large quantities of bronze from Hadadezer's cities Betah and Berothai.

⁹King Toi of Hamath heard that David had defeated the entire army of Hadadezer, ¹⁰and Toi sent his son Joram to King David to greet him and to bless him because he fought Hadadezer and defeated him, since Hadadezer had often waged war against Toi. Joram brought silver, gold, and bronze items with him. ¹¹King David also dedicated these to Yahweh with the silver and gold that he had dedicated from all the nations that he subdued: ¹²from Aram, from Moab, from the Ammonites, from the Philistines, from Amalek, and from the spoils of Hadadezer the son of Rehob, the king of Zobah.

¹³David made a name [for himself] when he returned from his striking down Edom in the Valley of Salt, (some) eighteen thousand (men). ¹⁴He placed garrisons in Edom; throughout Edom he placed garrisons. All the Edomites became David's servants.

So Yahweh gave David victory wherever he went.

Textual Notes

8:1 וַיַּךְ—"He defeated." This Hiphil (H) third masculine singular preterite (imperfect with *waw* consecutive) of נָכָה recurs in 8:2, 3, 5, and other Hiphil forms of this verb appear in 8:9, 10, 13. It is commonly rendered as "strike (down)," which is appropriate in 8:5 and 8:13, which specify a particular number of soldiers who were killed. In the other verses, "defeat" is more appropriate. See the third textual note on 1 Sam 4:8, which has the Hiphil of נָכָה as well as the cognate noun מַכָּה.[1] Likewise, the noun is sometimes appropriately translated as "a defeat," as in 1 Sam 14:30. In military contexts the Niphal (N) of נָגַף is translated with the corresponding passive meaning, "be defeated." See the textual note on 2 Sam 2:17 and the third textual note on 1 Sam 4:2.[2]

וַיַּכְנִיעֵם—"He humbled them." The Niphal (N) of כָּנַע in 1 Sam 7:13 signified that after being routed with divine intervention the Philistines "were humbled/subdued" so that they could no longer make incursions into Israel. Here the Hiphil (H) has the corresponding active, transitive meaning.

מֶתֶג הָאַמָּה—"Metheg-ammah" is literally "the one-cubit [הָאַמָּה] bridle [מֶתֶג]" or "the forearm bridle." The LXX reads the perfect passive participle τὴν ἀφωρισμένην, "that which was set aside." The parallel verse 1 Chr 18:1 reads גַּת וּבְנֹתֶיהָ, "Gath and its daughters [nearby villages]." While many English versions treat the phrase in 2 Sam 8:1 as an otherwise unknown place-name, "Metheg-ammah," there are many other suggestions as to what it means. Based on the LXX, McCarter suggests that its Vorlage read המגרש, "the common land"[3] (to be pointed הַמִּגְרָשׁ; see מִגְרָשׁ in, e.g., Josh 21:13–19). The Hebrew noun אֵם means "mother," and in 2 Sam 20:19, it refers to a "mother" city, a meaning supported by the Phoenician cognate ʾm, "mother [i.e., chief] city." On that basis some older commentators understood the Hebrew wording here to mean "control of the mother city [i.e., Gath]."[4] Keil understood it to mean "the bridle of the mother," meaning control of the government, that is, that David took control of the Philistine government and exacted tribute.[5] If מֶתֶג הָאַמָּה were a scribal accident with a metathesis of the gimel and taw (מתג in place of מגת), it may have originally read מִגַּת אַמָּה, "from Gath [to] Ammah" (cf. 2:24). If that were the case, then the Chronicler may have substituted "Gath and its villages" (1 Chr 18:1) as an explanation for his readers of a much later era.

מִיַּד פְּלִשְׁתִּים:—"From Philistine control" is literally "from the hand of (the) Philistines." See also יָד in the textual note on 8:3.

8:2 וַיְמַדְּדֵם בַּחֶבֶל ... וַיְמַדֵּד שְׁנֵי־חֲבָלִים—"He divided them into portions with a rope. ... He measured off two rope lengths." The noun חֶבֶל denotes a "rope," "chord," or "line." Here it has the definite article, marked by the patach under the preposition (-בַּ), which is commonly used with terms of measurement (GKC, § 126 n). Both verbs are a Piel (D) third masculine singular preterite (imperfect with waw consecutive) of מָדַד, and the first has a third masculine plural object suffix. In the Qal (G) it means "to measure." In the Piel it signifies "to measure off" a particular length or "to divide, apportion." Its Piel is used similarly in a clause repeated in Ps 60:8 (ET 60:6) and Ps 108:8 (ET 108:7), וְעֵמֶק סֻכּוֹת אֲמַדֵּד, "and I will apportion the Succoth Valley."

הַשְׁכֵּב אוֹתָם אַרְצָה—Literally "making them lie down to the ground." The Hiphil (H) infinitive absolute of שָׁכַב, "lie down," has a causative meaning and describes the

[1] Steinmann, *1 Samuel*, 121.
[2] Steinmann, *1 Samuel*, 119–20.
[3] McCarter, *II Samuel*, 243.
[4] As noted by McCarter, *II Samuel*, 243; see also Keil, *The Books of Samuel*, 356.
[5] Keil, *The Books of Samuel*, 355–56.

circumstances in which the preceding verb ("divided") was accomplished (Joüon, § 123 r).[6]

וּמְלֹא הַחֶבֶל לְהַחֲיוֹת—The noun מָלֹא denotes the "fullness" of something. The Hiphil (H) of חָיָה, "be alive," can have the causative meaning "to make someone alive," that is, to raise the dead (2 Ki 8:1, 5), but it usually has the nuance of "sparing," "preserving," or "keeping" a living person "alive" (e.g., Gen 6:19, 20; 45:7; Josh 2:13; 14:10).

וַתְּהִי מוֹאָב—"So Moab became." Names of countries usually are grammatically feminine (Joüon, § 134 g; Waltke-O'Connor, § 6.4.1c–d), and so the verb וַתְּהִי is feminine singular, even though the rest of the verse refers to the Moabites in the masculine plural, לַעֲבָדִים נֹשְׂאֵי מִנְחָה, literally "servants, bearers of tribute." (See the same wording, לַעֲבָדִים נוֹשְׂאֵי מִנְחָה, in the third textual note on 8:6 and עֲבָדִים in 8:14.) Feminine singular verbs are also used in 8:5, וַתָּבֹא אֲרַם, literally "and Aram came," and 8:6, וַתְּהִי אֲרַם, "so Aram became." The parallel verses in Chronicles have the same feminine singular country names, but the Chronicler changed the verbs to be masculine, either plural (1 Chr 18:2) or singular (1 Chr 18:5, 6).

8:3 [וּפְרָת] , בַּנָּהָר יָדוֹ לְהָשִׁיב—"To restore his control at the Euphrates River" is literally "to return his hand on the River of Perath." פְּרָת is the name for the "Euphrates" (e.g., Gen 2:14; 15:18). The Qere has the name, which is included in most Masoretic manuscripts, the parallel in 1 Chr 18:3, and LXX 2 Sam 8:3 (Εὐφράτην). The Kethib lacks the name; it is, therefore, an instance of what the Masoretes call קְרִי וְלֹא כְתִיב, "read but not written" (see GKC, § 17 b). Without it, the preceding word would be vocalized בַּנָּהָר, "on the River." The noun נָהָר, "river," by itself, without פְּרָת, often refers to the Euphrates, usually with the article (2 Sam 10:16; see also, e.g., Gen 31:21; Ex 23:31; Josh 24:2, 3, 14, 15), but sometimes without the article (e.g., Is 7:20; Jer 2:18). See BDB, s.v. נָהָר, 1.

8:4 אֶלֶף וּשְׁבַע־מֵאוֹת פָּרָשִׁים—The MT reads "a thousand and seven hundred charioteers." The translation "a thousand chariots, seven thousand charioteers" follows the LXX (χίλια ἅρματα καὶ ἑπτὰ χιλιάδας ἱππέων) and 1 Chr 18:4 (אֶלֶף רֶכֶב וְשִׁבְעַת אֲלָפִים פָּרָשִׁים). The reading in 4QSam[a] is largely reconstructed (אלף ר]נכב ושבעת אלפים פרשים]), but attests the first letter (ר) of the word רֶכֶב, "chariots," and supports this translation, as does Josephus in part (regarding the number of chariots).[7]

וַיְעַקֵּר דָּוִד אֶת־כָּל־הָרֶכֶב וַיּוֹתֵר מִמֶּנּוּ מֵאָה רָכֶב:—"David disabled all except a hundred of the chariot horses." The MT literally reads "and David disabled all the chariots, and/but he left from them a hundred chariots." The segholate noun רֶכֶב (pausal רָכֶב) usually refers to "chariots," but by metonymy here and in the parallel verse 1 Chr 18:4 it refers to the "horses" who drew them (BDB, s.v. רֶכֶב, 1). The verb וַיְעַקֵּר is a Piel (D) preterite (imperfect with *waw* consecutive) of עָקַר. This verb is always used in the Piel and only in Gen 49:6; Josh 11:6, 9; 2 Sam 8:4; 1 Chr 18:4, meaning "to hamstring" animals, that is, to disable them by severing hamstring muscles in their legs.

---

[6] Waltke-O'Connor, § 35.3.2a, interprets the infinitive as an adverbial infinitive or a verbal complement and translates it as *"by making* them *lie down"* (example 3).

[7] Josephus, *Antiquities*, 7.99.

The verb וַיּוֹתֵר is the only instance in Samuel of the Hiphil (H) of יָתַר, meaning "to leave over, let remain." Its Niphal (N), "be left, remain," is common in Samuel (1 Sam 2:36; 25:34; 30:9; 2 Sam 9:1; 13:30; 17:12), as is its cognate noun יֶתֶר, the "rest, remnant, what remains" (1 Sam 13:2; 2 Sam 10:10; 12:28; 21:2). Here and in the parallel verse 1 Chr 18:4, it is accented on the final syllable and pointed the same way as a jussive (יוֹתֵר). The expected form, which does not appear in the OT, would be וַיּוֹתֵר, accented on the penultimate syllable (-וֹ-) and with the *tsere* in the final syllable (-תֵר) reduced to *seghol* (-תֶר). See GKC, § 69 v. See the expected form of another first-*yod* verb, וַיִּסֶף, in 2:22.

8:6 נְצִבִים—This plural of the noun נְצִיב, "garrison," recurs twice in 8:14. See the second textual note on 1 Sam 10:5.[8]

בַּאֲרַם דַּמֶּשֶׂק—"In the Aramean kingdom of Damascus." This Hebrew construct phrase is literally "in Aram of Damascus." It signifies the portion of Aram that previously was under the domination of Damascus, as opposed to the territory of Aram that was under the control of Zobah (אֲרַם צוֹבָא in 10:6).

וַתְּהִי ... לַעֲבָדִים נוֹשְׂאֵי מִנְחָה—Literally "and he/it became ... servants who brought [him] tribute." See these same words in the fourth textual note on 8:2. Both here and in 8:2 the MT prefixes the preposition לְ to the plural noun עֲבָדִים as part of the idiom "to become" (הָיָה + לְ). The preposition לְ is absent from the reading in 4QSamᵃ (עבדים) and the parallel in 1 Chr 18:6, as well as in 2 Sam 8:14, where וַיְהִי ... עֲבָדִים would literally mean "were ... servants." However, both readings mean the same thing. Perhaps MT 2 Sam 8:6 with לְ was adapted to 2 Sam 8:2, or 4QSamᵃ and 1 Chr 18:6 without לְ were adapted to 2 Sam 8:14.

וַיֹּשַׁע יְהוָה אֶת־דָּוִד בְּכֹל אֲשֶׁר הָלָךְ׃—"So Yahweh gave David victory wherever he went." This clause is repeated in 8:14 (where the verb is spelled plene, or *maleʾ*, וַיּוֹשַׁע). When God is the subject of the Hiphil (H) of יָשַׁע, it is traditionally translated as "to save," which conveys the meaning well when God's people are under enemy attack (e.g., 1 Sam 4:3; 7:8; 2 Sam 3:18) and when the entirety of God's "salvation" (the noun יֶשַׁע in 2 Sam 22:3, 36, 47; 23:5) is intended (the Hiphil [H] of יָשַׁע in 2 Sam 22:3, 28; see also the Niphal [N] in 22:4: "to be saved"). When God's people are on the offensive, launching the attack, "give victory" is appropriate for God's action (8:6, 14). When human allies are the subject, "to rescue" (10:11) or "to help" (10:19) is suitable.

8:7 שִׁלְטֵי הַזָּהָב—"Gold quivers." שֶׁלֶט is traditionally translated as "shield" but here more likely denotes a quiver for carrying arrows (*CDCH*; see also Jer 51:11).[9] As early as Josephus, this phrase was understood to mean χρυσᾶς φαρέτρας, "gold quivers."[10] The same Hebrew construct phrase is in the parallel verse 1 Chr 18:7. David's "quivers" (שְׁלָטִים) are referenced, but without describing them as gold, also in 2 Ki 11:10; 2 Chr 23:9 (cf. Song 4:4).

---

[8] Steinmann, *1 Samuel*, 192.

[9] See Borger, "Die Waffenträger des Königs Darius," 397–98; Yadin, *The Art of Warfare in Biblical Lands*, 198, 296.

[10] Josephus, *Antiquities*, 7.104.

Based on 1 Ki 14:25–26, 4QSam^a and the LXX have a long expansion at the end of this verse:

גם] [אותם ל]נחק אחר שושק מלך מצרים ב]עלותו אל ירו]שלים]
בימי רחבעם בן שלו]מה]

καὶ ἔλαβεν αὐτὰ Σουσακιμ βασιλεὺς Αἰγύπτου ἐν τῷ ἀναβῆναι αὐτὸν εἰς Ιερουσαλημ ἐν ἡμέραις Ροβοαμ υἱοῦ Σολομῶντος.

And King Shishak of Egypt[11] took them when he went up to Jerusalem in the days of Solomon's son Rehoboam.

8:8 וּמִבֶּטַח וּמִבֵּרֹתָי—"And from Betah and from Berothai" is the reading in the MT, which is supported by the LXX (καὶ ἐκ τῆς Μασβακ ἐκ τῶν ἐκλεκτῶν πόλεων, "and from Masbak, from the chosen cities"). 1 Chr 18:8 reads וּמִטִּבְחַת וּמִכּוּן, "and from Tibhath and from Cun." However, in 1 Chr 18:8 וּמִטִּבְחַת appears to be a double scribal mistake in the transmission of the place-name. First, there is a metathesis of the *bet* and *tet*, making -טב- in place of -בט-. Second, there apparently was a dittography of the *chet* that is the final consonant of בֶּטַח, making בטחח, and then the second repeated letter was changed to a similarly shaped *taw* to make -חת. It appears as if Berothai and Cun were in the same vicinity.[12] The Chronicler may have substituted Cun for Berothai for the sake of his audience, who may have been familiar with Cun but not Berothai.

An expansion about the "bronze" (the feminine noun נְחֹשֶׁת) is present in this verse according to the LXX and similarly in the parallel verse 1 Chr 18:8, and most of it is supported by Josephus:

בָּהּ ׀ עָשָׂה שְׁלֹמֹה אֶת־יָם הַנְּחֹשֶׁת וְאֶת־הָעַמּוּדִים וְאֵת כְּלֵי הַנְּחֹשֶׁת׃

With it Solomon made the bronze sea, the pillars, and the bronze vessels. (1 Chr 18:8)

ἐν αὐτῷ ἐποίησεν Σαλωμων τὴν θάλασσαν τὴν χαλκῆν καὶ τοὺς στύλους καὶ τοὺς λουτῆρας καὶ πάντα τὰ σκεύη.

With it Solomon made the bronze sea, the pillars, the lavers, and all the vessels. (LXX 2 Sam 8:8)

… ἐξ οὗ καὶ Σολομὼν τὸ μέγα σκεῦος θάλασσαν δὲ καλούμενον ἐποίησε καὶ τοὺς καλλίστους ἐκείνους λουτῆρας.

… out of which Solomon made the great vessel called "sea" and those most beautiful lavers.[13]

Since this expansion appears similarly but not identically in LXX 2 Sam 8:8 and MT 1 Chr 18:8, it appears as if it was an ancient addition to the text, perhaps by a scribe in Solomon's court.

הַרְבֵּה מְאֹד׃—The Hiphil (H) infinitive absolute of רָבָה, "be(come) much," is often used adverbially together with מְאֹד (BDB, s.v. רָבָה, Hiphil, 1 e (3); this would mean

---

[11] "Shishak" is the Hebrew reflection of the Egyptian name "Shoshenq."

[12] Dahood, "Philological Observations on Five Biblical Texts," 390–91.

[13] Josephus, *Antiquities*, 7.106.

that David "very greatly took"). Here, however, these two words function adjectivally (BDB, s.v. רָבָה, Hiphil, 1 e (4)) to modify נְחֹשֶׁת, literally "exceedingly much" bronze.

8:9 תֹּעִי—"Toi" is the reading in the MT. The parallel in 1 Chr 18:9 records the name as תֹּעוּ, "Tou," which is supported by LXX 1 Sam 8:9 (Θοου). The different involves a graphic confusion of *yod* and *waw*.

הִכָּה—"He had defeated." See the first textual note on 8:1.

8:10 יוֹרָם—"Joram" is the reading in the MT. The parallel in 1 Chr 18:10 reads הֲדוֹרָם, "Hadoram." "Joram" means "Yahweh is exalted," as יוֹ is a hypocoristic form of יהוה, "Yahweh," used at the beginning of names, and רָם is a form of the verb רוּם, "be high, exalted." "Hadoram" means "Hadad is exalted," and "Hadad" was one of the names of the Canaanite fertility god Baal.[14] A later scribe may have altered הֲדוֹרָם to יוֹרָם in order to avoid the association of David's court with a pagan god. See the second textual note on 2:8, which discusses the alteration of the names of Saul's sons to eliminate pagan associations with royal names.

לִשְׁאָל־לֹו לְשָׁלוֹם—"To greet him" is literally "to ask him regarding peace," that is, to ask whether he is enjoying peace and prosperity. This idiom consists of the verb שָׁאַל, "to ask," which takes the preposition לְ with its object (here לֹו), and the noun שָׁלוֹם, "peace," prefixed with the preposition לְ in the sense of "concerning, regarding." See the first textual note on 1 Sam 10:4;[15] the idiom also appears in 1 Sam 17:22; 25:5; 30:21. In 2 Sam 11:7 the idiom uses three construct phrases (e.g., "the peace of Joab") instead of the preposition לְ with the objects of the verb.

וּלְבָרֲכֹו—"And to bless him." For the Piel (D) of בָּרַךְ, see the textual note on 2 Sam 6:11–12, as well as the first textual note on 1 Sam 2:20 and the third textual note on 1 Sam 9:13.[16]

וַיַּכֵּהוּ—"And he defeated him." See the first textual note on 8:1.

כִּי־אִישׁ מִלְחֲמוֹת תֹּעִי הָיָה הֲדַדְעֶזֶר—"Since Hadadezer had often waged war against Toi." The accents on the words אִישׁ מִלְחֲמוֹת תֹּעִי and the second word's reduced vowel -חֲ- (instead of -חָ-) indicate that these words form a construct chain, literally "a man-of-wars-of-Toi was Hadadezer," i.e., Hadadezer had waged many wars against Toi. See Waltke-O'Connor, § 9.5.2e, including example 17; it explains the *nomen rectum* תֹּעִי as a genitive of disadvantage: wars "*against* Toi."

וּבְיָדֹו הָיוּ כְּלֵי־כֶסֶף וּכְלֵי־זָהָב וּכְלֵי נְחֹשֶׁת:—"Joram brought silver, gold, and bronze items with him" is literally "and in his [Joram's] hand were items of silver and items of gold and items of bronze."

8:11 הִקְדִּישׁ ... הִקְדִּישׁ—"He dedicated ... he had dedicated." When God is the subject of the Hiphil (H) of קָדַשׁ, it literally means "to make holy" or "sanctify" (e.g., 1 Ki 9:3, 7; cf. Jer 1:5; Zeph 1:7). With people as the subject, it commonly refers to the

---

[14] In Ugaritic "Baal" and "Hadad" (*hadd-*) are interchangeable names for the male fertility god. He was often depicted as a bull and pictured with thunderbolts, symbolizing rainstorms. Cf. "Hadad" as a personal name of an Edomite enemy of Solomon (1 Ki 11:14–25) and "Hadad" also in Gen 36:35–36; 1 Chr 1:46–47, 50–51.

[15] Steinmann, *1 Samuel*, 192.

[16] Steinmann, *1 Samuel*, 90, 179, respectively.

consecration or dedication of offerings to Yahweh and his holy purposes, as here (also, e.g., Ex 28:38; Lev 22:2–3; 27:14–19).

כִּבֵּשׁ:—"He subdued." This perfect is the only instance of the Piel (D) of the verb כָּבַשׁ, "to subdue," in the OT and the only appearance of כָּבַשׁ in Samuel. It is used in a military sense here, as also in Josh 18:1; 1 Chr 22:18. Its Qal (G) is used in the creation narrative in Gen 1:28.

8:12 מֵאֲרָם—"From Aram" is the reading in Codex Leningradensis. "From Edom" (מֵאֱדוֹם) is the reading in some Masoretic manuscripts, the LXX (ἐκ τῆς Ἰδουμαίας), and the parallel in 1 Chr 18:11 (מֵאֱדוֹם; cf. Ps 60:2 [ET superscription]). "Edom" is most likely the correct reading since the immediate context is about David's conquest of "Edom" (8:13–14), not Aram, and "the Valley of Salt" (בְּגֵיא־מֶלַח, 8:13) is thought by some to have been south of the Dead Sea toward Edom. This valley was the site of other conflicts with the Edomites (2 Ki 14:7; 2 Chr 25:11). The reading in most Masoretic manuscripts, מֵאֲרָם, was probably a scribal error caused by a graphic confusion of *dalet* (אֱדֹם-) and *resh* (אֲרָם-).

8:13 מֵהַכּוֹתוֹ—"From his striking down." This is the Hiphil (H) infinitive construct of נָכָה with a prefixed preposition מִן and a third masculine singular object suffix. For the verb, see the first textual note on 8:1.

8:14 וַיִּהְיוּ ... עֲבָדִים—Literally "and he/it became ... servants." See the third textual note on 8:6.

Commentary

975–969 BC[17]

This chapter records David's expansion of his kingdom's hegemony in all directions following (וַיְהִי אַחֲרֵי־כֵן, "after this," 8:1) God's messianic promise to make a house for him (2 Samuel 7). Since David would not be directing his attention to building the temple,[18] he, instead, concentrated on enlarging his dominion in accord with Yahweh's pledge in 7:9–11. In contrast to David's earlier wars, where the enemies were the aggressors,[19] in these wars, David struck first. His activity, however, was not unrelated to building the temple, since from these wars he would gather more spoils to dedicate to Yahweh and his future temple (8:8, 11–12; see also 1 Ki 7:51; 1 Chr 18:8).

Some scholars have proposed that this section of Samuel was based on an inscription from a stele that David had erected to proclaim his victories.[20] If this was the case, David would have composed the inscription in the first person

---

[17] See "The Chronology of David's Reign" in the commentary on 5:1–5.

[18] See the commentary on 7:1–17.

[19] See, e.g., the Philistine conflicts (1002 BC) in 5:17–25 and the Ammonite war (998–997 BC) in 10:1–11:1; 12:26–31. Although 10:1–11:1 and 12:26–31 are later in the book, they precede 2 Samuel 8 (975–969 BC) chronologically. See "The Chronology of David's Reign" in the commentary on 5:1–5.

[20] Good, "2 Samuel 8." Similarly, Rudolph Kittel (1922; according to Hertzberg, *I and II Samuel*, 290) and Caquot and de Robert (*Les livres de Samuel*, 442) suggest that it is from David's royal annals.

and the author of Samuel would have converted it to the third person, often by supplying "David" as the subject of sentences. The Mesha Stele (c. 840 BC), e.g., begins in the first person, "I am Mesha, … king of Moab," and the king goes on to claim that his god, Chemosh, gave him victory over his enemies.[21] While this proposal about 2 Samuel 8 is possible, it has not been confirmed by any archaeological discoveries to date.

David's victories are not necessarily arranged chronologically. Instead, there is a geographic arrangement: first west (Philistia, 8:1), then east (Moab, 8:2), next north (Aram, 8:3–6), then south (Edom, 8:13–14). There is also a chiastic arrangement with the inner two conquered nations bringing David tribute (נֹשְׂאֵי מִנְחָה, Moab in 8:2 and Aram in 8:6), something not mentioned with the outer two (Philistia and Edom).

This account weaves together two themes about David: his subjugation of surrounding nations and his growing fame (see "heard that David … ," 8:9, and "David made a name," 8:13). The first theme is the topic of the first section (8:1–6), which covers three nations subdued by David and concludes with the notice that "Yahweh gave David victory wherever he went" (8:6). Then the second theme—David's fame—is introduced with the gifts brought to David and David's consecration of the gifts to Yahweh (8:9–12). The two themes are connected by the gold and bronze treasures that David seized from his enemies (8:7–8), and then the two themes are united in relating David's victory over Edom (8:13–14), which once again notes that "Yahweh gave David victory wherever he went" (8:14).

David Subjugates the Philistines (8:1)

Parallel: 2 Sam 8:1 ‖ 1 Chr 18:1

This record of David's war against the Philistines emphasizes their defeat. However, unlike the other three nations in this section, the Philistines are not said to have become David's "servants" (8:2, 6, 14). Instead, David "humbled" the Philistines and took territory from them (for "Metheg-ammah," see the third textual note on 8:1). This probably indicates that although they were subdued and would never again be a major threat to Israel, they retained a measure of independence.

David Subjugates Moab (8:2)

Parallel: 2 Sam 8:2 ‖ 1 Chr 18:2

David's defeat of Moab notes his unusual method of executing prisoners of war. Two-thirds were executed, while a third was allowed to live.[22] We do not know why David chose this method or why he did not execute all of the prisoners. Perhaps this was a sign of his mercy toward the Moabites as his

---

[21] See Gibson, *Textbook of Syrian Semitic Inscriptions*, 1:74–77.

[22] See the textual notes on 8:2. Interestingly, the parallel verse 1 Chr 18:2 omits any reference to the measuring, sparing, and execution of the Moabite prisoners of war.

distant cousins; they were descendants of Abraham's nephew Lot (Gen 11:27; 19:30–37).

David Subjugates Aram (8:3–6)

Parallel: 2 Sam 8:3–6 ‖ 1 Chr 18:3–6

David's war against Zobah pressed the advantage over Aram that he had initially established during the earlier Ammonite war (10:6–19).[23] The text is ambiguous as to who went to the Euphrates River—David or Hadadezer (8:3).[24] There are, however, two good reasons for understanding the text as describing Hadadezer's movements: First, Hadadezer is the closest antecedent to the pronoun on the infinitive construct (the Qal [G] of הָלַךְ), בְּלֶכְתּוֹ, "when he went." Second, the movement was intended to *restore* his control over the territory on the Euphrates; this makes more sense when speaking of an Aramean king and rules out David, who had no previous control of that region. In the earlier Ammonite war, a number of Hadadezer's vassals became David's vassals (10:19). 2 Sam 8:3 is probably noting that Hadadezer was moving on the territory near the Euphrates to reassert his authority over them. This would have brought David out to defend his vassals in Aram. Apparently David took advantage of Hadadezer's vulnerability on Zobah's southern flank created by the movement of the Aramean king's northward march. Those who argue that David was the one who advanced to the Euphrates usually understand the text as saying that David went to place a monument at the Euphrates (cf. יָד as "monument" in 1 Sam 15:12; 2 Sam 18:18; Is 56:5). This depends on positing that לְהָשִׁיב, "to restore," in 2 Sam 8:3 is the result of a scribal error and that the correct reading is לְהַצִּיב, "to establish" or "to erect," in 1 Chr 18:3. However, it is difficult to understand why David would advance an army large enough to defeat an impressive Aramaic force (8:4) simply for the purpose of erecting a monument on the Euphrates.[25]

David's disabling of all but a hundred of the captured chariot horses (8:4) served three purposes: First, it removed them from the enemy's arsenal.[26] Second, since chariots were not effective in the hill country of Israel, it removed the expense of David maintaining a large number of chariot horses. Finally, it enabled David to follow Yahweh's proscription against Israelite kings owning large numbers of horses (Deut 17:16).[27]

---

[23] For the dating of the Ammonite war in 10:1–11:1; 12:26–31, see figure 2, "Chronology of David's Reign," in the commentary on 5:1–5.

[24] Those who favor David as the one going to the Euphrates include Smith, *The Books of Samuel*, 305; Ackroyd, *The Second Book of Samuel*, 86; McCarter, *II Samuel*, 247; Bergen, *1, 2 Samuel*, 348; Auld, *I and II Samuel*, 428. Those who favor Hadadezer include Anderson, *2 Samuel*, 132; Baldwin, *1 and 2 Samuel*, 220; Hertzberg, *I and II Samuel*, 291.

[25] Bergen, *1, 2, Samuel*, 348, argues that David was extending Israel's claim on the land as far north as the Euphrates to fulfill the divine promises in Gen 15:18; Ex 23:31; Deut 1:7; 11:24.

[26] Compare the similar action by Joshua (Josh 11:6–9).

[27] Contrast Solomon (1 Ki 5:6 [ET 4:26]; 2 Chr 9:25, 28).

God provided David with victory over all Aram when the Damascene Arameans joined the conflict in support of Hadadezer (8:5). David's stationing of garrisons in or near Damascus (8:6) was probably meant to ensure the continued fealty of the defeated people, since they were far north of Israel.

David Takes the Spoils of War and His Fame Grows (8:7–12)

Parallel: 2 Sam 8:7–12 ‖ 1 Chr 18:7–11

David's victory over the Aramean kingdoms gave him the opportunity to add gold and large quantities of bronze to his treasury (8:7–8). It also brought him to the attention of Hamath's King Toi, who had been at war with Hadadezer. He apparently acknowledged David's growing empire by sending his son with items made of precious metals (8:9–10). However, David did not add any of these items or others that he had captured in his military triumphs to his personal treasury (8:11–12). By dedicating them to Yahweh, David accomplished two objectives: he was able to prepare for the building of the temple (cf. 1 Chr 18:8; see also 1 Ki 7:51), and he once again heeded the Law's limits on Israelite kings, who were not to amass great wealth (Deut 17:17).[28]

The list of nations from which David had captured precious metals appears to be a summary of the spoils from all of his military victories, beginning with his raids against the Amalekites when he was in the service of the king of Gath and living in Ziklag (1 Samuel 27; 30). These victories are cataloged at various places in the book of Samuel, as shown in figure 6.

Figure 6
___

Enemies Subdued by David

Defeated Enemy	David's Victory
Aram	2 Sam 10:6–19
Moab	2 Sam 8:2
Ammon	2 Sam 10:1–11:1; 12:26–31
Philistines	2 Sam 5:17–25; 8:1; 21:15–22
Amalek	1 Sam 30:1–31
Hadadezer	2 Sam 8:3–10

David's Fame: David Subjugates Edom (8:13–14)

Parallel: 2 Sam 8:13–14 ‖ 1 Chr 18:12–13

The uniqueness of David's victory over Edom is highlighted in several ways in this section:

___

[28] Contrast Solomon (1 Ki 9:28; 10:2, 10–11, 14–25; 2 Chr 8:18; 9:1, 9–10, 13–24).

- It does not begin with the formula "David defeated … ," which was used in earlier verses (see וַיַּךְ דָּוִד אֶת־ in 8:1, 3; וַיַּךְ אֶת־ in 8:2; and וַיַּךְ דָּוִד in 8:5).
- It alone is said to have enhanced David's reputation (8:13; see below).
- Although the Edomites became David's servants (8:14), they are not said to have brought him tribute, as did the Moabites (8:2) and the Arameans (8:6).

David's reputation or "name" (שֵׁם, 8:13), not the spoils of war, is the focus of his victory over Edom. McCarter argues that the Hebrew words that literally state "David made a name" (וַיַּעַשׂ דָּוִד שֵׁם, 8:13) ought to be understood as meaning "David built a monument," based on Is 55:13.[29] However, in Is 55:13, the noun שֵׁם does not mean "monument," but speaks of Yahweh's "name" or reputation as an everlasting sign or emblem (לְשֵׁם לְאוֹת עוֹלָם). In addition, elsewhere in the OT the combination of the Qal (G) of the verb עָשָׂה with the noun שֵׁם as its direct object normally means "to make a name," that is, to create or enhance one's reputation.[30]

David is said to have struck down eighteen thousand Edomites in the Valley of Salt (8:13). 1 Chr 18:12 credits this to David's nephew Abishai. However, this is not a discrepancy. Instead, Abishai, one of David's generals, probably led the attack (cf. 2 Sam 10:10; 18:2). However, David, as king, was credited with the overall victory. In addition, Ps 60:2 (ET superscription) credits striking down twelve thousand Edomites in the Valley of Salt to Joab. Since Joab was David's chief commander (2 Sam 8:16), that psalm probably credits him with the victory even though his brother Abishai probably led the troops into battle. The "twelve thousand" in Ps 60:2 (ET superscription) may be a simple scribal error, since numbers are often among the most easily corrupted features during the transmission of texts and only vowel letters and the transposition of two consonants differentiate the two numbers.[31]

David's garrisons in Edom are emphasized by repetition (8:14). This may indicate the rebellious nature of Edom, displayed repeatedly in history. Note Edom's later uprising against Israel and Judah (1 Ki 11:14–22; 2 Ki 8:20–22 ‖ 2 Chr 21:8–10).

---

[29] McCarter, *II Samuel*, 243, 251.

[30] Gen 11:4; 2 Sam 7:9, 23; Is 63:12, 14; Jer 32:20; Dan 9:15; Neh 9:20; 1 Chr 17:8 (cf. 2 Sam 23:22).

[31] The number "eighteen thousand" in 2 Sam 8:13 consists of three Hebrew words, שְׁמוֹנָה עָשָׂר אָלֶף. The second and third words are the same as in the number "twelve thousand" in Ps 60:2 (ET superscription), שְׁנֵים עָשָׂר אָלֶף. The three consonants (שׁ, מ, and נ) in the first word in Ps 60:2 (ET superscription), שְׁנֵים, *sheneym*, are also in the first word of 2 Sam 8:13, שְׁמוֹנָה, *shemonah*. Before the addition of vowel letters, the first number in 2 Sam 8:13 would have been written שמנ, *sh-m-n*, and the first number in Ps 60:2 (ET superscription) would have been written שנמ, *sh-n-m*.

David's Officials

Translation

8 **15**David reigned over all Israel. David was administering justice and righteousness for all his people.

16Joab the son of Zeruiah was over the army.

Jehoshaphat the son of Ahilud was [royal] historian.

17Zadok the son of Ahitub and Ahimelech the son of Abiathar were high priests.

Seraiah was [royal] scribe.

18Benaiah the son of Jehoiada was over the Cherethites and the Pelethites.

The sons of David were palace administrators.

Textual Notes

8:15 וַיְהִי דָוִד עֹשֶׂה מִשְׁפָּט וּצְדָקָה—"David was administering justice and righteousness" is literally "and David was doing justice and righteousness." The verbal construction is periphrastic: וַיְהִי (הָיָה, "and he was") with a participle (עֹשֶׂה, Qal [G] masculine singular of עָשָׂה, "to do") signifies durative action (Joüon, §§ 121 c and 154 m). David habitually and/or continually did this over a long period of past time. The same verb עָשָׂה will take as its object the same pair of nouns (מִשְׁפָּט וּצְדָקָה) to describe David's son Solomon as a king whom God installed "to do justice and righteousness" (1 Ki 10:9). These nouns are frequently paired or placed in parallel in the prophets and the psalms,[1] including prophecies of the Messiah, who will administer them on the throne of David (Is 9:6 [ET 9:7]; Jer 23:5; 33:15; cf. Ps 72:1).

The noun מִשְׁפָּט can refer to divine "justice" in terms of both Law ("judgment" against sin) and Gospel ("justification" of his people by grace and his "vindication" of them versus their enemies). It can refer to an "ordinance" in the Torah, which expresses his will both to condemn sin and to save his people from it (see מִשְׁפָּטָיו in 2 Sam 22:23). Here it refers to actions that accomplish God's will for his people by punishing the guilty and rescuing the innocent. It had a similar sense in 1 Sam 8:3, where, however, Samuel's sons, appointed as judges in Israel, perverted "justice" (מִשְׁפָּט) by not walking faithfully as did their father; see the commentary on 1 Sam 8:3.[2] Likewise, צְדָקָה, "righteousness," can denote an inherent attribute of God or the expression of it revealed in his Word and his actions to save his people (1 Sam 12:7). Those who are saved and justified by grace exhibit God's righteousness as they live by faith (see the pairing of צְדָקָה with מִשְׁפָּט for Abraham in Gen 18:19). They can, then, claim his "righteousness"

---

[1] See, e.g., Is 1:27; 5:16; 33:5; 56:1; Jer 4:2; Ezek 33:14, 16; Amos 5:24; Pss 33:5; 99:4; 106:3.

[2] Steinmann, *1 Samuel*, 169–70.

as their own, as does David (2 Sam 22:21, 25). See also the concluding paragraphs of the commentary on 1 Sam 12:1–25.[3]

8:16 וְיוֹאָב בֶּן־צְרוּיָה עַל־הַצָּבָא—Here the preposition עַל, "over," indicates the office of a superior rank (Waltke-O'Connor, § 11.2.13c, including example 8). The same prepositional phrase (עַל־הַצָּבָא) recurs in 2 Sam 17:25. The noun צָבָא can refer to Israel's "army" (e.g., 1 Sam 14:50; 2 Sam 20:23). It is also used in the plural in the title "Yahweh of armies" (see the fourth textual note on 1 Sam 1:3[4]).

מַזְכִּיר:—"[Royal] historian." In form this noun is the Hiphil (H) masculine singular participle of זָכַר, "to remember," and so it literally denotes "someone who reminds" others by way of the history he writes; he is a "recorder" (BDB, Hiphil, 4). This title refers to an official keeper of a record of the events in the royal court.[5] Note that this is different from the court secretary or "scribe" (סֹפֵר); see the fourth textual note on 8:17.

8:17 וַאֲחִימֶלֶךְ בֶּן־אֶבְיָתָר—"And Ahimelech the son of Abiathar." This may be a scribal transposition for "Abiathar the son of Ahimelech." See the commentary.

כֹּהֲנִים—"High priests." The noun כֹּהֵן, which is, in form, the Qal (G) participle of כָּהַן, usually denotes a "priest" but in some contexts the "high priest." See the third textual note on 1 Sam 1:9.[6] The construction with a proper name followed by הַכֹּהֵן with the definite article, "the priest," is used to designate the high priest.[7] This construction with the article, with כֹּהֵן in the singular or the plural, is an appositional construction: אֶבְיָתָר הַכֹּהֵן, "Abiathar the high priest,"[8] or צָדוֹק הַכֹּהֵן, "Zadok the high priest,"[9] or צָדוֹק וְאֶבְיָתָר הַכֹּהֲנִים, "Zadok and Abiathar the high priests."[10]

Since both men named in 8:17a apparently functioned as high priest, the construction here is slightly different: their names are followed by the plural without the definite article, כֹּהֲנִים. The construction without the article is always used in a nominal sentence: "Zadok the son of Ahitub and Ahimelech the son of Abiathar were high priests" (2 Sam 8:17 ‖ 1 Chr 18:16; similarly, "Zadok and Abiathar were high priests," 2 Sam 20:25; 1 Ki 4:4).

וּשְׂרָיָה—"(And) Seraiah." This is probably the correct reading; it is a fairly common name in the OT.[11] The LXX reads Ασα, "Asa." The parallel in 1 Chr 18:16 reads שַׁוְשָׁא, "Shavsha" (LXX 1 Chr 18:16: Σουσα). In 2 Sam 20:25 the name is שְׁיָא, "Sheya"

---

[3] Steinmann, *1 Samuel*, 229.

[4] Steinmann, *1 Samuel*, 44.

[5] Also in 2 Sam 20:24; 1 Ki 4:3; 2 Ki 18:18, 37; Is 36:3, 22; 1 Chr 18:15; 2 Chr 34:8.

[6] Steinmann, *1 Samuel*, 47–48.

[7] Examples of this construction in the book of Samuel are in 1 Sam 1:9; 2:11; 21:2, 3 (ET 21:1, 2); 22:11; 23:9; 30:7; 2 Sam 15:27. The only exceptions are in Persian-period books, where the construction designates an ordinary priest, not the high priest (Ezra in Ezra 7:11; 10:10, 16; Neh 8:2, 9; 12:26; Shelemiah in Neh 13:13).

[8] 1 Sam 23:9; 30:7; 1 Ki 1:7, 19, 25, 42; 2:22, 26.

[9] E.g., 2 Sam 15:27; 1 Ki 1:8, 26, 32, 34, 38, 39, 44, 45.

[10] 2 Sam 15:35a. Variations of that plural construction, with a preposition before each of the names, occur in 2 Sam 15:35b; 17:15; 19:12 (ET 19:11); 1 Chr 15:11.

[11] 2 Ki 25:18, 23; Jer 40:8; 51:59, 61; 52:24; Ezra 2:2; 7:1; Neh 10:3 (ET 10:2); 11:11; 12:1, 12; 1 Chr 4:13, 14, 35; 5:40 (ET 6:14); the longer form שְׂרָיָהוּ, "Seraiahu," occurs in Jer 36:26.

(Kethib) or שְׁוָא, "Sheva" (Qere). Regarding these other names, "Asa" (in Hebrew אָסָא) too is common, but there is little to recommend it here. "Shavsha" and "Sheya" occur nowhere else and appear to be scribal errors for "Seraiah." "Sheva" occurs one other time (1 Chr 2:49).

סוֹפֵר:—"[Royal] scribe." This refers to the royal court secretary, who probably was in charge of recording the royal decrees and correspondence, judging from other OT references to this office. This role is distinct from that of the מַזְכִּיר, "[royal] historian" (see the second textual note on 8:16). The title "scribe" recurs in 20:25 and clearly is related to the noun סֵפֶר, "scroll." It must have been an important office since other holders of this title are named in other OT books,[12] and some of them played key roles, including Shaphan, who read the newly rediscovered Torah to King Josiah, prompting his reformation (2 Ki 22:3, 8, 9, 10, 12), and especially the scribe Ezra, who read the Torah aloud and provided theological leadership for the reconstituted community after the exile.[13]

8:18 וְהַכְּרֵתִי וְהַפְּלֵתִי—The MT reads only these two gentilic nouns, "and the Cherethites and the Pelethites." The preposition עַל, "over," precedes these words in the parallel to this verse in 1 Chr 18:17 (עַל־הַכְּרֵתִי וְהַפְּלֵתִי; see also 2 Sam 20:23), and the translation follows that reading: "over the Cherethites and the Pelethites."

וּבְנֵי דָוִד כֹּהֲנִים הָיוּ:—The MT states "and the sons of David were priests." Among the ancient versions only the Vulgate (*sacerdotes*) and Aquila (ἱερεῖς) support "priests" in the MT (this passage is not extant in any of the Qumran Samuel scrolls). David was from the tribe of Judah, and only the descendants of Aaron within the tribe of Levi were allowed to be priests (Ex 28:1; 40:12–15). No other passage supports the idea that David's sons were priests. The reading in the MT appears to be a scribal corruption of some type, perhaps under the influence of כֹּהֲנִים, "(high) priests," in 8:17. Here in place of כֹּהֲנִים הָיוּ, "they were priests," the translation follows a conjectural emendation, סֹכְנֵי הַבָּיִת, "palace administrators" (the plural of סֹכֵן, "administrator," in construct with הַבַּיִת, "the house" [pausal: הַבָּיִת], referring to the palace). The LXX appears to have attempted a correction of the MT, reading καὶ υἱοὶ Δαυιδ αὐλάρχαι ἦσαν, "and the sons of David were court officials."[14] The reading in the parallel verse 1 Chr 18:17 is וּבְנֵי־דָוִיד הָרִאשֹׁנִים לְיַד הַמֶּלֶךְ, "and David's sons were the heads/chief officials at the king's side." If the original reading here in 2 Sam 8:18 was סֹכְנֵי הַבָּיִת, then the reading in 1 Chr 18:17 was possibly the Chronicler's effort to explain the obscure term סֹכֵן, "administrator," to postexilic readers. This possibility is supported by various ancient translations of 2 Sam 8:18 that have some representation of the Hebrew word in 1 Chr 18:17, הָרִאשֹׁנִים, "the heads/chiefs."[15] The Syriac Peshitta has ܘܗܘ ܪܫܐ and

---

[12] See the scribes named in 1 Ki 4:3; 2 Ki 18:18, 37; 19:2; 22:3, 8, 9, 10, 12; Is 36:3, 22; 37:2; Jer 36:10, 12a, 20, 21, 26, 32; 37:15, 20; Ezra 7:6, 11; Neh 8:1, 4, 9, 13; 12:26, 36; 13:13; 1 Chr 18:16; 24:6; 27:32; 2 Chr 26:11; 34:15, 18, 20. Scribes are referred to by their title only in 2 Ki 12:11 (ET 12:10); 25:19; Jer 36:12b, 23; 52:25; Esth 3:12; 8:9; 2 Chr 24:11; 34:13.

[13] Ezra 7:6, 11; Neh 8:1, 4, 9, 13; 12:26, 36. See Steinmann, *Ezra and Nehemiah*, 283–84.

[14] This is the only instance of the noun αὐλάρχης, "court official," in the LXX, but the related noun αὐλαρχία, referring to the function of a court official, is used in LXX 1 Ki 2:46. LXX Is 22:15 uses the noun ταμίας, "steward."

[15] Wenham, "Were David's Sons Priests?" 80.

the Targum רַבְרְבִין הֲווֹ, both meaning that David's sons "were great/important men." The Old Latin calls them *principes domus regis*, "heads of the king's house," and the Syro-Hexaplar *capita cantorum*, "heads of the singers."[16] Josephus also appears to support this: οἱ δὲ πρεσβύτεροι παῖδες αὐτοῦ περὶ τὸ σῶμα καὶ τὴν τούτου φυλακὴν ἦσαν, "but his [David's] older sons were near his body and were the guard of this man [David]."[17] The position of the perfect copulative verb הָיוּ at the end of the clause in the MT is unusual.[18] Some propose that it may be a later addition to the text.[19] Most often in Samuel הָיוּ appears after its subject and preceding its object or a prepositional phrase,[20] and twice it is placed before its subject (2 Sam 8:10; 10:5). However, for 2 Sam 8:18 both the Syriac and the Targum place the verb at the end of the clause. For further discussion, see the commentary.

Commentary

1002–969 BC[21]

Parallel: 2 Sam 8:15–18 ‖ 2 Chr 18:14–17

This short section speaks of David's administration of "justice" (מִשְׁפָּט) and "righteousness" (צְדָקָה) for the people (8:15). As king, David was to rule as God's regent and to reflect God's reign over Israel. The qualities of David's administration noted here are also God's (Deut 32:4; Pss 36:7 [ET 36:6]). The author lists David's high officials as an example of his administration.

"Joab" (2 Sam 8:16) would remain commander of the army throughout David's reign, although Solomon would have him executed per David's advice (1 Ki 2:5–6, 28–35). On the other hand, "Jehoshaphat" would continue to serve as court historian under Solomon (1 Ki 4:3).

During David's reign the office of high priest appears to have been shared (2 Sam 8:17). Under Solomon, "Zadok" would become the sole high priest (1 Ki 2:35). The high priest named "Ahimelech" here appears to have shared this name with his grandfather. The previous high priest mentioned in 1 Sam 30:7 is called "Abiathar the son of Ahimelech." In three places, however, the names are reversed, and the high priest is identified as "Ahimelech the son of Abiathar": here in 2 Sam 8:17, in the parallel in 1 Chr 18:16 (reading "Ahimelech" instead of "Abimelech"), and also in 1 Chr 24:6. The reversal of names in these verses may be the result of scribal transposition. Otherwise, it appears as if Abiathar's father and predecessor as well as his son was named Ahimelech. However, Ahimelech the son must have served concurrently with his father, Abiathar,

---

[16] See Wenham, "Were David's Sons Priests?" 80.

[17] Josephus, *Antiquities*, 7.110.

[18] The verb הָיוּ is placed at the end of some other verses in the OT: Ex 37:17; Num 1:44; Ezek 13:4; 22:18; 23:2; Hos 7:2; Obadiah 16; 1 Chr 4:14.

[19] Anderson, *2 Samuel*, 135, suggests that the verb may be "superfluous." However, if the verb was added later, why would it be placed in such an unconventional position in the sentence?

[20] E.g., 1 Sam 1:18; 13:2; 14:21; 25:7, 16; 2 Sam 2:10; 12:1 (cf. 2 Sam 4:2; 8:7).

[21] See "The Chronology of David's Reign" in the commentary on 5:1–5.

since Abiathar will be mentioned numerous times in the narrative to come.[22] Abiathar would be banished and removed from the high priesthood by Solomon (1 Ki 2:26–27, 35). Thus, Abiathar (and his son Ahimelech) would be the last of the descendants of Eli to serve as high priest in fulfillment of the prophecy against Eli's house (1 Sam 2:27–36).

Seraiah was the court scribe (2 Sam 8:17). Nothing more is known about him.

The final verse in this list (8:18) seems to have suffered from severe scribal corruption. Taken as it stands it literally reads "Benaiah the son of Jehoiada and the Cherethites and the Pelethites and the sons of David priests were." The Cherethites and Pelethites were foreign mercenaries and hardly qualified to be priests in Israel. Thus, it appears as if the information in this verse has been garbled in transmission.

Elsewhere, Benaiah is said to be "over" (עַל) the Cherethites and Pelethites, and most English versions assume that this preposition should be added to the first part of the verse (see the first textual note on 8:18). After the death of Joab, Solomon put Benaiah in charge of Israel's army (1 Ki 2:35).

The "Cherethites" (2 Sam 8:18) were probably related somehow to the Philistines—perhaps they were a Philistine clan (cf. Ezek 25:16; Zeph 2:5). They inhabited part of the Negev (1 Sam 30:14). In both Ezek 25:16 and Zeph 2:5, the LXX renders כְּרֵתִים as "Cretans" (Κρῆτες). However, this may simply be a guess based on the similar sounds of these Hebrew and Greek words. Perhaps the "Pelethites" were also a Philistine clan. These mercenaries may have been recruited by David during his time at Ziklag (1 Samuel 27; 30). They seem to have functioned as a palace guard (2 Sam 15:18; 1 Ki 1:38, 44), although at times they were mobilized to serve alongside the Israelite army under Joab (e.g., 2 Sam 20:7).

The thorniest problem presented by 2 Sam 8:18 is the role of David's sons. The Hebrew text appears to say that they were priests. Many critical commentators who believe the Levitical priesthood to have been a late convention originating in exilic or postexilic times simply argue that this notice about David's sons ought to be understood according to the normal meaning of the Hebrew word for "priest" used here (כֹּהֵן).[23] This verse supposedly demonstrates that the priesthood was not confined to Aaronides at this time and that there were priests, including members of the royal family, who served the royal court.[24] However, is more likely that the last two Hebrew words (כֹּהֲנִים הָיוּ, "they were priests") are a corruption of the original text (see the second textual note on 8:18).

---

[22] See Abiathar also in 1 Sam 22:20, 21, 22; 23:6, 9; 2 Sam 15:24, 27, 29, 35, 36; 17:15; 19:12 (ET 19:11); 20:25; 1 Ki 1:7, 19, 25, 42; 2:22, 26, 27, 35; 4:4; 1 Chr 15:11; 27:34.

[23] Smith, *The Books of Samuel*, 309; McCarter, *II Samuel*, 256–57; Anderson, *2 Samuel*, 137.

[24] Many scholars claim that Israelite kings (and therefore also their sons) functioned as priests, and for support they often point out that David wore a linen ephod (2 Sam 6:14). However, wearing the ephod did not mean that David was a priest or was functioning as one. See the commentary on 6:14.

Some conservative commentators seek to explain the noun for "priests" (כֹּהֲנִים) as carrying a different connotation in this context. Thus, it has been suggested that it means "priests" *after the order of Melchizedek*, a function supposedly given to Judahite kings in Jerusalem as successors to Melchizedek (cf. Gen 14:17–20; Ps 110:4; Heb 5:1–10; 6:20–7:28).[25] The problem with this suggestion is that while David, as king in Jerusalem, might possibly be considered a successor to Melchizedek, "king of Salem [that is, Jerusalem]" (Gen 14:18), it is not obvious how his sons, who were not kings, would have been considered Melchizedek's successors. Moreover, the book of Hebrews stresses that just as there was no predecessor in the priesthood of Melchizedek, so also he had no successor until Jesus Christ, the eternal High Priest, who is the only Priest to come from the tribe of Judah (Heb 7:3, 13–18).[26]

Another suggestion is that כֹּהֲנִים has the sense of "royal confidants."[27] This is based on the statement that Zabud, under King Solomon, was "priest, the king's friend" (כֹּהֵן רֵעֶה הַמֶּלֶךְ, 1 Ki 4:5). However, this statement does not necessarily define a "priest" (כֹּהֵן) as "the king's friend" (רֵעֶה הַמֶּלֶךְ). Instead, it simply states that this particular priest was also a royal confidant to Solomon. Note that Hushai, during the reign of King David, is said to be "the friend of David" (רֵעֶה דָוִד, 2 Sam 15:37; 16:16) and "the friend of the king" (רֵעַ הַמֶּלֶךְ, 1 Chr 27:33), but he is not called a "priest" (כֹּהֵן).

It is much more likely that the sense of the last two Hebrew words in 2 Sam 8:18 (where the text may be corrupt) is preserved in the parallel verse 1 Chr 18:17, which states that "David's sons were the heads/chief officials" (וּבְנֵי־דָוִיד הָרִאשֹׁנִים). Since most of the ancient versions translate the end of the verse so as to portray David's sons as "heads" over some administrative departments, it has been proposed that the text originally called the princes סֹכְנִים, "administrators of royal property"[28] (see the second textual note on 8:18). Similar office titles existed in Ugaritic (*skn*) and Neo-Assyrian (*šaknu*). In Is 22:15 Shebna is said to have held the position of "the steward/administrator … over the palace" (הַסֹּכֵן … עַל־הַבָּיִת). A viable conjecture for the Hebrew phrase at the end of 2 Sam 8:18 is that an original construct phrase using two of the Hebrew words in Is 22:15, סֹכְנֵי הַבַּיִת, "the administrators of the palace," was accidentally corrupted to כֹּהֲנִים הָיוּ, "they were priests." It is not difficult to imagine that a scribe accidentally substituted the more common word כֹּהֲנִים, "priests," from the previous verse (8:17) in place of the rare word סֹכְנֵי, since the only other instance of the noun סֹכֵן in the OT is in Is 22:15. Then the last word may have been converted from the noun (with the article and in pause) הַבָּיִת,

---

[25] Bergen, *1, 2 Samuel*, 352.

[26] See Kleinig, *Hebrews*, 344–51.

[27] Keil, *The Books of Samuel*, 368–69.

[28] Hitzig, *Psalmen*, 2:318; Cody, *A History of the Old Testament Priesthood*, 103–5; Wenham, "Were David's Sons Priests?"

"the house/palace," to the verb הָיוּ, "they were," with the accidental loss of the *bet* and the graphic confusion of Paleo-Hebrew *taw* (ת) and *waw* (ו).

This list of David's officials is similar to the one in 2 Sam 20:23–26. A quick comparison notes that the first five of the six offices listed in 8:15–18 are also found in 20:23–26, but in a slightly different order, while two of the seven offices in 20:23–26 are not mentioned here. (The name of the second high priest here is Ahimelech, whereas in 20:23–26 it is Abiathar; see the commentary on 8:17.)

Figure 7

David's Officials

(Officials not found in both lists are in *italics*.)

2 Samuel 8:15–18	2 Samuel 20:23–26
Joab, commander of the army	Joab, commander of the army
Jehoshaphat, royal historian	Benaiah, over the Cherethites and Pelethites
Zadok and Ahimelech, high priests	*Adoram, in charge of forced labor*
Seraiah, royal scribe	Jehoshaphat, royal historian
Benaiah, over the Cherethites and Pelethites	Sheva (i.e., Seraiah), royal scribe
David's sons, palace administrators	Zadok and Abiathar, high priests
	Ira, David's priest

2 Samuel 9:1–20:26

David's Failures and Struggles

Prelude: David Remembers His Promise to Jonathan

Translation

9 ¹David asked, "Is there still anyone left who belongs to the house of Saul so that I may show him kindness for Jonathan's sake?" ²Now the house of Saul (still) had a servant. His name was Ziba. They summoned him to David, and the king said to him, "Are you Ziba?"

He said, "I am your servant."

³The king said, "Is there no one still belonging to the house of Saul so that I may show God's kindness to him?"

Ziba said to the king, "There is still a son of Jonathan who is crippled."

⁴The king said to him, "Where is he?"

Ziba said to the king, "He is in the house of Machir the son of Ammiel in Lo-debar."

⁵So King David sent and took him from the house of Machir the son of Ammiel from Lo-debar. ⁶Mephibosheth the son of Jonathan, the son of Saul, came to David. He fell facedown and bowed. David said, "Mephibosheth."

He said, "I am your servant."

⁷David said to him, "Do not be afraid, because I will certainly show kindness to you for the sake of Jonathan, your father. I will restore the entire estate of your grandfather Saul to you. You will always eat meals at my table."

⁸He bowed [again] and said, "Who is your servant that you have noticed a dead dog like me?"

⁹The king summoned Ziba, Saul's attendant, and said to him, "Everything that belonged to Saul and to all his house I have given to your master's grandson. ¹⁰You are to work the land for him: you, your sons, and your slaves. You will bring [the produce], and it will be food for your master's grandson, and he will eat it. Your master's grandson Mephibosheth will always eat food at my table." (Ziba had fifteen sons and twenty slaves.)

¹¹Ziba said to the king, "According to all that my lord the king has commanded his servant, so your servant will do."

Mephibosheth ate at the king's table like one of the king's sons. ¹²Mephibosheth had a young son whose name was Mica. All the people living in Ziba's house were Mephibosheth's servants. ¹³However, Mephibosheth was living in Jerusalem since he always ate at the king's table. (He was lame in both of his feet.)

Textual Notes

9:1 הֲכִי יֶשׁ־עוֹד אֲשֶׁר נוֹתַר לְבֵית שָׁאוּל—"Is there still anyone left who belongs to the house of Saul?" is literally "is it (so) that there still exists (someone) who remains to the house of Saul?" The interrogative *he* is prefixed to the conjunction כִּי as a neutral question, הֲכִי, "is it that?" (see BDB, s.v. כִּי, 1 d (a)). This question introduces the subject clause (Joüon, § 161 j), יֶשׁ־עוֹד, which is the particle of existence, יֵשׁ, "there exists/is," joined to the adverb עוֹד, "yet, still." The verb נוֹתַר is the Niphal (N) third masculine singular perfect of יָתַר, "be left, remain" (see the second textual note on 8:4). The preposition לְ in the sense of possession, "belonging to," is often used for a kinship relationship to define a person's family or tribe (BDB, s.v. לְ, 5 a (c)). This preposition is used similarly in 9:2–3 (see the first textual note on 9:2 and the first and third textual notes on 9:3).

וְאֶעֱשֶׂה עִמּוֹ חֶסֶד—"So that I may show him kindness" is literally "and I will do with him kindness." A Hebrew imperfect (אֶעֱשֶׂה, the Qal [G] of עָשָׂה) with conjunctive *waw* can express purpose, "so that" (GKC, § 165 a; Joüon, § 115 a and c (1)). The same verb is used in the same way again in 9:3 (וְאֶעֱשֶׂה). The vocabulary here is the standard Hebrew idiom for "show mercy, kindness," or "act in faithfulness," the Qal (G) of עָשָׂה, "do," plus the preposition עִם, "with," and the object noun חֶסֶד. See the third textual note on 2:5. The idiom here is repeated in 9:3 and similarly in 9:7; see also 2:5; 10:2. This idiom with God/Yahweh as subject can refer to God displaying his own grace and fidelity, as in 2:6: "may Yahweh show you kindness and faithfulness."

9:2 וּלְבֵית שָׁאוּל עֶבֶד—"Now the house of Saul (still) had a servant." For the sense of the preposition לְ, see the first textual note on 9:1.

הַאַתָּה צִיבָא וַיֹּאמֶר עַבְדֶּךָ:—" 'Are you Ziba?' He said, '[I am] your servant.' " A single word (עַבְדֶּךָ, "your servant," pausal for עַבְדְּךָ) pertaining to the question may serve as its answer (Joüon, § 161 l). In 9:6 Mephibosheth's answer is the same word with the addition of the focus marker, הִנֵּה עַבְדֶּךָ, "behold, [I am] your servant." Again in 9:8 and 9:11 the one who is speaking with the king refers to himself in the third person as "your servant" (עַבְדְּךָ) as a term of self-deference and submission to the monarch's divine authority. For a much stronger self-deprecation, see the second textual note on 9:8.

9:3 הַאֶפֶס עוֹד אִישׁ לְבֵית שָׁאוּל—"Is there no one still belonging to the house of Saul?" The interrogative *he* is prefixed to אֶפֶס, a particle of nonexistence (see GKC, § 152 s), "nothing, no one," which is the antonym of the particle of existence, יֵשׁ, "there is," in the first textual note on 9:1. For the sense of the preposition לְ, see the first textual note on 9:1.

וְאֶעֱשֶׂה עִמּוֹ חֶסֶד אֱלֹהִים—"So that I may show God's kindness to him." See the second textual note on 9:2. There the noun חֶסֶד was in the absolute state. Here the construct phrase חֶסֶד אֱלֹהִים, literally "the faithfulness/mercy of God," shows that David is not merely displaying human kindness. Instead, as Israel's king, he is acting on behalf of his and the nation's gracious God, Yahweh. This is confirmed by the wording when David and Jonathan made a "covenant of/with Yahweh" (1 Sam 20:8; see also 1 Sam 18:3; 20:16, 42; 23:18), at which time Jonathan requested that David (literally) "do with me the kindness of Yahweh" (1 Sam 20:14; cf. 2 Sam 7:15). The use of the same idiom here (חֶסֶד + עִמּ- + עָשָׂה) indicates that David seeks to remain faithful to that covenant between them and Yahweh. God's gracious governance of this bond is also emphasized in 2 Sam 21:7, which refers to it as "*Yahweh's* oath … between David and Saul's son Jonathan."

עוֹד בֵּן לִיהוֹנָתָן—Literally "still a son to Jonathan." The particle of existence, יֵשׁ, "there is" (9:1), is implied. Here the preposition לְ (see the first textual note on 9:1) is used periphrastically in place of a construct phrase to express indefiniteness, "*a son*" (BDB, s.v. לְ, 5 c (*b*) α). A construct phrase, בֶּן־יְהוֹנָתָן, "*the son of Jonathan*," would imply that Jonathan had only this one son.

נְכֵה רַגְלָיִם:—"(Who is) crippled." See the first textual note on 4:4.

9:4 הִנֵּה־הוּא—Literally "behold/look, he." The particle הִנֵּה focuses attention on the answer but need not be translated.

בֵּית מָכִיר—The noun בַּיִת , "house," is often used in construct with a name as a local accusative, identifying a place, thus "*in* the house of Machir" (see Joüon, § 126 h).

9:6 מְפִיבֹשֶׁת—"Mephibosheth." See the third textual note on 4:4 and the second textual note on 2:8.

וַיִּשְׁתָּחוּ—"And he bowed." This verb form is pausal for וַיִּשְׁתַּחוּ, which is the first word of 9:8. It is the Hishtaphel third masculine singular preterite (imperfect with *waw* consecutive) of חָוָה, "to bow down, worship." See the third textual note on 1 Sam 1:3 and the second textual note on 1 Sam 1:28.[1]

9:7 עָשֹׂה אֶעֱשֶׂה עִמְּךָ חֶסֶד—This is the same idiom as in 9:1 (see the second textual note on 9:1) but strengthened with the addition of the Qal (G) infinitive absolute עָשֹׂה, "I will *certainly* show."

וַהֲשִׁבֹתִי—"I will restore." The accent on this first common singular Hiphil (H) perfect of שׁוּב, "to return," has shifted to the final syllable (תִי-), indicating that it has *waw* consecutive, thus "I will …" See GKC, § 49 h, and the third textual note on 6:21.

אֶת־כָּל־שְׂדֵה שָׁאוּל אָבִיךָ—"The entire estate of your grandfather Saul." The noun שָׂדֶה is often translated as "field." However, in this instance it denotes the landed "estate" of the former king (cf. הָאֲדָמָה, "the land," in 9:10). In the previous clause of 9:7, אָבִיךָ, "your father," referred to Jonathan, but the identical word here, אָבִיךָ, refers to Saul, requiring the translation "your grandfather." Cf. "grandson" in the third textual note on 9:9.

עַל־שֻׁלְחָנִי תָּמִיד:—Literally "at my table always." These words recur in a different order in 9:10 and (without a suffix on שֻׁלְחָן) in 9:13. See also the second textual note on 9:11. In 9:7, 10, 13 תָּמִיד serves as an adverb and refers to regular (repeated) meals, as also in 2 Ki 25:29 ‖ Jer 52:33. It is used most often as an adverb, "continually." It appears frequently in the legislation for the regular and continual worship at the tabernacle, including the showbread (Ex 25:30; Num 4:7), and sometimes as a substantive (e.g., Ex 29:42; 30:8; throughout Numbers 28).

9:8 וַיִּשְׁתַּחוּ—"(And) he bowed." See the second textual note on 9:6.

---

[1] Steinmann, *1 Samuel*, 44, 62.

מֶה עַבְדֶּךָ כִּי פָנִיתָ אֶל־הַכֶּלֶב הַמֵּת אֲשֶׁר כָּמוֹנִי—Literally "what is your servant that you faced toward the dead dog that is like me?" This expression of supreme humility shows that Mephibosheth considers David's treatment of him to be entirely by grace, unmerited by him but shown to him on account of another (his father, Jonathan), as is God's treatment of us on account of Jesus Christ. The use of the interrogative מָה, "what?" (usually used for a thing) instead of מִי, "who?" (for a person) and the reference to oneself in the third person strengthens the abject humility. The verb פָנִיתָ is the Qal (G) of פָּנָה, meaning "to turn (toward)" or "to face," as also in 1:7; 2:20. A speaker refers to himself or someone else metaphorically as a "dead dog" (כֶּלֶב with the Qal [G] participle of מוּת) elsewhere in the OT only in 1 Sam 24:15 (ET 24:14; see the fourth textual note there[2]) and 2 Sam 16:9, and in all three passages the speaker is addressing the king. For the explicative אֲשֶׁר, see Joüon, § 158 f. The suffix on כָּמוֹנִי (the preposition כְּ), "like me," is the only element of the clause that is first person instead of third person (see Joüon, § 151 b). This simile suggests that Mephibosheth does not even consider himself worthy to claim to "be" a dead dog, but only "like" one.

9:9 נַעַר—"Attendant." This word may denote a boy or young man and can also be used in reference to servants of various types (*HALOT*, 3). The author plays on this term in the initial chapters of the book; see the commentary on 1 Sam 2:12–17 and the first textual note on 1 Sam 3:1.[3]

לְשָׁאוּל וּלְכָל־בֵּיתוֹ—The preposition לְ, repeated with "Saul" and "all his house," denotes possession, "belonging to." Cf. the first textual note on 9:1.

לְבֶן־אֲדֹנֶיךָ—"To your master's grandson." In the phrase בֶּן־אֲדֹנֶיךָ, which occurs twice in 9:10, the noun בֵּן, "son," is used in the sense of "grandson." Cf. the use of אָב, "father," for "grandfather" in the third textual note on 9:7.

9:11 אֹכֵל—Most Masoretic manuscripts have this Qal (G) participle describing Mephibosheth, literally "(was) eating," denoting regular (habitual and recurring) action. This same participle is used for Mephibosheth in 9:13, תָּמִיד הוּא אֹכֵל, literally "always he (was) eating," meaning "he always ate." Here in 9:11 the Syriac Peshitta has a periphrastic perfect with the participle, ܠܥܣ ܗܘܐ, literally "was eating," and it uses the same construction (but with the participle of a different verb) in 9:13, ܣܡܝܟ ܗܘܐ, "was dining." Here two Masoretic manuscripts read יֹאכַל, "he would eat," the Qal (G) imperfect, which can refer to recurring action in the past (Joüon, § 113 e). The imperfect is supported by the future in the Vulgate, which translates this second half of the verse as a continuation of Ziba's speech to the king, *Mifiboseth comedet*, "Mephibosheth will eat" (see also the next textual note).

שֻׁלְחָנִי—The MT has "my table," which David used in 9:7, 10, but the quotation of David ceased in 9:10. The MT appears to have accidentally substituted this suffixed form from 9:7, 10. One Masoretic manuscript reads שֻׁלְחָנוֹ, "his [David's] table." The LXX reads τῆς τραπέζης Δαυιδ, "David's table." The translation above follows the Syriac Peshitta, ܦܬܘܪܐ ܕܡܠܟܐ, "the king's table," which fits with the reference to "the

---

2   Steinmann, *1 Samuel*, 456.

3   Steinmann, *1 Samuel*, 87, 109.

king's sons" (בְּנֵי הַמֶּלֶךְ) at the end of the verse. The Vulgate reads *mensam tuam*, "your table," as part of Ziba's speech to David.

כְּאַחַד מִבְּנֵי הַמֶּלֶךְ:—"Like one of the king's sons." The preposition מִן (on מִבְּנֵי) has a partitive sense here. When the genitive, or *nomen rectum*, in a construct phrase has the definite article (בְּנֵי הַמֶּלֶךְ), the entire phrase is definite, but the emphasis here is more on the particular king ("the sons of *the* king," David) than on specific sons of his. See Waltke-O'Connor, § 9.7a, including example 3.

9:12 וְכֹל מוֹשַׁב בֵּית־צִיבָא עֲבָדִים לִמְפִיבֹשֶׁת:—Literally "and every resident of the house of Ziba (were) servants belonging to Mephibosheth." The noun מוֹשָׁב is derived from the verb יָשַׁב, "to dwell, reside; sit." This noun denoted a "seat" at the royal table in 1 Sam 20:18, 25, and it often refers to a "dwelling place." This is the only OT passage where it denotes people, and its singular serves as a collective, "residents" or "those living" in a house (see BDB, s.v. מוֹשָׁב, 5).

9:13 וְהוּא פִּסֵּחַ שְׁתֵּי רַגְלָיו:—Hebrew generally employs a pronominal suffix when referring to limbs, thus "he was lame in both of *his* feet" (see Joüon, § 146 g). Contrast the lack of a suffix in נְכֵה רַגְלָיִם, literally "struck of (in respect to) feet," i.e., "crippled," in the fourth textual note on 9:3.

Commentary

c. 999 BC[4]

The list of David's officials (8:15–18) served to round out the first account of David's reign, showcasing him as a godly ruler (2 Samuel 5–8). Unlike the previous chapter (וַיְהִי אַחֲרֵי־כֵן, "after this," 8:1), this one does not begin with a chronological notice. This absence, combined with the administrative summary in 2 Samuel 8, is a subtle indication that this chapter and the subsequent ones are not arranged chronologically in relation to 2 Samuel 5–8. In fact, the narratives in 2 Samuel 5–8, which include several summary statements, are more or less in chronological order and cover all the years of David's reign, first over Judah (1009–1002 BC) and then over all Israel (1002–969 BC).[5] But the narratives in 2 Samuel 9–20 begin with a flashback to a time early in David's reign (chapter 9 in c. 999 BC) and then move forward in chronological order (the date of chapter 20 is 973 BC).[6]

The reason for a new beginning with the flashback to David's provision for Mephibosheth is so that this account can prepare readers for the roles played by Ziba (16:1–4; 19:18, 30 [ET 19:17, 29]) and Mephibosheth (19:25–31 [ET 19:24–30]) in connection with Absalom's rebellion (chapters 15–19; 978–974 BC). The final chapters of the book (2 Samuel 21–24) are a miscellany

---

[4] See "The Chronology of David's Reign" in the commentary on 5:1–5.

[5] The summary statements are in 5:4–5 (1009–969 BC); 5:10–12 (980–975 BC); 5:13–16 (1002–969 BC); 8:1–14 (975–969 BC); and 8:15–18 (1002–969 BC).

[6] The one exception to this chronological order is the narrative of Solomon's birth in 994 BC (12:24–25), which the author inserted into his description of the events of 997 BC (11:1–12:23, 26–31).

of items from David's reign, and except for 2 Samuel 24 they cannot be dated precisely. (For further details on the dating of the events of David's reign, see "The Chronology of David's Reign" in the commentary on 5:1–5.)

This narrative opens with David inquiring about showing kindness to Saul's house "for Jonathan's sake" (9:1). David is not displaying interest in showing kindness to Saul's entire progeny and will later allow other sons of Saul to perish (21:1–14). David's motivation is linked to his promises to Jonathan, as the two of them had established a covenant with Yahweh.[7] David had also sworn to Saul that he would not cut off his descendants (1 Sam 24:21–23 [ET 24:20–22]). David appears to be unaware of any survivors from Jonathan's family. David had fled Saul's court about 1015 BC. Mephibosheth was five years old when Jonathan died about 1009 BC (2 Sam 4:4), placing his birth in 1014 BC. The last contact between Jonathan and David took place at Horesh (1 Sam 23:16–18; c. 1013–c. 1012 BC). Therefore, David, even if he had learned of the birth of Mephibosheth from Jonathan at their final meeting, would not have known whether any son of Jonathan had survived since that time.

David's courtiers, however, knew about Saul's servant Ziba and summoned him to answer David's questions (9:2a). After confirming that the man was Ziba (9:2b), David inquired about members of Saul's house (9:3). Ziba identified only Mephibosheth. While Saul had sons by his concubine and grandsons through his daughter Merab and these relatives were also alive at this time (they are mentioned in 21:8), they would not have been considered part of Saul's house. Sons of a concubine or sons of a daughter normally were not eligible for dynastic succession.

David then inquired about Mephibosheth's whereabouts and learned that he was living with a certain Machir in Lo-debar (9:4). Machir, who was apparently maintaining loyalty to Saul's house, would later show that same kind of fidelity to David during Absalom's rebellion (17:27–29). It may have been David's kindness to Mephibosheth that won Machir's allegiance. The exact location of Lo-debar is not known, but from the notice in 17:27 it appears to be in the Transjordan; it is perhaps identical to "Lidbir" in the territory of Gad (לְדִבִר, Josh 13:26). It is likely that when Mephibosheth's uncle Ish-bosheth reigned over the northern tribes from the Transjordanian city of Mahanaim (2:8–4:12), Mephibosheth was also brought east of the Jordan and had remained there.

When David had Mephibosheth brought to Jerusalem (9:5), Jonathan's son showed due respect and humility before the king (9:6). It would have been quite a tense moment for the grandson[8] of the previous monarch, who may have wondered whether he was going to be accused of having treasonous designs on the throne held by his grandfather.[9] David reassured Mephibosheth that this was

---

[7] 1 Sam 18:3; 20:8, 16, 42; 23:18. See the second textual note on 2 Sam 9:3.

[8] See the third textual note on 9:9.

[9] See the third textual note on 9:7.

not the case (9:7). Instead, he promised two things: to restore the property to Mephibosheth that had belonged to Saul and to give Mephibosheth the privilege of eating at the royal table.

Some commentators suggest that Saul's estate had been confiscated by David as crown property and this is why the king could order it restored to Mephibosheth.[10] However, it may not have been crown property as much as it was abandoned property. After Saul's death the surviving heirs of Saul's house would have been Ish-bosheth and Mephibosheth.[11] Apparently both of them had moved to the Transjordan, and Mephibosheth—still a teen in 999 BC when David fetched him—had been living under the care of Machir. In this situation the property may have reverted to Saul's daughters (Num 27:1–11). Since his daughters were married and were living with their husbands—Michal with David in Jerusalem[12] and Merab with Adriel in Meholah[13]—the land may have been placed under the maintenance of a caretaker, perhaps Ziba. The produce of the land would have been given to the daughters' husbands (cf. 9:10). This would also explain how David's courtiers knew of and found Ziba. Now David was simply declaring that the property should be given to Mephibosheth as Saul's legitimate heir.

David's other kindness was to invite Mephibosheth to the king's table. This was tantamount to treating him like one of the princes (9:11) and was similar to David's privileges at Saul's table as the king's son-in-law (1 Sam 20:5, 18, 24–29). Some have suggested that David had an ulterior motive for bringing Mephibosheth to his table. According to this suggestion, the grandson of the former king would have been under the watchful eye of David to prevent him from seeking to seize the throne.[14] However, it would appear that David was taking a greater risk by bringing Mephibosheth to Jerusalem.[15] Had David allowed Mephibosheth to live in Lo-debar in relative obscurity, it is doubtful that this crippled grandson of Saul would have posed any threat. However, by placing Mephibosheth in Jerusalem and in the royal court, David was taking a chance that Mephibosheth could have observed and taken advantage of court intrigues to elevate himself to the throne. In fact, this is exactly the charge that

---

[10] Anderson, *2 Samuel*, 141; McCarter, *II Samuel*, 261.

[11] Saul's sons by his concubine Rizpah (21:8) would not have been considered heirs. A concubine was a wife for whom one paid no bride-price, and therefore her sons would not be considered her husband's heirs.

[12] Michal was King Saul's second daughter (1 Sam 14:49). David had married her with her father's approval (1 Sam 18:20–27). Saul, however, later rescinded his consent by giving Michal to another man (1 Sam 25:44). Subsequently, David retrieved her (2 Sam 3:13–16), and she resided with him in Jerusalem (2 Sam 6:16–23).

[13] Merab was Saul's older daughter (1 Sam 14:49). Saul had promised her to David but broke his promise by giving her to Adriel (1 Sam 18:17–19). Her marriage to Adriel and her five sons by him are noted in 2 Sam 21:8.

[14] E.g., Hertzberg, *I and II Samuel*, 300.

[15] Baldwin, *1 and 2 Samuel*, 227, n. 1.

Ziba would later level against Mephibosheth (16:3). Despite this risk, David was willing to keep his covenant pledge to Jonathan[16] and honor their friendship in a deeper way than he had been able to do while Jonathan was alive.[17]

In accepting David's kindness and generosity, Mephibosheth referred to himself with the self-deprecating phrase "dead dog" (see the second textual note on 9:8). Dogs were not kept as pets in antiquity, and they were viewed as less than noble beasts (Eccl 9:4). To refer to someone as a dog was to denigrate them (1 Sam 17:43; 2 Ki 8:13; see also 2 Sam 3:8). Even worse was a lifeless dog—now only a lowly animal that had even lost its seemingly miserable life (1 Sam 24:15 [ET 24:14]; 2 Sam 16:9). In referring to himself in this way, Mephibosheth was conceding that he had no royal claim. He acknowledged that in his current state as a ward of Machir, he was hardly noticeable to King David, much less worthy of the honor and kindness David had bestowed on him.

Since Mephibosheth would be living in Jerusalem, we are told that David again summoned Ziba, told him of the grant of Saul's land, and ordered him to tend it and bring its produce to Mephibosheth (9:9–10a). He also informed him that Mephibosheth would be an absentee landlord, since he would be eating at David's table. The parenthetical comment concerning the size of Ziba's household (9:10b) informs readers that Ziba was well able to fulfill David's order. Saul's servant had no choice other than to comply with David's order (9:11a).

The final verses in this account are a summary of Mephibosheth's time at David's court (9:11b–13). This probably encapsulates the years between David's grant (c. 999 BC) and Absalom's rebellion (974 BC), when Mephibosheth last appears in the narrative (19:25–31 [ET 19:24–30]).[18] This summary prepares the reader for the events involving Ziba and Mephibosheth during Absalom's rebellion. Mephibosheth lived in Jerusalem in the manner of a royal prince (9:11b).[19] He apparently married since he had a son, Mica (9:12a), who would still be young at the time of Absalom's rebellion (974 BC). Meanwhile, Ziba's entire household was obligated to work for him as his servants (9:12b). Mephibosheth, however, was absent from active oversight of Ziba and could not easily travel to Gibeah to monitor his activity, since he was lame (9:13). This eventually would allow an opportunistic Ziba to seek a way to remove his obligation to Mephibosheth (16:1–4).

Mephibosheth's son "Mica" (מִיכָא, 9:12) became the progenitor of a prodigious line of descendants. They are mentioned twice in Chronicles (1 Chr

---

[16] See the second textual note on 9:3.

[17] Saul continued to reign as long as Jonathan was alive. Their deaths in the same battle are recorded in 1 Sam 31:2–6. In 2 Samuel 1 David learned of and lamented Jonathan's death.

[18] Mephibosheth is also mentioned in 21:7, which records that David had compassion on him because of the oath between David, Jonathan, and Yahweh. 2 Sam 21:1–9 narrates an incident that probably took place before Absalom's rebellion, but Mephibosheth plays no role in the narrative at that point.

[19] See the third textual note on 9:11.

8:34–40; 9:40–44), where their forefather's name is spelled "Micah" (מִיכָה, 1 Chr 8:34–35; 9:40–41).

This short account of David's demonstration of Yahweh's grace to Mephibosheth illustrates David's character as a faithful follower of God. It shows David fulfilling his vow to Jonathan, which was sworn in Yahweh's name (1 Sam 20:42; see also 1 Sam 23:18) and so could even be called a "covenant of Yahweh" (1 Sam 20:8) and "*Yahweh's* oath" (2 Sam 21:7).[20] Although Jonathan had died a decade earlier (1 Sam 31:2), David neither overlooked nor forgot his obligation to both Jonathan and Yahweh to keep his pledge. As such, David serves as an example to Christians of faithful dealings with one's neighbor and fidelity to the true God, who has revealed his steadfast love for all, even the most disadvantaged, in Jesus Christ. David welcomed a disabled man (2 Sam 9:3, 13) to his royal table. The Son of David[21] came to heal the lame (e.g., Mt 11:4–5; 15:30–31; 21:14) and welcome all to feast at the royal banquet of God.[22]

---

[20]   See also 1 Sam 18:3; 20:8, 16, 42; 23:18 and the second textual note on 2 Sam 9:3.

[21]   See the commentary on 2 Samuel 7 as well as "The Promise to David (2 Samuel 7)" in "Christ in Samuel" in the introduction (Steinmann, *1 Samuel*, 23–24).

[22]   See, e.g., Is 25:6–9; Ps 23:5 (in a psalm of David); Mt 22:1–14; Lk 14:12–24; Rev 19:6–9. See also the Last Supper (Mt 26:17–30) and Holy Communion for those who are prepared (1 Cor 11:23–34).

David Defeats the Ammonites

Translation

10 ¹After this the king of the Ammonites died, and his son Hanun reigned in his place. ²David thought, "I will show kindness to Hanun the son of Nahash just as his father showed kindness to me." So David sent his servants to console him concerning his father.

When David's servants arrived in Ammonite territory, ³the Ammonite officials said to their master Hanun, "Is David showing respect for your father by sending men to console you? Didn't David send his servants to you for the purpose of searching the city, spying on it, and destroying it?" ⁴So Hanun took David's servants and shaved half of their beards, cut their clothes in half at the hips, and sent them away.

⁵When David was told about the men, he sent [someone] to meet them, since the men were very humiliated. The king said, "Stay in Jericho until your beards regrow and then return."

⁶Then the Ammonites realized that they had made themselves repulsive to David. The Ammonites sent and hired the Arameans of Beth-rehob and the Arameans of Zobah (twenty thousand foot soldiers) and the king of Maacah (a thousand men) and the men of Tob (twelve thousand men).

⁷When David heard [about this], he sent Joab and all the elite troops. ⁸The Ammonites came out and arranged their battle lines at the entrance of the city gate. The Arameans of Zobah and Rehob and the men of Tob and Maacah were in the open country by themselves. ⁹When Joab saw that he was under attack in front and in the rear, he chose all of the most skilled men from Israel and lined [them] up in battle formation to meet the Arameans. ¹⁰The rest of the troops he placed under the command of his brother Abishai and lined [them] up in battle formation to meet the Ammonites. ¹¹He said, "If the Arameans are too strong for me, then you come to my rescue, and if the Ammonites are too strong for you, I will come to rescue you. ¹²Be strong! Let us fight bravely for the sake of our people and for the sake of the cities of our God! May Yahweh do what is good in his eyes!" ¹³So Joab and the troops with him advanced to fight the Arameans, and they fled before him. ¹⁴When the Ammonites saw that the Arameans had fled, they fled before Abishai and entered the city. Joab stopped his campaign against the Ammonites and came to Jerusalem.

¹⁵When the Arameans saw that they had been defeated by Israel, they regrouped. ¹⁶Hadadezer sent [messengers] and brought the Arameans who were across the Euphrates River. They came to Helam, and Shobach, the commander of Hadadezer's army, was leading them.

¹⁷David was informed, so he gathered all Israel and crossed the Jordan River. He came to Helam, and the Arameans arranged their battle lines to meet David and fight him. ¹⁸The Arameans fled before Israel, and David killed seven thousand charioteers and forty thousand foot soldiers. He struck down Shobach, the commander of his [Hadadezer's] army, and he died there. ¹⁹When all the kings who were Hadadezer's vassals saw that they were defeated by Israel, they made peace with Israel and became their vassals. So the Arameans were afraid to help the Ammonites again.

Textual Notes

10:2 עִם ׀ אֶעֱשֶׂה־חֶסֶד—"I will show kindness to." For this idiom (repeated in the next clause of 10:2), see the second textual note on 9:1 as well as the third textual note on 2:5. For the noun חֶסֶד, see also the second textual note on 9:3. Here the imperfect אֶעֱשֶׂה has the volative nuance of intention (cf. Joüon, § 113 l, m, n): David desires to be gracious toward Hanun, just as Hanun's father, Nahash, was graciously disposed toward David, and he initiates action to display his intent. Therefore the following verb וַיִּשְׁלַח is translated with a final or telic nuance, "*so* he sent."

לְנַחֲמוֹ בְּיַד־עֲבָדָיו—"His servants to console him" is literally "to comfort him by the hand of his servants." The verb לְנַחֲמוֹ is the Piel (D) infinitive construct of נָחַם with לְ and a third masculine singular object suffix, forming a purpose clause. In the Piel, נָחַם has the transitive meaning "to comfort, console." Here it refers to consoling a person who is grieving over the death of a relative, as also in 10:3 (see the third textual note on 10:3) and in 12:24, where David consoles Bathsheba after the death their son. Elsewhere in Samuel נָחַם is used only in the Niphal (N), meaning "be comforted" (2 Sam 13:39), "regret" (1 Sam 15:11, 35), "change one's mind" (1 Sam 15:29 [twice]), or "relent" (2 Sam 24:16). God is the subject in the majority of these passages (1 Sam 15:11, 29 [first occurrence], 35; 2 Sam 24:16).

10:3 הַמְכַבֵּד דָּוִד אֶת־אָבִיךָ בְּעֵינֶיךָ—"Is David showing respect for your father?" This question (with an interrogative *he* on הַמְכַבֵּד) is literally "is David honoring your father in your eyes?" The verb מְכַבֵּד is the Piel (D) masculine singular participle of כָּבֵד. In the Piel, the verb means "to honor" and is an antonym of "to despise, disgrace, humiliate" (see 1 Sam 2:29–30; 15:30; see also the Niphal [N] in the context of 2 Sam 6:20–22).

כִּי־שָׁלַח—"By sending" is literally "because he sent." Here the conjunction כִּי is explicative (BDB, 3 c) since it introduces a clause that explains how or in what way David is (or claims to be) "honoring" Hanun's father.

מְנַחֲמִים—"Men to console you." This participle could also be translated as "consolers, comforters." For the meaning of the Piel (D) of נָחַם, see the second textual note on 10:2.

בַּעֲבוּר חֲקוֹר—"For the purpose of searching." The combination of prepositions (עֲבוּר + בְּ) בַּעֲבוּר is often used with an infinitive construct to denote purpose (BDB, s.v. עֲבוּר II, 1 b, under the root עבר). Three infinitives follow here. The first, חֲקוֹר, is the Qal (G) of חָקַר, "to search, explore, examine." In the parallel verse 1 Chr 19:3 it has been regularized to the form לַחְקֹר (as in Prov 23:30) since purpose is more commonly

179

expressed by an infinitive construct prefixed with the preposition לְ. See also the next textual note.

וּלְרַגְּלָהּ וּלְהָפְכָהּ—"Spying on it, and destroying it." These two infinitive constructs with לְ indicate purpose. Both have a third feminine singular suffix, referring back to the noun הָעִיר, "the city," since this noun is feminine (as are cities in general). The first infinitive construct is the Piel (D) of the denominative verb רָגַל, derived from the noun רֶגֶל, "foot." By etymology, then, this verb refers to travel by foot, but its Piel (D) most often means "to spy." Its plural Piel participle, מְרַגְּלִים, denotes "spies" in 1 Sam 26:4 or "agents" (see the textual note on 2 Sam 15:10). The second infinitive is the Qal (G) of הָפַךְ, "to turn, change." When it refers to cities it can mean "overturn, destroy" (e.g., Gen 19:25, 29; Deut 29:22 [ET 29:23]).

10:4 וַיְגַלַּח אֶת־חֲצִי זְקָנָם—"And he shaved half of their beards." This means he shaved off half of each man's beard. In the Piel (D), the verb גָּלַח means "to shave" (as here with the noun זָקָן, "beard") or "cut off" one's hair (three times in 14:26). The MT here is partially supported by the LXX, which reads καὶ ἐξύρησεν τοὺς πώγωνας αὐτῶν, "and he shaved their beards." The parallel verse 1 Chr 19:4 reads וַיְגַלְּחֵם, "and he shaved them," and the third masculine plural object suffix refers to the men, implying that he completely shaved off the full beard of each man.

וַיִּכְרֹת אֶת־מַדְוֵיהֶם בַּחֵצִי עַד שְׁתוֹתֵיהֶם—Literally "and he cut their garments at the half until their buttocks." The suffixed plural מַדְוֵיהֶם, "their garments," is a noun whose singular could be either מַדְוֶה or מַדּוּ. The identical form is in 1 Chr 19:4, but the noun appears nowhere else in the OT. בַּחֵצִי, "in the half," is a pausal form of the noun חֲצִי (as in the preceding textual note) with the preposition בְּ and the definite article. The only other OT occurrence of the noun שֵׁת, "buttocks," is in Is 20:4, which likewise refers to them as stripped or bare.[1] The parallel verse 1 Chr 19:4 uses the noun (with the article) הַמִּפְשָׂעָה, "the hip."

10:5 וַיַּגִּדוּ לְדָוִד—Literally "and they reported to David." The impersonal plural verb (the Hiphil [H] of נָגַד) with no stated subject can be translated as a passive, with its object as the subject: "when David was told" (see Joüon, §§ 128 b, 155 i). See the equivalent Hophal (Hp) clause at the start of 10:17: וַיֻּגַּד לְדָוִד, "and it was reported to David." In 10:5 the longer reading in 4QSam^a (וינגדו לדויד על [האנשים]) is "[when David was told *about*] the men," which is supported by the LXX (καὶ ἀνήγγειλαν τῷ Δαυιδ ὑπὲρ τῶν ἀνδρῶν) and the parallel in 1 Chr 19:5 (וַיַּגִּידוּ לְדָוִיד עַל־הָאֲנָשִׁים). The translation above follows the longer reading.

לִקְרָאתָם—"To meet them." For this Qal (G) infinitive construct of קָרָא II, "to meet, encounter," with the preposition לְ, see the second textual note on 1 Sam 4:1.[2] This form has a third masculine plural object suffix. The form without the suffix, לִקְרַאת, occurs in 10:9, 10, 17, where it refers to engaging in battle.

---

[1] *DCH* lists this noun as שֵׁת II. BDB includes it as שֵׁת III under the root שׁתה II and suggests that the root שׁתה II may be a parallel root of שִׁית and may mean "to set, sit."

[2] Steinmann, *1 Samuel*, 119.

נִכְלָמִים—This is the Niphal (N) masculine plural participle of כָּלַם, meaning "be ashamed, disgraced, humiliated." The same participle recurs (with the article) in 19:4 (ET 19:3). The Hiphil (H) or Hophal (Hp) of this verb was used in 1 Sam 20:34; 25:7, 15.

שְׁבוּ ... וְשַׁבְתֶּם—"Stay ... return." The first of these two Qal (G) verb forms is the imperative of יָשַׁב, while the second is the perfect of שׁוּב with *waw* consecutive.

יְצַמַּח—"They regrow." The Qal (G) of צָמַח often refers to the "sprouting" of plants (e.g., Gen 2:5; Ex 10:5). The verb is used in the Piel (D) specifically for the "growing" (Ezek 16:7) or "regrowing" (here and in the parallel verse 1 Chr 19:5, as well as Judg 16:22) of human hair. The verb's Hiphil (H), literally "to make sprout, cause to blossom," is used metaphorically in 2 Sam 23:5 for God bringing about salvation for David and fulfilling his desires.

10:6 נִבְאֲשׁוּ בְּדָוִד—"They had made themselves repulsive to David." In the Qal (G), the verb בָּאַשׁ literally means "to stink," e.g., the stench of rotting fish and frogs in Ex 7:18, 21; 8:10 (ET 8:14). In the Niphal (N), it has a reflexive and metaphorical meaning, "make oneself be repulsive," here and also in 2 Sam 16:21. See the second textual note on 1 Sam 13:4.[3] The parallel verse 1 Chr 19:6 has the Hithpael (HtD) הִתְבָּאֲשׁוּ with the same meaning. See Waltke-O'Connor, § 23.4h, including examples 24a and 24b.

רַגְלִי—For "foot soldiers" or "infantry troops," see the third textual note on 1 Sam 4:10.[4]

וְאִישׁ טוֹב—"And the men of Tob." The singular noun אִישׁ, "man," is used as a collective for soldiers. This is also evident in its use in 10:8.

The parallel in 1 Chr 19:6–7 has a much longer text:

וַיִּרְאוּ בְּנֵי עַמּוֹן כִּי הִתְבָּאֲשׁוּ עִם־דָּוִיד וַיִּשְׁלַח חָנוּן וּבְנֵי עַמּוֹן אֶלֶף כִּכַּר־כֶּסֶף לִשְׂכֹּר לָהֶם מִן־אֲרַם נַהֲרַיִם וּמִן־אֲרַם מַעֲכָה וּמִצּוֹבָה רֶכֶב וּפָרָשִׁים׃ וַיִּשְׂכְּרוּ לָהֶם שְׁנַיִם וּשְׁלֹשִׁים אֶלֶף רֶכֶב וְאֶת־מֶלֶךְ מַעֲכָה וְאֶת־עַמּוֹ וַיָּבֹאוּ וַיַּחֲנוּ לִפְנֵי מֵידְבָא וּבְנֵי עַמּוֹן נֶאֶסְפוּ מֵעָרֵיהֶם וַיָּבֹאוּ לַמִּלְחָמָה׃

When the Ammonites realized that they had made themselves repulsive to David, Hanun and the Ammonites sent a thousand talents of silver to hire for themselves chariots and charioteers from Aram Naharaim, from the Arameans of Maacah, and from Zobah. They hired for themselves thirty-two thousand chariots and the king of Maacah and his army. They came and camped in front of Medeba, and the Ammonites gathered from their cities and came for the battle.

4QSam[a], though fragmentary, appears to combine elements of 2 Sam 10:6 and 1 Chr 19:6–7. It contains אלף ככר כסף, "a thousand talents of silver"; רכב ופרשים, "chariots and charioteers"; and [ובני] עמון נאספו מן, "[and the Amm]onites gathered from," as in 1 Chr 19:6–7. Like 2 Sam 10:6 it also has the phrase [ואת א]ישטוב, "[and the m]en of Tob," or, since it is written as one word, "[and I]shtob" (cf. the LXX: Ιστωβ).

---

3 Steinmann, *1 Samuel*, 232.

4 Steinmann, *1 Samuel*, 122.

10:7 כָּל־הַצָּבָא הַגִּבֹּרִים—"All the elite troops" is literally "all the army, the mighty men." The articular plural substantive הַגִּבֹּרִים is in apposition to the articular singular noun הַצָּבָא, "the army." Later in the book הַגִּבֹּרִים will be used for David's most elite commandos (see the first textual note and the commentary on 23:8). The LXX reading here, τὴν δύναμιν, τοὺς δυνατούς, "the army, the mighty men," agrees with the appositional phrase in the MT. One Masoretic manuscript has the construct phrase צְבָא הַגִּבֹּרִים, "the army of the mighty men," which is supported by the Syriac Peshitta (ܚܝܠܐ ܕܓܢܒܪܐ) and the Vulgate (*omnem exercitum bellatorum*) and which is probably the correct Hebrew reading in the parallel verse 1 Chr 19:8 (as supported by the ancient versions there).

10:8 וַיַּעַרְכוּ מִלְחָמָה—"And they arranged their battle lines." This verb and object noun are literally "and they arranged a battle." In this context the Qal (G) of עָרַךְ, "to order, arrange," refers to the arraying of troops in a line to meet the enemy in combat (*HALOT*, 3), as again in 10:9, 10, 17. See the first textual note on 1 Sam 4:2.[5]

פֶּתַח הַשָּׁעַר—"At the entrance of the city gate." This is an accusative of location, so the translation adds "at." 1 Chr 19:9 reads פֶּתַח הָעִיר, "(at) the entrance of the city."

בַּשָּׂדֶה—"In the open country." The noun שָׂדֶה, "field," is often used of the open country as opposed the city, an urban area enclosed by a wall (see *HALOT*, 1).

10:9 כִּי־הָיְתָה אֵלָיו פְּנֵי הַמִּלְחָמָה מִפָּנִים וּמֵאָחוֹר—"That he was under attack in front and in the rear" is literally "that the face/front of the battle was to him, from front and from behind." The verb הָיְתָה is feminine singular, matching הַמִּלְחָמָה, "the battle," even though the subject of the verb is the (usually masculine) plural word in construct in the phrase פְּנֵי הַמִּלְחָמָה, "the face of the battle" (GKC, § 146 a; Joüon, § 150 i).

וַיִּבְחַר מִכֹּל בָּחוּרֵי יִשְׂרָאֵל—"He chose all of the most skilled men from Israel." This Qere literally says "and he chose from all the chosen men of Israel." For the Qal passive (Gp) participle בָּחוּר, literally "chosen, selected," see the second textual note on 6:1. The Kethib is grammatically awkward because the preposition בְּ is attached to the genitive/*nomen rectum* in the construct phrase, בָּחוּרֵי בְּיִשְׂרָאֵל, literally "the chosen men of *in* Israel." 1 Chr 19:10 reads בָּחוּר בְּיִשְׂרָאֵל, "chosen in Israel," with the singular בָּחוּר serving as a collective. If 1 Chr 19:10 preserves the correct reading, then the Qere in 2 Sam 10:9 may be a Masoretic attempt at a correction of the Kethib in 2 Sam 10:9, which might have arisen when a stray mark was interpreted as a *yod* after בָּחוּר. All three readings are approximately equivalent.

There is also a noun בָּחוּר, "young man," whose singular (as in 1 Sam 9:2) is indistinguishable from the singular of the Qal passive participle that is here, but its plural in construct would have a *patach* under its first consonant, בַּחוּרֵי (see 1 Sam 8:16), whereas the plural Qal passive participle in construct here has a *shewa* under the first consonant (-בְּ).

10:10 יֶתֶר הָעָם—"The rest of the troops." For the noun יֶתֶר, the "rest, remnant, what remains," see the second textual note on 8:4. The noun עַם usually refers to "people," as in 10:12, where עַמֵּנוּ denotes "our people" Israel, but in military contexts the definite

---

5 Steinmann, *1 Samuel*, 119.

noun often denotes "the troops," as here and in 10:13. See the second textual note on 1:4.

נָתַן בְּיַד אֲבִשַׁי—"He placed under the command of ... Abishai" is literally "he gave into the hand of Abishai."

10:11 אִם־תֶּחֱזַק אֲרָם מִמֶּנִּי—Literally "if Aram is strong from/than me." The preposition מִן, "from," is often used to form a comparative (Joüon, § 141 g, h). Here, however, תֶּחֱזַק ... מִמֶּנִּי forms an elliptical comparison, "it is too strong for me." See also יֶחֶזְקוּ מִמְּךָ, "they are too strong for you," later in 10:11. For elliptical comparisons, see Joüon, § 141 i.

In Hebrew a people and especially a land can be construed as feminine, and so here אֲרָם, "Aram," is the subject of the feminine singular verb תֶּחֱזַק (see also 8:5; cf. GKC, § 145 k). However, אֲרָם is also used as a masculine singular collective, and it can be the subject of either singular or plural masculine verbs. See Joüon, § 150 e; the textual note on 10:13–14; and second textual note on 10:17.

וְהָיְתָה לִּי לִישׁוּעָה—"Then you come to my rescue" is literally "and you will be for me for salvation." The Qal (G) perfect verb (here with *waw* consecutive), הָיְתָה, is a defective, or *ḥaser*, spelling of הָיִיתָ (as in 5:2) with a longer spelling of its second masculine singular ending, ־תָה, instead of the usual orthography ־תָ (GKC, § 44 g; Joüon, § 42 f). The noun יְשׁוּעָה, "salvation," is derived from the verb discussed in the next textual note.

לְהוֹשִׁיעַ לָךְ:—"To rescue you." The verb is the Hiphil (H) infinitive construct of יָשַׁע, "to save," with לְ. It recurs in 10:19. When this Hiphil verb has human allies as its subject, the translations "rescue" (10:11) or "help" (10:19; 14:4) are appropriate. לָךְ is pausal for לְךָ, with a second masculine (not feminine) singular suffix.

10:12 חֲזַק וְנִתְחַזַּק—"Be strong! Let us fight bravely." The first form of the stative verb חָזַק is the Qal (G) masculine singular imperative. The second form of חָזַק is the Hithpael (HtD) plural cohortative. In the Hithpael, this verb means to behave with courage and bravery (see *HALOT*, Hithpael, 1). The form נִתְחַזַּק retains the original *patach* in the final syllable (־זַּק) instead of the usual *tsere* of the Hithpael (GKC, § 54 k).

10:13–14 בָאֲרָם וַיָּנֻסוּ ... נָס אֲרָם—"The Arameans, and they fled. ... The Arameans had fled." Here the singular collective noun אֲרָם is first used with the masculine plural of the verb נוּס, "flee" (see also the second textual note on 10:17). In the second instance, it is the subject of the masculine singular of the same verb, as again in 10:18, וַיָּנָס אֲרָם (similarly, וַיִּרְא אֲרָם in 10:15).

10:14 וַיָּשָׁב יוֹאָב מֵעַל בְּנֵי עַמּוֹן—"Joab stopped his campaign against the Ammonites" is literally "and Joab returned from upon/against the sons of Ammon."

10:15 וַיִּנָּגֶף—For the Niphal (N) of נָגַף (this is the third masculine singular perfect) with the military meaning "be defeated," see the third textual note on 1 Sam 4:2[6] and the textual note on 2 Sam 2:17. See also the plural וַיִּנָּגְפוּ, "they were defeated," in 10:19.

וַיֵּאָסְפוּ יַחַד:—"They regrouped" is literally "and they gathered (themselves) together." For the Niphal (N) of אָסַף (as well as its active Qal [G]) for troops gathering

---

[6] Steinmann, *1 Samuel*, 119–20.

together for battle, see the first textual note on 6:1. יַחַד is the pausal form of the adverb יַחַד, "together" (also in 14:16; 21:9).

10:16 הַנָּהָר—Often "the river" is used to denote the Euphrates (e.g., Gen 31:21; Is 7:20). See the Kethib in the first textual note on 8:3.

10:17 וַיֶּאֱסֹף—"So he gathered." The Qal (G) of אָסַף often refers to gathering troops for battle. See the first textual note on 6:1 and also the Niphal (N) of אָסַף in the second textual note on 10:15.

וַיַּעַרְכוּ אֲרָם—"And the Arameans arranged." A singular collective noun such as אֲרָם can be the subject of a verb that is either in the singular or the plural, as here. See also in וַיִּרְאוּ אֲרָם in the third textual note on 10:19. Compare the textual note on 10:13–14, and contrast the first textual note on 10:11.

10:18 שְׁבַע מֵאוֹת רֶכֶב וְאַרְבָּעִים אֶלֶף פָּרָשִׁים—The reading in the MT is "seven hundred chariot[eer]s and forty thousand charioteers." The translation above follows the reading in 1 Chr 19:18, שִׁבְעַת אֲלָפִים רֶכֶב וְאַרְבָּעִים אֶלֶף אִישׁ רַגְלִי, "seven thousand chariot[eer]s and forty thousand foot soldiers." That reading is supported by the Lucianic recension of the LXX and the Old Latin here. It is also supported by Josephus, who reverses the order of the phrases: πεζῶν μὲν εἰς τέσσαρας μυριάδας ἱππέων δὲ εἰς ἑπτακισχιλίους, "forty thousand foot soldiers and seven thousand horsemen."[7]

שַׂר־צְבָאוֹ—"The commander of his [Hadadezer's] army." Shobach was identified as "the commander of Hadadezer's army" in 10:16. 1 Chr 19:18 reads שַׂר־הַצָּבָא, "the commander of the army."

10:19 כָל־הַמְּלָכִים עַבְדֵי הֲדַדְעֶזֶר—These two phrases are in apposition, literally "all the kings, the servants of Hadadezer." This has the meaning of a restrictive relative clause, "all the kings *who were* vassals of Hadadezer." Here the noun עֶבֶד, "slave, servant," denotes a king who is a subject of another king, thus a "vassal." The cognate verb later in the verse, וַיַּעַבְדוּם (the Qal [G] third masculine plural preterite [imperfect with *waw* consecutive] of עָבַד), literally "and they served them," is therefore translated as "and (they) became their vassals."

וַיַּשְׁלִמוּ אֶת־יִשְׂרָאֵל—"They made peace with Israel." The Hiphil (H) of the verb שָׁלֵם, a denominative from the noun שָׁלוֹם, "peace," often means "to make peace" (also in, e.g., Deut 20:12; Josh 11:19; 1 Ki 22:45 [ET 22:44]). This Hiphil verb takes the preposition אֵת, "with," here and also in Josh 10:1, 4.

וַיִּרְאוּ אֲרָם—"So the Arameans were afraid." The *metheg* accent with the *hireq* (-ִ֫- for -ִי-) indicates that this is a defective, or *ḥaser*, spelling of וַיִּירְאוּ, the Qal (G) third masculine plural preterite (imperfect with *waw* consecutive) of יָרֵא, "be afraid," rather than the Qal third masculine plural preterite (imperfect with *waw* consecutive) of רָאָה, "to see," whose consonants and vowels would be identical, וַיִּרְאוּ (the first word of 10:6, 19).

לְהוֹשִׁיעַ—For "to help," see the third textual note on 10:11.

---

[7] Josephus, *Antiquities*, 7.128.

Commentary

998 BC[8]

This chapter is the first of three devoted to events during the Ammonite war, 998–997 BC. David's leadership of Israel was only sporadic and minimal during this period, and much of the matters of war were delegated to Joab. It was David's inattention to his duty to lead Israel out to battle (1 Sam 8:20) that caused his attention to wander to Bathsheba and then necessitated his attempt to cover up his affair (11:1–12:25). His subsequent troubles were a consequence of it (13:1–20:26).

David's Ambassadors Are Humiliated by Hanun (10:1–5)

Parallel: 2 Sam 10:1–5 ‖ 1 Chr 19:1–5

This account once again begins with the clause "(and it came to pass) after this" (וַיְהִי אַחֲרֵי־כֵן, 10:1), the author's favorite general chronological indicator of a subsequent narrative.[9] The death of the Ammonite king Nahash sets the stage for this storyline. While there is no mention elsewhere of David's interaction with Nahash, it is reasonable to assume that Nahash favored David over his enemy Saul, who had defeated Nahash earlier (1 Samuel 11). In fact, Nahash may have been the grandfather of David's half sister Abigail (see the fifth textual note on 17:25). Thus, David may have felt a familial obligation to send a mourning delegation to honor his half sister's grandfather. Since Nahash's prior attack on Jabesh (1 Samuel 11) probably took place in 1049 BC, he must have had a long reign—at least fifty-one years.

David's motive is made clear by the author: the king wished to reciprocate for Nahash's kindness and maintain his relationship with Ammon (10:2). From the beginning David seems to have made a special effort to court the favor of the inhabitants of the Transjordan—not only the Israelite tribes living there (cf. 2:5–7), but in this case also the Ammonites. The effort aided him later during Absalom's rebellion when Transjordanians, including Nahash's son Shobi, came to his aid (17:27).

Despite David's good intentions, Hanun's advisors suspected David of seeking to expand his sphere of influence by using his ambassadors to spy on the city's defenses (10:3). "The city" is the Ammonite capital Rabbah, modern Amman, Jordan. Ironically, their fear and subsequent provocative action put into motion the series of events that resulted in David's capture of Rabbah (12:26–31).

The treatment of David's emissaries was designed to inflict maximum embarrassment (10:4). The beard was a sign of a mature man, and shaving half of it symbolically made them half men, while cutting off their clothes to expose

---

8   See "The Chronology of David's Reign" in the commentary on 5:1–5.

9   This clause occurs ten times in the OT, six times in Samuel (1 Sam 24:6 [ET 24:5]; 2 Sam 2:1; 8:1; 10:1; 13:1; 21:18) and twice in parallel verses in Chronicles (1 Chr 18:1; 19:1). The other two uses are in Judg 16:4; 2 Ki 6:24.

their hips, which would have exposed both their buttocks and genitals, adding further shame. David, however, spared them the humiliation of being seen in the royal court with half beards by allowing them to stay in Jericho until their beards grew out (10:5). David lost their services for a considerable period of time, but his compassion toward those who served him was more important. In this David is an example for others in authority—especially employers. Workers are to be treated with kindness and not simply viewed as sources of productivity. Christian employers and supervisors who show the compassion of Christ to those over whom they exercise authority imitate David's example.

Joab Defeats the Ammonites (10:6–14)

Parallel: 2 Sam 10:6–14 ‖ 1 Chr 19:6–15

Too late the Ammonites concluded that they had made an enemy of David (10:6), whom they deemed to be much more powerful than they were. To aid in their defense they hired armies from the various Aramean states. Beth-rehob lay on the northern border of the land of Israel (Num 13:21) and overlooked the valley in which the city of Dan was situated (Judg 18:28). The exact location of Zobah is not known, but from information in the OT and in surviving Assyrian texts, it appears to have been somewhere in the vicinity of Emesa (modern Homs, Syria). Maacah was a kingdom in the Golan Heights, north of Gilead, but south of Mount Hermon, and it was probably associated with the city Abel-beth-maacah (2 Sam 20:14, 15; 1 Ki 15:20; 2 Ki 15:29). Tob lay just north of Gilead (Judg 11:3, 5; 1 Macc 5:13).

In response to news of this coalition of Ammonites and Arameans, David mobilized his elite troops under Joab (2 Sam 10:7), apparently in an effort to strike before the Arameans could assemble their forces and march to Ammon. According to 1 Chr 19:7 Joab attacked at Medeba on Ammon's southern border with Moab (Num 21:30; Josh 13:9, 16; Is 15:2). Perhaps this was the beginning of a campaign to strip away Ammon's client cities before attacking Rabbah directly. Medeba would have been a good choice, since it was the most distant from Aram.

The Ammonites came out of the city, and Joab may have been able to attack them with impunity had the Arameans not arrived at Medeba in time to catch him in a pincers movement (10:8). The superior Aramean forces required Joab to place his best troops against them (10:9). Since both of his flanks were exposed, Joab had little choice but to divide his army into two commands, with the second under the control of his brother Abishai (10:10), with orders that they would come to each other's aid if needed (10:11). This was a risky strategy, since both contingents could have been overwhelmed, with neither being able to come to the aid of the other. However, Joab's words of encouragement to Abishai demonstrate his faith in God, who alone grants victory (10:12).[10] The phrase "cities

---

[10] See "Prosperity and Success Come Only from God" in "Other Theological Themes in Samuel" in the introduction (Steinmann, *1 Samuel*, 29).

of our God" is unique to Joab (2 Sam 10:12; 1 Chr 19:13). It most likely refers to Israel's cities as God's own personal possession and habitation. Joab invoked the gracious covenant name of Israel's saving God, "Yahweh," and trusted him to do what was "good in his eyes," which was to bless his people.[11]

The author relates Joab's victory with a few broad strokes—the Arameans fled, and the Ammonites retreated to the city (10:13–14). We are not told why Joab did not pursue his campaign and chose instead to return to Jerusalem. Perhaps it was not David's intent to expand his kingdom's reach at this time.

David Defeats Ammon's Aramaic Allies (10:15–19)

Parallel: 2 Sam 10:15–19 ‖ 1 Chr 19:16–19

The defeat of the Aramean army was not taken lightly. Hadadezer, whose territory David would later turn into an Israelite dependency (8:3–8),[12] rallied the more distant Arameans across the Euphrates to the northeast and sent them on a campaign under the command of Shobach (10:15–16). David was informed of Aram's military activities and met the Arameans at Helam, somewhere in the Transjordan (10:17). The location of Helam is otherwise unknown.

David's defeat of Aram included the death of a large number of Arameans as well as the death of Shobach (10:18), effectively neutralizing Aram. Now for the first time David saw his kingdom expand into an imperial power with the acquisition of all of Hadadezer's vassals (10:19). With the Arameans no longer a threat, David could turn his attention to the conquest of Ammon and the avenging of the insult to his emissaries. However, it must have been late in the autumn at this point, and that campaign would have to wait until the following spring (11:1).

---

[11] For God's revelation of his name, "Yahweh," as part of his redemption of his people through the exodus deliverance, see Exodus 3. The book of Samuel recounts or refers to Yahweh saving his people from "Egypt" in, e.g., 1 Sam 2:27–28; 4:8; 6:6; 8:8; 10:18–19; 12:6–8; 15:2, 6; 2 Sam 7:6, 23. See the textual note on 1 Sam 10:18–19 and the fourth textual note on 1 Sam 15:2 (Steinmann, *1 Samuel*, 200–201, 283). See also references to the "ark," where Yahweh dwelt in the midst of his people after their deliverance, in 1 Samuel 4–7; 2 Samuel 6–7 (also 11:11; 15:24–29).

[12] The events of 2 Samuel 8 are subsequent to the events in 2 Samuel 10. See "The Chronology of David's Reign" in the commentary on 5:1–5.

David Commits Adultery and Murder

Translation

11 ¹In the spring of the year, at the time when the kings go out [to war], David sent Joab with his servants and all Israel. They destroyed the Ammonites and laid siege against Rabbah, while David stayed in Jerusalem.

²At evening time David got up from his couch and was walking around on the roof of the palace, and from the roof he saw a woman bathing. The woman was very beautiful. ³David sent [someone], and he sought information about the woman. [The investigator] said, "Isn't this Bathsheba, Eliam's daughter, the wife of Uriah the Hittite?"

⁴So David sent messengers and fetched her. When she came to him, he lay with her (she had been purifying herself from her uncleanness). Then she returned to her home. ⁵The woman became pregnant, and she sent word to David, saying, "I am pregnant."

⁶David sent word to Joab, "Send Uriah the Hittite to me." So Joab sent Uriah to David. ⁷Uriah came to him, and David asked him about the welfare of Joab and the troops and about the progress of the war. ⁸David said to Uriah, "Go down to your house, and wash your feet." So Uriah went out of the palace, and a present from the king followed him.

⁹Now Uriah lay down in the entrance to the king's palace with all his master's servants and did not go down to his house. ¹⁰David was told, "Uriah did not go down to his house."

David said to Uriah, "Haven't you just come from a journey? Why didn't you go down to your house?"

¹¹Uriah said to David, "The ark and Israel and Judah are living in temporary shelters, and my master Joab and the servants of my maser are camping in the countryside. How can I go to my house to eat and drink and lie with my wife? I swear by your life, I will not do this!"

¹²David said to Uriah, "Stay here today too, and tomorrow I will send you away." So Uriah stayed in Jerusalem that day. On the next day, ¹³David invited him. He ate in his presence and drank, and [David] got him drunk. He went out in the evening to lie down on his bunk with his master's servants, but he did not go down to his house.

¹⁴In the morning David wrote a message to Joab and sent it with Uriah. ¹⁵He wrote in the message, "Put Uriah on the front where the battle is most fierce, then turn back from him so that he will be struck and die." ¹⁶When Joab had observed the city, he put Uriah in the place where he knew that the best soldiers were. ¹⁷The men of the city came out and attacked Joab. Some of the troops, some of David's servants, fell and died, including Uriah the Hittite.

[18]Joab sent word and informed David all the matters of the war. [19]He commanded the messenger, "As you conclude telling the king all the matters of the war, [20]if the king's anger arises, and he says to you, 'Why did you approach the city to fight? Didn't you know they would shoot down from the wall? [21]At Thebez who struck down Abimelech the son of Jerubbesheth? Wasn't it a woman who dropped an upper millstone down from the wall, and he died? Why did you approach the wall?' then say, 'Your servant Uriah the Hittite is also dead.'"

[22]The messenger left, came, and told David all that Joab had sent him [to say]. [23]The messenger said to David, "The men overwhelmed us and came outside the city to us, but we counterattacked them up to the entrance of the city. [24]The archers shot down at your servants from the wall, and some of the king's servants died. Also your servant Uriah the Hittite died."

[25]David said to the messenger, "Say this to Joab, 'Do not let this trouble you, because the sword will devour this way. Intensify your attack on the city and destroy it. Encourage him.'"

[26]When Uriah's wife heard that her husband Uriah was dead, she mourned for her husband. [27]When the time of mourning passed, David sent and brought her to his house. She became his wife and bore him a son, but what David had done was evil in Yahweh's eyes.

Textual Notes

11:1 וַיְהִי לִתְשׁוּבַת הַשָּׁנָה—"In the spring of the year" is literally "and it came to pass at the return of the year." The prepositional phrase לִתְשׁוּבַת הַשָּׁנָה is an expression for spring (1 Ki 20:22, 26; 2 Chr 36:10; similarly, 1 Chr 20:1). The preposition לְ is used in a temporal sense, "at (the time)," as again with לְעֵת, "at the time when," in the next clause and in 11:2 (BDB, s.v. לְ, 6 a). The feminine noun תְּשׁוּבָה is derived from the verb שׁוּב, "to return." The expression is based on a lunar calendar that began in autumn. With the coming of spring and the end of the rainy season in Palestine, the year began to return toward autumn. In Ex 23:16 autumn is called the season "at the going out of the year" (בְּצֵאת הַשָּׁנָה; for צֵאת, see the next textual note).

צֵאת—"Go out [to war]." The verb form here is a Qal (G) infinitive construct of יָצָא. The Qal (G) of the verb יָצָא is often used to denote going to war (see the first textual notes on 1 Sam 18:6[1] and 2 Sam 2:12; see also its Hiphil [H] in the second textual note on 5:2). For other instances of the Qal of יָצָא denoting going to war with "king" (מֶלֶךְ) as the subject, see Gen 14:8; Num 21:33; Deut 3:1; 29:6 (ET 29:7); Josh 8:14; 1 Sam 8:20; 1 Ki 20:21; 2 Ki 3:6; 24:7; Dan 11:11 (cf. 2 Ki 19:9; Is 37:9; 1 Chr 14:8; 19:9; 2 Chr 35:20).

הַמַּלְאָכִים—This is the reading in Codex Leningradensis. These consonants would normally be vocalized as הַמַּלְאָכִים, "the messengers," as in 11:4, which is the plural of the masculine noun מַלְאָךְ with the definite article. However, this pointing is different and has the *raphe'* accent over the *aleph* (-אָ-), meaning that the Masoretes

---

[1]   Steinmann, *1 Samuel*, 350.

considered the *aleph* in הַמַּלְאָכִים to be a vowel letter and not a consonant.[2] In that case, the expected vocalization would be הַמְּלָכִים as a variant spelling for הַמְּלָכִים, "the kings." Most Masoretic manuscripts have הַמְּלָאכִים with the marginal Masoretic note יתיר א, which means that the א is superfluous, and so the word in most manuscripts is a variant spelling of הַמְּלָכִים, "the kings." A considerable number of Masoretic manuscripts have the usual spelling for "the kings," הַמְּלָכִים. The translation above, "the kings," is also supported by the LXX, a number of Old Latin manuscripts, the Aramaic Targum, and the Vulgate.

Yet the reading הַמַּלְאָכִים, "the messengers," has its defenders.[3] They claim that "the messengers" are diplomats and that there was a time of the year when diplomats were normally sent out. This is a strange concept, since diplomacy is hardly something practiced at only one time of the year. In addition, there are two other words in this chapter with a confusing superfluous *aleph* (see the first textual note on 11:24). This is probably a third instance.

וַיַּשְׁחִתוּ—"They destroyed." The verb שָׁחַת can be used in either the Piel (D) stem (1 Sam 23:10; 2 Sam 1:14; 14:11; 24:16) or the Hiphil (H) stem, as here (also 1 Sam 6:5; 26:9, 15; 2 Sam 20:15, 20), for destroying or killing.

וַיָּצֻרוּ—"And they laid siege." The verb צוּר (one of several homographs) is used only in the Qal (G) and often refers to laying siege to a city (BDB, s.v. צוּר II, 2; *HALOT*, s.v. צוּר I, 3). It also occurs in 1 Sam 23:8; 2 Sam 20:15.

11:2 וַיִּתְהַלֵּךְ—"And he was walking around." In the Hithpael (HtD), הָלַךְ, "walk," denotes iterative or repeated action; see the third textual note on 7:6.

וַיַּרְא אִשָּׁה רֹחֶצֶת מֵעַל הַגָּג—"And from the roof he saw a woman bathing." The prepositional phrase מֵעַל הַגָּג, literally "from upon the roof," functions adverbially to modify the verb וַיַּרְא, "and he [David] saw," emphasizing David's vantage point of looking from the roof of his palace. It does not modify the Qal (G) feminine singular participle רֹחֶצֶת, "bathing," so the text does not say that Bathsheba was bathing on a roof. She may have been bathing inside and became visible to David through a window only because he was up on his roof.

Elsewhere in Samuel the verb רָחַץ refers to "washing" the feet in 1 Sam 25:41; 2 Sam 11:8 and to David washing his body before anointing himself with oil in 2 Sam 12:20. This verb is used often in the Torah in various stipulations for purification. These include ritual washings by priests[4] and washings to render an unclean person clean (e.g., Lev 14:8–9; twelve times in Lev 15:1–33). Most pertinent here are the regulations for a woman during her menstrual period (Lev 15:19–24). She was unclean for seven days, and during this time anyone or anything that came into contact with her blood was required to be washed in water. Lev 15:19–24 does not explicitly prescribe

---

[2] See Yeivin, *Introduction to the Tiberian Masorah*, §§ 395, 397.

[3] Fokkelman, *King David*, 51; Baldwin, *1 and 2 Samuel*, 231, n. 1; Bergen, *1, 2 Samuel*, 363, n. 100. Bergen claims that Garsiel, "The Story of David and Bathsheba," also supports this reading. However, pages 251–52 in Garsiel's article make clear that he reads "the kings" not "the messengers."

[4] See רָחַץ, "wash," in, e.g., Ex 29:4; 30:18–21; 40:12; Lev 16:4, 24; Num 19:7.

that she must bathe at the end of her period (on the eighth day) to become clean again, but the larger context implies that this was so.[5] Most likely, then, Bathsheba was washing herself to fulfill this divine commandment. See further the second textual note on 11:4 and the commentary.

וְהָאִשָּׁה טוֹבַת מַרְאֶה מְאֹד:—"The woman was very beautiful." See the commentary.

11:3 וַיִּשְׁלַח דָּוִד וַיִּדְרֹשׁ ... וַיֹּאמֶר—Literally "David sent, and he sought. ... And he said." There is no direct object of the first verb to indicate who or how many people David may have "sent" to investigate, but the singular verb used for the report, "and he said," suggests that a single investigator reported the results. The verb דָּרַשׁ can denote "seeking" information via an investigation (*HALOT*, 3 a, 3 b). The subject of the verb וַיִּדְרֹשׁ, "and he sought," could be David himself or the detective whom he sent.

בַּת־שֶׁבַע בַּת־אֱלִיעָם—"Bathsheba, Eliam's daughter" is literally "the daughter of Sheba, the daughter of Eliam." Even though she is identified as the "daughter" (בַּת) of Eliam, her name means "the daughter [בַּת] of Sheba." The name שֶׁבַע, "Sheba," may derive from the verb "to swear an oath" (the Niphal [N] of שָׁבַע), or it may be the number "seven" (שֶׁבַע), both of which are involved in the explanation of the place-name "Beersheba" in Gen 21:27–31.

אוּרִיָּה הַחִתִּי:—"Uriah the Hittite." He is called this in 11:3, 6, 17, 21, 24. For the gentilic designation הַחִתִּי, "the Hittite," see the commentary, as well as the second textual note on 1 Sam 26:6.[6] After it 4QSamᵃ adds [נושא כלי יואב] to identify Uriah as "Joab's armor [b]earer,"[7] but that is probably an interpretive gloss. See the textual note on 2 Sam 23:37.

11:4 וַתָּבוֹא אֵלָיו—"And/when she came to him" is the reading in the MT and 4QSamᵃ (ותבוא אליו). This is supported by most LXX manuscripts, which read καὶ εἰσῆλθεν πρὸς αὐτόν, "and she came to him," and by the Vulgate. Two LXX manuscripts (B, A) read καὶ εἰσῆλθεν πρὸς αὐτήν, "and he went in to her," in agreement with two Old Latin manuscripts. For the possible sexual significance of the Hebrew idiom with the verb בּוֹא and the preposition אֶל, see the fourth textual note on 3:7.

וְהִיא מִתְקַדֶּשֶׁת מִטֻּמְאָתָהּ—"She had been purifying herself from her uncleanness." In this parenthetical statement the feminine pronoun הִיא, "she," is the subject of the Hithpael (HtD) feminine singular participle of קָדַשׁ, "be holy, pure." In the Hithpael, it is factitive ("to make [something] be in a state of purity") and reflexive (action one does to oneself). This verb and the terminology of "clean" and "unclean" are key to the theology of sanctification in Leviticus: Yahweh himself is the one who sanctifies (קָדַשׁ) his people and purifies them from their uncleannesses. For an overview, see the discussion by Kleinig in the introduction to his Leviticus commentary.[8] According to the Torah a menstruating woman was ritually unclean for seven days (Lev 15:19–24). By ritual analogy to the larger context in Leviticus, presumably she became clean/pure after washing on the eighth day (see the second textual note on 11:2). In Leviticus טָמֵא is

---

[5] Kleinig, *Leviticus*, 320, citing Milgrom, *Leviticus 1–16*, 934–35. See further Kleinig, *Leviticus*, 311–24.

[6] Steinmann, *1 Samuel*, 492–93.

[7] Cf. Josephus, *Antiquities*, 7.131.

[8] Kleinig, *Leviticus*, 1–13.

the usual noun for "uncleanness," used in the context of the regulation for menstruation (see טֻמְאָה in Lev 15:3, 25, 26, 30, 31) and in other sacrificial provisions for the priestly mediation of cleanliness and purity for the people (e.g., Lev 14:19), including the Day of Atonement (Lev 16:16, 19). Apparently David perpetrated his sin against Bathsheba on the day she became clean again. If he had had sexual relations with her during her week of impurity, he himself would have become unclean for a week (Lev 15:24; see also Lev 15:19, 33; 18:19).[9] While David avoided transgressing the letter of that particular law, his adultery was an even greater violation of her sanctity. Legislation in the Torah provided means through which the unclean could become clean again, but adultery carried the death penalty (Lev 20:10; Deut 22:22; cf. Deut 22:25–27, where a rapist is to be put to death but his victim is to be spared). A violation of the Sixth Commandment (Ex 20:14; Deut 5:18) was tantamount to idolatry and was a violation also of the First Commandment and the entire Law.[10]

11:5 וַתַּהַר הָאִשָּׁה—"The woman conceived/became pregnant." The verb is the Qal (G) third feminine singular preterite (imperfect with *waw* consecutive) of הָרָה. The identical verb form is used twenty-eight times in the OT (e.g., 1 Sam 1:20; 2:21), most of which are in Genesis (e.g., Gen 4:1, 17; 21:2; 25:21). A woman is pregnant with a child from the moment of conception. See the cognate feminine adjective הָרָה, "pregnant," later in the verse where Bathsheba reports, הָרָה אָנֹכִי, "I am pregnant" (11:5).

וַתִּשְׁלַח וַתַּגֵּד לְדָוִד—"And she sent word to David" is literally "and she sent and she reported to David." Her reporting was through the intermediary she sent. Similarly, the verb וַיִּשְׁלַח at the start of 11:6 is translated as "David sent word."

11:7 וַיִּשְׁאַל דָּוִד לִשְׁלוֹם יוֹאָב וְלִשְׁלוֹם הָעָם וְלִשְׁלוֹם הַמִּלְחָמָה:—Literally "and David asked regarding the peace of Joab and regarding the peace of the people and regarding the peace of the war." For this idiom, see the second textual note on 8:10. The noun שָׁלוֹם can have a wide range of meanings, including "welfare" and "progress" (cf. *HALOT*).

In contexts of warfare, the definite noun הָעָם, literally "the people," often refers specifically to military personnel, as again in 11:17. See the second textual note on 1:4.

11:8 רֵד—"Go down." This is the Qal (G) masculine singular imperative of יָרַד, which suggests that the palace was higher in elevation than the other residences. Forms of יָרַד recur in 11:9, 10 (twice), 13.

וּרְחַץ רַגְלֶיךָ—"And wash your feet." For the verb רָחַץ, see the second textual note on 11:2 and the commentary.

מַשְׂאַת הַמֶּלֶךְ:—"A present from the king" is literally "the gift of the king." In this construct phrase, the genitive הַמֶּלֶךְ indicates the source, "*from* the king." מַשְׂאַת is the construct form of the feminine noun מַשְׂאֵת (derived from the verb נָשָׂא), which can denote a gift, offering, or tribute (see *DCH*, s.v. מַשְׂאֵת I). It is the subject of the preceding feminine verb וַתֵּצֵא.

---

[9] Cf. Num 5:19, where willful adultery renders a woman unclean, although in this case it was David who imposed himself upon her.

[10] The prophets often condemn sexual sin as a form of idolatry. See, e.g., Jer 5:7; 7:9; Ezek 16:38; 23:37; Hos 2:4 (ET 2:2). See also James 2:10–11.

11:9 אֵת—This is the preposition "with" rather than the marker of a definite direct object.

11:10 וַיַּגִּדוּ לְדָוִד—"David was told" is literally "and they reported to David." See the first textual note on 10:5.

הֲלוֹא מִדֶּרֶךְ אַתָּה בָא—"Haven't you just come from a journey?" is literally "are you not coming from a road?" The verb בָא must be the Qal (G) masculine singular participle (rather than the third masculine singular perfect) because the pronoun אַתָּה is its subject.

11:11 בַּסֻּכּוֹת—"In temporary shelters." The feminine noun סֻכָּה denotes a tent (or "booth"). Its plural, as here, סֻכּוֹת, "*succoth*," is used in the legislation for the Feast of Booths or Tabernacles, which commemorated the wilderness wandering after the exodus redemption (Lev 23:34, 42, 43; Deut 16:13, 16; Deut 31:10).

חֹנִים—"Are camping." In the book of Samuel the verb חָנָה, "encamp," usually refers to establishing a military camp for warfare. See the second textual note on 1 Sam 11:1.[11]

וַאֲנִי אָבוֹא—"How can I go?" is literally "and I, should I come?" Hebrew questions are not always marked with an interrogative. Sometimes a pronoun (here אֲנִי) preceding a verb (אָבוֹא) can indicate a question (Joüon, § 161 a). The imperfect of בּוֹא has a modal nuance, "*should* come" (cf. Joüon, § 113 l, m).

וְלִשְׁכַּב עִם־אִשְׁתִּי—"And (to) lie with my wife." For this and other sexual idioms, see the fourth textual note on 3:7.

חַיֶּךָ וְחֵי נַפְשֶׁךָ אִם־אֶעֱשֶׂה אֶת־הַדָּבָר הַזֶּה:—"I swear by your life, I will not do this!" This is a double oath formula,[12] literally "(by) your life and the life of your soul if I should do this thing." See the second textual notes on 1 Sam 1:26 and 1 Sam 14:45.[13] The two phrases here, חַי-, "the life of," and חֵי נַפְשׁ-, "the life of the soul of," are used together also in 1 Sam 20:3; 25:26.

11:12 וּמִמָּחֳרָת:—The feminine noun מָחֳרָת usually has the prefixed preposition מִן and means "the next day" (see the first textual note on 1 Sam 5:3[14]). In the MT this is the last word of 11:12, and most English versions translate it as such: Uriah stayed in Jerusalem that day "and the next" (e.g., NASB, ESV). However, that English translation would seem to conflict with David's promise earlier in the verse, "tomorrow I will send you away." This commentary's translation connects this Hebrew word to the following verse (11:13): "On the next day, David invited [וַיִּקְרָא] him." Often מִמָּחֳרָת follows the verb that refers to the action on the next day (e.g., 1 Sam 5:3, 4), but sometimes it precedes the verb (e.g., 1 Sam 11:11; 18:10; 20:27; 31:8). See further the commentary.

11:13 בְּמִשְׁכָּבוֹ—The noun מִשְׁכָּב often denotes a piece of furniture on which one lies down: a "couch" (11:2) or bed." In this verse, Uriah's מִשְׁכָּב is located in the place where David's servants slept, perhaps his servants who were part of the army, thus "on his bunk."

---

[11]   Steinmann, *1 Samuel*, 208–9.

[12]   *IBH*, § 64 D; Waltke-O'Connor, § 40.2.2b; Joüon, § 165 e.

[13]   Steinmann, *1 Samuel*, 61, 265.

[14]   Steinmann, *1 Samuel*, 135.

11:15 הָבוּ—This is the Qal (G) masculine plural imperative of יָהַב, "to give," "ascribe," here meaning to "place" (*DCH*). Only its imperative is used in the OT.

אֶל־מוּל פְּנֵי הַמִּלְחָמָה הַחֲזָקָה—Literally "to the front of the face of the strong battle." The construct chain אֶל־מוּל פְּנֵי־ can mean "on the forefront of" (BDB, s.v. מוּל I, 2 a). An adjective with the definite article (הַחֲזָקָה, the feminine of חָזָק, "strong") can form a superlative, thus "the fiercest battle," i.e., "where the battle is most fierce."

וְנִכָּה וָמֵת:—The perfect verb forms with *waw* consecutive (the Niphal [N] of נָכָה and the Qal [G] of מוּת) form a purpose clause: "*so that* he will be struck and will die." Usually נָכָה is used in the Hiphil (H) stem (ninety-eight times in Samuel), "strike (down)," as in 11:21, and for the passive meaning its Hophal (Hp) is used (e.g., 1 Sam 5:12). This is the only instance of its Niphal in the OT.

11:16 וַיְהִי בִּשְׁמוֹר יוֹאָב—"When Joab had observed." בִּשְׁמוֹר is the Qal (G) infinitive construct (with בְּ) of שָׁמַר, which often means "keep" in the sense of "keep watch over" and thereby also can mean "observe" (see *HALOT*, 1, 4, 6). There is no justification for translating it as "keep" in the sense of "besiege," that is, a hostile army's attempt to restrict movement in and out of a city (cf. HCSB, ESV, NIV).

אַנְשֵׁי־חַיִל—The context indicates that this construct phrase is a superlative: "(the) *best* soldiers." See the corresponding singular construct phrase אִישׁ חַיִל, "a skilled soldier," in the first textual notes on 1 Sam 31:12[15] and 2 Sam 23:20 (where it is the Qere), as well as the third textual note on 2 Sam 24:9. The book of Samuel uses similar construct phrases with חַיִל, "bravery, might; army," that have similar meanings, e.g., גִּבּוֹר חַיִל, literally "a mighty man of valor," in 1 Sam 9:1; 16:18, and בֶּן חַיִל, literally "a son of valor," in 1 Sam 14:52; 18:17; 2 Sam 2:7; 13:28; 17:10. See the second textual note on 2 Sam 2:7.

11:17 וַיִּלָּחֲמוּ אֶת־יוֹאָב—"And they attacked Joab" is literally "and they warred with Joab." The Niphal (N) of לָחַם can take the preposition אֶת, "with," as here and in 21:15. More often it takes the preposition בְּ, as in 2 Sam 8:10; 12:26, 27, 29.

מִן־הָעָם—"Some of the troops." The preposition מִן as a partitive meaning here, "some of" (BDB, 3 b (*a*); Waltke-O'Connor, § 4.4.1b (2), including note 11). See also the second textual note on 11:24. For הָעָם, "the troops," see the textual note on 11:7.

11:19 כְּכַלּוֹתְךָ אֵת כָּל־דִּבְרֵי הַמִּלְחָמָה לְדַבֵּר אֶל־הַמֶּלֶךְ:—The syntax employs two Piel (D) infinitive constructs (each with a prefixed preposition and the first with a subjective pronominal suffix), literally "when you finish all the words of the war, speaking to the king." The Piel (D) of כָּלָה often means "to finish" or "conclude" doing something, and the action is signified by another infinitive, which here is לְדַבֵּר, "speaking." See the first textual notes on 1 Sam 13:10 and 1 Sam 18:1.[16] 1 Sam 18:1 has the same two infinitives as here (וַיְהִי כְּכַלֹּתוֹ לְדַבֵּר), as also do 1 Sam 24:17 (ET 24:16) and 2 Sam 13:36.

---

[15] Steinmann, *1 Samuel*, 568.

[16] Steinmann, *1 Samuel*, 234, 344.

11:20 מַדּוּעַ נִגַּשְׁתֶּם—"Why did you approach?" This second masculine plural perfect of נָגַשׁ could be Piel (D), but this verb does not appear elsewhere in the OT in that stem. It is Niphal (N). The same form recurs in 11:21.

יֹרוּ—"They would shoot." This is the Hiphil (H) third masculine plural imperfect of יָרָה with a modal meaning that expresses expected customary action ("would"). The Hiphil (H) of יָרָה means "to shoot (arrows)" again in 11:24, as well as 1 Sam 20:20, 36a; 31:3. Its Qal (G) has that meaning in 1 Sam 20:36b, 37. In 1 Sam 12:23, however, its Hiphil (H) means "to teach, instruct."

מֵעַל הַחוֹמָה:—"Down from the wall" is literally "from on the wall." The combination of prepositions (עַל + מִן) indicates that the defenders are up on the wall and so can rain down arrows upon the attacking Israelites (see BDB, s.v. עַל, 7 a). The same prepositional phrase recurs in 11:21, 24. Cf. also מֵעַל in the second textual note on 11:2.

11:21 הִשְׁלִיכָה—"She dropped." Usually the Hiphil (H) of שָׁלַךְ means "to throw" something that is relatively light, such as a garment (20:12) or a head (20:22; but a body in 18:17). Since, however, an upper millstone had considerable weight, "dropped" better fits her action from the wall above.

פֶּלַח רֶכֶב—"An upper millstone" is literally "a millstone of riding/rotating." The context of each passage clarifies whether the noun פֶּלַח, "millstone," refers to the upper, relatively thinner one that was rotated or the lower, thicker, stationary one (Job 41:16 [ET 41:24]). Grain was milled by placing it between the stones. Here and in Judg 9:53 פֶּלַח is in construct with the noun רֶכֶב, "chariot; rider," and the phrase refers to the upper stone. In Deut 24:6 רֶכֶב alone (without פֶּלַח) refers to the upper stone.

בְּתֵבֵץ—"At Thebez" has been moved forward in the English sentence for clarity. This place-name recalls the account in Judg 9:50–57.

11:22 וַיֵּגֶד לְדָוִד אֵת כָּל־אֲשֶׁר שְׁלָחוֹ יוֹאָב:—"And he told David all that Joab had sent him [to say]." It is possible that the direct object (אֵת כָּל־אֲשֶׁר שְׁלָחוֹ יוֹאָב) refers to "the entire [*message*] that Joab had sent *to him*" (so Joüon, § 158 i, footnote 1). See שָׁלַח with the object כָּל־דָּבָר, "to send every/the whole word," in 2 Sam 15:36 (cf. also 1 Sam 21:3 [ET 21:2]; Pss 107:20; 147:18). Yet it is more likely that the third masculine singular object suffix on the verb שְׁלָחוֹ refers to the *messenger* (Joab "had sent *him*") and that a verb of speaking is implied ("to say to David").

The LXX contains a long expansion at the end of this verse:

> … πάντα τὰ ῥήματα τοῦ πολέμου. καὶ ἐθυμώθη Δαυιδ πρὸς Ιωαβ καὶ εἶπεν πρὸς τὸν ἄγγελον ἵνα τί προσηγάγετε πρὸς τὴν πόλιν τοῦ πολεμῆσαι; οὐκ ᾔδειτε ὅτι πληγήσεσθε ἀπὸ τοῦ τείχους; τίς ἐπάταξεν τὸν Αβιμελεχ υἱὸν Ιεροβααλ; οὐχὶ γυνὴ ἔρριψεν ἐπ' αὐτὸν κλάσμα μύλου ἀπὸ τοῦ τείχους καὶ ἀπέθανεν ἐν Θαμασι; ἵνα τί προσηγάγετε πρὸς τὸ τεῖχος;

> … all the news of the war. And David became angry at Joab and said to the messenger, "Why did you approach the city to fight? Didn't you know that you would be struck from the wall? Who struck Abimelech the son of Jerubbaal? Didn't a woman throw a piece of a millstone on him from the wall and he died at Thamasi? Why did you approach the wall?"

This appears to be a purposeful insertion to demonstrate that David reacted as Joab had anticipated in 11:19–21.

11:23 נִגְבְּרוּ עָלֵינוּ—"They overwhelmed us." The Qal (G) of גָּבַר, "be strong," with preposition עַל in the sense of hostility ("against," BDB, s.v. עַל, 7 d), means to "prevail over" someone (BDB, s.v. גָּבַר, Qal, 2 b). The preposition עַל signifies hostility again later in the verse (see the third textual note on 11:23).

הַשָּׂדֶה—"Outside the city" is literally "(in) the field." At times the noun שָׂדֶה refers simply to land not enclosed by city walls.

וַנִּהְיֶה עֲלֵיהֶם—"But we counterattacked them" is literally "and/but we were against/ over them." The preposition עַל indicates hostility (BDB, 7 d). The clause implies that the counterattack was successful in driving the enemy back to their city wall (cf. the first textual note on 11:23).

11:24 וַיֹּרוּ הַמֹּורִים—"The archers shot down." In this Qere, the subject, הַמֹּורִים, is the masculine plural Hiphil (H) participle of יָרָה, "to shoot (arrows)." See the second textual note on 11:20. It is the subject of the same verb's Hiphil (H) third masculine plural preterite (imperfect with *waw* consecutive). This Qere is supported by the LXX (καὶ ἐτόξευσαν οἱ τοξεύοντες), by the Vulgate (*et direxerunt iacula sagittarii*), and partially by the Syriac Peshitta (ܘ̣ܪܡܘ). The Kethib is probably to be vocalized as וַיִּרְאוּ הַמֹּורִאִים, and the words are to be parsed in the same way with the same meaning, but both words are spelled as if the verb were יָרָא, with a final *aleph*. See GKC, § 75 rr.

מֵעַבְדֵי הַמֶּלֶךְ—"Some of the king's servants." The preposition מִן as a partitive meaning here (BDB, 3 b (*a*)), as in 11:17 (see the second textual note on 11:17).

11:25 אַל־יֵרַע בְּעֵינֶיךָ אֶת־הַדָּבָר הַזֶּה—"Do not let this trouble you" is literally "may this thing not be evil in your eyes." The particle אֵת, which usually serves as the direct object marker, precedes the phrase הַדָּבָר הַזֶּה, "this word/thing/matter," even though the phrase is the subject of the verb (cf. GKC, § 117 i, l; Joüon, § 125 j (6)). The verb יֵרַע is the Qal (G) third masculine singular jussive of רָעַע, "be evil," which is a denomina- tive (derived from the noun רָעָה). For its form here, יֵרַע, see GKC, § 67 n. רָעַע occurs as a preterite (imperfect with *waw* consecutive) in 11:27 (וַיֵּרַע).

כָּזֹה וְכָזֶה—"This way." This idiom is literally "like this and like this." It is used elsewhere in the OT in Judg 18:4; 1 Ki 14:5. The first instance of the demonstrative, זֹה, "this," is feminine singular and a variant spelling of זֹאת. The second, זֶה, is masculine singular. See BDB, s.v. זֶה, 6 c (β).

תֹּאכַל הֶחָרֶב—"The sword will devour." Nearly identical wording was in 2:26, but with a modal nuance (see the first textual note on 2:26). The feminine noun חֶרֶב (in pause חָרֶב), "sword," is the subject of a feminine form of the verb אָכַל, "to eat," also in 18:8. A "sword" is also said to have a "mouth" (פֶּה) by which it devours or kills: לְפִי־חֶרֶב, "by (the) mouth/edge of (the) sword" (1 Sam 15:8; 22:19; 2 Sam 15:14). See the first textual note on 1 Sam 22:19.[17]

הַחֲזֵק ... וְחַזְּקֵהוּ—The verb חָזַק, whose Qal (G) means "be strong," has a causative meaning, "to make [something or someone] strong; strengthen," in both the Piel (D) and the Hiphil (H). The first form here is the Hiphil masculine singular imperative, trans- lated as "intensify," since its object is the phrase מִלְחַמְתְּךָ, literally "your battle." The

---

second form is the Piel masculine singular imperative with a third masculine singular suffix, and in this stem the verb can mean "encourage" (BDB, Piel, 2 and 3).

וְהָרְסָהּ—"And destroy it." The referent of the third feminine singular object suffix on the Qal (G) masculine singular imperative of הָרַס is the preceding definite noun, הָעִיר, "the city," which is grammatically feminine. Elsewhere in the OT הָרַס often refers to "tearing down" structures such as the altars of false gods. It refers to the destruction of cities also in, e.g., Is 14:17; Ezek 26:4; 1 Chr 20:1.

11:26 אִישָׁהּ ... בַּעְלָהּ—"Her husband ... her husband." The first noun here, אִישׁ, with a feminine suffix, is the most common way to designate a woman's "husband." The second noun here, בַּעַל, "lord," commonly refers to the god Baal (plural in 1 Sam 7:4; 12:10), but can be used to refer to Yahweh as "Lord" in Israelite personal names (see the second textual note on 2:8) and in place-names (see 2 Sam 5:20). The noun בַּעַל can also refer to a "husband," as here (see BDB, I 2). A participle of the verb בָּעַל refers to Yahweh as the "Husband" of his people in Is 54:5 (cf. Is 62:4–5). Hos 2:18 (ET 2:16) plays on the two different Hebrew nouns that are here in 2 Sam 11:26.

11:27 וַיַּאַסְפָהּ—"And he brought her" is literally "and he gathered her." The verb is the Qal (G) third masculine singular preterite (imperfect with *waw* consecutive) of אָסַף. The *patach* vowels (-יַּאַ-, from -יֶּאֱ-) are due to the initial guttural root letter א. See the similar forms וַיַּאַסְפוּ in 1 Sam 5:8, 11; 17:1; 2 Sam 21:13 and וַיַּאַסְפֵהוּ in 1 Sam 14:52. Cf. GKC, §§ 23 d; 68 b, h.

וַיֵּרַע—"But it was evil." See the first textual note on 11:25.

Commentary

997 BC[18]

This account of David's adultery and his murder of Uriah is the first place in the book of Samuel that portrays David as openly flouting God's Law. His scheming and duplicity show that his native cleverness could be bent to evil ends. This act caused a cascade of actions that adversely affected his family (13:1–39), his throne, and all Israel (14:1–20:22), the entire people of God. After David was later confronted by God's prophetic representative and confessed his transgression to him, he was forgiven all his sins (12:13). Nevertheless, David and those around him would still suffer from the temporal consequences of his violation of God's Word. The negative effects reflected the severity of the transgression (12:9–15). Yet David, like all penitent believers, received eternal life through faith and by grace alone.[19]

---

[18] See "The Chronology of David's Reign" in the commentary on 5:1–5.

[19] The apostle Paul discusses the consequences of various sins in, e.g., 1 Cor 6:9–20, and he stresses that sexual sins, which would include David's, are the most grievous. The Lutheran Confessions speak of both temporal and eternal consequences of sin, that is, earthly miseries in this life and eternal damnation to hell. God's forgiveness in Christ absolves all sins and grants eternal life, but does not necessarily alleviate all temporal consequences. See, e.g., Ap IV 128 and FC SD V 17–21. In the traditional Lutheran rite of confession and absolution, the confession includes the acknowledgment that "we justly deserve Your present [temporal] and eternal punishment" (*LSB* 151).

David Commits Adultery (11:1–5)

Parallel: 2 Sam 11:1 ‖ 1 Chr 20:1a

The chapter begins with a double chronological notice: it was spring, and it was the time when kings customarily go out to war (11:1). However, King David did not go out to war—he sent Joab to war while he stayed in Jerusalem. David did not always go out to battle with his army (e.g., 10:7), and in at least one instance his soldiers urged him not to join them in battle (21:17). Thus, some interpreters argue that the author is not implying that David's sin was the result of his idleness in Jerusalem when he did not go out to war.[20] However, the double chronological notice by the author makes the point that the expected behavior of kings was to go to war in the spring. Had the author wanted to give only a chronological note, the phrase "in the spring of the year" would have sufficed (cf. 1 Ki 20:22, 26; 2 Chr 36:10). The added note about kings going out is an understated way of injecting an ominous note into David's presence in Jerusalem. Israel's initial request for a king centered on the expectation that he would lead the fight in the nation's battles (1 Sam 8:19–20), and this military role was reiterated when the first king was anointed (1 Sam 10:1). David had displayed his prowess in his victory over Goliath (1 Samuel 17; see also, e.g., 1 Sam 16:18; 18:5; 19:8), but it seems that now his courage was flagging.

This ominous note expands into a complete tune in the next verse (11:2) when David arose from his couch. In the evening he began a walk on the roof of his palace that led him to see a bathing woman who was "very beautiful" (טוֹבַת מַרְאֶה מְאֹד, 11:2). Only one other woman in the OT is described by these same Hebrew words as "very beautiful": Rebekah (טֹבַת מַרְאֶה מְאֹד, Gen 24:16).[21] The author of Samuel notes the appealing appearance of several other persons, although the Hebrew wording is different (even when the translation gives "beautiful"). David already had a good-looking wife in Abigail (וִיפַת תֹּאַר, "beautiful," 1 Sam 25:3). He had attractive children in Tamar (יָפָה, "beautiful," 2 Sam 13:1) and Absalom (the masculine form יָפֶה, literally "handsome," 2 Sam 14:25) and a good-looking granddaughter, also named Tamar (יְפַת מַרְאֶה, "beautiful," 2 Sam 14:27). David himself had "a handsome appearance" (יְפֵה מַרְאֶה, 1 Sam 17:42), and his predecessor Saul was also "a handsome young man" (בָּחוּר וָטוֹב, 1 Sam 9:2). However, in the book of Samuel this is the first time when the appearance of someone becomes an occasion for lust. This pattern will be repeated in 2 Samuel 13, where David's children are ravaged in the aftermath of his own sin (cf. 2 Sam 12:10).

Although Bathsheba was bathing and David could see her, there is no indication that she was purposely enticing the king. Instead, David took the initiative

---

[20] McKenzie, "Why Did David Stay Home?"; Simon, "The Poor Man's Ewe Lamb," 209; Stoebe, "David und Uria," 388–89; Bergen, *1, 2 Samuel*, 364.

[21] The first two Hebrew words (but without the third word, "very," מְאֹד), are used to call Rebekah "beautiful" (טוֹבַת מַרְאֶה, Gen 26:7), and the same two-word appellation describes Queen Vashti (Esth 1:11) and Esther (Esth 2:7; cf. Esth 2:3).

toward her: he inquired about her (11:3), fetched her with messengers (11:4), and later brought her into his house as a wife (11:27).[22]

David's inquiry led to an identification of the woman by her association with two men (11:3). The first was her father Eliam. There was an Eliam among David's thirty prominent soldiers (23:34),[23] and it is tempting to identify that Eliam as Bathsheba's father, since the second man, "Uriah the Hittite" (11:3), was also among the Thirty (23:39). The Hebrew name Uriah (אוּרִיָּה) is appropriate for an Israelite and means "my light [אוּרִי] is Yahweh [יָהּ, *Yah*]" or "Yahweh is my light," yet Uriah is designated as "the Hittite" (הַחִתִּי) five times in this chapter (11:3, 6, 17, 21, 24) and in 12:9–10; 23:39. Scholars often identify Uriah as a Neo-Hittite, one of the Anatolian peoples who allegedly expanded into the northern Levant during the Iron Age.[24] In the last two centuries a considerable amount of archaeological and historical evidence has been discovered for a prosperous Hittite Empire in the second millennium BC, discrediting the skepticism of some older scholars. Nevertheless, some have challenged the identification of "Uriah" as "the Hittite" because they assume we should have been able to find more corroborating evidence for a population of Neo-Hittites living in Canaan in the early first millennium BC:

> There was a time when historians scoffed at the name "Hittite(s)" in the OT since it was not known outside the Bible. Archaeological discoveries in Egypt, Mesopotamia, Turkey, and Syria from the early nineteenth century [AD] on, however, have revealed an Indo-European group scholars have dubbed "Hittites" (as opposed to "Hethites"), who established an empire in Anatolia that became a major power in the ancient Near East. But a serious problem remains. The biblical references to Hittites living in Canaan appear to be unhistorical since there is no evidence—linguistic, historical, or archaeological—for a Hittite presence in Canaan. Kempinski attempted to establish an early twelfth-century migration of Hittites to Canaan, requiring Abraham to be placed in the thirteenth–twelfth century BC, but this scenario finds little support in the archaeological record.[25]

Singer also contends:

> The archaeological evidence seems hardly sufficient to prove a presence of northern Hittites in Palestine. After a century of intensive excavations, all that has surfaced is a handful of Hittite seals and about a dozen pottery vessels

---

[22] David's first marriage was to Saul's daughter Michal (1 Sam 18:20–27), but Saul later gave Michal to another man (1 Sam 25:44). David married Ahinoam (1 Sam 25:43), and she probably was his second wife. Abigail consented to his marriage proposal (1 Sam 25:39–42) and became his third wife. Thus, David had the two wives "Ahinoam" and "Abigail" (named in that order) in 1 Sam 27:3; 30:5; 2 Sam 2:2. Michal was returned to him in 2 Sam 3:14–16. Additional wives and concubines of David are noted in 2 Sam 3:2–5; 5:13.

[23] Eliam (אֱלִיעָם, 2 Sam 11:3) is called Ammiel (עַמִּיאֵל), a variant form of the name, in 1 Chr 3:5.

[24] McCarter, *II Samuel*, 285–86; Anderson, *2 Samuel*, 153.

[25] Wood, "Hittites and Hethites," 239, citing Kempinski, "Hittites in the Bible: What Does Archaeology Say?" especially 30–44.

that exhibit some northern artistic influences. The seals may have belonged to Hittite citizens who passed through Canaan, and the vessels may have filtered gradually into Palestine through various Syrian intermediaries. The paucity of tangible evidence becomes even more conspicuous in the face of the absence of two salient features of Hittite culture—the hieroglyphic script and the cremation burial—both of which seem to have extended only as far south as the region of Hama in central Syria.[26]

This challenge assumes that if Uriah were a Hittite, he must have been a part of a Neo-Hittite population in Canaan during the Israelite monarchy that was large enough to leave behind more artifacts than currently have been excavated. Since, however, extant evidence indicates that some Hittites did travel through Canaan, it is not unreasonable that at least one individual such as Uriah may have settled there. In the OT the Hebrew singular gentilic with the article, "the Hittite" (הַחִתִּי), is used both for individuals and for groups of people.[27] Wood proposes that these individuals and groups were not from the Hittite Empire in Anatolia but were native Canaanites and are to be identified with בְּנֵי־חֵת, "the sons of Heth."[28] Wood makes a strong argument, since several OT passages identify Hittites as one of the peoples of Canaan (e.g., Gen 15:20; Ex 7:1; Deut 20:17).[29] Whether Uriah was ethnically a member of the peoples of Canaan or traced his roots to the Anatolian Empire, his name, "my light is Yahweh," indicates that he (and probably his family, perhaps in earlier generations) had converted to the worship of the one true God, Yahweh, the God of Israel. This lends an ironic touch to the entire account, since "Uriah the Hittite" showed more piety and a stronger faith in Yahweh (11:11) than did David, a descendant of Abraham, the king over God's people Israel, and an ancestor of the Messiah (2 Samuel 7; Mt 1:1).[30] The Gospel record will even emphasize that the Christ is descended from "the wife of Uriah" (Mt 1:6).[31]

[26] Singer, "The Hittites and the Bible Revisited," 754, quoted by Wood, "Hittites and Hethites," 240.

[27] An individual man is called הַחִתִּי, "the Hittite," in Gen 23:10; 25:9; 26:34; 36:2; 49:29–30; 50:13; the ethnic group is so designated in, e.g., Gen 15:20; Ex 23:28; Deut 7:1; 20:17. The feminine adjective חִתִּית (without the article), "a Hittitess," refers to a woman in Ezek 16:3, 45.

[28] Gen 23:3, 5, 7, 10, 16, 18, 20; 25:10; 49:32. Heth was the second son of Canaan (Gen 10:15; 1 Chr 1:13).

[29] Also, compare Gen 26:34 with Gen 28:8–9. According to Wood ("Hittites and Hethites," 244, 248–49), Neo-Hittites are always referenced in the OT with the plural words הַחִתִּים (masculine: Josh 1:4; Judg 1:26; 1 Ki 10:29; 2 Ki 7:6; 2 Chr 1:17) or חִתִּיֹּת (feminine: 1 Ki 11:1).

[30] See "Jesus Is the 'Son of David'" and "Jesus Is the 'Son of Abraham'" in Gibbs, *Matthew 1:1–11:1*, 75–77.

[31] This way of referring to Bathsheba exposes David's sin of adultery with her. God's people have always been defined by faith in the messianic promise, not ethnic ancestry (Rom 4:1–25; Gal 3:1–29; 6:16). The genealogy of Jesus in Matthew 1 includes non-Israelites with checkered pasts who were converted to faith in Yahweh and became members of God's redeemed people by grace. See particularly the wives and mothers: Tamar (Mt 1:3), Rahab (Mt 1:5), and Ruth (Mt 1:5). See "The Women in Matthew's Genealogy" in Gibbs, *Matthew 1:1–11:1*, 86–89.

The account of David's dalliance with Bathsheba is told quickly (2 Sam 11:4). He "sent," he "fetched," he "lay"—then "she returned." The verbs all point to David as the guilty party and Bathsheba as the victim. Her only action in the text is to return to her house, where she properly was before and ought to have been. The parenthetical comment that "she had been purifying herself from her uncleanness" (11:4) explains why she was seen bathing—she had been keeping the Law of Moses by bathing to cleanse herself after her monthly period.[32] This comment serves several purposes. First, it contrasts David's sinful act of infidelity with the fidelity of Uriah's household—in this case Bathsheba's faithfulness to the Word of God. Second, it demonstrates that while David avoided transgressing the requirements for ceremonial purity, he committed a much more grievous sin against the Sixth Commandment (Ex 20:14; Deut 5:18) and thus became guilty of violating the entirety of God's Law.[33] Third, it hints that Bathsheba's pregnancy was not unexpected (2 Sam 11:5), since she would have been near the most fertile time of her monthly cycle. Fourth, since she had just menstruated, she was not carrying a child of Uriah, and therefore the child conceived must have been David's.

Bathsheba's pregnancy prompted her to send a message to David. This is the only quotation of her in the entire book of Samuel, and it consists of only two Hebrew words: הָרָה אָנֹכִי, "I am pregnant" (11:5).

David Tries to Cover Up His Sin (11:6–13)

David's reaction to Bathsheba's news was to avoid his responsibility and shame by attempting to cover up his sin. David ordered Joab to send Uriah to Jerusalem (11:6). Upon his arrival at the royal court, David interviewed him, and Uriah must have been puzzled by the questions (11:7)—reporting such items would normally have been part of regular dispatches brought by low-level couriers, not a task for one of the army's elite soldiers. David then sent Uriah home to "wash his feet" (11:8). Foot washing was part of entering a house for the evening and relaxing (Gen 19:2; 24:32; 43:24; Judg 19:21), and it certainly implied that Uriah would also sleep with his wife (as confirmed by Uriah's response to David, "and lie with my wife," in 11:11). Uriah left, apparently without revealing his intentions to David, since the king sent a present after him—probably food and wine (cf. "eat and drink" in 11:11).

Uriah, however, had other concerns. David's servants reported to him that Uriah did not follow orders (11:9–10a). This would have been obvious almost immediately, since his house was near the palace and within easy viewing distance of it. Perhaps when the messengers with the gift arrived, Uriah was not there. Thus, it is likely that the conversation between David and Uriah (11:10b–12) took place early in the nighttime. David simply asked why Uriah did not obey (11:10b). Uriah's answer once again contrasted his faith (expressed by

---

[32] See the second textual notes on 11:2 and 11:4.

[33] See the second textual note on 11:4.

his words as well as his actions) with David's sin (11:11). Uriah noted that Yahweh's ark (cf. 2 Samuel 6) and Israel's army were in temporary shelters, and as a soldier, he also ought not be in a permanent shelter. David's soldiers were to remain ritually clean while on military duty by abstaining from sexual intercourse (1 Sam 21:5 [ET 21:4]). Uriah, like Bathsheba, his wife, was determined to be ceremonially clean.[34] He even took a vow by David's life to remain so.

Upon hearing Uriah's oath, David had no choice but to acquiesce (11:12). He ordered him to stay that day and the next. On the second day, David invited him to a meal, got him drunk, and hoped that in his inebriated state he would forget his oath and the military requirement of abstention, go home, and sleep with Bathsheba (11:13). However, the drunk Uriah proved to be more righteous than the conniving David, and he did not go home.

This sequence of days can be somewhat confusing until one accounts for the fact that in ancient Israel the days began at sundown.[35] Thus, the first day that David told Uriah to stay had already begun by the time they had their nighttime conversation (11:10b–12). The second day began at the next sundown with the evening banquet where David got Uriah drunk. Uriah slept among David's servants that night (11:13), and in the morning—which was still counted as part of the second day—David sent Uriah back to Joab.[36]

David Commits Murder (11:14–27)

Since David could not make it appear as if the child to be born to Bathsheba might be Uriah's, he came up with a more sinister plan (11:14–15). He wrote a message to Joab, instructing him virtually to ensure that Uriah would be killed in battle. He sent the message with Uriah, most likely on a parchment or papyrus scroll with the royal seal, making Uriah the unwitting messenger of his own death.

Joab appears to have taken liberties with David's orders often, especially when he thought it was in David's best interest. See, for example, Joab's assassination of Abner in 3:22–27 (especially Joab's words in 3:24–25), his role in restoring Absalom to favor (14:1–24), and his killing of Absalom (18:5–17). In this case Joab partially carried out David's orders. He surveyed the Ammonite defenses of the city to determine where the enemy had likely stationed its "best soldiers" (11:16).[37] He advanced at that point, and the Ammonites came out of the city to attack (11:17). There is no mention of Joab following David's order

---

[34] According to Lev 15:16–18, a man and woman who engage in sexual intercourse are required to bathe and are unclean until the evening.

[35] In the account of creation, and hence in OT reckoning, a new day began at evening: "there was evening and there was morning" (e.g., Gen 1:5, 8).

[36] See also the textual note on 11:12.

[37] For the superlative, see the second textual note on 11:16. The suggestion of some (Wharton, "A Plausible Tale," 342; Eschelbach, *Has Joab Foiled David?* 27 and 94, n. 42) that "the best soldiers" mentioned here (11:16) were Joab's best does not comport with the immediately preceding statement that "Joab had observed the city" (11:16) and thus knew where its best soldiers were likely to be.

(11:15) to pull his forces back to expose Uriah alone to the Ammonite assault. Instead, according to the account of the battle later given to David (11:23), when Joab counterattacked, he pressed the battle up to the city's wall. The death of Uriah and others from Joab's men is attributed to archers from the wall (11:24). In this way Joab was able to fulfill David's wishes but conceal from his army David's command to have Uriah killed. In addition, Joab was able to preserve the morale of his troops. They certainly would have become dispirited if they thought that David might order their execution at the hands of the enemy as he had done to Uriah.

When Joab sent a report of the battle to David, he was careful to instruct the messenger how to respond if David became angry at Joab for pressing his assault up to the city wall (11:18–21). He expected to incur David's wrath for making the tactical mistake of coming within range of the defenders on the wall. He even anticipated that David would reference the case of the death of Abimelech (Judg 9:50–57). Intriguingly, Joab calls Abimelech "the son of Jerub*beseth*" (יְרֻבֶּשֶׁת, 2 Sam 11:21), whereas the book of Judges names Abimelech "the son of Jerub*baal*" (יְרֻבַּעַל, Judg 9:1, 28). Judges provides two names for Abimelech's father. Initially he is called "Gideon" (e.g., Judg 6:11, 13, 19, 22). After witnessing a theophany, he carried out Yahweh's instructions to tear down the altar of the male fertility god Baal and burn the pole of his female consort, the goddess Asherah (Judg 6:11–32). After that feat he received a second name, "Jerub*baal*," meaning, "let Baal contend [against him]," a taunt for the impotent non-god to exact revenge against him for destroying his altar (Judg 6:32; see also Judg 7:1; 8:29, 35). Here in 2 Sam 11:21 it appears that later scribes copying the book of Samuel bowdlerized the name "Jerub*baal*" to avoid any mention of the pagan god "Baal." They substituted -*besheth* (בֶּשֶׁת-), a form of the Hebrew noun for "shame" (בֹּשֶׁת, *bosheth*). For the significance of this substitution here and elsewhere in Samuel, see the second textual note on 2:8.

When the messenger came to David, he gave the report of the battle (11:22–24) Not wishing to bear the outburst of David's anger, he stated that Uriah had died in the battle (11:24) before David could question Joab's tactics.

David was then able to appear magnanimous by sending a message to encourage Joab (11:25). He noted that the loss of life was an inevitable consequence of war and ordered Joab to intensify the siege until he captured the city.

The narrator then turns his attention to Uriah's widow. She mourned for her husband (11:26), which probably involved a week's time.[38] Then she was taken into David's house as his wife and bore his child (11:27). Since the time

---

[38] Gen 50:10; 1 Sam 31:13; 1 Chr 10:12; Judith 16:24; Sirach 22:12. Only the most exceptional persons were mourned longer, e.g., thirty days for Aaron (Num 20:29) and Moses (Deut 34:8). The Torah stipulates that if a desirable woman is captured in war and an Israelite desires to marry her, he must allow her a full month to mourn before he takes her as his wife (Deut 21:10–13), but that was not Bathsheba's situation. Since she knew she was pregnant with David's child (2 Sam 11:5), she likely would have wanted to come under the protection of being a wife in his household as soon as possible.

from her conception to her marriage to David may have been only a month at most, it would have appeared as if David was able to cover up his dalliance with Uriah's wife by pretending that the child was conceived after he married her following Uriah's death. It is not unusual for a baby to be born a few weeks earlier than full term. Birth normally occurs when the baby's gestational age is about forty weeks. However, this is simply an average. A baby born in the range from thirty-seven to forty-two weeks can be perfectly healthy.[39]

At this point in the narrative it appears as if David's treachery had succeeded. However, the reader cannot help but see the terrible price that had been exacted by his infidelity. First was the cost to Bathsheba. A faithful wife living in obedience to God's Word was robbed of her husband and made a pawn of the king in whose service her husband was murdered. Note that her name is used only once and on the lips of one of David's servants (11:3). In the narrative in relation to David she is undignifiedly called "the woman" (11:2 [twice], 3, 5), is merely referenced by pronouns (11:4 [four times], 5, 27), or is the unstated subject of feminine verbs (11:4 [three times], 5 [three times], 27 [twice]). It is not until the very end of the chapter that David's relationship to her changes and she becomes "his wife" (11:27). Three times earlier she is the rightful "wife" of her husband, Uriah: she is "the wife of Uriah the Hittite" (11:3), "Uriah's wife" (11:26), and her husband, Uriah, calls her "my wife" (11:11), a title she never receives from David. In relation to David in the narrative, she is the object of lust and little more than chattel. These rhetorical touches are at least part of the literary condemnation that "what David had done was evil in Yahweh's eyes" (11:27).

A second price was the life of Uriah. Despite his identity as "the Hittite" (11:3, 6, 17, 21, 24), an ethnic foreigner grafted into Israel, he is portrayed as nothing other than a follower of Yahweh, a righteous member of God's people through faith, and a loyal soldier in David's army—so devoted to the cause that he refused the king's offer to take leave in his house from his military service (11:11). David had this brave soldier killed, and the collateral damage cost his army the lives of several other Israelite troops (11:17). This too is an implicit part of the author's comment that "what David had done was evil in Yahweh's eyes" (11:27).

A third price to be paid was less obvious, but nonetheless real: David corrupted Joab, the commander of his army, by making him an accomplice in the murder. Joab's part in Uriah's death was less than David had envisioned, since Joab had not strictly followed orders ("turn back from him," 11:15). Nonetheless, Joab was a willing party to David's plot to take Uriah's life, even if he had not been informed about the reason for David's order. The king's conscription of others into his web of turpitude is another proof that "what David had done was evil in Yahweh's eyes" (11:27).

---

[39] Modern medicine has increased the likelihood that babies born as early as twenty-two weeks may thrive.

In all of this the author of Samuel is demonstrating that sin is never simply a private matter. Whether or not we understand all of the consequences of our wrongdoing (and David surely did not foresee the results exposed in 13:1–20:22), we are reminded that sin always damages others, particularly those closest to us, and often in ways that are unseen. If it were not for the grace of God, sin would reign unchecked and destroy everyone. But God is gracious and sent his Son to bear the punishment for sin. That gracious impulse of God is the subject of the next chapter, which begins with Yahweh sending Nathan to speak his Word in confrontation with David (12:1).

Nathan Rebukes David

Translation

12 ¹Yahweh sent Nathan to David. He came to him and said to him, "There were two men in one city. One was rich, and one was poor. ²The rich man had very many sheep and cattle, ³while the poor man had nothing except one small ewe lamb that he had acquired. He raised her, and she grew with him and with his sons together. She would eat his morsel of food and drink from his cup. She would lie in his lap, and she was like a daughter to him. ⁴A traveler came to the rich man. He thought it a pity to take one of his sheep or cattle to prepare [a meal] for the traveler who came to him. So he took the poor man's ewe lamb and prepared it for the man who had come to him."

⁵David became very angry at the man and said to Nathan, "As Yahweh lives, the man who did this deserves to die! ⁶Moreover, he must repay the ewe lamb four-fold, because he did this thing and since he had no pity."

⁷Nathan said to David, "You are the man! Thus says Yahweh, the God of Israel: 'I anointed you to be king over Israel, and I rescued you from the hand of Saul. ⁸I gave you your master's house and your master's wives into your arms, and I gave you the house of Israel and Judah. If this had been too little I would have given you more. ⁹Why have you despised Yahweh's Word to do what is evil in my eyes? You struck down Uriah the Hittite with the sword and took his wife for yourself to be your wife. You killed him with the Ammonites' sword! ¹⁰Now the sword will never turn away from your house, because you despised me and took the wife of Uriah the Hittite for yourself to be your wife.'

¹¹"Thus says Yahweh: 'Look! I will raise a disaster against you from your house: As you watch I will take your wives and give them to your neighbor. He will lie with your wives in broad daylight. ¹²Although you acted in secret, I will do this thing publicly in front of all Israel.'"

¹³David said to Nathan, "I have sinned against Yahweh."

Nathan said to David, "Indeed, Yahweh has taken away your sin. You will not die. ¹⁴However, since you have treated Yahweh with utter contempt in this matter, the son who was born to you will certainly die."

¹⁵Nathan went home. Yahweh struck the child that Uriah's wife bore to David, and he became ill.

Textual Notes

12:1 וַיִּשְׁלַח יְהוָה אֶת־נָתָן—"Yahweh sent Nathan." God takes the initiative to repair his kingdom and bring David to repentance. After "Nathan," a few Masoretic manuscripts

206

add הַנָּבִיא, "the prophet" (see נָתָן הַנָּבִיא in 7:2; 12:25).[1] That longer reading is supported by the LXX (τὸν Ναθαν τὸν προφήτην) and the Syriac Peshitta (ܟܐܠܐ ܢܒܝܐ).

שְׁנֵי אֲנָשִׁים—"Two men." The Lucianic recension of the LXX prefaces Nathan's remarks with ἀνάγγειλον δή μοι (τὴν) κρίσιν ταύτην, "now pass judgment on this case for me," which, if original, might reflect a Hebrew text with הַגֶּד־נָא לִי אֶת הַמִּשְׁפָּט הַזֶּה (the first three of those words are in 2 Sam 1:4). Some understand the Lucianic reading to have been part of the original text.[2] However, it is more likely to be an explanatory addition.[3]

בְּעִיר אֶחָת—"In one city." The numeral אֶחָד (the form אֶחָת is the feminine אַחַת in pause) could also be translated as the "same" city (Joüon, § 147 a).

עָשִׁיר—"Rich." This adjective is used again in 12:2, 4 but nowhere else in the book of Samuel.

רָאשׁ:—"Poor." This form with א is an Aramaic-like Qal (G) masculine singular participle of רוּשׁ or רִישׁ, "be poor, needy." The same form recurs in 12:4. Its normal Hebrew form, רָשׁ (without א), is used in 12:3, as well as in 1 Sam 18:23. See GKC, § 72 p; Joüon, § 80 k.

12:2 לְעָשִׁיר הָיָה—"The rich man had." The preposition לְ is used in the sense of possession, "(belonging) to." The MT lacks the definite article and so would be translated literally as "*a* rich man had." See also the second textual note on 12:4, where the MT lacks an article that would be expected. The form with the article here would be לֶעָשִׁיר (cf. הֶעָשִׁיר, 12:4). Most English versions translate with "*the* rich man" (referring back to עָשִׁיר in 12:1).

12:3 וּלְרָשׁ אֵין־כֹּל—"The poor man had nothing" is literally "and (belonging) to the poor man there did not exist anything." This clause is intended to express the opposite of the rich man's situation (Joüon, § 160 k; cf. GKC, § 152 p).

כִּבְשָׂה—"Ewe lamb." This noun is feminine, so it is translated with "ewe." The following adjectives, pronouns (the suffix on וַיְחַיֶּהָ in the next textual note), and verbs for which it is the subject are feminine.

וַיְחַיֶּהָ—"He raised her." The Piel (D) of חָיָה, "be alive," usually has a causative meaning, "to make [someone] alive, resurrect" (1 Sam 2:6) or "keep someone alive" (1 Sam 27:9, 11). Here and in Is 7:21 it refers to animal husbandry, that is, nourishing and protecting a domesticated animal so that it will grow and thrive.

מִפִּתּוֹ תֹאכַל וּמִכֹּסוֹ תִשְׁתֶּה—"She would eat his morsel of food and drink from his cup." The verb אָכַל, "eat," can take the preposition מִן in the sense of source, "eat from" (Gen 2:16–17), or in a partitive sense, "eat some of" (see BDB, s.v. אָכַל, Qal, 1, and s.v. מִן, 2 c, 3). The noun פַּת denotes a small piece of food, as in 1 Sam 2:36; 28:22. The noun כּוֹס refers to a cup for drinking (e.g., Gen 40:11; Ps 23:5).

---

[1] Outside of Samuel, see "Nathan the prophet" also in 1 Ki 1:8, 10, 22, 23, 32, 34, 38, 44, 45; Ps 51:2 (ET superscription); 1 Chr 17:1; 29:29; 2 Chr 9:29.

[2] E.g., McCarter, *II Samuel*, 294.

[3] Anderson, *2 Samuel*, 158.

וּבְחֵיקוֹ תִשְׁכָּב—"She would lie in his lap." The noun חֵיק is commonly translated as "bosom." In Is 40:11 the Messiah comes as a Shepherd who carries his lambs in his חֵיק. The noun is commonly used in the context of an embrace within an intimate relationship, as for husbands and wives (2 Sam 12:8; also Deut 13:7 [ET 13:6]; 28:54, 56) and women with nursing infants (Num 11:12; 1 Ki 3:20; cf. Ruth 4:16).

12:4 הֵלֶךְ—This noun, "traveler," is clearly derived from the verb הָלַךְ, "walk." Its only other occurrence in the OT is in 1 Sam 14:26, where it refers to a "flow" of honey. Later this verse will refer to this wayfarer with אֹרֵחַ, the Qal (G) participle of אָרַח, "to journey, travel" (six times in the OT). Then he will be designated twice by הַבָּא, "who came/had come," the Qal masculine singular participle of בּוֹא with a definite article that functions as a relative pronoun.

לָאִישׁ הֶעָשִׁיר—The MT literally reads "to a man, the rich one." If the article were added to the noun with לְ (לְאִישׁ) in concord with the article on the adjective (הֶעָשִׁיר) its form would be לָאִישׁ. Most English versions translate the phrase as "to the rich man." See also the first textual note on 12:2.

וַיַּחְמֹל לָקַחַת—"He thought it a pity to take." The first verb is the Qal (G) third masculine singular preterite (imperfect with *waw* consecutive) of חָמַל, "to have pity, compassion." This verb recurs in 12:6 (see also, e.g., 1 Sam 15:3, 9; 2 Sam 21:7). The second verb is the Qal infinitive construct of לָקַח, "take," with the preposition לְ. It serves as a complement of the first verb, stating the action from which he refrained out of pity.

מִצֹּאנוֹ וּמִבְּקָרוֹ—"One of his sheep or cattle." The preposition מִן is used partitively here, "one of" (BDB, s.v. מִן, 3 b (*b*)).

12:5 וַיִּחַר־אַף דָּוִד—"David became angry." For this idiom, וַיִּחַר־אַף, literally "the anger [of someone] burned," see the first textual note on 6:7.

חַי־יְהוָה כִּי—"As Yahweh lives, (for)." For this oath formula appealing to Yahweh with the conjunction כִּי (untranslated), see the first textual note on 2:27 (also the second textual note on 1 Sam 14:45[4]); Waltke-O'Connor, § 40.2.2b, including example 5.

בֶן־מָוֶת—"He deserves to die" is literally "(he is) a son of death." The same construct phrase was in 1 Sam 20:31, and its plural equivalent is in 1 Sam 26:16. See *IBH*, § 15 A.

12:6 יְשַׁלֵּם—"He must repay." For the modal sense of "must" for the imperfect, see Joüon, § 113 m. Here the Piel (D) of שָׁלֵם refers to making restitution. Elsewhere it can denote "repaying" in the positive sense of God "rewarding" someone (1 Sam 24:20 [ET 24:19]) or a person "fulfilling" his vow to God (2 Sam 15:7), or it can have the negative sense of divine retribution or punishment (3:39).

אַרְבַּעְתָּיִם—"Fourfold." This is a feminine dual form of the number "four," whose feminine singular is אַרְבָּעָה. The Torah of Moses demanded the restitution of four sheep for every one stolen, but five oxen for one ox (Ex 21:37 [ET 22:1]). On the use of the dual form of numerals corresponding to the English suffix "-fold," see GKC, § 97 h; Joüon, § 100 o; Waltke-O'Connor, § 15.4a, including example 4. The LXX reads

---

[4]   Steinmann, *1 Samuel*, 265.

ἑπταπλασίονα, "sevenfold." Some passages speak of "sevenfold" restitution (Prov 6:30–31) or retribution (e.g., Gen 4:24; Lev 26:18–28; Ps 79:12).

עֵקֶב אֲשֶׁר עָשָׂה אֶת־הַדָּבָר הַזֶּה וְעַל אֲשֶׁר לֹא־חָמָל׃—"Because he did this thing and since he had no pity." These two clauses may serve as a hendiadys, "because he did this without pity," i.e., he acted ruthlessly or cruelly. The conjunction עֵקֶב, "because, as a consequence," appears in the book of Samuel only here and in 12:10. Cf. Joüon, § 170 g.

12:7 אַתָּה הָאִישׁ—"You are the man!" The wording of this accusation is unique in the OT. Cf. the questions with the interrogative *he*, (הָ)אִישׁ הַאַתָּה, in Judg 13:11; 1 Ki 13:14.

כֹּה־אָמַר יְהוָה—"Thus says Yahweh." This prophetic formula of divine revelation recurs in 12:11. See the second textual note on 7:5.

אָנֹכִי מְשַׁחְתִּיךָ—"I (myself) anointed you." The personal pronoun אָנֹכִי is emphatic, literally "I, I anointed you." For מָשַׁח, "anoint," see the second textual note and the commentary on 5:3. Yahweh himself (rather than his human agent) is the subject of this verb here and in 1 Sam 10:1; 15:17. This verb is used for the anointing of David in 1 Sam 16:12–13; 2 Sam 2:4, 7; 5:3, 17.

12:8 וָאֶתְּנָה ... וָאֶתְּנָה—"(And) I gave ... and I gave." When a first person singular (or plural) imperfect (here of נָתַן) is used with *waw* consecutive, the accent usually remains on the last syllable (is not retracted), and often its form is lengthened by the addition of the paragogic *he* ending, which is accented (הָ֫). See GKC, § 49 e. The form here is that of a cohortative, but without the cohortative's usual volitional meaning. See *IBH*, § 51 F.

בְּחֵיקֶךָ—"Into your arms." See the fifth textual note on 12:3.

מְעָט—"Too little." Here מְעַט (pausal: מְעָט) is used as a noun, "a little thing/amount," to form an elliptical comparison ("too"). See Joüon, § 141 i.

וְאֹסִפָה לְךָ כָּהֵנָּה וְכָהֵנָּה׃—Literally "and I would have added to you like they and like they." The verb אֹסִפָה is a defective, or *ḥaser*, spelling of אוֹסִיפָה, the singular Hiphil (H) cohortative (see Joüon, § 45) of יָסַף, meaning "to add, increase, do more." The cohortative expresses the speaker's desire and will to do something (Joüon, § 114 b). The repeated word כָּהֵנָּה is the preposition כְּ, "like," with the third feminine plural pronoun. It has a neuter sense as it refers not only to the (feminine plural) wives (נְשֵׁי אֲדֹנֶיךָ, "your master's wives") but to the other gifts as well (see BDB, s.v. הֵמָּה, 6 and 8 b).

12:9a מַדּוּעַ בָּזִיתָ ׀ אֶת־דְּבַר יְהוָה—"Why have you despised Yahweh's Word?" See also בְּזִתָנִי, "you despised me," in the next verse (12:10) and נִאֵץ, "treat with contempt," in the second textual note on 12:14. The Qal (G) of בָּזָה referred to "despising" Yahweh also in 1 Sam 2:30. David was the object of this verb as the person despised in 1 Sam 17:42; 2 Sam 6:16. When Saul "rejected Yahweh's Word," and then Yahweh consequently "rejected" Saul, the verb was מָאַס (1 Sam 15:23 [twice], 26 [twice]; 16:1), but that verb is not used in the case of David (it is absent from 2 Samuel). For "Yahweh's Word" as revelatory, theophanic, and Christological, see the third textual note on 1 Sam 3:1.[5] Cf. "the Word" in Jn 1:1, 14.

---

[5] Steinmann, *1 Samuel*, 109.

לַעֲשׂוֹת הָרַע—"To do what is evil" is literally "to do the evil." The infinitive construct (the Qal [G] of עָשָׂה) with לְ might express purpose: David despised the divine Word so that he could commit his sin, which was prohibited by it. Alternatively, the infinitive may serve as a gerund that provides further explanation of the preceding verb (בָּזִיתָ): he "despised" Yahweh's Word *by* doing evil. For this common usage of an infinitive, see Joüon, § 124 o.

בְּעֵינַי—"In my eyes." This is the Qere. Its first person suffix fits the larger context in that Yahweh is the speaker in 12:7b–12. The Kethib בעינו may be vocalized as בְּעֵינָו, a defective, or *ḥaser*, spelling of בְּעֵינָיו, the dual noun with a third masculine singular suffix, "in his eyes." The LXX supports the Kethib and that vocalization of it (ἐν ὀφθαλμοῖς αὐτοῦ). The Kethib fits the immediate context in that the first clause of the verse referred to Yahweh in the third person (see the first textual note on 12:9), and most English translations have "in his eyes" to consistently refer to Yahweh in the third person within this verse. The Kethib could also be vocalized as the singular noun with a third masculine singular suffix, בְּעֵינוֹ, "in his eye."

12:9b–10   בַּחֶרֶב ... בְּחֶרֶב בְּנֵי עַמּוֹן ... לֹא־תָסוּר חֶרֶב—"With the sword. ... with the Ammonites' sword. ... The sword will never turn away." The noun חֶרֶב is feminine and so is the subject of תָסוּר, the third feminine singular Qal (G) imperfect of סוּר, "depart, turn away." The noun appears twice in 12:9 as the instrument of David's crime, then in 12:10 as the instrument of his punishment. This expresses the *lex talionis*, or law of retribution: the punishment fits the crime.

12:11   הִנְנִי מֵקִים—"I will raise" is literally "behold, I (am) raising." The pronominal suffix on the particle הִנֵּה serves as the subject of the Hiphil (H) masculine singular participle of קוּם. The construction of הִנֵּה with a participle is a common way in which Yahweh announces imminent judgment or salvation in prophetic oracles (see GKC, § 116 p).

לְעֵינֶיךָ—"As you watch" is literally "to your eyes."

לְרֵעֶיךָ—"To your neighbor." The reading לְרֵעֶיךָ in Codex Leningradensis appears to be the masculine plural of the noun רֵעַ with לְ and a second masculine singular suffix, "to your friends." However, the *yod* (ֶי-) in the suffix, which normally indicates that the noun is plural, may instead be the original third root letter (רעי) of the noun, and so the noun is singular (so BDB s.v. רֵעַ II, citing GKC, § 93 ss): "to your neighbor." Many Masoretic manuscripts read לְרֵעֶךָ, without the *yod*, which is clearly the singular noun.

לְעֵינֵי הַשֶּׁמֶשׁ הַזֹּאת:—"In broad daylight" is literally "to the eyes of this sun." The noun שֶׁמֶשׁ is usually feminine; here it is modified by the feminine demonstrative pronoun זֹאת. See also שֶׁמֶשׁ in the second textual note on 12:12.

12:12   בַסָּתֶר—"In secret." This phrase is the preposition בְּ and the definite article attached to the segholate noun סֵתֶר (pausal: סָתֶר), "a covering; hiding place; secrecy." The phrase could be translated adverbially: "you acted *secretly*." For its antonym, see the next textual note.

וְנֶגֶד הַשָּׁמֶשׁ:—Literally "and before the sun." The prepositional phrase serves as an antonym of בַסָּתֶר and can be translated as an adverb: "publicly."

12:13   חָטָאתִי לַיהוָה—"I have sinned against Yahweh." The Qal (G) of חָטָא, "to sin," is used with the prepositional phrase לַיהוָה also in 1 Sam 2:25; 7:6; 12:23; 14:33, 34.

210

The verb is common in Leviticus as a technical term for committing an offense against God that requires sacrificial atonement.[6] David will use the verb חָטָאתִי again in his confessions in 24:10, 17.

יְהוָה הֶעֱבִיר חַטָּאתְךָ—"Yahweh has taken away your sin." The direct object noun חַטָּאת, "a sin," is cognate to the verb David used in his confession (see the prior textual note). The Hiphil (H) of עָבַר, "cause to pass over, across," can mean "cause to pass away, take away, remove" (see BDB, Hiphil, 4; *DCH*, Hiphil, 8), but its use for expressing forgiveness is rare. It is used for removing "sin" (חַטָּאת) only here and for taking away "iniquity" (עָוֹן) only in 2 Sam 24:10 ‖ 1 Chr 21:8; Zech 3:4; Job 7:21 (cf. Micah 7:18; Prov 19:11). The usage in 2 Sam 24:10 ‖ 1 Chr 21:8 is similar to 2 Sam 12:13 because the "iniquity" (עָוֹן) is described earlier in the verse as having been incurred by the verb חָטָא, "to sin."

12:14   אֶפֶס כִּי־—This combination, "however, since," clarifies that the plenary absolution in 12:13 does not mean that David's sin is inconsequential. See Waltke-O'Connor, § 39.3.5e, including example 23.

נִאֵץ נִאַצְתָּ—"You have treated … with utter contempt." This is the Piel (D) infinitive absolute[7] and the Piel second masculine singular perfect of נָאַץ. This verb was used for the sons of Eli who, as apostate priests, treated Yahweh's sacrificial offerings with contempt (1 Sam 2:17). Elsewhere it is a strong term since those who so despise Yahweh receive disastrous punishments; e.g., in Num 14:23 the contemptuous are excluded from the promised land, and in Num 16:30 they are swallowed alive into Sheol. In Is 1:4; 5:24 those who show contempt for the Holy One of Israel or his Word fall under his judgment (cf. Jer 23:17; Pss 10:3, 13; 74:10).

אֶת־אֹיְבֵי יְהוָה—In the MT the direct object of the contempt is "the enemies of Yahweh," and this reading is supported by the LXX (τοὺς ἐχθροὺς κυρίου). However, despising Yahweh's enemies would hardly seem to be a sin that would elicit his judgment. This reading probably is a euphemism for treating Yahweh himself with contempt, as if the direct object were אֶת־יְהוָה, and most English versions give "the LORD" as the direct object. Some scholars argue that the euphemism was used by the original author and so is the original reading, since there are literary parallels in ancient Egypt and Mari.[8] Others believe scribes created the euphemism by inserting אֹיְבֵי to make a construct phrase.[9] A similar euphemism is present in 1 Sam 25:22, which refers to "the enemies of David," but there the LXX lacks "the enemies of," whereas LXX 2 Sam 12:14 includes it. Here 4QSamª reads את דבר יהוה, "the Word of Yahweh" (cf. בָּזִיתָ ‖ אֶת־דְּבַר יְהוָה, 12:9).[10]

---

[6]   E.g., Lev 4:2, 3, 14, 22, 23, 27, 28, 35; 5:1, 5, 6, 7, 10, 11, 13, 15, 16, 17.

[7]   The Piel (D) infinitive absolute would normally be vocalized נָאֵץ, but the *patach* has been weakened to *hireq* for the sake of assonance (GKC, § 52 o; Joüon, § 52 c).

[8]   See the discussion in McCarter, *II Samuel*, 296.

[9]   E.g., McCarter, *II Samuel*, 296; Bergen, *1, 2 Samuel*, 373, including n. 115.

[10] See further the first textual note on 1 Sam 25:22 (Steinmann, *1 Samuel*, 475–76). See also Tov, *Textual Criticism of the Hebrew Bible*, 271–72.

הַבֵּן הַיִּלּוֹד—"The son who was born" is literally "the born son." For the adjective יִלּוֹד, see the textual note on 5:14. Cf. the cognate noun with the article הַיֶּלֶד, "the child," in 12:15.

12:15 וַיֵּאָנַשׁ:—"And he became ill." This is the Niphal (N) third masculine singular preterite (imperfect with *waw* consecutive) of the verb אָנַשׁ. It is in pause (GKC, § 51 m); otherwise it would be vocalized with *tsere* in the final syllable: וַיֵּאָנֵשׁ. This is the only instance of אָנַשׁ as a perfect or imperfect verb. Its Qal passive (Gp) participle, אָנוּשׁ, is used as an adjective, "incurable," often referring to diseases.[11]

Commentary

997 BC[12]

It had appeared as if David had successfully concealed his sins from his courtiers and his army (2 Samuel 11). However, he could not conceal anything from God, and we were told that what David had done was evil in God's eyes (11:27). Yet Yahweh is a gracious and merciful God who keeps his promises (2 Samuel 7). As a result, instead of rejecting David and destroying his dynasty, as he had done to Saul because of the first king's rejection of Yahweh's Word,[13] God sent Nathan to call David to repentance and then absolve him of his sin. Nathan's depiction of the case of the two men took the form of a typical appeal for justice by someone who had access to the king and was acting as a patron for someone who did not (12:1–4). Since antiquity this has been the understanding of the *form* of Nathan's words as presented to David.[14] Readers almost instantly understand Nathan's story to be a sort of parable whose application to David is obvious. Moreover, Nathan's short account of the poor man and the rich man contains several plays on words and subtle references that heighten the story's condemnation of David's actions. See figure 8. These connections add irony to Nathan's words and David's initial condemnatory reaction to them, making the entire narrative of Nathan's rebuke more vivid for the reader.

David's reaction of decreeing capital punishment for the perpetrator in Nathan's case (12:5) demonstrates that he assumed Nathan was presenting him with an actual situation to adjudicate. He not only swore that the offending rich man was worthy of death (12:5), but he also imposed the penalty required by the Law of Moses: fourfold repayment for theft of a sheep (see the second textual note on 12:6).

---

[11] Is 17:11; Jer 15:18; 17:9, 16; 30:12, 15; Micah 1:9; Job 34:6.

[12] See "The Chronology of David's Reign" in the commentary on 5:1–5.

[13] 1 Sam 15:23, 26; 16:1. See the first textual note on 2 Sam 12:9a.

[14] See the second textual note on 12:1. Gregory the Great also comments that Nathan "asked his [David's] judgment as if concerning the cause of a poor man against a rich one" (*The Book of Pastoral Rule*, 3.2 [*NPNF*² 12b:25]).

Figure 8

Nathan's Story and Reflection in the Surrounding Narrative

Nathan's Story	Reflection in the Surrounding Narrative
The ewe lamb would "lie" in her master's arms (the verb שָׁכַב, 12:3).	1. David "lay" with Bathsheba (the same verb, שָׁכַב, 11:4). 2. Uriah did not "lie" with his wife, but "lay" in the place where his master's servants were (the same verb, שָׁכַב, 11:9, 11, 13). 3. Someone will "lie" with David's wives (the same verb, שָׁכַב, 12:11).
The ewe lamb would lie in her master's "lap" or "arms" (the noun חֵיק; see the fifth textual note on 12:3).	God gave Saul's wives into David's "arms" (the noun, חֵיק, 12:8).
The ewe lamb was like a "daughter" to the poor man (the noun בַּת, 12:3).	The ewe lamb represents "Bathsheba" (בַּת־שֶׁבַע, "the daughter of Sheba"), who was "Eliam's daughter" (see the second textual note on 11:3).
The rich man "thought it a pity" to take one of his own sheep (the verb חָמַל, 12:4).	David condemned the story's rich man because "he had no pity" (the same verb, חָמַל, negated in 12:6).
The rich man "took" the poor man's lamb (the verb לָקַח, 12:4).	1. David "took" Uriah's wife (the same verb, לָקַח, 12:9, 10). 2. Yahweh "will take" David's wives (the same verb, לָקַח, 12:11).
The rich man "prepared" the lamb for his visitor (the verb עָשָׂה, literally "to do, make, act," 12:4).	1. David twice refers to the man who "did" this (the same verb עָשָׂה, 12:5, 6). 2. David despised Yahweh's Word "to do" evil (the same verb, עָשָׂה; see the second textual note on 12:9a). 3. David "acted" in secret, but God will "do" this (i.e., take David's wives) in public (the same verb, עָשָׂה, twice in 12:12).

David must have been stunned by Nathan's accusation: "*You* are the man!" (12:7a). At that point it became clear to David that Nathan's scenario was a parable. The rehearsal of what Yahweh had done for David (12:7b–8) emphasized what David had been given and that Yahweh would have given him much more—through legitimate means. While Yahweh stated that he gave David his "master's wives," this is probably not to be taken literally as if David had married the wives of former King Saul.[15] Instead, it is to be understood as a rhetorical flourish to make the point that David had inherited the kingdom forfeited by apostate Saul, and one of David's wives was the second daughter of Saul, so David had married into royalty.[16] Since David had his own wives and concubines, he did not need to seduce and steal another man's wife. After all, Yahweh would have given him more through lawful marriages.

Nathan's main accusation against David was that he "despised Yahweh's Word" (12:9; see also "you despised me [Yahweh]," 12:10). The actual evil acts of which David was accused were cited as evidence of this: he "struck down Uriah" with the sword and "took his [Uriah's] wife" as his own (12:9). The murder of Uriah was laid at David's feet, and he was given no way to deny it when Nathan stated that "the Ammonites' sword" was the instrument used by the adulterous king. While the acts themselves were serious transgressions of God's Law, the root cause identified by God was the disdain with which David had treated Yahweh and his Word.

Yahweh also told David that the consequences for his sins would correspond to them: just as David had taken Uriah's wife and lain with her, so Yahweh would take David's wives and give them to David's "neighbor," who would lie with them (12:11).[17] Moreover, while David had sought to conceal his acts, Yahweh would exact his justice in public (12:11b–12). This reversal was to demonstrate to David (and to the readers of the book of Samuel) that there are no acts concealed from God (see, e.g., Mt 6:4, 6, 18; Mk 4:22; Heb 4:12).

David's response to Nathan's accusation and prophecy was simple and yet extraordinary: "I have sinned against Yahweh" (two Hebrew words, חָטָאתִי לַיהוָה, 12:13). Most persons when confronted with their sin first seek to deny what they have done or to make excuses for their behavior (as did Saul in 1 Sam 13:11–12; 15:15, 20–21; 28:15). However, David knew that Nathan's accusation was a call to repentance, and his only recourse was to confess his

---

[15] There is no evidence that Saul had more than two wives—the mother of Jonathan and his brothers, and a concubine, Rizpah (2 Sam 3:7). Neither is said to have married David.

[16] King Saul two daughters, Merab and Michal (1 Sam 14:49). He had first promised that David could marry his older daughter, Merab, and David admitted that he did not deserve this honor, by which he would become a son-in-law to the king (1 Sam 18:17–18). However, Saul broke his promise by giving Merab to another man (1 Sam 18:19). Subsequently, Saul gave his consent for David to marry his second daughter, Michal (1 Sam 18:20–27), who became David's first wife. See further the footnote on David's wives and concubines in the commentary on 2 Sam 11:1–5.

[17] Re the "neighbor," see the third textual note on 12:11. This neighbor would be David's son Absalom (16:21–22).

sin and trust that God is merciful to penitent sinners (Psalm 51; see also 2 Sam 24:10, 17).[18] This illustrates that David, unlike Saul before him, was a man after God's own heart (1 Sam 13:14; see also 2 Sam 7:21). David had despised Yahweh's Word, but the same prophetic Word wrought in his heart contrition by the accusation of the Law and faith by the promise of the Gospel—the promise of the Messiah (2 Samuel 7). Such repentance (contrition and faith)[19] is a daily constant throughout the believer's life.[20]

God's gracious gifts of faith, courage, and intellect had brought David thus far in his office as God's anointed king, for Israel's benefit (2 Sam 7:8–9). Moreover, God promised to build a house for David to benefit his people eternally, and this would be fulfilled by the Son of David who would reign on his throne forever.[21] God chose and molded David to be a king as God envisioned royal service—not as Israel had envisioned it when they first requested a king (1 Samuel 8). This conclusion about David was drawn at least as early as St. Paul, who said:

καὶ μεταστήσας αὐτὸν ἤγειρεν τὸν Δαυὶδ αὐτοῖς εἰς βασιλέα ᾧ καὶ εἶπεν μαρτυρήσας· εὗρον Δαυὶδ τὸν τοῦ Ἰεσσαί, ἄνδρα κατὰ τὴν καρδίαν μου, ὃς ποιήσει πάντα τὰ θελήματά μου.

And after removing him [Saul], he [God] raised up David for them as a king, to whom he also testified, "I have found in David the [son] of Jesse a man **according to my own heart**, *who will do all the things I desire*." (Acts 13:22)

God's desire was, first of all, that David repent. Yahweh understood well that David, like all other people except the Messiah, was sinful (Gen 8:21).

---

[18] See especially Ps 51:19 (ET 51:17), where David uses the same verb for "despise" (בָּזָה) that Yahweh had used in the accusation against him in 2 Sam 12:9: "a broken and contrite heart, O God, you will *not despise*."

[19] Contrition and faith are the result of the Law and the Gospel, respectively. These correspond to other dialectics in Scripture such as mortifying (putting to death) and vivifying (being raised to new life), putting off sin and being clothed in Christ. These are essential to the daily renewal of the Christian. See Ap XII, "Penitence," 46–48, 56. David's confession of sin in 2 Sam 12:13 is quoted (§§ 48, 56) as an example of self-condemnation that results from the binding of the Law, that is, of contrition.

[20] See FC SD III 9–11:

A poor sinner is justified before God (that is, he is absolved and declared utterly free from all his sins, and from the verdict of well deserved damnation, and is adopted as a child of God and an heir of eternal life) without any merit or worthiness on our part, and without any preceding, present, or subsequent works, by sheer grace, solely through the merit of the total obedience, the bitter passion, the death, and the resurrection of Christ, our Lord, whose obedience is reckoned to us as righteousness. The Holy Spirit offers these treasures to us in the promise of the Gospel, and faith is the only means whereby we can apprehend, accept, apply them to ourselves, and make them our own. Faith is a gift of God whereby we rightly learn to know Christ as our redeemer in the Word of the Gospel and to trust in him, that solely for the sake of his obedience we have forgiveness of sins by grace, are accounted righteous and holy by God the Father, and are saved forever.

[21] See the commentary on 7:11–16 and the excursus "הָאָדָם as 'the Man' in 2 Samuel 7:19 and 1 Chronicles 17:17" following the commentary on 7:1–29.

What God desired most of all in a king was one who would repent (Ps 51:19 [ET 51:17]). Repentant kings would have the capacity to understand God's mercy and would show that compassion to the people they governed on behalf of the God of grace.

Nathan, as God's spokesman, immediately pronounced the appropriate words after David confessed. He did not accuse him further or test him to confirm that his confession was genuine and sincere. He did not require David to perform works of penance or vainly try to regain God's favor by his actions. He simply announced God's forgiveness: "Yahweh has taken away your sin" (12:13). In an added sign of God's mercy, David was promised, "You will not die" (12:13), although his sin of murder was a capital offense,[22] as also was his sin of adultery.[23] David was completely and wholly forgiven before Yahweh by sheer grace. Nevertheless, his acts would have temporal consequences. Nathan did not retract God's punitive actions announced in 12:11–12, and there would even be consequences for David's new son: he would die (12:14). David would learn that his sins would cause painful suffering for him and his family during the rest of his earthly life.

God's provision of forgiveness for David illustrates well that sinners cannot save themselves, earn God's favor by their own merits and efforts, or in any way pay for their sins before God. It demonstrates that as sinful beings, humans can be justified before God only by his grace and favor in Jesus Christ, the only sinless human. John Cassian (c. AD 360–435) notes this in commenting on David's penitence:

> For if we recall that thief who was by reason of a single confession admitted into paradise [Lk 23:39–43], we shall feel that he did not acquire such bliss by the merits of his life, but obtained it by the gift of a merciful God. Or if we bear in mind those two grievous and heinous sins of King David, blotted out by one word of penitence [2 Sam 12:13], we shall see that neither here were the merits of his works sufficient to obtain pardon for so great a sin, but that the grace of God superabounded [cf. Rom 5:20], as, when the opportunity for true penitence was taken, He removed the whole weight of sins through the full confession of but one word.[24]

We are told that Nathan went home, and the child became ill (12:15). The note that the child was the one *"Uriah's wife* bore to David" emphasizes the reason for God's judgment. The striking of the child with illness served several purposes:

---

[22] The mandate in Gen 9:6 was given to Noah and his family, that is, to all humanity on earth, not just to Israel. The verb רָצַח, "to murder," is used in the Fifth of the Ten Commandments (Ex 20:13; Deut 5:17). That verb's participle is also used for a "murderer," who is to be put to death in Num 35:16–21, 30–31.

[23] The verb נָאַף, "to commit adultery," used in the Sixth of the Ten Commandments (Ex 20:14; Deut 5:18), is also used in the statute for Israel to put to death those guilty of this sin (Lev 20:10).

[24] John Cassian, *The Institutes of the Cœnobia*, 12.11 (*NPNF*[2] 11:283).

- It showed the reliability and trustworthiness of Nathan as Yahweh's true prophet. The divine judgment he pronounced was visibly fulfilled (and so also the divine clemency he announced in 12:13, although presently invisible, was trustworthy and true).[25]

- It demonstrated to David that the later punishment concerning his wives (12:11–12) was certain to happen.

- It allowed David once again to exercise his faith, to practice his complete reliance on Yahweh and his mercy during this life and even in death in the hope of the resurrection (12:16, 22–23).

- It gave David a chance to teach others about God's grace, mercy, and favor (2 Sam 12:21–22; Ps 51:15 [ET 51:13]).

The illness and death of the child no doubt will strike modern readers as tragic to the point of calling God's justice into question. However, David did not question Yahweh's decision. He understood God's justice as working in the service of God's favor and trusted that his son would be taken to God, where he someday would also rest in his Savior's loving arms (12:23).

---

[25] God's forgiveness is received now through faith in the Word of the Gospel. The believer has eternal life already now, although this life is presently hidden with Christ (Col 3:3). It will be fully revealed in the life hereafter at the resurrection of the body. As Nathan was shown to be a true prophet, so also Christians trust that the pastor's word of absolution truly does bestow the forgiveness of God in Jesus Christ (Mt 16:19; 18:18; Jn 20:22–23; cf. 1 Jn 1:8–9). David's admission of sin and Nathan's pronouncement of forgiveness in 2 Sam 12:13 are cited as a biblical example of confession and absolution in Ap XII 56. Confession and absolution do not simply take place as a one-time act when a person is converted to faith; they are a regular and needed part of the life of faith. An explanation of Luther's Small Catechism cites 2 Sam 12:13 twice as a biblical basis for the office of the keys, exercised weekly (or more often) by the pastor in his congregation (*Luther's Small Catechism with Explanation* [St. Louis: Concordia, 1986, 1991], §§ 264, 268).

Bathsheba's Child Dies

Translation

12 ¹⁶David sought God on behalf of the child. David fasted, then came and spent the night sleeping on the ground. ¹⁷When the elders of his house stood over him to lift him up from the ground, he was unwilling, and he would not eat food with them.

¹⁸On the seventh day the child died. David's servants were afraid to tell him that the child was dead because they thought, "When the child was alive we spoke to him, and he would not listen to us. How can we tell him the child is dead? He may harm [himself]!" ¹⁹David saw that his servants were whispering among themselves, so David understood that the child was dead.

David said to his servants, "Is the child dead?"

They said, "He is dead."

²⁰David got up from the ground, washed, groomed, and changed his clothes. He went to Yahweh's house and worshiped. Then he came to his house and asked [to eat]. They brought him food, and he ate.

²¹His servants said to him, "What have you done? When the child was alive you fasted and wept. Now that the child is dead, you got up and ate!"

²²He said, "As long as the child was still alive I fasted and wept because I thought, 'Who knows? Yahweh may have mercy on me and the child will live.' ²³Now the child is dead. Why in the world should I fast? Am I able to bring him back again? I am going to him. He will not come back to me."

Textual Notes

12:16 וַיָּצָם דָּוִד צוֹם—Literally "and David fasted a fast." This is a cognate accusative construction. The direct object of the Qal (G) verb צוּם, "to fast," is the cognate noun צוֹם, "a fast." Hebrew is fond of such constructions (see *IBH*, § 17 B; GKC, § 117 p–r),[1] but English avoids them. The verb recurs in the perfect in 12:21 (צַמְתָּ) and 12:22 (צַמְתִּי) and as a participle in 12:23 (צָם).

וּבָא וְלָן וְשָׁכַב אָרְצָה:—These three Qal (G) verbs are perfects (of בּוֹא, לִין, and שָׁכַב, respectively) with *waw* consecutive. The first, וּבָא, indicates sequential action: after fasting all day David "then came," presumably to his sleeping quarters. The second and third, literally "and he spent the night, and he slept on the ground," are not separate but are contemporaneous actions: "and he spent the night sleeping on the ground."

---

[1] See, e.g., the first textual notes on 1 Sam 1:6, 11, 17, 21, the second textual note on 1 Sam 2:13, and the third textual note on 1 Sam 2:24 (Steinmann, *1 Samuel*, 45, 48, 51, 58, 84, 93).

4QSamᵃ reads וישכב בשק ארצה, probably to be vocalized as וַיִּשְׁכַּב בַּשַּׂק אָרְצָה,[2] "and he slept on the ground in sackcloth." This likely is an ideological expansion to make David appear more penitent (cf. the third textual note on 12:20). Here the donning of שַׂק, "sackcloth," is a gesture of repentance in the hope that someone will live and not die, as also in, e.g., 1 Ki 20:31–32; Jonah 3:5–8. (It is a ritual in mourning for the dead in, e.g., 2 Sam 3:31; 21:10.)

12:17 וַיָּקֻמוּ זִקְנֵי בֵיתוֹ עָלָיו—"When the elders of his house stood over him." Here the verb קוּם has the pregnant meaning "to (arise and) stand," and the preposition עַל commonly means "over." See BDB, s.v. קוּם, Qal, 1 e.

וְלֹא־בָרָא—"And he would not eat." The verb בָּרָה means "to eat." Here in Codex Leningradensis, it is spelled with a final *aleph*, בָרָא (see GKC, § 75 rr). Many other Masoretic manuscripts spell it here as בָּרָה, as does 4QSamᵃ (ולו[א ברה). Forms of final *he* verbs and final *aleph* verbs often interchange (GKC, § 75 nn).

12:18 וַיִּרְאוּ—"They were afraid." The *metheg* (or *gaʿya*) accent beside the *hireq* (-ִ-) indicates that this is a defective, or *ḥaser*, spelling of וַיִּירְאוּ, a Qal (G) form of יָרֵא, "be afraid," and not a form of רָאָה, "to see." See the third textual note on 10:19.

חַי—This adjective, "alive," recurs in 12:21, 22. Cf. the third textual note on 12:22.

וְעָשָׂה רָעָה:—"He may harm [himself]!" is literally "and he will do evil."

12:19 מִתְלַחֲשִׁים—"Were whispering among themselves." This is the Hithpael (HtD) masculine plural participle of the rare verb לָחַשׁ (which occurs elsewhere only in Pss 41:8 [ET 41:7]; 58:6 [ET 58:5]). The force of its Hithpael is reciprocal (see Waltke-O'Connor, § 26.2g), "whisper to one another."

וַיָּבֶן—"So he understood." This is the Qal (G) third masculine singular preterite (imperfect with *waw* consecutive) of בִּין, "perceive, discern."

וַיֹּאמֶר דָּוִד אֶל־עֲבָדָיו הֲמֵת הַיֶּלֶד וַיֹּאמְרוּ מֵת:—Literally "and David said to his servants, 'Is the child dead?' and they said, 'Dead.'" A question can be answered in the affirmative simply by repeating a word from the question (Joüon, § 161 l).

12:20 וַיִּרְחַץ—"He washed." For רָחַץ, "wash," see the second textual note on 11:2. As in the context there, its use here may relate to the Torah stipulations for bathing as an act of purification. While David may have simply been washing as part of putting on new clothes and attending to his appearance, his washing comes as a result of the death of the child born to Bathsheba. The entire incident began when David saw Bathsheba bathing, probably as cleansing after her menstruation (see the second textual note on 11:2). David's bathing closes the account of his adultery and its immediate aftermath. A man who had sexual relations with a woman that led to an emission of semen was required to wash (Lev 15:18). While David probably bathed immediately after having sexual relations with Bathsheba, here his bathing may be an admission that his act that began with his assignation with Bathsheba had led to the tragic death of this child. Alternately, the author may be noting David's bathing to signal to readers the connection of David's

---

[2] When the noun שַׂק, "sackcloth," is prefixed with the preposition בְּ, it usually has the article, בַּשַּׂק, instead of lacking it, בְּשַׂק. The vocalization of אָרְצָה is pausal for אַרְצָה.

act and the child's death even if David was not purposely bathing to acknowledge that the child was conceived by his adulterous liaison.

וַיָּסֶךְ—"He groomed." This is the Qal (G) third masculine singular preterite (imperfect with *waw* consecutive) of סוּךְ, "apply oil." This is often translated as "anoint," but this verb is not used for ceremonial anointing.[3] It denotes the application of olive oil as part of one's grooming for a fragrance and for cosmetic treatment of the skin (e.g., Deut 28:40). It is used again in 2 Sam 14:2, where a woman is not to apply oil to herself because she feigns to be in mourning. In contrast, then, David's application of oil to himself here is a sign that his penitential mourning is over.

שִׂמְלֹתָיו—"His clothes." This suffixed plural noun is the Qere and is supported by the plural in the LXX (τὰ ἱμάτια αὐτοῦ). The Kethib is the same noun in the singular, שִׂמְלָתוֹ, "his (outer) garment." That David "changed his clothes" may suggest that he had been wearing "sackcloth," a noun that 4QSam[a] includes in 12:16; see the second textual note on 12:16.

וַיִּשְׁתָּחוּ—"And he worshiped." This verb is the Hishtaphel of חָוָה, "to bow down, worship." See the third textual note on 1 Sam 1:3.[4] For the form here (וַיִּשְׁתָּחוּ is pausal for וַיִּשְׁתַּחוּ), see the second textual note on 1 Sam 1:28.[5] When this verb refers to worship at the tabernacle, it is sometimes accompanied by the offering of a sacrifice (1 Sam 1:3).

וַיִּשְׁאַל וַיָּשִׂימוּ לוֹ לֶחֶם—"And he asked [to eat]. They brought him food" is literally "and he asked, and they set food for him."

12:21 מָה־הַדָּבָר הַזֶּה אֲשֶׁר עָשִׂיתָה—Literally "what is this word/matter which you did?" Here on עָשִׂיתָה, and occasionally elsewhere, the second masculine singular ending (suffix) of a Qal (G) perfect verb is written with *he*, ־תָה, instead of the usual orthography ־תָ (GKC, § 44 g; Joüon, § 42 f). See such forms also in, e.g., 2 Sam 2:26; 3:7; 10:11.

בַּעֲבוּר—This combination of בְּ and עֲבוּר is often used as a preposition meaning "because of, on account of." Here in the clause "because of the child being alive," it has the temporal meaning "when." See BDB, s.v. עֲבוּר II, 1 a. It is equivalent to בְּעוֹד (בְּ + עוֹד), "as long as," in 12:22.

וַתֵּבְךְּ—"And you wept." The form of this Qal (G) preterite (imperfect with *waw* consecutive) of בָּכָה, "to weep," could be third feminine singular (as it is in, e.g., Gen 21:16; Judg 11:38), but the context here requires it to be second masculine singular, as also in 2 Chr 34:27. בָּכָה recurs in the next verse (וָאֶבְכֶּה, 2 Sam 12:22).

12:22 מִי יוֹדֵעַ—"Who knows?" This question with the Qal (G) masculine singular participle of יָדַע, "to know," appears in prophetic calls for repentance that express the Gospel hope that God will act with blessing (Joel 2:14) and relent from a pronouncement

---

[3] Instead, the verb מָשַׁח, "anoint," is used for liturgical anointings in the Torah (e.g., Ex 28:41; 30:26) and for the anointing of kings (e.g., 2 Sam 2:4, 7; 5:3, 17; 1 Ki 1:34). See the first textual note on 1 Sam 9:16 (Steinmann, *1 Samuel*, 180). See also the discussion of the cognate noun מָשִׁיחַ, "Anointed One," in the commentary on 1 Sam 2:10, 35 (Steinmann, *1 Samuel*, 80–81, 105–6).

[4] Steinmann, *1 Samuel*, 44.

[5] Steinmann, *1 Samuel*, 62.

of impending death (Jonah 3:9), and he does relent (Jonah 3:10). It is also used in, e.g., Ps 90:11; Prov 24:22; Eccl 3:21; 6:12.

וְחַנַּנִי—"He may have mercy on me." This Qere is the Qal (G) third masculine singular perfect of חָנַן, "be gracious, show favor," with *waw* consecutive and a first common singular pronominal suffix. In the Qal, God is usually the subject of this verb, and it refers to him bestowing "redemption from enemies, evils, and sins" (BDB, Qal, 2 b). The Kethib, יחנני, would probably be vocalized as יְחָנֵּנִי, the Qal third masculine singular imperfect with a first common singular pronominal suffix (cf. יְחָנֵּנוּ in Pss 67:2 [ET 67:1]; 123:2). The modal meaning "he *may* have mercy" would customarily be expressed with an imperfect (Joüon, § 113 l), whereas such a meaning for a perfect with *waw* consecutive would be rare (cf. the second textual note on 12:23). The future verb in the LXX appears to support the Kethib: εἰ ἐλεήσει με κύριος, "whether the Lord will have mercy on me."

וְחַי הַיֶּלֶד:—"And the child will live." The word וְחַי is a verb, the Qal (G) third masculine singular perfect of חָיָה, "to live," with *waw* consecutive. It is to be distinguished from the homographic adjective חַי, "alive," in 12:18, 21, 22.

12:23 לָמָּה זֶּה—For "why in the world?" see the first textual note on 3:24.

אֲנִי צָם—"[Why] should I be fasting?" Such a modal meaning ("should") would customarily be expressed by an imperfect (Joüon, § 113 l). Here, unusually, it is expressed with a participle, the masculine singular Qal (G) participle of צוּם, "to fast," with the pronoun אֲנִי, "I," as its subject.

Commentary

997 BC[6]

David's immediate reaction to the child's illness was to beg God for mercy (12:16). Once again, David demonstrated that he understood Yahweh by faith; he knew that Yahweh was a gracious and merciful God (Ex 34:6; Pss 86:15; 103:8; 145:8). As a sign of his repentance for his sins (2 Samuel 11), as well as his mourning for the child, who, God had declared, would die (12:14), David fasted and slept on the ground. The elder leaders among David's courtiers sought to get him to abandon this mourning, but David remained resolute (12:17).

We are told that the child died "on the seventh day" (12:18). Commentators are divided as to whether this was the seventh day of the child's life or the seventh day of the child's illness.[7] It was most likely both. That is, as soon as the child was born (11:27), Nathan was sent to David with his prophecy (12:1), and the child became ill that same day, immediately after Nathan left David (12:15). The child's death on the seventh day was tragic: the child died before he could be circumcised, which was prescribed on the eighth day (Lev 12:3; cf. Lk 1:59; 2:21; Acts 7:8; Phil 3:5). Thus, the child did not receive the sign of God's covenant with Israel (Gen 17:10–14). Yet this does not necessarily mean

---

[6] See "The Chronology of David's Reign" in the commentary on 5:1–5.

[7] For instance, Anderson understands it to be the seventh day of the child's illness (*2 Samuel*, 163–64), whereas Bergen takes it to be the seventh day of the child's life (*1, 2 Samuel*, 375).

that he perished eternally, for Abraham was declared righteous through faith (Gen 15:6) before God prescribed circumcision as the sign of the Abrahamic covenant (Gen 17:10–14),[8] and David trusted that he would go to be with his child (2 Sam 12:23).[9]

David's servants found his behavior so odd that they were afraid to tell him of the child's death. They dreaded what he might do in reaction to the news (12:18). However, from their whispering, David inferred that the child was dead and forced them to confirm his conclusion (12:19). Then David's behavior seemed even more bizarre to them (12:20). He abandoned the mourning rituals that normally would have been performed after a loved one's death. He worshiped and ate. These were not signs that he had abandoned hope and surrendered himself to a view of God as an uncaring Judge. Rather, these are hints of David's faith that death is not the end of life with God.[10]

David's worship is said to have taken place in "Yahweh's house" (בֵּית־יהוה, 12:20), the same place where David trusted that he would live with God forever (בֵּית־יהוה, Ps 23:6). Later this will be a common phrase for the temple,[11] but no temple had yet been built in Jerusalem. However, it ought to be noted that the author of Samuel has already used this phrase to refer to the tabernacle.[12] Here too it refers to the tabernacle. According to Chronicles the tabernacle was kept in Gibeon during David's reign (1 Chr 16:39). Gibeon was about seven miles (eleven kilometers) northwest of Jerusalem.

Finally, David's servants could no longer hold back their consternation at his behavior and asked him why his conduct seemed to be the reverse of what it ought to have been (12:21). His reply explains that his comportment was prompted by Yahweh's merciful character, not by cultural norms (12:22–23).[13]

---

[8] The justification of Abraham by faith before the giving of the law of circumcision is the topic of Romans 4.

[9] The eighth day was counted inclusively, so it was the same day of the week as the birth, but one week later. Circumcision, therefore, was on the first day of the new week of life. In Christian thought, it correlates with the resurrection of our Lord on the first day of the week (Mt 28:1; Mk 16:2; Lk 24:1; Jn 20:1), which became the day of Christian congregational worship (1 Cor 16:2; cf. Rev 1:10). In place of circumcision, Baptism is the sacrament of initiation into God's covenant people by his grace in Jesus Christ, and it is a death and burial and also a resurrection in Christ. See Rom 6:1–6; Col 2:11–13; Titus 3:4–7, and the "eight souls" saved through the flood as a type of Baptism into the resurrection of Christ (1 Pet 3:20–21). The original creation was accomplished in one week (Gen 1:1–2:3), and the first day of the new week signifies a new creation (cf. 2 Cor 5:17; Gal 6:15).

[10] See Pss 16:9–11; 22:20–32 (ET 22:19–31); 23:6 in the psalms of David.

[11] E.g., 1 Ki 6:37; 7:12, 40; 8:10–11.

[12] 1 Sam 1:7, 24; 3:15. See also Ex 23:19; 34:26; Deut 23:19 (ET 23:18); Josh 6:24; Judg 19:18.

[13] Scholars have attempted various explanations for David's behavior and often conclude that his actions are ambiguous. For a review and summary of the approaches to understanding David's words and acts, see Pyper, "Reading David's Mind," 74–75. Many interpreters claim that David's words about his reasons are enigmatic. However, his words are not as unclear as claimed when one takes seriously the statements that he was seeking God's mercy for the child (12:16, 22).

David was acknowledging that Yahweh's mercy was served by taking the child and no further amount of fasting would bring him back to temporal life. Instead, David acknowledged that he was going to the child (12:23). This was not simply an admission of his own mortality but also an assertion of his confidence that his son was now in Yahweh's gracious presence, where David himself would also be someday, and so they would be reunited in the joy of eternal life together.[14]

As a pastoral application, David's confidence (12:22–23) provides great comfort for parents of children who tragically die in utero or shortly after birth. God promises to grant salvation through his means of grace, e.g., "Baptism now saves you" (1 Pet 3:21; see also, e.g., Acts 2:38–39; Rom 6:3–4; Col 2:11–12), but God is also able to work in other ways as he pleases. Thus, the response of John the Baptist to the presence of Christ while both were still in utero suggests that John was already saved by faith (Lk 1:41, 44; cf. Jer 1:5). Nevertheless, these passages should not be misused to postpone (and certainly not to omit) the Sacrament of Holy Baptism, which in emergency situations can be administered by a parent or any other Christian.[15]

It has been noted that although David did not mourn for his child after the child died, David had lamented others after they died. David mourned for Saul and Jonathan (1:17–27) and Abner (3:31–35), as he would for Amnon (13:36–37) and Absalom (18:33). Here David mourned *before* the child died, since he was warned by a prophet of Yahweh of the impending death (12:14). In the other cases where David grieved, he had not received any such forewarning. He had no opportunity to bewail and ask God to spare the life of Saul, Jonathan, Abner, Amnon, or Absalom.[16] David turned accepted societal norms on their head because God had revealed in advance the impending death of his son. David's behavior signaled his respect for Yahweh's Word given through Nathan. He had been guilty of despising Yahweh's Word (12:9–10), but now he displayed his repentance[17] by his changed attitude of trust in God's Word.

---

[14] Again, see Pss 16:9–11; 22:20–32 (ET 22:19–31); 23:6 in the psalms of David.

[15] See "Holy Baptism in Cases of Emergency" (*LSB* 1023).

[16] Note that David tried other means to spare Absalom's life (18:5, 12).

[17] "Repentance" can be defined as both contrition for one's sin and faith in God's forgiveness. See Ap XII, "Penitence," 46–48, 56. See further the commentary on 12:1–15.

Solomon Is Born

Translation

12 **²⁴David comforted his wife Bathsheba. He came to her and lay with her. She bore a son, and she called his name Solomon. Yahweh loved him, ²⁵so he sent word through the prophet Nathan. He called his name Jedidiah on account of Yahweh.**

Textual Notes

12:24 וַיְנַחֵם—"He comforted." For the Piel (D) of the verb נָחַם, see the second textual note on 10:2.

וַיָּבֹא אֵלֶיהָ—"He came (in) to her." This Hebrew idiom with the verb בּוֹא and preposition אֶל, literally "to come in to," can by itself refer to sexual intercourse (see the fourth textual note on 3:7). That meaning is confirmed here by the following two clauses (see the next two textual notes). The account of David's adultery with Bathsheba used the same clause but with the genders reversed (although probably not in a sexual sense): the verb was feminine and the pronominal suffix on the preposition was masculine: וַתָּבוֹא אֵלָיו, "and/when she came to him" (see the first textual note on 11:4).

וַיִּשְׁכַּב עִמָּהּ—"And he lay with her." The identical clause was in the account of David's adultery (11:4). The same verb (שָׁכַב) and preposition (עִם) were used by Uriah to refer to sleeping with his wife in 11:11; see them also in 12:11; 13:11.

וַתֵּלֶד בֵּן—"She bore a son." See the identical clause in 1 Sam 1:20 (cf. 1 Sam 2:21; 2 Sam 11:27).

וַתִּקְרָא—"And she called" is the Qere and the sole reading in a number of other Masoretic manuscripts. It is supported by the Syriac and the Targum. The Kethib is וַיִּקְרָא, "and he called." Elsewhere in the book of Samuel naming children appears to be the mother's prerogative (1 Sam 1:20; 4:21). Mothers name their children (with the verb קָרָא) also in, e.g., Gen 4:25; 19:37, 38; 29:32, 33, 35; Judg 13:24; Is 7:14 (cf. Ex 2:10).

שְׁלֹמֹה—"Solomon." This name is almost certainly based on the noun שָׁלוֹם, *shalom* (derived from the verb שָׁלֵם), whose meanings include God-given "peace," "wholeness," "health," and "prosperity," and which can be a synonym of "deliverance, salvation" (*HALOT*, s.v. שָׁלוֹם, 7). In Num 6:24–27 *shalom* encapsulates the divine gifts of blessing, protection, illumination, grace, favor, and the bestowal of Yahweh's "name." The simplest explanation of the form שְׁלֹמֹה is that the ending ה- is a third masculine singular pronominal suffix (GKC, § 7 c) and so the name means "his peace." Most likely the pronoun "his" refers to Yahweh as the giver, but it could also refer to David as the recipient (the son is "his [David's] peace"). Thus, the gift of Solomon signifies the restoration of Yahweh's salvation to David after his confession and absolution (12:1–15) from his sin, which had been evil in Yahweh's eyes (11:27). Solomon is also "his [David's] wholeness" in that he fills the void in David's dynasty left by the death of his prior son

(12:18–19). Other nuances are possible. For example, Solomon's name is used in conjunction with the cognate verb שָׁלֵם to state that the work of building the temple was "finished, completed" (1 Ki 7:51 ‖ 2 Chr 5:1). This may suggest that שְׁלֹמֹה may be interpreted as "its [the temple's] completion" or "its [the prophecy's] fulfillment," as Solomon literally fulfills the prophetic promise of a son of David in 2 Sam 7:12–15.[1]

וַיהוָה אֲהֵבוֹ:—"Yahweh loved him." Yahweh's free choice to love Solomon highlights the baby's significance as a gift of grace. The verb אָהַב is stative and here refers to a past action (Joüon, § 112 b) but also signifies ongoing love. This verb is used for the "love" of a son elsewhere,[2] including Mal 1:2, quoted by Paul in Rom 9:13 to help explain divine election by grace alone. Cf. Jesus as God's "beloved" Son in Mt 3:17; 12:18; 17:5 and baptized believers as God's "beloved" children in 1 Jn 3:2; 4:7.

12:25 וַיִּשְׁלַח בְּיַד נָתָן הַנָּבִיא—"So he [Yahweh] sent word through the prophet Nathan" is literally "and he sent by the hand of Nathan the prophet." See וַיִּשְׁלַח בְּיַד- also in 1 Sam 16:20; 2 Sam 11:14 (cf. 15:36). That is, Nathan was made responsible for delivering the message of God's love for the child. This contrasts starkly with the use of the same idiom for the delivery of the death note in 2 Sam 11:14 and Yahweh's sending (וַיִּשְׁלַח) of the same prophet, Nathan, to David for the purpose of exposing his sin in 12:1.

יְדִידְיָה בַּעֲבוּר יְהוָה:—"Jedidiah on account of Yahweh." The first part of the name, יְדִיד-, *jedid*, appears to be a construct form of the adjective יָדִיד, "beloved," which can refer to Yahweh himself (Is 5:1) or to those he loves (Deut 33:12; Pss 60:7 [ET 60:5]; 108:7 [ET 108:6]; 127:2). It is also related to the noun דּוֹד, "(male) lover; love." Both may derive from an original biliteral root דד that was expanded to a typical triliteral root in two different ways: first, the initial consonant *yod* was added to make ידד as the root of יָדִיד, "beloved," and, second, a medial *waw* was added to make דוד, the root of דּוֹד, "lover," and דָּוִד, "David." In the Song of Songs, Solomon frequently uses דּוֹד autobiographically for himself as the (male protagonist) "lover" and also uses it as an abstract plural for "love" itself.[3] The name of Solomon's father, דָּוִד, "David," meaning "beloved," is derived from דּוֹד. "Jedidiah" (יְדִידְיָה) ends with the theophoric element יָה-, *yah*, a short form of "Yahweh" (יהוה). The significance of "Jedidiah" as a reference to Yahweh is reinforced by the following prepositional phrase בַּעֲבוּר יְהוָה, "on account of Yahweh." Nothing about the child himself nor his father David elicited or merited this love. Rather, the child was loved by Yahweh (12:24) and received this beloved name solely on account of Yahweh's grace and his gracious promise of the Messiah (2 Samuel 7).

---

[1] See various suggestions in, e.g., *HALOT*, s.v. שְׁלֹמֹה, D 1–5.

[2] E.g., Gen 22:2; 25:28; 37:3–4; 44:20.

[3] See Mitchell, *The Song of Songs*, 386–93.

Commentary

994 BC[4]

Finally the author turns his attention to Bathsheba and her role in the narrative. She had lost a husband (11:17) and a son (12:18–19), and at last David comforted her (12:24). The comfort included their sexual relationship as husband and wife. Bathsheba became David's "wife" in 11:27, and here the author first recalls her status as "his wife" (12:24) before noting their intercourse. While sex outside of marriage is an abuse (11:4), David's comforting of his wife reminds us that God designed the sexual dimension of marriage not simply for procreation but also for the expression of intimacy and affection, as Solomon would write (Prov 5:18–19; Song of Songs).

Bathsheba named her son "Solomon" (2 Sam 12:24), a named derived from the Hebrew root signifying "peace," "welfare," and "well-being." While there are various explanations for the exact meaning of the name,[5] it is clear that Bathsheba was expressing her prayer for a more prosperous and blessed future for her new son as well as her marriage.

Once again Yahweh revealed his gracious disposition toward David through the prophecy of Nathan, who gave the boy a second name: "Jedidiah," "beloved of Yah(weh)." This name signaled to David that God was no longer ill-disposed toward him or his progeny by Bathsheba (contrast 11:27–12:15). The name is also a play on David's name since the adjective יָדִיד, "beloved," derives from the same root as דָּוִד, "David."[6]

---

[4] See "The Chronology of David's Reign" in the commentary on 5:1–5.

[5] See the sixth textual note on 12:24.

[6] See the second textual note on 12:25.

Rabbah Is Captured

Translation

12 **26**Joab attacked Rabbah of the Ammonites and captured the royal precinct. **27**Joab sent messengers to David and said, "I have attacked Rabbah, and I have also captured the water district. **28**Now gather the rest of the troops, encamp against the city, and capture it. Otherwise, I myself will capture the city, and it will be named after me."

29So David gathered all the troops and went to Rabbah. He attacked it and captured it. **30**He took their king's crown from his head. It weighed a talent of gold and had a precious stone. It was [placed] on David's head. He took away very much plunder from the city. **31**He removed the people who were in it and put them to work tearing it down with iron picks and iron axes. He made them work with brick molds. He did this to all the Ammonite cities. Then David and all of the troops returned to Jerusalem.

Textual Notes

12:26 וַיִּלָּחֶם יוֹאָב בְּרַבַּת בְּנֵי עַמּוֹן—Literally "and Joab made war on Rabbah of the sons of Ammon." The Niphal (N) of לָחַם, "wage war," commonly takes the preposition בְּ on those who are attacked, as here (בְּרַבַּת) and again in 12:27 (בְרַבָּה) and 12:29 (בָּהּ).[1]

וַיִּלְכֹּד—"And he captured." The Qal (G) of לָכַד recurs in 12:27, 28 (twice), 29, and these are the last instances of לָכַד in the book of Samuel.

עִיר הַמְּלוּכָה:—"The royal precinct." This construct phrase is literally "the city of kingship." The noun עִיר may denote a district or precinct within a larger city (*HALOT*, s.v. עִיר I, A 2).

12:27 עִיר הַמָּיִם:—"Water district" is literally "the city of water." This is probably another name for the royal precinct. See the previous textual note.

12:28–29 אֱסֹף אֶת־יֶתֶר הָעָם ... וַיֶּאֱסֹף דָּוִד אֶת־כָּל־הָעָם—"Gather the rest of the troops. ... So David gathered all the troops." For the use of the Qal (G) of אָסַף for "gathering" troops for battle, see the first textual note on 6:1. In military contexts the noun with the article הָעָם, "the people," often denotes "the troops." See the first textual note on 1 Sam 4:3[2] and the second textual note on 2 Sam 1:4. For the noun יֶתֶר, the "rest, remnant, what remains," see the second textual note on 8:4.

---

[1] See also 1 Sam 12:9; 14:47; 15:18; 19:8; 23:1, 5; 28:1, 15; 29:8; 31:1; 2 Sam 8:10.

[2] Steinmann, *1 Samuel*, 120.

וְלָכְדָה ... עָלֶיהָ ... בָּהּ וַיִּלְכְּדָהּ:—The feminine singular pronominal suffix ("it") on each of these four words refers to the city Rabbah. Both the noun עִיר, "city," and city names, including רַבָּה, "Rabbah," are feminine.

12:28 וַחֲנֵה עַל־—For "encamp against," see the second textual note on 1 Sam 11:1.[3]

פֶּן־אֶלְכֹּד אֲנִי—"Otherwise, I myself will capture." The use of the redundant first common singular pronoun אֲנִי, "I," after the first common singular verb אֶלְכֹּד, "I will capture," is emphatic (GKC, § 135 a). The conjunction פֶּן, "lest, otherwise," governs both this clause and the next one (see the next textual note; GKC, § 150 m, note 2).

וְנִקְרָא שְׁמִי עָלֶיהָ:—"And it will be named after me" is literally "and my name will be called upon it." The noun שֵׁם, "name," is the subject of the Niphal (N) of קָרָא, "be called," also in 6:2.

12:30 עֲטֶרֶת ... וּמִשְׁקָלָהּ כִּכַּר זָהָב וְאֶבֶן יְקָרָה—"The crown. ... It weighed a talent of gold and had a precious stone." The noun עֲטָרָה is feminine and thus is the referent of the feminine singular suffix on the noun מִשְׁקָלָהּ, literally "its weight (was)."[4] The "talent of gold" (כִּכַּר זָהָב) may imply not only that the crown weighed that much but also that a talent of gold was used to make it. The adjectival phrase וְאֶבֶן יְקָרָה, "and a precious stone," is not an additional part of the weight, but a statement that, in addition to the gold, the crown also had a gemstone. The feminine noun אֶבֶן, "stone," is usually used in the plural for gemstones (e.g., Ex 25:7; 28:9), but its singular is sometimes used as a collective (e.g., Ex 28:17), and so it is possible that the crown may have had a number of jewels. The identical adjectival phrase אֶבֶן יְקָרָה is used in other passages to refer to a quantity of precious stones.[5]

מַלְכָּם—"Their king." This is the segholate noun מֶלֶךְ with a third masculine plural suffix. Some scholars suggest that it ought to be vocalized as מִלְכֹּם, "Milcom," the Ammonite god.[6] This is a distinct possibility and would imply that the crown David seized had been a crown on an idol's head.[7] The LXX reads Μελχολ τοῦ βασιλέως αὐτῶν, "Milcom their king," perhaps reflecting an accidental duplication of this word or uncertainty about whether it meant "Milcom" or "their king" (and so both possible translations were included).

12:31 וַיֶּשֶׂם בַּמְּגֵרָה וּבַחֲרִצֵי הַבַּרְזֶל וּבְמַגְזְרֹת הַבַּרְזֶל וְהֶעֱבִיר אוֹתָם בַּמַּלְבֵּן—"And he put them to work tearing it down with iron picks and iron axes. He made them work with brick molds." The Hebrew text is difficult. It literally reads "and he set with a saw and with picks of iron and with axes of iron, and he caused them to pass by with a brick

---

3 Steinmann, *1 Samuel*, 208–9.

4 This is the only instance in the OT where the weight of an object is given in a circumstantial clause introduced by *waw*. Usually the weight of an object is given in a circumstantial clause without *waw* and the suffixed noun מִשְׁקָל-, "[its] weight," is at the end of the circumstantial clause, rather than at its beginning, as here. See Joüon, § 158 b, including note 1.

5 1 Ki 10:2, 10, 11; Dan 11:38; 1 Chr 29:2; 2 Chr 3:6; 9:1, 9, 10; 32:27 (cf. Ezek 27:22; 28:13).

6 "Milcom" (מִלְכֹּם) is named in 1 Ki 11:5, 33; 2 Ki 23:13; his name should possibly be the reading also in Jer 49:1, 3; Zeph 1:5, which have מַלְכָּם.

7 O'Ceallaigh, " 'And So David Did to *All the Cities* of Ammon,' " 186, including n. 2; McCarter, *II Samuel*, 311; Bergen, *1, 2 Samuel*, 377; see the discussion in Anderson, *2 Samuel*, 168, and Baldwin, *1 and 2 Samuel*, 246, n. 1.

mold." The singular nouns מְגֵרָה and the Qere מַלְבֵּן are collectives, corresponding to the English plurals "saws" and "brick molds." The problems presented in understanding this text are as follows:

1. וַיָּשֶׂם, literally "and he set, placed."[8] It is translated as "and he put them to work" in view of the following word (see the discussion of בַּמְּגֵרָה in point 2). In the Qal (G), the verb שִׂים (or שׂוּם) can have a variety of connotations. Here it most likely refers to putting someone in an office or role in order to carry out a task (see BDB, s.v. שׂוּם, שִׂים, Qal, 3 d, 4 a). It is preferable to follow the reading וַיָּשֶׂם with such a meaning than to adopt the reading וַיָּשַׂר in the parallel verse 1 Chr 20:3. וַיָּשַׂר is usually taken to be a form of the verb שׂוּר, "to saw," and translated as "and he sawed them apart," based on LXX 1 Chr 20:3 (καὶ διέπρισεν). However, 1 Chr 20:3 is the only verse where שׂוּר apparently means "to saw." This verb appears elsewhere in the OT only in Hosea and with other meanings. The Hiphil (H) of שׂוּר in Hos 8:4 probably is a by-form of the verb שָׂרַר, which is a denominative from שַׂר, "prince," and means "set up princes." In Hos 9:12 שׂוּר is an alternate spelling for סוּר, "turn aside/away." In Hos 12:5 (ET 12:4) שׂוּר is a by-form of שָׂרָה, "to wrestle" (see שָׂרָה in Gen 32:29 [ET 32:28]; Hos 12:4 [ET 12:3]). Therefore, the reading וַיָּשַׂר in 1 Chr 20:3 may be a corruption of the reading וַיָּשֶׂם here in 2 Sam 12:31. The verb apparently suffered from a graphic confusion of the final *mem* (of וַיָּשֶׂם here) and *resh*, resulting in וַיָּשַׂר (1 Chr 20:3). Perhaps a poorly formed or incomplete final *mem* was misread by a later scribe as *resh*.

2. בַּמְּגֵרָה, literally "with a saw," translated as "tearing it down." The noun מְגֵרָה appears only four times in the OT: here; the parallel verse 1 Chr 20:3 (twice; see point 4); and 1 Ki 7:9. In 1 Ki 7:9 it clearly denotes "a saw" for cutting stone. The translation above follows the suggestion of O'Ceallaigh that בַּמְּגֵרָה is mispointed and ought to be read as בְּמַגְּרָה, the Piel (D) infinitive construct of מָגַר, "to throw (down)," with the preposition בְּ and a third feminine singular pronominal suffix (referring to the city, Rabbah), meaning (to work) "at tearing it down."[9] The verb מָגַר occurs twice elsewhere in the OT: its Qal passive (Gp) participle in Ezek 21:17 (ET 21:12) means "thrown (to the sword)," and its Piel (D) in Ps 89:45 (ET 89:44) means "to throw down (to earth)." The construction resulting from this emendation is a Qal (G) form of שִׂים (see point 1) followed by a coordinating infinitive construct denoting purpose (בְּמַגְּרָה): "to place" a person in a position or role "in order to do" something. Although this construction is not common, it is used a couple times in the OT with this meaning (1 Sam 8:5; 1 Ki 10:9), and the construction of שִׂים with an infinitive construct can also express various other meanings.[10]

3. וּבַחֲרִצֵי הַבַּרְזֶל, "(and) with picks of iron." The noun חָרִיץ is derived from the verb חָרַץ, "to cut, sharpen." This noun is used in 1 Sam 17:18, apparently to denote a (cut) slice of cheese. Here it probably denotes a type of slicing or chiseling iron tool, such as a "pick." Its only other occurrence is in the parallel in 1 Chr 20:3. It is related to the noun חָרוּץ, which refers to a sharp threshing sledge in Is 41:15, said to be made of iron in Amos 1:3.

---

[8] This verb with this meaning is supported by the LXX's verb ἔθηκεν.

[9] O'Ceallaigh, "'And *So* David Did to *All the Cities* of Ammon,'" 183, whose translation of the word is "at tearing her (the city) down"; cf. Anderson, *2 Samuel*, 167.

[10] See Is 51:10; Jer 42:15; 44:12; Ezek 21:25 (ET 21:20); 30:21; Zech 7:12; Dan 11:17.

4. וּבְמַגְזְרֹת הַבַּרְזֶל, "and (with) axes of iron." The noun מַגְזֵרָה is from the verb גָּזַר, "cut in two," and is often taken to denote an iron tool for cutting, such as an "axe." It is related to the noun גַּרְזֶן, "axe, pickaxe" (Deut 19:5; 20:19; 1 Ki 6:7; Is 10:15; and in the Siloam Inscription [see *DCH*]). The only OT occurrence of מַגְזֵרָה is here. The parallel verse 1 Chr 20:3 has וּבַמְּגֵרוֹת, the plural of מְגֵרָה (with וְ and בְּ; see point 2).

5. וְהֶעֱבִיר, "(and) he made them work." In the Hiphil (H) the verb עָבַר usually has the causative meaning of making someone to cross over, pass by, or pass through, but such a meaning does not appear to fit the context here.[11] The translation follows the suggestion that וְהֶעֱבִיר is the result of the common graphic confusion of *resh* in place of *dalet*, and so it ought to be emended to וְהֶעֱבִיד, the Hiphil of עָבַד, "to work, serve."[12] The verb עָבַד is commonly used in the Qal (G), but its Hiphil appears in Ex 1:13; 6:5 with the meaning that the Egyptians "enslaved" or "made" the Israelites "work" at hard labor. Its Hiphil has similar meanings in Jer 17:4; Ezek 29:18; 2 Chr 2:17 (ET 2:18).

6. בַּמַּלְבֵּן, "with brick mold(s)." This is the reading of the Qere and many Masoretic manuscripts. The Kethib is בַּמַּלְכֵּן, but the noun מַלְכֵּן is otherwise unknown. The noun מַלְבֵּן is rare, but clearly denotes a brick mold (Nah 3:14) or a brick pavement (Jer 43:9). It is derived from the verb לָבַן, whose Qal (G) means "make bricks" (Gen 11:3; Ex 5:7, 14). It is related to the noun לְבֵנָה, "brick, paving stone."[13]

Beginning with the LXX, 2 Sam 12:31 was interpreted to mean that David ordered the Ammonites to be hacked to pieces or burned in brick kilns. Josephus also says that David tormented and killed the Ammonites.[14] Luther's translation likewise renders this part of the verse as follows: *und legt sie unter eisern segen und zacken, und eisern keile, und verbrand sie in Zigelöfen*,[15] "and he laid them under iron saws and spikes and iron picks and burned them in brick kilns." KJV followed this tradition: "and put them under saws, and under harrows of iron, and under axes of iron, and made them pass through the brickkiln." From the eighteenth century AD onward, however, scholars began to argue that this passage did not depict torture inflicted upon the Ammonites, but instead spoke of David putting them to work in forced labor.[16] The translation above endorses this view. This makes better sense of the rest of the verse, since וְכֵן יַעֲשֶׂה לְכֹל עָרֵי בְנֵי־עַמּוֹן states that David "did so to all the Ammonite *cities*," implying that David was tearing

---

[11] Nevertheless, the MT reading וְהֶעֱבִיר is supported by καὶ διήγαγεν in LXX 2 Sam 12:31.

[12] McCarter, *II Samuel*, 311; Anderson, *2 Samuel*, 167; Baldwin, *1 and 2 Samuel*, 246; Ackroyd, *The Second Book of Samuel*, 117; Hertzberg, *I and II Samuel*, 320; Smith, *The Books of Samuel*, 327. McCarter, Baldwin, and Smith credit this suggestion to Hoffmann. See Hoffmann, "Lexikalisches," 66–67.

[13] E.g., Gen 11:3; Ex 1:14; 5:7; 24:10; Is 65:3; Ezek 4:1.

[14] Josephus, *Antiquities*, 7.161.

[15] WA DB 9/1.333. In modern German it is translated as *und legte sie unter eiserne Sägen und Zacken und eiserne Keile und verbrannte sie in Ziegelöfen* (*Die Bibel: Oder die ganze Heilige Schrift, Alten und Neuen Testaments nach der deutschen Übersetzung D. Martin Luthers* [St. Louis: Concordia, n.d.]).

[16] For the history of this interpretation, see Sawyer, "King David's Treatment of the Ammonites (2 Samuel 12:31)."

down the fortifications around all the Ammonite cities, not taking punitive measures against the captured Ammonites.

Commentary

997 BC[17]

Parallel 2 Sam 12:30–31 ‖ 1 Chr 20:2–3

The author has completed his account of David's adultery and its aftermath, including the birth of Solomon (11:1–12:25). He now regresses in time to the end of the Ammonite war, probably about three years before the birth of Solomon.[18] The account opens with Joab's capture of the royal precinct of the city (12:26), what Joab will call "the water district," that is, the place where the city had a source of water to sustain it during the siege (12:27). Joab urged David to come and complete the conquest (12:28). Otherwise, the city would be "named after" Joab. This probably means that, should David not join the final battle for the city, Joab would get credit for the conquest.

David's capture of the city is not given in detail (12:29). However, we are told that David took the crown of the king (or of the god Milcom; see the second textual note on 12:30) and that it was placed on his head. Since this crown weighed a talent—about seventy-five pounds (thirty-four kilograms)—it was too heavy to wear for an extended period of time (cf. 1 Sam 17:5, 38–39). Most likely the crown was ceremonially placed on David's head by some of his men and then removed after the ceremony.

The final verse (2 Sam 12:31) relates David's conscription of captured Ammonites. He forced them to tear down the city—probably to destroy its fortifications—and make bricks, perhaps for David's building projects (see the textual note on 12:31). We are told that David did this to all the Ammonite cities, thereby rendering the inhabitants incapable of rebellion, since they would have no defensive walls around their cities.

---

[17] See "The Chronology of David's Reign" in the commentary on 5:1–5.

[18] See figure 2, "Chronology of David's Reign," in the commentary on 5:1–5.

Amnon Rapes Tamar

Translation

13 ¹After this David's son Absalom had a beautiful sister, and her name was Tamar. David's son Amnon loved her. ²Amnon was frustrated to the point of making himself sick on account of his sister Tamar, since she was a virgin, and it appeared to Amnon to be impossible to do anything to her.

³Now Amnon had a friend, and his name was Jonadab the son of Shimeah, David's brother. Jonadab was a very clever man. ⁴He said to him, "Why are you, the king's son, dejected like this every morning? Will you not tell me?"

Amnon said to him, "Tamar, the sister of my brother Absalom—I love [her]!"

⁵Jonadab said to him, "Lie on your bed and pretend to be sick. When your father comes to see you, say to him, 'Please let my sister Tamar come and give me something to eat. She can prepare the food in front of me, so I can watch, and she can feed me.'"

⁶So Amnon lay down and pretended to be sick. When the king came to see him, Amnon said to the king, "Please let my sister Tamar come and make a couple of pastries in front of me, and she can feed me."

⁷David sent [a message] to Tamar at the palace, "Please go to the home of your brother Amnon and prepare food for him."

⁸So Tamar went to the home of her brother Amnon. He was lying down. She took dough, kneaded it, made pastries in front of him, and cooked the pastries. ⁹Then she took the pan and set [it] in front of him, but he refused to eat. Amnon said, "Have everyone leave me." So everyone left. ¹⁰Then Amnon said to Tamar, "Bring the food to the bedroom and feed me." Then Tamar took the pastries that she had made and brought them to her brother Amnon in the bedroom.

¹¹When she brought [them] to him to eat, he grabbed her and said to her, "Come, lie with me, my sister."

¹²She said to him, "No, my brother! Do not humiliate me, because this should never be done in Israel. Do not do this stupid thing! ¹³Where could I take my shame? You would become like one of the stupid fools in Israel! Now please speak to the king, because he will not refuse your request to marry me."

¹⁴But he would not listen to her. Since he was stronger than she was, he overpowered her and lay with her. ¹⁵Then Amnon developed a very great hatred for her, because the hatred that he had for her was greater than the love that he had had for her. Amnon said to her, "Get up! Get out!"

¹⁶She said to him, "No—because sending me away is much worse than the other thing that you did to me!" But he would not listen to her.

¹⁷He called his servant who assisted him and said, "Send this (woman) away from me, outside, and bolt the door after her!" ¹⁸(She was wearing a long tunic,

because the virgin daughters of the king wore such garments.) His assistant brought her outside and bolted the door after her.

¹⁹Tamar put ashes on her head and tore the long tunic she wore. She put her hands on her head and went away wailing. ²⁰Her brother Absalom said to her, "Has your brother Amnon been with you? Now, my sister, be silent. He is your brother. Do not dwell on this matter." So Tamar lived as a desolate woman in her brother Absalom's house.

²¹When David heard all of this, he was very angry. He did not discipline his son Amnon, since he loved him because he was his firstborn. ²²Absalom did not speak with Amnon—either good or bad—because Absalom hated Amnon since he had raped his sister Tamar.

Textual Notes

13:1 וַיְהִי אַחֲרֵי־כֵן—"After this" is literally "and it came to pass after thus." The author frequently opens a new episode in the narrative with this clause. See the commentary on 2:1.

וּלְאַבְשָׁלוֹם—"Absalom had" is literally "and (there was) to Absalom." The preposition לְ is used in the sense of possession (BDB, s.v. לְ, 5 b (a)), "belonging to," thus "had." Similarly, see וּלְאַמְנוֹן רֵעַ, "now Amnon had a friend," in 13:3.

אָחוֹת יָפָה—"A beautiful sister." In the book of Samuel the feminine noun אָחוֹת, "sister," appears only in this chapter (nine times) and in 17:25. In this chapter it refers to Tamar, who was the full sister of Absalom (13:1, 4, 20, 22, 32) and the half sister of Amnon (13:2, 5, 6, 11). The feminine adjective יָפָה, "beautiful," also describes Abigail (1 Sam 25:3) and another Tamar, Absalom's daughter (2 Sam 14:27). Different Hebrew terminology portrayed Bathsheba as "beautiful" (see the third textual note on 11:2). For a discussion of such terminology in Samuel, see the commentary on 11:2.

וּשְׁמָהּ תָּמָר—"And her name was Tamar." When used as a common noun תָּמָר means "palm tree" (e.g., Ex 15:27; Deut 34:3), which is a suitable simile for an attractive woman (Song 7:8–9 [ET 7:7–8]).

13:2 וַיֵּצֶר לְאַמְנוֹן—"Amnon was frustrated" is literally "and it was constrained for Amnon." In this impersonal construction (the Hebrew verb has no stated subject), the verb can be translated as a passive with its object (לְאַמְנוֹן) as its subject (Joüon, §§ 128 b, 152 d, 155 i (3)). The verb is the Qal (G) preterite (imperfect with *waw* consecutive) of צָרַר I in the intransitive sense, "be cramped, restricted, constricted, depressed" (see *HALOT*, s.v. צרר I, B).

לְהִתְחַלּוֹת—"To the point of making himself sick." This verb is the Hithpael (HtD) infinitive construct of חָלָה, "be sick, ill." Its Hithpael stem has a reflexive meaning, "make oneself ill." With the preposition לְ it forms a result clause, expressing the result of his frustration.

כִּי בְתוּלָה הִיא—"Since she was a virgin." The noun בְּתוּלָה recurs in the plural in 13:18. It denotes a young woman who may be betrothed (e.g., Deut 22:23) or unbetrothed (e.g., Deut 22:28) but is not yet married, and some contexts emphasize her virginity.[1] If the emphasis here is on her marriageable age rather than her virginity,[2] Amnon was heartsick because Tamar was old enough to be married, but as her half brother, he could not marry her (Lev 18:9, 11; 20:17).

וַיִּפָּלֵא בְעֵינֵי אַמְנוֹן לַעֲשׂוֹת לָהּ מְאוּמָה:—"And it appeared to Amnon to be impossible to do anything to her." The verb is a Niphal (N) preterite (imperfect with *waw* consecutive) of פָּלָא, which could mean "be beyond one's power, difficult, extraordinary, miraculous." In context it may form an elliptical comparison (see Joüon, § 141 i): "and it was *too* difficult in Amnon's eyes to do anything to her."

13:3 וְיוֹנָדָב ... יוֹנָדָב—"Jonadab ... and Jonadab" is the reading in the MT and the LXX. 4QSam[a] reads [ויהונתן] ... [י]הונתן], "[J]onathan ... [and Jonathan]."

13:4 מַדּוּעַ אַתָּה כָּכָה דַּל—"Why are you ... dejected like this?" For the adverb כָּכָה, "thus," see also 1 Sam 2:14; 19:17; 2 Sam 17:21. The adjective דַּל can mean "low, weak, poor, helpless" (1 Sam 2:8; 2 Sam 3:1).

בַּבֹּקֶר בַּבֹּקֶר—"Every morning" is literally "in the morning, in the morning." The repetition conveys a distributive sense.[3]

אֶת־תָּמָר אֲחוֹת אַבְשָׁלֹם אָחִי אֲנִי אֹהֵב:—"Tamar, the sister of my brother Absalom—I love [her]!" The translation reflects the emphasis of the unusual Hebrew syntax. "Tamar" is placed first and marked as the direct object (אֶת־תָּמָר). The next three words describe her relationship to Amnon (אֲחוֹת אַבְשָׁלֹם אָחִי), literally "the sister of Absalom my brother." The verb (the participle אֹהֵב) is placed last of all and is preceded by the pronoun אֲנִי, "I," as its subject.

13:5 שְׁכַב—"Lie." This is the Qal (G) masculine singular imperative of שָׁכַב, "to lie down." It may seem to have its ordinary physical meaning here and in 13:6, 8, but its three uses in these early verses of the chapter prepare the reader for its sexual sense in 13:11, 14. Its sexual meaning in those verses is made explicit by the prepositions it governs, עִמִּי, "with me," in 13:11, and אֹתָהּ "with her," in 13:14. In form אֹתָהּ appears to be the direct object marker אֵת with a third feminine singular suffix. The expected form of the suffixed preposition would be אִתָּהּ (as in 3:16). However, suffixed forms of the direct object marker are often substituted for suffixed forms of the preposition (Joüon, § 103 j). For שָׁכַב, see also the fourth textual note on 3:7 and the third textual note on 12:24.

וְהִתְחָל—"And pretend to be sick." This is an apocopated (GKC, § 75 cc) Hithpael (HtD) masculine singular imperative (with the conjunction *waw*) of חָלָה, "be sick." Its Hithpael had a reflexive meaning in 13:2 (see the second textual note on 13:2), but here it is reflexive-declarative,[4] as again in 13:6 (וַיִּתְחָל). Verbs in the Hithpael stem can mean that the actor is disguising himself, thus "to pretend illness" (Joüon, § 53 i).

---

[1] E.g., Gen 24:16; Lev 21:3, 14; Judg 21:12 (cf. 1 Ki 1:2–4). See *DCH*, s.v. בְּתוּלָה. *DCH* is wrong to cite Joel 1:8 as proof that a בְּתוּלָה could be married. The lamenting woman in the simile in Joel 1:8 could have been betrothed but not yet married when "the bridegroom of her youth" died.

[2] See Wenham, "*Bᵉtûlāh* 'A Girl of Marriageable Age.' "

[3] Waltke-O'Connor, § 12.5a.

[4] *IBH*, § 42 A; Waltke-O'Connor, § 26.2f.

תָּבֹא נָא—"Let her come, please." The Qal (G) third feminine singular imperfect would normally be written with *waw*: תָּבוֹא. This shortened form is the jussive, and the context implies that it has a jussive meaning ("may/let come"), as confirmed by the particle of entreaty נָא, "please." However, sometimes a jussive form does not have a jussive meaning. Also, a regular imperfect form can have a jussive meaning. The context of 13:6 implies that the regular form in the clause תָּבוֹא־נָא has a jussive meaning, "let her come, please." See Joüon, § 114 g, including note 1.

וְתַבְרֵנִי לֶחֶם ... אֶת־הַבִּרְיָה—"And let her give me something to eat ... the food." The verb תַבְרֵנִי is the Hiphil (H) third feminine singular jussive of בָּרָה, "to eat," with a causative meaning. In the OT this rare verb appears only in 2 Sam 3:35; 12:17; 13:5, 6, 10; Lam 4:10, and its feminine cognate noun בִּרְיָה, "food," occurs only in 2 Sam 13:5, 7, 10.

וְעָשְׂתָה—"She can prepare" could also be translated as "and let her prepare." This perfect with *waw* consecutive continues the volitive force of the preceding jussive verbs (see the third and fourth textual notes on 13:5; Joüon, § 119 k; *IBH*, § 53 B 3).

וְאָכַלְתִּי מִיָּדָהּ:—"And she can feed me" is literally "and I can eat from her hand." The same idiom recurs in 13:6, 10, but with the Qal (G) of the verb בָּרָה, "eat," in place of the Qal of אָכַל here.

13:6 וּתְלַבֵּב ... שְׁתֵּי לְבִבוֹת—Literally "and let her make ... two pastries." The Piel (D) of לָבַב, "make cakes," is a denominative from the noun לְבִבָה, "cake, pastry," which is the cognate accusative here.[5] In the OT the verb is used only in 13:6, 8, and the noun appears only in 13:6, 8, 10, always plural. The number שְׁנַיִם, "two" (שְׁתֵּי is its feminine in construct), probably does not mean no more than two pastries, but denotes "some" or "a few" (see Joüon, § 142 c).

13:7 אָחִיךְ—"Your brother." Amnon is called the "brother" (אָח) of Tamar in 13:7, 8, 10, 12, 20, although he is her half brother (13:1).

13:8 הַבָּצֵק—"(The) dough." The noun בָּצֵק may refer to leavened dough here. The context of Ex 12:34, 39 requires it to be unleavened there.

וַתָּלְשׁ—"She kneaded it." This Qere and the Kethib וַתָּלוֹשׁ are alternate spellings of the same form, a Qal (G) preterite (imperfect with *waw* consecutive) of לוּשׁ.

וַתְּבַשֵּׁל—"And she cooked." The verb בָּשַׁל is usually used in the Piel (D), in which it often means "to boil," but it can also be used more generally for any manner of cooking, as here (BDB, Piel, 2).

13:9 הַמַּשְׂרֵת—"The pan." The noun מַשְׂרֵת occurs only here. Its exact meaning is uncertain, but it must refer to a vessel or utensil for cooking.

וַתִּצֹק—"And she set." This is the Qal (G) preterite (imperfect with *waw* consecutive) of יָצַק. In imperfect forms of this verb, the initial *yod* consonant is regularly assimilated. Rarely the assimilated *yod* is marked by *daghesh* (-צַּ-, Is 44:3), but usually the *daghesh* is omitted (see GKC, § 71). Normally יָצַק means "to pour out" liquids (oil, as in 1 Sam 10:1; water; molten metal; stew in 2 Ki 4:40–41). Here it apparently has a more general meaning, similar to that of its Hiphil (H) in 2 Sam 15:24. Its implied direct object probably is the pan ("set [it]") but might be the pastries ("set [them]").

---

5 The verb is a "productive" Piel (Waltke-O'Connor, § 24.4e, including example 4).

הוֹצִיאוּ כָל־אִישׁ מֵעָלַי—"Have everyone leave me." The Hiphil (H) imperative of יָצָא, "go out," with the combination of prepositions מֵעָלַי (the preposition מִן prefixed to עַל) literally means "make every man go out from over me." See מֵעָלַי also in 13:17. Royal attendants normally stood in readiness to serve a king or prince seated on his throne, so they are said to be "over" him, and here Amnon is lying down. See attendants described with עַל עָמַד, literally "to stand over" to serve a seated or reclining superior, in, e.g., Gen 18:8; 1 Ki 22:19; Zech 4:14.

13:10 הַחֶדֶר ... הֶחָדְרָה:—"To the bedroom ... in the bedroom." The noun חֶדֶר commonly denotes a "bedroom" or other "inner room" within a large building. The first instance, הַחֶדֶר, is an accusative of place or destination (Joüon, § 125 n), hence "to," while the second instance, הֶחָדְרָה, has the directional *he*, reflected in English idiom with "in."

13:11 וַתַּגֵּשׁ אֵלָיו לֶאֱכֹל—"When she brought [them] to him to eat" is literally "and she brought near to him to eat." There is no stated object of the Hiphil (H) of נָגַשׁ, "bring [something] near." It must be supplied from the context. Likewise, the implied subject of the infinitive construct (with לֶאֱכֹל (לְ, "to eat," must be determined from the context (Joüon, § 124 s).

וַיַּחֲזֶק־בָּהּ—"He grabbed her." For the Hiphil (H) of חָזַק with the preposition בְּ, see the first textual note on 1 Sam 15:27[6] and the textual note on 2 Sam 1:11.

בּוֹאִי שִׁכְבִי עִמִּי—"Come, lie with me." See the fourth textual note on 3:7 and the second and third textual notes on 12:24. Here the verb בּוֹא, "come" (Qal [G] feminine singular imperative) is not accompanied by the preposition אֶל, "to," so by itself it might not have sexual connotations, but the following clause with the Qal feminine singular imperative of שָׁכַב, "lie," governing the suffixed preposition עִם, "with," clarifies the intent of Amnon's imperative for her to "come." For שָׁכַב, "lie," see the first textual note on 13:5.

אֲחוֹתִי:—"My sister." See the third textual note on 13:1. In this context Amnon's use of this term for her is shocking because it highlights that he is fully aware that his request is incestuous and an abomination (Lev 18:9, 11, 26–30; 20:17). See further the commentary.

13:12 אַל־אָחִי—"No, my brother!" The negative אַל is used as an exclamation, "no!" as also in 13:16. Her designation of him as her "brother" emphasizes the incestuousness of his intended sin; see also the preceding textual note.

אַל־תְּעַנֵּנִי—"Do not humiliate me." Here this verb is translated as "humiliate" to correspond to Tamar's use of the noun חֶרְפָּה, "shame, humiliation," in 13:13 (see the first textual note on 13:13). For the Piel (D) of עָנָה III, "to afflict, oppress, abuse," see the third textual note on 7:10. It recurs in 13:14, 22, 32, where again it refers to Amnon's rape of Tamar. In these verses it could also be translated as "(sexually) abuse," "violate," or "rape." It is rendered as "overpower" in 13:14 because of its immediate context there, but as "rape" in 13:22, 32. In the Piel this verb denotes rape also in Gen 34:2; Judg 19:24; 20:5; Lam 5:11.

---

[6] Steinmann, *1 Samuel*, 288.

לֹא־יֵעָשֶׂה כֵן—"This should never be done." The force of the imperfect (the Niphal [N] of עָשָׂה, "to do") could also be "this must never be done." See *IBH*, § 47 D; Joüon, § 113 m.

13:12–13 הַנְּבָלִים ... הַנְּבָלָה הַזֹּאת—"This stupid thing ... the stupid fools." In 1 Samuel 25 the narrative played on the adjective and substantive נָבָל, *nabal*, "foolish/stupid fool," the name of the antagonist Nabal, and the noun נְבָלָה, *nebalah*, "foolishness, stupidity." See the first textual note on 1 Sam 25:3 and the second textual note on 1 Sam 25:25,[7] as well as the second textual note on 2 Sam 3:33. These terms denote the most extreme kind of foolishness. Such fools reject the very existence of God and mock him as if he were powerless (Pss 14:1; 53:2 [ET 53:1]; 74:22). When such people are given prosperity, as was Nabal, they are insufferable (Prov 30:21–22).

13:13 וַאֲנִי אָנָה אוֹלִיךְ אֶת־חֶרְפָּתִי—Literally "and I, where could I take my shame?" Note the alliteration caused by the similarity of the first and second words, וַאֲנִי אָנָה, and the fact that the first four words begin with *aleph*. The verb is the Hiphil (H) first common singular imperfect of הָלַךְ, which can mean "lead away, carry, take, take away." There is no place Tamar could go to rid herself of her shame. The noun חֶרְפָּה refers to a "disgrace," "shame," or "humiliation" for all Israel in 1 Sam 11:2; 17:26 and for an individual in 1 Sam 25:39, as here.

לֹא יִמְנָעֵנִי מִמֶּךָ:—"He will not refuse your request to marry me" is literally "he will not withhold me from you."

13:14 וְלֹא אָבָה לִשְׁמֹעַ בְּקוֹלָהּ—"But he would not listen to her" is literally "but he was not willing to hear by her voice." The same clause recurs in 13:16 but with לָהּ in place of בְּקוֹלָהּ. In this construction the Qal (G) verb אָבָה, "be willing," takes an infinitive construct with לְ (לִשְׁמֹעַ) as a complement to specify the action the person is (or is not) willing to do. See this construction also in 1 Sam 22:17; 26:23; 2 Sam 2:21; 6:10; 13:25; 14:29; 23:16, 17.

וַיֶּחֱזַק מִמֶּנָּה—The Qal (G) of חָזַק, "be strong," with the preposition מִן, "from, than" (with a third feminine singular suffix), forms a comparative clause: literally "and he was stronger than her."

וַיְעַנֶּהָ—"He overpowered her." This translation corresponds to the preceding clause with "stronger" (see the preceding textual note). It is the Piel (D) preterite (imperfect with *waw* consecutive) with a third feminine singular object suffix of the same verb עָנָה III discussed in the second textual note on 13:12.

וַיִּשְׁכַּב אֹתָהּ:—"And he lay with her." See the first textual note on 13:5.

13:15 וַיִּשְׂנָאֶהָ אַמְנוֹן שִׂנְאָה גְּדוֹלָה מְאֹד—"Then Amnon developed a very great hatred for her" is literally "and Amnon hated her (with) a very great hatred." The verb takes a double accusative construction. The first accusative is the direct object: the third feminine singular pronominal suffix on the verb וַיִּשְׂנָאֶהָ, "and he hated *her*." The second accusative is the cognate accusative noun שִׂנְאָה, "hatred," derived from the verb, thus forming a cognate accusative construction. The cognate accusative can be called an internal object of the verb (see GKC, § 117 q). Cf. the next textual note.

---

[7] Steinmann, *1 Samuel*, 472, 477.

גְּדוֹלָה הַשִּׂנְאָה אֲשֶׁר שְׂנֵאָהּ—"The hatred that he had for her was greater" is literally "greater (was) the hatred (with) which he hated her." This is similar to the construction in the prior textual note in that the verb has a suffix that is its accusative direct object (שְׂנֵאָהּ, "he hated her") and a cognate noun is used (הַשִּׂנְאָה, "the hatred"). Here, however, rather than being a second accusative, the cognate noun is the subject of a nominal clause ("the hatred … was greater") and is modified by a relative clause that includes the cognate verb (אֲשֶׁר שְׂנֵאָהּ, "[with] which he hated her").

מֵאַהֲבָה אֲשֶׁר אֲהֵבָהּ—"Than the love that he had had for her" is literally "than (the) love (with) which he loved her." The מִן is comparative, and the rest of the wording forms a construction like the one in the preceding textual note in which a relative clause with a cognate verb modifies a cognate noun.

13:16 אַל־—The negative אַל is used as an exclamation, "no!" as in 13:12 (אַל־אָחִי, "no, my brother!").

אוֹדֹת הָרָעָה הַגְּדוֹלָה הַזֹּאת … לְשַׁלְּחֵנִי—"Because sending me away is much worse" is literally "because of this great evil … to send me away." The syntax is unusual. The word אוֹדָה is always used in the plural (אוֹדֹת) to signify cause: "because." (This is its only instance in the OT where it is not preceded by the preposition עַל.) The phrase הָרָעָה הַגְּדוֹלָה הַזֹּאת, "this great evil," is translated comparatively as "much worse," that is, "more evil," because of the comparative מִן that begins the next clause (see the next textual note). The Piel (D) infinitive construct of שָׁלַח, "to send away," with the preposition לְ and a first common singular object suffix, explains the action ("to send me away") that constitutes "this great evil."

מֵאַחֶרֶת אֲשֶׁר־עָשִׂיתָ עִמִּי—"Than the other thing that you did to me" is literally "from another which you did with me." The adjective אַחֶרֶת is the feminine form of אַחֵר, "other, another." The feminine gender can be used for abstract ideas, such as actions (see GKC, § 122 p, q).

וְלֹא אָבָה לִשְׁמֹעַ לָהּ:—See the first textual note on 13:14.

13:17 וַיִּקְרָא אֶת־נַעֲרוֹ מְשָׁרְתוֹ וַיֹּאמֶר שִׁלְחוּ־נָא—"He called his servant who assisted him and said, 'Send … !'" The words נַעֲרוֹ מְשָׁרְתוֹ are masculine singular, and the second is in apposition to the first: literally "his servant, the one who assisted him." The first imperative directed at the servant (שִׁלְחוּ, "send" this woman away) is masculine plural, suggesting that other attendants would also enforce this action against Tamar, while the next imperative, נְעֹל, "bolt," is singular (see the fourth textual note on 13:17), apparently since it would require only one servant to bolt the door.

אֶת־זֹאת—"This (woman)" is literally "this (one)." At times the demonstrative pronoun (masculine זֶה or feminine זֹאת) is used to express contempt (1 Sam 10:27; 21:16 [ET 21:15]; 29:4; cf. Joüon, § 143 b). This pronoun is definite, and so it is marked by the definite direct object marker אֵת (Joüon, §§ 125 g; 137 e; 143 b).

הַחוּצָה—"Outside." Here the noun חוּץ, "outside," has the article and the directional *he*, literally "to the outside." It recurs in 13:18 without the directional *he*, הַחוּץ, as an accusative of direction (Joüon, § 125 n) with the same meaning.

וּנְעֹל—"And bolt." נְעֹל is the Qal (G) masculine singular imperative of the II-guttural (ע-) verb נָעַל (Joüon, § 69 b). In 13:18 its perfect with a conjunctive *waw* is used (וְנָעַל, "and he bolted [the door]") where a preterite (imperfect with *waw* consecutive) would be more expected (Joüon, § 119 z), continuing the preterite (imperfect with *waw* consecutive) וַיֹּצֵא, "and he brought [her outside]" (see Joüon, § 118 c).

13:18 כְּתֹנֶת פַּסִּים—"A long tunic" is literally "a tunic of the soles." The noun פַּס denotes the palm of a hand or the sole of a foot. The same construct phrase denotes Joseph's garment (Gen 37:3). It recurs with the definite article (כְּתֹנֶת הַפַּסִּים) in 2 Sam 13:19, as for Joseph's in Gen 37:23, 32.

כֵּן תִּלְבַּשְׁןָ בְנוֹת־הַמֶּלֶךְ הַבְּתוּלֹת מְעִילִים—"The virgin daughters of the king wore such garments" is literally "thus the daughters of the king, the virgins, wore robes." The verb is the third feminine plural Qal (G) imperfect of לָבֵשׁ, "to wear" (on the form of the verb, see GKC, § 47 l). Here the imperfect denotes customary action in the past, "they used to wear," probably extending to the present time from the standpoint of the author (see Joüon, § 113 a).

13:19 יָדָהּ—In the MT the suffixed noun יָד is singular, "her hand." The translation "her hands" follows the plural reading of the LXX (τὰς χεῖρας αὐτῆς).

וַתֵּלֶךְ הָלוֹךְ וְזָעָקָה—"And she went away wailing" is literally "and she went, going, and she was wailing." The Qal (G) infinitive absolute of הָלַךְ, "walk," is often used with a second infinitive absolute to express simultaneous and continuing action. Here, instead of a second infinitive absolute, the idiom uses the Qal (G) third feminine singular perfect with *waw* consecutive of זָעַק, "to cry out, wail" (וְזָעָקָה is pausal for וְזָעְקָה). See Waltke-O'Connor, § 32.2.5d, including example 25; GKC, § 113 t.[8] See also the second textual note on 16:13.

13:20 הַאֲמִינוֹן—This word in Codex Leningradensis is the interrogative *he* prefixed to the name אֲמִינוֹן: "has Aminon?" The translation follows the reading הַאַמְנוֹן, found in a number of Masoretic manuscripts, which is supported by the LXX (Αμνων), the Syriac Peshitta, and the Vulgate.

הַחֲרִישִׁי—"Be silent." This is the feminine singular Hiphil (H) imperative of חָרֵשׁ, "be silent, keep quiet." The Hiphil of חָרֵשׁ is also in 1 Sam 7:8; 10:27; 2 Sam 19:11 (ET 19:10).

אַל־תָּשִׁיתִי אֶת־לִבֵּךְ לַדָּבָר הַזֶּה—"Do not dwell on this matter" is literally "do not set your heart to this word." The Qal (G) of שִׁית, "set, place," is used idiomatically with the direct object לֵב, "heart," and the preposition לְ (see BDB, s.v. שִׁית, Qal, 2 b).

וַתֵּשֶׁב ... וְשֹׁמֵמָה—"So she lived ... as a desolate woman." The Qal (G) of יָשַׁב, "live, dwell," is modified adverbially (GKC, § 118 p) by a participle with *waw*, וְשֹׁמֵמָה (pausal for וְשֹׁמְמָה; GKC, § 84ᵃ s). This Qal (G) feminine singular participle of שָׁמֵם may signify that she was abandoned. It could also mean "appalled" or have a sexual meaning, "deflowered" (BDB, Qal, 1), that is, her virginity was violated by rape.

13:21 וַיִּחַר לוֹ מְאֹד—"He was very angry." See the second textual note on 1 Sam 20:7[9] and the first textual note on 2 Sam 3:8.

---

[8] Cf. Joüon, § 123 n, which cites 1 Sam 19:23 and 2 Sam 16:13 as similar examples but is unjustified in claiming that the second verb is to be emended to another infinitive absolute.

[9] Steinmann, *1 Samuel*, 390.

At the end of 13:21 the LXX has a long addition: καὶ οὐκ ἐλύπησεν τὸ πνεῦμα Αμνων τοῦ υἱοῦ αὐτοῦ, ὅτι ἠγάπα αὐτόν, ὅτι πρωτότοκος αὐτοῦ ἦν, "and he [David] did not discipline [literally 'grieve the spirit of'] Amnon his son since he loved him, because he was his firstborn." Several Old Latin manuscripts have a similar reading. Josephus also knew of this reading.[10] These versions, then, may reflect a Hebrew reading like this:

וְלֹא עָצַב אֶת־רוּחַ אַמְנוֹן בְּנוֹ כִּי אֲהֵבוֹ כִּי בְכֹרוֹ הוּא

4QSam[a], though fragmentary, appears to support this reading, since it includes [אה]בו כי בכורו הוא[א], "[he lo]ved him because [he was his] firstborn." If this Hebrew reading is original, it was probably lost in the MT due to homoioarchton when a scribe's eye skipped from וְלֹא at the beginning of this text to וְלֹא at the beginning of 13:22. The translation above follows this reading.

13:22 לְמֵרָע וְעַד־טוֹב—"Either good or bad." This phrase with the adjectives רַע and טוֹב, respectively, is literally "from evil and until good." The prepositions לְ and מִן are prefixed to רַע.

עַל־דְּבַר אֲשֶׁר—This compound conjunction is formed by the causal preposition עַל, "because of," followed by the construct chain דְּבַר אֲשֶׁר, "the word/matter (of) which." The phrase can be translated as "because of the fact that" (Joüon, § 170 h; cf. Joüon, § 129 q) or "since."

עִנָּה—"He had raped." For this Piel (D) of עָנָה III, see the second textual note on 13:12.

Commentary

985 BC[11]

The judgment pronounced on David's house (2 Sam 12:10–12) continues to unfold. This chapter opens with an introduction to Tamar, who is described as Absalom's sister (2 Sam 13:1; cf. 1 Chr 3:9), rather than David's daughter, which was also true of her. This not only serves to distance David from the events of this narrative (cf. 13:21) but also moves Absalom to the center. He will be a major focus of the next few chapters (2 Samuel 13–18).

Tamar, however, is defined in this chapter by her relationship to two men: "David's son Absalom" and "David's son Amnon" (13:1). In relation to Absalom she is a (full) "sister" (13:1), and her violation elicits his protective jealous anger (13:22). The same Hebrew noun is used to call her Amnon's (half) "sister" (see the third textual note on 13:1), but to Amnon she is merely an object of lust and, ultimately, contempt (cf. 13:16–18). Amnon's obsession with Tamar was so intense that he made himself sick over her (13:2). His frustration is characterized as his viewing her as impossible to have, even though she was a woman of marriageable age (see the third textual note on 13:2). The Law of Moses

---

[10] Josephus, *Antiquities*, 7.173.

[11] See "The Chronology of David's Reign" in the commentary on 5:1–5.

forbade sexual relations and marriage between close relatives, including half siblings (Lev 18:6, 9, 11; 20:17).

Amnon's friend Jonadab came to his aid by inquiring about Amnon's health and offering advice (13:3–5). Jonadab was Amnon's cousin, the son of Shimeah, one of David's older brothers. Shimeah (שִׁמְעָה, 13:3, 32) is called Shammah (שַׁמָּה) in 1 Sam 16:9; 17:13 and Shimea (שִׁמְעָא) in 1 Chr 2:13. Jonadab's advice was designed to bring Tamar from the palace, where she was almost certainly under the eye of someone assigned to care for David's daughters (cf. 13:7). It is unclear whether Jonadab intended for Amnon to assault Tamar or whether he simply intended that Amnon be allowed to enjoy her company for a while without her minders present. Perhaps he thought that after Amnon saw Tamar and simply spent some time in her presence, he would give up his obsession with his half sister. Jonadab appears again later in the chapter where he is depicted as a member of David's court who has insight into the dynamics of the relationship between Amnon and Absalom (13:32–33, 35).[12]

Amnon followed Jonadab's advice (13:6). David certainly would have come to see Amnon when he was ill, since Amnon was David's eldest son and probably the heir apparent to the throne. In the days before antibiotics and other modern therapies, any illness that confined someone to bed would have been considered life threatening and was to be taken seriously. Perhaps David was moved to grant Amnon's request and have Tamar come from the safe confines of the palace (13:7) because he feared that he might soon lose another son.

The pace of the author's narrative slows when Tamar arrives at Amnon's house (13:8a). We are given the details of her preparation of the food, with Amnon apparently watching from his bed (13:8b), then Amnon's refusal to eat and his order for his attendants to leave (13:9), his request for Tamar to bring the food to him in the bedroom, and Tamar's compliance (13:10). The narrative becomes even more detailed as Amnon's propositioning of Tamar and her plea for him to desist are reported (13:11–13). Tamar used "no," "not," or "never" (אַל or לֹא) four times in 13:12 and made five appeals to Amnon:

1. At first Tamar simply refused, calling Amnon her "brother" and implying that such incest was forbidden (2 Sam 13:12a). Sexual intercourse between a brother and sister or half sister is prohibited by the Law of Moses (Lev 18:6, 9, 11; 20:17). It is one of the "abominations" for which a person is to be excommunicated from

---

[12] Hill, "A Jonadab Connection in the Absalom Conspiracy," theorizes that Jonadab was actually in league with Absalom and that his advice to Amnon was designed to have Amnon commit a crime that would eventually eliminate him from succeeding to the throne. This would then leave Absalom as the heir apparent. If this were the case, then Absalom was complicit in his sister's rape. According to Hill, his suggestion would also explain why Jonadab later knew that Absalom had killed only Amnon and not all of the king's sons (13:32–33). As intriguing as this theory is, it is based on speculation and is not supported by any explicit statements in the text. Moreover, if Jonadab had reasoned that David would be forced to punish Amnon for the rape of Tamar, thereby eliminating him as first in line for the throne, he badly miscalculated. Such miscalculation would hardly have qualified him as "clever" or "wise" (חָכָם, 13:3).

God's people (cf. 1 Corinthians 5) and cut off from God eternally (Lev 18:26–30; cf. 1 Cor 6:9–10).

2. Then she appealed to the humiliation to which he would subject her, a degradation that was not to be done in Israel (2 Sam 13:12b). This was an implication that no true follower of Yahweh would commit such an act. Certainly no believer would do this to another member of God's people. Note the parallel language concerning the rape of Dinah (Gen 34:7). In NT language, no one who does such things will inherit the kingdom of God (1 Cor 6:9–10; Gal 5:19–21; Eph 5:5).

3. Such a violation would be a "stupid thing," such an outrageous crime that everyone would recognize its heinous and godless character (2 Sam 13:12c). Once again note the parallel language with the rape of Dinah (Gen 34:7).

4. Then she called Amnon's attention to the consequences for herself and for him: she would be utterly disgraced, and he would be seen as a stupid fool, implying that he would be jeopardizing his position as heir to David's throne (2 Sam 13:13a).

5. Finally, she appealed to Amnon to ask David for her, arguing that the king would not refuse this request from his eldest son (2 Sam 13:13b). This last appeal appears to be a desperate grasping at straws, since such marriages were forbidden by the Law of Moses (Lev 18:9, 11; 20:17). Except for David's affair with Bathsheba and his subsequent murder of Uriah (2 Samuel 11), he had always been scrupulous about keeping Yahweh's laws. Even while carrying out his surreptitious adultery and murder, he had tried to appear publicly to be keeping the Law.

We are told that Amnon would listen to none of Tamar's words, and the narrative pace quickens as the act of rape is described (2 Sam 13:14). Amnon's change of heart toward Tamar (13:15) not only revealed that his love for her was nothing more than lust but also that his humiliation of her by rape also debased him and made him nothing more than a coldhearted criminal. He contemptuously ordered her out of his house.

Tamar's refusal to leave (13:16) corresponds to the Law of Moses. A man who seduced a virgin was obligated to marry her, and his rejection of her was even worse than the rape itself (13:16; see also Ex 22:15–16 [ET 22:16–17]; Deut 22:28–29). But Amnon's disgust and hatred for her was complete. He ordered his staff to eject her from the house (2 Sam 13:17). He had called her his "sister" (13:11), but now he dismissed her as "this (one)" (זֹאת; see the second textual note on 13:17).

The parenthetical note concerning Tamar's tunic calls the reader's attention to Amnon's callous treatment of a virgin daughter of the king and his servant's compliance with his cruel order (13:18). Tamar's reaction, however, was one of shock and dismay as displayed by her putting ashes on her head, tearing her tunic, putting her hands on her head, and wailing plaintively (13:19). We are not told how Absalom found her, but his reaction was to offer some inadequate words (13:20). She was the victim of sexual assault, but Absalom compounded her shame by commanding her not to report the crime. The reader will learn that Absalom's request for her to "be silent" about her "brother" (13:20) was to provide Absalom with cover to plot his revenge (13:22). Most important, Absalom granted his sister the sanctuary that Amnon would not provide for her (13:20).

David's reaction was anger, but lack of action (13:21). The reason for his inaction is elaborated in ancient versions of this verse (see the textual note on 13:21). David failed in his vocations as the king of Israel and as a father by not disciplining Amnon, not even demanding the fifty shekels of silver prescribed by Moses' Law (Deut 22:29). Perhaps David's sense of guilt because of his sexual sin with Bathsheba made it all the more difficult for him to punish Amnon for a similar crime. In this respect David had become like the high priest Eli— unable to correct his errant sons, and they would suffer as a result (cf. 1 Sam 2:22–25). If David had confronted Amnon with his sin, as Nathan had done to David (2 Sam 12:1–12), Amnon might have repented and received forgiveness, as had David (2 Sam 12:13). Instead, his sin remained unconfessed, and so he remained unabsolved. Concealed sin only festers and triggers further sinning.

Absalom, however, did respond. At first he simply refused to speak to Amnon (13:22), but as the subsequent narrative unfolds, we find that he had further plans for his recalcitrant half brother.

Absalom Murders Amnon

Translation

13 ²³After two years when Absalom was shearing sheep in Baal-hazor, which is near Ephraim, Absalom invited all the king's sons. ²⁴Absalom came to the king and said, "Your servant is shearing sheep. Please, have the king and his servants come with your servant."

²⁵The king said to Absalom, "No, my son. All of us should not go, so that we will not burden you." Although Absalom urged him, he was not willing to go, but he gave him his blessing.

²⁶Absalom said, "If not, let my brother Amnon come with us."

The king said, "Why should he go with you?" ²⁷But Absalom urged him, so the king sent Amnon and all the king's sons with him. So Absalom made a feast like a king's feast.

²⁸Absalom commanded his servants, "Watch. When Amnon is in a good mood from drinking wine, I will say to you, 'Strike Amnon,' and then you shall kill him. Do not be afraid. Haven't I commanded you? Be strong and courageous." ²⁹Absalom's servants did to Amnon as Absalom had commanded. All the king's sons arose, and each of them mounted his mule and fled.

³⁰While they were on their way, a rumor came to David: "Absalom has struck down all the king's sons, and not one of them is left." ³¹The king stood and tore his clothes and lay on the ground. All his servants were standing with their clothes torn.

³²Jonadab, the son of David's brother Shimea said, "My lord should not assume that they have killed all the young men, the king's sons, since only Amnon is dead, because Absalom was determined to do this since the day he [Amnon] raped his sister Tamar. ³³The king ought not be too concerned about this matter and think that all the king's sons are dead, since Amnon alone is dead."

³⁴Absalom fled. When the young man who was on watch looked up, he saw a large crowd coming from the road west of him by the side of the mountain. ³⁵Jonadab said to the king, "The king's sons have come! As the word of your servant, so it is." ³⁶As he finished speaking, the king's sons came and wept loudly. The king and his servants also wept very bitterly. ³⁷But Absalom fled and went to Talmai the son of Ammihud, the king of Geshur. And he [David] mourned his son every day.

³⁸Now Absalom had fled and gone to Geshur, and he was there three years. ³⁹The king's [anger] ceased to be directed toward Absalom, because he had been comforted concerning Amnon, although he was dead.

Textual Notes

13:23 לִשְׁנָתַיִם יָמִים—"After two years" is literally "to two years, days." The preposition לְ can serve temporally to indicate a point in time (BDB, 6; see the first textual note on 11:1), and here it denotes the close or end of a period (BDB, 6 b; Waltke-O'Connor, § 11.2.10c, including example 10), hence "after." The noun שְׁנָתַיִם is the dual form of שָׁנָה, "year," thus "two years." The plural of יוֹם is used in apposition to a preceding designation of time (BDB, s.v. יוֹם, 6 b; GKC, § 131 d). In English such a use of "days" is redundant, and so יָמִים is not translated. The phrase שְׁנָתַיִם יָמִים recurs in 14:28.

13:23–24 וַיִּהְיוּ גֹזְזִים לְאַבְשָׁלוֹם ... וַיֹּאמֶר הִנֵּה־נָא גֹזְזִים לְעַבְדֶּךָ—"When Absalom was shearing sheep ... And he said, 'Your servant is shearing sheep'" is literally "And there were shearers belonging to Absalom. ... And he said, 'Behold please, shearers belong to your servant.'" The clauses with the masculine plural Qal (G) participle of גָּזַז, "to shear sheep," and the preposition לְ denoting possession, emphasize the activity in progress for the sheep owned by Absalom rather than the identity of the persons actually doing it. See the similar clause in the first textual note on 1 Sam 25:7.[1]

13:24 יֵלֶךְ־נָא—"Please, have/let [them] ... come." The verb is the masculine singular Qal (G) jussive of הָלַךְ, "walk, go," expressing a request (Joüon, § 114 h). In contrast, the imperfect would be accented on the final syllable, יֵלֵךְ (the imperfect יֵלֵךְ is in 13:26b). The retraction of the accent to the first syllable (יֵלֶךְ) and the consequent shortening of the second *tsere* vowel (-לֵ-) to *seghol* (-לֶ-) mark this form as a jussive. This is reinforced by the particle of entreaty נָא, "please," which is normally used only with a volitive form. See the same clause, יֵלֶךְ־נָא, in 13:26a. Cf. נָא with another volitive verb in the second textual note on 13:25.

עִם־עַבְדֶּךָ—Instead of the MT's "with your servant," 4QSam[a] reads אל עבדך, "to your servant." The Lucianic recension of the LXX, the Old Latin, and the Vulgate support 4QSam[a].[2]

13:25 אַל־בְּנִי—"No, my son." The negative אַל is used as an exclamation, "no!" as also in 13:12, 16, which is much less common than its usage with a verb (see GKC, § 152 g).

אַל־נָא נֵלֵךְ כֻּלָּנוּ—"All of us should not go." The usage of נָא with a volitive verb form (here a cohortative) is common (Joüon, § 114 b, f). See the first textual note on 13:24, where נָא was used with a jussive. Here the volitive form נֵלֵךְ is the cohortative of הָלַךְ, "walk, go," negated by אַל, "not." Initially the force of this statement seems to be "none of us should go," since at first David did not want Amnon (or any other son) to go (13:26). But David then relented and allowed all of his sons to go (13:27), although he himself did not go, so the force of the statement here could be interpreted as "not all of us should go."

וְלֹא נִכְבַּד עָלֶיךָ—"So that we will not burden you" is literally "and we will not be heavy upon you." This clause introduced by *waw* expresses purpose ("so that"; see GKC, § 165 a). In form the verb נִכְבַּד could be the Niphal (N) third masculine singular

---

[1] Steinmann, *1 Samuel*, 473.

[2] McCarter, *II Samuel*, 330.

perfect of כָּבֵד (as in 2 Sam 6:20), but the context indicates that it is the Qal (G) first common plural imperfect of כָּבֵד, "be heavy." See the Qal of כָּבֵד also in 1 Sam 5:6, 11; 31:3.

וַיִּפְרָץ־בּוֹ—"Although he urged him." This clause is repeated in 13:27 (where it is translated as "but he urged him"). In 2 Sam 5:20; 6:8 the Qal (G) of פָּרַץ means "to burst through." Four times in the OT (here in 2 Sam 13:25, 27; also in 1 Sam 28:23; 2 Ki 5:23), פָּרַץ takes the suffixed preposition בְּ as its object and means "to urge, apply pressure to." The reading in 4QSamᵃ is ויפצר בו, to be vocalized as וַיִּפְצַר־בּוֹ, the Qal (G) of פָּצַר with the suffixed preposition בְּ. That combination, פָּצַר + בְּ, has the same meaning, "to urge," in Gen 19:3; 33:11; Judg 19:7; 2 Ki 2:17; 5:16 and the physical meaning "to push on" in Gen 19:9. Most likely פָּצַר is related to פָּרַץ, "urge," and one is a by-form of the other by metathesis (צר- for רצ- or vice versa). Consequently, the reading in 4QSamᵃ 13:25 is equivalent to the MT. LXX 2 Sam 13:25 and 13:27 read ἐβιάσατο, "he forced, urged forcefully," which is similar to παρεβιάζοντο in LXX 1 Sam 28:23. See the first textual note on 1 Sam 28:23.[3]

וְלֹא־אָבָה לָלֶכֶת—"He was not willing to go." In this construction, the Qal (G) of the verb אָבָה, "be willing," takes an infinitive construct as a complement to specify the action the person is (or is not) willing to do. See the first textual note on 13:14.

וַיְבָרֲכֵהוּ:—"But he gave him his blessing" is literally "and/but he blessed him." For the Piel (D) of בָּרַךְ, see the textual note on 2 Sam 6:11–12, as well as the first textual note on 1 Sam 2:20 and the third textual note on 1 Sam 9:13.[4]

13:26 וְלֹא—"If not" is literally "and not." This is an elliptical protasis of a conditional sentence (GKC, § 159 dd; Joüon, § 167 o; for the vocalization with *qamets*, וְלֹא, instead of *shewa*, וְלֹא, see Joüon, § 104 d, including note 1). By it Absalom concedes David's response (see the second textual note on 13:25) that not *all* of the people Absalom invited (the king and all his sons) would come, but he hopes that the king will permit one other son to come.

יֵלֶךְ־נָא—"Let [him] … come." See the first textual note on 13:24.

אִתָּנוּ—"With us." This suffixed preposition is omitted from 4QSamᵃ, probably due to homoioarchton with the following word, the name אַמְנוֹן. The presence of the preposition here in the MT is supported by its repetition in 13:27, וַיִּשְׁלַח אִתּוֹ, "so he sent [them] … *with him*."

עִמָּךְ:—"With you." This is the pausal form of עִמְּךָ, the preposition עִם with the second masculine singular suffix (not the second feminine singular suffix, which would be spelled identically, ךְ-).

13:27 וַיִּפְרָץ־בּוֹ—"But he urged him." See the fourth textual note on 13:25.

---

[3] Steinmann, *1 Samuel*, 524. BDB (s.v. פָּצַר, Qal) asserts that פָּרַץ, "urge," is a scribal error for פָּצַר. That might be a plausible assertion if there were only one or two instances where פָּרַץ means "urge" or if it occurred with that meaning in other syntactical constructions besides taking בְּ with its object. However, since the OT has four passages in which פָּרַץ + בְּ means "to urge" and five passages in which פָּצַר + בְּ has the identical meaning, it is more likely that these verbs are by-forms. *HALOT*, s.v. פרץ II, recognizes that פָּרַץ, "urge," in 1 Sam 28:23; 2 Sam 13:25, 27; 2 Ki 5:23 is likely a by-form of פָּצַר.

[4] Steinmann, *1 Samuel*, 90, 179.

אַמְנוֹן וְאֵת כָּל־בְּנֵי הַמֶּלֶךְ:—In the MT, 13:27 ends with these words: literally "Amnon and all the sons of the king." After that phrase, the translation includes another sentence: "so Absalom made a feast like a king's feast," which is lacking in the MT. It translates a Hebrew reading like this (cf. 1 Sam 25:36):

$$\text{וַיַּעַשׂ אַבְשָׁלוֹם מִשְׁתֶּה כְּמִשְׁתֵּה הַמֶּלֶךְ}$$

This Hebrew reading is suggested by the LXX (καὶ ἐποίησεν Αβεσσαλωμ πότον κατὰ τὸν πότον τοῦ βασιλέως), the Old Latin, and 4QSamᵃ, which only partially preserves the last word (ה[מ]ל[ך], "[the] ki[n]g") but has space for this missing text.[5] If original, this text was lost in the MT due to homoioteleuton, since MT 13:27 ends with הַמֶּלֶךְ, "the king."

13:28 כְּטוֹב לֵב־אַמְנוֹן בַּיַּיִן—"When Amnon is in a good mood from drinking wine" is literally "when the heart of Amnon is good with wine." The word כְּטוֹב is the Qal (G) infinitive construct of טוֹב, "be good," with the preposition כְּ, forming a temporal clause. The verb טוֹב can have the nuance "be glad, joyful" (BDB, 2). The same wording is in Esth 1:10 (cf. Judg 16:25 [Qere]; Eccl 9:7).

וַהֲמִתֶּם—"And then you shall kill him." This form (GKC, § 72 w) is the Hiphil (H) second masculine plural perfect of מוּת, "die," with *waw* consecutive, denoting a subsequent action ("and then"; see GKC, § 159 g). In the Hiphil, מוּת has a causative meaning, "put to death." See also the third common plural perfect הֵמִיתוּ in 13:32. Qal (G) perfect forms of the verb appear later: מֵת, "he is/was dead," in 13:32, 33, 39 and מֵתוּ, "they are dead," in 13:33.

חִזְקוּ—"Be strong." This is the Qal (G) masculine plural imperative of חָזַק with an intransitive meaning. For a similar exhortation with חָזַק, see the first textual note on 2:7.

וִהְיוּ לִבְנֵי־חָיִל:—"And be ... courageous." See the second textual note on 2:7.

13:29 וַיִּרְכְּבוּ אִישׁ עַל־פִּרְדּוֹ—"And each of them mounted his mule" is literally "and they mounted/rode, (each) man on his mule." The noun אִישׁ is used in a distributive sense here. The noun פֶּרֶד denotes a "mule" used for transportation, as in 18:9, where Absalom is literally רֹכֵב עַל־הַפֶּרֶד, "riding on the mule."

13:30 וְהַשְּׁמֻעָה בָאָה—"A rumor came." The feminine noun שְׁמוּעָה is derived from the verb שָׁמַע, "to hear," and so literally refers to something heard, that is, "a report" or "news" of an event, as also in 1 Sam 2:24; 4:19; 2 Sam 4:4. Because of the inaccuracy of "all" in the report here in 13:30, it is translated as "a rumor." It is used with the verb בּוֹא, "to come," also in 4:4. The verb form בָּאָה is the Qal (G) third feminine singular perfect, as indicated by the accent on the first syllable (בָּאָה). (The Qal feminine singular participle would be spelled identically but accented on the last syllable: בָּאָה.)

וְלֹא־נוֹתַר מֵהֶם אֶחָד:—"And not one of them is left" is literally "and one from them is not left." The masculine numeral אֶחָד, "one," is the subject of the Niphal (N) third masculine singular perfect of יָתַר, "be left, remain." See the second textual note on 8:4. The preposition מִן (on מֵהֶם, literally "from them") is used partitively.

13:31 וַיִּקְרַע אֶת־בְּגָדָיו—"And he tore his clothes." For the "tearing" (קָרַע) of clothes as an act of grief and/or mourning in the book of Samuel, see also 1 Sam 4:12; 2 Sam 1:2, 11; 3:31; 13:19 (Tamar); 15:32. See further the commentary.

וַיִּשְׁכַּב אָרְצָה—"And he lay on the ground." David had performed this same action in 2 Sam 12:16 to attempt to avert the death of his first son by Bathsheba.

וְכָל־עֲבָדָיו נִצָּבִים קְרֻעֵי בְגָדִים:—"All his servants were standing with their clothes torn." The form קְרֻעֵי is the Qal passive (Gp) participle of קָרַע, "tear" (masculine plural in construct with בְגָדִים, "clothes"), which has a passive meaning, literally "torn of clothes." It is common for a passive participle to be in construct with a noun that serves as a genitive of specification, thus "torn in respect to clothes" (see GKC, § 116 k; Joüon, § 121 o; Waltke-O'Connor, § 37.3c, example 24). The LXX translates the verb as an active form and with a suffixed form of "clothes" as its direct object: καὶ πάντες οἱ παῖδες αὐτοῦ οἱ περιεστῶτες αὐτῷ διέρρηξαν τὰ ἱμάτια αὐτῶν, "and all his servants who were standing around him *tore* their clothes." This may reflect a Hebrew Vorlage which had an (active) Qal (G) form of קָרַע and a third masculine plural suffix on "clothes," that is, בִּגְדֵיהֶם, "their clothes" (cf. קָרְעוּ בִגְדֵיכֶם in 3:31). Apparently, 4QSamᵃ had a third variation, but the only extant word is בגדיו, "his clothes" (בְּגָדָיו, with a third masculine singular suffix).

13:32 אַל־יֹאמַר אֲדֹנִי—"My lord should not assume" is literally "let my lord not think." The verb יֹאמַר is the jussive of אָמַר, meaning "say to oneself" or "think" rather than "speak aloud."

עַל־פִּי אַבְשָׁלוֹם הָיְתָה שׂוּמָה–"Absalom was determined to do this" is literally "a set thing was upon the mouth of Absalom." The verb שׂוּמָה is the feminine singular Qal passive (Gp) participle of שִׂים, "to set, place," in a metaphorical sense for an established plan. Cf. the jussive of שִׂים for performing a mental act in the textual note on 13:33. (In place of שׂוּמָה here many Masoretic manuscripts have שִׂימָה, which is a different spelling of the same form; cf. Joüon, § 81 b.) This participle is the subject of the third feminine singular perfect הָיְתָה, "was." Since this is an unusual idiom, there have been several proposals to emend the text or understand שׂוּמָה differently.[6] However, Hebrew can use a feminine singular form for an abstract idea or action (GKC, § 122 p, q), and so no emendation is needed.

עַנֹּתוֹ—"He [Amnon] raped." This is the Piel (D) infinitive construct of עָנָה III with a third masculine singular pronominal suffix that serves as its subject. For this Piel verb, see the second textual note on 13:12.

אֲחֹתוֹ:—"His sister." Tamar was the half sister of Amnon and the full sister of Absalom. Earlier in the chapter אָחוֹת was used for Tamar as the "sister" of each of them. See the third textual note on 13:1.

13:33 וְעַתָּה אַל־יָשֵׂם אֲדֹנִי הַמֶּלֶךְ אֶל־לִבּוֹ דָּבָר—"The king ought not be too concerned about this matter" is literally "and now, may my lord the king not set into his heart a word." The verb יָשֵׂם is the Qal (G) jussive of שִׂים, "to set, place." This verb is used idiomatically with the preposition אֶל and the noun לֵב, "to set [something] into one's

---

[6] See the discussion in Joo, "שׂוּמָה (2 Sam xiii 32)."

heart," for thinking intensely or pondering something. The same construction is used in 2 Sam 19:20 (ET 19:19). (The similar idiom שִׂים לֵב אֶל/לְ, "to set one's heart to" a matter, is used in Ex 9:21; 1 Sam 9:20; 25:25; 2 Sam 18:3; Ezek 40:4; 44:5; Job 2:3; 34:14.) Here the direct object of the verb שִׂים is the noun דָּבָר, "a word/matter," which is explicated by the following clause introduced by the infinitive construct (with לְ) לֵאמֹר, "and think that."

13:34 וַיִּשָּׂא ... עֵינָיו—"When he looked up" is literally "and he lifted up ... his eyes." The Qere is the suffixed dual עֵינָיו, "his (two) eyes," which is the sole reading in many Masoretic manuscripts and is supported by the LXX (τοὺς ὀφθαλμοὺς αὐτοῦ). The Kethib is probably to be vocalized as the suffixed singular עֵינוֹ, "his eye" (if not a defective, or *ḥaser*, spelling of the suffixed dual, עֵינָו).

הַצֹּפֶה—"(The one) who was on watch." The Qal (G) participle of צָפָה, "gaze," often denotes a "watchman" or a "lookout" (1 Sam 14:16; five times in 2 Sam 18:24–27), usually stationed in a tower on the city wall. Metaphorically it can refer to a prophet as a watchman stationed by God to protect and save his people (Is 52:8; Jer 6:17; Ezek 3:17; 33:7; Hos 9:8).

מִדֶּרֶךְ אַחֲרָיו—"From the road west of him" is literally "from the road behind him," which is the literal translation of the LXX (ἐν τῇ ὁδῷ ὄπισθεν αὐτοῦ). Directions in Hebrew are oriented as if an observer is standing on the shore of the Mediterranean facing inland. Therefore "in front" is to the east and "behind" is to the west. North is "left," and south is "right." Some scholars propose emending אַחֲרָיו to חֹרֹנַיִם, "Horonaim" (Is 15:5; Jer 48:3, 5, 34), based on "the road of Horonaim" in the longer LXX. At the end of this verse, after "by the side of the mountain," the LXX contains additional text:

… ἐν τῇ καταβάσει· καὶ παρεγένετο ὁ σκοπὸς καὶ ἀπήγγειλεν τῷ βασιλεῖ καὶ εἶπεν ἄνδρας ἑώρακα ἐκ τῆς ὁδοῦ τῆς Ωρωνην ἐκ μέρους τοῦ ὄρους.

… in the descent, and the watchman came and reported to the king and said, "I have seen men from the road of Horonaim from the region of the mountain."

This may reflect an underlying Hebrew text such as this:

בַּמּוֹרָד וַיָּבֹא הַצֹּפֶה וַיַּגֵּד לַמֶּלֶךְ וַיֹּאמֶר אֲנָשִׁים רָאִיתִי מִדֶּרֶךְ חֹרֹנַיִם מִצַּד הָהָר

There is a distinct possibility that this additional text was original to this verse and was lost in the MT due to homoioteleuton, when a scribe's eye skipped from מִצַּד הָהָר at the end of MT 13:34 to the same phrase at the end of the verse as reconstructed. Note that Jonadab's words in 13:35 assume that the watchman relayed his observations to David, though nothing is said about this in the MT.

13:36 כְּכַלֹּתוֹ לְדַבֵּר—"As he finished speaking." See the explanation of the syntax of the identically inflected pair of infinitives in the first textual note on 1 Sam 18:1.[7] See also the textual note on 2 Sam 11:19.

וַיִּשְׂאוּ קוֹלָם וַיִּבְכּוּ—"And they wept loudly" is literally "and they lifted up their voice and wept." See the first textual note on 3:32. The identical wording as here is also in Judg 21:2; Job 2:12; see also Judg 2:4; 1 Sam 11:4.

---

[7] Steinmann, *1 Samuel*, 344.

בָּכֽוּ בְכִי גָדֽוֹל מְאֹֽד:—"They wept very bitterly" is literally "they wept a very great weeping." Hebrew is fond of such cognate accusative constructions (*IBH*, § 17 B; GKC, § 117 p–r). See, e.g., the first textual notes on 1 Sam 1:6, 11, 17, 21, the second textual note on 1 Sam 2:13, and the third textual note on 1 Sam 2:24.[8]

13:37 עַמִּיהֽוּד—"Ammihud" is the reading of the Qere, is the sole reading in many Masoretic manuscripts, and is supported by the LXX (Εμιουδ). For this name elsewhere, see Num 1:10; 2:18; 7:48, 53; 10:22; 34:20, 28; 1 Chr 7:26; 9:4. The Kethib is the otherwise unattested עַמִּיחֽוּר, "Ammihur."

וַיִּתְאַבֵּל—"And he mourned." The Hithpael (HtD) of אָבַל, "to mourn," refers to grieving over deaths also in 1 Sam 6:19; 2 Sam 14:2; 19:2 (ET 19:1). It refers to Samuel grieving over Saul in 1 Sam 15:35; 16:1.

כָּל־הַיָּמִֽים:—"Every day" is literally "all of the days." Other options for translating this are "day after day," "continually," and "for the rest of his life."

13:39 וַתְּכַל דָּוִד הַמֶּלֶךְ לָצֵאת אֶל־אַבְשָׁלֹום—For "the king's [anger] ceased to be directed toward Absalom," the MT literally reads "[the ? of] David the king finished going out to Absalom." The first verb, וַתְּכַל, is the third feminine singular Piel (D) preterite (imperfect with *waw* consecutive) of כָּלָה, whose Qal (G) means "be complete, finished." In the Piel it has a causative meaning. The most suitable meaning in the syntactical context here (before לָצֵאת) is "to finish" doing an action that is denoted by an infinitive construct with the preposition לְ (see BDB, s.v. כָּלָה, Piel, 1 c). Also possible would be "to complete" something such as a period of time (see BDB, Piel, 1 b) or "to cause something to cease" (see BDB, Piel, 2 a). However, the context in the MT has no feminine singular noun that could serve as the subject of וַתְּכַל. Its subject, whatever it may be, is also the implied subject of the second verb, לָצֵאת, the Qal (G) infinitive construct of יָצָא, "go out," with the preposition לְ.

The phrase דָּוִד הַמֶּלֶךְ, "David the king," never appears elsewhere in the MT among the preexilic and exilic books of the OT.[9] Among the postexilic books, דָּוִיד הַמֶּלֶךְ, "David the king," occurs only in Chronicles.[10] The uniqueness of this phrase outside of Chronicles and the fact that the clause contains no feminine noun to serve as the subject of the verb וַתְּכַל raise suspicions about its genuineness. Most likely the original Hebrew reading was רוּחַ הַמֶּלֶךְ, literally "the spirit of the king," meaning "the king's anger." The feminine noun רוּחַ can denote or be associated with "anger," either God's anger, as in 2 Sam 22:16 ‖ Ps 18:16 (ET 18:15; see BDB, 1 d (1)), or human anger (see BDB, 1 d (2), 3 c). This feminine noun fits the context admirably as the subject of both verbs in the sentence. Apparently דָּוִד, "David," in the MT is the result of a double graphic confusion of the first and last consonants of רוּחַ, "spirit; anger": *dalet* was substituted

---

[8]   Steinmann, *1 Samuel*, 45, 48, 51, 58, 84, 93.

[9]   Cf. GKC, § 131 g. The usual phrase is הַמֶּלֶךְ דָּוִד, literally "the king, David," translated as "King David" (2 Sam 3:31; 5:3; 6:16; 7:18; 8:8, 10, 11; 9:5; 13:21; 16:5, 6; 19:12, 17 [ET 19:11, 16]; 1 Ki 1:1, 13, 28, 31, 32, 37, 38, 43, 47; also 1 Chr 15:29; 17:16; 18:10, 11; 21:24; 29:24). Some LXX manuscripts read ὁ βασιλεὺς Δαυιδ, "the king, David," in 2 Sam 13:39, but this does not strictly correspond to דָּוִד הַמֶּלֶךְ, "David the king," in MT 2 Sam 13:39.

[10] 1 Chr 24:31; 26:26, 32; 28:2; 29:1, 9, 29; 2 Chr 2:11 (ET 2:12); 7:6.

for *resh* and *dalet* for *chet* (which perhaps was partially formed). Some LXX manuscripts read τὸ πνεῦμα τοῦ βασιλέως, "the spirit/anger of the king," and this reading is partially confirmed by 4QSamᵃ, which reads רו[ח] המלך [רון], to be vocalized as רוּחַ הַמֶּלֶךְ. (The Targum apparently conflates that reading with the MT: נַפְשָׁא דְדָוִיד מַלְכָּא, "the soul of David the king.")

נִחָם—"He had been comforted." The verb נָחַם in the Niphal (N) here has the passive meaning "be comforted," which corresponds to the active Piel (D) meaning "to comfort." See the second textual note on 10:2.

כִּי־מֵת:—Here כִּי is concessive: "*although* he was dead."

Commentary

Absalom's murder of Amnon for the rape of his sister Tamar two years earlier (13:1–22) visited another consequence of David's sin upon his house. David had abused his royal power to commit sexual sin and murder (2 Samuel 11), and although he was forgiven (12:13), the prophet had announced the earthly consequence: "now the sword will never turn away from your house, because you despised me and took the wife of Uriah the Hittite for yourself to be your wife" (12:10). David had established the pattern of committing sexual sin and then murder in the attempt to cover it up (2 Samuel 11). David's son Amnon had committed the sins of incest and rape against his sister (13:1–22), and now his abomination would be requited with murder (13:23–39), which brought further grief to the king and his royal court (13:31).

However, there was another sin of David that contributed to Amnon's death at the hand of his brother Absalom. Earlier his adultery was facilitated by his neglect of his duty to lead Israel's troops out to battle (11:1–2). David again failed to act as Israel's king by not punishing Amnon for raping Tamar (13:21). Neither had he carried out his vocation as the head of his household. David had not acted as father by disciplining his eldest son, Amnon, nor had he been a father to his daughter Tamar in providing for her in the wake of her sexual assault at the hands of Amnon. Those two actions were left to David's son Absalom, who brought his sister Tamar into his own household (13:20) and now would exact revenge against his brother Amnon.

God has established authorities in the world in order to restrain sin and reward good behavior (Rom 13:1–5). When those authorities do not carry out those functions but instead neglect their duty to inhibit acts that tear apart the fabric of civil order, they sin by abandoning their responsibility to God and society. In addition, they also risk further public chaos as those who feel aggrieved by the misdeeds of others fill the vacuum left by sovereigns who have been inattentive to their divine vocations. David's incapacity to deal with Amnon was a contributing factor in Absalom's violence against his brother.

The Murder of Amnon (13:23–33)

983 BC[11]

The author picks up the narrative after a two-year wait by Absalom (13:23). Sheepshearing was also a time for feasting. Since shearing was labor intensive and required a large number of workers, it was also a time for assembling large amounts of food to feed them. For this reason it also became a time of revelry (cf. 1 Sam 25:2–8, 11, 36–37). The estate where Absalom was shearing was in Baal-hazor, which is said to be near "Ephraim" (13:23). This is not the territory of the Israelite tribe by that name, but a town. "Ephraim" (Jn 11:54) is probably to be identified with Ephron, which lay about four miles (six kilometers) northeast of Bethel (2 Chr 13:19).[12] This would suggest that modern Jebel el-ʿAṣur, about five miles (eight kilometers) northeast of Bethel, may be the site of Baal-hazor.

Absalom first came to David to invite him to the feast (13:24). David declined, saying he did not want to be a burden to his son (13:25). Feeding the king and his court in royal style could be quite expensive. Absalom, we are told, urged David to reconsider despite the king's initial refusal. Instead, David gave Absalom his blessing for holding the feast (13:25). Then Absalom asked for Amnon to attend (13:26). The author has crafted the narrative in such a way that the perceptive reader may discern that the invitation to David was a ruse. Absalom may have anticipated David's refusal, and after having made a demonstration of his disappointment by continuing to urge David to attend, he could then ask for Amnon, David's eldest son and heir apparent, to attend in David's stead. Thus, Absalom was able to credibly disguise his true motive for seeking Amnon's attendance. David, apparently suspecting nothing, not only sent Amnon but also the rest of his sons (13:27).[13]

The author quickly transitions to the feast at Baal-hazor. Absalom was already beginning to show his pretentions to the throne by throwing "a feast like a king's feast" (13:27). Just as Absalom proved to be clever and cunning in dealing with David, so now he was also calculating when dealing with Amnon. He instructed his servants to kill Amnon when it was obvious that he was feeling the effects of the wine and would have let down his guard (13:28). Moreover, Absalom encouraged his servants. He even appealed to his own authority and stature: "Haven't I commanded you?" (13:28).

---

[11] See "The Chronology of David's Reign" in the commentary on 5:1–5.

[12] Seebass, "Ephraim in 2 Sam xiii 23."

[13] David may have had ulterior motives. First, it would be perilous for David and all of his sons to be together in one place, far away from the military capital, since an enemy force could obliterate the entire Davidic dynasty in one swift attack. Second, if David went along, he himself would be vulnerable; he might have suspected that one of his sons would attempt to usurp his throne (as Absalom would do later in 15:1–18:18). Third, as David's negligent slothfulness had prevented him from going into battle (11:1–2) and from punishing Amnon (13:21), perhaps once again he was displaying his indolence by foregoing his duty as the head of the household to accompany his sons.

At this point the narrative pace quickens: Absalom's order was carried out, and the rest of David's sons fled (13:29). The aside that each mounted his "mule" (פֶּרֶד) is the first reference to these creatures in the Scriptures. Crossbreeding of animals was forbidden by the Law of Moses (Lev 19:19). Assuming that the royal household observed that command, the mules must have been imported (cf. Ezek 27:14) or obtained from Canaanites still residing in the land. It would appear that the "mule" (פֶּרֶד or its feminine cognate פִּרְדָּה) became a favorite mount for Israelite royalty (2 Sam 18:9; 1 Ki 1:33, 38, 44; 10:25; 18:5; cf. Is 66:20; contrast ὄνος, "donkey," in Mt 21:2, 5, 7; Jn 12:15).

A rumor with misinformation reached David that all of his sons had been killed by Absalom (2 Sam 13:30). David instantly arose from his throne and went into mourning (13:31). With the death of Amnon, David finally behaved as he ought to have when Tamar tore her robe (13:19). This tearing was a common outward sign of mourning, loss, shock, and extreme dismay.[14] Once again David lay on the ground to mourn the loss or imminent loss of progeny (see 12:16).

For the second time in this chapter, Jonadab is quoted as offering advice (13:32–33; earlier, see 13:5). Apparently this nephew of David was keenly aware of the internal strife in the royal family, and he had inflamed it by his successful counsel as to how Amnon could entrap Tamar to violate her (13:5). Since he was complicit in the crime that was now avenged, he bore some responsibility for the ensuing murder. Now he advised David that Absalom had been determined to exact revenge on Amnon because he raped his sister Tamar. Based on his intimate knowledge of the motives of the perpetrators, he counseled the king not to be unduly alarmed (see the textual note on 13:33). Jonadab knew that Absalom was not treacherously seeking the lives of all of David's sons— this was not a palace coup. Only Amnon was the target of Absalom's vengeance.

Absalom Flees to Geshur (13:34–39)

983–980 BC[15]

The flight of Absalom from Israel is mentioned three times in this short passage (13:34, 37, 38) to emphasize that David had now lost both him and Amnon (as well as his first son by Bathsheba [12:14–18]). With the first notice of Absalom's flight we are also told that a watchman observed the return of the royal crowd (13:34). Jonadab's prediction that only Amnon had been killed was proved correct, and he sought to encourage David by noting the arrival of David's other sons (13:35). Their survival, however, was not a sufficient reason for rejoicing. Instead, it was an occasion for the sons as well as the king and his entourage to mourn Amnon's death bitterly (13:36).

---

[14] Gen 37:29, 34; 44:13; Num 14:6; Josh 7:6; Judg 11:35; 1 Sam 4:12; 2 Sam 1:2, 11; 1 Ki 21:27; 2 Ki 2:12; 5:7, 8; 6:30; 11:14; 18:37; 19:1; 22:11; 22:19; Is 36:22; 37:1; Jer 41:5; Job 1:20; Esth 4:1; Ezra 9:3; 2 Chr 23:13; 34:19, 27; Mk 14:63; Acts 14:14.

[15] See "The Chronology of David's Reign" in the commentary on 5:1–5.

Once again we are told that Absalom fled, this time noting his destination (13:37). Geshur was a small kingdom that bordered the Sea of Galilee on the northeast. David had formed an alliance with this small state, probably to seek a buffer between himself and the Arameans, when he married Absalom's mother, the daughter of Talmai (2 Sam 3:3). Now Absalom, Talmai's grandson, found refuge there. Meanwhile, David mourned "his son" (בְּנוֹ, 13:37). The text is ambiguous, and it is not clear which son David was mourning—the murdered Amnon or the estranged Absalom. Perhaps this ambiguity was intentional and the author is signaling that David's emotions were mixed concerning these two sons. Amnon had been heir apparent, and Absalom normally would have become heir to the throne upon the firstborn son's death.[16]

For a third time we are told that Absalom fled—this time with the additional information that he was in Geshur for three years (13:38).[17] This notice serves as a transition to the change in David's attitude concerning his two sons: he lost his animus toward Absalom as he was comforted over the dead Amnon (13:39).

---

[16] Amnon was David's firstborn son (2 Sam 3:2; 1 Chr 3:1). His second son was Chileab/Daniel, who is mentioned only in genealogical lists (2 Sam 3:3; 1 Chr 3:1). This suggests that Chileab/Daniel died while still young. His third son, Absalom (2 Sam 3:3; 1 Chr 3:2), would then be the next in line for the throne. The flight of Absalom also explains why later the fourth son, Adonijah (2 Sam 3:4; 1 Chr 3:2), felt that he had a legitimate claim to the throne (1 Ki 1:5–10). However, both Yahweh and David apparently had promised the kingdom to Solomon, his oldest surviving Jerusalem-born son (1 Ki 1:13, 17, 29–30; 1 Chr 22:9–13; cf. 1 Ki 1:10).

[17] Since sheepshearing was done in the springtime, Absalom's first year in Geshur was from spring 983 to spring 982. This means that his third and final year in Geshur lasted until spring 980.

Absalom Returns to Jerusalem

Translation

14 ¹Zeruiah's son Joab knew that the king thought about Absalom. ²So Joab sent to Tekoa and brought a wise woman from there. He said to her, "Pretend to be in mourning. Dress in mourning clothes. Do not groom. Pretend to be a woman who has been in mourning over a dead person for many days. ³Then go to the king and speak these words to him." Joab put the words in her mouth.

⁴The woman from Tekoa spoke to the king. She fell facedown on the ground and bowed and said, "Help me, Your Majesty."

⁵The king said to her, "What is your concern?"

She said, "I am indeed a widow. My husband is dead. ⁶Your servant had two sons. The two of them were fighting in the countryside. There was no one to intervene. The one struck the other, and he killed him. ⁷Now the entire clan has risen against your servant. They said, 'Give [us] the one who struck his brother, and let us kill him for the life of the brother whom he killed. We will also destroy the heir.' They would extinguish my ember which remains, so as not to place a name and remnant for my husband on the land."

⁸The king said to the woman, "Go home. I will issue a command concerning you."

⁹The woman from Tekoa said to the king, "My lord, Your Majesty, let the guilt lie with me and my father's house, and let the king and his throne be innocent!"

¹⁰The king said, "Whoever speaks to you, bring him to me, and he will not bother you again."

¹¹She said, "Please, Your Majesty, invoke Yahweh your God so that the blood avenger will not destroy again and they will not obliterate my son."

He said, "As Yahweh lives, not a hair of your son will fall to the ground."

¹²The woman said, "Let your servant tell my lord the king a matter."

He said, "Speak."

¹³The woman asked, "Why have you devised something similar against the people of God? When the king spoke this way, he condemned himself, because he has not brought back his own banished person. ¹⁴For we are certainly going to die and be like water that is spilled on the ground and which cannot be collected [again]. God would not remove a life. He makes plans so that a banished person will no longer be alienated from him. ¹⁵Now, I have come to speak this matter to the king, my lord, because the people have frightened me. Your servant thought, 'I must speak to the king. Perhaps the king will do something for his servant. ¹⁶The king will certainly listen in order to save his servant from the hand of the man who would destroy me and my son together from God's inheritance.' ¹⁷Your servant thought, 'May the word of my lord, Your Majesty, bring relief because, like

the Angel of God, my lord, Your Majesty, is able to discern good and evil.' May Yahweh your God be with you!"

¹⁸The king answered the woman, "Please do not conceal from me the matter that I am about to ask you."

The woman said, "Let my lord, Your Majesty, speak."

¹⁹The king said, "Did Joab put you up to all this?"

The woman solemnly answered, "As you live, my lord, Your Majesty, there is no escaping what you have said, my lord, Your Majesty, because your servant Joab commanded me. He also put all these words in the mouth of your servant. ²⁰Your servant Joab did this in order to portray the matter in a different light. My lord has wisdom like the wisdom of the Angel of God, knowing everything on earth."

²¹The king said to Joab, "I made my decision: go, bring back the young man Absalom."

²²Joab fell facedown on the ground and bowed. He blessed the king, and Joab said, "Today your servant knows that I have found favor in your eyes, my lord, Your Majesty, because Your Majesty has granted the request of your servant." ²³Joab got up and went to Geshur and brought Absalom to Jerusalem.

²⁴The king said, "Let him go to his house. I will not grant him an audience." So Absalom went to his house and was not granted a royal audience.

²⁵Now there was no man so highly praised for his good looks in all Israel as Absalom. From the sole of his foot to the top of his head he had no flaw. ²⁶When he shaved his head—he shaved it at the end of every year because it got heavy, and he shaved it—he weighed the hair of his head as two hundred shekels according to the royal standard. ²⁷Three sons were born to Absalom, as well as one daughter—her name was Tamar. She was beautiful.

²⁸Absalom lived in Jerusalem two years without being granted a royal audience. ²⁹Absalom sent (word) to Joab that he might send him to the king, but he [Joab] did not wish to come to him. He sent (word) again a second time, but he did not wish to come. ³⁰He said to his servants, "Look! Joab has a plot of land next to mine, and he has barley there. Go and set it on fire." So Absalom's servants set the plot of land on fire.

Joab's young men came to him with their clothes torn and said, "Absalom's servants have set your plot of land on fire."

³¹Then Joab got up and came to Absalom's house and said to him, "Why have your servants set my plot of land on fire?"

³²Absalom said to Joab, "Look, I sent (word) to you, saying, 'Come here, I want to send you to the king to say, "Why did I come from Geshur? It would have been better for me [if] I were still there."' Now let me have a royal audience, and if I am guilty, then he should put me to death." ³³So Joab went to the king and told him. He called Absalom, and he came to the king and bowed down to him with his face on the ground before the king. Then the king kissed Absalom.

Textual Notes

14:1 לֵב הַמֶּלֶךְ עַל־אַבְשָׁלוֹם:—"The king thought about Absalom" is literally "the heart of the king (was) upon/concerning Absalom." This has been understood in various ways, from David longing for Absalom (NET, NIV) to the king as still hostile to Absalom.[1] Given that David refused to grant Absalom an audience upon his return to Jerusalem (14:24, 28), it is best to understand this statement to mean that David's thoughts were preoccupied with Absalom, perhaps to the point of distraction from his other responsibilities.

14:2 תְּקוֹעָה—"To Tekoa." This is the place-name תְּקוֹעַ, "Tekoa," with the directional *he* ending.

הִתְאַבְּלִי־נָא—"Pretend to be in mourning." For the Hithpael (HtD) of אָבַל, "to mourn," see the second textual note on 13:37. The form here is the feminine singular Hithpael imperative. In this case the Hithpael is reflexive-declarative. See also the feminine singular Hithpael participle מִתְאַבֶּלֶת in the fourth textual note on 14:2. The particle of entreaty נָא is commonly used after a verb when making a request; see the first textual note on 13:24. It is used again in the next clause after a Qal (G) feminine singular imperative, וְלִבְשִׁי־נָא, "dress."

וְאַל־תָּסוּכִי שֶׁמֶן—"Do not groom" is literally "and do not groom (with) olive oil." This could also be rendered as "do not apply olive oil" or "do not perfume (yourself) with olive oil." Olive oil was used as a skin moistener, a perfume base, and a hair ointment. For the verb סוּךְ, see the second textual note on 12:20. Syntactically the noun שֶׁמֶן, "oil," is an accusative that functions adverbially since it denotes the substance applied for grooming.

וְהָיִית כְּאִשָּׁה ... מִתְאַבֶּלֶת עַל־מֵת—"Pretend to be a woman who has been in mourning over a dead person" is literally "and you shall be as a woman ... who has been mourning over a dead man." See the second textual note on 14:2. The masculine singular Qal (G) participle מֵת, from מוּת, "die," is used as a substantive. See other Qal (G) forms of מוּת in 14:5 (וַיָּמָת) and 14:14 (מוֹת נָמוּת) and the Hiphil (H) forms discussed in the fifth textual note on 14:6.

זֶה יָמִים רַבִּים—"For many days" is literally "this many days." See Joüon, § 143 a; Waltke-O'Connor, § 17.4.2b, including example 8.

14:3 וְדִבַּרְתְּ אֵלָיו כַּדָּבָר הַזֶּה—"And speak these words to him" is literally "and speak to him according to this word."

וַיָּשֶׂם יוֹאָב אֶת־הַדְּבָרִים בְּפִיהָ:—"Joab put the words in her mouth." This means that Joab told her what to say. The Hebrew idiom recurs in 14:19.[2]

14:4 הָאִשָּׁה הַתְּקֹעִית—"The woman from Tekoa" is literally "the woman, the Tekoaite." This phrase recurs in 14:9. תְּקֹעִית is a feminine form of the gentilic adjective תְּקוֹעִי (2 Sam 23:26), which associates a person with the town of "Tekoa" (תְּקוֹעַ, 14:2).

וַתִּפֹּל עַל־אַפֶּיהָ אַרְצָה—"She fell facedown on the ground" is literally "and she fell on her nostrils to the ground." This idiom employs the Qal (G) of נָפַל, "fall"; the

---

[1] Anderson, *2 Samuel*, 187.

[2] See this idiom also in Ex 4:15; Num 22:38; 23:5, 12, 16; Is 51:16; 59:21; Ezra 8:17.

suffixed dual of אַף, "nostril, nose," whose dual often means "face" (BDB, s.v. אַף I, 2, under the root אנף); and the noun אֶרֶץ, "earth, ground," with a directional *he* suffix. See also 1 Sam 20:41 and עַל־אַפָּיו אַרְצָה, "on his nostrils/face to the ground," in 2 Sam 14:33. In the OT this idiom more commonly uses the suffixed dual of פָּנֶה, "face," as in 14:22, וַיִּפֹּל יוֹאָב אֶל־פָּנָיו אַרְצָה, literally "and Joab fell on his face to the ground" (see also 1 Sam 5:3–4; 17:49; and, without אַרְצָה, 1 Sam 25:23; 2 Sam 9:6).

וַתִּשְׁתָּחוּ—"And she bowed." For the Hishtaphel of חָוָה, "to bow down, worship," see the third textual note on 1 Sam 1:3.[3] This form is its third feminine singular preterite (imperfect with *waw* consecutive). See the second textual note on 1 Sam 1:28,[4] which has the corresponding masculine form וַיִּשְׁתָּחוּ. That masculine form appears in 2 Sam 14:22, 33.

הוֹשִׁעָה הַמֶּלֶךְ:—"Help me, Your Majesty." The verb is the Hiphil (H) masculine singular imperative of יָשַׁע, "to save, rescue," with a paragogic *he* ending. With a human subject, "rescue" (10:11) or "help" (10:19; 14:4) is suitable; see the third textual note on 10:11. The article on הַמֶּלֶךְ marks it as a vocative (*IBH*, § 20 D). It is translated as "Your Majesty" here, as in 1 Sam 17:55; 22:15; 23:20; 24:9 (ET 24:8); 26:17; and again in this chapter in 2 Sam 14:9, 11, 17, 18, 19, 22.

14:5 מַה־לָּךְ—"What is your concern?" is literally "what pertains to you?" This could also be rendered as "what do you want?" (see BDB, s.v. מָה, 1 a (c)). The preposition לְ has the nuance of relationship (BDB, 5 a) or possession (BDB, 5 b). See also 1 Sam 11:5 and the expression with a suffix preposition לְ in 2 Sam 16:10; 19:23 (ET 19:22).

אֲבָל—This adverb has an asseverative force, "indeed, surely, truly," which is ironic in the context of "pretend" (14:2).

14:6 וּלְשִׁפְחָתְךָ—"Your servant had." Here לְ is used in the sense of possession. The feminine noun שִׁפְחָה denotes a "slave girl" or female household "servant." See the first textual note on 1 Sam 1:18.[5] It recurs in 2 Sam 14:7, 12, 15, 17, 19; also 17:17. The feminine noun אָמָה is a close synonym and is also translated as "servant"; see the second textual note on 14:15.

וַיִּנָּצוּ—"They were fighting." This is the third masculine plural Niphal (N) preterite (imperfect with *waw* consecutive) of נָצָה. The Niphal indicates reciprocal action, i.e., they were fighting with each other. This verb is used in the Niphal for two people fighting against each other also in, e.g., Ex 2:13; Lev 24:10; Deut 25:11.

וְאֵין מַצִּיל בֵּינֵיהֶם—"There was no one to intervene" is literally "and there was no savior between them." The Hiphil (H) participle of נָצַל is used as a substantive and so is negated by אֵין rather than לֹא or אַל. See also the second textual note on 14:16.

וַיַּכּוֹ הָאֶחָד אֶת־הָאֶחָד—"The one struck the other" is literally "and he struck him—the one [struck] the (other) one." The third masculine singular object suffix on the verb וַיַּכּוֹ is proleptic and refers to the direct object אֶת־הָאֶחָד, "the (other) one." Such a redundant pronoun (more commonly retrospective than prospective, as here) is frequent in

---

[3]   Steinmann, *1 Samuel*, 44.

[4]   Steinmann, *1 Samuel*, 62.

[5]   Steinmann, *1 Samuel*, 51.

Hebrew but is redundant in English. It is omitted in translation by the LXX, the Syriac, the Targum, and the Vulgate.[6]

וַיָּמֶת אֹתוֹ:—"And he killed him." The verb is the Hiphil (H) third masculine singular preterite (imperfect with *waw* consecutive) of מוּת, "die," with a causative meaning, "put to death." Its Hiphil is indicated by the *seghol* (-ֶ-) as well as by its use with a direct object (אֹתוֹ). Contrast the corresponding Qal (G) form וַיָּמָת in the preceding verse (14:5). In this chapter, other Hiphil forms of מוּת appear in 14:7 (וּנְמִתֵהוּ), a first common plural imperfect with a conjunctive *waw* and a third masculine singular object suffix, literally "and we will put him to death") and 14:32 (וֶהֱמִתָנִי, a second masculine singular perfect with *waw* consecutive and a first common singular object suffix, literally "and you will put me to death").

14:7 תְּנִי—"Give [us]." This verb is the Qal (G) feminine singular imperative of נָתַן, "give." English usage requires supplying an indirect object, "(to) us."

אֶת־מַכֵּה אָחִיו—"The one who struck his brother." The Hiphil (H) masculine singular participle of נָכָה is joined to אָחִיו as an objective genitive, literally "(the) striker of his brother." The participle is normally pointed with *seghol*, מַכֶּה, and its bound/construct form is indicated by the *tsere* vowel (-ֵּ-).

וְנַשְׁמִידָה גַּם אֶת־הַיּוֹרֵשׁ—"We will also destroy the heir." The verb וְנַשְׁמִידָה is the Hiphil (H) cohortative of שָׁמַד, meaning "to annihilate, exterminate." This clause with its first person verb ends the woman's quotation of the speech of her clansmen.[7] The Hiphil third masculine plural imperfect of שָׁמַד is negated in 14:11 (וְלֹא יַשְׁמִידוּ, "and they will not obliterate"), and its Hiphil infinitive construct (with לְ) is used in 14:16 (לְהַשְׁמִיד, "who would destroy").

וְכִבּוּ—"They would extinguish." In the Qal (G), כָּבָה usually refers to extinguishing a literal fire. However, its Piel (D) is almost always used figuratively, as here, for the snuffing out of a person's life. The form is the Piel third common plural perfect with *waw* consecutive. This clause begins the woman's commentary on the plans of her clansmen. The volitive translation "they would/intend to extinguish" is appropriate for this context because it refers to an action that is planned but not yet accomplished.

גַּחַלְתִּי—"My ember." The feminine segholate noun גַּחֶלֶת literally refers to a burning "coal" or a smoldering "ember." Its figurative sense here is that the woman's family line could easily be extinguished, but if her one "ember" (son) is allowed to live, he may eventually ignite a blazing fire (be the progenitor of a large number of descendants).

אֲשֶׁר נִשְׁאָרָה—"Which remains." As pointed, נִשְׁאָרָה is the Niphal (N) third feminine singular perfect of שָׁאַר, "remain, be left (over)," in pause. Cf. the cognate noun שְׁאֵרִית, "remnant," later in this verse. (Note that the *aleph* in the penultimate syllable of נִשְׁאָרָה has *qamets* and is accented, -אָ-. If this perfect verb were not in pause, the *aleph* would have *chateph patach* and the accent would be on the final syllable, נִשְׁאֲרָה, as in Josh 13:1; Dan 10:17. If the verb were the Niphal feminine singular participle,

---

6 McCarter, *II Samuel*, 338.

7 ESV unnecessarily changes this first person verb to the third person, "and so they would destroy ... ," so that this clause begins the woman's own commentary on the intended actions of her clansmen.

the *aleph* would have *qamets*, but the accent would be on the final syllable, נִשְׁאָרָה, as in 2 Ki 19:30; Is 37:31.) Instead of נִשְׁאָרָה, 4QSamᶜ reads ה[שׁ]ארתי, which could be parsed either as the Hiphil (H) first common singular perfect (הִשְׁאַרְתִּי) or the Niphal (N) feminine singular participle with a first common singular suffix (נִשְׁאַרְתִּי). The Hiphil perfect could have a causative meaning, "which I have caused to remain," or an intransitive meaning, "which I have remaining." The Niphal feminine singular participle with the suffix would mean "my remaining [ember]."[8]

שִׂים—"To place." This Qere is the Qal (G) infinitive construct of שִׂים, which is sometimes spelled שׂום. The Kethib is שׂום, which is the Qal infinitive construct of the alternate spelling. See GKC, § 73 b.

14:9 עָלַי ... הֶעָוֹן—"Let the guilt lie with me" is literally "upon me ... (be) the iniquity." Note the emphatic fronted position of the prepositional phrase "upon me." The noun עָוֹן, literally "iniquity," recurs in 14:32. The context implies that this nominal sentence is an expression of the woman's desire or will as part of her petition to the king, so the translation supplies the optative verb "let ... lie."

וְהַמֶּלֶךְ וְכִסְאוֹ נָקִי:—"And let the king and his throne be innocent." This is another nominal sentence expressing her desire, and so again the translation supplies a verb, "let ... be." A singular adjective (נָקִי, "innocent") can modify a plural phrase that consists of closely related words ("the king and his throne"; cf. Joüon, § 148 d).

14:10 וְלֹא־יֹסִיף עוֹד לָגַעַת בָּךְ—"And he will not bother you again." In this construction the Hiphil (H) imperfect of יָסַף, "to do again," takes an infinitive construct (see Joüon, §§ 102 g, 124 c, 177 b). See the first textual note on 1 Sam 3:6.[9] The infinitive construct with the preposition לְ here, לָגַעַת, is the Qal (G) of נָגַע, "to touch," which can have the nuance of doing "harm" (BDB, Qal, 3). In the Qal, נָגַע regularly takes the preposition בְּ, as here (בָּךְ, "you").

14:11 יִזְכָּר־נָא הַמֶּלֶךְ אֶת־יְהוָה אֱלֹהֶיךָ—"Please, Your Majesty, invoke Yahweh your God." This is a request for David to use Yahweh's name in an oath. With the pronominal suffix on אֱלֹהֶיךָ, "*your* God," the woman emphasizes that David (in contrast to apostate Saul) continues to believe in Yahweh, the gracious God who saved Israel through the exodus redemption, and that, as king, he rules on behalf of Yahweh and so is bound to act mercifully. The verb יִזְכָּר is the third masculine singular Qal (G) jussive of זָכַר, "to remember." In the Hiphil (H), it commonly means to "invoke" God and his name, Yahweh. This seems to be the only instance in the OT where the Qal has that meaning (see BDB, Qal, I 3 a). For the vocative הַמֶּלֶךְ, "Your Majesty," see the fourth textual note on 14:4.

מֵהַרְבִּת גֹּאֵל הַדָּם לְשַׁחֵת—"So that the blood avenger will not destroy again" is literally "from the avenger of blood doing more to destroy." The participial phrase גֹּאֵל הַדָּם, "the redeemer of blood" or perhaps "the avenger of the [shed] blood," is a technical term in the legislation of the Torah for a relative of a murder victim who executes capital

---

[8] For the possible interpretations of the reading in 4QSamᶜ, see Cross et al., *Qumran Cave 4.XII*, 257.

[9] Steinmann, *1 Samuel*, 110.

punishment on the murderer.[10] The Hiphil (H) infinitive construct of רָבָה, "make many; do much" (here with the preposition מִן), is often used with another infinitive construct as its complement, specifying the action that is repeated or increased (see BDB, s.v. רָבָה, Hiphil, 1 d (1)). The spelling of its infinitive here is unique, whether one reads the Qere, הַרְבַּת, or the Kethib, הַרְבִית. Normally it is spelled הַרְבּוֹת. The second infinitive construct (with לְ), לְשַׁחֵת, is the Piel (D) of שָׁחַת, meaning "to destroy" or "kill" in either the Piel (D) stem (as here) or the Hiphil (H) stem. See the fourth textual note on 11:1.

חַי־יְהוָה אִם־יִפֹּל מִשַּׂעֲרַת בְּנֵךְ אָרְצָה:—"As Yahweh lives, not a hair of your son will fall to the ground." Israel's troops uttered almost the same oath regarding Jonathan in 1 Sam 14:45. See the second textual note on 1 Sam 14:45[11] and the first textual note on 2 Sam 2:27. In such an oath, the particle אִם, "if," is used as a negative, "not."

14:13 וְלָמָּה חָשַׁבְתָּה—"Why have you devised?" Occasionally the second masculine singular ending (suffix) of a perfect verb is written as תָה- instead of the usual orthography תָ- (GKC, § 44 g; Joüon, § 42 f). The verb חָשַׁב recurs in 14:14; see the second textual note on 14:14.

כָּזֹאת—"Something similar" is literally "[something] like this."

וּמִדַּבֵּר הַמֶּלֶךְ הַדָּבָר הַזֶּה כְּאָשֵׁם—"When the king spoke this way, he condemned himself." The verb מִדַּבֵּר can be parsed either as a Piel (D) infinitive construct with the prefixed preposition מִן, in which case a literal translation is "from the king speaking this word, [he is] like a guilty man," or a Hithpael (HtD) masculine singular participle (from מִתְדַּבֵּר with an assimilation of the *taw*) with a reciprocal meaning, literally "the king, speaking together [with another person] this word, [is] like a guilty man." The masculine singular adjective אָשֵׁם, "guilty," is used as a substantive. It is cognate to the noun אָשָׁם, "guilt offering," in 1 Sam 6:3, 4, 8, 17.

נִדְחוֹ:—"His own banished person." This is the masculine singular Niphal (N) participle of נָדַח, which in the Niphal means "be scattered, be driven away," with a third masculine singular pronominal suffix. The same participle but without a suffix, נִדָּח, is used at the end of 14:14.

14:14 הַנִּגָּרִים—"That is spilled." This is the masculine plural Niphal (N) participle of נָגַר, "to pour (out)." Other Niphal forms of it appear in Ps 77:3 (ET 77:2); Lam 3:49. Elsewhere in the OT it is used only in the Hiphil (H; five times) and the Hophal (Hp; once).

וְחָשַׁב מַחֲשָׁבוֹת—"He makes plans." This cognate accusative construction could be rendered literally as "and he thinks thoughts" or "and he devises devices."

לְבִלְתִּי יִדַּח מִמֶּנּוּ נִדָּח:—"So that a banished person will no longer be alienated from him." The combination לְבִלְתִּי introduces a negative purpose clause, "so that not/no." Usually לְבִלְתִּי is used to negate an infinitive construct; this is a rare example of its use with an imperfect (יִדַּח); see Joüon, § 160 l. The verb יִדַּח is a Niphal (N) third masculine singular imperfect from one of two by-forms, either דָּחַח or דָּחָה, both meaning "to

---

[10] See Num 35:9–34; Deut 19:4–13; see also Josh 20:1–9. Its only other use in the OT is here in 2 Sam 14:11.

[11] Steinmann, *1 Samuel*, 265.

push, drive away." The only other instance of דָּחַח in the OT is in Jer 23:12, whereas דָּחָה occurs elsewhere seven times in six verses. Both can have an eschatological sense of eternal separation from God, which is the fate of the wicked (Jer 23:12; Ps 36:13 [ET 36:12]; Prov 14:32), but Yahweh's help rescues the believer from that fate (Ps 118:13).

14:15 יֵרְאֻנִי הָעָם—"The people have frightened me." The noun עָם, "people," is singular but a collective, and so it can be the subject of a plural verb, as here. The verb יֵרְאֻנִי is the third masculine plural Piel (D) imperfect of יָרֵא, "be afraid," with a first common singular pronominal suffix. In the Piel, which occurs four other times in the OT (Neh 6:9, 14, 19; 2 Chr 32:18), it has a causative meaning, "to frighten." Here the LXX reads ὄψεταί με ὁ λαός, "the people will see me," and so its translators apparently supplied the unpointed verb יראני with the vocalization יִרְאֻנִי, the third masculine plural Qal (G) imperfect of רָאָה, "to see," with a first common singular suffix.

אוּלַי יַעֲשֶׂה הַמֶּלֶךְ אֶת־דְּבַר אֲמָתוֹ:—"Perhaps the king will do something for his servant" is literally "perhaps the king will do the word/matter of his servant." For the feminine noun אָמָה, "(female) servant," see the third and fourth textual notes on 1 Sam 1:11.[12] It recurs in 14:16 and is a close synonym of the feminine noun שִׁפְחָה, "slave girl" or female household "servant" (see the first textual note on 14:6).

14:16 כִּי—Here this conjunction is translated as an asseverative: "certainly."

לְהַצִּיל—"To save." This is the Hiphil (H) infinitive construct of נָצַל with the preposition לְ expressing purpose (from her point of view) and result (from the king's point of view). She appeals to him so that he will save her (purpose), and he acts in response to hearing her petition (result). The Hiphil of נָצַל, "save, deliver, rescue," refers to action by the king (as Yahweh's anointed) again in 19:10 (ET 19:9). It is often associated with Yahweh's redemption of his people from Egypt through the exodus; see the textual note on 1 Sam 10:18–19.[13] It refers to Yahweh's saving action also in 2 Sam 12:7; 22:1, 18, 49 (cf. 23:12).

לְהַשְׁמִיד—"Who would destroy." This is the Hiphil (H) infinitive construct of שָׁמַד, "destroy" (see the third textual note on 14:7), with the preposition לְ. Here the infinitive with לְ is used in a modal sense ("would") and does not require another verb that it complements.[14] However, based on the LXX (τοῦ ζητοῦντος ἐξᾶραί), some scholars propose adding the masculine singular Piel (D) participle with the article הַמְבַקֵּשׁ before this infinitive.[15] The clause would then be translated as "who is seeking to destroy."

14:17 יְהִיֶה־נָּא דְבַר־אֲדֹנִי הַמֶּלֶךְ לִמְנוּחָה—"May the word of my lord, Your Majesty, bring relief." In form יִהְיֶה is the Qal (G) imperfect of הָיָה, literally "it will be," rather than the jussive, יְהִי, "may/let it be" (see the fifth textual note on 14:17), but sometimes an imperfect is used with a jussive meaning (see Joüon, § 114 g, note 1). The noun

---

[12] Steinmann, *1 Samuel*, 48.

[13] Steinmann, *1 Samuel*, 200–201.

[14] Such modal uses of the infinitive construct with לְ tend to be found in poetry but are not exclusive to poetry. See Waltke-O'Connor, § 36.2.3f.

[15] McCarter, *II Samuel*, 339; Anderson, *2 Samuel*, 185. There also seems to be space in the lacunae in 4QSam^c for המבקש.

מְנוּחָה, "rest, peace," with the preposition לְ, literally "for rest," is translated together with the verb as "may it bring relief."

כְּמַלְאַךְ הָאֱלֹהִים—Three times in the book of Samuel, David is said to be "like" (כְּ) "an angel of God" (1 Sam 29:9)[16] or "the Angel of God" (2 Sam 14:17; 19:28 [ET 19:27]; see also 2 Sam 14:20).[17] Other than 2 Sam 14:17, 20; 19:28 (ET 19:27), the only other instances of this construct phrase with the definite article (מַלְאַךְ הָאֱלֹהִים) are in references to the theophanic Angel of Yahweh in Gen 31:11; Ex 14:19; Judg 6:20; 13:6, 9. The phrase is used without the article in Gen 21:17 also in reference to the Angel of Yahweh. Traditionally these appearances of the Angel of Yahweh have been interpreted as appearances of the preincarnate Christ, the Son of God. The comparison of David to him fits the prophetic emphasis on him as the Son of David. See the commentary on 2 Samuel 7, as well as the excursus following it, "הָאָדָם as 'the Man' in 2 Samuel 7:19 and 1 Chronicles 17:17."

לִשְׁמֹעַ—"To discern" is literally "to hear." At times the verb שָׁמַע in the Qal (G) can denote being able to hear and understand with insight (HALOT, Qal, 6).

הַטּוֹב וְהָרָע—"Good and evil" is literally "the good and the evil." The article is used with nouns that express abstract ideas (BDB, s.v. הַ, 1 h). The word טוֹב can be a noun or an adjective. The adjective רַע is used here as a substantive. See this pair of words without articles in, e.g., Gen 2:9, 17; 3:5, 22; 2 Sam 13:22; 19:36 (ET 19:35).

וַיהוָה אֱלֹהֶיךָ יְהִי עִמָּךְ:—"May Yahweh your God be with you!" The verb יְהִי is jussive in both form and meaning (cf. the first textual note on 14:17). Sometimes this expression, "may Yahweh (your God) be with you," occurs without an explicit verb (see the textual note on 7:3). When it occurs with a verb, it is unusual for the subject to precede the verb, as it does here (cf., e.g., Ex 10:10; 1 Sam 20:13; 1 Chr 22:11, 16). עִמָּךְ is pausal for עִמְּךָ, and so the suffix ךָ-, which appears to be feminine (second singular), is actually masculine (second singular).

14:18 אַל־נָא תְכַחֲדִי—"Please do not conceal." The negative אַל with an imperfect (תְכַחֲדִי, Piel [D] second feminine singular of כָּחַד) forms a command, but its force here is softened by the particle of entreaty נָא, "please."

14:19 הֲיַד יוֹאָב אִתָּךְ בְּכָל־זֹאת—"Did Joab put you up to all this?" This question with the interrogative he is literally "(was) the hand of Joab with you in all this?"

וַתַּעַן הָאִשָּׁה וַתֹּאמֶר—"The woman solemnly answered" is literally "and the woman answered and said." In the context of the following oath, the two verbs here combine to express a solemn declaration.

חֵי־נַפְשְׁךָ—"As you live." See the second textual note on 1 Sam 1:26.[18]

אִם־אִשׁ ׀ לְהֵמִין וּלְהַשְׂמִיל מִכֹּל אֲשֶׁר־דִּבֶּר—"There is no escaping what you have said" is literally "if there is going/there is no going to the right or to the left from all that you have said." The translation substitutes an equivalent English idiom for the Hebrew idiom. For the use of the particle אִם, "if," as a negative, "no/not," in an oath, see the

---

[16] See the textual note on 1 Sam 29:9 (Steinmann, *1 Samuel*, 544).

[17] In 2 Sam 14:20 David is said to be wise like the wisdom of the Angel of God (see the second textual note on 14:20).

[18] Steinmann, *1 Samuel*, 61.

third textual note on 14:11. The two verbs are Hiphil (H) infinitive constructs, each with לְ. The first, הֵמִין, is of the denominative verb יָמַן (GKC, § 70 c), which occurs only in the Hiphil and means "go to the right." The second, הַשְׂמִיל, is of the denominative verb שְׂמֹאל, which also occurs only in the Hiphil and means "go to the left." The word אֵשׁ is most likely a variant spelling of יֵשׁ, "there is/exists," which is the reading in a few Hebrew manuscripts and 4QSamᶜ (יש) and which is supported by the LXX (ἔστιν). This variant spelling is also used in Micah 6:10 (see BDB, s.v. אֵשׁ). It could also be a defective, or *ḥaser*, spelling of אִישׁ ("a *person* cannot go to the right …"), which is the reading in other Masoretic manuscripts.

וְהוּא שָׁם בְּפִי שִׁפְחָתְךָ אֵת כָּל־הַדְּבָרִים הָאֵלֶּה:—"He also put all these words in the mouth of your servant." See the second textual note on 14:3.

14:20 לְבַעֲבוּר סַבֵּב אֶת־פְּנֵי הַדָּבָר—"In order to portray the matter in a different light" is literally "for the purpose of turning the face of the matter/word." The translation substitutes an equivalent English idiom for the Hebrew idiom. The verb סַבֵּב is the Piel (D) infinitive construct of סָבַב, with a transitive meaning. Cf. its intransitive Qal (G) in the first textual note on 14:24.

וַאדֹנִי חָכָם כְּחָכְמַת מַלְאַךְ הָאֱלֹהִים—"My lord has wisdom like the wisdom of the Angel of God" is literally "and my lord (is) wise/a wise man like the wisdom of the Angel of God." The first two words are a nominal clause; the adjective חָכָם, "wise," may be used as a substantive, "a wise man" (see Joüon, § 154 d). This clause is translated with the verb "has" and חָכָם, "wise," is translated as "wisdom" in order to fit with the rest of the sentence. For "the Angel of God," see the second textual note on 14:17.

14:21 הִנֵּה־נָא עָשִׂיתִי אֶת־הַדָּבָר הַזֶּה—"I have made my decision" is literally "now behold, I have done this thing/word." A speaker with authority (God, or in this case, the king) can use a perfect verb (here עָשִׂיתִי) to refer to an action that he has decreed even if its accomplishment still lies in the future (GKC, § 106 m).

14:22 וַיִּפֹּל יוֹאָב אֶל־פָּנָיו אַרְצָה—"Joab fell facedown on the ground." See the second textual note on 14:4.

וַיִּשְׁתָּחוּ—"And he bowed." See the third textual note on 14:4.

וַיְבָרֶךְ—"He blessed." For the Piel (D) of בָּרַךְ, see the textual note on 2 Sam 6:11–12, as well as the first textual note on 1 Sam 2:20 and the third textual note on 1 Sam 9:13.[19]

עַבְדֶּךָ:—"Your servant." This form with a second masculine singular suffix is the reading of the Qere and 4QSamᶜ (עבדכה). It is the second occurrence of עַבְדְּךָ in the verse. The Kethib (עַבְדּוֹ) and the LXX (τοῦ δούλου αὐτοῦ) read "his servant." It is more formal to refer to the king in the third person when addressing him. It is also formal and customary for a supplicant to use the third person to refer to himself. Joab's use of the first person verb מָצָאתִי, "I have found," earlier in the verse presumes familiarity with the king.

14:24 יִסֹּב … וַיִּסֹּב—" 'Let him go. …' So he went" is literally " 'Let him turn. …' And he turned." The first form, translated as a jussive, could be either the Qal (G) imperfect

---

[19] Steinmann, *1 Samuel*, 90, 179.

or the Qal jussive third masculine singular of סָבַב. The second is its preterite (imperfect with *waw* consecutive).

וּפָנַי לֹא יִרְאֶה—"I will not grant him an audience" is literally "and my face he shall not see." The same Hebrew idiom with the Qal (G) of רָאָה, "to see," recurs later in this verse and also in 14:28, 32.

14:25 וּכְאַבְשָׁלוֹם לֹא־הָיָה אִישׁ־יָפֶה בְּכָל־יִשְׂרָאֵל לְהַלֵּל מְאֹד—The Hebrew word order emphasizes Absalom by placing his name first, literally "and as Absalom there was not a man handsome in all Israel to praise greatly." The Piel (D) infinitive construct (with לְ) לְהַלֵּל, "to praise," indicates the result of his good looks (cf. Joüon, § 124 l). Its implied subject may be the preceding proper noun יִשְׂרָאֵל, "... in all Israel, so that [Israel] praised him greatly," or it may be used impersonally with an indefinite subject (anyone, everyone), in which case the active verb can be translated as a passive, "so that he was praised." The masculine form of the adjective יָפֶה, "handsome, beautiful," was used for David in 1 Sam 16:12; 17:42. Its feminine form, יָפָה, "beautiful," describes Tamar in 2 Sam 13:1, as well as Abigail (1 Sam 25:3) and Absalom's daughter Tamar (2 Sam 14:27). For a discussion of such terminology in Samuel, see the commentary on 2 Sam 11:2.

לֹא־הָיָה בוֹ מוּם:—"He had no flaw" is literally "there was not in him a blemish." A "blemish" (מוּם) disqualified an Aaronide from serving as a priest (Lev 21:17–23) and an animal from being sacrificed to God (Lev 22:20–25; Deut 15:21; 17:1). Solomon will describe his bride in similar terms: "all of you is beautiful [יָפָה] ... , and a blemish [מוּם] is not in you" (Song 4:7). Cf. the description of the church as "holy and without blemish" (ἁγία καὶ ἄμωμος, Eph 5:27) because of the Sacrament of Baptism ("the washing of water with the Word," Eph 5:26).

14:26 וּבְגַלְּחוֹ—"When he shaved." This is the Piel (D) infinitive construct of גָּלַח, whose Piel means "shave," with the conjunction *waw* and a third masculine singular pronominal suffix that serves as the subject of the infinitive. The verb גָּלַח is used three times in this verse and previously in 10:4, all in the Piel (D). See further the commentary.

מִקֵּץ יָמִים ׀ לַיָּמִים—"At the end of every year" is literally "from the end of days to the days." This is a variation of the idiom for "annually," מִיָּמִים יָמִימָה (Ex 13:10; Judg 11:40; 21:19; 1 Sam 1:3; 2:19).

כִּי־כָבֵד עָלָיו—"Because it got heavy" is literally "because it was heavy on him." The word כָּבֵד could be the adjective כָּבֵד, "heavy" (so BDB, כָּבֵד adjective, 1 a), as in, e.g., 1 Sam 4:18,[20] in which case the clause here would be a nominal clause, "(it was) heavy." Or כָּבֵד could be the Qal (G) of the stative verb כָּבֵד, "be heavy," as in, e.g., 1 Sam 5:6, 11.

וְשָׁקַל אֶת־שְׂעַר רֹאשׁוֹ מָאתַיִם שְׁקָלִים—"He weighed the hair of his head as two hundred shekels." Two hundred shekels is equivalent to about five pounds (two kilograms). The Qal (G) of שָׁקַל has the transitive meaning "to weigh [something]" and takes two direct objects. The first direct object is the thing weighed, אֶת־שְׂעַר רֹאשׁוֹ, "the hair of his head," and the second is what it weighed, מָאתַיִם שְׁקָלִים, "two hundred shekels"

---

[20] See the third textual note on 1 Sam 4:18 (Steinmann, *1 Samuel*, 129).

(Joüon, § 125 v; cf. GKC, § 118 h). The verb שָׁקַל is cognate to the noun שֶׁקֶל, "shekel," used here as a measure of weight.

בְּאֶבֶן הַמֶּלֶךְ:—"According to the royal standard" is literally "with the stone of the king." Usually a balance or pair of scales was used for weighing. The item to be weighed was placed in one of the pans and enough stones or other weights were place in the other pan to balance it.

14:27   וַתְּהִי הָיְתָה אִשָּׁה יְפַת מַרְאֶה—"She was beautiful" is literally "she was a woman (who was) beautiful of appearance." For the adjective יָפֶה (feminine יָפָה, here in construct, יְפַת), "handsome, beautiful," see the first textual note on 14:25. The same construct phrase with the feminine adjective, יְפַת מַרְאֶה, "beautiful of appearance," is used elsewhere in the OT only for Sarah (Gen 12:11) and Rachel (Gen 29:17) as attractive women. This construct phrase but with the masculine form of the adjective (יְפֵה מַרְאֶה) is used to refer only to Joseph in Gen 39:6 and to David in 1 Sam 17:42.

14:28   שְׁנָתַיִם יָמִים—"Two years." See the textual note on 13:23.

14:29   לִשְׁלֹחַ אֹתוֹ—"That he [Joab] might send him [Absalom]" is literally "to send him." The Qal (G) infinitive construct of שָׁלַח with לְ expresses the purpose of Absalom's request to Joab.

וְלֹא אָבָה לָבוֹא ... וְלֹא אָבָה לָבוֹא:—"But he did not wish to come. … But he did not wish to come." For the Qal (G) verb אָבָה, "be willing," with an infinitive construct (with לְ) as a complement to specify the action the person is (or is not) willing to do, see the first textual note on 13:14.

14:30   חֶלְקַת יוֹאָב אֶל־יָדִי—"Joab has a plot of land next to mine" is literally "a plot of Joab (is) to my hand."

וְלוֹ־שָׁם שְׂעֹרִים—"And he has barley there." The suffixed preposition לוֹ indicates possession. שְׂעֹרִים is the plural of the feminine noun שְׂעֹרָה, "barley," to be distinguished from the nouns שַׂעֲרָה in 14:11 and שֵׂעָר in 14:26, both meaning "hair."

וְהַצִּיתוּהָ בָאֵשׁ—"And set it on fire" is literally "and ignite it with the fire." The Qere וְהַצִּיתוּהָ, which agrees with the reading in 4QSamᶜ (ו[]הציתוה) and the LXX (καὶ ἐμπρήσατε αὐτήν), is the Hiphil (H) masculine plural imperative of יָצַת, "kindle," with the conjunction *waw* and a third feminine singular object suffix, referring back to the feminine noun חֶלְקָה, "a plot." This reading is also supported by the statement at the end of the verse in the MT: וַיַּצִּתוּ עַבְדֵי אַבְשָׁלוֹם אֶת־הַחֶלְקָה בָּאֵשׁ, "so Absalom's servants set the plot of land on fire."

In forms of the verb יָצַת, the first consonant, *yod*, is regularly assimilated into the second consonant, the sibilant *tsade*, and is marked by the daghesh in the *tsade* (-צַּ-; see GKC, § 71). The Kethib, והוצתיה, probably is to be vocalized as וְהוֹצַתִּיהָ, the first common singular Hiphil perfect of יָצַת with *waw* consecutive and a third feminine singular object suffix, "and I will ignite it." Its form would suggest that the verb's first consonant, *yod*, was originally *waw* and that the *waw* reappears in this form (-וֹ-), and so the *yod* is not assimilated.

The translation includes the following sentence at the end of 4:30: "Joab's young men came to him with their clothes torn and said, 'Absalom's servants have set your plot of land on fire.' " This sentence is restored from 4QSam^c, the LXX, and the Old Latin. 4QSam^c reads:

[וַיּבאו י]לדי יואב אלו קרועי בנגדיהם ויאומרו הציתו עב[די אבשלום
אתן ה]חלקה באש

In this sentence the construct phrase קרועי בנ[גדיהם] is to be vocalized as קְרוּעֵי־בְגְדֵיהֶם, literally "torn with respect to their garments," which is comparable to the construct phrase קְרֻעֵי בְגָדִים, discussed in the third textual note on 13:31. The verb הציתו is to be vocalized as הִצִּיתוּ ("they burned," the third common plural Hiphil perfect of יָצַת), the same form that is in 14:31.

The LXX reads:

καὶ παραγίνονται οἱ δοῦλοι Ιωαβ πρὸς αὐτὸν διερρηχότες τὰ ἱμάτια αὐτῶν καὶ εἶπαν ἐνεπύρισαν οἱ δοῦλοι Αβεσσαλωμ τὴν μερίδα ἐν πυρί.

In the MT this text apparently was lost by homoioteleuton when a scribe's eye skipped from בָּאֵשׁ ("with the fire") at the end of MT 14:30 to the same word, בָּאֵשׁ, at the end of this additional sentence.

14:31 אֶל־אַבְשָׁלוֹם הַבָּיְתָה—"To Absalom's house" is literally "to Absalom, toward the house."

לָמָה הִצִּיתוּ עֲבָדֶךָ ... בָּאֵשׁ—"Why have your servants set ... on fire?" 4QSam^c has the singular of the noun עֶבֶד with an alternate spelling of the second masculine singular suffix, עבדכה, "your servant." Codex Leningradensis reads עֲבָדֶךָ, which is a defective, or *haser*, spelling of the suffixed plural, "your servants."[21] The plene, or *male'*, spelling would be עֲבָדֶיךָ, which is the reading in many Masoretic manuscripts and which is supported by the LXX (οἱ παῖδές σου). Since the verb הִצִּיתוּ is plural (the third common Hiphil perfect of יָצַת), its subject ought to be plural.

הַחֶלְקָה אֲשֶׁר־לִי—"My plot of land." In the Hebrew, Joab's ownership of the land is emphasized by these three words, including the relative clause (beginning with אֲשֶׁר) with the preposition לְ in the sense of possession, literally "the plot which is to me/mine." The idea could have been expressed more concisely by one word, the suffixed noun חֶלְקָתִי, "my plot," as in Jer 12:10. Cf. Joüon, § 130 e.

14:32 וְאֶשְׁלְחָה—The volitive force of this cohortative (Qal [G] singular of שָׁלַח) is expressed by "I *want* to send."

טוֹב לִי עֹד אֲנִי־שָׁם—This nominal expression with the adjective טוֹב, "good," is literally "good for me [if] still I (were) there." In context it has a comparative force: "it would have been *better* for me [if] I were still there" (Joüon, §§ 141 g; 157 a).

וְעַתָּה אֶרְאֶה פְּנֵי הַמֶּלֶךְ—"Now let me have a royal audience" is literally "and now I will see the face of the king." For this idiom, see the second textual note on 14:24. The imperfect (אֶרְאֶה) can have the volitive force of a request or even a demand ("let me …").

וְאִם־יֶשׁ־בִּי עָוֹן—"And if I am guilty" is literally "and if there is in me iniquity."

---

[21] If the consonants in Codex Leningradensis were not already pointed, עבדך could be vocalized as singular, עַבְדְּךָ.

וַהֲמִתֻנִי:—"Then he should put me to death." For the modal force of this perfect with *waw* consecutive verb, see Joüon, § 119 w.

14:33 וַיִּשְׁתַּחוּ—"And he bowed down." See the third textual note on 14:4.

עַל־אַפָּיו אָרְצָה—"With his face on the ground." See the second textual note on 14:4.

וַיִּשַּׁק—"Then he kissed." This is the Qal (G) third masculine singular preterite (imperfect with *waw* consecutive) of נָשַׁק. Here the king kisses his son, who is also a subject under him in his kingdom, to signify forgiveness and acceptance. Elsewhere this Hebrew verb is used in 2 Sam 19:40 (ET 19:39) when King David kisses his subject Barzillai for being loyal to him. In 2 Sam 15:5, where Absalom conspires to usurp the throne of King David, he will kiss those who pay homage to him as if he were king. The prophet Samuel had kissed Saul when anointing him as Israel's first king (1 Sam 10:1). David (Saul's son-in-law) and Jonathan (Saul's son) kissed upon departing after establishing their mutual covenant with Yahweh (1 Sam 20:41). Compare a son kissing his father and/or mother in Gen 27:26–27; 50:1; 1 Ki 19:20; a father kissing his nephew and future son-in-law in Gen 29:13; a father kissing his daughters and/or grandchildren in Gen 32:1 (ET 31:55); 48:10; a brother kissing his brother(s) in Gen 33:4; 45:15; Ex 4:27; a husband kissing his wife in Gen 29:11 (cf. Song 1:2; 8:1); and someone kissing another family member in Ex 18:7; Ruth 1:9, 14. "Kissing" (נָשַׁק) refers to an act of worshiping a false god in 1 Ki 19:18; Hos 13:2. In contrast, in Ps 2:12 rulers are exhorted to "kiss the Son" (the Messiah [Ps 2:6–7]) in worship lest they perish under his wrath. Contrast the feigned kiss of betrayal into death in 2 Sam 20:9 and Judas' betrayal of Jesus with a kiss (Mt 26:48–49; Lk 22:47–48).

Commentary

This narrative of the stepwise restoration of Absalom to Jerusalem and to royal approval serves as an immediate prelude to Absalom's rebellion (2 Samuel 15–19). Since it is Joab who initiated the action that resulted in Absalom's return from exile, it is tempting to hold him culpable for Absalom's subsequent attempt to usurp David's throne. In this view Joab was simply a troublesome meddler in royal affairs. However, there are factors that weigh against this.[22] No matter what his faults were, Joab was always loyal to David, as evidenced by his concern that David receive the honor for capturing Rabbah (12:27–28) and, in this chapter, his reticence to obtain an audience with David for Absalom (14:29). Rather, the action he undertook to move David to bring Absalom back to Jerusalem was prompted by David's preoccupation with Absalom (see the textual note on 14:1). Moreover, Joab had nothing to gain from Absalom's return and eventually suffered loss because of it (14:30–31). The blame for the insurrection lies with David himself, as Eschelbach notes:

> David failed to protect the safety of Tamar, failed to administer justice against Amnon, and failed to deal with Absalom, either for punishment or reconciliation [2 Samuel 13]. If anything predisposed Absalom's rebellion it was David's disposition to him, not the fact that Joab effected his return. In comparison

---

[22] See Eschelbach, *Has Joab Foiled David?* 70.

to Joab, the complexity of David's human character makes trouble for the kingdom, both actively and passively. Sometimes, David's character drives him to *do what is wrong* [e.g., 2 Samuel 11]. At other times, as in this case, David demonstrates that his emotions and feelings cause a paralysis that makes things go wrong because *he will not do what is right.*[23]

David's inaction in the face of injustice (2 Samuel 13) endangered the stability of God's kingdom. The king's vocation was to administer justice on behalf of Israel's God,[24] so much so that he was "like the Angel of God" (see the second textual note on 14:17). His failure to do so also left open the question of who would succeed him on the throne. Would Absalom come back from exile to claim the throne upon David's death? As the king's oldest living heir he could have asserted a strong claim on the crown. David had "thought about" Absalom for three years without determining a course of action (14:1).

Wise leaders need to know the difference between making a beneficial decision not to take action and the inability to be decisive, which leads to deleterious dithering. When authorities are paralyzed—whether by circumstance, the fear of making a bad move, or the inability to discern between good and evil (cf. 14:17)—the result is often that unfolding events or actions by their subordinates (or insubordinates) will make the decision for them. Since David did not punish the malefactors and deal with their sins (perhaps because of nagging guilt over his own behavior), he left God's people vulnerable in an unstable and iniquitous environment.

Before proceeding to the actual narrative, it ought to be noted that critical scholars often hold that 14:15–17 has been displaced from its original spot, which they suppose was after 14:7.[25] Under their view of the woman's words to David, she must have discussed her fictitious case completely before challenging David's inaction concerning Absalom (14:13–14). This solves what they perceive to be a number of exegetical problems with her presentation to David. Such scholars claim that she revealed the fictitious nature of her case when she challenged David in 14:13–14 and that after doing so she would no longer have been able to maintain her masquerade, as she does in 14:15–17.

There are several problems with this theory however. The strongest argument against this proposal is that it is completely without textual evidence. No ancient version places 14:15–17 after 14:7 or has it in any other location. In addition, we ought to note both the similarity and differences between the woman's fictional appeal to the king and two other similar fabricated appeals to regents: those of Nathan to David (2 Sam 12:1–4) and an unnamed prophet to

---

[23] Eschelbach, *Has Joab Foiled David?* 70.

[24] See 2 Sam 7:10 and the description of the messianic kingdom and King in 2 Samuel 7; see also, e.g., Is 9:5–6 (ET 9:6–7); 11:1–5.

[25] McCarter, *II Samuel*, 345–46; Anderson, *2 Samuel*, 185; Ackroyd, *The Second Book of Samuel*, 128.

King Ahab (1 Ki 20:35–43). In all three cases the person presenting the appeal prompted a judicial ruling. In all three cases after the king had ruled, the applicability of the case to a royal transgression was revealed. In the cases in 2 Samuel 12 and 1 Kings 20, the unreal case was dropped. Here the woman attempted to maintain the fiction before the king in 14:15–17. Why did she do that? Note that in the two other cases, the kings clearly recognized that the presenters were prophets (2 Sam 7:2; 12:25; 1 Ki 20:41). Their status afforded them a measure of protection from the wrath of the king whom they had deceived. However, the woman from Tekoa had no such security. Thus, she had to maintain the fiction and hope that either the king would accept her case as genuine or not challenge it even if he suspected it to be illusory. In this case, David came to suspect that her appeal was based on a fabrication, but he also intuited that Joab was the culprit behind it (14:19). It was ultimately Joab's status that protected the woman. Therefore, we may conclude that 14:15–17 has not been displaced from earlier in the chapter. Instead, this passage is designed to be in its present location as a significant element in the woman's strategy during her audience with David.

Joab Succeeds in Bringing Absalom Back to Jerusalem (14:1–23)

980 BC[26]

The author begins this story with a notice about Joab's knowledge. He noticed that the king seemed to be thinking about the situation with Absalom but never arriving at a course of action concerning him (14:1). When either Abishai or Joab is first introduced into a narrative, he is often identified as the son of David's sister Zeruiah, as is Joab here.[27]

Joab decided that he needed to take action to break David's internal stalemate. He must have had some acquaintance with a wise woman who lived in Tekoa, since it appears that he sent and specifically requested her to come to Jerusalem (14:2). Tekoa was a city in Judah about ten miles (sixteen kilometers) south of Jerusalem at the modern site known as Khirbet Tequʿ. Joab gave her specific instructions as to how to present herself to David and told her exactly what to say (14:2–3). Thus, the plan was Joab's, and the woman was simply an actor recruited to play a role.

The woman's initial conversation with David is reported in 14:4–11. Bergen notes that the tale the woman presents contains parallels to the story of Cain's murder of Abel:[28]

---

[26] See "The Chronology of David's Reign" in the commentary on 5:1–5.

[27] 1 Sam 26:6; 2 Sam 2:13; 8:16; 16:9; 18:2; 19:22 (ET 19:21); 21:17; 23:18.

[28] Adapted from Bergen, *1, 2 Samuel*, 390.

	Cain and Abel	Joab's Parable
Two brothers were alone together in the countryside.	Gen 4:8	2 Sam 14:6
One killed the other.	Gen 4:8	2 Sam 14:6
Someone in authority needed to intervene to protect the murderer from vengeance.	Gen 4:13–15	2 Sam 14:7–8
There was a threat of retaliation if someone should kill the murderer.	Gen 4:15	2 Sam 14:10

Bergen notes:

> The parallels suggest that Joab deliberately crafted the tale in order to compel David to render the same verdict that the Lord issued in Cain's behalf. …
>
> Implicit in Joab's use of this parallel is the assumption that David had a masterful knowledge of the Torah, and that Joab—like Nathan before him (cf. 12:6)—counted on the king using it as an authoritative guide in formulating his legal decisions.[29]

Upon hearing about the woman's plight, David promised to issue a command on her behalf (14:8). While David's words may seem cryptic to a modern reader, they are indeed a promise to protect her son from the clan. She replied with an interesting prayer or allowance that "the guilt" (הֶעָוֺן; see the first textual note on 14:9) should be hers and that the king should be held innocent in the matter (14:9). Some interpreters suggest that this was actually a plea for mercy.[30] There is a close parallel in Abigail's words to David in 1 Sam 25:24, after which Abigail pleaded that David not destroy her household (1 Sam 25:25–31). Based on that, it is probably best to understand the woman as begging for protection for her son and holding David guiltless if any accusation of injustice were leveled at the throne. David appears to have understood this and promised such protection (14:10).

Perhaps to add verisimilitude to her desperate plight, she begged David to take an oath invoking Yahweh by name to keep an avenger of blood from killing her son (14:11).[31] David complied with an oath calling upon the covenant name of Israel's redeeming God ("as Yahweh lives") that not a single hair on her son's head would fall to the ground (14:11). This was the ultimate promise of protection, similar in wording and theology to the oath pledged by Israel's army to Jonathan when Saul would have had him executed (1 Sam 14:45).

---

[29] Bergen, *1, 2 Samuel*, 390.

[30] Hoftijzer, "David and the Tekoite Woman," 424–27. Her plea may be a fuller version of the simple plea בִּי אֲדֹנִי, literally "in me, my lord/Lord" (Gen 43:20; 44:18; Num 12:11; Judg 6:13; 1 Sam 1:26; 1 Ki 3:17, 26), or בִּי אֲדֹנִי, "in me, O Lord" (Ex 4:10, 13; Josh 7:8; Judg 6:15; 13:8). However, most regard בִּי in these contexts to be a particle of entreaty (so BDB, s.v. בִּי) rather than the suffixed preposition בְּ, "in."

[31] See the first and second textual notes on 14:11.

With David's decree in place, the audience with the king ought to have been concluded. However, the woman pressed on, asking for permission to tell David something else (2 Sam 14:12). She then proceeded to accuse David of devising something similar against God's people (14:13). That is, just as she was in danger of having her burning ember extinguished, which would have deprived her husband from leaving his name and a remnant in the promised land (14:7), the people of Israel were in danger of having their lamp—the line of the Messiah (7:11–16; cf. 1 Sam 2:10, 35)—extinguished by David's failing to resolve the issue with Absalom. Should Absalom attempt to succeed to the throne, this could lead to further fratricide and the possible end to David's "house" or "dynasty," which God had promised to build to last forever (7:11, 16, 19, 25–27). Nothing less than God's promise of the Savior was at stake. However, if David brought Absalom back, he could eventually resolve the matter. David had established a judicial precedent with his ruling for the woman (14:8, 10, 11), and he ought to follow that precedent in preserving an even more important "ember" (14:7), the "lamp" of David,[32] who would be "the light to the nations" (Is 42:6; 49:6; cf. Is 60:3; Rev 21:24), "the light of the world" (Jn 8:12; 9:5). After all, as the woman noted, "we are [all] certainly going to die and be like water that is spilled on the ground" (2 Sam 14:14)—and that included David. He must resolve the issue before he too would die. Moreover, she also noted that God would not remove a life—such as Absalom, who had murdered Amnon, or more pointedly, such as David, who had murdered Uriah—without preparing a way for that life no longer to be alienated from him. David ought to have mercy on Absalom just as God had mercy on him. Adam and Eve were banished from God's presence because of their fall into sin, and the way back to him was blocked (Gen 3:23–24). In the fullness of time God carried out his plan to reconcile us to himself, even while we were still his enemies (Rom 5:6–11), through the new Adam (Rom 5:12–17). Our reconciliation to him and to one another is entirely his doing and has been accomplished through the Son of David (2 Cor 5:18–21).

The woman then returned to her tale and revealed to David the thoughts she claimed to have had while preparing for her audience with the king (2 Sam 14:15–17). She magnanimously trusted that David would be a merciful king who would understand her alarm at the prospect of losing God's inheritance. She compared David to "the Angel of God" in his ability to discern what is good and what is evil (see the second textual note on 14:17).

By this time David had begun to suspect her story, as is obvious from their next exchange (14:18–20). When confronted, the woman admitted there was no use denying Joab's involvement, and so she confessed everything (14:18–19). She also demonstrated why she was regarded as "wise" (14:2). She quickly

---

[32] 1 Ki 11:36; 15:4; 2 Ki 8:19; Ps 132:17; 2 Chr 21:7.

formulated an explanation for Joab's scheme: it was to help portray the matter in a different light (14:20). In this way she was able to reveal Joab's plot while describing his actions in the most defensible way. She realized that it would do her no good simply to shift the blame to Joab; she needed him as her patron. At the same time, she once again sought to placate David by comparing him to "the Angel of God" (14:20, as in 14:17), which was a proper recognition of his divine office (see the second textual note on 14:17).

David immediately spoke to Joab in person and gave him permission to bring Absalom back from exile (14:21). Since the precedent had been set by his ruling on the woman's fictitious story, he used it as a template for his verdict to allow his eldest surviving son to receive mercy despite the murder he had committed.

When not on a campaign, Joab, as the commander of Israel's army, would have normally been at the royal court when the king held audiences and conducted other business. Like the woman, Joab knew when to show humility before the king (14:22). Joab then carried out David's decision (14:23).

Absalom in Jerusalem (14:24–27)

980 BC[33]

When Joab arrived in Jerusalem with Absalom, the king refused to grant his son an audience (14:24), which may have been tantamount to receiving him back into the royal court. By this refusal David denied him a claim on the throne. This son could again live in the royal city, but his actions cost him his standing as David's heir.

Despite his loss of favor in the royal palace, Absalom retained a measure of esteem in public because of his good looks (14:25). The author's seeming digression about Absalom's hair uses the Piel of the verb גָּלַח, "shave," three times (14:26). While David's emissaries to Hanun were shamed by someone "shaving" them (the Piel of גָּלַח, 10:4), Absalom seems to have taken pride in having to shave his head of heavy hair every year. It weighed about five pounds (two kilograms). It was Absalom's head, in which he took such pride, that was his ultimate undoing when it was caught in a tree, making him easy prey for Joab (18:9, 14–15).

We are also told about Absalom's three sons and one daughter (14:27). He apparently named his beautiful daughter after his lovely sister Tamar (cf. 13:1). His sons must have died early—perhaps succumbing to childhood diseases that ravaged so many children before modern medicine could offer preventions and cures. We are told that at a later time Absalom had no sons, which prompted him to set up a monument to preserve his memory (18:18).

---

[33] See "The Chronology of David's Reign" in the commentary on 5:1–5.

Absalom Forces Joab to Obtain an Audience for Him with the King (14:28–33)

978 BC[34]

Absalom was not content with simply being allowed to live in Jerusalem without readmission to the royal court and reinstatement to a claim as David's successor. After two years he decided that Joab, who had engineered his return from Geshur, was the appropriate person to use in order to change his status (14:28–29). However, Joab's loyalty lay with David, not Absalom, so he twice refused to even consult with David's estranged son.

Desperate to obtain a measure of public recognition from David, Absalom decided to force Joab to come to him by burning a nearby field owned by the head of Israel's army (14:30). This brought Joab to confront Absalom (14:31), but he also found himself in a rather uncomfortable position. Joab could hardly ask the king for relief from Absalom's action, since he had manipulated David into bringing the murderous son back from exile. Surely David would have pointed out that Joab had to live with the consequences of his actions.

When confronted, Absalom told Joab to obtain for him an audience with David (14:32). Absalom's request included his argument to David that he ought to be granted a meeting with the king: He would have been better off in Geshur. There he could have at least maintained a position in the royal court of his maternal grandfather. If David wished to execute his son for avenging Amnon's rape of Tamar (2 Samuel 13), then he ought to find him guilty of murder and have him executed. However, Absalom may have been implying that David could not find him guilty without also indicting himself as culpable in the entire affair, since he had failed to discipline Amnon (2 Samuel 13). Absalom might also have been insinuating David's comparable guilt for his own sexual sin with Bathsheba and his murder of her husband (2 Samuel 11).

Absalom thus obtained his royal audience, showing himself properly subservient to the king (14:33). David's kiss was an affectionate greeting that acknowledged Absalom.[35] In the public setting of the palace's throne room, it signaled to all of David's courtiers that Absalom was once again restored to the good graces of the throne and as a full member of the king's family.

---

[34] See "The Chronology of David's Reign" in the commentary on 5:1–5.

[35] See the third textual note on 14:33.

Absalom Conspires against David

Translation

15 ¹After this Absalom obtained for himself a chariot and horses and fifty men running ahead of him. ²Absalom would get up early and stand beside the road through the city gate. Whenever any man who had a grievance to bring to the king to adjudicate [came], Absalom would call out to him, "From which city are you?"

He would reply, "Your servant is from one of the tribes of Israel."

³Absalom would say to him, "See, your case is good and correct, but the king has not provided someone to hear it for you." ⁴Then Absalom would say, "Who might appoint me judge in the land? Then any man who had a grievance or a judicial case would come to me, and I would justify him!" ⁵Whenever a man approached in order to bow down to him, Absalom would reach out, take hold of him, and kiss him. ⁶Absalom did this type of thing for all Israelites who would come to the king for justice. So Absalom stole the loyalty of the men of Israel.

⁷At the end of four years Absalom said to the king, "I would like to go to pay the vow at Hebron that I made to Yahweh, ⁸since your servant made a vow when I was living in Geshur in Aram: 'If Yahweh indeed brings me back to Jerusalem, I will worship Yahweh.'"

⁹The king said, "Go in peace." So he went to Hebron.

¹⁰Absalom had sent agents throughout all the tribes of Israel instructing them, "When you hear the sound of the ram's horn, you will say, 'Absalom has become king in Hebron!'" ¹¹Two hundred men went with Absalom from Jerusalem. They had been invited and went innocently. They did not know the entire situation. ¹²While he was offering sacrifices, Absalom sent [for] David's advisor Ahithophel the Gilonite [to come] from his city Giloh. The conspiracy grew stronger, and the people supporting Absalom kept increasing.

Textual Notes

15:1 וַיְהִי֙ מֵאַחֲרֵי כֵ֔ן—"After this" is literally "and it came to pass from after thus." This construction (see GKC, § 111 g) is unusual because it includes the preposition מִן, "from." 4QSamᶜ has the corresponding construction without it, ויהי אחרי כן (to be vocalized וַיְהִ֣י אַחֲרֵי כֵ֔ן), which is common in Samuel and appears elsewhere in the OT.[1]

וַיַּ֩עַשׂ ל֨וֹ—"He obtained for himself" is literally "and he made for himself." The verb is the preterite (imperfect with *waw* consecutive) of עָשָׂה.

15:2 וְהִשְׁכִּים֙ אַבְשָׁל֔וֹם וְעָמַ֗ד—"Absalom would get up early and stand." After a preterite (imperfect with *waw* consecutive), וַיַּ֫עַשׂ in 15:1 (see the preceding textual note), the

---

[1] Judg 16:4; 1 Sam 24:6 (ET 24:5); 2 Sam 2:1; 8:1; 10:1; 13:1; 21:18; 2 Ki 6:24; 1 Chr 18:1; 19:1.

two perfect verbs here (the Hiphil [H] of שָׁכַם and the Qal [G] of עָמַד), each with *waw* consecutive, express habitual or frequentative action in the past ("would …"; see Joüon, § 119 v). So do the preterite (imperfect with *waw* consecutive) verbs later in the verse, וַיֹּאמֶר … וַיִּקְרָא (cf. Joüon, § 118 n), as well as verbs in 15:3–6.

עַל־יַד דֶּרֶךְ הַשַּׁעַר—"Beside the road through the city gate" is literally "at the hand of the way of the city gate." 4QSamᵃ omits the noun with the article, הַשַּׁעַר, "the city gate."

לָבוֹא אֶל־הַמֶּלֶךְ לַמִּשְׁפָּט—"To bring to the king to adjudicate" is literally "to come to the king for the justice." The implied subject of the Qal (G) infinitive construct (with לְ) לָבוֹא, "to come," is "any man" (כָּל־הָאִישׁ) who had a "grievance" (רִיב). Here and in 15:6, the noun מִשְׁפָּט, "judgment, justice," refers to "justice" meted out by the king. See 8:15, where King David administered "justice and righteousness" (מִשְׁפָּט וּצְדָקָה), and the verb from which it is derived, שָׁפַט, "to judge, carry out justice," in, e.g., 1 Sam 4:18; 7:15–17; 8:5–6. The contexts of 2 Sam 15:2, 6 imply that the people who brought their cases to the king anticipated that he would rule in their favor and condemn their antagonists.

15:3 דְּבָרֶךָ טוֹבִים וּנְכֹחִים—"Your case is good and correct" is literally "your words are good and right." In Codex Leningradensis the suffixed masculine plural noun דְּבָרֶךָ, "your words," is written defectively, without *yod*. Many Masoretic manuscripts have the usual plene, or *male᾿*, spelling, דְּבָרֶיךָ.

וְשֹׁמֵעַ אֵין־לְךָ מֵאֵת הַמֶּלֶךְ:—"But the king has not provided someone to hear it for you" is literally "but a listening person is not for you from with the king."

15:4 מִי־יְשִׂמֵנִי שֹׁפֵט בָּאָרֶץ—"Who might appoint me [to be the] judge in the land?" A rhetorical question with the interrogative pronoun מִי, "who?" and an imperfect verb (here יְשִׂמֵנִי) often expresses a wish, desire, or aspiration, i.e., "I wish people would appoint me to be the judge of the land!" See GKC, § 151 a 1; Joüon, § 163 d; Waltke-O'Connor, § 18.2f, including example 35.

וְעָלַי יָבוֹא כָל־אִישׁ—"Then any man … would come to me." The prepositional phrase וְעָלַי is placed first for emphasis, literally "and *to me* would come any man."

אֲשֶׁר־יִהְיֶה־לּוֹ־רִיב וּמִשְׁפָּט—"Who had a grievance or a judicial case." In 15:2, 6 the noun מִשְׁפָּט refers to "justice" adjudicated by the king (see the third textual note on 15:2). Here, however, it refers to "a judicial case" that would be brought to the judge to be adjudicated.

וְהִצְדַּקְתִּיו:—"And I would justify him!" Absalom promises to judge every person who comes to him to be in the right and the opponent to be in the wrong. Of course, Absalom would not be able to fulfill this promise if two opposing parties both bring their cases before him. This perfect verb with *waw* consecutive expresses what he (claims he) "would" do if his preceding wish were fulfilled (see GKC, § 112 p). The Hiphil (H) of צָדֵק, "be righteous," is used forensically for "justifying" a person, that is, declaring him to be righteous (in common legal parlance, to pronounce him innocent or right). In a legal dispute, the person who wins the case is justified. See the Hiphil of צָדֵק in Deut 25:1; 1 Ki 8:32; Is 50:8; Ps 82:3; with the Messiah as subject, Is 53:11; unjustly in Is 5:23; Prov 17:15; and negated in Ex 23:7. The judge condemns the opposing party with the Hiphil of רָשַׁע, "declare [someone] to be wicked" (e.g., Ex 22:8 [ET 22:9];

Is 50:9; Ps 37:33). Both of these verbs are used with their corresponding adjectives in Deut 25:1; 1 Ki 8:32, literally "to declare the righteous to be righteous" and "to declare the wicked to be wicked."

15:5 לְהִשְׁתַּחֲוֺת לוֹ—"In order to bow down to him." The verb is the Hishtaphel infinitive construct of חָוָה, "to bow down, worship." See the third textual note on 1 Sam 1:3,[2] which has this same infinitive construct with the preposition לְ. In both passages it expresses purpose (*IBH*, § 29 H).

וְנָשַׁק לוֹ:—"And he would kiss him." See the third textual note on 14:33.

15:6 כַּדָּבָר הַזֶּה—"This type of thing" is literally "like this word/matter."

לְכָל־יִשְׂרָאֵל אֲשֶׁר־יָבֹאוּ—"For all Israelites who would come." The translation with the plural "Israelites" smooths the grammar. The prepositional phrase לְכָל־יִשְׂרָאֵל is literally "for all *Israel*," but the verb יָבֹאוּ in the following relative clause is plural, literally "who *they* would come."

וַיְגַנֵּב ... אֶת־לֵב אַנְשֵׁי יִשְׂרָאֵל:—"So he stole the loyalty of the men of Israel" is literally "and he stole the heart of the men of Israel." This connotes deception; see Gen 31:20 and the commentary below. At times לֵב, "heart," denotes an inclination or disposition (see *HALOT*, 4; *CDCH*, 1 a). It signifies "loyalty" again in 15:13. The verb גָּנַב is commonly used in the Qal (G) with a literal meaning, "to steal" something, as in the Seventh Commandment (Ex 20:15; Deut 5:19) and in 2 Sam 21:12; similarly, 19:42 (ET 19:41). Its Piel (D) appears only twice in the OT (here and in Jer 23:30) and has a metaphorical meaning, "to steal [something] away," that is, to alienate something from the person who rightfully claims it, in this case, from King David (in Jer 23:30, from God). Its Hithpael (HtD) will be used twice in 2 Sam 19:4 (ET 19:3) meaning "to steal into" a place, that is to enter stealthily, not wanting to be detected (see the textual note on it there).

15:7 אַרְבָּעִים שָׁנָה—This reading in the MT is "forty years," which is supported by the LXX (τεσσαράκοντα ἐτῶν). However, David reigned for a total of "forty years" (5:4), beginning in 1009 BC, and Absalom's rebellion was likely in 974 BC, so the insertion of a forty-year span of time at this point in the narrative doesn't fit with the chronology of David's reign as detailed elsewhere.[3] The translation "four years" is supported by the Lucianic recension of the LXX, the Syriac, the Vulgate, and Josephus.[4] In Hebrew this reading would be אַרְבַּע שָׁנָה (cf. 1 Ki 15:33), which differs from the MT by omitting the last two consonants of the numeral, ־ים. "Four years" is a much more reasonable period and is adopted in most English translations. Two Masoretic manuscripts read אַרְבָּעִים יוֹם, "forty days," which some scholars advocate,[5] but that seems to be too short of a time for Absalom to gather political support for his rebellion by stealing "the loyalty of the men of Israel" (15:6).

---

[2] Steinmann, *1 Samuel*, 44.

[3] See "The Chronology of David's Reign" in the commentary on 5:1–5.

[4] Josephus, *Antiquities*, 7.196. See McCarter, *II Samuel*, 355.

[5] See Althann, "The Meaning of ארבעים שנה in 2 Sam 15,7."

אֵלְכָה נָּא—"I would like to go." This singular cohortative of הָלַךְ with the particle of entreaty נָא is translated as an expression of the speaker's will. It could also have the force of a request for permission (Joüon, § 114 d, n): "please allow me to go."

וַאֲשַׁלֵּם אֶת־נִדְרִי אֲשֶׁר־נָדַרְתִּי—"To pay the vow … that I made" is literally "and I will fulfill my vow, which I vowed." The imperfect with conjunctive *waw* וַאֲשַׁלֵּם expresses the purpose of the prior verb (see the previous textual note), the ostensible reason for his travel. The Piel (D) of שָׁלֵם often has the positive meaning of a person "fulfilling" or "paying in full" his vow to God. For its other meanings, see the first textual note on 12:6. The use of the verb נָדַר, "to vow," with the direct object noun נֶדֶר, "a vow," is yet another example of the Hebrew preference for cognate accusative constructions.[6] The same construction is also at the start of the next verse (נָדַר נֶדֶר, 15:8).

15:8 אִם־יָשׁוֹב יְשִׁיבֵנִי יְהוָה—"If Yahweh indeed brings me back." The second verb form, יְשִׁיבֵנִי, is the Hiphil (H) third masculine singular imperfect of שׁוּב, "return," with a first common singular suffix. The preceding form of שׁוּב reinforces the second verb, thus "indeed." Its Kethib is יָשִׁיב, the same Hiphil verb but without a suffix. The Qere, יָשׁוֹב, which is the sole reading in many Masoretic manuscripts, is a Qal (G) infinitive absolute.

וְעָבַדְתִּי—"I will worship." When the Qal (G) of עָבַד, "serve," has God or a false god as its object, it connotes faith and worship (e.g., God in 1 Sam 7:3–4; 12:14, 20, 24; false gods in 1 Sam 8:8; 26:19; both in 1 Sam 12:10).

15:9 וַיָּקָם וַיֵּלֶךְ—"So he went" is literally "and he arose and he went." This verbal hendiadys can be represented by one verb in English.

15:10 מְרַגְּלִים—"Agents." The Piel (D) participle of רָגַל elsewhere denotes "spies."[7] See the first textual note on 1 Sam 26:4[8] and the fifth textual note on 2 Sam 10:3. However, here the context requires that these are agents who surreptitiously facilitate Absalom's rebellion. Instead of מְרַגְּלִים, 4QSamᶜ has מירושלם, "from Jerusalem," which is probably a scribal error that substitutes the more familiar form in the next verse (מִירוּשָׁלַ‍ִם, 15:11) for a less familiar one.

15:11 וְאֶת־אַבְשָׁלוֹם—"With Absalom." Here אֵת is the preposition, "with," rather than the more common direct object marker. The same prepositional phrase recurs at the end of 15:12.

קְרֻאִים וְהֹלְכִים לְתֻמָּם—"They had been invited and went innocently" is literally "[they were] called and walking (according) to their integrity." The Qal (G) of הָלַךְ, "walk," is used idiomatically with the noun תֹּם, "completeness, perfection, integrity," to denote the manner of life of a believer in 1 Ki 9:4 (David); Ps 26:1, 11 (David again); Prov 2:7; 10:9; 19:1; 28:6. The same expression but with the verb in the Hithpael (HtD) occurs in Ps 101:2; Prov 20:7.

---

[6] *IBH*, § 17 B. See, e.g., the first textual notes on 1 Sam 1:6, 11, 17, 21 (Steinmann, *1 Samuel*, 45, 48, 51, 58).

[7] Gen 42:9, 11, 14, 16, 30, 31, 34; Josh 2:1; 6:22, 23; 1 Sam 26:4.

[8] Steinmann, *1 Samuel*, 492.

וְלֹא יָדְעוּ כָּל־דָּבָר׃—"They did not know the entire situation" is literally "and they did not know any word/matter."

15:12 בְּזָבְחוֹ אֶת־הַזְּבָחִים—"While he was offering sacrifices" is literally "in his sacrificing the sacrifices." The translation of this temporal clause, formed by the suffixed infinitive construct of זָבַח with the preposition בְּ, is placed first in the verse because it probably describes the action of Absalom (named at the start of the verse), rather than Ahithophel (the closer antecedent). Yet the Hebrew text appears to be ambiguous. It could be read as if Ahithophel was offering sacrifices. However, since Absalom was making a show of repaying a vow (2 Sam 15:7–8), which usually involved sacrifices (Lev 7:16; 22:21, 23; Num 15:3, 8; 1 Sam 1:21), and since accession to the throne was also accompanied by sacrifices (e.g., 1 Ki 1:9), Absalom was most likely the one presenting offerings to Yahweh.

וַיְהִי הַקֶּשֶׁר אַמִּץ—"The conspiracy grew stronger" is literally "and the conspiracy was/became mighty." The noun קֶשֶׁר denotes a treasonous "conspiracy" against a monarchy also in 1 Ki 16:20; 2 Ki 11:14 (‖ 2 Chr 23:13); 2 Ki 12:21 (ET 12:20); 14:19 (‖ 2 Chr 25:27); 2 Ki 15:15, 30; 17:4. Elsewhere the adjective אַמִּיץ, "mighty," almost always refers to God (Is 28:2; 40:26; Job 9:4, 19; but to a person in Amos 2:16).

וְהָעָם הוֹלֵךְ וָרָב—"And the people … kept increasing" is literally "and the people were going and many." The Qal (G) participle of הָלַךְ is coordinated with the adjective רָב, "much, many," to denote continuous action. Occasionally elsewhere it is coordinated with another adjective or a second participle (see GKC, § 113 u; Joüon, § 123 s).

Commentary

To the reader it appears that David must have been hopelessly clueless about Absalom's activities. Everything Absalom is reported to have done in this chapter clearly was aimed at claiming the throne for himself. When the events of this chapter are placed in chronological sequence with the other events during David's reign, it becomes obvious that David was preoccupied with other things: he was completing the construction of his palace (979–976 BC) and then moving the ark to Jerusalem (975 BC).[9]

However much David's projects may have distracted him, there was certainly another factor that also contributed to his inability to recognize the incipient uprising that Absalom was planning: David had abdicated his responsibility to discipline his own sons.[10] He failed to punish Amnon for raping Tamar (13:21). Then he did not punish Absalom for murdering Amnon (13:23–37) and opted instead petulantly to refuse Absalom a royal audience upon his return from exile in Geshur (14:24). Later, even after Absalom would rebel and dishonor David by sleeping with his wives (16:21–23), an incestuous abomination (Lev 18:8; 20:11), David would order his commanders to treat Absalom kindly (2 Sam 18:5). He also failed to discipline Adonijah (1 Ki 1:6). In this respect

---

[9] See "The Chronology of David's Reign" in the commentary on 5:1–5, including figure 2.

[10] Thus, David at this point lacked a prerequisite for a Christian pastor (1 Tim 3:4–5; Titus 1:6).

David resembled the high priest Eli, who refrained from disciplining his sons in the priesthood, and so Yahweh terminated his lineage (1 Sam 2:22–36). Nevertheless, Yahweh had promised that he himself would discipline David's son (Solomon) for his wrongdoing, and, moreover, Yahweh would never remove his favor from the dynasty of David, from which the messianic King would be born. Therefore David's kingdom and throne would endure forever (2 Sam 7:14–16).

Parents are often prone to overlook the faults of their children. Yet parents are responsible for disciplining their children (Prov 23:13–14; 29:15) whenever they violate the Law of God, and this is part of training them in the Lord's ways (Eph 6:4). Of course, parents are also to teach their children the Lord's way by the Gospel, showing them mercy and kindness as a reflection of God's grace to them through Christ (Eph 4:32–5:2; Col 3:21; see also 1 Jn 2:12–13; 3 Jn 4).

Absalom Lays the Groundwork for Rebellion (15:1–6)

978–974 BC[11]

Once Absalom had been publicly received back into the favor of the royal court, he began to display his regal pretentions. His assembling a chariot and horses and retinue to run before him was an obvious signal of his claim on the throne (15:1). Samuel had warned Israel that kings would do this (1 Sam 8:11). Later when Adonijah would claim the throne, he would also assemble chariots and fifty runners (1 Ki 1:5). Subsequent Israelite kings would regularly have their own royal chariots.[12] However, in David's day, Absalom's use of a chariot as a sign of royal pretentions appears to be an innovation for Israel.

Simply displaying royal trappings was not, by itself, going to allow Absalom to usurp the throne while David was alive. Absalom pursued political popularity and support by stationing himself at the city gate, where those who were bringing grievances to the king would be entering Jerusalem (15:2). It is unlikely that every Israelite had access to the king.[13] Instead, the most prominent men of the kingdom as well as leaders of clans and tribes were most likely those few who were admitted to the throne room to bring the grievances of their constituencies to David.[14] Absalom's engagement with such influential men of the kingdom was designed to convince them that they ought to support his desire to be Israel's judge (15:3–4). Absalom's claim that he would give justice to these claimants[15] implied that David did not grant justice. Absalom certainly had evidence that

---

[11] See "The Chronology of David's Reign" in the commentary on 5:1–5.

[12] 1 Ki 12:18; 18:44–45; 20:33; 22:34–35, 38; 2 Ki 9:21, 24, 27; 2 Chr 10:18; 18:34; 35:24.

[13] Prov 30:28 notes animals that are small but wise. A lizard appears to be subject to the whims of ordinary humans, who can pick it up in their hands. However, it can gain access to the king—something most of the king's subjects cannot do.

[14] Note 2 Sam 12:1–6, where Nathan appears to be presenting the case of a poor man who does not have direct access to the royal court.

[15] See the fourth textual note on 15:4.

David had not acted justly: Where was justice for Uriah (2 Samuel 11)? When did David grant a measure of justice for his own daughter Tamar after Amnon raped her (2 Samuel 13)? It was *Absalom* who had given her justice when he took vengeance on Amnon (13:23–37)!

Moreover, Absalom presented himself as a man of the people (15:5). When someone came to bow down to him, he prevented the man from such abasement by taking hold of him and greeting him with a kiss, the ancient equivalent of a modern politician's hearty egalitarian handshake, and a recognition of the man as a brother (cf. Ex 4:27; see the third textual note on 2 Sam 14:33).

By these acts Absalom was able to gain the loyalty of all the influential men in the land (15:6). The author says that the prince "stole the loyalty of the men of Israel." The Hebrew expression is literally "and he stole the heart" (אֶת־לֵב ... וַיְגַנֵּב). This expression occurs only one other time in the OT, in Gen 31:20, where it notes Jacob's deception of Laban. Here Absalom deceived the men of Israel into granting their loyalty to him.

The Beginning of Absalom's Rebellion (15:7–12)

974 BC[16]

After four years of carefully cultivating his political base,[17] Absalom was ready to overthrow David and seize the throne. He appealed to David to be given permission to go to Hebron and repay a vow he had taken in Geshur (15:7–8). Apparently David had been unconcerned about Absalom's regal chariot display, even though the prince was under the watchful eye of the court in Jerusalem and needed permission to travel outside of the city. Absalom's extravagant chariot parades may have been regarded as harmless affectations of a prince who hoped to be king someday. David ought to have been concerned, however, about Absalom's request, since the prince had been living in Jerusalem for six years without keeping what he now claimed to have been a vow to Yahweh. The Law of Moses required prompt repayment of vows (Deut 23:22 [ET 23:21]). Notwithstanding the conflict between Absalom's show of piety and his impious life up to this point, the king allowed Absalom to go with his blessing, apparently suspecting nothing (2 Sam 15:9).

The author informs us that Absalom had sent agents to infiltrate the tribes and stand ready to announce his accession to the throne (15:10). The blowing of a ram's horn to accompany the declaration that someone had claimed the kingdom is also recorded in 1 Ki 1:34, 39 (King Solomon) and 2 Ki 9:13 (King Jehu). Apparently it was intended to announce an unexpected accession while the throne was still occupied by someone else.

Absalom was accompanied by two hundred men whom he had invited to Hebron, making the repayment of Absalom's vow part of a great public display (15:11). We are told that these men did not know the entire situation. They

---

[16] See "The Chronology of David's Reign" in the commentary on 5:1–5.

[17] See the first textual note on 15:7.

had been deceived into becoming part of Absalom's conspiracy to capture the throne. Most likely these were prominent men in Jerusalem, men in David's service. This would have served to weaken David's position in Jerusalem. While safely ensconced in Hebron, some twenty miles (thirty-two kilometers) south of Jerusalem, Absalom offered sacrifices in payment of his vow (15:12).[18] Meanwhile, he had sent for David's advisor Ahithophel, who lived in Giloh. The exact location of Giloh is unknown. However, according to the information in Josh 15:48–54, it was situated in the Judean hill country in the vicinity of Hebron.

The reader is immediately struck with the incongruence of someone who is described as one of David's advisors and yet willingly joins Absalom's insurrection. However, a close reading of the rest of the book of Samuel reveals that Ahithophel was the father of Eliam (2 Sam 23:34), who in turn was the father of Bathsheba (11:3). It is likely that Ahithophel was disenchanted with David because the king had defiled his granddaughter by seducing her while she was married to Uriah (2 Samuel 11).[19] Ahithophel's grudge against David would be made clearer in his advice to Absalom as he later proposed personally to lead an armed force to defeat the king and kill him (17:1–3). With Ahithophel's support, Absalom's conspiracy gained strength and momentum.

The name "Ahithophel" (אֲחִיתֹפֶל) means "brother of foolishness." Since it is unlikely that anyone would give this name to a son, it has been proposed that this is the author's bowdlerization of his actual name.[20] If this is the case, it serves as an ironic rejection of his legendary sagacity that made his advice seem to be as trustworthy as an oracle from God (16:23). The most cogent proposal for his actual name is "Ahiphelet" (אֲחִיפֶלֶט), "brother of deliverance," virtually making "Ahithophel" a mocking anagram of his name.[21]

---

[18] See the first textual note on 15:12.

[19] For a comprehensive analysis of Ahithophel's motives and actions, see Bodner, "Motives for Defection." Also see Bergen, *1, 2 Samuel*, 398–99.

[20] The current text of the book of Samuel appears to have other bowdlerized personal names that had the theophoric element *ba'al*. See the second textual note on 2:8.

[21] McCarter, *II Samuel*, 357; Hertzberg, *I and II Samuel*, 338. Compare the name "Eliphelet" (אֱלִיפֶלֶט), meaning "God of deliverance" (2 Sam 5:16; 23:34; Ezra 8:13; 10:33; 1 Chr 3:6, 8; 8:39; 14:7), and "Elpelet" (אֶלְפֶּלֶט), likely meaning the same, "God of deliverance" (1 Chr 14:5).

David Flees Jerusalem

Translation

15 ¹³An informer came to David, saying, "The loyalty of the men of Israel is with Absalom."

¹⁴David said to all his servants who were with him in Jerusalem, "Get up! Let's flee, since there will be no escape for us from Absalom. Leave quickly; otherwise he will quickly overtake us, bring disaster on us, and strike the city with a sword."

¹⁵The king's servants said to the king, "Whatever my lord the king chooses [to do], we will remain your servants."

¹⁶The king left, and his entire household followed him. The king left behind ten concubines to take care of the palace. ¹⁷The king and all the troops under his command left. They stopped at the last house, ¹⁸and all his servants were passing beside him, including all the Cherethites, all the Pelethites, and all the Gittites: six hundred men who had come from Gath under his command. They were passing in front of the king.

¹⁹The king said to Ittai the Gittite, "Why are you also going with us? Go back and stay with the [new] king, because you are a foreigner and you are an exile from your homeland. ²⁰Yesterday you arrived, and today should I make you wander around by going with us? I am going wherever I can go. Go back, and take back your countrymen with you. May Yahweh show you true kindness."

²¹Ittai replied to the king, "As Yahweh lives and as my lord the king lives, wherever my lord the king is—whether for death or for life—your servant will be there."

²²David said to Ittai, "Go, pass by." So Ittai the Gittite and all his men and all the (women and) children with him passed by.

²³The entire land was weeping loudly while all the troops were marching by. The king was crossing in the Kidron Valley, and all the troops were passing by on the Wilderness Road. ²⁴Moreover, Zadok and all the Levites with him were carrying God's ark of the covenant. They set God's ark down, and Abiathar offered [sacrifices] until all the troops finished passing out of the city. ²⁵The king said to Zadok, "Take God's ark back to the city. If I find favor in Yahweh's sight, he will bring me back and allow me to see it and its resting place. ²⁶However, if he says, 'I am not pleased with you,' then I am at his service; he may do to me whatever he considers to be right."

²⁷The king also said to the high priest Zadok, "Aren't you an observer? Return to the city in peace along with your son Ahimaaz and Abiathar's son Jonathan—your two sons [will go] with you. ²⁸Look, I will be waiting at the fords in the wilderness until word comes from you to inform me." ²⁹So Zadok and Abiathar returned God's ark to Jerusalem, and they remained there.

³⁰**David was going up the Mount of Olives, weeping as he went up. His head was covered, and he was walking barefoot. Each man of the troops who were with him covered his head and was weeping as he went.** ³¹**Someone informed David, "Ahithophel is among those conspiring with Absalom."**

David said, "Yahweh, please make Ahithophel's advice foolish."

³²**As David came to the summit, where he used to worship God, Hushai the Archite was there to meet him. His tunic was torn, and dirt was on his head.** ³³**David said to him, "If you leave with me, you will be a burden to me.** ³⁴**However, if you return to the city and say to Absalom, 'I will be your servant, Your Majesty. I was your father's servant before, and now I am your servant,' then you can foil for me Ahithophel's advice.** ³⁵**Won't the high priests Zadok and Abiathar be with you there? Then you can tell everything that you hear from the king's palace to the high priests Zadok and Abiathar.** ³⁶**Moreover, their two sons—Zadok's Ahimaaz and Abiathar's Jonathan—are there with them. Through them you can send to me everything that you hear."** ³⁷**So David's friend Hushai went to the city as Absalom was entering Jerusalem.**

Textual Notes

15:13 הַמַּגִּיד—"An informer." This is the Hiphil (H) masculine singular participle of נָגַד, "to report, inform," with the definite article. Hebrew commonly uses the article when the narrator has a specific individual in mind, even if not named or identified further (*IBH*, § 20 A; Joüon, § 137 n). English uses an indefinite article in such cases.

לֶב־אִישׁ יִשְׂרָאֵל אַחֲרֵי אַבְשָׁלוֹם:—"The loyalty of the men of Israel is with Absalom" is literally "the heart of the man of Israel (is) after Absalom." For this use of לֵב, "heart," see the third textual note on 15:6. The noun אִישׁ, "man," is used in a collective sense.

15:14 וְנִבְרָחָה—"Let's flee." This form with the accent and the *qamets* in the penultimate syllable (-רָ-) is pausal for וְנִבְרְחָה, the plural Qal (G) cohortative of בָּרַח with a conjunctive *waw*. A cohortative can be used to encourage or instigate an action (*IBH*, § 51 D).

מַהֲרוּ לָלֶכֶת—"Leave quickly" is literally "hurry to go." The Piel (D) masculine plural imperative of מָהַר, "to hurry, do (something) quickly," takes the Qal (G) infinitive construct of הָלַךְ, "walk, go" (with לְ), as its verbal complement to specify the action that is to be done in haste. See also the next textual note.

יְמַהֵר וְהִשִּׂגָנוּ—"He will quickly overtake us" is literally "he will hurry and he will reach us." As in the preceding textual note, the Piel (D) of מָהַר, "to hurry," takes another verb as its complement to signify the action that is rapid. The complement is the Hiphil (H) third masculine singular perfect of נָשַׂג with *waw* consecutive and a first common plural object suffix. In the OT נָשַׂג is used only in the Hiphil and commonly refers to a pursuer "overtaking" the party fleeing from him (see BDB, 1 a).

וְהִדִּיחַ עָלֵינוּ אֶת־הָרָעָה—"Bring disaster on us" is literally "and he will thrust upon us the evil." Usually the Hiphil (H) of נָדַח means "thrust away" or "banish" someone into exile (BDB, Hiphil, 2). This is the only instance where it refers to imposition rather than expulsion. In 14:13, 14, its Niphal (N) participle referred to Absalom as "banished," and the Niphal of the by-form דָּחָה in 14:14 similarly meant "be banished, alienated."

לְפִי־חָרֶב׃—"With a sword" is literally "by the mouth/edge of a sword." See the first textual note on 1 Sam 22:19[1] and the third textual note on 2 Sam 11:25.

15:15 הִנֵּה עֲבָדֶיךָ—"We will remain your servants" is literally "behold, your servants." Such an expression with the particle הִנֵּה, "look, behold," can denote readiness to serve (1 Sam 3:4–8, 16; 22:12; 2 Sam 1:7; see BDB, a). See the textual note on 1 Sam 22:12.[2] See also הִנְנִי in the first textual note on 15:26.

15:16 וְכָל־בֵּיתוֹ בְּרַגְלָיו—"And his entire household followed him" is literally "and all his house (was) at his feet." This expresses that they were under David's authority and following his instructions. See also the second textual note on 15:17.

נָשִׁים פִּלַגְשִׁים—"Concubines" is literally "wives, concubines." This refers to those wives whose status was that of concubines. The second, more specific noun is in apposition to the first, more general noun (Joüon, § 131 b). Compare the archaic colloquial English expression "widow woman." See further the footnote about David's wives and concubines in the commentary on 11:1–5. For the status of concubines compared to wives, see the commentary on 5:13.

15:17 וְכָל־הָעָם—"And all the troops." In military contexts the noun with the article הָעָם, "the people," often denotes "the troops." See the first textual note on 1 Sam 4:3[3] and the second textual note on 2 Sam 1:4. Here a few Masoretic manuscripts read וְכָל־עֲבָדָיו, "and all his servants," which is supported by the LXX (καὶ πάντες οἱ παῖδες αὐτοῦ). Two Masoretic manuscripts read וְכָל־בֵּיתוֹ, "and his entire household."

בְּרַגְלָיו—"Under his command" is literally "at his feet." This expression is used to denote a contingent of soldiers under the authority of a commander or a group following someone as their leader. It recurs in the same sense in 15:18, but with the noun in the singular, בְּרַגְלוֹ. See also Judg 4:10; 8:5; 1 Sam 25:27; 1 Ki 20:10; 2 Ki 3:9.

בֵּית הַמֶּרְחָק׃—"(At) the last house" is literally "the house of the distance," that is, the most distant one. The construct phrase forms a superlative.

15:19 שׁוּב וְשֵׁב—"Go back and stay." Note the wordplay. Both words have the same consonants (including the conjunction *waw*), but in a different order. Both are Qal (G) masculine singular imperatives. The first is of שׁוּב, "return," while the second is of יָשַׁב, "live, reside." See also the fourth textual note on 15:20.

גֹּלֶה—"An exile." The Qal (G) participle of the verb גָּלָה, "go into exile," is used as a noun, referring to a person who is "an exile," as also in 2 Ki 24:14; Is 49:21; Amos 6:7.

15:20 תְּמוֹל l בּוֹאֶךָ—"Yesterday you arrived" is literally "yesterday (was the day of) your coming." The verb is the suffixed Qal (G) infinitive construct of בּוֹא.

וְהַיּוֹם אֲנִיעֲךָ עִמָּנוּ לָלֶכֶת—"And today should I make you wander around by going with us?" The context implies that this is a question even though it is not marked as such (see GKC, § 150 a). The translation follows the Qere, אֲנִיעֲךָ, which is the Hiphil (H) first common singular imperfect of נוּעַ with a second masculine singular object suffix. Usually the Hiphil of נוּעַ means "to shake [something]," but it can also mean "to

---

[1] Steinmann, *1 Samuel*, 428.

[2] Steinmann, *1 Samuel*, 426.

[3] Steinmann, *1 Samuel*, 120.

make [someone] wander" (see BDB, 4, citing also Num 32:13; Ps 59:12 [ET 59:11]). This reading is supported by the LXX: κινήσω σε, "shall I move you?" The Kethib is אֲנוּעֶךָ, the Qal (G) first common singular imperfect of נוּעַ with a second masculine singular suffix, but the meaning of the Qal is "to wave, shake" in an intransitive sense, so one would not expect the Qal to have a direct object such as the suffix. The infinitive construct with לְ, לָלֶכֶת (the Qal of הָלַךְ), further explains the preceding verb and means "by going" (see Joüon, § 124 o).

וַאֲנִי הוֹלֵךְ עַל אֲשֶׁר־אֲנִי הוֹלֵךְ—"I am going wherever I can go" is literally "and I am going to (the place) where I am going." The repetition of the words אֲנִי הוֹלֵךְ in the main clause and then in the relative clause (... אֲשֶׁר) is a kind of paronomasia that expresses indefiniteness (Joüon, § 158 o). David is unsure of where he may be going (cf. Gen 12:1).

שׁוּב וְהָשֵׁב—"Go back, and take back." Again the author engages in wordplay with a pair of masculine singular imperatives (one with the conjunction *waw*) that share three consonants (see also the first textual note on 15:19). Here both are of שׁוּב, "return." The first is Qal (G), and the second is Hiphil (H).

אַחֶיךָ עִמָּךְ—"Your countrymen with you" is literally "your brothers with you."

חֶסֶד וֶאֱמֶת:—The MT simply has a pair of nouns that can be translated literally as "grace and truth" (cf. Jn 1:14, 17). The first noun, חֶסֶד, could also be rendered as "loving kindness" or "(covenant) faithfulness,"[4] and, depending on the first, the second could also be rendered as "faithfulness." These nouns are commonly paired as divine attributes of Yahweh and are used to describe how Yahweh treats his people.[5] They are paired in 2 Sam 2:6: יַעַשׂ־יְהוָה עִמָּכֶם חֶסֶד וֶאֱמֶת, "may Yahweh show you loving kindness and faithfulness," which is translated by the LXX as ποιήσαι κύριος μεθ᾽ ὑμῶν ἔλεος καὶ ἀλήθειαν. Similarly, here the LXX reads καὶ κύριος ποιήσει μετὰ σοῦ ἔλεος καὶ ἀλήθειαν, "and Yahweh will show you loving kindness and faithfulness" (but with "you" in the singular). The translation above and most English versions follow the LXX reading.[6] If such a reading was originally in the Hebrew, i.e., יַעַשׂ־יהוה עִמְּךָ חֶסֶד וֶאֱמֶת, then the MT suffered haplography due to the eye of a scribe (perhaps copying the text in an era before it was pointed) skipping from the preceding word עִמָּךְ ("with you [singular]," pausal for עִמְּךָ) to the same word (but not in pause), עִמְּךָ, in this reconstructed reading.

15:21 וַיַּעַן אִתַּי אֶת־הַמֶּלֶךְ וַיֹּאמֶר—"Ittai replied to the king" is literally "and Ittai answered the king and he said." When combined in a response, the two verbs עָנָה, "answer," and אָמַר, "say," can be translated as one, "reply." See the first textual note on 1 Sam 1:15.[7]

חַי־יְהוָה וְחֵי אֲדֹנִי הַמֶּלֶךְ—"As Yahweh lives and as my lord the king lives." See the fifth textual note on 11:11, which has a similar double oath formula. For חַי־יְהוָה, "as

---

4   See the third textual note on 2:5; the second textual note on 9:1; and the second textual note on 9:3.

5   See also, e.g., Gen 32:11 (ET 32:10); Ex 34:6; Micah 7:20; Pss 25:10; 26:3; 40:11–12 (ET 40:10–11); 57:4, 11 (ET 57:3, 10); 69:14 (69:13).

6   HCSB, ESV, GW.

7   Steinmann, *1 Samuel*, 49–50.

Yahweh lives," see the first textual note on 2:27 (see also the second textual note on 1 Sam 14:45[8]).

כִּי בִמְקוֹם אֲשֶׁר יִהְיֶה־שָּׁם ׀ אֲדֹנִי הַמֶּלֶךְ—"Wherever my lord the king is" is literally "for in the place of where he will be there—my lord the king." The force of בִמְקוֹם אֲשֶׁר—the preposition בְּ, the noun מְקוֹם in construct, and the relative particle אֲשֶׁר—is "wherever" (Joüon, § 129 q; see also GKC, § 130 c). This reading without the particle אִם is the Qere, which is the sole reading in a few Masoretic manuscripts. The Kethib in Codex Leningradensis reads כִּי אִם instead of כִּי alone. The Kethib, כִּי אִם, would have to be an emphatic assurance (see GKC, § 163 d) rather than a negative (as in 2 Sam 3:35; see BDB, s.v. כִּי אִם, 1 a).

אִם־לְמָוֶת אִם־לְחַיִּים—"Whether for death or for life." For such a disjunction, אִם is repeated before each alternative (Joüon, § 175 c). These two nouns, "death" and "life," stand as opposite alternatives also in, e.g., Deut 30:15, 19; Jer 8:3; 21:8; Prov 11:19; 12:28; 18:21. See also 2 Sam 1:23. In some of these passages, the words have an eschatological sense, God's blessing of life that will endure forever versus eternal death under God's curse (Deut 30:15, 19). Also when used without "death," the noun חַיִּים can refer to eternal "life" (e.g., Pss 21:5 [ET 21:4]; 133:3; Dan 12:2). Compare Ittai's oath and invocation of Yahweh to the oath and confession of faith by Ruth in which she pledges to remain with Naomi, confesses faith in Yahweh as her own God too, and expresses the confidence that not even death will separate them, i.e., that they will be together in the afterlife (Ruth 1:16–17).[9]

15:22 וְכָל־הַטַּף—"And all the (women and) children." The noun טַף commonly refers to "children," who would naturally be accompanied by their mothers. Many passages use נָשִׁים, "women," together with this noun to refer to mothers and their children (e.g., Gen 34:29; 45:19; Deut 3:6).

15:23 וְכָל־הָאָרֶץ בּוֹכִים קוֹל גָּדוֹל—"The entire land was weeping loudly" is literally "and all the land—they were weeping (with a) great voice." For the construction, see Joüon, § 125 s. The feminine singular noun אֶרֶץ, "land," can stand as the subject of the masculine plural participle בּוֹכִים, "weeping" (from בָּכָה), because the "land," by metonymy, refers to its inhabitants.

15:24 אֲרוֹן בְּרִית הָאֱלֹהִים—Literally "the ark of the covenant of God." This exact construct chain refers to the ark in 1 Sam 4:4b and occurs elsewhere only in Judg 20:27; 1 Chr 16:6. More common (thirty times in the OT) is the designation אֲרוֹן בְּרִית יהוה, "the ark of the covenant of Yahweh," in 1 Sam 4:3, 4a, 5.[10]

וַיַּצִּקוּ—"They set ... down." This is the Hiphil (H) third masculine plural preterite (imperfect with *waw* consecutive) of יָצַק. Normally יָצַק is used in the Qal (G) and means "pour out" (as in 1 Sam 10:1), but its Qal can mean "set before/down" (see the second textual note on 2 Sam 13:9), and its Hiphil has that meaning here (also in Josh

---

8 Steinmann, *1 Samuel*, 265.

9 See Wilch, *Ruth*, 143–44, 168–75.

10 See also, e.g., Num 10:33; Deut 10:8; 31:9, 25; Josh 6:8; 1 Ki 8:1; 1 Chr 15:25, 26, 28, 29; 22:19; 28:2.

7:23). Some have suggested that when יָצַק is used to mean "set down," it is a dialectical variation of יָצַג, whose Hiphil commonly means "to set" down or before (fifteen times in the OT).[11]

וַיַּעַל—"And he offered [sacrifices]." This verb is translated as the Hiphil (H) third masculine singular preterite (imperfect with *waw* consecutive) of עָלָה. The Hiphil of עָלָה is often used with the cognate noun עֹלָה, "sacrifice, burnt offering," as its direct object,[12] and the context here suggests that the plural of עֹלָה is the implied object. However, the verb form is ambiguous. It could also be the same form but in the Qal (G), in which case it would mean Abiathar "went up."

עַד־תֹּם ... לַעֲבוֹר—"Until ... finished passing out." The verb תֹּם is the Qal (G) infinitive construct of תָּמַם, "to be complete, finished," here used in a temporal clause. The Qal infinitive construct (with לְ) לַעֲבוֹר, "to cross over, pass out," serves as its verbal complement, specifying the action that is finished.

15:25 הָשֵׁב ... וֶהֱשִׁבַנִי—"Take back. ... He will bring me back." Both verbs are Hiphil (H) forms of שׁוּב, "to return." The first is the masculine singular imperative, and the second is the third masculine singular perfect with *waw* consecutive and a first common singular object suffix. Thus, if David finds favor in Yahweh's eyes, both the ark of God and his anointed king will be restored to their proper location together in Jerusalem. The Hiphil of שׁוּב is used again for returning the ark in 15:29 (וַיָּשֶׁב).

וְהִרְאַנִי אֹתוֹ וְאֶת־נָוֵהוּ—"And he will allow me to see it and its resting place" is literally "and he will cause me to see it and its resting place." In the Hiphil (H), רָאָה, "see," commonly takes a double accusative, "to show [someone] [something else]." Here the first accusative is the pronominal suffix on the verb וְהִרְאַנִי, and the second accusative is the compound phrase with the repeated definite object marker (אֹתוֹ וְאֶת־). See GKC, § 117 e; Joüon, § 125 e. For the noun נָוֶה, "resting place," see the first textual note on 7:8.

15:26 הִנְנִי—"Then I am at his service" is literally "behold me." This could also be rendered as "then I am at his disposal." For this nuance of הִנֵּה, see the textual note on 15:15.

יַעֲשֶׂה־לִּי כַּאֲשֶׁר טוֹב בְּעֵינָיו—Literally "may he do to me just as (it is) good in his eyes." See this idiom with God as the subject also in 1 Sam 3:18; 2 Sam 10:12.

15:27 צָדוֹק הַכֹּהֵן—"The high priest Zadok." For כֹּהֵן, "priest," meaning "*high* priest," see the second textual note on 8:17. This noun recurs in the plural twice in 15:35 and is translated as "high priests" there. Zadok and Abiathar shared the high priesthood under David (see, e.g., 17:15). Abiathar offers sacrifices in 15:24.

הֲרוֹאֶה אַתָּה—"Aren't you an observer?" This question with an interrogative *he* is rhetorical and so is translated in the negative ("aren't ... ?") to bring out its force. Some versions translate it as something like "aren't you a seer [i.e., a prophet]?"[13] While that is possible, the context appears to be saying that Zadok is able to observe the goings on in the city and report them to David. For the Qal (G) participle רֹאֶה, "seer," referring to

---

11 McCarter, *II Samuel*, 371; Anderson, *2 Samuel*, 200.

12 E.g., Gen 8:20; 22:2; 1 Sam 6:14–15; 7:9–10; 2 Sam 6:17–18; 24:24–25.

13 GW; similarly, ESV, NET.

288

a prophetic visionary, see the commentary on 1 Sam 9:9[14] (cf. the second textual note on 2 Sam 7:17).

שֻׁבָה—This is the Qal (G) masculine singular imperative of שׁוּב, "return," with paragogic *he*.

שְׁנֵי בְנֵיכֶם אִתְּכֶם:—"Your two sons [will go] with you." In English this might be misunderstood as meaning that both of the sons were Zadok's, since King David is speaking to him alone (and not to Abiathar). However, the second masculine pronominal suffix ("your") on בְנֵיכֶם is plural. Therefore "your two sons" are the two sons just named, Zadok's son Ahimaaz (see also 1 Chr 5:34–35 [ET 6:8–9]; 6:38 [ET 6:53]) and Abiathar's son Jonathan. Ahimaaz is named in conjunction with Jonathan in 2 Sam 15:27, 36; 17:17, 20. A similar phrase, but with a third masculine plural suffix, appears in 15:36: עִמָּם שְׁנֵי בְנֵיהֶם, literally "with them (are) their two sons." See the first textual note on 15:36.

15:28 מִתְמַהְמֵהַּ—"Waiting." This is the Hithpalpel (HtD) masculine singular participle of מָהַהּ. This verb appears nine times in the OT, always in this stem. Instead of doubling the middle root letter, as is usual in the Piel (D) and Hithpael (HtD) stems, the whole root, which originally was biliteral (מה), is reduplicated.

בְּעַרְבוֹת—This Qere, meaning "on the steppes of," is the preposition בְּ with the construct form of the plural of עֲרָבָה, "plain, steppe," which often refers to an area near a river or the Dead Sea (see BDB, s.v. עֲרָבָה I, under the root ערב IV). The Qere is supported by the LXX, which transliterates the noun as if it were a place-name, ἐν Αραβωθ. The reading of the Kethib (with a transposition of the consonants ער) is בְּעַבְרוֹת, "at the fords of," which is the corresponding plural form of עֲבָרָה, "a ford," derived from the verb עָבַר, "to cross over." Most English versions follow the Kethib.[15] The same textual issue with divided evidence recurs in 17:16, where Hushai urges Zadok and Abiathar to pass information to David. In that verse many Masoretic manuscripts read בְּעַבְרוֹת, "at the fords of," in agreement with the Kethib here in 15:28. In 17:16 Codex Leningradensis reads בְּעַרְבוֹת, "on the steppes of," which again is transliterated by the LXX (ἐν Αραβωθ) in agreement with the Qere and the LXX in 15:28. There are two contextual reasons to favor the Kethib. First, the fords would be a much more specific designation of David's location, and such specificity would be needed for a messenger to locate him. Second, David forded the Jordan (17:16, 21–22), and the battle where Absalom's forces were defeated took place in the Transjordan in the forest of Ephraim (18:6), and this is confirmed when David again forded the Jordan in the opposite direction on his return to Jerusalem (19:19 [ET 19:18]).

15:30 עֹלֶה בְמַעֲלֵה הַזֵּיתִים—"Going up the Mount of Olives" is literally "ascending on the ascent of the olive trees." The masculine noun מַעֲלֶה, "ascent," is derived from the verb עָלָה, "go up, ascend."

עֹלֶה וּבוֹכֶה—"Weeping as he went up." The masculine singular Qal (G) participle עֹלֶה is repeated (see the previous textual note) and here is coordinated with another

[14] Steinmann, *1 Samuel*, 184–85.

[15] HCSB, ESV, GW, NET, NIV. See also Anderson, *2 Samuel*, 199, 201.

Qal participle, בּוֹכֶה, from בָּכָה, "to weep" (used previously in 15:23). See the coordinated infinitives of these two verbs in the fifth textual note on 15:30.

וְרֹאשׁ לוֹ חָפוּי—"His head was covered" is literally "and a head (belonging) to him (was) covered." The verb חָפוּי is the masculine singular Qal passive (Gp) participle of חָפָה, which is used for "covering" the head also in Jer 14:3–4. The same Qal passive participle (but in construct) is used similarly in Esth 6:12. Most III-ה roots were originally III-י, and this form preserves the original final letter י.

הֹלֵךְ יָחֵף—"Walking barefoot." The verb הָלַךְ and the adjective יָחֵף are paired also in Is 20:2–3 (cf. Jer 2:25).

עָלֹה וּבָכֹה:—"Weeping as he went up." As earlier in the verse (see the second textual note on 15:30), the verbs עָלָה, "to ascend," and בָּכָה, "to weep," are coordinated, but here their forms are infinitive absolutes.

15:31 וְדָוִד הִגִּיד—"Someone informed David." The MT appears to state "and David declared." The verb is the Hiphil (H) perfect third masculine singular of נָגַד, "to report, declare." The MT can be understood to mean "someone reported to David" if the verb has an unstated impersonal subject with "David" as its object, but this would be an unusual syntactical construction. Two Masoretic manuscripts read וּלְדָוִד, "and *to* David," which is more customary syntax, since the Hiphil of נָגַד usually takes the preposition לְ with its indirect object. 4QSamᵃ preserves a similar reading, [ו]לדוי[ד הוגד], "[it was reported] to David," although only the prepositional phrase ("to David") is (mostly) extant. Its reconstructed verb הוגד would be pointed הוּגַד, plene, or *maleʾ*, spelling of the Hophal (Hp) perfect, which is spelled הֻגַּד in the OT. Likewise, the LXX reads καὶ ἀνηγγέλη Δαυιδ, "and it was reported to David."

בַּקֹּשְׁרִים—"Among those conspiring." This is the Qal (G) masculine plural participle of קָשַׁר, "to conspire," often used for treason (cf. 1 Sam 22:8, 13). See the cognate noun קֶשֶׁר, "conspiracy," in the second textual note on 2 Sam 15:12.

סַכֶּל־נָא—"Please make … foolish." This is the masculine singular Piel (D) imperative of סָכַל with the particle of entreaty נָא, "please." In the Qal (G) this verb means "be foolish." Its Piel has a causative meaning. Elsewhere in Samuel its Niphal (N; 1 Sam 13:13; 2 Sam 24:10) and Hiphil (H; 1 Sam 26:21) forms mean "to act foolishly." The Piel of the by-form שָׂכַל is used in Is 44:25, where Yahweh "makes foolish" the knowledge of "wise men" who are associated with false prophecy and occult practices. Cf. the cognate nouns סָכָל, "foolish person" (e.g., Eccl 2:19; 10:3, 14); סֶכֶל, "folly" (Eccl 10:6); and סִכְלוּת, "foolishness" (e.g., Eccl 1:17; 2:3, 12–13).

אֶת־עֲצַת אֲחִיתֹפֶל—"Ahithophel's advice." The noun עֵצָה can refer to an advisor's formal "counsel" as a recommended course of action for a king (e.g., 1 Ki 1:12; 12:8, 13, 14). It often denotes God's own counsel.[16] This is the first appearance of this noun in the book of Samuel, and it will recur in the same sense in 15:34; 16:20, 23; 17:7, 14 (twice), 23, then nowhere later in the book. In all these passages except one occurrence in 17:14, it refers to "advice" given by Ahithophel, whose advice to the aspirant king Absalom is confounded by Yahweh. For the cognate verb יָעַץ, "to counsel, advise," see the first

---

[16] E.g., Is 5:19; 11:2; 19:17; 25:1; 28:29; Ps 73:24; Prov 8:14.

textual note on 16:23. As here, Yahweh confounds human counsel (עֵצָה) also in, e.g., Is 19:3; Jer 19:7; Ps 33:10; Job 5:13; Neh 4:9 (ET 4:15; cf. Is 19:11; 30:1; Jer 18:23).

15:32 יִשְׁתַּחֲוֶה—"He used to worship." The imperfect is used for habitual past action (Joüon, § 113 c). This is the Hishtaphel of חָוָה, "to bow down, worship." See the third textual note on 1 Sam 1:3.[17]

לִקְרָאתוֹ—"To meet him." This is the Qal (G) infinitive construct of קָרָא II, "to meet, encounter," with the preposition לְ and a third masculine singular object suffix. See the second textual note on 1 Sam 4:1.[18]

קָרוּעַ כֻּתָּנְתּוֹ—"His tunic was torn" is literally "he was torn (with respect to) his tunic." The masculine form of the Qal passive (Gp) participle of קָרַע, "tear," refers back to Hushai. The feminine noun כֻּתֹּנֶת, "tunic," with a suffix is an accusative of respect or limitation (see Joüon, §§ 121 o; 127 b). Cf. the masculine plural Qal passive participle of קָרַע in 1 Sam 4:12; 2 Sam 1:2; 13:31.

15:33 וְהָיִתָ עָלַי לְמַשָּׂא:—"You will be a burden to me." A similar expression with the verb הָיָה and the preposition לְ prefixed to the noun מַשָּׂא, "burden" (derived from the verb נָשָׂא, "bear, carry"), recurs in 19:36 (ET 19:35).

15:34 הַמֶּלֶךְ—For "Your Majesty," see the fourth textual note on 14:4 and *IBH*, § 20 D.

עֶבֶד אָבִיךָ וַאֲנִי מֵאָז—"I was your father's servant before" is literally "a servant of your father, and I (was) from then." Like the preceding verbal clause (עֲבַדְךָ אָנִי ... אֶהְיֶה), this nominal clause begins with the noun עֶבֶד, "servant," placed first for emphasis. The *waw* on the pronoun וַאֲנִי ("and I") may introduce an apodosis, as it does when the identical word is repeated in the next clause, וְעַתָּה וַאֲנִי עַבְדֶּךָ, literally "and now, and I (am/will be) your servant" (see GKC, § 143 d).

וְהֵפַרְתָּה—"Then you can foil." This begins the apodosis of the conditional sentence that began at the beginning of the verse ("however, if you return to the city …"). The verb is the Hiphil (H) second masculine singular perfect of פָּרַר with *waw* consecutive and the ending תָּה- instead of the usual תָּ- (GKC, § 44 g; Joüon, § 42 f). Elsewhere in the OT the Hiphil of פָּרַר is often used for "breaking" a covenant (e.g., Gen 17:14; Lev 26:15, 44; Deut 31:16, 20), but here it has the nuance "undo, frustrate, counteract." Again in 2 Sam 17:14 this verb is used in the sense of "foil" with the direct object "the advice of Ahithophel" (אֶת־עֲצַת אֲחִיתֹפֶל).

15:35 צָדוֹק וְאֶבְיָתָר הַכֹּהֲנִים—"The high priests Zadok and Abiathar." See the first textual note on 15:27.

וְהָיָה כָּל־הַדָּבָר אֲשֶׁר תִּשְׁמַע מִבֵּית הַמֶּלֶךְ תַּגִּיד—"Then you can tell everything that you hear from the king's palace" is literally "and it will be [if you, Hushai, return to Jerusalem that] all the word that you will hear from the house of the king you can report." The imperfect תַּגִּיד has the nuance "you can/may/will be able to report." See the similar force of the verb in the second textual note on 15:36.

---

[17] Steinmann, *1 Samuel*, 44.

[18] Steinmann, *1 Samuel*, 119.

15:36 עִמָּם֙ שְׁנֵ֣י בְנֵיהֶ֔ם אֲחִימַ֣עַץ לְצָד֔וֹק וִיהוֹנָתָ֖ן לְאֶבְיָתָ֑ר—Literally "with them (are) their two sons—Ahimaaz (belonging) to Zadok and Jonathan (belonging) to Abiathar." See the similar phrase in the fourth textual note on 15:27.

וּשְׁלַחְתֶּ֥ם בְּיָדָֽם—"Through them you can send" is literally "and you will send by their hand." For the idiom שָׁלַח בְּיַד־, see the first textual note on 12:25. Here David switches from the previous second person singular forms to a second person plural verb form (although in translation, the English "you" is used for plural as well as singular forms). See also the second plural תִּשְׁמָ֑עוּ, "you hear," at the end of this verse.

15:37 רֵעֶ֣ה דָוִ֑ד—This construct phrase is literally "the friend of David." The expected pointing for the construct state of a noun such as רֵעֶה (from a III-ה root) would be רֵעֵה, with *tsere* in the final syllable (cf., e.g., שְׂדֵה עֶפְר֔וֹן, "the field of Ephron," Gen 23:17). The form here is exceptional (GKC, § 93 ll), although all four occurrences in the OT of רֵעֶה in the singular construct state have that pointing (also 2 Sam 16:16; 1 Ki 4:5; Prov 27:10 [Kethib]).

וְאַבְשָׁל֖וֹם יָבֹ֥א—"As Absalom was entering." Here the imperfect יָבֹא denotes action simultaneous with the preceding verb, וַיָּבֹא, "so he [Hushai] went" (see Joüon, § 113 ga).

Commentary

974 BC[19]

The account of David's flight from Absalom begins with the first stages of his escape from the city of Jerusalem shortly before Absalom's forces entered it. Here David interacted with several persons from his court in Jerusalem—his immediate courtiers (15:14–15), Ittai the Gittite (15:19–22), the high priest Zadok (15:25–29), Ahithophel the Gilonite (in absentia; 15:31), and Hushai the Archite (15:32–37).

David Orders His Court to Evacuate Jerusalem (15:13–15)

David's first recorded warning about Absalom's true intentions came from an unnamed informant who reported that Absalom was a real threat since he had widespread support (15:13). There is no mention of Absalom marching on Jerusalem. Either the author has given us only the part of the message that he wanted to emphasize—David's vulnerable political and military position—or David simply assumed that Absalom would attack. David noted that there was "no escape" from Absalom (15:14). He was not implying that he and his court could not hope to escape even if they fled Jerusalem. Instead, he meant that had they stayed in Jerusalem, the city certainly would have fallen to Absalom's army. They had to move quickly before they were trapped in a besieged city. In the face of this crisis, David's courtiers pledge their loyalty to the king they have been serving (15:15).

---

[19] See "The Chronology of David's Reign" in the commentary on 5:1–5.

Ittai Pledges His Support for David (15:16–22)

David departed with his entire household—presumably his wives and children—except for ten concubines whom he placed in charge of maintaining the palace (15:16).[20] This paved the way for the fulfillment of Nathan's prophecy that an insurgent from his own household would violate his wives in public (12:11–12; fulfilled in 16:21–22), though David probably did not realize this at the time. In his departure David was accompanied by his standing army (15:17–18). As they came to the last house before leaving the city, David stopped and reviewed the troops as they passed by. They are identified as three groups: Cherethites, Pelethites, and Gittites, totaling six hundred men (15:18). Later we are told that the Gittites' "children" (probably with their mothers) were exiting (see the textual note on 15:22), which implies that the families of all six hundred men were also evacuating Jerusalem.

On the identity of the Cherethites and Pelethites, see the commentary on 8:18. The "Gittites" were men from Gath, which was one of the cities of the Philistine pentapolis (Josh 13:3; 1 Sam 6:17; cf. 1 Sam 7:14). David had spent time there (1 Sam 27:1–11) along with his earlier company of six hundred men (1 Sam 27:2). While there, David may have recruited the "Gittites" who are mentioned here. All of the Cherethites, Pelethites, and Gittites under David's command may have formed a single military unit. Some scholars have argued that six hundred was the size of a troop referred to as a גְּדוּד, *gedud*, a "raiding party."[21] Others simply see it as a standard size for a military unit (Judg 18:16–17; 1 Sam 13:15).[22]

David specifically addressed Ittai, the commander of the Gittites, inviting him to stay in Jerusalem to offer his services to the new king (2 Sam 15:19–20). The name "Ittai" (אִתַּי) may be of Semitic origin and mean "with me." It is probably a hypocoristic form of a longer name that included a theophoric element and signified that the deity is "with me." It could be a shortened form of "Ithiel" (אִיתִיאֵל, Neh 11:7), which means "God is with me."[23]

Since earlier in David's administration "the Cherethites" and "the Pelethites" had been mentioned, but without the Gittites (2 Sam 8:18 ‖ 1 Chr 18:17),[24] Ittai's contingent must have been a relatively recent addition to David's personal army of mercenaries. David's comment that Ittai had come only "yesterday" (תְּמוֹל, 2 Sam 15:20) is not to be understood literally but as indicating

---

[20] See the footnote about David's wives and concubines in the commentary on 11:1–5.

[21] Malamat, "The Danite Migration," 9, including n. 3; Naʾaman, "Ittai the Gittite," 23. See גְּדוּד, *gedud*, "a raiding party," in, e.g., 2 Sam 22:30 ‖ Ps 18:30 (ET 18:29); 1 Ki 11:24; Jer 18:22; Hos 7:1; Micah 4:14 (ET 5:1).

[22] Mazar, "The Military Élite of King David," 314.

[23] Delcor, "Les Kerethim et les Cretois," 411–13. Other scholars suggest that the name "Ittai" has a Hittite or Hurrian origin and means "father." See the discussion in McCarter, *II Samuel*, 370.

[24] "Obed-edom the Gittite" had been mentioned in 2 Sam 6:10–11.

that Ittai had arrived more recently than the Cherethites and Pelethites. Since Ittai was a foreigner from Philistine Gath and a recent supplement to David's mercenary force, David was suggesting that his interests might lie in backing the new claimant to the throne, Absalom, rather than siding with David, who appeared headed for certain exile. To encourage Ittai to consider this option and also to retain his faith in the one true God, David added a prayer for Yahweh's grace to attend Ittai.[25]

However, Ittai took an oath by Yahweh, the living God, and by David's life that he would serve David throughout life and even die with him (15:21), which may suggest a bond that would endure into eternal life.[26] As a result, David ordered him to pass on with the other troops (15:22). In the subsequent battle against Absalom's forces in the forest of Ephraim, David rewarded Ittai's loyalty by making him one of three commanders on the battlefield (18:2).

David Sends the Ark and the High Priests Back to Jerusalem (15:23–29)

The author suggests a lament by the creation itself as "the entire land" wept while David's troops left the city (15:23). David himself departed eastward across the Kidron Valley on the road that led to the wilderness. The Kidron Valley, which separated the city from the Mount of Olives, was considered the eastern border of Jerusalem.

The high priest Zadok and the Levites brought the ark out with David (15:24). Earlier David had allowed unauthorized persons to transport the ark in an unorthodox manner, with a disastrous result (see the commentary on 6:1–7), but here he adhered to the Torah of Moses, which specified that the ark was to be carried by hand by the Kohathite Levites (Num 4:1–15; cf. Deut 10:8). While the troops were passing out of the city, the high priest Abiathar officiated at the offering of sacrifices.[27] When the troops had exited Jerusalem, David ordered the high priest Zadok to return the ark to the city (15:25–26). Unlike Israel's earlier mistake of thinking that the ark could be used to ensure victory in battle in an *ex opere* fashion, that is, without proper faith in Yahweh and due respect for his throne (1 Samuel 4),[28] David refused to attempt such manipulation of God. Instead, he trusted that God would do what was best and right. The ark belonged in its resting place in the city where God had chosen to dwell (see the commentary on 6:12).

---

[25] See the sixth textual note on 15:20.

[26] See the fourth textual note on 15:21. Such an everlasting bond with the kingship of David can be interpreted messianically in light of the messianic promise given to David and his dynasty in 2 Samuel 7. See the commentary there.

[27] Zadok and Abiathar shared the high priesthood under David. See the first textual note on 17:15.

[28] Since Yahweh was enthroned over the cherubim that overshadowed the mercy seat of the ark (1 Sam 4:4), the ark can be said to be his throne.

However, David also noted Zadok's loyalty and recruited him to perform a dangerous task—to be David's spy in Jerusalem, along with Abiathar, and the two sons of the high priests (15:27–29).[29] They were to send an intelligence report concerning Absalom's activity to David, who would wait for it at the fords of the Jordan River.[30] It is interesting to note that Zadok is mentioned four times in 15:24–29, and David spoke only to him. Abiathar, in contrast, is mentioned just twice, and David assumed that Abiathar would follow David's instructions given to Zadok. Therefore Zadok was treated as first among the two high priests.[31] This may be an indication that even at this time the prophecy against Eli's house (1 Sam 2:27–36), which would ultimately be fulfilled when Zadok alone would be made high priest under Solomon (1 Ki 2:26–27, 35), was already partially fulfilled.

David's Prays That Yahweh Will Make Ahithophel's Advice Be Foolish (15:30–31)

Having crossed the Kidron Valley, David ascended the Mount of Olives (15:30). David was weeping with his head covered while walking barefoot. These were signs of disgrace and humiliation.[32] Elsewhere in the OT, the covering of a person's head signaled his shame (Esth 6:12; 7:8; Jer 14:3–4). Here the troops followed David's example, sharing their king's dishonor.

David received word that his advisor Ahithophel (15:12) had joined Absalom's conspiracy (15:31). David offered a prayer that Yahweh would frustrate Ahithophel's "advice" and cause it to be "foolish."[33] This anticipates Ahithophel's suicide after the failure of his "advice" (17:23) and also prepares for David's conversation with Hushai (15:32–37).

David Sends Hushai Back to Jerusalem (15:32–37)

David came to the summit of the Mount of Olives (15:32). We are told that he used to worship God there, perhaps before the ark was moved to Jerusalem (2 Samuel 6). At the summit David encountered Hushai the Archite. To demonstrate his continued loyalty to the king, Hushai showed the expected outward signs of grief with a torn robe and with dirt on his head. David told Hushai that he ought not accompany him into exile, since he would only "be a burden" (15:33). Perhaps this was an indication that Hushai was quite old and in no shape physically to be on the run from a pursuing army. Instead, David suggested that Hushai become a double agent in Absalom's court and seek to undermine Ahithophel's counsel (15:34). David divulged that Zadok and Abiathar and their two sons were also his spies in Jerusalem. Hushai could

---

[29] See the fourth textual note on 15:27.

[30] See the second textual note on 15:28.

[31] See the first textual note on 15:27.

[32] See the textual notes on 15:30.

[33] See the third and fourth textual notes on 15:31.

transmit enemy intelligence to them, and they would pass along the message to David (15:35–36).

Hushai was introduced as an "Archite" (15:32), that is, he was not an Israelite by descent, but was from a Canaanite tribe from the vicinity of Ataroth in the territory of Ephraim.[34] While he may well have been a worshiper of Yahweh, given his loyalty to the king whom Yahweh had anointed,[35] his ethnic identity may have given him credible cover to claim to have switched his loyalty from David to the new king, thereby making him the perfect mole to place among the advisors of Absalom.

The last verse in the chapter (15:37) reveals two interesting facts. First, Hushai is characterized as "David's friend." This indicates more than an informal, close bond between the two men. The title "the king's friend" signified a position in the royal court, perhaps that of a trusted counselor.[36] Thus, Hushai is listed among David's officers in 1 Chr 27:33. Second, we are told that Absalom was arriving in the city as Hushai entered it. Since the Mount of Olives is close to Jerusalem, it appears that David and his entourage had escaped just in time, perhaps only a half hour or so ahead of Absalom's forces. God's timing is always perfect (cf. Gal 4:4).

---

[34] Josh 16:1–2 places the border between Ephraim and Benjamin in the territory of the Archites. This would seemingly make the Archites residents in the land when it was divided among the tribes of Israel. Thus, the most likely construal is that they were Canaanites in the land when Israel entered it.

[35] Hushai might also have been familiar with the messianic promise given to David in 2 Samuel 7. In 12:7 Yahweh, speaking through the prophet Nathan, stated that he himself had "anointed" (מָשַׁח) David. That verb (מָשַׁח) is used for Samuel anointing David in 1 Sam 16:3, 12, 13; for the men of Judah anointing him in 2 Sam 2:4, 7; and for Israel anointing him in 2 Sam 5:3, 17.

[36] See the title "the king's friend" for Zabud among Solomon's officials (1 Ki 4:5).

David Deals with Members
of Saul's Clan

Translation

16 ¹When David had crossed a little over the summit, there was Ziba, Mephibosheth's servant, to meet him with a pair of saddled donkeys. On them were two hundred loaves of bread, a hundred bunches of raisins, a hundred portions of summer fruit, and a container full of wine. ²The king said to Ziba, "Why do you have these things?"

Ziba said, "The donkeys are for the king's household to ride. And the bread and summer fruit are for the young men to eat. The wine is for those who become exhausted in the wilderness to drink."

³The king said, "Where is your master's son?"

Ziba said to the king, "Look, he is staying in Jerusalem, since he thought, 'Today the house of Israel will restore my father's kingdom to me.'"

⁴The king said to Ziba, "Now all that is Mephibosheth's is yours."

Ziba said, "I bow [before you]. May I always find favor in your eyes, my lord, Your Majesty."

⁵When King David came to Bahurim, there was a man going out from there. He was from the clan of the house of Saul. His name was Shimei the son of Gera. As he came out, he was cursing as he came. ⁶He threw rocks at David and all King David's servants. However, the entire army and all the elite troops were on his right and his left. ⁷This is what Shimei said when he cursed: "Go out! Go out, you man of bloodshed and good-for-nothing man! ⁸Yahweh has paid you back for all of the shed blood of the house of Saul, in whose place you rule. Yahweh has given the kingdom to your son Absalom. Look, you are in your evil because you are a man of bloodshed!"

⁹Zeruiah's son Abishai said to the king, "Why should this dead dog curse my lord, Your Majesty? Let me go over there and lop off his head!"

¹⁰The king said, "Why do I put up with you, sons of Zeruiah? Let him curse this way because Yahweh said to him, 'Curse David.' So who can say, 'Why have you done so?'" ¹¹The king said to Abishai and to all of his servants, "Look, my own son who came out from my body is seeking my life! How much more now this Benjaminite? Leave him alone, and let him curse, because Yahweh spoke to him. ¹²Perhaps Yahweh will see my affliction, and Yahweh will repay good to me in place of his curses this day." ¹³David and his men went along the road. Shimei was going parallel to him along the ridge of the hill, cursing and throwing stones as he went beside him. He also kept throwing dirt [at David]. ¹⁴The king and the entire army that was with him arrived exhausted, but they were refreshed there.

Textual Notes

16:1 וְדָוִד עָבַר מְעַט מֵהָרֹאשׁ—"When David had crossed a little over the summit." The word מְעַט, "a little," is often used as a substantive to refer to a small quantity. Here, however, it is used as an adverb of place, modifying the verb עָבַר, hence "had crossed a little." The prepositional phrase מֵהָרֹאשׁ, literally "from the head," uses the noun רֹאשׁ to refer to a geographical "summit," as in 15:32.

לִקְרָאתוֹ—"To meet him." This is the suffixed Qal (G) infinitive construct of קָרָא II, "to meet, encounter," with לְ. See the second textual note on 1 Sam 4:1.[1]

וְצֶמֶד חֲמֹרִים חֲבֻשִׁים—"With a pair of saddled donkeys." The identical phrase (without the conjunction *waw*) is used in Judg 19:10. The noun צֶמֶד often denotes a "(yoked) pair" of "donkeys" (חֲמֹרִים, as here; also Judg 19:3, 10) or "oxen" (1 Sam 11:7; 1 Ki 19:21; Job 1:3; 42:12). The Qal passive (Gp) masculine plural participle חֲבֻשִׁים is of חָבַשׁ, "to bind, tie," which can refer to saddling an animal (e.g., Num 22:21; a חֲמוֹר, "donkey," in, e.g., Gen 22:3; 2 Sam 17:23; 19:27 [ET 19:26]).

צִמּוּקִים—"Bunches of raisins." The noun צִמּוּק denotes a cluster of raisins. In the OT it appears only in the plural, and three of its four instances are in the book of Samuel (1 Sam 25:18; 30:12; 2 Sam 16:1; also 1 Chr 12:41 [ET 12:40]).

קַיִץ—"Summer fruit." This noun can refer to the season of "summer" or to fruit that ripens at that time of year. It recurs in the same sense in 16:2. This term is vague, and no unit of measure is given. It probably consisted of figs and pomegranates, the two major summer fruits cultivated in ancient Israel.

וְנֵבֶל יָיִן:—"And a container full of wine." For this construct phrase, see the third textual note on 1 Sam 1:24 and the fourth textual note on 1 Sam 10:3, as well as the plural phrase נִבְלֵי־יַיִן in the second textual note on 1 Sam 25:18.[2] See also the similar construct phrase נֹאד יַיִן, "a skin full of wine," in 1 Sam 16:20. The noun יַיִן, "wine," is used as a genitive of material.[3] The noun נֵבֶל, often translated as a "skin," is most likely a jar or other hard container (cf. Lam 4:2; see *CDCH*, s.v. נֵבֶל I).

16:2 מָה־אֵלֶּה לָּךְ—"Why do you have these things?" is literally "what are these (in relation) to you?" The prepositional phrase לָּךְ is pausal for לְךָ, with a second masculine singular suffix.

וְהַלֶּחֶם—"And the bread." This is the reading of the Qere, which is supported by the LXX (καὶ οἱ ἄρτοι). The Kethib וְלְהַלֶּחֶם includes the preposition לְ, "and regarding the bread."

הַיָּעֵף—"Those who become exhausted" is literally "the exhausted (man)." The adjective יָעֵף, "tired, weary, exhausted," appears four times in the OT and is always used as a substantive (also Judg 8:15; Is 40:29; 50:4). Hebrew can use the definite article for a specific person who is in mind even though the reference is indefinite ("a, anyone"); see the first textual note on 15:13. The adjective עָיֵף, "weary … fr[om] exertion and hunger" (BDB), whose plural in 16:14 is translated as "exhausted," is a more

---

[1] Steinmann, *1 Samuel*, 119.

[2] Steinmann, *1 Samuel*, 60, 191, 474.

[3] *IBH*, § 51 c; Waltke-O'Connor, § 9.5.3d; Joüon, § 129 f; GKC, § 128 o.

common by-form with a transposition of the first and second consonants (עי versus יע). The use of that word in 16:14 shows that Ziba's provisions were needed for the purpose he stated in 16:2. The cognate verb meaning "be(come) weary, exhausted" is spelled with the same consonants as the adjective יָעֵף here, either in the same order, יָעֵף (e.g., Is 40:28, 30–31), or, with a transposition of the first two consonants, עִיֵף (e.g., 1 Sam 14:28, 31; 2 Sam 21:15).

16:3 יָשִׁיבוּ לִי בֵּית יִשְׂרָאֵל—"The house of Israel will restore … to me." The subject is the construct phrase בֵּית יִשְׂרָאֵל, "the house of Israel," which is grammatically singular, but the verb יָשִׁיבוּ, "will restore," is plural (third masculine Hiphil [H] imperfect of שׁוּב) since the "house" is comprised of many individuals and the action is not by unanimous consensus.

16:4 הִנֵּה לְךָ כֹּל אֲשֶׁר לִמְפִי־בֹשֶׁת—Literally "look, yours (is) everything which (belongs) to Mephibosheth." The prepositional phrase לְךָ, "(belonging) to you, yours," which serves as the predicate of the nominal sentence, is placed first for emphasis.

הִשְׁתַּחֲוֵיתִי—"I bow." This is the Hishtaphel first common singular perfect of חָוָה, "to bow down, worship." See the third textual note on 1 Sam 1:3.[4] This perfect expresses present-tense action (Joüon, § 112 f; Waltke-O'Connor, § 30.5.1d, including example 27).

אֶמְצָא־חֵן—"May I (always) find favor." Since Ziba has already found favor with David (16:4a), the sense is probably a petition to the king or a prayer to God that he would always find such favor. The verb אֶמְצָא is a first common singular form of the Qal (G) of מָצָא, "find." The meaning determined by the context ("may") probably indicates that it is a cohortative, whose form theoretically would be אֶמְצָאָה, but for third-*aleph* verbs such as מָצָא that cohortative form is almost always avoided (Joüon, § 114 b, note 1). The form could also be an imperfect with that same modal meaning, "may" (Joüon, § 113 l).

הַמֶּלֶךְ:—For "Your Majesty," see the fourth textual note on 14:4.

16:5 יֹצֵא יָצוֹא וּמְקַלֵּל:—"As he came out, he was cursing as he came" is literally "coming out, to come out and cursing." The Qal participle of יָצָא, "come out," is followed by a Qal infinitive absolute of the same verb, יָצוֹא. The infinitive is coordinated with מְקַלֵּל, the Piel participle of קָלַל, "to belittle, curse." This use of an infinitive absolute with a participle is a rare construction (Joüon, § 123 n); usually two infinitive absolutes are coordinated to emphasize continuing action. The Piel of קָלַל is used again for Shimei's cursing of David in 16:7, 9, 10 (twice), 11, 13 (see also the cognate noun קְלָלָה, "a curse," in the third textual note on 16:12). The Piel of קָלַל can refer to a person "cursing" or blaspheming God (the likely reading in 1 Sam 3:13) or to "cursing" another person in the name of one's God or gods (1 Sam 17:43). In this passage Shimei invokes the gracious covenant name of Israel's God, "Yahweh," as he curses Yahweh's anointed (16:8 [twice]). His cursing, then, is a prime example of the violation of the Second Commandment (Ex 20:7; Deut 5:11) as well as a transgression of the injunction

---

[4] Steinmann, *1 Samuel*, 44.

against cursing a ruler of Israel (Ex 22:27b [ET 22:28b], which uses the stronger verb אָרַר).

16:6 וַיְסַקֵּל בָּאֲבָנִים—"He threw rocks" is literally "and he pelted with the stones." The Qal (G) of סָקַל often is used with בָּאֲבָנִים to mean "to stone" someone to death "with (the) stones."[5] In the OT its Piel (D) is used with בָּאֲבָנִים only here and in 16:13, both times for throwing stones but without inflicting death.

הַגִּבֹּרִים—For "the elite troops," see the textual note on 10:7.

16:7 בְּקַלְלוֹ—"When he cursed." This is the Piel (D) infinitive construct of קָלַל (see the textual note on 16:5) with בְּ and a third masculine singular suffix, forming a temporal clause. The translation "when he [Shimei] cursed" assumes that the suffix serves as the subject of the infinitive, but the suffix could also be its object, in which case the clause would be translated as "while cursing him [David]." For its ambiguity, see Joüon, § 124 i, note 2.

אִישׁ הַדָּמִים—"You man of bloodshed." The article is used to mark the construct phrase as a vocative,[6] literally "O man of *the* blood." This and the following phrase use a construct phrase with אִישׁ to describe the character or quality of a person (Waltke-O'Connor, § 9.5.3b, including example 8). In Hebrew the plural for human "blood" (דָּם) is a plural of result[7] that denotes shed blood, as again in 16:8; 21:1. The same construct phrase recurs in 16:8 but without the article, as also in Ps 5:7 (ET 5:6). See also the plural אַנְשֵׁי דָמִים, "men of bloodshed," in Pss 26:9; 55:24 (ET 55:23); 59:3 (ET 59:2); 139:19; Prov 29:10.

וְאִישׁ הַבְּלִיָּעַל:—"And good-for-nothing man." As in the prior textual note, the article is used to mark the construct phrase as a vocative, literally "O man of *the* worthlessness." בְּלִיָּעַל (here in pause and with the article: הַבְּלִיָּעַל) is a compound noun from בְּלִי, "not, without," and a nominal form of the verb יָעַל, which occurs only in the Hiphil (H) and means "to avail, be beneficial" (see the verb in 1 Sam 12:21). בְּלִיָּעַל is often used to characterize people who are not simply useless but actively malicious and destructive. It recurs often in Samuel.[8] A Greek variant of this Hebrew word, Βελιάρ, is used by Paul as a term for Satan in 2 Cor 6:15.

16:8 הֵשִׁיב עָלֶיךָ יְהוָה—"Yahweh has paid you back" is literally "Yahweh returned upon you." The Hiphil (H) of שׁוּב can be used with various prepositions, including עַל (as here), with Yahweh as the subject in the sense of either "paying back" (divine retribution), as here (also 1 Sam 25:39), or bestowing a good reward, as in 2 Sam 16:12 (also 1 Sam 26:23; 2 Sam 22:21, 25; cf. 1 Sam 25:21).

אֲשֶׁר מָלַכְתָּ תַּחְתָּיו—"In whose place you rule" is literally "whom you rule in his place." The Qere תַּחְתָּיו is the usual plene, or *male'*, spelling of the plural form of the preposition תַּחַת with a third masculine singular suffix. The Kethib תחתו probably is to

---

5. Deut 13:11 (ET 13:10); 17:5; 22:21, 24; Josh 7:25; 1 Ki 21:13; without בָּאֲבָנִים in 1 Sam 30:6.

6. *IBH*, § 19 B; Waltke-O'Connor, § 13.5.2a.

7. *IBH*, § 11 C; GKC, § 124 n; Waltke-O'Connor, § 7.4.1b; Joüon, § 136 b.

8. 1 Sam 1:16; 2:12; 10:27; 25:17, 25; 30:22; 2 Sam 16:7; 20:1; 22:5; 23:6. See also, e.g., Deut 13:14 (ET 13:13); 15:9; Judg 19:22; 20:13; 1 Ki 21:10, 13; Nah 1:11; 2:1 (ET 1:15); Job 34:18; Prov 6:12; 16:27; 19:28; 2 Chr 13:7.

be pointed as the same word but spelled defectively, תַּחְתָּו (as in 2 Sam 2:23; 3:12; Job 9:13), since the singular form of the preposition with a suffix, תַּחְתּוֹ, never appears in the OT. Cf. the unsuffixed preposition תַּחַת, "in place of," in 16:12.

וְהִנְּךָ בְּרָעָתֶךָ—"Look, you are in your evil." Most likely the preposition בְּ has the locative sense "in," i.e., David is "in" the evil situation for which he is responsible. As he shed blood, so now his blood is in danger of being shed (see Gen 9:6). Cf. NKJV: "you are caught in your own evil," and NASB. The suffix on the noun רָעָתֶךָ is subjective, and so the word could be rendered as "the punishment which you deserve" (Joüon, § 129 d).

16:9 הַכֶּלֶב הַמֵּת הַזֶּה—For "this dead dog," see the fourth textual note on 1 Sam 24:15 (ET 24:14)[9] and the second textual note on 2 Sam 9:8.

אֶעְבְּרָה־נָּא וְאָסִירָה אֶת־רֹאשׁוֹ:—Literally "please let me cross over, and let me remove his head." The verbs are singular cohortatives, the Qal (G) of עָבַר and the Hiphil (H) of סוּר, respectively (see Joüon, § 114 d).

16:10 מַה־לִּי וְלָכֶם—"Why do I put up with you?" is literally "what (is) to me and to you [plural]?" or "what belongs to both me and you [plural]," that is, "what do we have in common?" (see BDB, s.v. מָה, 1 d (*c*), and s.v. לְ, 5 b). This expression, with either a singular or plural "you," expresses exasperation and is a formula for repudiation, a denial that the two parties have anything in common or any relationship to each other.[10]

כֹּה יְקַלֵּל כִּי—"Let him curse this way because." This reading with the Qere of the first and the third words, literally "thus may he curse because," is supported by the LXX (οὕτως καταράσθω ὅτι). The reading with the Kethib of those words is כִּי יְקַלֵּל וְכִי, which could mean "because he will curse, and because" or "surely he will curse, and [he will do that] because." The Piel (D) third masculine singular verb could be either the jussive or the imperfect of קָלַל (see the textual note on 16:5).

16:11 אֲשֶׁר־יָצָא מִמֵּעַי—"Who came out from my body." Ironically, the same wording (the verb יָצָא and the suffixed plural of the noun מֵעֶה with the preposition מִן) was used in the divine promise of a son who would come from David in 7:12, but Absalom is not that son whose kingdom Yahweh promised to establish.

הַנִּחוּ לוֹ—"Leave him alone." This form of נוּחַ is from its second Hiphil (H) paradigm, in which the forms appear as if from a root נָנַח and mean "set; leave" (BDB, s.v. נוּחַ, Hiphil B), as also in 16:21; 20:3. For its first Hiphil paradigm, see the textual note on 7:1.

וִיקַלֵּל—"And let him curse/keep on cursing." In this context the jussive has a durative force (cf. Joüon, § 113 d, commenting on יְקַלֵּל in 16:9). This jussive is bound to the preceding imperative with *waw* (Joüon, § 177 k).

16:12 יִרְאֶה יְהוָה בְּעֵינִי—"Yahweh will see my affliction." The verb רָאָה, "see," can take the preposition בְּ in the sense of "look into" or "look at" with particular care or compassion (see BDB, s.v. רָאָה, Qal, 8 a (2)). The object with בְּ is, according to the Qere, בְּעֵינִי, literally "in/with my eyes," which is the sole reading in some Masoretic manuscripts. It might mean that David hopes that Yahweh will see the situation through

---

9 Steinmann, *1 Samuel*, 456.

10 Also Judg 11:12; 2 Sam 19:23 (ET 19:22); 1 Ki 17:18; 2 Ki 3:13; 2 Chr 35:21 (cf. Jn 2:4).

his eyes, that is, from David's perspective or point of view. The Kethib, בעוני, could be pointed בְּעֲוֹנִי, "on my iniquity," and the noun עָוֹן can also refer to the "punishment" one suffers because of one's iniquity (cf. ESV: "on the wrong done to me"). A few Masoretic manuscripts read בְּעָנְיִי, "on my affliction" (the suffixed noun עֳנִי), which is supported by the LXX (ἐν τῇ ταπεινώσει μου, "on my humiliation") as well as the Syriac and the Vulgate. This reading is followed by most English versions.[11]

וְהֵשִׁיב יְהוָה לִי טוֹבָה—"And Yahweh will repay good to me." See the first textual note on 16:8.

קִלְלָתוֹ—Literally "his curse." This is the suffixed noun קְלָלָה, "a curse," which is cognate to the verb קָלַל, discussed in the textual note on 16:5.

16:13 בְּצֵלַע הָהָר לְעֻמָּתוֹ ... לְעֻמָּתוֹ—"Parallel to him along the ridge of the hill ... beside him" is literally "on the rib of the mountain, parallel to him ... beside him." The word עֻמָּה is always used as a preposition and almost always with the prefixed preposition לְ. It often indicates proximity "close by" or motion in "parallel" (BDB, s.v. עֻמָּה, a, under the root עמם I). In both instances of לְעֻמָּתוֹ here, its third masculine singular suffix refers back to "David" at the start of the verse. It was not necessarily the ridge itself but the movement of Shimei on the ridge that was "parallel" to David and "beside him."

הָלוֹךְ וַיְקַלֵּל וַיְסַקֵּל בָּאֲבָנִים—"Cursing and throwing stones as he went." This construction emphasizes continuing action. Usually frequentative or iterative action is signified by the Qal (G) infinitive absolute הָלוֹךְ, "going," followed by an infinitive absolute of the verb denoting the action that continued (Joüon, § 123 s). The syntax of the construction here is atypical. The Qal infinitive absolute הָלוֹךְ, "going," is followed by two Piel (D) preterite (imperfect with *waw* consecutive) verbs that denote the actions Shimei continued to perform (and a prepositional phrase with the second verb): וַיְקַלֵּל וַיְסַקֵּל בָּאֲבָנִים, "cursing and throwing stones," literally "and he cursed and he threw with the stones." See GKC, § 113 t. The same construction with הָלוֹךְ, but followed by only one preterite (imperfect with *waw* consecutive), appears in 1 Sam 19:23. A similar construction with הָלוֹךְ, but with a perfect verb with *waw* consecutive, is used in Josh 6:13a; 2 Sam 13:19. Is 31:5 has two other infinitive absolutes, each followed by one perfect verb with *waw* consecutive. Since, then, the OT attests a total of six infinitive absolutes followed by finite tenses with *waw* consecutive to denote continuing action and three of them with הָלוֹךְ are in the book of Samuel (1 Sam 19:23; 2 Sam 13:19; 16:13), Joüon, § 123 n, is unjustified in calling for the finite tenses in these five verses to be emended to infinitive absolutes.

וְעִפַּר בֶּעָפָר:—"He also kept throwing dirt" is literally "and he kept dusting [David] with the dust." This cognate accusative construction uses the Piel (D) perfect with *waw* consecutive, denoting continuing action (GKC, § 112 f), of the denominative verb עָפַר, which is derived from the accusative noun here, עָפָר, "dust (of the earth), dirt." This is the only OT instance of the verb, and it is a denominative productive Piel (Waltke-O'Connor, § 24.4e, including example 6). This action was intended to shame David by

---

[11] HCSB, GW, NET, NIV.

forcibly applying dirt on his head. A person would voluntarily throw dirt on his head to signify lamentation, mourning (a death), or repentance.[12] Man was made out of "dust" (עָפָר, Gen 2:7), and upon death he will return to "dust" (עָפָר, Gen 3:19).

16:14 עֲיֵפִים—This spelling of the adjective, עָיֵף (also in 17:29), "exhausted," is more common (seventeen times in the OT) than the spelling יָעֵף. See the third textual note on 16:2.

וַיִּנָּפֵשׁ שָׁם:—"But they were refreshed there." The verb נָפַשׁ appears only three times in the OT, always in the Niphal, one other time for God's people (Ex 23:12) and once for God himself on the seventh day (Ex 31:17). Since it is a denominative from the noun נֶפֶשׁ, "soul," in reference to people, it could be translated literally as "their soul was restored" (cf. Ps 23:3; also, e.g., Pss 19:8 [ET 19:7]; 35:17; Ruth 4:15).

Commentary

974 BC[13]

After David crossed the summit of the Mount of Olives on his way to the fords of the Jordan, he encountered two persons related to the house of Saul. The first was Saul's former servant Ziba, who was now serving Saul's grandson Mephibosheth. The second was Shimei, a member of Saul's clan. In David's encounters with these two men, we are given insight into his faith and state of mind as he fled from his renegade son Absalom.

These interactions with the house of Saul also serve to contrast David's reaction to adversity with Saul's response to adversity earlier in the book of Samuel. When apostate Saul[14] was told that, because of his infidelity to the divine Word, God would take the kingdom from him and give it to another (1 Sam 15:23–16:1), he became murderously desperate and sought to kill David, whom he suspected as being God's new chosen king (1 Sam 18:6–26:25). Shortly before his death (1 Sam 31:1–6), Saul resorted to the occult when he surmised that God had abandoned him (1 Sam 28:4–20). David was also desperate as he fled from Absalom, who was murderously conspiring to seize the throne from him. However, David did not attempt to take the life of anyone. He even commanded the preservation of the life of his harshest heckler, Shimei (2 Sam 16:9–10). Nor did he turn away from God, but obeyed his Word in faith. He humbly submitted to whatever Yahweh may have spoken (2 Sam 16:11) and trusted in Yahweh for righteousness and ultimate vindication (2 Sam 16:12; 22:21, 25; see also, e.g., 1 Sam 26:23). While he may have used his judicial powers to recruit an ally in Ziba (see the commentary on 2 Sam 16:1–4), he did not break his covenant oath, sworn by Yahweh, to show Yahweh's "gracious

---

[12] See 2 Sam 1:2; 15:32; see also Josh 7:6; Ezek 27:30; Job 2:12; Lam 2:10 (cf. 2 Sam 13:19).

[13] See "The Chronology of David's Reign" in the commentary on 5:1–5.

[14] See the commentary on 1 Sam 10:7–8 and figure 16, "Saul's Faltering Accession," in "Samuel Anoints Saul (9:26–10:8)" in the commentary on 1 Sam 9:26–10:16, as well as the beginning of the commentary on 1 Sam 10:17–27a (Steinmann, *1 Samuel*, 196–98, 203). Saul and most of his troops lacked trust in Yahweh's deliverance and so were terrified of the Philistines (1 Sam 13:7, 12; 17:11; 28:5).

love" (חֶסֶד, 1 Sam 20:8, 14–15) to Jonathan's posterity (1 Sam 18:3; 20:8, 14–16; 22:8; 23:18).

Ziba Brings Supplies for David (16:1–4)

David's encounter with Ziba, the caretaker of Mephibosheth's estate (see 9:1–11), is presented as unexpected—this is probably the force of "there was" (וְהִנֵּה, 16:1). Ziba's provision of supplies for David's troops (see the textual notes on 16:1) is somewhat reminiscent of Abigail's gifts when she encountered David (1 Sam 25:18).

The unexpected nature of Ziba's presence is reflected in David's question "why do you have these things?" (16:2). Ziba's reply focuses on the intended benefits of the items he was bringing, not his reason for bringing them. Therefore, David probed again, asking about Mephibosheth's whereabouts (16:3a). Ziba's reply (16:3b) is not simply information; it is also an accusation that Saul's grandson saw Absalom's rebellion as an opportunity for he himself to ascend to the throne. Mephibosheth thought he could usurp Absalom's usurpation. The text does not inform readers whether Ziba's allegation is true. There are several possibilities:

1. Ziba is reporting Mephibosheth's aspirations correctly.
2. Mephibosheth sent the supplies to David, and Ziba is taking advantage of the situation to undercut his master and ingratiate himself with David.
3. Ziba came without Mephibosheth's knowledge and hoped to damage Mephibosheth's standing with David in order to gain favors from the king.

While the author does not resolve these issues here or even later (19:25–31 [ET 19:24–30]), there are good reasons to suspect that Ziba is deceiving David and slandering Mephibosheth:[15]

1. It is difficult, if not impossible, to imagine that the permanently disabled Mephibosheth (2 Sam 4:4; 9:13) thought he could ascend to the throne. At most he could count on the support of some Benjaminites who were still loyal to the house of Saul. His former patron Machir was a supporter of David (2 Sam 9:4, 5; 17:27–29). Absalom seemed to enjoy popular support at this point, and should Absalom fail, David had military forces at his disposal and most likely could have easily dealt with any threat from Saulide sympathizers.
2. Ziba reported to David Mephibosheth's thoughts (or perhaps an oral statement).[16] It is difficult to understand why Mephibosheth would have shared his ambitions with anyone, much less a servant. Were Saul's grandson hoping to be able to somehow seize the throne, it would have been dangerously foolish for him to plot in

---

[15] Similarly, in 1 Sam 28:11–19, the text, on its surface, reports an interaction with Samuel from beyond the grave. A more careful consideration, however, leads the reader to conclude that the interaction is actually with an evil spirit who intends to deceive, not with Samuel. See the commentary there. The author also leaves the reader to wonder about the target of David's anger at the death of Uzziah (see commentary on 2 Sam 6:8).

[16] In 16:3 the verb אָמַר is translated as "he thought." It could be understood to introduce either Mephibosheth's internal dialogue (thought) or a statement that he uttered. The verb most commonly means "to say (aloud)," but often in narrative it conveys unspoken thoughts.

front of Ziba, whom David had appointed—perhaps forced—to look after his estate (9:9–11).

3. No text in the book of Samuel ever portrays Mephibosheth as disloyal to David or as having a desire to regain the kingdom for the house of Saul.

For these reasons, most expositors from antiquity onward have suspected Ziba of deception and fraud. For instance, John Chrysostom (c. AD 349–407) stated: "Ziba flattered David out of season, and falsely slandered his master (2 Sam. xvi. 1–3)."[17]

However, this incident is less about Ziba and more about David. David took Ziba at his word and immediately decreed that Mephibosheth's estate was now Ziba's (16:4). Such a judicial verdict appears ill-considered and precipitous on the king's part. He had not allowed Mephibosheth to defend himself (cf. Prov 18:17). He did not need to hand down a decision at this juncture—he could have postponed it until a later time, should he regain Jerusalem and secure his position on the throne once more. Since the author of Samuel relates that David felt the compulsion to grant Ziba the estate, he is also implying something about David's state of mind. David was not at all certain that he would survive Absalom's challenge for the kingdom. He needed every useful and influential ally he could possibly find. A lame Mephibosheth in occupied Jerusalem would be of no use to him. However, the able-bodied and capable Ziba, head of a large family ("fifteen sons and twenty slaves," 9:10), may have proven strategic to David's survival.

Therefore, this encounter between David and Ziba reveals David's desperation and gloom as he considered the powers arrayed against him. This was the situation in which David wrote Ps 3:2–3 (ET 3:1–2; see also Ps 2:1–3). While David trusted God to defend him (Ps 3:4–9 [ET 3:3–8]; see also Ps 2:12b), he also understood that God worked through persons.[18] Thus, he calculated that it was best to garner Ziba's support now and perhaps work out any problems later, should he gain victory over his mutinous son.

Shimei Curses David (16:5–14)

On his way to the Jordan River, David passed by the Benjaminite city of Bahurim, modern Ras eṭ-Ṭmim, just east of Mount Scopus (2 Sam 16:5; cf. 19:17 [ET 19:16]; 1 Ki 2:8). Here he encountered the cursing Shimei, who is identified as a man from a clan of the house of Saul; Saul's clan was that of Matri (1 Sam 10:21).[19] Shimei's attack on David was not simply verbal. It also involved an attempt to stone David and his servants, although they were protected by the army on both sides (2 Sam 16:6).

---

[17] John Chrysostom, *Homilies on Philippians*, 5 (*NPNF*[1] 13:205).

[18] Note that David had asked Yahweh to turn Ahithophel's advice into foolishness while also recruiting Hushai to be his agent to counteract Ahithophel's counsel (15:31–37).

[19] Shimei is called "the son of Gera" (2 Sam 16:5). Gera is not a reference to the Benjaminite clan of Gera (1 Chr 8:3, 5, 7) but is the name of Shimei's father.

Shimei's curse welcomed David's exit from Jerusalem and accused him of "bloodshed" and godlessness as a "good-for-nothing man" (אִישׁ הַבְּלִיָּעַל, 16:7).[20] He claimed that Yahweh was paying David back for the bloodshed he inflicted on the house of Saul (16:8). He was most likely referring to the execution of seven Saulides at Gibeon, which David had allowed (21:1–14).[21] Since he also linked David's troubles with Absalom's rebellion (16:8), he may have included Uriah's death (11:14–24) as part of David's bloody deeds. The seeds of Absalom's rebellion were sown in David's adultery with Bathsheba and in his order to let Uriah be killed. This led to an entire sequence of events: the rape of Tamar by Amnon (13:1–20), Absalom's killing of his half brother Amnon (13:21–39), and now Absalom's attempted palace coup.

David's nephew Abishai was indignant that David gave no orders to stop Shimei's curses (16:9). He characterized the Benjaminite with the extremely deprecating phrase "dead dog" (see the commentary on 9:8) and offered to execute him. Abishai's suggestion was not unreasonable, since the Law of Moses prohibited anyone from cursing a ruler (Ex 22:27 [ET 22:28]; cf. Job 34:17–18; see the textual note on 2 Sam 16:5).

David, however, overruled Abishai. He conceded that Shimei may have been acting on Yahweh's behalf, and no one ought to gainsay what Yahweh has done (16:10). David was acutely aware that his troubles stemmed from his sin, especially his adultery with Bathsheba and his murder of her innocent husband Uriah (2 Samuel 11). He did not deny that he had shed blood and behaved like a godless good-for-nothing man, and he would not have Shimei punished for stating what was at least partially true. However, Shimei would eventually be punished for cursing the king (1 Ki 2:8, 36–46).

David also pointed out that his own son sought his life, so there was no reason to punish this Matrite for similar acts (2 Sam 16:11). David's reference to Absalom as one "who came out from my body" (אֲשֶׁר־יָצָא מִמֵּעַי) echoes God's promise that someone from David's "body" (אֲשֶׁר יֵצֵא מִמֵּעֶיךָ, "who will come from your own body") would build Yahweh's temple in Jerusalem (7:12–13). Perhaps at this low point David was assuming that Absalom might well succeed in seizing the throne and would, therefore, be the one to build the temple. Nevertheless, David held out hope that Yahweh would have pity on him because of his afflictions and turn Shimei's curses into good for him (16:12). However, in the present, Shimei's cursing, stoning, and hurling of dirt was a reminder of David's sin and self-inflicted misery (16:13).

---

[20] See the third textual note on 16:7.

[21] This execution of the seven descendants of Saul took place sometime between 996 and 980 BC, at least six years before Absalom's insurgency; see "The Chronology of David's Reign" in the commentary on 5:1–5. There is no reason to believe that Shimei was accusing David of being complicit in the death of Ishbosheth (4:5–12), though he may have believed that David had a part in Abner's murder at the hands of Joab (3:22–27).

Very quickly the scene moves to the goal of David's flight on that first day. His party arrived (presumably at the Jordan River), exhausted from their forced march, and they were rejuvenated (16:14). This allows the author to shift the scene to Jerusalem and Absalom's acts there as David was fleeing.

Absalom Follows Ahithophel's Advice

Translation

16 **15**Now Absalom and all the army of the men of Israel came to Jerusalem, and Ahithophel was with him. **16**As David's friend Hushai the Archite came to Absalom, Hushai said to Absalom, "Long live the king! Long live the king!"

17Absalom said to Hushai, "This is your loyalty to your friend? Why didn't you go with your friend?"

18Hushai said to Absalom, "No, for the one whom Yahweh and this people and all the men of Israel have chosen—I will be for him, and I will remain with him. **19**Furthermore, whom shall I serve? Should I not [serve] before his son? As I served before your father, so also I will be before you."

20Then Absalom said to Ahithophel, "Give your advice: what should we do?"

21Ahithophel said to Absalom, "Go in to your father's concubines whom he left to take care of the palace. All Israel will hear that you have made yourself repulsive to your father, and they will support everyone who is with you." **22**So they pitched a tent for Absalom on the roof, and Absalom went in to his father's concubines in the sight of all Israel. **23**The advice that Ahithophel gave in those days was as if someone would ask for a word from God. Thus was all of Ahithophel's advice, both to David and to Absalom.

Textual Notes

16:15 וְכָל־הָעָם֙ אִ֣ישׁ יִשְׂרָאֵ֔ל—In military contexts, the noun עַם, "people," with the definite article can denote "the troops" or "the army." See the first textual note on 1 Sam 4:3[1] and the second textual note on 2 Sam 1:4. The construct phrase אִ֣ישׁ יִשְׂרָאֵ֔ל is in apposition to הָעָם֙, literally "the army, the man of Israel," and it identifies what kind of soldiers comprised the army. In English, the appositional phrase is best translated as if all four words were a construct chain, with the singular noun אִישׁ being used as a collective: "all of the army of the men of Israel."

16:16 רֵעֶ֥ה דָוִ֖ד—This construct phrase is literally "the friend of David." See the first textual note on 15:37. It does not merely signify an informal friendship but is a title for a royal official; in Solomon's administration Zabud will bear the title "the king's friend" (1 Ki 4:5). The masculine noun here is רֵעֶה. The shorter masculine noun רֵעַ will be used with a suffix, רֵעֶ֫ךָ, "your friend," twice in 16:17, referring to David as the king to whom Hushai had been loyal.

יְחִ֣י הַמֶּ֔לֶךְ יְחִ֖י הַמֶּֽלֶךְ׃—The acclamation יְחִ֣י הַמֶּ֔לֶךְ, repeated here, is literally "may the king live!" The verb יְחִי is the Qal (G) third masculine singular jussive of חָיָה, "to live." The Israelites used this acclamation when Saul was chosen as their first king

---

[1] Steinmann, *1 Samuel*, 120.

(1 Sam 10:24). It will also be used for Adonijah (1 Ki 1:25), Solomon (1 Ki 1:34, 39), and Joash (2 Ki 11:12 ‖ 2 Chr 23:11).

16:17 חַסְדְּךָ—"Your loyalty." The noun חֶסֶד can refer to God's faithful love, bestowed according to his covenant of grace. This love can be shown by a king to God's people. The noun can also refer to a person's loyalty to Yahweh's anointed king. See 1 Sam 20:8, 14–15; 2 Sam 2:5–6; 3:8; 7:15; 9:1, 3 (see the second textual note on 9:3), 7; 22:51. See also the cognate terms in 2 Sam 22:26.

אֶת־רֵעֶךָ ... אֶת־רֵעֶךָ‎—"To your friend … with your friend." In both instances אֶת is the preposition "with" rather than the direct object marker. Both רֵעֶךָ and רֵעֶךָ are pausal forms of רֵעֲךָ. For "friend," see the first textual note on 16:16.

16:18 כִּי אֲשֶׁר בָּחַר יְהוָה וְהָעָם הַזֶּה וְכָל־אִישׁ יִשְׂרָאֵל—Literally "for (the one) whom Yahweh chose, and this people and every man of Israel." This relative clause is a *casus pendens* (see Joüon, § 156 k). The third masculine singular pronominal suffix on the later words לוֹ, "for *him*," and אִתּוֹ, "with *him*," refer back to the person described here. The verb בָּחַר is singular, in agreement with its most important subject, "Yahweh," emphasizing the primacy of Yahweh's choice of this person; that the person is also the choice of "this people" and "all the men of Israel" is of secondary importance. Elsewhere in Samuel the verb בָּחַר, "choose," is used both for Yahweh choosing a king (Saul in 1 Sam 10:24; the verb is negated for the other sons of Jesse in 1 Sam 16:8–10, which implies a positive use for David; and David in 2 Sam 6:21) and also for the people's choice of a king (Saul in 1 Sam 8:18; 12:13).

לוֹ אֶהְיֶה—"I will be for him." This is the reading of the Qere, which is supported by the LXX (αὐτῷ ἔσομαι). The Kethib is לֹא אֶהְיֶה, "I will not be."

16:19 וְהַשֵּׁנִית—"Furthermore" is literally "and the second (thing)." This is the feminine form of the adjective שֵׁנִי, which is the ordinal "second."

כַּאֲשֶׁר עָבַדְתִּי לִפְנֵי אָבִיךָ—"As I served before your father." See the commentary.

16:20 הָבוּ לָכֶם עֵצָה—"Give your advice" is literally "give for yourselves counsel." This may be equivalent to an English question that indirectly asks for advice: "what would you do?" Note that plural forms are used both for the Qal (G) imperative of יָהַב, "give," and for the pronominal suffix (כֶם-) on the preposition לְ, "yourselves." Apparently Absalom was asking all of his advisors while addressing Ahithophel as his chief advisor. For the noun עֵצָה, "advice, counsel," which recurs in 16:23, see the fourth textual note on 15:31.

16:21–22 בּוֹא אֶל־פִּלַגְשֵׁי אָבִיךָ ... וַיָּבֹא אַבְשָׁלוֹם אֶל־פִּלַגְשֵׁי אָבִיו—"Go in to your father's concubines. … And Absalom went in to his father's concubines." The Hebrew idiom with the verb בּוֹא and the preposition אֶל, literally "to go in to," means "to have sexual intercourse with" or "to sleep with." See the fourth textual note on 3:7 and the second textual note on 12:24.

16:21 אֲשֶׁר הִנִּיחַ—"Whom he left." This refers to David's action in 15:16. This third masculine singular perfect of נוּחַ is from its second Hiphil (H) paradigm, whose forms appear as if they were from a root ננח and mean "set; leave" (BDB, s.v. נוּחַ, Hiphil B). The identical form הִנִּיחַ recurs in 20:3. For the first Hiphil paradigm of נוּחַ, see the textual note on 7:1.

לִשְׁמֹר הַבָּֽיִת—"To take care of the palace." The identical purpose clause was in 15:16, where David left behind ten of his concubines to do this.

נִבְאַשְׁתָּ אֶת־—"You have made yourself repulsive to" is literally "you have made yourself stinky with." For the Niphal (N) of בָּאַשׁ, see the second textual note on 1 Sam 13:4[2] and the first textual note on 2 Sam 10:6. In those verses it took the preposition בְּ, but here it takes the preposition אֶת, "with."

וְחָזְקוּ יְדֵי כָּל־אֲשֶׁר אִתָּֽךְ׃—"And they will support everyone who is with you" is literally "and they will strengthen the hands of everyone who (is) with you." אִתָּךְ is pausal for אִתְּךָ.

16:22 וַיַּטּוּ ... הָאֹהֶל—"So they pitched a tent." The verb is the Hiphil (H) third masculine plural preterite (imperfect with *waw* consecutive) of נָטָה, "to stretch out." Usually נָטָה is used in the Qal (G) to refer to pitching a tent (BDB, Qal, 2). Its Hiphil is used with this meaning only here and, metaphorically, in Is 54:2. In 2 Sam 21:10 it refers to spreading out a cloth. Hebrew commonly uses the definite article on a noun (הָאֹהֶל, "*the* tent") when the narrator has in mind a specific one; see the first textual note on 15:13.

16:23 וַעֲצַת אֲחִיתֹפֶל אֲשֶׁר יָעַץ—"The advice that Ahithophel gave." This cognate accusative construction is literally "and the counsel of Ahithophel that he counseled." The verb יָעַץ, "to counsel, advise," takes as its object the noun that is derived from it, עֵצָה (here in construct: עֲצַת). For the noun, see the fourth textual note on 15:31. This is the first instance of the verb in the book of Samuel; it recurs in 17:7, 11, 15 (twice), 21. Ahithophel is the one who counsels in 17:7, 15a, 21, while Hushai advises in 17:11, 15b.

יִשְׁאַל־אִישׁ—"Someone would ask" is literally "a man will/would ask." This is the Qere. The Kethib has only the verb יִשְׁאַל, used impersonally with no stated subject, which would have almost the same meaning, "one would ask." The LXX (ἐπερωτήσῃ) supports the Kethib. Therefore אִישׁ, "a man," may be a scribal addition to the Hebrew text.

Commentary

974 BC[3]

The author now takes his readers back in time to the entry of Absalom into Jerusalem as Hushai also entered the city (16:15; cf. 15:37). Hushai greeted Absalom with the customary acclamation used at coronations as a pledge of loyalty and repeated it as if to emphasize his sincerity: "Long live the king! Long live the king!" (יְחִי הַמֶּלֶךְ יְחִי הַמֶּלֶךְ, 16:16).[4] However, readers will immediately perceive that Hushai was concealing his loyalty to David, since he did not state to *which* king he was promising his allegiance. The author intends readers to interpret the double acclamation in light of his prior affirmation that Hushai was, in actuality, "David's friend" (16:16a).

---

[2] Steinmann, *1 Samuel*, 232.

[3] See "The Chronology of David's Reign" in the commentary on 5:1–5.

[4] See the second textual note on 16:16.

Absalom appears to have accepted Hushai's acclamation as a pledge of loyalty to him. However, he questioned Hushai's quick abandonment of David—was Hushai simply a political opportunist (16:17)? Absalom's challenge contained a sarcastic rebuke with a double entendre: Hushai was the king's friend—a trusted official (1 Chr 27:33; cf. 1 Ki 4:5), but he appeared to be a traitor to his friend David, whom Absalom twice labeled "*your* friend" (רֵעֶךָ ... רֵעֶךָ, 2 Sam 16:17).

Hushai explained that he was simply being loyal to the king chosen by Yahweh and the people (16:18). However, Hushai once again found a way to flatter Absalom while concealing his true fidelity to David. While Absalom may have wanted to believe he was God's choice as king, there was no evidence for it—no prophetic pronouncement, no vision, no sign. Instead, David was the one whom Yahweh had chosen (see the discussion of בָּחַר, "choose," in the first textual note on 16:18). David had been anointed as king three times: first, by the prophet Samuel (1 Sam 16:12–13), then by the men of Judah (2 Sam 2:4, 7), and finally by the elders of Israel (2 Sam 5:3, 17). Since these actions were by Yahweh's choice, the prophet Nathan could affirm that Yahweh himself had anointed David (2 Sam 12:7). Moreover, there was no indication that Israel had chosen Absalom. He had engineered his acclamation as king (15:10). The elders of Israel had not come to Hebron to recognize him as king, as they had done for David (5:1–3), and as the men of Judah had done for David earlier (2:1–4). Thus, Hushai was able to proclaim his loyalty to David while making the narcissistic Absalom (cf. 14:25–26) believe that Hushai had shifted his allegiance to him.

Hushai then asked two rhetorical questions about whom he should serve (16:19). Again, he chose his words judiciously. First, Hushai asked, "Whom shall I serve?" Absalom assumed that the answer to the question was himself, but Hushai did not state that. Second, Hushai asked, "Should I not [serve] before his [David's] son?" Then Hushai said that as he had "served before" (עָבַדְתִּי לִפְנֵי) Absalom's father, so also he would "be before" Absalom. The expression "to serve before" (עָבַד לִפְנֵי) is unique in the OT. It is so unusual that in some Masoretic manuscripts a scribe apparently sought to correct it by changing the preposition לִפְנֵי, "before," to the direct object marker אֵת, to match the usual construction. Usually "to serve someone" is expressed by the Qal (G) of עָבַד with the direct object marker (אֵת) introducing the person served.[5] Hushai was carefully avoiding a forthright statement of whom he would be serving by instead stating in whose presence he would be functioning. Moreover, his final statement that he would "be before you [Absalom]" (אֶהְיֶה לִפְנֶיךָ) said nothing about service.

Hushai's carefully crafted reply to Absalom managed to convince this particular son of David that Hushai was his ally. However, Hushai had said no such thing. In fact, he entirely avoided using Absalom's name. While Ahithophel was

---

[5] In Samuel, see this construction, עָבַד אֵת, in 1 Sam 7:4; 12:10, 14, 20, 24; 17:9; 2 Sam 15:8.

known for his wisdom (16:23), Hushai proved to be wise, cunning, and wily enough to insert himself among Absalom's advisors as David's covert agent.

Having accepted Hushai into his circle of counselors, Absalom next asked them their advice, directly addressing Ahithophel as chief advisor (16:20; see the textual note). Ahithophel's advice was that Absalom ought to do the unthinkable—sleep with his father's concubines—thereby making himself detestable to his father (16:21). Ahithophel was hoping that Absalom would thereby gain the support of the populace or at least of the Israelite leaders whom Ahithophel assumed had been scandalized by David's acts in regard to Bathsheba and Uriah (2 Samuel 11). Ahithophel's advice, however, was not in Absalom's best interest, but served his own agenda. He wanted to get vengeance on David for corrupting his granddaughter and killing his grandson-in-law.[6] For Absalom, sleeping with David's concubines was a claim to the throne (cf. 1 Ki 2:22–23).[7] However, Ahithophel's guidance was sinister for Absalom. Absalom was not only ruining his relationship with his father, David, but he was also turning his back on Yahweh, whose Law condemned a man who had sexual relations with his father's wife. This was an incestuous abomination for which the death penalty was prescribed.[8] In the NT a man who does such a thing is to be delivered over to Satan for the destruction of his flesh (1 Cor 5:5), that is, excommunicated from the church of Christ (1 Cor 5:1–13). The concubines of David whom Absalom defiled were most likely Jebusite women whom David had married when he settled in Jerusalem (see the commentary on 2 Sam 5:13). By violating these women, Absalom fulfilled Nathan's condemnatory prophecy to David (12:11), while Ahithophel's advice that he should do so was a partial answer to David's prayer that Yahweh turn Ahithophel's advice into foolishness (15:31). Fools deny the existence of God, defy his Law, ignore his commands, and despise and dishonor their parents.[9]

Why did Absalom follow Ahithophel's evil and godless advice and publicly disgrace David (16:22)? The author tells us that at that time Ahithophel's pronouncements—both to David and to Absalom—were considered as good as God's own Word (16:23). Thus, Absalom was not afraid to defy God's Law because he valued Ahithophel's words as much as—even more than—the Word of God. David also knew that Ahithophel's advice had been as valuable as an oracle from God, which is why he prayed that it would be turned to folly (15:31). The author of Samuel is subtly warning his readers that they must not rely on human words alone, no matter how persuasive, or place them on a par with

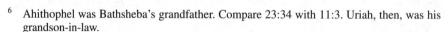

[6] Ahithophel was Bathsheba's grandfather. Compare 23:34 with 11:3. Uriah, then, was his grandson-in-law.

[7] Note that God had stated that when he made David king, he had given Saul's wives to him (12:8). However, there is no evidence that David slept with Saul's wives. This may simply be the rhetoric of kingship: the new king inherits his predecessor's household.

[8] Lev 18:8; 20:11; Deut 23:1 (ET 22:30); cf. Gen 35:22; 49:3–4. For the status of concubines as wives, see the commentary on 2 Sam 5:13.

[9] Pss 14:1; 53:2 (ET 53:1); Prov 10:23; 15:20; 17:25; 30:17.

God's Word. While even the most trusted Christian friend, parent, teacher, or pastor may often speak advice that is based on Scripture, we must always compare each piece of advice with the Word of God, which is the living voice of the perfect and holy God and is designed to point us to Christ (1 Thess 5:21–23; 2 Pet 2:1; 1 Jn 4:1–3). The Lutheran Confessions note:

> Christ commanded, "Beware of false prophets" (Matt. 7:15). Paul also commanded that ungodly teachers should be shunned and execrated as accursed [Titus 3:10], and he wrote in II Cor. 6:14, "Do not be mismated with unbelievers, for what fellowship has light with darkness?"[10]

---

[10] Treatise, 41.

Absalom Follows Hushai's Advice

Translation

17 [1]Ahithophel said to Absalom, "Let me choose twelve thousand men, leave, and pursue David tonight. [2]I will come upon him while he is exhausted and tired and cause him to panic. All the people who are with him will flee, and I will strike down the king alone. [3]Let me bring all the people back to you as a bride returns to her husband. It is only the life of one man whom you are seeking. All the people will be unharmed." [4]The plan seemed good to Absalom and all of Israel's elders.

[5]Absalom said, "Summon Hushai the Archite also. Let's hear what he has to say as well." [6]Hushai came to Absalom, and Absalom said to him, "Ahithophel spoke this plan. Should we follow his plan? If not, you should speak up."

[7]Hushai said to Absalom, "The advice that Ahithophel gave is not good this time." [8]Hushai said, "You yourself know your father and his men: they are skilled soldiers and enraged like a bear robbed of her cubs in the wild. Your father is an experienced soldier. He will not spend the night with the people. [9]Look, now he is (probably) hiding in one of the caves or one of the (other) places. As some among them fall at the beginning, someone is certain to hear [about it] and say, 'There has been a slaughter among the troops under Absalom.' [10]Then also the most skilled soldier whose heart is like a lion's heart will completely lose courage, because all Israel knows that your father is an experienced soldier and skilled soldiers are with him. [11]Therefore, I advise that all Israel from Dan to Beersheba be gathered to you as numerous as the sand that is beside the sea and that you personally go into battle. [12]We will come upon him in whatever place he is found, and we will descend on him like dew on the ground. Not even one of all the men who are with him will be left. [13]If he withdraws into a city, all Israel will bring ropes to that city, and we will drag it into the valley until not even a pebble could be found there."

[14]Absalom and all the men of Israel said, "The advice of Hushai the Archite is better than Ahithophel's advice." (Yahweh had decreed to foil Ahithophel's better advice in order for Yahweh to bring disaster on Absalom.)

[15]Hushai said to the high priests Zadok and Abiathar, "Here is what Ahithophel advised Absalom and the elders of Israel, and here is what I myself advised. [16]Now quickly send and report to David, 'Do not spend the night at the fords in the wilderness. Instead, cross over [the Jordan River], otherwise the king and all the people with him will be devoured.'"

[17]Now Jonathan and Ahimaaz were staying in En-rogel. A female servant would come and tell them, and they would go and report to King David, since they could not risk being seen going into the city. [18]A young man saw them and told Absalom.

The two of them quickly left and came to a man's house in Bahurim. He had a cistern in his courtyard, and they went down into it. [19]The wife took [a cloth] and spread [it] out as a covering over the mouth of the cistern and spread around grain on it, and no one knew about it. [20]Absalom's servants came to the woman at the house and said, "Where are Ahimaaz and Jonathan?"

The woman said to them, "They passed on to the water." So they searched, but did not find [them]. Then they returned to Jerusalem.

[21]After they left, they [Jonathan and Ahimaaz] came up from the cistern and went and reported to King David. They said to David, "Get up and cross the water quickly because Ahithophel has advised immediate action against you." [22]So David and all the people with him got up and crossed the Jordan River. By the morning light there was no one who had not crossed the Jordan River.

[23]Ahithophel saw that his advice was not followed, so he saddled his donkey, mounted [it], and went to his home in his city. He put his affairs in order and hanged himself. He died and was interred in his father's tomb.

[24]David came to Mahanaim while Absalom and all the men of Israel with him crossed the Jordan River. [25]Absalom had placed Amasa over the army in place of Joab. Amasa was the son of a man whose name was Ithra the Israelite, who had slept with Abigail, the granddaughter of Nahash, the sister of Zeruiah, the mother of Joab. [26]Israel and Absalom camped in the land of Gilead.

[27]As David came to Mahanaim, Nahash's son Shobi from Ammonite Rabbah, Ammiel's son Machir from Lo-dibbar, and Barzillai the Gileadite from Rogelim [28]brought beds, basins, pottery, wheat, barley, flour, roasted grain, beans, lentils, [29]honey, buttermilk, sheep, and cheese from cows' milk to David and the people with him to eat. [They did this] because they thought, "The people are hungry, exhausted, and thirsty in the wilderness."

Textual Notes

17:1 אֶבְחֲרָה נָּא ... וְאָקוּמָה וְאֶרְדְּפָה—"(Please) let me choose, ... leave, and pursue." These three verbs are singular Qal (G) cohortatives (of בָּחַר, קוּם, and רָדַף, respectively), spoken by a subordinate to a superior, asking permission to undertake an action (see Joüon, § 114 b, d, f). The first has the particle of entreaty נָּא (and the second two have a conjunctive *waw*). The second, וְאָקוּמָה, literally "and let me arise," is translated as "(let me) leave." Another singular cohortative (with a conjunctive *waw*), וְאָשִׁיבָה (the Hiphil [H] of שׁוּב), "(and) let me bring back," begins 17:3.

17:2 יָגֵעַ—"Exhausted." This adjective is a synonym of the adjectives יָעֵף and עָיֵף (see the third textual note on 16:2). This is the only instance of the adjective יָגֵעַ in the book of Samuel. Its cognate verb, יָגַע, "be exhausted, weary from exertion," is used in 23:10 with יָד, "hand," as its subject. Cf. the next textual note here.

וּרְפֵה יָדַיִם—"And tired." This construct phrase with the adjective רָפֶה is literally "and slack/limp of hands." The affected body part ("hands") is the genitive (GKC, § 128 y; see also the first textual note on 4:4). The adjective רָפֶה is used similarly in the phrase יָדַיִם רָפוֹת, "limp hands," in Is 35:3. Its cognate verb, רָפָה, is used in the comparable expression וַיִּרְפּוּ יָדָיו, "and his hands drooped"; see the second textual note on 2 Sam 4:1.

17:3 כְּשׁוּב הַכֹּל הָאִישׁ אֲשֶׁר אַתָּה מְבַקֵּשׁ—The MT reads literally "as the whole returns. The man whom you are seeking …" The first verb, כְּשׁוּב, is the Qal (G) infinitive construct of שׁוּב, "return," with the preposition כְּ. Its subject is the noun with the article הַכֹּל, "the whole/all" (two Masoretic manuscripts read כֹּל). Three other passages in the OT have an infinitive construct followed by הַכֹּל, but in all of them, הַכֹּל is the object of the verb, rather than its subject (Is 65:8; Ezek 7:14; 1 Chr 29:19).

The reading of the LXX here is ὃν τρόπον ἐπιστρέφει ἡ νύμφη πρὸς τὸν ἄνδρα αὐτῆς· πλὴν ψυχὴν ἑνὸς ἀνδρὸς σὺ ζητεῖς, "[and I will return all the people to you] in the manner in which a bride returns to her husband. It is only the life of one man you are seeking." The LXX suggests a Hebrew reading like this:

כְּשׁוּב הַכַּלָּה אֶל אִישָׁהּ רַק נֶפֶשׁ אִישׁ אֶחָד אַתָּה מְבַקֵּשׁ

This Hebrew reading is partially supported by 4QSamᵃ: נפ[שׁ] [ר]ק שׁ. The LXX reading is followed by most modern English versions (ESV, GW, NRSV), although some follow the MT (e.g., HCSB).

כָּל־הָעָם יִהְיֶה שָׁלוֹם:—"All the people will be unharmed" is literally "all the people will be (at) peace." The noun שָׁלוֹם denotes not only "peace" in terms of absence of conflict but also wholeness and being intact.

17:4 וַיִּישַׁר הַדָּבָר—"The plan seemed good" is literally "and the word/matter was straight." The Qal (G) of יָשַׁר, "go straight" (1 Sam 6:12), can have the metaphorical meaning "be pleasing, agreeable, right."

17:5 וְנִשְׁמְעָה מַה־בְּפִיו גַּם־הוּא:—"Let's hear what he has to say as well" is literally "and let us hear what is in his mouth—also he." The verb וְנִשְׁמְעָה is the plural Qal (G) cohortative of שָׁמַע, "hear" (with a conjunctive *waw*). It is the fifth and final cohortative in this chapter (see also the first textual note on 17:1). The personal pronoun הוּא, "he," stands in apposition to the third masculine singular pronominal suffix on בְּפִיו, "in *his* mouth" (Joüon, § 146 d (6)) and lends emphasis to it (GKC, § 135 f).

17:6 כַּדָּבָר הַזֶּה—"This plan" is literally "as this word/matter." This phrase indicates that at this point Absalom recounted Ahithophel's plan to Hushai. The same phrase is used similarly in, e.g., 1 Sam 17:27, 30; 2 Sam 14:3.

17:7 הָעֵצָה אֲשֶׁר־יָעַץ אֲחִיתֹפֶל—"The advice that Ahithophel gave." This is a cognate accusative construction, literally "the counsel that Ahithophel counseled." The verb יָעַץ, "to advise, counsel," recurs in 17:11, 15 (twice), 21. Ahithophel is the one who counsels in 17:7, 15a, 21, while Hushai does so in 17:11, 15b. The cognate noun עֵצָה, "advice, counsel," recurs in 17:14 (three times), 23. The noun refers to "advice" given by Ahithophel to Absalom in all these occurrences except the first one in 17:14, which refers to advice given by Hushai.

17:8 גִּבֹּרִים—"Skilled soldiers." This noun will recur but in the singular, גִּבּוֹר, describing David in 17:10.

וּמָרֵי נֶפֶשׁ הֵמָּה—"And (they are) enraged" is literally "and bitter of soul are they." This could also be translated as "and (they are) fierce." The adjective מַר, "bitter," is used in construct with the noun נֶפֶשׁ, "soul," to describe a temper or temperament of various emotions (BDB, s.v. מַר, 2 b, under the root מרר I). The same construct phrase, מַר נֶפֶשׁ, is in 1 Sam 1:10; 22:2. It describes angry and violent men also in Judg 18:25.

כְּדֹב שַׁכּוּל בַּשָּׂדֶה—"Like a bear robbed of her cubs in the wild" is literally "like a bear bereaved in the field." The adjective שַׁכּוּל, "bereaved, robbed of offspring," modifies the noun דֹּב, "a bear," also in Hos 13:8; Prov 17:12. The noun and adjective are masculine in form, but the reference is probably to a mother bear ("her") because female bears raise their cubs and defend them ferociously. The adjective is cognate to the verb שָׁכַל, "be bereaved," used twice in 1 Sam 15:33 in reference to women whose children had been killed.[1] See another animal simile in 2 Sam 17:10. Here the LXX supplies a Hellenistic addition to clarify the animal simile for its readers: καὶ ὡς ὗς τραχεῖα ἐν τῷ πεδίῳ, "and like a savage sow in the plain."

אִישׁ מִלְחָמָה—"An experienced soldier" is literally "a man of war." See this construct phrase also in 1 Sam 16:18; 17:33; 2 Sam 8:10; see also, e.g., Josh 17:1; Judg 20:17. Cf. בֶּן־חַיִל in the first textual note on 2 Sam 17:10.

וְלֹא יָלִין—"He will not spend the night." The Qal (G) of לִין, which refers to lodging overnight, recurs in 17:16; see also 12:16; 19:8 (ET 19:7).

17:9 נֶחְבָּא—"Hiding." This is the Niphal (N) masculine singular participle of חָבָא. In the Hiphil (H), this verb corresponds to "hide" in the transitive sense: "to hide [something]." In the Niphal, it corresponds to the intransitive and implicitly reflexive sense "to hide (oneself)."[2]

בְּאַחַת הַפְּחָתִים—"In one of the caves." The noun is the plural of פַּחַת, "pit, cave," which recurs in the singular in 18:17.

כִּנְפֹל בָּהֶם בַּתְּחִלָּה—"As some among them fall at the beginning." This translation of the temporal clause assumes that the third masculine plural suffix on בָּהֶם, "among them," refers to Absalom's troops, being led by Ahithophel. In their (hypothetical) initial attack against David, some of the attackers would fall; the Qal (G) of נָפַל, "fall," often refers to dying in battle (see BDB, Qal, 2 a). Alternatively and theoretically, the suffix on בָּהֶם could refer to David and his men, in which case the clause would mean "when [Absalom's troops] fall upon them [David and his men] at the beginning." The Qal of נָפַל can be used with various prepositions, including בְּ, to mean "to fall upon," that is, "to attack" (Josh 11:7; cf. Is 9:7 [ET 9:8]; see BDB, Qal, 4 a). However, the end of the verse clarifies that the first option is meant.

וְשָׁמַע הַשֹּׁמֵעַ—"Someone is certain to hear" is literally "and the hearer will hear." Both verbs are forms of שָׁמַע, "hear." The first is the Qal (G) third masculine singular perfect with *waw* consecutive, followed by its subject, which is the Qal masculine singular participle. Although the definite article is used with the participle, the participle has an indefinite sense, "someone." See Joüon, § 155 d, and the first textual note on 15:13.

---

[1] See the first textual note on 1 Sam 15:33 (Steinmann, *1 Samuel*, 290).

[2] Note the English usages of "hid" in the transitive sense, "I hid the treasure," and the intransitive sense, "when the police were searching for the escaped felon, he hid in the woods."

הָיְתָה֙ מַגֵּפָ֔ה—"There has been a slaughter." The feminine noun מַגֵּפָה denotes a "slaughter" or military "defeat" also in, e.g., 1 Sam 4:17; 2 Sam 18:7.

בָּעָ֕ם אֲשֶׁ֖ר אַחֲרֵ֥י אַבְשָׁלֹֽם׃—"Among the troops under Absalom" is literally "among the people who [follow] after Absalom." In military contexts the noun with the article הָעָם, "the people," often denotes "the troops." See the first textual note on 1 Sam 4:3[3] and the second textual note on 2 Sam 1:4.

17:10 וְה֤וּא גַם־בֶּן־חַ֨יִל֙ ... וּבְנֵי־חַ֔יִל—"Then also the most skilled soldier ... and skilled soldiers." The construct phrase בֶּן־חַיִל denotes a man who is well-trained and competent. In military contexts it indicates someone who is skilled at the art of war; see the second textual note on 2 Sam 2:7.[4] It is a synonym of the construct phrases אִישׁ־חַיִל, discussed in the first textual notes on 1 Sam 31:12[5] and 2 Sam 23:20, and אִישׁ מִלְחָמָה, "an experienced soldier," discussed in the fourth textual note on 2 Sam 17:8.

הִמֵּ֥ס יִמָּֽס—"He will completely lose courage." This is the Niphal (N) infinitive absolute (GKC, § 67 t) and the Niphal third masculine singular imperfect of מָסַס, literally "to melt." This verb is often used in connection with לֵב or לֵבָב, "heart," and denotes incapacitating fear (see BDB, Niphal, 2).

17:11 יָעַ֗צְתִּי—"I advise." Here the perfect (Qal [G] first common singular) refers to what Hushai is about to say (Waltke-O'Connor, § 30.5.1d, including example 22; cf. GKC, § 106 i). In 17:15 the perfect of the same verb (יָעַץ, the Qal [G] third masculine singular) will refer back to what Ahithophel had "advised."

הֵאָסֹ֨ף יֵאָסֵ֥ף—"(That) it be gathered." This is the Niphal (N) infinitive absolute and the Niphal third masculine singular imperfect of אָסַף, "gather." For the Niphal of אָסַף denoting troops gathering together for battle (as well as its active Qal [G]), see the first textual note on 6:1. For an opposite meaning, see the first textual note on 17:13.

כַּח֛וֹל אֲשֶׁר־עַל־הַיָּ֖ם—"As the sand that is beside the sea." A number of Masoretic manuscripts include the noun שָׂפָה, "lip, edge, shore," in construct and read as follows: כַּח֛וֹל אֲשֶׁר־עַל־שְׂפַת־הַיָּ֖ם, "as the sand that is on the shore of the sea," an expression used elsewhere in the OT.[6]

לָרֹ֑ב—"As numerous." The noun רֹב, "multitude; (numerical) abundance," with the preposition לְ is often used adverbially (BDB, s.v. רֹב, 1, under the root רבב I).

וּפָנֶ֥יךָ הֹלְכִ֖ים בַּקְרָֽב׃—"And that you personally go into battle" is literally "and your face going in the battle." The plural noun פָּנִים with a second masculine singular suffix is the subject of the Qal (G) masculine plural participle of הָלַךְ. Hushai's way of referring to Absalom's personal presence emphasized the need for Absalom himself to lead his army against David, in contrast to Ahithophel's plan (17:1–3), which did not involve Absalom on the battlefield.

17:12 בְּאַחַ֤ד הַמְּקוֹמֹת֙ אֲשֶׁ֣ר נִמְצָ֣א שָׁ֔ם—"In whatever place he is found" is literally "in one of the places where he is found there." The numeral "one" is used in construct

---

[3] Steinmann, *1 Samuel*, 120.

[4] The phrase is also used in, e.g., Deut 3:18; Judg 18:2; 1 Sam 14:52; 18:17; 1 Chr 5:18.

[5] Steinmann, *1 Samuel*, 568.

[6] See Gen 22:17; Josh 11:4; Judg 7:12; 1 Sam 13:5; 1 Ki 5:9 (ET 4:29).

with the noun to signify indetermination ("any, whatever"; see Joüon, § 137 v; Waltke-O'Connor, § 13.8a, including example 11). The masculine form of the numeral in construct (with the preposition בְּ), בְּאַחַד, "in one of," is the reading of the Qere. The Kethib has its feminine form in construct (also with the preposition בְּ), בְּאַחַת, "in one of" (as once in 17:9). The noun מָקוֹם, "place," is usually masculine, even though its plural מְקוֹמֹת corresponds to the usual form of feminine plurals, but here the Kethib, because of the numeral, construes it as feminine (GKC, § 122 l; cf. Joüon, § 134 m). The same plural form with the article was in 17:9 (הַמְּקוֹמֹת), where the masculine form of the numeral one was in construct with it (בְּאַחַד). The context here indicates that the form of the verb נִמְצָא is the Niphal (N) third masculine singular perfect of מָצָא, "to find." The identical verb recurs toward the end of 17:13. In other contexts this form (נִמְצָא) is to be parsed as the Qal (G) first common plural imperfect of מָצָא (Gen 47:25; 1 Ki 18:5; Prov 1:13).

וְנַחְנוּ עָלָיו—"And we will descend on him." The verb וְנַחְנוּ is the Qal (G) first common plural perfect of נוּחַ, "to rest, settle down" (so BDB, s.v. נָחַח, under אֲנַחְנוּ), with waw consecutive. In most contexts the connotations of נוּחַ are peaceful. Here it likely denotes surrounding the place where David is in a gradual and quiet manner that will escape the notice of those in that place. The word וְנַחְנוּ could also be a conjunctive waw with a variant spelling of the first plural pronoun "we," which is usually spelled אֲנַחְנוּ; but the shortened variant spelling נַחְנוּ appears elsewhere in the OT five times. The LXX translates וְנַחְנוּ with καὶ παρεμβαλοῦμεν, "and we will encamp."

וְלֹא־נוֹתַר בּוֹ ... גַּם־אֶחָד:—"Not even one ... will be left" is literally "and there will not be left with him ... even one." For a similar expression with three of the words here (וְלֹא־נוֹתַר ... אֶחָד), see the second textual note on 13:30. The translation takes נוֹתַר as the Niphal (N) third masculine singular perfect of יָתַר, meaning "be left over, remain," as do many modern English versions (e.g., ESV, NASB, NKJV). The form נוֹתַר could also be parsed as the Hiphil (H) first common plural jussive of יָתַר, which, negated, means "we will not let remain/leave behind." This is how the LXX understood it (οὐχ ὑπολειψόμεθα), as does GKC, § 109 d. If so, this would be a fourth first person plural verb used by Hushai in 17:12–13. See also the commentary.

17:13 וְאִם־אֶל־עִיר יֵאָסֵף—"If he withdraws into a city." In 17:11 the same verb יֵאָסֵף, the Niphal (N) third masculine singular imperfect of אָסַף, referred to troops "gathering" to launch an offensive (see the second textual note on 17:11). Ironically, here the verb denotes the defensive maneuver of David "withdrawing" from the battlefield.

וְהִשִּׂיאוּ כָל־יִשְׂרָאֵל אֶל־הָעִיר הַהִיא חֲבָלִים—"All Israel will bring ropes to that city." The verb וְהִשִּׂיאוּ is one of only two instances of the Hiphil (H) of נָשָׂא, "to carry, bear," in the OT. The other is in Lev 22:16, where it takes a double accusative and means "cause [someone] to bear [something]." Here it may have a causative meaning (so BDB, Hiphil, 2) if other Israelites who possess ropes are implied as the first accusative and the noun חֲבָלִים, "ropes," is the second accusative: "all Israel will cause (people who have ropes) to carry/bring ropes to that city." Alternatively, the Hiphil may simply have the transitive meaning "bring" (so *DCH*, Hiphil, 2).

וְסָחַבְנוּ אֹתוֹ—"And we will drag it." The verb סָחַב, "drag," occurs only in the Qal (G) and connotes violent hostility, e.g., "dragging" captives from a town (Jer 49:20;

319

50:45) or a body through the streets (Jer 22:19). Here the direct object marker has a third masculine singular suffix, אֹתוֹ, even though the pronoun's antecedent is the feminine definite noun הָעִיר, "the city."

לֹא־נִמְצָא שָׁם גַּם־צְרוֹר׃—"Not even a pebble could be found there." The same Niphal (N) third masculine singular perfect verb נִמְצָא, "be found," and the adverb שָׁם, "there," were used in 17:12 for David being discovered.[7] Here the perfect may indicate what will be a completed state in the future (so GKC, § 106 o). The noun צְרוֹר II, "pebble," appears two or three times in the OT and is a by-form of the noun צֹר, "flint" (so *DCH*). It is to be distinguished from the homographic noun צְרוֹר I, "a bundle, pouch," discussed in the first textual note on 1 Sam 25:29.[8] It is also possible to parse נִמְצָא as the Qal (G) first common plural imperfect of מָצָא, in which case this would mean "we will not find there even a pebble." If so, this would be the fifth first person plural verb Hushai uses in 17:12–13. See also the commentary.

17:14 טוֹבָה עֲצַת ... מֵעֲצַת—"The advice of ... is better than the advice of ..." The adjective טוֹב, "good," with the preposition מִן, "from, than," forms a comparative, "better than." The feminine form of the adjective, טוֹבָה, is used to match the gender of the feminine noun עֵצָה, "advice." See also the third textual note on 17:14.

וַיהוָה צִוָּה לְהָפֵר—"Yahweh had decreed to foil." The unusual placement of a subject in front of a perfect verb (וַיהוָה צִוָּה) often signals an anterior construction, which corresponds to a pluperfect tense, "*had* decreed." The Hiphil (H) infinitive construct with the preposition לְ, לְהָפֵר, literally "to break/frustrate," is from פָּרַר, whose Hiphil (H) was used in 15:34 in the sense of "foil" with the direct object "the advice of Ahithophel" (אֵת עֲצַת אֲחִיתֹפֶל; see the third textual note on 15:34).

אֶת־עֲצַת אֲחִיתֹפֶל הַטּוֹבָה—"The better advice of Ahithophel." Since Hebrew has no separate forms for adjectives in the absolute, comparative, or superlative degrees, טוֹב can mean "good," "better," or "best," depending on the context and construction (see also the first textual note on 17:14). Here there is an implied comparison between Ahithophel's advice and Hushai's advice. An adjective alone with the definite article can express a comparative, as here, הַטּוֹבָה, "the better [advice]" (see also, e.g., 1 Sam 15:28) or a superlative, "best," as does הַטּוֹב in, e.g., 1 Sam 8:14, 16.

לְבַעֲבוּר הָבִיא יְהוָה—"In order for Yahweh to bring." The combination of prepositions לְ + בְּ + עֲבוּר is regularly used with an infinitive construct (here הָבִיא, the Hiphil [H] of בּוֹא, "come") to express purpose (see BDB, s.v. עֲבוּר II, 1 b).

הָרָעָה׃—"Disaster." While this might be translated literally as "the evil," God is not the originator of evil. The noun רָעָה can denote a "disaster" or "calamity" that God imposes on people as well-deserved punishment for their evildoing.[9]

17:15 הַכֹּהֲנִים—"The high priests." For כֹּהֵן in the sense of "*high* priest," see the second textual note on 8:17. Zadok and Abiathar apparently shared the high priesthood

---

[7] See the first textual note on 17:12.

[8] Steinmann, *1 Samuel*, 478–79.

[9] E.g., 1 Sam 6:9; 25:39; 2 Sam 3:39; 12:11; 24:16.

under David, and the plural of כֹּהֵן is used for the two of them here and in 2 Sam 15:35; 19:12 (ET 19:11); 20:25.

כָּזֹאת וְכָזֹאת ... וְכָזֹאת וְכָזֹאת—"Here is what ... here is what." The idiom with the repeated feminine demonstrative pronoun, literally "like this and like this," is used twice here. It means that at this point in the narrative Hushai provided the details of what Ahithophel had advised and what he himself had advised. This idiom is also in Josh 7:20; 2 Ki 5:4; 9:12.[10]

17:16 מְהֵרָה—This feminine noun, meaning "speed, haste," is used most often as an adverbial accusative, "quickly," as again in 17:18, 21.

אַל־תָּלֶן—"Do not spend the night." The negated verb תָּלֶן is the Qal (G) second masculine singular jussive (see Joüon, § 114 i) of לִין (see the last textual note on 17:8). The corresponding imperfect form would be תָּלִין.

בְּעַרְבוֹת—This word in Codex Leningradensis means "on the steppes of," which is supported by the LXX's transliteration of it as a place-name (ἐν Αραβωθ). Many Masoretic manuscripts read בְּעַבְרוֹת, "at the fords of," and this commentary follows that reading. See the same issue in the second textual note on 15:28.

וְגַם עָבוֹר תַּעֲבוֹר—"Instead, cross over." The infinitive absolute can be used to emphasize an opposition or contrasting action, to do something else "instead of" or "rather than" the alternative ("spend the night at the fords"). See Joüon, § 123 i.

יְבֻלַּע לַמֶּלֶךְ וּלְכָל־הָעָם—"The king and all the people ... will be devoured" is literally "it will be swallowed for the king and for all the people." The verb יְבֻלַּע is the Pual (Dp) third masculine singular imperfect of בָּלַע I, "to swallow." Here it is used impersonally, with no grammatically nominative subject, and the prepositional phrases with לְ function as its compound subject.[11]

17:17 עֹמְדִים—"Were staying." This Qal (G) masculine plural participle, literally "standing," expresses durative action in the past (Joüon, § 119 v; Waltke-O'Connor, § 37.6d, including example 10). After this participle the next four verbs (וְהָלְכָה ... וְהִגִּידָה ... יֵלְכוּ וְהִגִּידוּ) express habitual or iterative past action, "would come and (would) tell, ... would go and (would) report." This system of communication was used whenever military intelligence was transmitted to David. See Waltke-O'Connor, § 32.2.5b, including example 12.

הַשִּׁפְחָה—"A female servant." The feminine noun שִׁפְחָה denotes a "slave girl" or female household "servant." See the first textual note on 1 Sam 1:18[12] and the first textual note on 2 Sam 14:6. Hebrew commonly uses the definite article on a noun when the narrator has in mind a specific person or thing (Joüon, § 137 m, n), but English expresses this with an indefinite article. See the first textual note on 15:13 and the fourth textual note on 17:9. See also הַמָּסָךְ in the first textual note on 17:19.

---

[10] See *IBH*, § 25 A; Joüon, § 147 f; Waltke-O'Connor, § 17.4.3b, including example 3.

[11] GKC, § 121 a; Joüon, § 152 fa; Waltke-O'Connor, §§ 10.4c, including example 7; 11.2.10g, including example 61.

[12] Steinmann, *1 Samuel*, 51.

לֹא יוּכְלוּ לְהֵרָאוֹת לָבוֹא הָעִירָה:—"They could not risk being seen going into the city" is literally "they would not able to be seen to go city-ward." The Qal (G) of יָכֹל, "be able," is used in the imperfect (cf. Joüon, § 113 ga). לְהֵרָאוֹת is the Niphal (N) infinitive construct of רָאָה, "to see," with the preposition לְ. The author's point is not that no one was able to see them, but that if they were seen going into the city, Absalom's supporters would suspect that they and their fathers were sending military intelligence to David. Despite their caution, their movements arouse such suspicion in the following verses (17:18–20).

17:18 וַיֵּרְדוּ שָׁם:—"And they went down into it" is literally "and they descended there."

17:19 וַתִּקַּח הָאִשָּׁה וַתִּפְרֹשׂ אֶת־הַמָּסָךְ—"The wife took [a cloth] and spread [it] out as a covering." The two verbs refer to the first and last parts of her action with, presumably, a large cloth (so BDB, s.v. מָסָךְ, 1, under the root סכך). The noun מָסָךְ, "a covering, screen," is derived from the verb סָכַךְ, "to cover (over), to screen."

עַל־פְּנֵי הַבְּאֵר—"Over the mouth of the cistern" is literally "over the face of the cistern." This is the reading in most Masoretic manuscripts, and it is supported by most versions of the LXX. Some Masoretic manuscripts read עַל־פִּי הַבְּאֵר, "over the mouth of the cistern" (cf. Gen 29:2, 3, 8, 10), which is supported by the Lucianic version of the LXX. Either way, the corresponding English idiom is "the mouth of the cistern."

וַתִּשְׁטַח עָלָיו הָרִפוֹת—"And she spread around grain on it." The rare verb שָׁטַח means "to spread around" or "disperse" many individual things (quail in Num 11:32; bones in Jer 8:2), whereas the verb פָּרַשׂ earlier in the verse meant to "spread out" one thing (a cloth). The object here, הָרִפוֹת, is the plural of the feminine noun רִיפָה (with the article), which apparently refers to some kind of grain (*DCH*, s.v. רִיפוֹת: "barley groats") or perhaps fruit or grit. Its only other instance in the OT is in Prov 27:22.

וְלֹא נוֹדַע דָּבָר:—"And no one knew about it" is literally "and a word/matter was not known." The verb נוֹדַע is the Niphal (N) perfect third masculine singular of יָדַע, "to know."

17:20 עָבְרוּ מִיכַל הַמַּיִם—"They passed on to the water." This could literally mean "they crossed Michal, the water." The word מִיכַל is used elsewhere in the book of Samuel as the name of Saul's younger daughter.[13] Suggestions for understanding this word are tenuous at best. Some propose that this is the construct form of a noun מִיכָל, meaning a "pool, stream" (see *DCH*, s.v. מִיכָל I) or a "collection, container" (*DCH*, s.v. מִיכָל II), derived from the verb כּוּל, "to comprehend," which in the Hiphil (H) can mean "to contain [a liquid]."[14] Some translations assume that, based on context, it means a "brook" (ESV, NASB, NKJV). If מִיכַל here is due to a transcription error, the original text seems unrecoverable. The translation above ignores the word. When the same phraseology recurs in 17:21, מִיכַל is absent: וְעָבְרוּ מְהֵרָה אֶת־הַמַּיִם, "and cross the water quickly."

---

13 1 Sam 14:49; 18:20, 27, 28; 19:11, 12, 13, 17; 25:44; 2 Sam 3:13, 14; 6:16, 20, 21, 23; 21:8.

14 1 Ki 7:26, 38; Jer 2:13; Ezek 23:32; see *HALOT*, s.v. כול, Hiphil, 1.

17:21 עֲלֵיכֶם ... וְעִבְרוּ קוּמוּ—"Get up and cross … against you." The verbs and the pronoun "you" are plural in Hebrew, referring to David and those fleeing with him.

כָּכָה—"Immediate action." This adverb (seemingly a combination of כְּ + כֹּה) literally means "as thus." It functions as a stand-in for a summary of what Ahithophel had said. See this adverb also in 1 Sam 2:14; 19:17; 2 Sam 13:4.

17:22 עַד־אוֹר הַבֹּקֶר עַד־אַחַד לֹא נֶעְדָּר אֲשֶׁר לֹא־עָבַר אֶת־הַיַּרְדֵּן:—"By the morning light there was no one who had not crossed the Jordan River" is literally "until the light of the morning, until one was not left who had not crossed the Jordan." The construct form אַחַד of the numeral אֶחָד, "one," is used; even though it is not strictly speaking in a construct phrase, it is closely bound to the following words (GKC, § 130 g). The verb נֶעְדָּר is the Niphal (N) third masculine singular perfect of עָדַר III, "to be missing, lacking." Cf. 1 Sam 30:19, where the same form was negated (וְלֹא נֶעְדָּר, "no one was missing").

17:23 לֹא נֶעֶשְׂתָה עֲצָתוֹ—"His advice was not followed" is literally "his advice was not done." The verb נֶעֶשְׂתָה is the Niphal (N) third feminine singular perfect of עָשָׂה, "do." Its subject is the feminine suffixed noun עֲצָתוֹ, "his advice."

וַיַּחֲבֹשׁ אֶת־הַחֲמוֹר—"So he saddled his donkey." The Qal (G) of חָבַשׁ, "to bind, tie," can refer to saddling an animal, including a חֲמוֹר, "donkey" (2 Sam 17:23; 19:27 [ET 19:26]). See the third textual note on 2 Sam 16:1. The definite article on הַחֲמוֹר, "*the* donkey," indicates the specific donkey that would be designated in English by a possessive pronoun, "his."

וַיְצַו אֶל־בֵּיתוֹ—"He put his affairs in order" is literally "and he commanded his house." This idiom is used for making arrangements to dispose of one's property in view of one's expected death, akin to the modern practice of making a will (see 2 Ki 20:1 ‖ Is 38:1).

וַיֵּחָנַק—"And he hanged himself." This is the Niphal (N) third masculine singular preterite (imperfect with *waw* consecutive) of חָנַק. This form with *patach* (-ַ-) is pausal for the expected form with *tsere* (-ֵ-); see GKC, § 51 m. This verb appears elsewhere in the OT only in Nah 2:13 (ET 2:12), where its Piel (D) means "to strangle." The Niphal (N) was originally a reflexive mode of the Qal (G), and it has retained this meaning for a number of verbs.

17:25 עַל־הַצָּבָא—"Over the army." For this prepositional phrase, see the first textual note on 8:16, which records that David installed Joab in this position.

יִתְרָא—This name, "Ithra," is a variant of the name יֶתֶר, "Jether" (1 Chr 2:17).[15]

הַיִּשְׂרְאֵלִי—Instead of "the Israelite," some LXX manuscripts and some English translations (e.g., ESV, RSV, NRSV) follow the reading in 1 Chr 2:17: הַיִּשְׁמְעֵאלִי, "the Ishmaelite."

אֲשֶׁר־בָּא אֶל־אֲבִיגַיִל—"Who had slept with Abigail." For the Hebrew idiom with the verb בּוֹא and the preposition אֶל, literally "to go in to," see the fourth textual note on 3:7. The use of this idiom, rather than a regular idiom for marriage (e.g., לָקַח לְאִשָּׁה, "take as a wife" [e.g., 1 Sam 25:39], or אֵשֶׁת־, "the wife of" [e.g., 1 Sam 4:19]), probably

---

[15] The name also occurs in Ex 4:18; Judg 8:20; 1 Ki 2:5, 32; 1 Chr 2:32; 4:17; 7:38.

indicates that Amasa was born of an illicit union between Ithra and Abigail, even if Ithra later married Abigail. Here her name is spelled אֲבִיגַל, "Abigal" (cf. 1 Sam 25:32; but in 1 Chr 2:16–17 her name is spelled אֲבִיגַיִל, "Abigail." She is to be distinguished from the "Abigail" who became one of David's wives (1 Samuel 25; 27:3; 30:5; 2 Sam 2:2; 3:3; 1 Chr 3:1).

בַּת־נָחָשׁ—"The granddaughter of Nahash." The interrelated issues involved in the translation and interpretation of this phrase are the meaning of בַּת, the identity of נָחָשׁ, and how to reconcile the information given here about Abigail's lineage with 1 Chr 2:13–17.

The noun בַּת normally denotes a "daughter," but may at times denote a "grand-daughter" (*HALOT*, s.v. בַּת I, 1). For instance, in 2 Ki 8:26 Athaliah is said to be בַּת־עָמְרִי מֶלֶךְ יִשְׂרָאֵל, which must mean "the granddaughter of King Omri of Israel,"[16] as translated by most modern English versions.[17] For reasons discussed below, this commentary advocates the view that Abigail was the granddaughter, rather than the daughter, of Nahash.

In the MT the (grand)father's name is נָחָשׁ, "Nahash," which is supported by most LXX manuscripts (Ναας). 4QSamᵃ (ש[י]) and some LXX manuscripts (Ιεσσαι) read "Jesse," which is probably an attempt to correct what was perceived to be a mistake: if David was the son of Jesse (1 Chr 2:13–15) and if Zeruiah and Abigail were his sisters (1 Chr 2:16), then Jesse should be the father of Abigail (and Zeruiah) as well as David.

However, this commentary follows the MT's more difficult reading נָחָשׁ, "Nahash." A man named Nahash is thus mentioned twice in this pericope, here in 17:25 and then in 17:27. 2 Sam 17:27 lists Shobi the son of Nahash from the Ammonite city Rabbah as one of the people who brought provisions for David and those fleeing with him. The mention of Rabbah, the capital of the Ammonite kingdom, makes it likely that Shobi was the son of the Ammonite king named Nahash who is mentioned also in 1 Sam 11:1–2; 12:12; 2 Sam 10:2; 1 Chr 19:1–2. The most natural reading of the text, then, is that the Nahash mentioned without any other designation two verses earlier, here in 2 Sam 17:25, is also this Ammonite king. If David had a familial connection to the Ammonite king Nahash (see below), it would help explain David's ill-fated attempt to console Nahash's son Hanun when Nahash died (10:1–4), as well as Shobi's support for David in 17:27.

As touched upon briefly above, the third issue involved in how to translate and interpret the phrase בַּת־נָחָשׁ here in 17:25 is how to reconcile the information given here, that Abigail the sister of Zeruiah was the daughter or granddaughter of Nahash, with 1 Chr 2:13–17, which lists the names of Jesse's sons, including David, and then says that their sisters were Zeruiah and Abigail. The question most pertinent to this

---

[16] Athaliah was the mother of King Ahaziah of Judah (2 Ki 8:26) and, therefore, the wife of King Jehoram of Judah, Ahaziah's father (2 Ki 8:25). Although Athaliah's name is not used in 2 Ki 8:18, that verse says that Jehoram's wife was the daughter of King Ahab of Israel (2 Ki 8:18), the son of King Omri of Israel (1 Ki 16:28). Therefore, Jehoram's wife, Athaliah, was Omri's granddaughter.

[17] E.g., HCSB, ESV, GW, NET, NIV.

pericope is how Abigail was related to David.[18] Theoretically there are three possibilities: (1) that Abigail was the full sister of David; (2) that Abigail was the half sister of David with both sharing a common mother; and (3) that Abigail was the half sister of David with Jesse as the father of both. This commentary advocates the third possibility.

Regarding the first possibility, Abigail could have been the full sister of David only if she were the daughter of Jesse. Thus, בַּת־נָחָשׁ here in 17:25 would have to mean "the granddaughter of Nahash," making Abigail's mother the daughter of Nahash. Although Nahash could have been someone other than the Ammonite king, as discussed above, that is an unlikely reading of 17:25 in light of 17:27. If, on the other hand, Nahash was the Ammonite king and if, as this scenario posits, Abigail and David were full siblings, that would mean that David's mother was an Ammonite. This commentary views that possibility as unlikely.

Some commentators advocate the second possibility, that Abigail and David had the same mother but different fathers. In this scenario, בַּת־נָחָשׁ would mean "the daughter of Nahash." Abigail would be the daughter (not the granddaughter) of a man named Nahash, who was the first husband of Abigail and David's mother. Their mother later married Jesse.[19] However, in this scenario, Nahash was most likely not the Ammonite king. Abigail and David's mother could not have been the widow of the Ammonite king Nahash because his death, which precipitated the Ammonite war, occurred in c. 998 BC,[20] when David was about forty-one years old.[21] And it is unlikely that the Ammonite king had divorced Abigail's mother because kings did not divorce wives with whom they were displeased or who were otherwise out of favor. They simply favored other wives they had married and placed out-of-favor wives in the royal harem, where they would live without again seeing the king (see, e.g., 2 Sam 20:3; Esth 1:19).

Thus, the solution that best accounts for all of the data posits this scenario: Abigail and David were both children of Jesse but had different mothers. Abigail's mother was the daughter of the Ammonite king Nahash, making Abigail his "granddaughter" (17:25).

17:28 מִשְׁכָּב—"(They brought) beds." In the MT 17:28 begins with the singular noun מִשְׁכָּב, "bed," apparently serving as a collective, "beds," since many of the following items are plural or other collectives. The Hebrew of 17:27–28 lacks a verb. The translation includes "brought" here to represent the verb הִגִּישׁוּ in 17:29 (see the third textual note on 17:29). The LXX supplies a verb and a numeral at the beginning of 17:28,

---

[18] The discussion will focus on the relationship of Abigail to David (and not his brothers also) since it is possible that David had a different mother than some of his brothers. And it will focus on the relationship of Abigail (and not Zeruiah also) to David since Abigail is the one listed in 17:25 as the daughter or granddaughter of Nahash. If Zeruiah and Abigail shared both of the same parents, Zeruiah would have had the same relationship to David as Abigail did. If Zeruiah, the mother of Joab, Abishai, and Asahel, had a different mother or father than David, that might explain David's complaints about his nephews not being of like mind with him (3:39; 16:10; 19:23 [ET 19:22]).

[19] See Hertzberg, *I and II Samuel*, 357, and Baldwin, *1 and 2 Samuel*, 268.

[20] See "The Chronology of David's Reign" in the commentary on 5:1–5.

[21] David was born in c. 1039 BC (see Steinmann, *1 Samuel*, 16–17).

ἤνεγκαν δέκα κοίτας, "they brought *ten* beds." Then LXX 17:29 also includes the verb προσήνεγκαν, "they brought forward," to translate the Hebrew verb הִגִּישׁוּ in MT 17:29.

וּכְלִי יוֹצֵר—"(And) pottery." This construct phrase is literally "and vessel(s) of a potter."

וְקָלִי וּפוֹל וַעֲדָשִׁים וְקָלִי:—"(And) roasted grain, beans, lentils, roasted grain." The noun קָלִי, "roasted grain," is repeated at the end of the verse in the MT. However, its second occurrence is missing in the LXX, the Old Latin Napoli codex, and the Syriac. Probably it was accidentally reproduced in the MT. Note that the list of the grain items concluded with the first וְקָלִי, "(and) roasted grain." Most modern English versions omit the second instance of the word.

17:29 וְחֶמְאָה—"(And) buttermilk." The feminine noun חֶמְאָה denotes some type of cultured milk product that is liquid and can be drunk (Deut 32:13–14; Judg 5:25; Job 20:17; 29:6). Therefore the traditional translation "curds" is inaccurate, since it implies a semisolid substance, nor is this "butter," as translated in the LXX (βούτυρον) and some modern versions.

וּשְׁפוֹת בָּקָר—"And cheese from cows' milk." This construct phrase is literally "and cheese(s) of cattle."

הִגִּישׁוּ—"They brought" is literally "they brought near." This is the Hiphil (H) third common plural perfect of נָגַשׁ. Its translation is placed at the start of 17:28 because of the requirements of English syntax.

וְעָיֵף—For this adjective, עָיֵף, "exhausted," see the third textual note on 16:2.

Commentary

974 BC[22]

The events recorded in this chapter were central to the outcome of the struggle between David and his rebellious son Absalom. The author highlights one of these—the favoring of Hushai's advice over Ahithophel's (17:14). However, there are two others that also turned the tide in favor of David: the escape of Ahimaaz and Jonathan from Absalom's servants (17:18–20) and David's Transjordanian allies bringing him supplies at Mahanaim (17:27–29).

Ahithophel's Offer to Attack David (17:1–4)

Since Ahithophel had previously given Absalom advice that he had accepted (see 15:31–34; 16:20–23), he went on to offer unsolicited aid to the usurper (17:1). His description of his military plan (17:1–3) used seven first person forms referring to himself and only twice used second person forms referring to Absalom. Ahithophel volunteered to personally lead a force of twelve thousand men that very evening. The plan was deceptively simple: to catch David and his forces exhausted and unprepared (17:2). However, it was also extremely optimistic: it relied on everyone abandoning David because of a display of overwhelming force and assumed that a surgical strike would be capable of killing only the king.

---

[22] See "The Chronology of David's Reign" in the commentary on 5:1–5.

Ahithophel offered to bring the people back to Absalom "as a bride returns to her husband" (17:3). Some commentators reject this clause, which is found in the LXX and supported by 4QSam[a] (see the first textual note on 17:3).[23] They see it as not appropriate to Ahithophel's speech, which they characterize as direct and prosaic. However, this characterization is based on Ahithophel's only other recorded speech, his advice in 16:21, which is only twenty words (in Hebrew). The problem with this conclusion is twofold: First, it assumes that everything Ahithophel said to Absalom previously was recorded by the author of the book of Samuel. However, the previous quotation of Ahithophel may simply be a condensation of a longer speech, and many other dialogues likely took place but were not recorded. Second, a short twenty-word quotation is hardly a sufficient basis for asserting that Ahithophel must always have employed its style.

There are good reasons why many commentators and English versions include Ahithophel's bride simile as original. First, the syntax of the MT is unusual.[24] Second, the figure of Israel as a bride dovetails nicely with Ahithophel's previous advice to Absalom. There he urged Absalom to take his father's concubines (16:21), that is, his wives (see the commentary on 5:13). Here he is offering to bring Israel, pictured as the bride of the Israelite king, to Absalom. As Absalom was to sleep with his father's actual wives, he was also to receive his father's metaphorical bride, Israel. Absalom, Ahithophel said, was seeking the life of only one man (17:3)—just as David had sought only the life of Uriah so that he could take Ahithophel's granddaughter Bathsheba as his bride (11:15).[25]

Ahithophel's proposal smacks of personal animus against David. He wished to lead the army, and his plan was designed to eliminate only David. He attempted to cast David as the man whom Absalom was seeking to kill, but his frequent use of first person forms betrays his personal hostility toward the legitimate king. Would his plan have been successful if it had been implemented? It is impossible to say, but there are a number of reasons to be less sanguine about it than Ahithophel was. As far as we know, Ahithophel was not a seasoned fighter, like David and Joab were. His success on the battlefield against David—despite the weary and tired state of the retreating troops—was far from assured. David had also recruited spies in Jerusalem and may have not been caught as unaware as Ahithophel had assumed. Finally, the author of the book of Samuel has indicated that Yahweh has shown his everlasting grace toward David,[26] making the outcome assured (see 2 Sam 17:14; Prov 21:31).

---

[23] Baldwin, *1 and 2 Samuel*, 265; Fokkelman, *King David*, 214, n. 10.

[24] See the first textual note on 17:3.

[25] Ahithophel was the father of Eliam (23:34), and Eliam was the father of Bathsheba (11:3).

[26] See especially 2 Sam 7:15 and the rest of 2 Samuel 7, where Yahweh promised to establish David's throne and dynasty forever through the messianic King, the Son of David. See also, e.g., 1 Sam 17:37, 45; 18:12, 14, 28; 20:15–16, 42; 30:6; 2 Sam 6:21; 22:51; 1 Ki 3:6; Is 55:3; Pss 18:51(ET 18:50); 89:50 (ET 89:49); 2 Chr 7:6.

Ahithophel's plan may have resulted in greater casualties among the people with David—perhaps also the deaths of noncombatants—but David, not Absalom, was God's chosen king.[27]

The plan presented by Ahithophel seemed good to Absalom and his men (17:4). However, this was an unsolicited piece of advice, and Absalom was not ready to follow it without further consideration.

Hushai's Advice for Attacking David (17:5–14)

Since Ahithophel had proposed a strategy to defeat David, which Absalom had not requested, he had Hushai summoned (17:5). He asked whether Ahithophel's scheme ought to be implemented (17:6). Hushai's reply (17:7–13) contains masterfully worded rhetoric designed to seduce the vainglorious Absalom into rejecting Ahithophel's advice. Hushai focused on what Absalom and Israel knew and would do. Instead of letting Ahithophel claim the victory, Absalom would be credited with the triumph because of his personal presence (17:11). Hushai used four similes compared to Ahithophel's one (17:3). He employed a first person singular form to refer to himself only once ("I advise," 17:11). He used at least three, and perhaps five, first person plural verb forms to include Absalom in his alternate plan for dealing with David.[28] He avoided directly criticizing Ahithophel's untested leadership of an attack force on the battlefield,[29] opting instead to emphasize the combat experience of David and his troops (17:8, 10). David's utter defeat was envisioned with catastrophic hyperbole (17:13). In short, Hushai successfully counteracted Ahithophel's advice first by fooling Absalom with his ruse of loyalty in 16:16–19 and then by his persuasive speech as a tested veteran of combat. He appealed to his and Absalom's shared knowledge of the enemy's character (17:8, 10). The rhetorical features of his address made his advice more diplomatic and vivid.

Hushai speech can be divided into three parts:

- A short rejoinder stating that Ahithophel's advice in this instance was not good (17:7)
- A longer rationale that argued against an immediate attack on David and used two similes of animals (17:8–10) that had been associated with David earlier in the narrative ("bear" and "lion" in 1 Sam 17:34–37)[30]

---

[27] 1 Sam 16:12–13; 2 Sam 5:10–12. David had been anointed king by Samuel (1 Sam 16:13), Judah (2 Sam 2:4), and Israel (2 Sam 5:3).

[28] These include three first person plural perfect verbs with *waw* consecutive: "(and) we will come" (וּבָאנוּ, 17:12); "and we will descend" (וְנַחְנוּ, 17:12); "and we will drag" (וְסָחַבְנוּ, 17:13). For the fourth possible first person plural verb, נוֹתַר, see the third textual note on 17:12. For the fifth possible first person plural verb, נִמְצָא, see the fourth textual note on 17:13.

[29] Hushai's comment that "the most skilled soldier whose heart is like a lion's heart will completely lose courage" (17:10) may imply that Ahithophel's bravado in the royal court would turn into cowardice on the battlefield.

[30] See also a "lion" defeated by one of David's men in 2 Sam 23:20. 1 Sam 17:34–37 records how David, by Yahweh's deliverance, fought off both the lion and the bear. 2 Sam 17:8 likens

- An alternate plan for defeating David using two terrestrial similes (17:11–12) and rhetorical exaggeration (17:13)

Hushai's short reply prudently did not call into question Ahithophel's wisdom in general, which was revered (16:23). Hushai opined only that Ahithophel's counsel was not good in this case, "this time" (17:7). Hushai did not engage in a debate about the merits of Ahithophel's previous advice to Absalom, nor did he attack Ahithophel's highly regarded reputation.

In his argument against moving immediately to attack David, Hushai first appealed to Absalom's knowledge: "*you yourself know* your father and his men" (17:8). He characterized them as skilled soldiers and David as an experienced soldier. In addition, he characterized them as "like a bear robbed of her cubs in the wild"—a simile designed not only to highlight their ferocity as a fighting force but also to subtly raise Absalom's apprehension by hinting that David viewed him as a usurper who had bereaved him of his own children, that is, the kingdom.

Next Hushai appealed to David's reputation as a military strategist. He would not sleep in the camp. Instead, he would be in one of the caves or some other out-of-the-way place (17:9). Therefore, if Ahithophel were to carry out his plan of attack, when some of the combatants would be slain, a rumor would spread in the confusion that Absalom's forces had been routed, and this would cause a panic among Absalom's troops (17:9). To make Absalom more fearful of this prospect, Hushai referred to "the troops under Absalom," although Ahithophel's plan called for no personal participation by Absalom, who would remain in Jerusalem with David's concubines on the roof of the palace (cf. 16:21–22). Once again Hushai used an animal simile, this time characterizing Absalom's soldiers as having a heart like the heart of a lion (17:10). This simile simultaneously invests Absalom's men with great character but also robs them of courage because of the widespread regard they had for the superior military skill of David and his men. By Yahweh's salvation, David had fought off and killed lions (1 Sam 17:34–37).

As Hushai had begun his rationale with what Absalom knew (7:8), he ended it with "*all Israel* knows" (17:10). This double appeal to common knowledge was a delicate and indirect way of saying what Hushai wanted to communicate: only an idiot—a novice such as Ahithophel, who lacked military experience—would attack David without having made more extensive preparations.

This led then to Hushai's counsel: First, he urged Absalom to gather a militia from all Israel (17:11). Israel's extent "from Dan to Beersheba" is a common expression that covers the land from northernmost to southernmost.[31] Absalom would then have command of a vast army that Hushai compared to the sand

---

David to a bereaved and enraged bear, and 2 Sam 17:10 likens the hearts of Absalom's best soldiers to the hearts of lions.

[31] See "from Dan to Beersheba" also in Judg 20:1; 1 Sam 3:20; 2 Sam 3:10; 24:2, 15; 1 Ki 5:5 (ET 4:25) and "from Beersheba to Dan" in 1 Chr 21:2; 2 Chr 30:5 (cf. Amos 8:14).

beside the sea. This comparison slyly placed Absalom in the position of the heir of the promises to Abraham (Gen 22:17; 32:13 [ET 32:12]).[32] David had been granted that status by God through Nathan's prophecy (see the commentary on 2 Sam 7:9–11). Absalom in his vanity would have been flattered by such a statement, since Hushai urged him personally to lead Israel into battle (see the last textual note on 17:11).

Hushai then spoke about the implementation of his plan: David would certainly be defeated in open battle, since he would be met with an overwhelming force that would completely wipe out his army (17:12). The meteorological simile for this overwhelming army attacking David's men—"we will descend on him like dew [טַל] on the ground"—recalls God's blessing on Jacob through Isaac (Gen 27:28) and his blessing on the tribes of Joseph through Moses (Deut 33:13).[33] Hushai was calling on Absalom to accept his advice because it would bring prosperity and success from Yahweh as in the divine promises made long ago.

However, Hushai also spoke of the implementation of his plan should David decide to take refuge in a fortified city (17:13). Again, Absalom's troops would be so numerous that they could level the city so that "not even a pebble could be found there." Ending his speech with this rhetorical flourish—using vivid hyperbole—Hushai had offered a plan that covered all possibilities. By implication he had said that Ahithophel did not offer a plan that took into account all of David's options, since it did not consider that David might act more strategically than Ahithophel imagined (see 17:8–9).

Because of Hushai's persuasive presentation, Absalom and his men declared Hushai's advice better (17:14). The author notes that Yahweh had decreed that Ahithophel's advice would be frustrated, and this would fulfill David's prayer in 15:31. In the book of Samuel, the narrator's voice seldom provides explicit theological commentary, as it does here (for other examples, see 11:27; 12:24–25). The author wished to note emphatically that God accomplished his will through the words of Hushai, which were more eloquent and appealing. They proved more convincing despite the fact that Ahithophel's stratagem was superior, according to the author ("Ahithophel's better advice," 17:14).

Hushai Sends David a Warning (17:15–22)

Though Hushai appeared to have won Absalom over to his plan, he took no chances that Absalom might reconsider. He sent word about both plans to Zadok and Abiathar, to be relayed to David with the advice that David move his people across the Jordan without delay (17:15–16).

---

[32] The image of being as numerous as the sand beside the sea also describes Israel in, e.g., 1 Ki 4:20; Hos 1:10 (cf. Is 10:22; 48:19). It portrays the offspring of David in the promise of Jer 33:22. Contrast its use for the Philistine army in 1 Sam 13:5.

[33] "Dew" (טַל) was also involved in the gift of the manna (Ex 16:13–14; Num 11:9). To be deprived of "dew" was a curse (Gen 27:39; 2 Sam 1:21; 1 Ki 17:1).

We are told that Jonathan and Ahimaaz, the high priests' sons, were staying in En-rogel (17:17), the spring southeast of Jerusalem in the Kidron Valley near where the Kidron and Hinnom Valleys join. This site is usually identified with modern Bir Ayyub, "the well of Job." It lay on the border between the territories of Judah and Benjamin (Josh 15:7; 18:16). To get word to them, a woman was sent to the well (2 Sam 17:17)—fetching water was a woman's job (cf. Jn 4:4–15). Jonathan and Ahimaaz avoided coming and going to Jerusalem, since this would have raised suspicions about their activity. However, they were seen with the woman, and Absalom was informed (17:18). To get to the fords of the Jordan River, Ahimaaz and Jonathan followed the same route as David, which took them to Bahurim, where Shimei had cursed the king (16:5–13). Fortunately, they had a place to hide at a house of someone who must have been sympathetic to David's cause. Their escape was aided by the man's wife, who hid them from Absalom's men in a cistern that she covered and concealed (17:19). When Absalom's men asked where Ahimaaz and Jonathan were, the woman told them that Ahimaaz and Jonathan had passed on to the water (17:20). Absalom's men searched but did not find Ahimaaz and Jonathan. The woman's actions are reminiscent of Rahab hiding the Israelite spies on her roof in Jericho (Joshua 2).

Ahimaaz and Jonathan were able to report Ahithophel's advice to David, who immediately moved his people across the Jordan River by morning (17:21–22). Since David had escaped to a safer position, Absalom was now in no position to follow Ahithophel's advice even if he had changed his mind.

The woman's participation in concealing Ahimaaz and Jonathan involved telling a lie in order to protect the lives of David, his men, and the women and children with them. It followed Hushai's deception of Absalom (16:16–19). The Scriptures are quite harsh in their depiction of lies that would bring harm to innocent persons, such as deceiving a neighbor in order to defraud him or lead him into sin, or lies that give false testimony in judicial proceedings, as condemned in the Eighth Commandment.[34] However, some lies, like this woman's fabrication, and especially falsehoods that protect the innocent or obtain justice, are portrayed in a more favorable light in the OT. These include the trickeries by Michal in 1 Sam 19:11–17 and by Jonathan in 1 Sam 20:28–29.[35] Rahab is saved and justified for her misdirection.[36] This is, in fact, in keeping with the spirit of admonitions such as Prov 31:8–9.[37] Shemesh notes:

---

[34] Ex 20:16; Deut 5:20. See also, e.g., Gen 37:31–32; 39:14–15, 17–18; Lev 19:11–12, 18–19; 1 Ki 21:13; 2 Ki 5:22–27; Is 59:3–4; Jer 9:4 (ET 9:5); 23:14; Pss 5:7 (ET 5:6); 7:15–16 (ET 7:14–15); 144:7–8, 11; Prov 6:16–19; 14:5, 25; 19:5, 9; Mt 26:59–61; Acts 6:11–14.

[35] See the commentary on those passages, as well as on David's apparent deceptions in 1 Sam 21:3–4, 13–14 (ET 21:2–3, 12–13); 27:10–11 (cf. 1 Sam 28:1–2).

[36] Rahab's misdirection saved the Israelite spies in Joshua 2, and subsequently she and her household were saved in Josh 6:17–25. The NT declares her righteous (Heb 11:31; James 2:25).

[37] "Speak out for those who cannot speak, for the rights of all those who are defenseless. Speak out, judge fairly, and defend the oppressed and needy" (Steinmann, *Proverbs*, 618).

The Hebrew Bible recognizes that under certain circumstances lying is unavoidable, particularly when it serves the weak as their only weapon against some force seeking to harm them or other persons. Included in this category are various instances of lies intended to save the liar's life or altruistic lies (mainly on the part of women).

Thus, for example, David lies to Ahimelech (1 Sam. 21:3 [ET 21:2]) and misleads King Achish of Gath (1 Sam. 21:14 [ET 21:13]) in order to save his own life. Saul's daughter Michal lies to her father's messengers in order to save her husband David's life (1 Sam. 19:11–16), and then lies to her father in order to escape his rage (1 Sam. 19:17). Jonathan, too, lies to his father to save his friend David's life (1 Sam. 20:28–29), and the woman from Bahurim lies to Absalom's servants to save David's spies Ahimaaz and Jonathan, hidden in the well in her courtyard (2 Sam. 17:18–20). Proof that God may actually approve of such lies may be derived from His rewarding of the midwives in Egypt, who lied to Pharaoh out of compassion for the lives of the male children born to the Hebrew women (Ex. 1:15–21). A further indication to that effect is the narrator's comment concerning Hushai's deception of Absalom by pretending to support him: "The Lord had decreed that Ahithophel's sound advice be nullified, in order that the Lord might bring ruin upon Absalom" (2 Sam. 17:14).

A forgiving view of deception may also be discerned in cases where persons lie to secure what belongs to them by right but has been unjustly withheld. Thus, the initiative taken by Judah's daughter-in-law Tamar, who disguises herself as a prostitute in order to become pregnant by him after his failure to marry her to his son Shelah, is described in a favorable light, and indeed justified by Judah himself in the narrative (Gen. 38:26). Tamar is rewarded for her subterfuge by the birth of the twins Perez and Zerah, through whom the tribe of Judah is established (Gen. 38:27–30). The biblical narrator also takes a favorable view of fraud when the object is some religious goal in keeping with the general outlook of the Bible. An example is Jehu's lying to the worshipers of Baal, which is aimed at killing all the prophets of Baal and eradicating his worship from the country (2 Ki. 10:18–28).[38]

Thus, Christians may at times find themselves in positions where they may have to lie or deceive to protect themselves or innocent people from injustice. In such cases one may have to choose to honor God by disobeying men (Acts 5:29) and keep the Fifth Commandment's prohibition against murder (Ex 20:13; Deut 5:17) even if it involves a violation of the Eighth Commandment (Ex 20:16; Deut 5:20), since God places a high value on the sanctity of all human life and is especially concerned about protecting the innocent, the weak, and the helpless.[39] In this case, Hushai's deception protected not only David, bearer of the messianic promise (2 Samuel 7), but also the noncombatants with David and his men.

---

[38] Shemesh, "Lies by Prophets and Other Lies in the Hebrew Bible," 84–85.

[39] Deut 10:17–19; 24:17; 27:19; Is 1:16–17; Jer 7:6–7; 22:3; Zech 7:10; Pss 10:14, 17–18; 68:6 (ET 68:5); 82:3; 146:9.

The Immediate Consequences of Absalom Following Hushai's Advice (17:23–29)

The rest of the chapter relates three direct aftereffects of Absalom being convinced to take Hushai's advice:

- Ahithophel committed suicide (17:23).
- David was able to travel all the way to safety in the Transjordanian town of Mahanaim by the time Absalom had gathered an army and crossed the Jordan River (17:24–25). Eventually Absalom would make camp in Gilead (17:26).
- David was able to be resupplied by his Transjordanian allies before having to engage Absalom's army in battle (17:27–29).

Ahithophel's suicide was his reaction to having his advice rejected (17:23). He now surmised that Absalom would be defeated and did not want to face execution for treason. He may have had an additional reason to avoid execution for treason, since in that case his property may have reverted to the crown.[40] He resolutely returned to his hometown and put his affairs in order. Although he committed suicide by hanging, he was permitted to be interred in his family tomb. His method of suicide can be compared to the accursed death of Absalom as he hung from a tree (see the textual notes and the commentary on 18:9–10). Suicide is a choosing of death over life and a sign of absence of faith in God, who promises to preserve his people through and beyond all of life's travails. In the NT Judas hanged himself in despair after realizing that he had betrayed the innocent blood of Jesus Christ (Mt 27:3–10).

David's escape to Mahanaim was facilitated by Absalom's dalliance with the king's wives in Jerusalem (16:21–22) as a militia was assembled from all Israel. Upon assembling his army, Absalom appointed his cousin Amasa, David's nephew, as his commander (17:25). Thus, two cousins, Joab and Amasa, would command opposing armies in the subsequent battle.

David was greeted by three allies in the Transjordan. Shobi was a son of the former Ammonite king Nahash, who may have been related to David through David's half sister Abigail (see the fifth textual note on 17:25). Machir had taken Mephibosheth as his ward after the death of Saul and Jonathan (9:4–5). He may have been loyal to David because of his appreciation for David's kindness to this crippled son of Jonathan (4:4; 9:3–10).[41] Barzillai the Gileadite is first introduced here. He may have been won to David's cause early on when David had first courted the Transjordanian tribes and especially the men of Jabesh-gilead following Saul's death (see the commentary on 2:5–7). David would use Mahanaim as his base of operations for the coming battle. Interestingly, Mahanaim had earlier served as the capital for Ish-bosheth's reign over the Transjordanian Israelites (2:8–9), testifying to its strategic importance. See figure 9.

---

[40] Shemesh, "Suicide in the Bible," 164. Shemesh notes that it can be inferred from Ahab taking possession of Naboth's vineyard after his execution (1 Ki 21:15–16) that the property of executed criminals fell to the crown and that this was the view of the rabbis (Babylonian Talmud, *Sanhedrin*, 48b).

[41] Bergen, *1, 2 Samuel*, 417; Hertzberg, *I and II Samuel*, 357.

Figure 9

The Rebellions of Absalom (2 Samuel 15–19) and Sheba (2 Samuel 20)

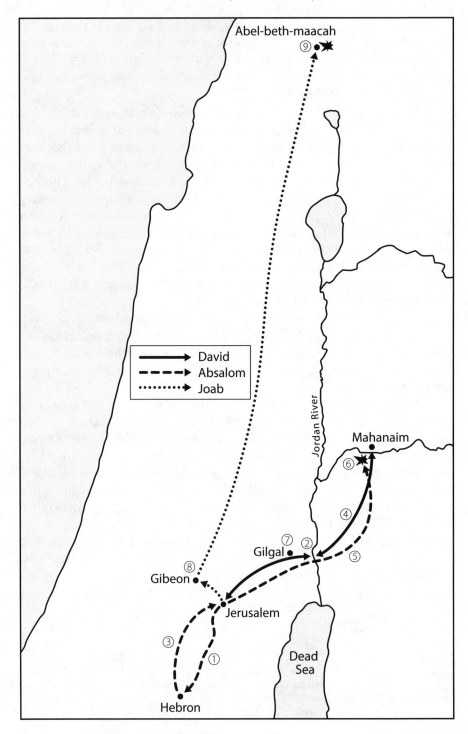

Key for Figure 9

1. Absalom goes to Hebron with two hundred men.
2. David flees Jerusalem and goes to the fords.
3. Absalom returns to Jerusalem.
4. David fords the Jordan River and goes to Mahanaim.
5. Absalom pursues David.
6. Absalom is defeated in the forest of Ephraim.
7. David returns. At Gilgal he is greeted by the tribes. Sheba foments rebellion.
8. Joab kills Amasa at Gibeon.
9. Joab pursues Sheba to Abel-beth-maacah, where the people of Abel-beth-maacah behead him and throw his head to Joab from the city wall.

Absalom Is Killed in Battle

Translation

18 ¹David organized the troops who were with him and placed officers in charge of a thousand men and officers in charge of a hundred men over them. ²David sent out the troops: a third under the command of Joab, a third under the command of Zeruiah's son Abishai, Joab's brother, and a third under the command of Ittai the Gittite.

The king said to the troops, "I am determined to go [into battle] with you."

³The troops said, "You should not go out [to battle], because if we flee, they will not be concerned about us. Even if half of us die, they will not be concerned about us, because you are like ten thousand of us. So it would be better for you to support us from the city."

⁴The king said to them, "I will do what you think is best." The king stood beside the city gate as all the troops went out to battle by hundreds and thousands. ⁵The king commanded Joab, Abishai, and Ittai, "For my sake be gentle with the young man Absalom." All the troops were listening when the king ordered all the commanders concerning Absalom.

⁶The troops when out to the countryside to engage Israel [in battle]. The battle was in the forest of Ephraim. ⁷The people of Israel were defeated there by David's servants. The slaughter there was great on that day: twenty thousand [men]. ⁸As the battle was spreading there over the entire region, the forest consumed more of the troops than the sword consumed on that day.

⁹Absalom happened to encounter David's servants while he was riding a mule. The mule went under the tangled branches of a large terebinth, and his head caught firmly in the terebinth. He was hanging in midair, and the mule under him moved on. ¹⁰A man saw this and told Joab. He said, "I saw Absalom hanging in a terebinth!"

¹¹Joab said to the man who told him, "You saw him? Why didn't you strike him to the ground there? It would have been my pleasure to give you ten [shekels] of silver and a belt!"

¹²The man said to Joab, "Even if I had the weight of a thousand [shekels] of silver in my hand, I would not reach out my hand against the king's son, because we heard the king command you and Abishai and Ittai, 'Protect the young man Absalom for me.' ¹³Or if I had acted treacherously at the cost of my life—and nothing is hidden from the king—you would have distanced yourself from me."

¹⁴Joab said, "I'm not going to waste time with you." He took three spears and thrust them into Absalom's heart while he was still alive in the interior of the terebinth. ¹⁵Ten young men—Joab's armor bearers—surrounded and struck Absalom and killed him. ¹⁶Then Joab blew a ram's horn, and the troops turned away from

pursuing Israel, because Joab restrained the troops. ¹⁷They took Absalom and

pursuing Israel, because Joab restrained the troops. **¹⁷They took Absalom and threw him into a large pit in the forest and piled a very large mound of stones on top of him while all Israel fled, each man to his tent. (¹⁸While he was alive Absalom had erected for himself a pillar which is in the King's Valley, because he had said, "I have no son to preserve the memory of my name." So he called the pillar by his name. It is still called Absalom's Monument to this day.)**

Textual Notes

18:1 וַיִּפְקֹד—"He organized." In military contexts the Qal (G) of פָּקַד can mean "to muster" troops for battle, i.e., "to count, number" (as in 2 Sam 24:2, 4) or "organize" them. See the textual note on 1 Sam 14:17;[1] see also 1 Sam 15:4.

אֶת־הָעָם אֲשֶׁר אִתּוֹ—"The troops who were with him." In military contexts the noun with the article הָעָם, "the people," often denotes "the troops." See the first textual note on 1 Sam 4:3[2] and the second textual note on 2 Sam 1:4.

שָׂרֵי אֲלָפִים וְשָׂרֵי מֵאוֹת:—"Officers in charge of a thousand men and officers in charge of a hundred men" is literally "officers of thousands and officers of hundreds." Standard military organization consisted of smaller units of fifty or a hundred men collected into larger units of a thousand men.[3]

18:2 יָצֹא אֵצֵא גַם־אֲנִי עִמָּכֶם:—"I am determined to go [into battle] with you" is literally "I will certainly go out, also I, with you." The combination of the Qal (G) infinitive absolute and the Qal (G) imperfect first common singular of יָצָא, "go out," with the particle and the redundant subject pronoun גַם־אֲנִי, "also I," is emphatic, expressing determination. The verb יָצָא in military contexts often denotes going into battle. See the first textual note on 1 Sam 18:6[4] and the first textual note on 2 Sam 2:12.

18:3 לֹא־יָשִׂימוּ אֵלֵינוּ לֵב ... לֹא־יָשִׂימוּ אֵלֵינוּ לֵב—"They will not be concerned about us. ... They will not be concerned about us." This repeated clause is literally "they will not set to us a [their] heart." This idiom is the second idiom discussed in the textual note on 13:33. For the second occurrence of this clause, 4QSam^a reads instead וְלֹא יְשִׂ[ין]ם לנו לב, "he [one, anyone] will not set to us a heart," i.e., "no one will be concerned about us."

וְאִם־יָמֻתוּ חֶצְיֵנוּ—"Even if half of us die." The noun חֲצִי, "half," has a first common plural suffix in a genitival sense, חֶצְיֵנוּ, "half *of* us." It is the subject of the Qal (G) third masculine plural imperfect of מוּת, "die."

כִּי־עַתָּה כָמֹנוּ עֲשָׂרָה אֲלָפִים—This is the reading in Codex Leningradensis and most other Masoretic manuscripts, literally "because now like us ten thousand." In place of the temporal adverb עַתָּה, "now," two Masoretic manuscripts read the personal pronoun אַתָּה, "you," which is supported by the LXX (σύ). That reading is the basis of the translation "because you are like ten thousand of us."

---

1. Steinmann, *1 Samuel*, 250.

2. Steinmann, *1 Samuel*, 120.

3. Ex 18:21, 25; Deut 1:15; 1 Sam 8:12; 17:18; 18:13; 22:7; 2 Ki 1:9, 11, 13.

4. Steinmann, *1 Samuel*, 350.

וְעַתָּה טֹוב—"So it would be better" is literally "and now good." In this context the adjective טֹוב, "good," functions as a comparative, "better" (Joüon, § 141 g). See the second textual note on 14:32 and the third textual note on 17:14.

כִּי־תִהְיֶה־לָּנוּ מֵעִיר לַעְזֹור:—Literally "for you will be for us from the city to help." For the second verb, the Qere and the sole reading in many Masoretic manuscripts is לַעְזֹור, a Qal (G) infinitive construct (see GKC, § 63 i) of עָזַר, "to help, aid." As in 2 Sam 8:5, this infinitive has the preposition לְ and also takes the preposition לְ in the sense of advantage (here on לָנוּ, "for us, for our benefit"). The Kethib is לַעְזִיר, the Hiphil (H) infinitive construct of the same verb with the preposition לְ and with the *he* preformative elided (-לַ for -לְהַ). Such elision is rare for infinitive constructs, suggesting that the Kethib is a transcription error.[5] Moreover, there is only one other example of this verb in the Hiphil (H) stem (2 Chr 28:23).

18:4 אֲשֶׁר־יִיטַב בְּעֵינֵיכֶם אֶעֱשֶׂה—The Hebrew word order emphasizes David's deference to their preference, literally "that which is good in your eyes I will do."

18:5 לְאַט־לִי—"For my sake be gentle" is literally "gently for me." The word לְאַט is often understood to be the preposition לְ and the substantive אַט, "gentleness" (1 Ki 21:27),[6] functioning adverbially. However, some have argued that it should be repointed as a form of the verb לוּט, "cover," and would translate David's command as "cover [i.e., protect]" Absalom.[7]

שָׁמְעוּ—This is the Qal (G) third common plural perfect of שָׁמַע, meaning "they heard," which is supported by the LXX (ἤκουσεν). The translation "were listening" follows the reading in 4QSamª, שמעים, to be vocalized שֹׁמְעִים, the Qal (G) masculine plural participle.

18:6 לִקְרַאת—"To engage [in battle]." This is the Qal (G) infinitive construct of קָרָא II, "to meet, encounter" (with the preposition לְ). See the second textual note on 1 Sam 4:1.[8] The verb קָרָא II recurs in the Niphal (N) in 18:9 (see the first textual note on 18:9).

18:7 וַיִּנָּגְפוּ ... הַמַּגֵּפָה—"They were defeated. ... The slaughter ..." The verb and the cognate noun could be translated similarly, either "they were defeated ... the defeat" or "they were slaughtered ... the slaughter," which fits better with the number of dead men at the end of the verse. For the Niphal (N) of נָגַף with the military meaning "be defeated," see the third textual note on 1 Sam 4:2[9] and the textual note on 2 Sam 2:17. The feminine noun מַגֵּפָה is derived from the verb and denotes a military "slaughter" or "defeat" also in 1 Sam 4:17; 2 Sam 17:9.

18:8 נָפֹצֶת—"Was spreading." This Qere, which is the sole reading in many Masoretic manuscripts, is the Niphal (N) feminine singular participle of פּוּץ. This verb means "be

---

[5] GKC, § 53 q.

[6] BDB, s.v. אַט, b; *HALOT*, s.v. אַט I, 2; see HCSB, ESV, GW, NET, NIV.

[7] Haupt, "Deal Gently with the Young Man"; McCarter, *II Samuel*, 405.

[8] Steinmann, *1 Samuel*, 119.

[9] Steinmann, *1 Samuel*, 119–20.

scattered" in both the Niphal and the Qal (used for soldiers retreating in defeat in 1 Sam 11:11). The Kethib here is the anomalous form נפצית.

וַיֶּרֶב הַיַּעַר לֶאֱכֹל—"The forest consumed more" is literally "the forest multiplied to eat." The Hiphil (H) third masculine singular preterite (imperfect with *waw* consecutive) of רָבָה, "be many," expresses the adverbial notion "more" (see Joüon, §§ 102 g; 141 h) in conjunction with לֶאֱכֹל, the Qal (G) infinitive construct of אָכַל, "to eat" (with לְ). For the construction, see BDB, s.v. רָבָה I, Hiphil, 1 d (1).

מֵאֲשֶׁר אָכְלָה הַחֶרֶב—"Than the sword consumed" is literally "than (the people) whom the sword ate." The preposition מִן expresses a comparative ("than"). The noun חֶרֶב, "sword," is feminine, and is the subject of the Qal (G) third feminine singular perfect of אָכַל, "eat." For the expression that a "sword" (חֶרֶב) "eats" or "devours" (אָכַל), see the first textual note on 2:26 and the third textual note on 11:25.

18:9 וַיִּקָּרֵא אַבְשָׁלוֹם לִפְנֵי עַבְדֵי דָוִד—"Absalom happened to encounter David's servants" is literally "and Absalom happened to be before David's servants." The verb וַיִּקָּרֵא is the Niphal (N) third masculine singular preterite (imperfect with *waw* consecutive) of קָרָא II, "meet, encounter." Compare the Qal (G) of this verb in the textual note on 18:6.

וְאַבְשָׁלוֹם רֹכֵב—Literally "and Absalom was riding." This is translated with a pronoun, "while *he* was riding," because of English stylistic considerations.

הַפֶּרֶד—"A mule." For the noun פֶּרֶד, "mule," see the textual note on 13:29. Hebrew commonly uses the definite article on a noun when the narrator has in mind a specific one. See Joüon, § 137 o, which cites the following הָאֵלָה הַגְּדוֹלָה (see the next textual note) and הַפַּחַת הַגָּדוֹל in 18:17. See also the first textual note on 15:13; the fourth textual note on 17:9; and the second textual note on 17:17.

שׂוֹבֶךְ הָאֵלָה הַגְּדוֹלָה—"The tangled branches of a large terebinth." The noun שׂוֹבֶךְ is a hapax legomenon. The related feminine noun שְׂבָכָה denotes a webbed net (Job 18:8) or a network or lattice (e.g., 1 Ki 7:17–18, 20; 2 Ki 1:2). The LXX translates the word here as τὸ δάσος, "the thicket." The noun אֵלָה, "terebinth," while traditionally translated as "oak," is the tree *Pistacia palaestina*, a member of the cashew family. The word recurs in 18:10, 14.

וַיֶּחֱזַק רֹאשׁוֹ בָאֵלָה—"And his head caught firmly in the terebinth." The Qal (G) of חָזַק, "be strong," with the preposition בְּ, "in," means "be caught fast" (BDB, s.v. חָזַק, Qal, 2 a) or "be firmly stuck." Absalom's extensive hair (14:26) may have contributed to his entanglement.

וַיֻּתַּן—"He was hanging" is literally "and he was placed." This verb is the Qal passive (Gp) third masculine singular preterite (imperfect with *waw* consecutive) of נָתַן, "give, put, set." 4QSamᵃ reads ויתל, which could be vocalized as וַיִּתָּל, the Niphal (N) third masculine singular preterite (imperfect with *waw* consecutive) of תָּלָה (see BDB, s.v. תָּלָה, Niphal). Alternatively, the 4QSamᵃ reading ויתל could be vocalized as a Qal passive (Gp) third masculine singular preterite (imperfect with *waw* consecutive), וַיֻּתַּל, "and he (was) hung." Qal (G) forms of תָּלָה (as in 2 Sam 4:12; 21:12) have the transitive meaning "hang [someone or something]." Qal passive (Gp) and Niphal (N) forms normally would have a passive meaning, "be hung," but possibly here such a form could have the intransitive meaning "be hanging." The LXX translation ἐκρεμάσθη, "(it)

339

was hung," apparently reflects a passive form of תָּלָה here. See also תָּלוּי in the textual note on 18:10. If the original reading here was וַיִּתָּל or וַיֵּתָל, then the verb וַיִּתֵּן in the MT would be the result of a graphic confusion between *lamed* and final *nun*.

בֵּין הַשָּׁמַיִם וּבֵין הָאָרֶץ—"In midair" is literally "between the sky and between the ground."

18:10 תָּלוּי—"Hanging." This is the Qal passive (Gp) masculine singular participle of תָּלָה, "to hang" (see the sixth textual note on 18:9). The identical form is used in Deut 21:23 to state that "(anyone) hanging" (on a tree, Deut 21:22) is "a curse of God," that is, accursed by God.

18:11 וְעָלַי לָתֶת לְךָ—"It would have been my pleasure to give you" is literally "and to give to you (would have been incumbent) upon me." The infinitive construct לָתֶת (the Qal [G] of נָתַן) is used nominally as the subject (Joüon, § 124 b). An infinitive construct with לְ can express an action that is one's duty or will (GKC, § 114 l), and that sense is reinforced here by the preposition עַל for an obligation "upon" someone to do something.[10] Here, however, Joab, rather than begrudging an obligation, is expressing what he would have preferred to do.

עֲשָׂרָה—"Ten" is the reading in the MT. The reading in 4QSamᵃ ([חמ]שים), the Lucianic recension of the LXX, and Josephus[11] is "fifty."[12]

18:12 וְלוּא—"Even if" is the reading of the Qere. The particle לוּ or לוּא indicates an unreal condition (Joüon, § 167 f, k). The Kethib is וְלֹא, "and not."

אָנֹכִי שֹׁקֵל—"I had the weight." The pronoun with the Qal (G) masculine singular participle is literally "I (were) weighing."

בְּאָזְנֵינוּ צִוָּה הַמֶּלֶךְ—"We heard the king command" is literally "in our ears the king commanded."

שִׁמְרוּ־מִי—This reading with the Qal (G) imperative of שָׁמַר and the interrogative pronoun מִי, "who?" in an indefinite sense ("whoever") could mean "whoever you are, protect" (Waltke-O'Connor, § 18.2e, including example 31; cf. GKC, § 137 c). In place of the interrogative pronoun מִי, "who?" two Masoretic manuscripts have the prepositional phrase לִי, "for me," an easier reading which is supported by the LXX, the Syriac, the Targum, and the Vulgate. The king's command in 18:5, לְאַט־לִי, used that prepositional phrase (see the first textual note on 18:5).

18:13 אוֹ־עָשִׂיתִי בְנַפְשׁוֹ שֶׁקֶר—"Or if I had acted treacherously at the cost of my life" is literally "or I did falsehood/treachery with my life/soul." The conjunction אוֹ introduces a hypothetical scenario that is the converse of the scenario in 18:12 (GKC, § 159 cc). In the Qere בְנַפְשִׁי, the preposition בְּ on נַפְשִׁי has the sense of price or cost (BDB, s.v. בְּ I, III 3). See בְּ on נֶפֶשׁ in a similar sense in 2 Sam 23:17 ‖ 1 Chr 11:19; 1 Ki 2:23; see also Num 17:3 (ET 16:38); Jer 42:20; Prov 7:23. The man is saying that if he had violated the king's command by killing Absalom, that action would have cost him his life.

---

[10] GKC, § 119 aa; Joüon, § 133 f; Waltke-O'Connor, §§ 11.2.13c, including example 7; 36.2.3f, including example 39.

[11] Josephus, *Antiquities*, 7.240.

[12] McCarter, *II Samuel*, 401.

The Kethib reads בְּנַפְשׁוֹ, "with his [Absalom's] life": the man would have acted treacherously if he had taken Absalom's life.

וְכָל־דָּבָר לֹא־יִכָּחֵד מִן־הַמֶּלֶךְ—"And nothing is hidden from the king" is literally "and every word/matter will not be hidden from the king." The verb יִכָּחֵד is the Niphal (N) third masculine singular imperfect of כָּחַד, whose Piel (D) means "to hide" in 1 Sam 3:17–18; 2 Sam 14:18.

וְאַתָּה תִּתְיַצֵּב מִנֶּגֶד:—"You would have distanced yourself from me" is literally "and you would have taken your stand from beside." The verb תִּתְיַצֵּב is the Hithpael (HtD) second masculine singular imperfect of יָצַב, which is used only in the Hithpael and means "position oneself, stand firm, take one's stand."

18:14 לֹא־כֵן אֹחִילָה לְפָנֶיךָ—"I'm not going to waste time with you" is literally "not thus let me wait before you." The verb אֹחִילָה is the Hiphil (H) singular cohortative of יָחַל, "to wait; hope." The cohortative could express a request for permission (GKC, § 108 c), but since a commander is speaking to a subordinate soldier, it has the force of a declaration of intent.

שְׁבָטִים—"Spears." The noun שֵׁבֶט usually refers to a "rod," "staff," or royal "scepter." The LXX reads βέλη, "arrows," perhaps reading a Hebrew Vorlage of שְׁלָחִים, "weapons" (cf. Neh 4:11, 17 [ET 4:17, 23]).

וַיִּתְקָעֵם—"And he thrust them." With this verb and the verb וַיִּתְקַע in 18:16, the author creates a sense of irony by repetition: וַיִּתְקָעֵם ... וַיִּתְקַע, "And he thrust them. ... Then he blew." (For other uses of repetition to create irony, see the next textual note and the second textual note on 18:17.) In 18:14, 16, the author repeats a Qal (G) third masculine singular preterite (imperfect with *waw* consecutive) of תָּקַע, each with Joab as the subject, but in quite different senses in 18:14 versus 18:16. The first instance (וַיִּתְקָעֵם, 18:14, with a third masculine plural object suffix, referring to the "spears") has the sense of "thrust, drive" (*DCH*, Qal, 1), while the second (וַיִּתְקַע, 18:16) means "blow, give a blast" (*DCH*, Qal, 5). Joab's spear thrusts enable him to blow the shofar to proclaim the victory.

בְּלֵב אַבְשָׁלוֹם ... בְּלֵב הָאֵלָה:—Literally "in the heart of Absalom ... in the heart of the terebinth." The repetition of the prepositional phrase with the noun לֵב, "heart," may be ironic. The spears easily find their target "in the heart of" Absalom because he is stuck, vulnerable and helpless, "in the heart of" the tree.

18:15 עֲשָׂרָה נְעָרִים נֹשְׂאֵי כְּלֵי יוֹאָב—"Ten young men—Joab's armor bearers." The noun נַעַר, "young man," can be used with the Qal (G) participle of נָשָׂא, "to carry, bear," and the object noun כְּלִי, "equipment," to denote an "armor bearer," although the participle and the object noun by themselves have the same meaning. See the second textual note on 1 Sam 14:1.[13] Thus, this could also be translated as "ten of Joab's armor bearers."

וַיְמִתְהוּ:—"And they killed him." This Hiphil (H) of מוּת, "die" (third masculine plural preterite [imperfect with *waw* consecutive] with a third masculine singular object suffix), makes Joab's armor bearers complicit in the killing of Absalom. Perhaps Joab's

---

[13] Steinmann, *1 Samuel*, 247.

spears mortally wounded Absalom, who remained alive until the armor bearers finished him off. The Polel (D) of מוּת often has the nuance of killing off someone who is already wounded (e.g., 1 Sam 14:13; 17:51; 2 Sam 1:9, 10, 16), and here the Hiphil (H) may have that same nuance.

18:16 וַיִּתְקַע יוֹאָב בַּשֹּׁפָר—"Then Joab blew a ram's horn." The transliteration of the noun שׁוֹפָר, *shofar*, has made its way into English. The verb תָּקַע (see the third textual note on 18:14) is used with the noun שׁוֹפָר prefixed with the preposition בְּ and the definite article, literally "to blow with the shofar." Usually this signals the winning of a victory and therefore calls the soldiers to cease their warfare, as here and also in 1 Sam 13:3; 2 Sam 2:28; 20:22. However, it is a treasonous call to rebel against King David in 20:1, as is the sounding of the shofar in 15:10.

18:17 אֶל־הַפַּחַת הַגָּדוֹל—Literally "into the large pit." For the noun פַּחַת, "pit, cave," see also the second textual note on 17:9. For the use of the definite article on a noun corresponding to an English indefinite expression ("a"), see the third textual note on 18:9.

וַיַּצִּבוּ—"And they piled." With this verb and the verb וַיַּצֶּב in 18:18, the author again creates irony by verbal repetition: וַיַּצִּבוּ ... וַיַּצֶּב, "And they piled. ... He had erected." (For the earlier uses of verbal repetition to create irony, see the third and fourth textual notes on 18:14.) Both verbs are Hiphil (H) preterites (imperfects with *waw* consecutive) of נָצַב, "to set up, pile up, erect." The irony is that Absalom during his lifetime "had erected" a monument for his own glory (וַיַּצֶּב, 18:18), but after his death David's troops "piled" stones upon his body (וַיַּצִּבוּ, 18:17), and the heap of stones also served as a historical monument to his inglorious defeat. The Hiphil (H) participle (מַצִּיב) of the same verb, נָצַב, referred to narcissistic Saul erecting a monument for himself in 1 Sam 15:12 before his ignominious defeat (1 Samuel 31).

אִישׁ לְאֹהָלָיו׃—"Each man to his tent." This reading with the Qere is the normal wording of this phrase, literally "each man to his tents [plural]."[14] The Kethib reads the noun as singular, לְאָהֳלוֹ, "to his tent"; that wording appears elsewhere only in Judg 20:8; 2 Ki 14:12 (Kethib).

18:18 וְאַבְשָׁלֹם לָקַח וַיַּצֶּב ... אֶת־מַצֶּבֶת—"Absalom had erected ... a pillar" is literally "and Absalom took and set up ... the pillar." The construction with a subject (with the conjunction *waw*) preceding a perfect verb (וְאַבְשָׁלֹם לָקַח) often expresses a pluperfect, "Absalom *had* ..." (Joüon, § 118 d). For וַיַּצֶּב (the Hiphil [H] of נָצַב), see the second textual note on 18:17. The feminine noun מַצֶּבֶת, "pillar, memorial stone" (*DCH*, s.v. מַצֵּבָה, 1), recurs later in the verse and is more often spelled מַצֵּבָה. Here this object noun forms a cognate accusative construction because it is derived from the second verb, נָצַב. This is an uncommon instance of the use of the definite direct object marker, אֵת, with an indefinite noun, מַצֶּבֶת.[15]

בְּחַיָּו—"While he was alive" is literally "in his life." This Qere (the sole reading in many Masoretic manuscripts) is the plural of the noun חַי, "life," with the preposition בְּ

---

[14] Judg 7:8; 1 Sam 4:10; 13:2; 2 Sam 19:9 (ET 19:8); 20:1, 22; 2 Ki 14:12 (Qere); 2 Chr 25:22.

[15] GKC, § 117 d, unjustifiably requires an emendation, either the addition of the definite article to make הַמַּצֶּבֶת or the omission of both אֵת and אֲשֶׁר.

and a third masculine singular suffix (see also Judg 16:30; Ps 49:19 [ET 49:18]; Eccl 3:12). This word is used in the plural as an abstract substantive to denote "life." The Kethib בחיו probably should be pointed בְּחַיָּו, a defective, or *ḥaser*, spelling of the same word, apparently with haplography of one *yod*.

בַּעֲבוּר הַזְכִּיר שְׁמִי—"To preserve the memory of my name" is literally "with the purpose to cause to remember/commemorate my name." The combination of prepositions בַּעֲבוּר (בְּ + עֲבוּר) indicates purpose here, as also in, e.g., 2 Sam 10:3, and with the further prefixing of לְ (לְ + בְּ + עֲבוּר) in 2 Sam 14:20; 17:14. The verb הַזְכִּיר is the Hiphil (H) infinitive construct of זָכַר, "to remember."

וַיִּקְרָא לָהֹ יַד אַבְשָׁלֹם—"It is still called Absalom's monument" is literally " 'the hand of Absalom' is called to it." The construct phrase יַד אַבְשָׁלֹם is the subject of the Niphal (N) of קָרָא with a passive meaning, "be called." The third feminine singular suffix on לָהֹ, "to it," refers back to the feminine noun מַצֶּבֶת (used twice earlier in the verse; see the first textual note on 18:18). The noun יָד is used twice in the book of Samuel, here and in 1 Sam 15:12, to mean "monument" (*HALOT*, 6 a).

Commentary

974 BC[16]

The account of the battle that results in Absalom's death begins with David arranging his troops (18:1–2a). The organization is standard: units of a hundred men subsumed into larger units of a thousand (see the third textual note on 18:1). The splitting of the army into three large commands is also standard (Judg 7:16; 9:43; 1 Sam 11:11; 13:17). The author may be emphasizing David's skill as a tactician as opposed to Absalom's inexperience. He simply relates that Absalom had placed Amasa in charge of his forces (17:25). In addition, by mentioning that Ittai the Gittite was one of David's three commanders, the author may be demonstrating David's trust in this foreign mercenary who had demonstrated faithfulness to the king (15:18–22). This believing Gittite[17] was placed on par with David's two nephews Joab and Abishai.

David's determination to go into battle with his troops is undermined by their argument as to his value (18:2b–4). Their statement that he is like ten thousand of them is a hyperbolic way of stating that his death in battle would be equivalent to a sweeping defeat of the army. Their judgment is proven to be correct when Absalom's death leads to immediate orders by Joab to cease fighting (18:16). The real battle was between David, Yahweh's anointed king,[18] and the rebellious claimant Absalom, and the death of either meant the end of the

---

[16] See "The Chronology of David's Reign" in the commentary on 5:1–5.

[17] David must have known that Ittai was a fellow believer in Yahweh before he entrusted him with the command of a third of his army.

[18] Yahweh himself had anointed David (2 Sam 12:7). He had done this through the prophet Samuel (1 Sam 16:3, 12, 13), the men of Judah (2 Sam 2:4, 7), and the elders of Israel (2 Sam 5:3, 17).

war. As a result, David stayed near the gate of the city—presumably Mahanaim (17:24, 27; 19:33 [ET 19:32])—to review his troops as they marched into battle.

David's order that Absalom be treated gently (18:5) demonstrated that despite all the evil Absalom had done (murdering Amnon in 13:23–37 and subsequently usurping the throne of his father), the king was still concerned about his son. It does not appear that Absalom was similarly concerned about David. The author emphasizes that although the order was given to Joab, Abishai, and Ittai, the entire army was aware of it (18:5).

The account of the battle begins with David's troops engaging Absalom's forces in the forest of Ephraim (18:6). The forest's name, "Ephraim," is also the name of a tribe situated west of the Jordan, which is a bit of a conundrum, since it is clear that the battle took place in the Transjordan. The tactic of drawing Absalom's army into the forest enabled David's smaller but more skilled force to gain the upper hand and use the forest itself as a weapon to consume Absalom's army (18:7–8).

As proof that God's creation itself had become an ally of David, the focus shifts to Absalom and his encounter with David's troops (18:9). He too was defeated by the forest as his head was caught in a tree. From antiquity readers have surmised that handsome Absalom's luxurious hair, to which he devoted his attention (14:25–26), became entangled in the tree's branches.[19] However, the text leaves to the readers' imagination exactly how Absalom's head was ensnared by the tree (18:9). What is clear is that the head in which Absalom took such pride had become his downfall (cf. Prov 16:18). Moreover, Absalom's mule left him. Since mules were often connected with Israelite royalty (2 Sam 13:29; 1 Ki 1:33, 38, 44; 10:25; 18:5), Absalom had lost his visible trappings of kingship.

Absalom was left hanging in a tree (18:9–10; see the textual note on וַיִּתַּן in 18:9). The Law of Moses used the identical verb form that is used in 18:10 (תָּלוּי, "hanging") to declare that anyone hung on a tree is accursed by God (Deut 21:22–23).[20] Absalom had made himself cursed by dishonoring his father (Deut 27:16), especially when he slept with his father's concubines (2 Sam 16:21–22), an abomination that was a capital crime.[21] His death as he hung on the tree may be compared to the accursed death of Ahithophel, who "hanged himself" (וַיֵּחָנַק; see the fourth textual note and the commentary on 17:23).

When Absalom's predicament was reported to Joab, the commander asked the soldier who had seen the prince why he had not killed him, stating that he

---

[19] Josephus, *Antiquities*, 7.239; Mishnah, *Sotah*, 1:8.

[20] See the textual note on 18:10.

[21] A person who dishonored his father or mother was "cursed" by God (Deut 27:16). The same judgment of being "cursed" was pronounced upon anyone who had sexual relations with his father's wife (Deut 27:20; see also Deut 23:1 [ET 22:30]). This incest was a lewd abomination that warranted the death penalty (Lev 18:8; 20:11; this crime is among the "abominations" labeled as such in Lev 18:26–29; see also "abomination" in Lev 18:22; 20:13). See also 1 Cor 5:1–5 and the commentary on 2 Sam 16:20–23. For the status of concubines as wives, see the commentary on 5:13.

would have given the man a reward (18:10–11). The man, however, had heard David's orders and did not trust Joab to defend him if he had disobeyed David (18:12–13). Joab had been known for his perfidious behavior in killing Abner (3:23–39), and this soldier was not about to put his faith in Joab to shield anyone from the king's wrath.

So Joab did what he thought was necessary: he struck Absalom fatally and had his armor bearers finish off the rebel (18:14–15). It is interesting to note that later in the narrative David never condemned Joab for this act. Perhaps David realized that a living Absalom would have continued to be a threat to his kingdom, which had received the messianic promise in 2 Samuel 7. David also knew that the death of Absalom spared the lives of more of his troops since Joab was then able to call an end to the battle (18:16). David would replace Joab as commander of the army, but in doing so he did not directly or indirectly criticize Joab's execution of Absalom (19:14 [ET 19:13]). Eschelbach has observed:

> Preceding narratives have shown how David himself felt about those who raised their hands against the king (1:14–15). Joab recognized this inconsistency in David's attitude toward Absalom. … Joab always acted to minimize bloodshed and to protect the lives of the innocent. … Joab has demonstrated that he would only raise his hand against bona fide threats to king and kingdom. …
>
> In light of this evidence I submit that Joab is here again simple and true to king and country. His concern for the lives of many innocent soldiers caused him to terminate Absalom and endanger his own position with the king in order to prevent a bloody civil war.[22]

In fact, when David later advised Solomon to dispatch Joab, he did not mention the killing of Absalom (1 Ki 2:5). David must have understood, even when he mandated that Absalom be shown mercy (2 Sam 18:5), that such a mandate was ill-advised despite his obvious fatherly affection (and feelings of guilt?) toward Absalom.[23]

We are next told of Absalom's inglorious internment (18:17). After Joab and his men took his dead body down from the tree, they threw him in a pit and covered it with stones. Part of their concern was to bury him on the same day, as was required by Deut 21:22–23,[24] but they treated him as if he were a disgraced Canaanite king who had hung on a tree. Earlier in Israel's history, the king of Ai (Josh 8:29) and five Canaanite kings defeated by Joshua—including

---

[22] Eschelbach, *Has Joab Foiled David?* 71.

[23] Shimei attributed Absalom's rebellion to David's bloodshed (16:8), which included Uriah's death (11:14–24) after David's adultery with Bathsheba (11:1–13). David harbored the guilt of knowing that his sins caused the sequence of tragedies in his family, as the prophet Nathan had declared (12:10): the rape of Tamar by Amnon (13:1–20), Absalom's killing of his half brother Amnon (13:21–39), and now Absalom's attempted coup.

[24] Jesus was buried in a nearby tomb, as he died on the cross late in the day and needed to be buried before the day ended (cf. Mk 15:42–46; Jn 19:38–42).

the kings of Hebron and Jerusalem (Josh 10:23–27)—had been hung on trees and then interned in graves covered with stones.[25]

The pile of stones over Absalom's grave made a sort of monument to his disgrace. The author then reminds us of a different monument—one that Absalom had set up for himself, since he had no sons to preserve his memory (18:18).[26] Though Absalom had three sons (14:27), they are never named in the OT and probably died while they were still young. So Absalom set up a pillar in the King's Valley, also called the Valley of Shaveh (Gen 14:17). The location of this valley is unknown, but it must have been in the vicinity of Jerusalem. It is often identified with some portion of the Kidron Valley. The author notes that in his day the pillar was still known as Absalom's Monument. It was, therefore, still serving the purpose for which it was erected, to serve as a warning against rebelling against God and his anointed king (cf. Psalm 2). Ironically, the only other person to erect a "monument" (יָד) to himself in the book of Samuel was Saul (1 Sam 15:12), who also died an ignominious death (1 Sam 31:4).

---

[25] Achan and his family were also buried and covered with stones after his crime, though they had not been hung on trees (Josh 7:24–26).

[26] Having sons to preserve one's memory is also a concern of the Law of Moses (Deut 25:5–10) and an important part of the dramatic climax in the book of Ruth (Ruth 4:5–17). This leads to the genealogy of David (Ruth 4:18–22; דָּוִד, "David," is the last Hebrew word in the book of Ruth) and, subsequently, the genealogy of Jesus Christ, "the Son of David" (Mt 1:1; his lineage from Boaz to David is given in Mt 1:5–6).

2 Samuel 18:19–19:9 (ET 18:19–19:8)

David Turns a Victory Celebration into Mourning

Translation

18 ¹⁹Ahimaaz, Zadok's son, said, "Please let me run and bring the good news to the king that Yahweh has vindicated him from the hand of his enemies."

²⁰Joab said to him, "You would not be a man with good news this day. You might bring good news another day, but this day you would not bring good news, since the king's son has died." ²¹Then Joab said to a Cushite, "Go, and tell the king what you have seen." So the Cushite bowed to Joab and ran.

²²Ahimaaz, Zadok's son, again said to Joab, "No matter what, please let me also run after the Cushite."

Joab said, "Why in the world do you want to run, my son? Go, but you will receive no reward for good news."

²³[Ahimaaz said,] "No matter what, I want to run."

So he said to him, "Run." Ahimaaz ran on the road of the plain and passed the Cushite.

²⁴Now David was sitting between the two gates. A watchman went to the roof of the gate at the wall. He looked out and saw that there was a lone runner. ²⁵The watchman called out and told the king. The king said, "If he is alone, he has good news." And he kept getting closer.

²⁶The watchman saw another man running. The watchman called to the gatekeeper, "There is a[nother] man running by himself."

The king said, "This man too is bringing good news."

²⁷The watchman said, "I see that the running style of the first man is like the running style of Ahimaaz, Zadok's son."

The king said, "He is a good man. He is coming with good news."

²⁸Ahimaaz called out to the king, "Peace!" and he bowed face down on the ground to the king. He said, "May Yahweh your God, who has handed over the men who rebelled against my lord the king, be blessed!"

²⁹The king said, "Is the young man Absalom safe?"

Ahimaaz said, "I saw a great commotion when Joab sent the king's servant and your servant, but I don't know what (it was)."

³⁰The king said, "Come around and stand here." So he turned aside and stood.

³¹Then the Cushite came, and the Cushite said, "May my lord the king receive good news that Yahweh today has vindicated you from the hand of everyone who rose up against you."

³²The king said to the Cushite, "Is the young man Absalom safe?"

347

The Cushite said, "May the enemies of my lord the king and all who rise up against you for evil be like the young man."

19 ¹The king trembled and went up to the room above the gate and wept. This is what he said as he went: "My son Absalom! My son! My son Absalom! I wish I myself had died instead of you, Absalom my son, my son!"

²Joab was told, "The king is weeping." He mourned over Absalom. ³That day the victory became mourning for all the troops, because the troops heard that day: "The king grieved over his son." ⁴The troops stole into the city that day as humiliated troops steal in when they flee from battle.

⁵The king covered his face and cried loudly, "My son Absalom! Absalom my son! My son! My son!"

⁶So Joab went into the house to the king and said, "Today you have openly shamed all of your servants—the ones who rescued your life today as well as the life of your sons and your daughters, the life of your wives, and the life of your concubines. ⁷[You did this by] loving those who hate you and hating those who love you. You have announced today that commanders and servants are nothing to you. For I know that today were Absalom alive and all of us dead that would be all right with you! ⁸Now get up! Go out and encourage your servants, because I swear by Yahweh that if you do not go out, not a [single] man will stay with you overnight, and this will be more trouble for you than all the trouble that has come upon you from your youth until now."

⁹The king got up and sat in the city gate. All the troops were told, "Look! The king is sitting in the city gate." All the troops came before David.

Meanwhile Israel had fled—each man to his tent.

Textual Notes

18:19 אָרוּצָה נָּא וַאֲבַשְּׂרָה—"Please let me run and bring the good news." The two verbs are singular cohortatives: the Qal (G) of רוּץ, "run," and the Piel (D) of בָּשַׂר, "report news." The verb רוּץ, "run," is used a total of ten times in this passage, all Qal. The same cohortative will recur in 18:22, but written defectively (אָרֻצָה־נָּא). The other forms are the imperfect אָרוּץ, "I want to run" (18:23); the preterites (imperfects with *waw* consecutive) "and he ran" (וַיָּרָץ, pausal, in 18:21 and וַיָּרָץ in 18:23); the participle רָץ, literally "running," in 18:22, 24, 26 (twice); and the imperative רוּץ, "run," in 18:23.

The verb בָּשַׂר, "to report news," appears five times in this passage, four in the Piel (D) stem (18:19, 20 [twice], 26) with an active meaning and once in the Hithpael (HtD) stem (18:31) in a passive sense, literally "to be (good-)newsed," that is, "to receive (good) news." In some contexts the Piel of בָּשַׂר refers to the delivery of a message that Israel has been defeated (1 Sam 4:17). In others, unbelievers consider the news to be a joyful triumph, while it is devastating to Israel (1 Sam 31:9; 2 Sam 1:20; 4:10). In this passage both the verb (18:19, 20 [twice], 26, 31) and the cognate noun בְּשׂוֹרָה, "(good) news" (18:20, 22, 25, 27) relate to delivering the news of victory, news, however, that David receives as tragic. See also the second and third textual notes on 4:10.

כִּי־שְׁפָטוֹ יְהוָה מִיַּד אֹיְבָיו:—"That Yahweh has vindicated him from the hand of his enemies." This is a pregnant construction with an implied verb, "vindicated him *by saving him* from the hand of his enemies" (see GKC, § 119 ff). The verb שְׁפָטוֹ is the Qal (G) third masculine singular perfect of שָׁפַט, "to judge," with a third masculine singular pronominal suffix. שָׁפַט refers to the administration of justice, resulting in condemnation of the wicked and/or justification/vindication of those who are righteous by grace. The perfect of שָׁפַט recurs in the same sense in a similar context in 18:31.

18:20 אִישׁ בְּשֹׂרָה—"A man with good news." The relationship between the two words in this construct phrase (as in all Hebrew construct phrases) must be determined from context. Here it clearly means "a man *with/bearing* good news." The messenger believes that he would be reporting news of victory, but Joab knows that King David will deem the death of his son to be bad news. See the first textual note on 18:19.

כִּי־עַל־כֵּן—This Qere, which is the sole reading in a number of Masoretic manuscripts, is literally "because on thus." It has a causal meaning, "since, because."[1] The Kethib lacks the third word, כֵּן, "thus," and only reads כִּי־עַל, "for on," which occurs elsewhere,[2] but not always with a causal meaning. In the Kethib כֵּן may have been omitted by homoioteleuton as a scribe's eye skipped over כֵּן to the similarly shaped בֶּן, "the son of."

מֵת—"He has died." This masculine singular Qal (G) form of מוּת could be parsed either as the third person perfect, "he (has) died," or the participle.

18:21 לֵךְ הַגֵּד—"Go, and tell." These two masculine singular imperatives are asyndetic (not joined with וְ). The first is the Qal (G) of הָלַךְ, "walk," and the second is the Hiphil (H) of נָגַד, "inform, report."

רָאִיתָה—"You have seen." This Qal (G) perfect of רָאָה has the longer form of the second masculine singular ending, תָה-, instead of the usual תָ- (GKC, § 44 g; Joüon, § 42 f). See the second textual note on 2:26.

וַיִּשְׁתָּחוּ—"So he bowed." This is the Hishtaphel of חָוָה, "to bow down, worship." See the third textual note on 1 Sam 1:3.[3] For the form here (וַיִּשְׁתָּחוּ), see the second textual note on 1 Sam 1:28.[4] The identical form recurs in 18:28.

18:22 וַיֹּסֶף עוֹד ... וַיֹּאמֶר—"Again he said" is literally "and he did more still ... and he said." The Hiphil (H) of יָסַף is often used idiomatically in combination with a second verb to signify a continuation or repetition of the action denoted by the other verb (Joüon, § 177 b, c). The second verb, וַיֹּאמֶר, is a Qal (G) preterite (imperfect with *waw* consecutive) of אָמַר.

וִיהִי מָה—"No matter what" is literally "and let whatever be." This clause recurs at the start of 18:23. The subject is the interrogative pronoun מָה, "what?" used in an indefinite sense (Joüon, § 144 f); see also וְלֹא יָדַעְתִּי מָה, "but I don't know what (it was)," in 18:29. The verb וִיהִי is the Qal (G) jussive of הָיָה with a conjunctive *waw*.

[1] See Joüon, § 170 h, note 1. See the same expression also in Gen 18:5; 19:8; 33:10; 38:26; Num 10:31; 14:43; Judg 6:22; Jer 29:28; 38:4.

[2] E.g., Ex 16:8; 34:27; Deut 8:3; 1 Sam 25:8; 2 Sam 9:13; 13:32.

[3] Steinmann, *1 Samuel*, 44.

[4] Steinmann, *1 Samuel*, 62.

אֶרֲצָה־נָּא גַם־אָנִי—"Please let me also run" is literally "please let me run, also I." For the cohortative אֶרֲצָה, see the first textual note on 18:19. The pronoun אָנִי is emphatic.

לָמָּה־זֶּה אַתָּה רָץ בְּנִי—"Why in the world do you want to run, my son?" is literally "why this [that] you are running, my son?" For לָמָּה־זֶּה, see the first textual note on 3:24. For the participle רָץ, see the first textual note on 18:19.

אֵין־בְּשׂוֹרָה מֹצֵאת:—"You will receive no reward for good news" is literally "there is no reward for good news [that will be] finding [you]." Here and in 4:10 the feminine noun בְּשׂוֹרָה, which usually denotes "(good) news" (see the first textual note on 18:19), has the nuance of a "reward" for bringing such news (BDB, 3). The feminine noun is the subject of מֹצֵאת, the feminine singular Qal (G) participle of מָצָא, "to find" (contracted; see GKC, § 74 i). The implied direct object of the participle probably is Ahimaaz, i.e., no reward is "finding [you]." Alternatively, מָצָא may have the sense "to secure," and the clause would then mean "there is no news securing gain [for you]" (see BDB, Qal, 1 a).

18:23 "Ahimaaz said" is supplied at the beginning of the verse. Possibly a verb such as וַיֹּאמֶר, "and he said" (e.g., 18:20), the common introduction for a quotation, has been lost. A verb of speaking is present in the LXX (καὶ εἶπεν), the Syriac, and the Vulgate. If the MT has the original reading, then these versions have supplied the verb to fill out the sense.

וִיהִי־מָה אָרוּץ—"No matter what, I want to run." The first two words were spoken by Ahimaaz in 18:22, and the third word (אָרוּץ) summarizes four words spoken by Ahimaaz in 18:22 (see the second and third textual notes on 18:22).

רוּץ וַיָּרָץ—" 'Run.' (And) he ran." The imperative רוּץ gives Ahimaaz permission to carry out his desire (GKC, § 110 b; Joüon, § 114 n), which he then does. For the verb, see the first textual note on 18:19.

הַכִּכָּר—"The plain." This noun with the article literally means "the circle." This was a descriptive name for the plain north of the Dead Sea (Gen 13:10–12; 19:17, 25, 28, 29; Deut 34:3).

18:24–27 הַצֹּפֶה—"A watchman." Five times in these verses the Qal (G) participle of צָפָה, "gaze," denotes a "watchman" or a "lookout," as also in 1 Sam 14:16; 2 Sam 13:34. See the second textual note on 13:34. Here in 18:24–27 it always has the definite article, used when the narrator has in mind a specific person, but corresponding to an indefinite article in English. See Joüon, § 137 o; the first textual note on 15:13; and the fourth textual note on 17:9.

18:24 וְהִנֵּה־אִישׁ רָץ לְבַדּוֹ:—"That there was a lone runner" is literally "and look, a man running by himself." This clause recurs in 18:26, but there it refers to Ahimaaz, rather than to the Cushite, as here. For the participle רָץ, see the first textual note on 18:19. The prepositional phrase with a suffix לְבַדּוֹ, "by himself; alone," recurs in 18:25 as well as 18:26.

18:25 בְּשׂוֹרָה בְּפִיו—"He has good news" is literally "good news is in his mouth." For the noun בְּשׂוֹרָה, see the first textual note on 18:19.

וַיֵּלֶךְ הָלוֹךְ וְקָרֵב:—"And he kept getting closer" is literally "and he went, going and drawing near." The Qal (G) infinitive absolute הָלוֹךְ is often used idiomatically with a second infinitive absolute to signify the continuation of the action denoted by the second verb (Joüon, § 123 m). Here, instead of a second infinitive absolute (which would be קָרוֹב), the idiom employs the verbal adjective קָרֵב, "approaching," derived from the verb קָרַב, "come near." For this construction, see Joüon, § 123 s.

18:26 הַשֹּׁעֵר—"The gatekeeper." This noun or Qal (G) participle is a denominative derived from the segholate noun שַׁעַר, "gate," used in 18:24 (twice); 19:1 (ET 18:33); 19:9 (ET 19:8; twice).

מְבַשֵּׂר:—"Bringing good news." This participle could also serve as a substantive (as also in 1 Sam 4:17; 2 Sam 4:10), "a bringer of good news" or even "an evangelist," as in Is 40:9, 41:27; 52:7; Nah 2:1 (ET 1:15); cf. Ps 68:12 (ET 68:11).

18:27 מְרוּצַת הָרִאשׁוֹן כִּמְרֻצַת אֲחִימַעַץ—"The running style of the first man is like the running style of Ahimaaz." The feminine noun מְרוּצָה, used in construct twice here, is derived from the verb רוּץ, "run," for which, see the first textual note on 18:19. It could also be rendered as "gait." Its only other OT occurrences are in Jer 8:6; 23:10, where a "course" of running metaphorically denotes one's way of life.

וְאֶל־בְּשׂוֹרָה טוֹבָה יָבוֹא:—The Hebrew word order emphasizes the content of the message David expects Ahimaaz to bring, literally "and for (the purpose of bringing) good news he comes."

18:28 שָׁלוֹם—"Peace!" This noun can be used in a greeting, as here,[5] or in a benediction for a departure (1 Sam 1:17; 20:42). In 2 Sam 18:29, 32 it will be used in David's question about Absalom's well-being/safety.

וַיִּשְׁתַּחוּ ... לְאַפָּיו אָרְצָה—"And he bowed face down on the ground" is literally "and he bowed ... to his face to the ground." See similar clauses in, e.g., 1 Sam 20:41; 24:9 (ET 24:8); 25:41; 2 Sam 14:4, 33; 24:20. For the verb וַיִּשְׁתַּחוּ, see the third textual note on 1 Sam 1:3[6] and the second textual note on 1 Sam 1:28.[7]

בָּרוּךְ יְהוָה אֱלֹהֶיךָ—Literally "blessed be Yahweh your God." In context this salutation with the Qal passive (Gp) participle of בָּרַךְ, "to bless," expresses a prayer: "may Yahweh your God ... be blessed!" Similar formulas with בָּרוּךְ laud Yahweh in 1 Sam 25:32, 39; cf. 2 Sam 22:47. See also the discussion of the Piel (D) of בָּרַךְ in the textual note on 2 Sam 6:11–12, as well as the first textual note on 1 Sam 2:20 and the third textual note on 1 Sam 9:13.[8]

אֲשֶׁר סִגַּר—"Who has handed over." The verb is the Piel (D) third masculine singular perfect of סָגַר, literally "to enclose, shut up." The Piel (D) and Hiphil (H) forms of this verb that mean "hand over" are usually followed by בְּיַד־, "into the hand of" (Piel, 1 Sam 17:46; 24:19 (ET 24:18); 26:8; Hiphil, 1 Sam 23:11, 12, 20; 30:15).

אֲשֶׁר־נָשְׂאוּ אֶת־יָדָם בַּאדֹנִי הַמֶּלֶךְ:—"Who rebelled against my lord the king" is literally "who raised their hand against my lord the king." See the same idiom in 20:21.

18:29 שָׁלוֹם לַנַּעַר לְאַבְשָׁלוֹם—"Is the young man Absalom safe?" is literally "(is there) peace to the young man, to Absalom?" These words are not marked as a question.

---

5   Also 1 Sam 25:5, 6; 30:21; 2 Sam 8:10; 20:9; cf. 1 Sam 10:4; 16:4–5; 17:22; 2 Sam 11:7.

6   Steinmann, *1 Samuel*, 44.

7   Steinmann, *1 Samuel*, 62.

8   Steinmann, *1 Samuel*, 90, 179.

Hebrew commonly omits such a marker (*IBH*, § 66; Joüon, § 161 a; GKC, § 150 a). However, a number of Masoretic manuscripts include the interrogative *he*, הֲשָׁלוֹם, as in 18:32, where David asks the Cushite the identical question.

לִשְׁלֹחַ אֶת־עֶבֶד הַמֶּלֶךְ יוֹאָב וְאֶת־עַבְדֶּךָ—"When Joab sent the king's servant and your servant." "Joab" (יוֹאָב) is the subject of the Qal (G) infinitive construct (with לְ) לִשְׁלֹחַ, which has a temporal meaning, "*when* Joab sent" (GKC, § 114 f, note 1). The infinitive has two direct objects, each marked with אֶת־. "The king's servant" refers to the Cushite and Ahimaaz uses "your servant" to refer to himself.

18:30 סֹב הִתְיַצֵּב—"Come around and stand." The first imperative is the Qal (G) of סָבַב, "turn about." Ahimaaz was probably facing the king and keeping a respectful distance. David invites him to come closer and face in the same direction as he is facing. The second imperative is the Hithpael (HtD) of יָצַב, which often has the nuance "stand still" (1 Sam 12:7, 16) or "take one's stand" (1 Sam 17:16); cf. 18:13. It is a synonym of the Qal (G) of עָמַד, used at the end of the verse.

18:31 יִתְבַּשֵּׂר—"May he receive good news." This is a Hithpael (HtD) jussive. See the first textual note on 18:19.

כִּי־שְׁפָטְךָ יְהוָה הַיּוֹם מִיַּד—"That Yahweh today has vindicated you from the hand of …" See almost the same wording in the second textual note on 18:19.

כָּל־הַקָּמִים עָלֶיךָ:—"Everyone who rose up against you" is literally "all the ones who arose against you." The Qal (G) participle of קוּם, "arise," can be used in the plural as a substantive denoting adversaries (see BDB, Qal, 2). Here it is a synonym of the plurals of the participle (used as a noun) אֹיֵב, denoting "enemies," in 18:19, 32. See also the Qal (G) perfect in קָמוּ עָלֶיךָ, "(they) rise up against you," in 18:32.

18:32 יִהְיוּ כַנַּעַר—"May they be like the young man." In the Hebrew word order, the comparison כַנַּעַר, "like the young man," is emphasized by its placement immediately after the plural jussive יִהְיוּ and before the two expressions describing enemies. English word order requires it to be placed last in the translation of the verse.

19:1 וַיַּעַל עַל־עֲלִיַּת הַשַּׁעַר—Literally "and he went up up to the upper room of the gate." Note the assonance with the trifold עַל.

וַיֵּבְךְּ—"And he wept." This is the Qal (G) third masculine singular preterite (imperfect with *waw* consecutive) of בָּכָה. The same form was in 1 Sam 24:17 (ET 24:16); 2 Sam 3:32. See also the participle בֹּכֶה, "weeping," in 19:2 (ET 19:1) and the variant reading in the next textual note.

בְּלֶכְתּוֹ—"As he went." This reading in the MT is the Qal (G) infinitive construct of הָלַךְ with בְּ and a third masculine singular suffix, which is supported by most LXX manuscripts (ἐν τῷ πορεύεσθαι αὐτόν). The Lucian version of the LXX (καὶ ἐδάκρυσεν) implies an underlying Hebrew text that read בִּבְכֹתוֹ, "as he wept," the Qal (G) infinitive construct of בָּכָה (see the preceding textual note) with בְּ and a third masculine singular suffix. This variant reading is favored by some.[9] The only difference in the consonants would be a graphic confusion of *lamed* and the second *bet*.

---

[9] E.g., McCarter, *II Samuel*, 403.

מִי־יִתֵּן מוּתִי אֲנִי תַחְתֶּךָ—"I wish I myself had died instead of you" is literally "who would give my dying—I in place of you?" The idiom מִי־יִתֵּן expresses a wish or prayer (*IBH*, § 26 C; Joüon, § 163 d; GKC, § 151 b; BDB, s.v. נָתַן, Qal, 1 f). The use of the first common singular pronoun אֲנִי after the first common singular suffix on the verb מוּתִי is emphatic, "I *myself*" (see *IBH*, § 24 E; GKC, § 135 f). The first three words (but with a different suffix on the Qal infinitive construct of מות, "to die") were uttered as a wish of despair by the grumbling Israelites in the wilderness (Ex 16:3).

19:2 וַיֻּגַּד לְיוֹאָב—"Joab was told" is literally "and it was told to Joab." The impersonal Hophal (Hp), with no stated subject, can be translated with its indirect object, Joab, as its subject. See the same construction in, e.g., 6:12; 10:17; 21:11.

וַיִּתְאַבֵּל עַל־אַבְשָׁלֹם:—"He mourned over Absalom." This Hithpael (HtD) preterite (imperfect with *waw* consecutive) is the reading of most Masoretic manuscripts and is to be preferred.[10] For the Hithpael of אָבַל, "to mourn," see the second textual note on 2 Sam 13:37. It is translated as the beginning of a new sentence, although it could continue the preceding sentence, have a present sense ("and mourns"), and be part of the quote (see Joüon, § 118 r; Waltke-O'Connor, § 33.3.5c, including example 9; and most English versions). Many scholars prefer to read the Hithpael participle, וּמִתְאַבֵּל, "and mourning," which is the reading of two Masoretic manuscripts, followed by the Syriac and the Targum (cf. the LXX: ὁ βασιλεὺς κλαίει καὶ πενθεῖ). The participle clearly would continue the preceding participial clause, הַמֶּלֶךְ בֹּכֶה וּמִתְאַבֵּל, "the king is weeping and mourning over Absalom," and all those words would be part of the quotation of the report told to Joab. However, this reading appears to be an attempt to smooth out a perceived syntactical problem of a participle followed by a preterite (imperfect with *waw* consecutive), under the assumption that both verbs should be part of the quote. Without that assumption, the syntax is normal.

19:3 הַתְּשֻׁעָה—"The victory." The feminine noun תְּשׁוּעָה is derived from the verb יָשַׁע, "to save," used with Yahweh as its subject in, e.g., 1 Sam 4:3; 14:23; 2 Sam 3:18; 8:6, 14. The noun could also be translated as "salvation." Yahweh is the one who "performs" or "accomplishes" (עָשָׂה) "salvation" (תְּשׁוּעָה) in 1 Sam 11:13; 19:5; 2 Sam 23:10, 12.

הָעָם—In military contexts this noun with the article, literally "the people," can refer to the armed forces, "the troops." See the first textual note on 1 Sam 4:3[11] and the second textual note on 2 Sam 1:4.

נֶעֱצַב הַמֶּלֶךְ—"The king grieved." The Niphal (N) third masculine singular perfect of עָצַב was also in 1 Sam 20:34 (but pointed נֶעְצַב), where Jonathan grieved over David's expulsion.

19:4 וַיִּתְגַּנֵּב הָעָם ... כַּאֲשֶׁר יִתְגַּנֵּב הָעָם—"The troops stole into ... as troops steal in ..." Both verbs are Hithpael (HtD) forms of גָּנַב, which, in the Qal (G), means "to steal, rob," as in the Seventh Commandment (Ex 20:15; Deut 5:19). These are the only two occurrences of this verb in the Hithpael. By context they must denote entering quietly or stealthily, which is one meaning of the verb "steal" in English. For the Qal (G) and Piel

---

[10] Washburn, "The King Is Weeping."

[11] Steinmann, *1 Samuel*, 120.

(D) of גֶּנֶב, see the third textual note on 15:6. For the use of הָעָם to mean "the troops," see the second textual note on 19:3 (ET 19:2).

הַנִּכְלָמִים—"Humiliated" or "ashamed." For this Niphal (N) participle, see the third textual note on 10:5.

19:5 לָאַט—"He covered." This is the only OT instance of this verb, spelled לָאַט. It is a by-form of the verb לוט, "enwrap, cover," used three times in the OT (1 Sam 21:10 [ET 21:9]; 1 Ki 19:13, also of covering the face), including a burial shroud in Is 25:7. Hence, the verb here may connote mourning a death. Ironically, David used the same consonants in his mandate for his commanders to "be gentle" with Absalom (לְאַט; see the first textual note on 18:5). Joab's disobedience of that command (לְאַט) now causes David to "cover" his face (לָאַט).

19:6 הֹבַשְׁתָּ ... אֶת־פְּנֵי כָל־עֲבָדֶיךָ—"You have openly shamed all of your servants" is literally "you have shamed the face of all of your servants." The verb הֹבַשְׁתָּ is the Hiphil (H) second masculine singular perfect of בּוֹשׁ, meaning "put to shame" (BDB, Hiphil, 2 a). In form it could also be parsed as the Hiphil (H) of יָבֵשׁ, "be dry" (so GKC, § 70 c), meaning "to make dry, wither," but that meaning is not as suitable here.

הַמְמַלְּטִים—"The ones who rescued." In the Piel (D), מָלַט can mean "to rescue, deliver." This is the masculine plural participle (with the article). See also the perfect מִלְּטָנוּ in 19:10 (ET 19:9) and the singular participle in 1 Sam 19:11.

19:7 וְלִשְׂנֹא ...לְאַהֲבָה—"By loving ... by hating." Each verb is a Qal (G) infinitive construct with the preposition לְ. The first is of אָהַב, "to love" (with a so-called feminine ending; see Joüon, 49 d), and the second is of שָׂנֵא, "to hate." They elaborate the preceding verb הֹבַשְׁתָּ (19:6 [ET 19:5]) by explaining how David "shamed" his servants. See Joüon, § 124 o.

אֵין לְךָ שָׂרִים וַעֲבָדִים—"Commanders and servants are nothing to you." This statement with the particle of negation (אַיִן in construct) and לְ in the sense of reference or relation (BDB, 5 a (d)) is literally "in relation to you commanders and servants do not exist."

לוּ אַבְשָׁלוֹם חַי—"Were Absalom alive." This is the reading of the Qere, the sole reading in many Masoretic manuscripts, and the reading of 4QSamᵃ (לו אבשלום חין). It is supported by the LXX (εἰ Αβεσσαλωμ ἔζη). The Kethib is לֹא אַבְשָׁלוֹם חַי, "not Absalom alive." See the first textual note on 18:12, which has nearly the same Qere and Kethib.

כִּי־אָז יָשָׁר בְּעֵינֶיךָ:—"That would be all right with you!" is literally "for then (that would be) straight in your eyes."

19:8 וְדַבֵּר עַל־לֵב—"And encourage" is literally "and speak upon the heart of." This idiom means to speak lovingly or to encourage (e.g., Gen 34:3; Is 40:2; Ruth 2:13; 2 Chr 30:22).

בַיהוָה נִשְׁבַּעְתִּי—"By Yahweh I swear." The Niphal (N) of שָׁבַע, "to swear," is used with this prepositional phrase, בַיהוָה, also in 1 Sam 24:22 (ET 24:21); 28:10.

כִּי־אֵינְךָ יוֹצֵא—Most Masoretic manuscripts have this participial clause, literally "that you are not going out." In context it must be conditional, "that *if* you do not go out" (Joüon, § 167 i). One Masoretic manuscript reads כִּי אִם, "that if," as does 4QSam[a] (כי אם), and this reading is supported by the LXX (ὅτι εἰ).

אִם־יָלִין אִישׁ אִתְּךָ הַלַּיְלָה—"Not a [single] man will stay with you overnight" is literally "if a man will lodge with you the night." After the conditional clause (see the prior textual note), the particle אִם functions as a negative (Joüon, § 165 d). The verb יָלִין is the Qal (G) third masculine singular imperfect of לִין, "lodge, spend the night," which was used with הַלַּיְלָה, "the night," also in 17:16. This clause does not refer to anyone literally sleeping beside David. Instead, it means that no one would remain loyal to David overnight; by the next day all of his troops would have defected.

וְרָעָה ... הָרָעָה—"And ... trouble ... the trouble." The feminine noun רָעָה, literally "evil," can also denote misery, distress, and harm. Joab probably intends it to allude to the sins David had committed as well as the sufferings that resulted from them.

19:9 הִגִּידוּ—"They were told." An impersonal verb with no subject (literally "they told") is often best translated as a passive (see Joüon, § 155 b).

וְיִשְׂרָאֵל נָס אִישׁ לְאֹהָלָיו:—Literally "and Israel fled, each man to his tents." Here Israel is the subject of the singular Qal (G) perfect of נוּס, as in 1 Sam 4:17. Cf. 1 Sam 4:10, where יִשְׂרָאֵל is followed by the plural verb וַיָּנֻסוּ, and 2 Sam 18:17, where כָל־יִשְׂרָאֵל, "all Israel," was the subject of the plural נָסוּ, "fled." For the phrase אִישׁ לְאֹהָלָיו, see the third textual note on 18:17.

Commentary

974 BC[12]

This section relates perhaps the lowest point in David's troubles[13] that were part of a cascading chain of events triggered by his adultery and murder (2 Samuel 11). It portrays David's most flawed attributes and exhibits his most self-centered behavior. Here David reaped what he sowed as an indulgent father unable to discipline his sons. He also jeopardized his relationship with his most devoted subjects by his misplaced devotion and affection for the rebellious Absalom as he mourned his death.

David Receives News of Absalom's Death
(18:19–19:1 [ET 18:19–33])

With the hostilities ended, Ahimaaz volunteered to take word of the victory to David (18:19). Apparently Ahimaaz and Jonathan had stayed with David after delivering Abishai's message (17:17–21). Now Ahimaaz was anxious to deliver much better news to David.

Joab's reaction was born of greater knowledge of the king and his feelings. David would not receive the victory as good news because of the death of Absalom (18:20). So he ordered a Cushite, a man from Nubia in what is now southern Egypt or northern Sudan, to take word to David. The Cushite was probably among the mercenaries who served David. Joab's orders were quite

---

[12] See "The Chronology of David's Reign" in the commentary on 5:1–5.

[13] See the fifth textual note on 19:8 (ET 19:7).

specific: the Cushite was to tell David *what he had seen* (18:21). As the Cushite left, Ahimaaz again asked to take the news to the king, and this time, after once again warning him that he would not be bringing news that the king would consider good, Joab allowed Ahimaaz to go (18:22–23). We are told that Ahimaaz took a route through the plain and passed the Cushite (18:23). The author does not tell us whether the Cushite took a different route or whether Ahimaaz simply ran faster on the same route as the Cushite.

The scene immediately shifts to David, who was between the two gates of the city (18:24). Apparently Mahanaim had a double gate at the entrance to the city with a courtyard between the two. The exchange between David and the watchman on the top of the gate tower allowed David to surmise that good news was being brought (18:25–26). Had the army been routed by Absalom's forces, the retreating troops would not have come home as individual runners but as groups fleeing to the city for refuge.

Once the first runner was close enough to be recognized, David was confident that the news would be good from "a good man"—someone who was reliable (18:27). Ahimaaz brought news of the victory couched in the form of praise for Yahweh (18:28). David, however, did not join in the praise but rather asked about Absalom (18:29). Ahimaaz did not answer David's question about his son. Some have viewed Ahimaaz's answer as deceptive.[14] Others view it as evasive.[15] Still others understand Ahimaaz as simply pretending as if he did not know what had happened to Absalom.[16] However, Ahimaaz's answer hewed closely to Joab's instructions to the Cushite (18:21). Ahimaaz did not say whether Absalom was alive because he was to report only what he had seen, and as his words reveal, he did not see what had happened to Absalom.[17]

David then told Ahimaaz to step aside as he awaited the second runner, whose initial message was essentially the same as Ahimaaz's (18:30–31). Once again, David revealed that he was more interested in Absalom's safety than that of his troops or news of a victory given by Yahweh (18:32). The Cushite answered the king's question obliquely, seeking to avoid David's wrath and hoping to soothe his grief. David, however, was not to be calmed by such diplomatic language. His reaction of deepest anguish used "my son" (בְּנִי) five times and "Absalom" three times in exclamations of grief and despair (19:1 [ET 18:33]). However, most telling were his words "I wish I myself had died instead of you." With these words David betrayed his loyal army who had put their lives on the line for him (cf. 18:3). They also are an insight into David's failings as a father who had an overly indulgent attitude toward his sons. He could neither discipline them nor properly grieve while also acknowledging that they may have been culpable in their own demise (cf. his reactions to Amnon in 13:21, 37).

---

[14] E.g., Bergen, *1, 2 Samuel*, 424.

[15] E.g., Hertzberg, *I and II Samuel*, 361; Auld, *I and II Samuel*, 545; Anderson, *2 Samuel*, 226.

[16] E.g., Baldwin, *1 and 2 Samuel*, 272; Brueggemann, *First and Second Samuel*, 322.

[17] See Ackroyd, *The Second Book of Samuel*, 172.

In expounding on the Fourth Commandment, Luther notes that such indulgent parenting is contrary to God's will:

> Think what deadly harm you do when you are negligent in this respect and fail to bring up your children to usefulness and piety. You bring upon yourself sin and wrath, thus earning hell by the way you have reared your own children, *no matter how devout and holy you may be in other respects.* Because this commandment is disregarded, God terribly punishes the world; hence there is no longer any civil order, peace, or respect for authority. We all complain about this state of things, but we do not see that it is our own fault. Because of the way we train them, we have unruly and disobedient subjects.
>
> This is enough to serve as a warning; a more extensive explanation will have to await another occasion.[18]

Joab Censures David (19:2–9 [ET 19:1–8])

The news of David's public weeping over Absalom came to Joab and the troops, turning what ought to have been a celebration of victory and Yahweh's salvation[19] into the equivalent of a defeat (19:2–4 [ET 19:1–3]). David, like any leader, set the tone for those who served him. David's example was loud mourning over Absalom, which the author quotes for a second time in order to emphasize the dampening effect the king's weeping had on the victorious troops' joy (19:5 [ET 19:4]; cf. 19:1 [ET 18:33]). This is in sharp contrast to the music and dancing by women who join in celebrating an army's triumph.[20]

Joab wasted no time in sharply upbraiding David for his behavior (19:6–8 [ET 19:5–7]). His rebuke is quite long—seventy-five Hebrew words—making it by far the longest quotation of Joab in the book of Samuel. His words accused David of having misplaced loyalty, and they told the king what he ought to do:

1. David's open grieving had brought shame on his troops, who were loyal to him and who had rescued the king's family (19:6 [ET 19:5]).

2. David's loyalties were reversed from what was appropriate (19:7a [ET 19:6a]), and they were the exact opposite of his army's loyalty to him (cf. 18:3).

3. He had treated his troops as worthless nonentities[21] compared to Absalom's life (19:7b [ET 19:6b]).

4. David immediately needed to change his behavior and encourage his troops, or they would abandon him as he had abandoned them (19:8 [ET 19:7]).

The author relates that after Joab's reprimand David complied without even a single recorded word in reply to Joab (19:9 [ET 19:8]). The troops were then told a different message from the one they had heard earlier. Now the king was available to receive his troops and restore their dignity. The proper order was

---

[18] LC I 176–78 (emphasis added).

[19] See the first textual note on 19:3 (ET 19:2).

[20] See Ex 15:1, 20–21; Judg 5:1–31; 11:34; 1 Sam 18:6–7; cf. 2 Sam 6:5, 12–19.

[21] See the second textual note on 19:7 (ET 19:6).

reestablished: the accomplishment of David's victorious troops was recognized, while the defeated Israelite troops fled from the battlefield to their tents.

In modern times as well as ancient, leaders have social responsibilities that require them to behave appropriately in public. This social bond between the leader and those led was categorized in terms of covenant in ancient Israel. The noun "covenant" (בְּרִית, 3:12, 13, 21; 5:3) was integral to the history of David's rise to the throne over all Israel, and it was not just a covenant between David and the people but a covenant that carried out Yahweh's will that David be the anointed king over his people (see 3:9–13 and 5:2–3).[22] Olyan has noted David's breach of covenant responsibility:

> In the eyes of the people, victory was turned into defeat, a state associated both with mourning and with shame. Thus, David's act constituted covenant violation: he loves those who hate him (his rebellious son Absalom) and hates those who love him (his loyal servants). To "hate" in a treaty context means to violate covenant; to "love" means to conform to covenant stipulations. Exod 20:5–6//Deut 5:9–10 illustrate the covenant associations of such love/hate language nicely; there Yhwh characterizes himself as a [G]od who punishes those who "hate" him and acts with covenant loyalty (חסד) toward those who "love" him (glossed in the text as "those who keep my commandments," i.e., serve the suzerain). Human treaty partners "love" and "hate" in the same manner. In 1 Kgs 5:15 [ET 5:1] we are told that Hiram of Tyre, wishing to confirm covenant relations with Israel at Solomon's accession to the throne, sends representatives to Solomon "for Hiram had always been a lover of David" (that is, loyal in covenant to David). Because David did not act appropriately toward his loyal servants, the legitimate covenant expectations of a victorious army were not met. There was no public rejoicing to confirm victory and honor, no sacrifices to reward the army for their loyalty to the beleaguered king. David's intentions—innocent to be sure—were irrelevant; only his ritual actions had significance. Through these actions, he effectively honored his enemy while shaming his loyal supporters. …
>
> By honoring the enemy—who should be diminished or shamed—and shaming his whole army, David has apparently gone beyond his rights as suzerain and broken covenant.[23]

David's behavior was entirely out of place, and Joab was right in scolding the king. While it would have been appropriate for David to have privately mourned Absalom's death, his role as king required him to lead his troops publicly by example and to be a support to them in the city (18:3), including when they returned to Mahanaim after defeating the rebellion. This is nothing more than part of a very real (even if unwritten) social contract between leaders and those whom they lead. If leaders fail to show appreciation for the accomplishments of the persons and organizations they lead, they signal that they do not

---

[22] See the earlier covenants between David and Jonathan in 1 Sam 18:3; 20:8, 14–17, 42; 23:18, some of which explicitly invoked Yahweh.

[23] Olyan, "Honor, Shame, and Covenant Relations," 210–11; see also Kruger, " 'Liminality' in 2 Samuel 19:1–9."

value those persons, their efforts, or their loyalty. At times leaders must put aside personal needs and desires in order to publicly acknowledge corporate successes. David's behavior was selfish and self-absorbed. Joab was correct in stating that had David not rectified this situation, his example of selfishness would have been imitated by his troops. They would have looked after their own self-interests and abandoned him.

David Returns to the Throne

Translation

19 ¹⁰All the people among all the tribes of Israel were arguing with one another: "The king delivered us from the grasp of our enemies. He rescued us from the grasp of the Philistines. Now he has fled from the land because of Absalom, ¹¹and Absalom, whom we anointed [to rule] over us, died in battle. So now, why are you staying silent about restoring the king?"

¹²King David sent (word) to the high priests Zadok and Abiathar: "Say to Judah's elders, 'Why should you be the last ones to restore the king to his palace? The talk of all Israel has come to the king at his house. ¹³You are my brothers. You are my flesh and blood. Why should you be the last ones to restore the king?' ¹⁴Say to Amasa, 'Are you not my flesh and blood? Thus may God do to me and thus may he add if you do not become commander of the army before me from now on in place of Joab.'"

¹⁵So he persuaded all the men in Judah collectively. They sent (word) to the king: "Return—you and all of your servants."

¹⁶The king returned. He came to the Jordan River, and Judah came to Gilgal to come meet the king and to bring the king across the Jordan River. ¹⁷Shimei the son of Gera the Benjaminite, who was from Bahurim, hurriedly came down with the men of Judah to meet King David, ¹⁸and a thousand men (came) with him from Benjamin. Ziba, the attendant for Saul's house, his fifteen sons, and his twenty servants (came) with him. They had rushed to the Jordan River before the king. ¹⁹They crossed the ford to bring the king's household across and to do what he desired.

Gera's son Shimei fell before the king when he had crossed the Jordan River. ²⁰He said to the king, "May my lord not charge me with [my] wrongdoing. Do not remember that your servant did wrong on the day when my lord the king left Jerusalem. May the king not take it to heart. ²¹For your servant knows that I myself sinned. Look! Today I am the first from the entire house of Joseph to come down to meet my lord, Your Majesty."

²²Zeruiah's son Abishai replied, "Should not Shimei be put to death for this, since he cursed Yahweh's anointed one?"

²³David said, "Why should I put up with you, sons of Zeruiah, that you should become a courtroom prosecutor on my behalf today? Should anyone be put to death in Israel today? Am I not aware that today I am [again] king over Israel?" ²⁴The king said to Shimei, "You will not die," and the king promised him by oath.

²⁵Now Saul's grandson Mephibosheth had come down to meet the king. He had not taken care of his feet nor trimmed his mustache, and he had not washed his clothes from the day the king left until the day when he came back safely. ²⁶When

he came to Jerusalem to meet the king, the king said to him, "Why didn't you go with me, Mephibosheth?"

²⁷He said, "My lord, Your Majesty, my servant betrayed me. Indeed, your servant thought, 'I should saddle my donkey for myself, ride on it, and go with the king, for your servant is lame.' ²⁸He slandered your servant to my lord the king. Yet my lord, Your Majesty, is like the Angel of God. Do what you think is right, ²⁹since my grandfather's entire house was nothing but dead men to my lord, Your Majesty. But you put your servant among those who eat at your table. What further right do I have to appeal to the king anymore?"

³⁰The king said to him, "Why should you continue to speak about these things? I declare (that) you and Ziba should divide the farmland."

³¹Mephibosheth said to the king, "So let him take all of it, after my lord, Your Majesty, has come to his palace safely."

³²Barzillai the Gileadite came down from Rogelim and crossed the Jordan River with the king, to escort him over the Jordan River. (³³Now Barzillai was very old—eighty years old. He had provided for the king while he stayed in Mahanaim, for he was a very rich man.) ³⁴The king said to Barzillai, "You cross over with me, and I will provide for you [when you are] with me in Jerusalem."

³⁵Barzillai said to the king, "How long will my life last that I ought to go up with the king to Jerusalem? ³⁶Presently I am eighty years old. Can I tell the difference between what is enjoyable and what is distasteful? Can your servant taste what I eat and what I drink? Can I still hear the sound of male and female singers? Why should your servant still be a burden to my lord, Your Majesty? ³⁷Since your servant is only going a little way across the Jordan River with the king, why should he repay me with so much? ³⁸Please let your servant return so that I can die in my city with the tomb of my father and my mother. Here is your servant Chimham. Let him cross [the river] with my lord, Your Majesty, and do for him what you desire."

³⁹The king said, "Chimham will cross with me, and I'll do what you desire for him. Whatever you request from me I'll do for you." ⁴⁰When all the people had crossed the Jordan River and the king had crossed, the king kissed Barzillai and blessed him. Then he returned him to his place.

⁴¹The king went on to Gilgal, and Chimham went on with him. All the people of Judah as well as half of the people of Israel escorted the king. ⁴²Now all the men of Israel were coming to the king. They said to the king, "Why have our brothers the men of Judah stolen you and brought Your Majesty and your household across the Jordan River, along with all of David's men?"

⁴³All the men of Judah replied to the men of Israel, "Because the king is closer to us! Why in the world are you angry about this? Have we ever eaten [provisions] from the king? Or have we ever been honored?"

⁴⁴The men of Israel answered the men of Judah, "We have ten shares in the king, so we have a greater claim on David than you. Why have you belittled us? Didn't we speak first about returning our king?" But the words of the men of Judah were harsher than the words of the men of Israel.

Textual Notes

19:10 כָּל־הָעָם נָדוֹן—"All the people … were arguing with one another." The verb is the Niphal (N) masculine singular participle of דִּין, "to plead" or "prosecute" a legal case. The Niphal at times denotes reciprocal action.[1] This is the only instance of the Niphal of דִּין in the OT, and it could also be translated as "were at strife with one another." The cognate noun דִּין can refer to "strife" (Prov 22:10).

הַמֶּלֶךְ הִצִּילָנוּ—"The king delivered us." The Hiphil (H) of נָצַל can refer to Yahweh saving his people (see the textual note on 1 Sam 10:18–19[2]) and here refers to his action through his anointed king (see this verb also in 2 Sam 12:7; 14:16; 22:1, 18, 49).

מִלְּטָנוּ—"He rescued us." For the Piel (D) of מָלַט, see the second textual note on 19:6 (ET 19:5).

19:11 מָשַׁחְנוּ—"We anointed." For מָשַׁח, "to anoint," see the second textual note and the commentary on 5:3 and the third textual note on 12:7. The book of Samuel contains no record of an anointing of Absalom.

מַחֲרִשִׁים—"Staying silent." This is the Hiphil (H) masculine plural participle of חָרַשׁ, whose Hiphil means "be silent, keep quiet." See the second textual note on 13:20. The participle denotes continuing action.

19:12 הַכֹּהֲנִים—This plural noun denotes "the *high* priests" Zadok and Abiathar, who shared the high priesthood under David. See the second textual note on 8:17 and the first textual note on 17:15.

לָמָּה תִהְיוּ אַחֲרֹנִים לְהָשִׁיב אֶת־הַמֶּלֶךְ—"Why should you be the last ones to restore the king?" This question recurs in 19:13 (ET 19:12). The adjective אַחֲרוֹן, "coming behind, later," is used here as a superlative substantive, "(the) last (of all)."

19:13 עַצְמִי וּבְשָׂרִי—The English idiom "my flesh and blood" conveys the sense of the Hebrew, literally "my bone and my flesh" (cf. Gen 2:23; Judg 9:2). The same Hebrew idiom recurs in 2 Sam 19:14 (ET 19:13).

19:14 וְלַעֲמָשָׂא תֹּמְרוּ הֲלוֹא … אַתָּה—"Say to Amasa, 'Are you not … ?'" The verb תֹּמְרוּ is an unusual spelling of תֹּאמְרוּ, "you shall say," with the omission of the quiescent *aleph* (GKC, § 68 h). The combination הֲלוֹא (הֲ- + לֹא), "are not?" expects a positive answer.

כֹּה יַעֲשֶׂה־לִּי אֱלֹהִים וְכֹה יוֹסִיף אִם־לֹא … תִּהְיֶה—"Thus may God do to me and thus may he add if you do not become." This is an oath by which the speaker swears to perform an action (here make Amasa his commander) and calls on God to punish him אִם־לֹא, "if" he does "not" perform it. See the textual note on 1 Sam 3:17.[3] See also 2 Sam 3:35.

לְפָנַי כָּל־הַיָּמִים—"Before me from now on." See the identical wording in Jer 31:36; 35:19. The prepositional phrase לְפָנַי, "before me," means that Amasa will stand before the king in readiness to do what he commands. In this context the construct phrase

---

[1] *IBH*, § 39 C; Waltke-O'Connor, § 23.4e.

[2] Steinmann, *1 Samuel*, 200–201.

[3] Steinmann, *1 Samuel*, 111–12.

כָּל־הַיָּמִים, literally "all the days," means "from now on," that is, for the remainder of David's reign.

19:15   וַיֵּט אֶת־לְבַב כָּל־אִישׁ־יְהוּדָה כְּאִישׁ אֶחָד—"So he persuaded all the men in Judah collectively" is literally "and he turned the heart of every man of Judah as one man." The idiom with the Hiphil (H) of נָטָה, "(cause to) turn, direct, incline," and the object noun לֵבָב, "heart," means to change someone's attitude or religion (Josh 24:23; 1 Ki 8:58; 11:2, 4). The verb וַיֵּט is the Hiphil (H) preterite (imperfect with *waw* consecutive) of נָטָה, whose Qal (G) means "stretch out, bend," or "turn" (usually intransitively, but sometimes transitively). A few Masoretic manuscripts point the verb as וַיֵּט, which is the identical form but in the Qal. With that pointing, the noun לְבַב, "heart," would be the subject of the verb, and so the noun would not (normally) have before it אֶת, the direct object marker.

19:16   לָלֶכֶת לִקְרַאת—"To come (to) meet." This construction has two Qal (G) infinitive constructs, each with the preposition לְ. The first is of הָלַךְ, but in place of לָלֶכֶת, a number of Masoretic manuscripts read לָרֶדֶת, "to come down," the Qal infinitive construct of יָרַד (see its Qal perfect in the next textual note and its Qal infinitive construct in 19:21 [ET 19:20]). The second is of קָרָא II, "to meet." Its infinitive construct with לְ is often used for engaging in battle (see the second textual note on 1 Sam 4:1[4]), but here it denotes peaceful military support.

19:17   וַיְמַהֵר ... וַיֵּרֶד—"He hurriedly came down" is literally "and he hurried … and he came down." When two verbs are coordinated in Hebrew, the first verb often functions adverbially and the second verb denotes the principal action.

19:18   וְצִיבָא נַעַר בֵּית שָׁאוּל וַחֲמֵשֶׁת עָשָׂר בָּנָיו וְעֶשְׂרִים עֲבָדָיו אִתּוֹ—"Ziba, the attendant for Saul's house, his fifteen sons, and his twenty servants (came) with him." See 9:9–10. In חֲמֵשֶׁת עָשָׂר, "fifteen" here, the construct form of the first numeral is used (contrast חֲמִשָּׁה עָשָׂר in 9:10; see Joüon, § 100 e).

וְצָלְחוּ הַיַּרְדֵּן—"They had rushed to the Jordan River." Since 19:16 (ET 19:15) states that the king had arrived at the Jordan, the perfect verb here, referring to action before the king's arrival, must have a pluperfect meaning, "*had* rushed" (Waltke-O'Connor, § 32.3e, including example 15). Elsewhere in the book of Samuel, the verb צָלַח, "to rush," always refers to the action of the Holy Spirit (1 Sam 10:6, 10; 11:6; 16:13) or an evil spirit (1 Sam 18:10). The noun הַיַּרְדֵּן is an accusative of destination (Joüon, § 125 n), thus "*to* the Jordan."

19:19   וְעָבְרָה הָעֲבָרָה לַעֲבִיר—"They crossed the ford to bring … across." Note the assonance as all three words have the same three root letters, עבר. The first word in the MT, וְעָבְרָה, is the Qal (G) third feminine singular perfect of עָבַר with conjunctive *waw*, meaning "and she/it crossed over/forded." The only feminine singular noun in the context that could serve as its subject is the second word, הָעֲבָרָה, "the ford" (see the second textual note on 15:28), but that would mean "the ford forded," unless perhaps הָעֲבָרָה refers to the group of people amassed for the crossing. The translation "they crossed the ford to bring … across" follows the Vulgate (*transierunt vada ut transducerent*)

---

and the Targum (וְאַעְבַּרוּ מְגִזְתָא לְאַעְבָּרָא), both of which imply the Hebrew reading וְעָבְרוּ הָעֲבָרָה לַעֲבִיר, in which the first word is the Qal (G) third common plural perfect with conjunctive *waw*, "and they crossed," and the noun הָעֲבָרָה, "the ford," is the object of the verb. The third word, לַעֲבִיר, is the Hiphil (H) infinitive construct of עָבַר with לְ, forming a purpose clause, "to bring across." The expected form would be לְהַעֲבִיר, but the *he* is elided (GKC, § 53 q; Joüon, § 54 b). The LXX reads καὶ ἐλειτούργησαν τὴν λειτουργίαν τοῦ διαβιβάσαι, "and they served the service to bring across," which reflects a Hebrew *Vorlage* of וְעָבְדוּ הָעֲבָדָה לַעֲבִיר, with the common graphic confusion of *dalet* in place of *resh* in the first two words. The Syriac Peshitta is similar to the LXX.

וְלַעֲשׂוֹת הַטּוֹב בְּעֵינָיו—"And to do what he desired." This infinitive clause denoting purpose is literally "and to do the good in his eyes." See similar clauses with טוֹב and עַיִן in 19:28, 39 (ET 19:27, 38). The Qere בְּעֵינָיו is the usual spelling of the dual noun with a third masculine singular suffix and the preposition בְּ. The Kethib, בעינו, should be vocalized as the same word but spelled defectively, בְּעֵינָו. See the same Qere/Kethib readings in 2 Sam 24:22; see also similar Qere/Kethib readings in the first textual note on 1 Sam 3:2 and the second textual note on 1 Sam 3:18,[5] as well as the first textual note on 2 Sam 13:34.

19:20–21 In most of his plea Shimei deferentially addresses the king in the third person rather than the second person. However, he does, perhaps out of desperation, refer to himself twice as עַבְדְּךָ, "*your* servant" (19:20, 21 [ET 19:19, 20]), instead of the customary עַבְדּוֹ, "*his* servant" (e.g., 1 Sam 22:15; 26:18–19; 2 Sam 9:11; 24:21). He also uses one second person verb; see the second textual note on 2 Sam 19:20 (ET 19:19).

19:20 אַל־יַחֲשָׁב־לִי אֲדֹנִי עָוֹן—"May my lord not charge me with [my] wrongdoing" is literally "may my lord not reckon to me iniquity." The verb חָשַׁב can be used for accounting or deeming a person to be righteous (Gen 15:6; Ps 32:2) or guilty (as here). The noun עָוֹן, "iniquity," is cognate to the verb עָוָה; see the third textual note on 19:20 (ET 19:19).

וְאַל־תִּזְכֹּר—"Do not remember." The negative with the imperfect forms a negative command. When God is the subject, "remembering" (זָכַר) a sin involves punishing the person who committed it (see BDB, Qal, II 4).

הֶעֱוָה—"He did wrong" is literally "he committed iniquity." For the Hiphil (H) of עָוָה, see the second textual note on 7:14. See the synonym חָטָא, "to sin," in the textual note on 19:21 (ET 19:20). David uses both verbs in his confession in 24:17.

לָשׂוּם הַמֶּלֶךְ אֶל־לִבּוֹ:—"May the king not take it to heart" is literally "the king to set into his heart." The verb לָשׂוּם is the Qal (G) infinitive construct of שִׂים with לְ, and the *qamets* under the *lamed*, לָ-, indicates that הַמֶּלֶךְ is its subject (GKC, § 115 g; Joüon, § 124 g). Instead of forming a separate clause, it could function adverbially to modify the preceding וְאַל־תִּזְכֹּר, i.e., "do not remember ... by (the king) taking it to heart." For the idiom שִׂים + אֶל + לֵב, see the textual note on 13:33.

---

[5] Steinmann, *1 Samuel*, 109, 112.

19:21 יָדַע עַבְדְּךָ כִּי אֲנִי חָטָאתִי—Shimei switches from the second person, "*your* servant knows," to the first person, "that *I myself* sinned," to confess his personal culpability. David confesses with the same first common singular Qal (G) perfect חָטָאתִי, "I have sinned," in 2 Sam 12:13; 24:10, 17, as did Saul in 1 Sam 15:24, 30; 26:21.

19:22 הֲתַחַת זֹאת לֹא יוּמַת שִׁמְעִי—"Should not Shimei be put to death for this?" The verb יוּמַת, "he will/should be put to death," is the Hophal (Hp) third masculine singular imperfect of מוּת, "die." The same form recurs in 19:23 (ET 19:22). In both verses it is translated literally by the LXX as θανατωθήσεται. A few Masoretic manuscripts read the more common form יָמוּת, "he will/should die," the Qal (G) third masculine singular imperfect, which resulted from an accidental metathesis of the *mem* and the *waw*. Cf. the Qal (G) imperfect תָּמוּת in 19:24 (ET 19:23).

קִלֵּל—"He cursed." The Piel (D) of קָלַל denoted Shimei's action also in 16:5–13. See the textual note on 16:5. See the Piel also in 1 Sam 3:13; 17:43. See further the third textual note on 19:44 (ET 19:43).

מְשִׁיחַ יְהוָה:—"Yahweh's anointed one" is literally "the messiah of Yahweh." This is the only time in the book of Samuel that this construct phrase refers to David. It referred to Saul in 1 Sam 24:7, 11 (ET 24:6, 10); 26:9, 11, 16, 23; 2 Sam 1:14, 16. See the discussion of the noun מָשִׁיחַ, "anointed one," in the commentary on 1 Sam 2:10, 35.[6]

19:23 מַה־לִּי וְלָכֶם—"Why should I put up with you?" is literally "what (is) to me and to you?" See the first textual note on 16:10. The pronominal suffix "you" (כֶם-) is plural. Next David will refer to the "sons of" (בְּנֵי) Zeruiah and use the plural verb תִּהְיוּ, "you should be/become," for them.

כִּי־תִהְיוּ־לִי הַיּוֹם לְשָׂטָן—"That you should become a courtroom prosecutor on my behalf today?" The Qal (G) of הָיָה is commonly used with the preposition לְ (here on לְשָׂטָן) to mean "to become." The other preposition לְ (with a suffix, לִי) has the sense of advantage, "for me/my sake" or "on my behalf." Given Shimei's request for a pardon (19:20–21 [ET 19:19–20]), David is accusing Abishai of taking the part of a courtroom "accuser" or "prosecutor" (שָׂטָן) who advocates the imposition of the death penalty on Shimei.[7]

19:24 וַיִּשָּׁבַע—Literally "and he swore an oath." It is possible that the oath may have invoked "Yahweh" or "God," as when the Niphal (N) of שָׁבַע is used in, e.g., 1 Sam 19:6; 20:42; 24:22 (ET 24:21); 28:10; 2 Sam 3:35; 19:8 (ET 19:7). This verb is used in oaths that a person will not be put to death in 1 Sam 19:6; 28:10; 30:15; cf. also 1 Sam 24:22 (ET 24:21).

19:25 וּמְפִבֹשֶׁת בֶּן־שָׁאוּל יָרַד—"Now Saul's grandson Mephibosheth had come down." The placement of a subject noun (מְפִבֹשֶׁת) before a perfect verb (יָרַד) can be an anterior construction with a pluperfect sense (see Joüon, § 118 d), "*had* come down." In 19:25–31 (ET 19:24–30), the narrative seems to skip ahead to David's interaction with Mephibosheth when the king returned to Jerusalem before returning back in 19:32–40 (ET 19:31–39) to events that took place at the Jordan. Mephibosheth most likely had

---

6 Steinmann, *1 Samuel*, 80–81, 105–6.

7 Day, "Abishai the *śāṭān* in 2 Samuel 19:17–24"; Anderson, *2 Samuel*, 237.

not traveled to the Jordan to meet David (cf. 19:16–19 [ET 19:15–18]). But he may have gone a short distance from Jerusalem to join the king's procession as it was nearing the city. He then met with David once the king reached the city (19:26 [ET 19:25]).

Usually the noun בֵּן means "son," but here it means "grandson." Mephibosheth was the son of Saul's son Jonathan. See 4:4; 9:6. See also "grandfather" in the first textual note on 19:29 (ET 19:28).

וְלֹא־עָשָׂה רַגְלָיו וְלֹא־עָשָׂה שְׂפָמוֹ—"He had not taken care of his feet nor trimmed his mustache" is literally "and he did not do his feet, and he did not do his mustache."

19:26 וַיְהִי כִּי־בָא יְרוּשָׁלַ͏ִם—"When he came to Jerusalem." The terminus of a motion is often presented in the accusative (Joüon, § 125 n), without a directive *he* suffix.[8] This is also the understanding of the LXX: εἰς Ιερουσαλημ. Many English versions read "from Jerusalem," which would require מִירוּשָׁלַ͏ִם (e.g., 5:13; 15:11). On the sequence of events, see the first textual note on (19:25 [ET 19:24]).

19:27 עַבְדִּי רִמָּנִי—"My servant betrayed me." Previously the Piel (D) of רָמָה, "to deceive," referred to deceptions by Michal (1 Sam 19:17) and Saul (1 Sam 28:12). Mephibosheth's servant was Ziba. David had ordered Ziba and his sons and servants to serve Mephibosheth and care for his estate (2 Sam 9:9–11). When Mephibosheth here makes the charge that Ziba had "betrayed" him, he is also accusing Ziba of having betrayed David. In 16:1–4 Ziba had convinced David that Mephibosheth aspired to the throne, and David rewarded Ziba by giving him Mephibosheth's estate. Now Mephibosheth asserts that Ziba's successful effort to gain David's favor in 16:1–4 was fraudulent. See also the first textual note on 19:28 (ET 19:27).

אֶחְבְּשָׁה־לִּי הַחֲמוֹר—"I should saddle my donkey for myself." Mephibosheth uses the Qal (G) cohortative אֶחְבְּשָׁה (and then the Qal imperfects with conjunctive *waw* וְאֵלֵךְ and וְאֶרְכַּב) to state what his intentions were before he was deceived by Ziba: he had wanted to travel by donkey to David and accompany him. For חָבַשׁ, "to bind, tie," which can refer to saddling an animal, see the third textual note on 16:1, where, ironically, it was Mephibosheth's deceitful servant Ziba who had saddled donkeys and traveled to meet David.

כִּי פִסֵּחַ עַבְדֶּךָ:—"For your servant is lame." This explains Mephibosheth's reliance on his donkey. The adjective פִּסֵּחַ, "lame," is cognate to the verb פָּסַח, which was used to describe the cause of Mephibosheth's disability in 4:4.

19:28 וַיְרַגֵּל בְּעַבְדְּךָ אֶל־אֲדֹנִי הַמֶּלֶךְ—"He slandered your servant to my lord the king." Elsewhere in the OT the Piel (D) of רָגַל often refers to the deceptive activity of "spying," as in 1 Sam 26:4; 2 Sam 10:3 (see also 2 Sam 15:10).[9] Here it means "to slander" and is used with the preposition בְּ in a hostile sense ("against"). The prepositional phrase with אֶל ("to my lord") refers to the slanderous words Ziba spoke to David in 2 Sam 16:2–3.

---

[8] See יְרוּשָׁלַ͏ִם, "to Jerusalem," in, e.g., 1 Sam 17:54; 2 Sam 5:6; 8:7; 10:14; 12:31; 14:23; 15:8, 29; 16:15; 17:20; 19:35 (ET 19:34); 20:2; 24:8.

[9] See the first textual note on 1 Sam 26:4 (Steinmann, *1 Samuel*, 492) and the fifth textual note on 2 Sam 10:3. See also the textual note on 2 Sam 15:10.

כְּמַלְאַךְ הָאֱלֹהִים—"Like the Angel of God." See the second textual note on 14:17 and the commentary on 14:17, 20.

19:29 כָּל־בֵּית אָבִי—"My grandfather's entire house." Usually the noun אָב refers to a "father," but here it refers to Saul as Mephibosheth's "grandfather." See the first textual note on 19:25 (ET 19:24).

אַנְשֵׁי־מָוֶת לַאדֹנִי—This could also be translated as "men deserving death in relation to my lord." In this construct phrase the genitive מָוֶת, "death," could signify the punishment the men deserved because of their actions "toward" or "in relation to" (לְ) David. See Joüon, § 129 j, and the singular construct phrase אִישׁ־מָוֶת, "a man deserving death," in 1 Ki 2:26.

וַתָּשֶׁת אֶת־עַבְדְּךָ בְּאֹכְלֵי שֻׁלְחָנֶךָ—"But you put your servant among those who eat at your table." See 9:7–13. Cf. the men at Saul's "table" in 1 Sam 20:29, 34.

וּמַה־יֶּשׁ־לִי עוֹד צְדָקָה וְלִזְעֹק עוֹד אֶל־הַמֶּלֶךְ—"What further right do I have to appeal to the king anymore?" The Hebrew syntax consists of two clauses joined by *waw*, literally "and what righteousness still exists for me, *and* to cry still to the king?" Alternatively, the noun צְדָקָה can be taken as an accusative of respect, "*what (with respect to) right* do I yet have?" (Waltke-O'Connor, § 18.1e, example 31).

19:30 לָמָּה תְּדַבֵּר עוֹד דְּבָרֶיךָ—Literally "why should you still speak your words?"

הַשָּׂדֶה:—"The farmland." The noun שָׂדֶה is often translated as "field," but it is used in various ways to denote land outside of cities. Here it refers to the farmland that Mephibosheth had inherited from Saul through Jonathan.

19:32 וַיַּעֲבֹר אֶת־הַמֶּלֶךְ הַיַּרְדֵּן—"And he crossed the Jordan River with the king." The verb וַיַּעֲבֹר is the Qal (G) third masculine singular preterite (imperfect with *waw* consecutive) of עָבַר, "to cross over." The word אֶת is most likely the preposition "with"; see Qal forms of עָבַר with the preposition אֵת, "cross (over) with," in 19:34, 37, 39 (ET 19:33, 36, 38); see also 15:33. The direct object of the verb is a definite noun (place-name) with the article, הַיַּרְדֵּן, "the Jordan." Some manuscripts include the direct object marker אֶת before the object, which is the construction used in 19:40 (ET 19:39; וַיַּעֲבֹר ... אֶת־הַיַּרְדֵּן, "and he crossed ... the Jordan"); see also the next textual note. If the verb here were Hiphil (וַיַּעֲבֵר, as in, e.g., 1 Sam 16:9, 10; see the textual note on 19:41 [ET 19:40]), then it would have a causative meaning and take a double accusative construction, "bring the king over the Jordan," as translated by the Vulgate (*transduxit regem Iordanem*). Then the second word, אֶת, would mark "the king" as the first accusative (direct object).

לְשַׁלְּחוֹ אֶת־הַיַּרְדֵּן:—"To escort him over the Jordan River." The Piel (D) infinitive construct with the preposition לְ and a third masculine singular suffix לְשַׁלְּחוֹ, is literally "to send him." The Piel of שָׁלַח can mean "to send (a person) off, away," and sometimes involves escorting the person part of the way (BDB, s.v. שָׁלַח I, Piel, 1 d, citing also, e.g., Gen 18:16; 1 Sam 9:26). The suffix on the infinitive is its direct object ("him"). The Piel of שָׁלַח normally does not take a double accusative construction, but it apparently does so here with אֶת־הַיַּרְדֵּן (in which אֶת must be the direct object marker, although it is omitted in a few Masoretic manuscripts). The Qere is הַיַּרְדֵּן, literally "the Jordan." The place-name is prefixed with the preposition בְּ in the Kethib, בַּיַּרְדֵּן, "in the Jordan."

19:33 בֶּן־שְׁמֹנִים שָׁנָה—"Eighty years old." Hebrew uses the noun בֵּן, "son," in construct with a numeral and the noun שָׁנָה, "year," to express a person's age in years. See the same phrase in 19:36 (ET 19:35).

וְהוּא־כִלְכַּל—"He had provided." The verb is the Pilpel (D) of כּוּל, "to sustain, support, nourish." It recurs in this stem in 19:34 (ET 19:33); 20:3.

בְשִׁיבָתוֹ—"While he stayed" is literally "in his staying." The feminine noun שִׁיבָה I, "(a period of) staying, living," is derived from the verb יָשַׁב, "to dwell, live." This is the only instance of this noun in the OT. In its place some Masoretic manuscripts have בְשִׁבְתּוֹ, which is the common Qal (G) infinitive construct of יָשַׁב with the preposition בְּ and a third masculine singular subjective suffix, with the same meaning.

כִּי־אִישׁ גָּדוֹל הוּא מְאֹד:—"For he was a very rich man." This nominal sentence explains why Barzillai was able to provide for David. The adjective גָּדוֹל, "great," can have the nuance "rich, wealthy" (1 Sam 25:2; Dan 11:2; see also the cognate verb גָּדַל in Gen 26:13).

19:34 וְכִלְכַּלְתִּי אֹתְךָ—"And I will provide for you" is literally "and I will sustain/nourish you." For the verb, see the second textual note on 19:33 (ET 19:32). Its direct object is the suffixed direct object marker אֹתְךָ. The LXX reads καὶ διαθρέψω τὸ γῆράς σου, "and I will sustain your old age."[10] This implies a Hebrew reading וְכִלְכַּלְתִּי אֶת־שֵׂיבָתְךָ.

19:35 כַּמָּה יְמֵי שְׁנֵי חַיַּי—"How long will my life last?" The interrogative מָה, "what?" is prefixed with the preposition כְּ, "as," in a temporal sense, literally "as what are the years of my life?"

19:36 הַיּוֹם—In this context "the day" is translated as the adverb "presently."

הַאֵדַע ׀ בֵּין־טוֹב לְרָע—"Can I tell the difference between what is enjoyable and what is distasteful?" is literally "can I know between good and evil?" For the combination of טוֹב and רַע, see also 13:22 and the fourth textual note on 14:17. For בֵּין ... לְ, as "between [one thing] and [another thing]," see BDB, s.v. בֵּין, 1 b.

אִם ... אִם—After the interrogative he that began the previous question, אִם functions twice in this verse as an interrogative particle that begins a (merely formal) alternative question (BDB, 2 a (b) (α)). It has the same function in 19:43 (ET 19:42).

וְלָמָּה יִהְיֶה עַבְדְּךָ עוֹד לְמַשָּׂא—"Why should your servant still be a burden?" See the textual note on 15:33.

19:37 וְלָמָּה יִגְמְלֵנִי הַמֶּלֶךְ הַגְּמוּלָה הַזֹּאת:—This cognate accusative construction is literally "and why should the king recompense me (with) this recompense?" See the verb גָּמַל, "repay, requite," also in 1 Sam 24:18 (ET 24:17); 2 Sam 22:21.

19:38 יָשָׁב־נָא עַבְדְּךָ וְאָמֻת—"Please let your servant return so that I can die." The first verb, יָשָׁב, is the Qal (G) third masculine singular jussive of שׁוּב. Barzillai deferentially refers to himself in the third person. However, for the second verb he switches to the first person (see Joüon, § 151 b, referring to the same feature in 19:36 [ET 19:35]): וְאָמֻת is a Qal (G) first common singular imperfect with conjunctive waw of מוּת, "to die." It is a defective, or *ḥaser*, spelling of וְאָמוּת and expresses purpose, "so that" (Waltke-O'Connor, § 39.2.2a, including example 2). (It is not a first person jussive, which would

---

[10] Cf. Josephus, *Antiquities*, 7.272: γηροκομήσειν.

be extremely rare [Joüon, § 114 g] and be pointed וְאָמֹת, nor is it a cohortative singular, which would be וְאָמוּתָה, as in Gen 46:30.)

19:39 וְכֹל אֲשֶׁר־תִּבְחַר עָלַי—"Whatever you request from me" is literally "and all that you choose (to be incumbent) upon me."

19:40 וַיִּשַּׁק הַמֶּלֶךְ לְבַרְזִלַּי וַיְבָרֲכֵהוּ—"The king kissed Barzillai and blessed him." Here the verb נָשַׁק, "to kiss," signifies a king's act of recognizing and thanking a loyal subject. The verb is used similarly in 14:33; 15:5. See the third textual note on 14:33. For the Piel (D) of בָּרַךְ, "to bless," see the textual note on 2 Sam 6:11–12, as well as the first textual note on 1 Sam 2:20 and the third textual note on 1 Sam 9:13.[11]

19:41 הֶעֱבִירוּ אֶת־הַמֶּלֶךְ—"They escorted the king." The verb הֶעֱבִירוּ, which is the Qere and the sole reading in many Masoretic manuscripts, is the Hiphil (H) third common plural perfect of עָבַר, and so אֵת is the direct object marker,[12] literally "they brought the king across." The Kethib, ויעברו, is a third masculine plural preterite (imperfect with *waw* consecutive). It could be pointed either as Qal (G), וַיַּעַבְרוּ, in which case אֵת is the preposition, "and they crossed with the king," or as Hiphil (H), וַיַּעֲבִרוּ (as in 19:42 [ET 19:41]), in which case אֵת is the direct object marker, "they escorted the king." The LXX translates the verb with a participle, διαβαίνοντες, which implies a Hebrew reading with the Qal (G) masculine plural participle עֹבְרִים, "were crossing."

19:42 גְּנָבוּךָ—For the Qal (G) of גָּנַב, "to steal," see the third textual note on 15:6.

19:43–44 Much of the dialogue between the men of Judah and the men of Israel in these two verses uses first and second person singular forms, as if each individual man of Judah spoke to an individual man of Israel and vice versa.

19:43 כִּי־קָרוֹב הַמֶּלֶךְ אֵלַי—"Because the king is closer to us!" is literally "because the king is closer to me." In this context the adjective קָרוֹב, "close," functions as a comparative, "closer."

וְלָמָּה זֶּה—"Why in the world?" See the first textual note on 3:24.

חָרָה לְךָ—"You are angry" is literally "it is hot/angry for you [singular]." For this construction, see the second textual note on 1 Sam 20:7[13] and the first textual note on 2 Sam 3:8.

הֶאָכוֹל אָכַלְנוּ—"Have we ever eaten?" The first form of אָכַל, "to eat," is the Qal (G) infinitive absolute with a prefixed interrogative *he*, and the second is the Qal first common plural perfect. Usually an infinitive absolute is used for emphasis, but in a question expecting a negative answer, it can reinforce the sense of doubt (Joüon, § 123 f; Waltke-O'Connor, § 35.3.1g, including example 17).

אִם־נִשֵּׂאת נִשָּׂא לָנוּ—"Or have we ever been honored?" For the use of אִם as an interrogative particle, see the third textual note on 19:36 (ET 19:35). The word נִשֵּׂאת can be parsed as a Niphal (N) infinitive absolute of נָשָׂא, "to carry, bear" (see GKC, § 76 b; cf. Joüon, § 123 f). The next word, נִשָּׂא, is the Niphal third masculine singular perfect of the same verb. In the Niphal, נָשָׂא can mean "be lifted up, be exalted" (see BDB,

---

[11] Steinmann, *1 Samuel*, 90, 179.

[12] Cf. the discussion of אֵת in the two textual notes on 19:32 (ET 19:31).

[13] Steinmann, *1 Samuel*, 390.

Niphal, 1 a–b, and *DCH*, Niphal, 1 a–b), and here it is translated as "be honored." The perfect נִשָּׂא is used impersonally, with no stated subject. The force of לָנוּ, the suffixed preposition לְ, may be a dative of advantage, literally "has it ever been exalted for us?" Such an impersonal translation is often best translated as a passive, hence "or have we ever been honored?" Alternatively נִשֵּׂאת can be parsed as a Niphal (N) feminine singular participle (so BDB, s.v. נָשָׂא, Niphal, on the form's use in other verses). The participle would refer to something "taken away." It could denote a portion from the king given as a gift (as the cognate feminine noun מַשְׂאֵת can mean): "has a gift ever been given to us?" (cf. KJV, ESV). The participle could also refer to something "taken away" as "stolen," in which case לָנוּ would be the agent of the passive: "has anything been carried away by us?" (see *DCH*, Niphal, 3; cf. NIV).

19:44 עֶשֶׂר־יָדוֹת לִי בַמֶּלֶךְ—"We have ten shares in the king" is literally "(there are) ten hands (belonging) to me in the king" (cf. *HALOT*, s.v. יָד I, 7 b i).

וְגַם־בְּדָוִד אֲנִי מִמְּךָ—"So we have a greater claim on David than you" is literally "and also in David I (have more) than you [singular]." The suffixed preposition מִן, "from, than," is used in a comparative sense: "(greater/more) than you."

וּמַדּוּעַ הֱקִלֹּתַנִי—"Why have you belittled us?" is literally "and/so why have you belittled me?" The verb is the Hiphil (H) second masculine singular perfect of קָלַל, "be light, little," with a first common singular object suffix (cf. GKC, § 67 w). For the Qal (G) of קָלַל, see the third textual note on 1 Sam 2:30.[14] For its Niphal (N), see the second textual note on 1 Sam 18:23[15] and the first textual note on 2 Sam 6:22. For its Piel (D), "to curse," see the second textual note on 2 Sam 19:22 (ET 19:21).

וְלֹא־הָיָה דְבָרִי רִאשׁוֹן לִי לְהָשִׁיב אֶת־מַלְכִּי—"Didn't we speak first about returning our king?" is literally "and was not my word first for me to return my king?" The first person pronouns ("my … me … my") emphasize the claim of priority of the speaker(s).

וַיִּקֶשׁ—"But it was harsher." This is the Qal (G) of קָשָׁה, "be hard." See this verb also in 1 Sam 5:7, and see the cognate adjective קָשֶׁה describing persons as "harsh" in 1 Sam 25:3; 2 Sam 3:39.

Commentary

974 BC[16]

The account of David's return to Jerusalem to occupy the throne of Israel once again focuses on his relationship with the tribes of Israel as well as with several individuals who had interacted with him previously: Shimei (16:5–13), Ziba (9:2–11; 16:1–4), Mephibosheth (9:6–13), and Barzillai (17:27–29). David resolved the issues with the two men from the house of Saul, Ziba and Mephibosheth. However, in all the other cases David's acts did not settle matters but instead left them unresolved. In each instance he or his successors would have to deal with the consequences of these royal indecisions. David's actions would set the tribe of Judah against the other tribes. This would precipitate

---

[14] Steinmann, *1 Samuel*, 100.

[15] Steinmann, *1 Samuel*, 359.

[16] See "The Chronology of David's Reign" in the commentary on 5:1–5.

Sheba's rebellion (20:1–26) and expose a rift in Israel that would eventually lead to the division of the kingdom (1 Ki 12:1–19; compare 2 Sam 20:1 with 1 Ki 12:16). Although David pardoned Shimei, he did not forget this Saulide's actions and would later instruct Solomon to deal with him (1 Ki 2:8–9, 36–46). By assuming care of Chimham at Barzillai's request (19:38–39 [ET 19:37–38]), David took on a responsibility that he would later pass on to Solomon (1 Ki 2:7). This passage, therefore, reveals the continuing turmoil that beset David's house because of his sins with Bathsheba and Uriah (2 Samuel 11), as foretold by the prophet Nathan (12:10–12).

Judah and Benjamin Welcome David Back to the Throne (19:10–19a [ET 19:9–18a])

With David east of the Jordan River and Absalom dead (2 Samuel 18), the tribes began to have a dispute about bringing David back as king (19:10–11 [ET 19:9–10]). The author reports only the two points in favor of David: he was successful in ridding Israel of the Philistine threat, and with the power vacuum left after Absalom's death, he was the logical choice as king. In the quote the tribes mention that they had "anointed" Absalom (19:11 [ET 19:10]), though the author had not reported any such event. Perhaps it took place after David fled Jerusalem (15:14), since it appears that there was no time for it to have taken place before that.

When David learned of the dispute, he sent word to his allies in Jerusalem, the high priests Zadok and Abiathar (19:12–13 [ET 19:11–12]). He decided to have them appeal to the elders of Judah, the tribe that had first recognized him as king (2:4; the northern tribes of Israel did so later in 5:3). His appeal was that the Judahites again ought to be first to recognize him since they were his tribe—his "flesh and blood." In order to placate any in Judah who had supported Absalom, David offered to place Amasa, Absalom's commander (17:25), over the army instead of Joab (19:14 [ET 19:13]). This was probably also a way for David to punish Joab for disobeying his order concerning Absalom (18:5, 14–15) and for Joab's direct words correcting the king for his public mourning for the slain prince (19:1–8 [ET 18:33–19:7]). However, this indirect way of dealing with Joab would lead to problems later. Moreover, Amasa had little experience as a commander, and in his only major battle he had been badly defeated (18:6–17). He would prove to be an ineffective choice for the chief commander of Israel's army (20:4–6). Nevertheless, David's offer proved successful in at least one aspect: he managed to elicit an invitation from the tribe of Judah to return to Israel as king (19:15 [ET 19:14]). His overture to them may have been designed to allay fears that since many of them had supported Absalom, they might be punished for their treasonous acts.

David returned, and Judah came to Gilgal, which was in the vicinity of Jericho (Josh 4:19), so that they could bring David's entourage across the Jordan River (19:16 [ET 19:15]). However, word must have spread to the other tribes, since men from Benjamin, including Shimei and Ziba's household, also came down to the river and crossed it to aid David (19:17–19a [ET 19:16–18a]).

David Pardons Shimei (19:19b–24 [ET 19:18b–23])

Shimei rushed to fling himself at David's feet as soon as the king had crossed the river (19:19b [ET 19:18b]). Shimei begged for mercy, calling his behavior an iniquitous crime of "wrongdoing" (עָוֺן, 19:20 [ET 19:19]). He admitted his misconduct by saying he had done "wrong" (הֶעֱוֵה, 19:20 [ET 19:19]) and "sinned" (חָטָאתִי, 19:21 [ET 19:20]). He neither sought to downplay his actions nor offer a defense for them. The only thing he cited in favor of a pardon was that he was the first of "the entire house of Joseph" to meet David. "The house of Joseph" is a phrase that is used to signify the tribes of Israel other than Judah (Josh 18:5; Zech 10:6).

Earlier when Shimei had been cursing David (16:5–13), Abishai had offered to execute him (16:9). Now, before David could reply to Shimei's appeal for pardon, Abishai stepped in with the obvious question: since Shimei had cursed "Yahweh's anointed one," why should he not be put to death (19:22 [ET 19:21]; see Ex 22:27 [ET 22:28])? David's reaction to Abishai's question was one of frustration with Zeruiah's "sons," Abishai in particular (19:23 [ET 19:22]; for Joab, see below). The king accused Abishai of taking on the role of a "courtroom prosecutor" (שָׂטָן, satan) on his "behalf" (לִי; see the second textual note on 19:23 [ET 19:22]; for "Satan" [1 Chr 21:1], see the commentary on 2 Sam 24:1–3). Many interpreters consider David to be saying that Abishai had become David's "adversary"; they understand שָׂטָן in a more general sense and take לִי to mean "to me."[17] However, it is more likely that David was noting once again that, like his brother Joab, Abishai was assuming the role of acting for David even when David had not requested such assistance and did not appreciate it. Joab had taken upon himself to countermand David's order concerning Absalom (18:5). He had killed David's rebellious son to protect the king, presuming to act in David's best interest (18:11–15).[18] Now Abishai was presuming to argue on David's behalf for the death penalty for Shimei. These "sons of Zeruiah" had driven David to exasperation because of their presumption and because they were at the same time too useful for him to banish them from his service.

David, however, believed it was the wrong day for executions. Since it was the day for his restoration to the throne, the execution of one of David's enemies might make some in Israel reconsider their welcoming of David back as their monarch. Moreover, David asked the rhetorical question whether he himself was aware that he was king once more. That is, David as sovereign could adjudicate cases without Abishai's aid, and Abishai ought to allow the king to

---

[17] This is the sense found in most English versions (e.g., HCSB, ESV, GW, NET).

[18] Joab's action was most likely in David's best interest. However, David did not appreciate it. He was unable to see that Absalom could not have been allowed to commit the capital crime of treason without suffering the appropriate punishment.

function as the king. David's decision was to grant a pardon to Shimei, and he made his clemency certain by taking an oath (19:24 [ET 19:23]).

David Deals with Mephibosheth and Ziba
(19:25–31 [ET 19:24–30])

The narration next skips ahead in sequence to Mephibosheth's interaction with David as the king returned to Jerusalem before returning back to events at the Jordan (19:32–40 [ET 19:31–39]). This order is prompted by the previous note that Ziba, Mephibosheth's servant, had come to the Jordan River to welcome David back (19:18 [ET 19:17]), a note that immediately followed the mention of Shimei's presence there.

Mephibosheth's appearance characterized someone who was in mourning (19:25 [ET 19:24]). His display of sorrow over David's loss of the kingdom had given every appearance of being sincere—such behavior would have been risky while Absalom was in power in Jerusalem. Nevertheless, David questioned Mephibosheth over his reasons for not leaving Jerusalem with him (19:26 [ET 19:25]). Perhaps he was suspicious because of his previous encounter with Ziba (16:1–4).

Mephibosheth immediately reported that Ziba had betrayed him (19:27 [ET 19:26]). Ziba had probably abandoned him both when David fled Jerusalem and again in going to the Jordan River to accompany David back to the city. Mephibosheth noted that he would have had to mount his donkey by himself, which might have been impossible for a lame man to do. After noting that Ziba had slandered him, Mephibosheth relied on David to make a ruling, noting that he had been dependent on David's kindness previously (19:28–29 [ET 19:27–28]; cf. 9:1–13). Mephibosheth wisely supposed that David, after his recent experience, might have been especially sensitive to any threat to his realm. He sought to acknowledge David's absolute authority by comparing the king to "the Angel of God." Three times in the book of Samuel, David is said to be like "an angel of God" (1 Sam 29:9) or "the Angel of God" (2 Sam 14:17; 19:28 [ET 19:27]; see also 2 Sam 14:20).

David promptly cut Mephibosheth's words short (19:30 [ET 19:29]). The king probably now realized that his initial response to Ziba may have been precipitous (16:4). He now partially reversed his previous ruling by decreeing that Ziba and Mephibosheth ought to divide Saul's estate. Mephibosheth replied that Ziba could have the entire property (19:31 [ET 19:30]). Mephibosheth was glad that David had safely come back to the palace, and his safe return was dearer to him than any portion of Saul's estate.

Did Ziba take possession of all of Saul's land, as David had decreed earlier (16:4) and as Mephibosheth now allowed (19:31 [ET 19:30]) by relinquishing the portion David had just offered to give him (19:30 [ET 19:29])? Ziba is never mentioned again in Scripture, so we do not know which of David's decrees was implemented. The author of the book of Samuel was more interested in David's interaction with Mephibosheth and what it demonstrated. There are a number of interesting parallels between David's ruling on the contentions of Ziba and Mephibosheth and Solomon's ruling on the contentions of the two prostitutes who claimed the same baby:

David: The Dispute between Mephibosheth and Ziba	Solomon: The Dispute between Two Prostitutes
Seemingly irresolvable claims about Mephibosheth's motives (2 Sam 16:3; 19:27 [ET 19:26])	Seemingly irresolvable claims about a baby (1 Ki 3:16–22)
Ziba had obtained the right to Mephibosheth's property (2 Sam 16:4)	One woman had supposedly obtained (stolen) the baby from the other (1 Ki 3:20)
The king decreed the property to be divided between Ziba and Mephibosheth (2 Sam 19:30 [ET 19:29])	The king decreed the baby to be divided between the two women (1 Ki 3:25)
Mephibosheth ceded all the property to Ziba (2 Sam 19:31 [ET 19:30])	One woman ceded the whole (unharmed) baby to the other (1 Ki 3:26)

Since the book of Samuel was composed sometime after the reign of Solomon,[19] the author may have presented Mephibosheth's words to David and the king's reply in such a way as to evoke the well-known story of Solomon's wisdom. In 1 Ki 3:16–27 Solomon successfully discerned which woman rightfully claimed to be the baby's mother and which claimant had attempted to defraud the other by slander. Here, instead of presenting the conclusion that Mephibosheth must have been the injured party, the author of Samuel allows his readers to draw that conclusion. From antiquity most who have commented on this dispute have concluded that Ziba had indeed slandered Mephibosheth (see the commentary of 16:1–4).

David Grants Barzillai's Request (19:32–40 [ET 19:31–39])

Next the author moves from Jerusalem (19:25–31 [ET 19:24–30]) back in sequence to note Barzillai's presence at David's crossing of the Jordan River (19:32–40 [ET 19:31–39]). This regression in time is prompted by the connection between Mephibosheth and Chimham: both are among those who eat at David's table (9:10–11; 19:39 [ET 19:38]; cf. 1 Ki 2:7).

Once again (as in 17:27) the author identifies Barzillai as hailing from Rogelim in Gilead (19:32 [ET 19:31]). He now adds a parenthetical note about Barzillai's age, the aid he had given to David (see 17:27–28), and his prominence (19:33 [ET 19:32]). All of these explain David's offer to provide for Barzillai in Jerusalem (19:34 [ET 19:33]). Barzillai's reply to David diplomatically declined

---

[19] See "The Composition of Samuel" in Steinmann, *1 Samuel*, 1–3.

the king's offer (19:35–38 [ET 19:34–37]). The author relates an extensive quotation (seventy-five Hebrew words) that gives three reasons that Barzillai should be allowed to return to Rogelim:

1. He was old and had little time left in life. He would not enjoy the king's table because of his failing senses (19:35–36a [ET 19:34–35a]).
2. He would simply be a burden for David (19:36b [ET 19:35b]).
3. Barzillai intended to go only a little way across the river with David, so why should David repay him so much for the little he had given the king (19:37 [ET 19:36])?

Barzillai then followed his reasons with two requests:

1. That he be allowed to return to the city where his parents' tomb was located and die there, implying a desire to be interred with them (19:38a [ET 19:37a]).
2. That Chimham be granted whatever favor David had wanted to give to Barzillai (19:38b [ET 19:37b]).

Chimham is identified only as David's "servant" (19:38 [ET 19:37]), that is, a loyal subject of the king. However, 1 Ki 2:7 may imply that he was one of Barzillai's sons, and this may have influenced Josephus later to state this identification explicitly.[20]

David acceded to Barzillai's request and granted Chimham what he had originally offered to Barzillai (19:39 [ET 19:38]). Chimham's residence may have become a place just outside of Jerusalem toward Bethlehem that was later known as Geruth-chimham, "the residence of Chimham" (גֵּרוּת כִּמְהָם, Jer 41:17). David then sent Barzillai on his way with a kiss (19:40 [ET 19:39]), a sign of affection often reserved for family members.[21] Barzillai was, therefore, like a father to David. In addition, David was kissing one of his supporters as Absalom had kissed those whose support he had sought (15:5).

Israel Disputes David's Welcome Back to the Throne (19:41–44 [ET 19:40–43])

David's next stop was Gilgal, where we are told he was now accompanied by all of Judah but only half of Israel (19:41 [ET 19:40]). This probably reflects the dispute within the northern tribes over whether David ought to be returned to the throne (see 19:10–11 [ET 19:9–10], which reports only *one side* of the dispute).

At Gilgal the men from Israel (i.e., the tribes other than Judah) complained that Judah had "stolen" the king (19:42 [ET 19:41]). Of course, this was David's doing, since he had intervened and suggested to Judah that it preempt Israel's initiative (19:12–14 [ET 19:11–13]).

The men of Judah took offense at the accusation of theft. They offered what they thought was a good reason for their taking the lead in bringing David back as sovereign: they were closer to him, since he was from their tribe

---

[20] Josephus, *Antiquities*, 7.274.

[21] See the third textual note on 14:33.

(19:43 [ET 19:42]; cf. 19:13 [ET 19:12]). Moreover, they leveled their own accusations by raising some questions: Had they eaten from the king's provisions or been honored by David? The other tribes had or would, as evidenced by Mephibosheth from Benjamin and Chimham from one of the Transjordanian tribes (Gad, Reuben, or half of Manasseh).[22]

The retort from the men of Israel also asserted a greater right to bring David back (19:44 [ET 19:43]). They had "ten shares in the king," meaning that they consisted of ten tribes, as opposed to the tribe of Judah and Simeon, which had been absorbed into Judah. They felt that Judah's claim belittled their importance to the kingdom. Moreover, they had been first in entertaining the idea of restoring David (19:10–11 [ET 19:9–10]), so they felt that their right to escort him was greater. However, the author states that the men of Judah were "harsher," or more vociferous, thereby alienating the rest of Israel all the more (19:44 [ET 19:43]).

This argument revealed a rift in the nation of Israel and showed that the tactics David had employed in manipulating the tribes into welcoming him back as king were less effective than he might have anticipated. The rift between Judah and Israel would not only lead to immediate trouble during David's reign (2 Samuel 20) but would also linger to be exposed again after Solomon's death (1 Ki 12:1–19).

---

[22] Chimham was called "your [David's] servant" by Barzillai (19:38 [ET 19:37]), and Barzillai also called himself that (19:36–38 [ET 19:35–37]). Thus, Barzillai was implying that Chimham was from his household. Since Barzillai assumed that Chimham was in line to get whatever David had promised Barzillai, most likely Barzillai was Chimham's father (otherwise Barzillai's assumption would have been presumptuous). Since Barzillai was a Gileadite (19:32 [ET 19:31]), Chimham would have also been one, and thus he would have been from one of the Transjordanian tribes since Gilead was in the Transjordan.

Sheba Rebels

Translation

20 ¹Now a certain good-for-nothing man happened to be there. His name was Sheba the son of Bichri, a Benjaminite man. He sounded a ram's horn and said:

"We have no portion in David!

We have no inheritance in Jesse's son!

Each man to his tent, Israel!"

²So all the men of Israel quit following David and followed Sheba the son of Bichri, but the men of Judah clung to [David,] their king, from the Jordan River to Jerusalem.

³David came to his palace in Jerusalem. The king took the ten concubines whom he had left to take care of the palace and put them in a secure house and provided for them. But he did not go in to them, and they were confined until the day of their death, living as widows.

⁴The king said to Amasa, "Summon the men of Judah for me within three days, and you report here." ⁵Amasa went to summon Judah, and he took longer than the time allotted to him. ⁶So David said to Abishai, "Now Sheba the son of Bichri will do more harm to us than Absalom. You take your master's servants and pursue him. Otherwise he will find fortified cities for himself and escape from us."

⁷Joab's men and the Cherethites and the Pelethites and all the elite troops went out following Abishai. They left Jerusalem to pursue Sheba the son of Bichri. ⁸When they were at the large rock in Gibeon, Amasa came before them. Now Joab was wearing an outer garment with a belt strapped over it on his waist with a sword in its sheath. As he went out it fell.

⁹Joab said to Amasa, "Are you well, my brother?" Joab's right hand grabbed Amasa's beard so that he could kiss him. ¹⁰Amasa was not on guard against the sword that was in Joab's hand. He struck him with it in the stomach, and he spilled his intestines on the ground (he did not do it to him [strike him] again), and he died. Then Joab and his brother Abishai pursued Sheba the son of Bichri.

¹¹One of Joab's young men stood over him and said, "Whoever favors Joab and whoever is for David, follow Joab!" ¹²Amasa was writhing in [his own] blood in the middle of the highway, and the man saw that all the troops stopped. So he moved Amasa from the highway to the field and threw a garment over him as he saw that everyone who came upon him stopped. ¹³When he removed [him] from the highway, every man passed by after Joab to pursue Sheba the son of Bichri.

¹⁴He [Sheba] passed through all the tribes of Israel to Abel-beth-maacah and all the Berites. They gathered and also followed him. ¹⁵They [Joab's troops] came and besieged him in Abel-beth-maacah. They built a siege ramp against the city—it

was located at the rampart—and all the troops with Joab were trying to destroy the wall to make it collapse.

¹⁶A wise woman called from within the city, "Listen! Listen! Please say to Joab, 'Come here, and let me speak to you.'" ¹⁷So he [Joab] came to her, and the woman said, "Are you Joab?"

He said, "I am."

She said to him, "Listen to the words of your servant."

He said, "I'm listening."

¹⁸She said, "They used to say in the past, 'Be sure to ask in Abel.' So they resolved matters. ¹⁹I am one of the peaceful, faithful persons in Israel. You are seeking to kill a city—a mother in Israel. Why would you swallow up Yahweh's inheritance?"

²⁰Joab answered, "I would never, ever swallow up or destroy! ²¹That isn't the case. There is a man from the hill country of Ephraim—Sheba the son of Bichri is his name. He rebelled against King David. Give only him [to me], and I'll leave the city."

The woman said to Joab, "All right. His head will be thrown to you from the wall." ²²The woman went to all the people with her wisdom, and they cut off the head of Sheba the son of Bichri and threw it to Joab. He blew the ram's horn, and every man dispersed from the city to his home. Joab returned to Jerusalem to the king.

²³Joab was over the entire army of Israel.

Benaiah the son of Jehoiada was over the Cherethites and the Pelethites.

²⁴Adoram was over the forced labor.

Jehoshaphat the son of Ahilud was the [royal] historian.

²⁵Sheva was the [royal] scribe.

Zadok and Abiathar were high priests.

²⁶In addition, Ira the Jairite was a priest of David.

Textual Notes

20:1 וְשָׁם נִקְרָא—"Now he happened to be there." The Niphal (N) third masculine singular perfect verb נִקְרָא is of קָרָא II, "to meet, happen," meaning "happen to be" somewhere (*DCH*, Niphal, 2). The word could also be the same form from קָרָא I, which would mean "and he was called, named," but his name is not given until later in the verse.

אִישׁ בְּלִיַּעַל—For "a good for nothing man," see the third textual note on 16:7.

שֶׁבַע בֶּן־בִּכְרִי—"Sheba the son of Bichri." This man is identified this way again in 20:2, 6, 7, 10, 13, 21, 22. The only other verse in the OT with the personal name שֶׁבַע, "Sheba," is 1 Chr 5:13 (for a different man). This is the only OT verse that has the personal name בִּכְרִי, "Bichri."

וַיִּתְקַע בַּשֹּׁפָר—"He blew a ram's horn." For the identical wording, see the textual note on 18:16, where, as usual, the sounding of the shofar signaled victory. Here, however, the horn blast is a treasonous call for the northern tribes of Israel to secede from

David and the tribe of Judah. The shofar was similarly used to announce Absalom's rebellion against his father, King David, in 15:10.

אֵין־לָנוּ חֵלֶק בְּדָוִד וְלֹא נַחֲלָה־לָנוּ בְּבֶן־יִשַׁי—"We have no portion in David! We have no inheritance in Jesse's son!" These two clauses are nominal sentences that stand in synonymous parallelism. In both, a negative (וְלֹא ... אֵין) negates the prepositional phrase לָנוּ, with לְ in the sense of possession, literally "(belonging) to us," thus "we have no."

אִישׁ לְאֹהָלָיו—Literally "(each) man to his tents." See the third textual note on 18:17. This phrase normally occurs after a battle and indicates that each soldier returns home, either in victory (2 Sam 20:22) or fleeing in defeat (1 Sam 4:10; 2 Sam 18:17; 19:9 [ET 19:8]). Here it is spoken as a call for David's soldiers to desert his army (cf. GKC, § 147 c).

20:2 וַיַּעַל כָּל־אִישׁ יִשְׂרָאֵל מֵאַחֲרֵי דָוִד אַחֲרֵי שֶׁבַע—Literally "every man of Israel went up from after David (and went) after Sheba." The preposition אַחַר can be used without a verb (as in its second instance here) in the pregnant sense of following "after" someone. See also 20:11. See the second textual note on 1 Sam 12:14.[1]

דָּבְקוּ בְמַלְכָּם—"They clung to [David,] their king." The idiom דָּבַק בְּ, "cling to," can refer to acting in loyalty to Yahweh (e.g., Deut 10:20; 11:22; 30:20; Josh 22:5; 2 Ki 18:6) or to a person (Ruth 1:14). It is also used for the union of a man with his wife in marriage (Gen 2:24). Similarly, it is used here in a nonliteral, idiomatic sense for the men of Judah remaining loyal to David, their king.

20:3 נָשִׁים ׀ פִּלַגְשִׁים—"Concubines." For this appositional phrase, see the second textual note on 15:16.

הִנִּיחַ—"He had left." This third masculine singular perfect form of נוּחַ is from its second Hiphil (H) paradigm, in which the forms appear as if from a root נָנַח and mean "set; leave" (BDB, s.v. נוּחַ, Hiphil B), as also in 16:11, 21. For its first Hiphil (H) paradigm, see the textual note on 7:1.

לִשְׁמֹר הַבָּיִת—"To take care of the palace." This same infinitive clause expressed David's purpose for leaving these concubines in 15:16.

וַיְכַלְכְּלֵם—"And he provided for them" is literally "and he nourished them." For the Pilpel (D) of כּוּל, "to sustain, support, nourish," see the second textual note on 19:33 (ET 19:32).

וַאֲלֵיהֶם לֹא־בָא—"But he did not go in to them." The Hebrew idiom with the verb בּוֹא and the preposition אֶל, literally "to come in to," refers to sexual intercourse. See the fourth textual note on 3:7.

צְרֻרוֹת עַד־יוֹם מֻתָן—"Confined until the day of their death." The first word is the feminine plural Qal passive (Gp) participle of the verb צָרַר I, "to bind, tie up," meaning "be locked up, be confined" (*DCH*, Qal, 4 c). The last word, מֻתָן, is the Qal (G) infinitive construct of מוּת, "to die," with a third feminine plural suffix.

אַלְמְנוּת חַיּוּת:—"Living as widows." This construct phrase is literally "a widow-hood of livingness." The noun אַלְמְנוּת, with the feminine abstract ending וּת-, signifies "widowhood" (cf. אַלְמָנָה, "widow"). It appears also in Gen 38:14, 19; Is 54:4. Here it

---

is in construct with another feminine abstract noun, חַיּוּת, a hapax legomenon denoting the state of being alive, derived from the verb חָיָה, "to live."

20:4 הַזְעֶק־לִי—"Summon … for me." The verb הַזְעֶק is a bound form of הַזְעֵק, the Hiphil (H) masculine singular imperative of זָעַק, "to cry out." Its Hiphil, literally "to cause a cry," refers to a leader issuing a proclamation that calls men to report for military service, as also in Judg 4:10, 13. The Hiphil (H) infinitive construct (with לְ) לְהַזְעִיק expresses purpose in 20:5, "to summon."

עֲמֹד:—"Report." This masculine singular Qal (G) imperative is literally "stand." David was ordering Amasa to raise an army and report back to David within three days.

20:5 וַיֹּוחֶר—"And he took longer." This Qere, which is the sole reading in a number of Masoretic manuscripts, is the Hiphil (H) third masculine singular preterite (imperfect with *waw* consecutive) of אָחַר, "be late, delay." The verb is spelled phonetically, without the quiescent *aleph* (GKC, § 68 i). The Kethib is another form of the same verb, with the same meaning, "and he delayed." It would apparently be vocalized as וַיֵּיחַר, a Qal (G) preterite (imperfect with *waw* consecutive), or as a Piel (D), וַיְיַחֵר (so GKC, § 68 i).

מִן־הַמּוֹעֵד אֲשֶׁר יְעָדוֹ:—"Than the time allotted to him" is literally "from/than the appointed time which he appointed (for) him." This is a cognate accusative construction. The object noun מוֹעֵד, "appointed time," is derived from the verb יָעַד, "to appoint, designate, assign." The preposition מִן is used in a comparative sense.

20:6 יֵרַע לָנוּ … מִן־אַבְשָׁלוֹם—"He will do more harm to us than Absalom." The Qal (G) of רָעַע, "to be evil, injurious," is used with the preposition מִן in a comparative sense.

וְרָדַף אַחֲרָיו—"And pursue him." The Qal (G) of רָדַף, "chase, pursue," is used with the preposition אַחֲרֵי, "after" someone, again in 20:7, 10, 13.

פֶּן־מָצָא לוֹ—Literally "lest he find for himself." The Qal (G) of מָצָא, "find," can have the nuance "attain, arrive at," or "reach" a place of safety (see BDB, 1 a). Most Masoretic manuscripts have the perfect מָצָא, but two read the imperfect, יִמְצָא.

וְהִצִּיל עֵינֵנוּ:—"And he will escape from us." The Hiphil (H) of נָצַל can mean "take away," and so this clause with the perfect with *waw* consecutive is literally "and he will take away our eye," meaning "elude our sight" (BDB, Hiphil, 1).

20:7 הַגִּבֹּרִים—For "the elite troops," see the textual note on 10:7.

20:8 וְיוֹאָב חָגוּר ׀ מִדּוֹ לְבֻשׁוּ—"Now Joab was wearing an outer garment" is literally "and Joab was girded (with) his outer garment (as) his clothing." For the Qal passive (Gp) participle חָגוּר, indicating the "wearing" of clothing (see Joüon, § 121 o), see the second textual note on 6:14. See also the cognate noun חֲגוֹר, "a belt" for a sword, in the next textual note. The noun מַד can refer to a military "outer garment" worn during warfare, as also in 1 Sam 17:38–39; 18:4.

וְעָלָיו חֲגוֹר חֶרֶב מְצֻמֶּדֶת עַל־מָתְנָיו בְּתַעְרָהּ—"With a belt strapped over it on his waist with a sword in its sheath" is literally "and over it [his outer garment] was a belt of a sword (which was) bound on his waist in its sheath." The noun חֶרֶב, "sword," is feminine and is the implied subject of the Pual (Dp) feminine singular participle מְצֻמֶּדֶת, "bound," from צָמַד, "to bind, join." The third feminine singular suffix on the noun תַּעַר,

"sheath" (בְּתַעְרָהּ, "in *its* sheath") refers back to חֶרֶב, "sword." See also בָהּ, "with it," in 20:10.

וְהוּא יָצָא וַתִּפֹּל:—Literally "he went out, and it fell." The implied subject of the Qal (G) third feminine singular preterite (imperfect with *waw* consecutive) of נָפַל, "fall," is the feminine noun חֶרֶב, "sword" (see the preceding textual note).

20:9 הֲשָׁלוֹם אַתָּה אָחִי—"Are you well, my brother?" is literally "are you peace, my brother?" The pronoun אַתָּה is the subject, and the noun שָׁלוֹם is the predicate in this nominal sentence (see GKC, § 141 c). For the use of שָׁלוֹם, "peace," in a greeting, see the first textual note on 18:28.

וַתֹּחֶז יַד־יְמִין יוֹאָב בִּזְקַן עֲמָשָׂא—"Joab's right hand grabbed Amasa's beard." The verb וַתֹּחֶז is the Qal (G) third feminine singular preterite (imperfect with *waw* consecutive) of אָחַז, "grasp," written phonetically, without the quiescent *aleph* (GKC, § 68 h). This verb commonly takes the preposition בְּ, here on בִּזְקַן. Some Masoretic manuscripts (וַתֹּאחֶז) and 1QSam (ותאחז) spell it in its fuller form. It is feminine because its subject is the feminine noun יָד, "hand," in the construct chain יַד־יְמִין יוֹאָב, literally "the hand of the right of Joab."

לִנְשָׁק־לוֹ:—"So that he could kiss him." The Qal (G) infinitive construct of נָשַׁק with the prefixed preposition לְ forms a purpose clause. The verb "kiss" (נָשַׁק) usually demonstrates a bond of friendship and loyalty under God and his king, but here it is a feigned kiss of betrayal into death. Compare Judas' betrayal of Jesus with a kiss (Mt 26:48–49; Lk 22:47–48). See further the third textual note on 14:33.

20:10 וַעֲמָשָׂא לֹא־נִשְׁמַר בַּחֶרֶב—"Amasa was not on guard against the sword." The Niphal (N) of שָׁמַר here means "be on one's guard" and takes the preposition בְּ (on בַּחֶרֶב) in the sense of "against" (BDB, s.v. שָׁמַר, Niphal, 1; Waltke-O'Connor, § 23.1j, example 1b).

אֶל־הַחֹמֶשׁ—For this prepositional phrase, "in the stomach," see the second textual note on 2:23 (see also 4:6).

וַיִּשְׁפֹּךְ מֵעָיו אַרְצָה—"And he spilled his intestines on the ground." The Qal (G) of שָׁפַךְ has the transitive meaning "to pour [something] out." It can be used for shedding someone's blood (1 Sam 25:31) and has a similar sense here as Joab spills "his [Amasa's] intestines" (מֵעָיו) to the ground.

רָדַף—"He pursued" is a Qal (G) third masculine singular perfect. It is not unusual in Biblical Hebrew for the verb to exhibit concord with only the first element in a compound subject (here וְיוֹאָב וַאֲבִישַׁי אָחִיו), especially when that element is a proper noun. One Masoretic manuscript (רָדְפוּ) and 4QSamᵃ (רדפו) have the plural form.

20:11 מִי אֲשֶׁר חָפֵץ בְּיוֹאָב וּמִי אֲשֶׁר־לְדָוִד—"Whoever favors Joab and whoever is for David." The interrogative pronoun מִי (with אֲשֶׁר) is used twice in an indefinite sense: "whoever" (see BDB, s.v. מִי, g; *IBH*, § 26 A). For the verb חָפֵץ with the preposition בְּ, meaning "to favor [someone]," see the third textual note on 1 Sam 18:22.[2]

אַחֲרֵי יוֹאָב:—"Follow Joab!" is literally "after Joab." A verb of motion is implied with this prepositional phrase. Cf. the second textual note on 20:13.

---

[2] Steinmann, *1 Samuel*, 359.

20:12 מִתְגֹּלֵל—"(Was) writing." This is the Hithpolel (HtD) participle of גָּלַל, "to roll," with a reflexive and iterative sense, "roll oneself over and over."

כָּל־הָעָם—"All the troops." This same construct phrase recurs in 20:15, 22. In military contexts the noun with the article הָעָם, "the people," often denotes "the troops." See the first textual note on 1 Sam 4:3[3] and the second textual note on 2 Sam 1:4.

20:13 הֹגָה—"He removed [him]." This is translated as the Hiphil (H) third masculine singular perfect of יָנָה II (so BDB), meaning "remove" or "expel." This is the only OT instance of this verb, but the Syriac cognate ܓ in the Aphel stem attests the meaning "expel." The form could also be parsed as the Hophal (Hp) third masculine singular perfect of the same verb (so GKC, § 69 w), in which case it would mean "he was removed."

עָבַר כָּל־אִישׁ אַחֲרֵי יוֹאָב—"Every man passed by after Joab." This translation takes כָּל־אִישׁ as the subject and interprets the prepositional phrase אַחֲרֵי יוֹאָב to indicate the direction of motion after passing by Amasa. It is also possible that the prepositional phrase אַחֲרֵי יוֹאָב could modify the subject, כָּל־אִישׁ, in which case the meaning would be "every man (who was following) after Joab passed by [Amasa]." Cf. the second textual note on 20:11.

20:14 This verse is difficult. It has been subjected to many emendations by scholars seeking to make sense of it. The following four textual notes highlight the difficulties.

וַיַּעֲבֹר בְּכָל־שִׁבְטֵי יִשְׂרָאֵל—"He [Sheba] passed through all the tribes of Israel." The subject ("Sheba") of the singular verb is supplied in English for clarity. The verse must be about "Sheba" (שֶׁבַע), named at the end of the preceding verse (20:13), rather than Joab or his followers, who were mentioned earlier in the previous verse. In Biblical Hebrew it is unusual for a noun that is the object of a preposition ending a previous sentence (אַחֲרֵי שֶׁבַע) to become the unstated subject of a preterite (imperfect with *waw* consecutive) verb at the beginning of the next sentence. Normally the subject is made explicit. However, 20:15 begins in a similar way with plural preterite (imperfect with *waw* consecutive) verbs (וַיָּבֹאוּ וַיָּצֻרוּ … וַיִּשְׁפְּכוּ). The subjects of those verbs are not stated but are implied to be Joab and his troops even though Joab and his men are not mentioned in the preceding verse (this verse, 20:14). They are mentioned later in 20:15: וְכָל־הָעָם אֲשֶׁר אֶת־יוֹאָב, "and all the troops (who were) with Joab."

אָבֵלָה וּבֵית מַעֲכָה—The MT reads "to Abel and Beth-maacah."[4] The place-name אָבֵל, "Abel," stands by itself in 20:18 as a short form of the longer place-name in 20:14–15. אָבֵל, "Abel," is used with a directional *he* suffix ("to/at Abel") here in 20:14 and again in 20:15 (אָבֵלָה בֵּית הַמַּעֲכָה). However, the place-name in 20:14–15 most likely should be the construct chain אָבֵל בֵּית־מַעֲכָה, "Abel-beth-maacah." That is its name in 1 Ki 15:20; 2 Ki 15:29. There are five other place-names with "Abel" ("stream"

---

[3] Steinmann, *1 Samuel*, 120.

[4] Some scholars suggest that the conjunction *waw*, "and," indicates that these were twin cities: a walled "Abel" ("stream" or "mourning") and an unwalled "Beth-maacah," one on each side of a stream (e.g., Bergen, *1, 2 Samuel*, 437; similarly, Baldwin, *1 and 2 Samuel*, 279–80; MacLaurin, "Qrt-ʾAblm"). However, there is little to recommend this suggestion. Since the town of Abel was "a mother in Israel" (20:19), it certainly had associated "daughters," i.e., outlying villages (cf., e.g., בָּנוֹת in Josh 15:47; Judg 1:27; 2 Chr 13:19).

or "mourning") in the OT:[5] Abel-mizraim (אָבֵל מִצְרַיִם, "the stream of Egypt" or "the mourning of the Egyptians" [a play on words], Gen 50:11); Abel-meholah (אָבֵל מְחוֹלָה, "stream of dancing," Judg 7:22; 1 Ki 4:12; 19:16); Abel-keramim (אָבֵל כְּרָמִים, "stream of vineyards," Judg 11:33); Abel-maim (אָבֵל מַיִם, "stream of water," 2 Chr 16:4);[6] and Abel-shittim (אָבֵל הַשִּׁטִּים, "the stream of the acacia trees," Num 33:49).[7] None of these passages refer to "Abel *and* [another place-name]," as does the MT here in 2 Sam 20:14. Moreover, of the numerous places named "house of [name]" (... בֵּית‎), none are spelled with an article on the following noun in only some occurrences (as in 20:15: אָבֵלָה בֵּית הַמַּעֲכָה) and without the article in others (as would be the case if אָבֵלָה וּבֵית מַעֲכָה in 20:14 is emended to אָבֵלָה בֵּית מַעֲכָה or to אָבֵל בֵּית מַעֲכָה). Some never have an article (e.g., בֵּית־עֲנָת, "Beth-anath," Josh 19:38; Judg 1:33), and others always have an article (e.g., בֵּית הַיְשִׁמוֹת, "Beth-jeshimoth," Num 33:49; Josh 12:3; 13:20; Ezek 25:9).[8] Thus, it is likely that both of the variations of the place-name here, which is spelled differently in 2 Sam 20:14 than in 20:15, have suffered some corruption in transmission.

וְכָל־הַבֵּרִים—"And all the Berites." This ethnic group is otherwise unattested in the OT. Some English versions and some commentators would emend הַבֵּרִים to הַבִּכְרִים, "the Bichrites," which would refer to the relatives of Sheba "the son of Bichri" (see the third textual note on 20:1).[9] However, no other passage refers to הַבִּכְרִים, "the Bichrites," and this emendation has no textual support.[10]

וַיִּקָּהֲלוּ—"(And) they gathered." This Qere is the sole reading in many Masoretic manuscripts. It is the Niphal (N) third masculine plural preterite (imperfect with *waw*

---

[5] For "stream, brook," see *HALOT*, s.v. אָבֵל II; for "mourning," see *HALOT*, s.v. אָבֵל I. Interestingly, the six places whose names started with "Abel" were probably all located in the Transjordan (although the location of Abel-meholah is debated), which may account for the word אָבֵל, "stream." It has an Aramaic derivation and is not used in the OT with that meaning except in place-names. The cognate Hebrew word is אָבֵל, "watercourse, canal" (Dan 8:2, 3, 6; see *HALOT*, s.v. אָבֵל I). The Hebrew words אָבֵל, "stream," and אָבֵל, "watercourse," are probably from the Aramaic root יבל (see *CAL*, s.v. *ybl, ybl'*, "stream") and exhibit a common interchange of *aleph* for an initial *yod* (see also *HALOT*, s.v. יָבֵל I, "watercourse").

[6] Abel-maim appears to be an alternate name for Abel-beth-maacah. See the parallel, 1 Ki 15:20.

[7] Abel-shittim was probably the place more commonly known as just Shittim (הַשִּׁטִּים, "the acacia trees," Num 25:1; Josh 2:1; 3:1; Micah 6:5; see BDB, s.v. שִׁטִּים, 1). Shittim was the location of the final encampment of the Israelites in the plains of Moab before they entered the promised land.

[8] Note, however, that Beth-shemesh (בֵּית־שֶׁמֶשׁ; twenty occurrences, e.g., Josh 15:10) never has an article. However, when it is converted to a gentilic, "the Beth-shemeshite," an article is added (בֵּית־הַשִּׁמְשִׁי, 1 Sam 6:14, 18).

[9] ESV; NIV; NRSV; Hertzberg, *I and II Samuel*, 369; McCarter, *II Samuel*, 429; Anderson, *2 Samuel*, 234; Baldwin, *1 and 2 Samuel*, 280.

[10] McCarter, *II Samuel*, 428, and Anderson, *2 Samuel*, 234, claim that the LXX reading καὶ πάντες ἐν Χαρρι, "and all those in Charri," is support for reading the Hebrew text as וְכָל־הַבִּכְרִים, "and all the Bichrites." However, the LXX actually implies a Hebrew reading וְכֹל בְּכָרִי (the second word would be the preposition בְּ prefixed to the place-name כָּרִי). It is difficult to see how the Hebrew reading implied by the LXX, וְכֹל בְּכָרִי, could have become the MT reading וְכָל־הַבֵּרִים, since that would require a loss of the *kaph* in בְּכָרִי as well as the addition of *he* and *mem* to make הַבֵּרִים.

consecutive) of קָהַל, meaning "to gather" in an intransitive sense. The Qere, meaning "and they gathered," makes sense with the following clause, וַיָּבֹאוּ אַף־אַחֲרָיו, literally "and they too came after him," i.e., "and they also followed him." It is also supported by the LXX, which reads καὶ ἐξεκκλησιάσθησαν, "and they were gathered."[11]

If the Kethib, ויקלהו, were pointed as וַיְקַלְּהוּ, then it could be a Hiphil (H) third masculine plural preterite (imperfect with *waw* consecutive) of קָלַל, "to curse," with a third masculine singular object suffix, meaning "and they treated him with contempt" (cf. הֵקַלֹּתַנִי in 19:44 [ET 19:43]). However, that meaning would not fit with the following clause, which states that they became followers of Sheba. The Kethib probably suffered from an accidental metathesis of the *lamed* and *he*.

Both readings are somewhat difficult. No explicit subject is given for this and the following verb (וַיִּקָּהֲלוּ וַיָּבֹאוּ). An explicit subject would have to follow (not precede) these preterite (imperfect with *waw* consecutive) verbs. Who "gathered and came"? (Or, for the Kethib, who treated Sheba with contempt?) The preceding clause referred to "all the tribes of Israel" and then "all the Berites," so one or both of those groups (or some of their members) may be implied as the subjects.

20:15 וַיָּצֻרוּ עָלָיו—"And they besieged him." See the fifth textual note on 11:1, which has the identical verb form and the same preposition, עַל, indicating a hostile action against someone/something. See also the preposition in אֶל־הָעִיר, "against the city," later in this verse.

וַיִּשְׁפְּכוּ סֹלְלָה—"They built a siege ramp" is literally "and they poured out a siege ramp." The verb שָׁפַךְ, "pour out," is used idiomatically with the noun סֹלְלָה, "siege ramp," for constructing a ramp against some fortification.[12]

וַתַּעֲמֹד בַּחֵל—"It was located at the rampart." The implied subject of the Qal (G) third feminine singular preterite (imperfect with *waw* consecutive) וַתַּעֲמֹד, literally "and it stood," is the preceding feminine noun סֹלְלָה, "siege ramp."

מַשְׁחִיתִם—"(Were) trying to destroy." The verb שָׁחַת is used in the Hiphil (H) here and in 20:20 to mean "destroy." See the fourth textual note on 11:1. Here it may imply that Joab's men were using battering rams against the wall.

20:17 אֲמָתֶךָ—"Your servant." For the feminine noun אָמָה, "(female) servant," see the third and fourth textual notes on 1 Sam 1:11[13] and the second textual note on 2 Sam 14:15. It is a close synonym of the feminine noun שִׁפְחָה, "slave girl" or female household "servant" (see the first textual note on 2 Sam 14:6).

20:18 שָׁאֹל יְשָׁאֲלוּ—"Be sure to ask." The Qal (G) infinitive absolute of שָׁאַל is used for emphasis with its Piel (D) third masculine plural imperfect (GKC, § 113 w; Joüon,

---

11 Some scholars propose on the basis of the LXX verb ἐξεκκλησιάσθησαν, "they were gathered," that the verb originally was נִקְהֲלוּ, a Niphal (N) third common plural perfect, and that it follows its explicit subject (McCarter, *II Samuel*, 425, 428; see also Anderson, *2 Samuel*, 231, 234). However, because of the conjunction καί, the LXX actually implies the reading of the Qere.

12 See the idiom also in 2 Ki 19:32; Is 37:33; Jer 6:6; Ezek 4:2; 17:17; 21:27 (ET 21:22); 26:8; Dan 11:15.

13 Steinmann, *1 Samuel*, 48.

§ 123 p). This is one of only two instances of the Piel of שָׁאַל in the OT, and it apparently has the nuance "inquire carefully" (BDB, Piel, 1). (The other instance is in Ps 109:10, where it refers to begging.)

הֵתַמּוּ:—"They resolved matters." This is the Hiphil (H) third common plural perfect of תָּמַם, whose Qal (G) means "be complete, perfect."

20:19 אָנֹכִי שְׁלֻמֵי אֱמוּנֵי יִשְׂרָאֵל—"I am one of the peaceful, faithful persons in Israel." The first word in the three-word construct chain, שְׁלֻמֵי, is the construct form of the masculine plural Qal passive (Gp) participle of שָׁלֵם, "be at peace." The second is the construct form of the masculine plural Qal passive (Gp) participle of אָמַן, which has the intransitive meaning "faithful" (BDB, Qal, 4 b).

עִיר וְאֵם—Literally "a city and a mother." The woman may allude to mothers in the city, including herself, or mean "a city which is a mother," or both. See the commentary.

תְבַלַּע—"You would swallow up." Another Piel (D) imperfect of בָּלַע is used in 20:20. Cf. the Pual (Dp) in the fifth textual note on 17:16.

20:20 חָלִילָה חָלִילָה לִי אִם־—See the second textual note on 1 Sam 2:30.[14] After the oathlike formula, the particle אִם serves as a negative (GKC, § 149 a, e; cf. Joüon, § 165 k).

20:21 לֹא־כֵן הַדָּבָר כִּי—Literally "the word/matter is not thus, but" (see Joüon, § 172 c).

נָשָׂא יָדוֹ בַּמֶּלֶךְ בְּדָוִד—"He rebelled against King David" is literally "he lifted up his hand against the king, against David." See this idiom also in the fifth textual note on 18:28.

וְאֵלְכָה מֵעַל הָעִיר—"And I'll leave the city." The combination of prepositions מֵעַל (מִן + עַל), literally "from against," means that Joab will abandon his assault against the city. Cf. עַל in the first textual note on 20:15.

הִנֵּה רֹאשׁוֹ מֻשְׁלָךְ—Literally "look, his head is being thrown." The verb is the masculine singular Hophal (Hp) participle of שָׁלַךְ (GKC, § 53 s), whose Hiphil (H) means "to throw" (11:21; 18:17; 20:12, 22). The particle הִנֵּה with a participle can refer to an action in the imminent future that is so certain that it can be described as if it is already taking place (GKC, § 116 p; Joüon, § 121 e).

בְּעַד הַחוֹמָה:—"From the wall." The combination of prepositions בְּעַד (בְּ + עַד) can refer to action "through" a window (1 Sam 19:12; 2 Sam 6:16). This could imply that Sheba's head will be thrown "through" a window or opening in the city wall.

20:22 The statements in the next two textual notes were also used earlier in 20:1 to refer to Sheba's actions that initiated his revolt. Ironically, they form an inclusio around the battle by signaling his defeat by decapitation here.

וַיִּתְקַע בַּשּׁוֹפָר—Literally "and he blew with the ram's horn." See the fourth textual note on 20:1 and also the textual note on 18:16.

אִישׁ לְאֹהָלָיו—Literally "(each) man to his tents." Here, as usual, this phrase marks the conclusion of a battle, in contrast to Sheba's use of it in his summons (see the sixth textual note on 20:1).

---

[14] Steinmann, *1 Samuel*, 100.

20:23 אֶל—"Over." Samuel is one of the OT books in which the preposition אֶל (usually meaning "to") is often used in place of עַל ("over"). See the first textual note on 2 Sam 2:9 and the second textual note on 2 Sam 3:29.

וּבְנָיָה בֶּן־יְהוֹיָדָע עַל־הַכְּרֵתִי וְעַל־הַפְּלֵתִי—"Benaiah the son of Jehoiada was over the Cherethites and the Pelethites." This was also stated in 8:18 (cf. 1 Ki 1:38, 44).

20:24 הַמַּס—The noun מַס is a singular collective that refers to a body of forced laborers.[15]

הַמַּזְכִּיר:—For this title, "the [royal] historian," see the second textual note on 8:16.

20:25 וּשְׁיָא—"(And) Sheva" is the Qere. The Kethib is וְשֵׁיָא, "(and) Sheya." In 8:17 this man was called שְׂרָיָה, "Seraiah." See the third textual note on 8:17.

סֹפֵר—For "scribe," see the fourth textual note on 8:17.

כֹּהֲנִים:—Zadok and Abiathar apparently shared the high priesthood under David. For this plural meaning "*high* priests," see the second textual note on 8:17 and the first textual note on 17:15.

20:26 עִירָא הַיָּאִרִי—"Ira the Jairite." There is no known Jairite clan among the Aaronides, so this name has become the subject of some discussion.[16] Two LXX manuscripts call him ὁ Ιεθερ, "the Ither(ite)," and there is some support for this in the Syriac.[17] However, this appears to be an assimilation to another Ira—Ira the Ithrite (עִירָא הַיִּתְרִי) among David's thirty prominent soldiers (2 Sam 23:38 ‖ 1 Chr 11:40).

כֹּהֵן לְדָוִד:—This circumlocution, "a priest (belonging) to David," is used to name a priest in addition to the two named in 20:25. If a construct phrase had been used here, כֹּהֵן דָּוִד, it would mean that Ira was "David's priest" or "*the* priest of David," as if he were the sole priest for David.

Commentary

973 BC[18]

This chapter brings to a close the third major section of 2 Samuel: David's failures and struggles (9:1–20:26). The major character in this chapter is not David or Sheba, but Joab. This focus on David's nephew enables the author to underscore two struggles David faced. The first was his struggle to resecure his grasp on Israel's kingship after his sins in 2 Samuel 11 had precipitated the turmoil and insurrection recorded in 2 Samuel 12–19. This effort was concluded successfully by Joab obtaining the head of Sheba (20:22). The other struggle, which David was unable to resolve successfully, involved his inability to restrain Joab and remove him from the command of Israel's army. By relating the events surrounding Sheba's rebellion, the author demonstrates that David's need for a secure position as monarch ran counter to his desire to remove Joab. Joab's skill as a military leader was essential for the stability of David's throne.

---

[15] Also, e.g., in Gen 49:15; Ex 1:11; Deut 20:11; Josh 16:10; 1 Ki 5:27–28 (ET 5:13–14).

[16] See, e.g., Elitzur, "Ira ha-Yairi and the Sons of David."

[17] McCarter, *II Samuel*, 434.

[18] See "The Chronology of David's Reign" in the commentary on 5:1–5.

While Joab's methods were at times insubordinate, violent, and immoral, he often understood more clearly than David what threats to the king's position needed to be handled swiftly and effectively. Thus, in the end, although David had demoted Joab and promoted Amasa to fill his position (19:14 [ET 19:13]), the king was forced to reinstate Joab as commander of the army (20:23). David would not be able to deal with the misdeeds of this son of Zeruiah directly,[19] but he would have to use Solomon to rid the palace of Joab (1 Ki 2:5–6, 28–34).

Sheba Foments Rebellion (20:1–2)

When the quarrel over David broke out between Judah and the rest of the tribes at Gilgal, Sheba was there (19:42–20:1 [ET 19:41–20:1]). The strident words of the Judahites led to Sheba's call for secession from David's kingdom. His call took for a fact that Judah had "stolen" the king (19:42 [ET 19:41]) and that the rest of Israel had no vested interest in David. This rallying cry would be revived later when Israel broke away from Rehoboam (1 Ki 12:16).

The antagonist is introduced as "Sheba the son of Bichri," and this full name is always used for him.[20] His father is never mentioned elsewhere in the OT. Some view "the son of Bichri" as a reference to his relationship to a more distant ancestor, a man from Saul's clan named Becorath (בְּכוֹרַת, 1 Sam 9:1).[21] If that were the case his full name would perhaps have been "Sheba the son of a Bichrite." However, Joab would later clearly identify the man whom he sought as "a man from the hill country of Ephraim—Sheba the son of Bichri" (20:21). Therefore, Sheba was an Ephraimite, not a Saulide from the tribe of Benjamin. David's troubles had become so severe that he no longer simply faced rivals from his own family (e.g., Absalom) and from Saul's house (e.g., Shimei). Now opposition had spread to the point where other Israelite clans were bold enough to challenge his rule.

We are told that the men of Israel followed Sheba and that only the men of Judah stayed with David on his trip back to Jerusalem (20:2). However, it appears as if Sheba's active followers were not numerous, since Joab would be able to suppress the rebellion by obtaining only Sheba's head (20:22).

David Takes Charge Again in Jerusalem (20:3–6)

David's only reported activity during the rebellion consists of two decisions. The first was his sequestering of the ten concubines he had left in charge of the palace and with whom Absalom had slept (20:3; cf. 15:16; 16:21–22). David continued to protect and provide for them, but they were confined and had no further contact with David. He refrained from intimacy with them, and they were treated as if they had been widowed. His son Absalom had taken them as

---

[19] Joab, Abishai, and Asahel were the three sons of Zeruiah (2 Sam 2:18). For Joab and Abishai, see also, e.g., 1 Sam 26:6; 2 Sam 2:24; 3:30; 18:2.

[20] 2 Sam 20:1, 2, 6, 7, 10, 13, 21, 22.

[21] Hertzberg, *I and II Samuel*, 371; Anderson, *2 Samuel*, 240.

his own concubines before he was killed (16:21–22). The Law of Moses forbade a father from intimacy with a daughter-in-law (Lev 18:15; cf. Lev 20:12).

David's second decision was to move quickly to suppress Sheba's revolt. Unlike Absalom, whose delay in attacking David enabled David to mount a successful defense against the insurgent prince, David knew that he had to nip the rebellion in the bud. Since Amasa had been appointed as the new commander of the army (19:14 [ET 19:13]), David told him to raise an army quickly—in just three days—and report back (20:4). However, apparently the inexperienced Amasa was unable to recruit a fighting force or took longer to do it than David had given him or simply did nothing (20:5). David next turned to his nephew Abishai, Joab's brother, and ordered him to take the standing army ("your master's servants") and pursue Sheba (20:6). David said that given the delay in responding to Sheba, Sheba could do more harm than Absalom. The longer David's army delayed in taking the field, the weaker he appeared and the more emboldened Sheba's supporters would be. If Sheba found several fortified cities to support him, he could construct a formidable network of resistance to David.

That David turned to Abishai and did not reinstate Joab hints that he was seeking to permanently demote his former commander. Joab had failed to comply with David's command that he not kill Absalom (18:5, 14–17) and then had reproved the king for mourning his slain son (19:2–8 [ET 19:1–7]). It was problematic that David had few experienced Israelite field generals whom he could appoint as chief commander. Abishai was the most experienced and in some ways was the logical choice (10:10; 18:2). However, Abishai was Joab's brother, and this left Joab just one step away from his former office.

Joab Assassinates Amasa at Gibeon (20:7–10)

Abishai led David's immediately available troops out after Sheba (20:7). They were David's small standing army and consisted of four units. One of these consisted of "Joab's men," as the author identifies them, hinting that Joab still had the loyalty of the unit he commanded directly. "The Cherethites" and "the Pelethites" were units of David's mercenary forces (see the commentary on 8:18). "All the elite troops" were probably a mostly native Israelite unit (cf. 23:8–39), as opposed to the foreign mercenaries that made up the Cherethites and Pelethites.

Pursuit of Sheba led Abishai and the army to Gibeon in Benjamin,[22] perhaps as a gateway to Sheba's territory, the hill country of Ephraim (20:21). There at a large rock, which must have been an important landmark since it is used as a reference point by the author of the book of Samuel, Amasa finally presented himself before the troops (20:8). No mention is made of Amasa arriving with troops he had conscripted from Judah (per David's command in 20:4), though

---

[22] See figure 9, "The Rebellions of Absalom (2 Samuel 15–19) and Sheba (2 Samuel 20)," at the end of the commentary on 17:1–29.

apparently Josephus later assumed that he had brought men with him.[23] Amasa may well have assumed that he would now take command of the Judean armed forces. However, Joab had other ideas.

While the text is not clear as to the details of Joab's greeting and execution of Amasa, Neiderhiser has presented perhaps the most cogent explanation of 20:8–10:

> Joab is girded and attired like any soldier on his way to war. As he goes out to meet Amasa, who is belatedly joining the army, his sword falls out of its sheath. One can assume that even a seasoned veteran such as Joab could have an equipment malfunction at an unguarded moment. Probably an embarrassment similar to that of a modern soldier whose rifle slips off his shoulder but an occasional happening nonetheless, it is certainly in this case contrived by Joab. With a natural motion, given such circumstances, he picks it up with his left hand and continues to greet Amasa. The specific reference of the text to the right hand is intentional. The right hand is the hand with which one does battle. It is empty here, and thus no threat is implied. In fact it is used to grasp the beard as part of the greeting kiss so common among kinsmen and friends. The "accidentally" dropped sword dangling idly in the left hand is not a recognizable danger. Such is not a posture of combat or offense. Amasa, completely taken in by the ruse of Joab and by the friendly greeting, pays no attention[6] to the weapon that with a single blow works his demise. The narrator by telling us that the sword fell out and that Joab used his right hand to grasp the beard of Amasa and that Amasa paid no attention to the sword in Joab's hand (the left hand is the only one available since the right one is occupied) tells us clearly what happened. For him to explain further would be to insult the intelligence of his reader.[24]

Joab's unexpected use of his left hand to wield a weapon is reminiscent of Ehud's assassination of Eglon (Judg 3:21). In Semitic cultures the left hand was often thought of as inferior[25] and nearly useless, if not inherently deleterious (cf. Eccl 10:2), explaining Amasa's lack of alarm at Joab's approach with a sword.

The Troops Rally behind Joab and Pursue Sheba (20:11–15)

One of Joab's loyal men stood over the slain Amasa and rallied the troops behind Joab, equating allegiance to Joab with allegiance to David (20:11). Since he saw that the writhing of Amasa in his death throes in the middle of the highway caused the men to hesitate, he moved him and covered him as the army now followed Joab (20:12–13). Now Joab had regained his position of leadership, at least in the eyes of the troops. From this point on, the author portrays

---

[23] Josephus, *Antiquities*, 7.283.

[24] Neiderhiser, "2 Samuel 20:8–10," 210.

[25] See, e.g., Gen 48:13–14. The right hand is used for the main activity, while the left hand plays a supporting role in Judg 7:20; Ezek 39:3; Song 2:6; 8:3. To be ambidextrous was remarkable (1 Chr 12:1–2). Some English terms that are derived from Latin preserve the preference for the "right hand" (*dextera*), including "dexterity" and "ambidextrous" (both hands are "right hands") and the evil connotation of the word for the "left," *sinister*.

Joab as the leader of the expedition to end Sheba's rebellion, even though David had entrusted the task to Abishai (20:6).

As the Judeans tracked Sheba, he passed northward through Israel until he came to Abel-beth-maacah in the extreme north (20:14).[26] The modern site of this city is called Abil el-Kamh. It lies to the northwest of Lake Huleh on the eastern side of the Derdara River. There, apparently exhausted and no longer able to flee, Sheba took refuge in the city. In keeping with ancient tactics, Joab mounted a siege of the city with a siege ramp and attempted to breach the city's defensive wall (20:15).[27]

A Wise Woman's Intervention Saves Abel-beth-maacah (20:16–22)

As the city appeared to be susceptible to Joab's forces, a woman called out to the troops and asked for Joab (20:16). The author calls her "wise," perhaps rendering in advance his verdict about her successful negotiation with Joab. It has been noted that this woman was rhetorically skilled; she hastily deployed "a barrage of wordy weapons including four commands, two questions, one proverb, an accusation, and a promise."[28]

She deftly engaged Joab in a conversation, first asking whether it was Joab that she was addressing and then requesting that he consider her offer as coming from one of his humble servants (20:17). Joab must have been doubly flattered by her opening. First of all, she assumed that he would be in charge, thereby acknowledging his reputation. She probably did not know of David's change in commanders (19:14 [ET 19:13]; 20:6) and may have been ignorant of the outcome of Absalom's rebellion. Second, she used the deferential language of a person of inferior status speaking to a superior.

The woman then moved on to quote an aphorism: "be sure to ask in Abel" (20:18). While there have been a number of suggestions as to what this saying might have meant, it is best to understand it in light of her next statement: Israelites "resolved matters" there. That is, just ask for what you want or need, and it can be negotiated. Her indictment of Joab was that he did not seek first to make an offer of peace—demanding that the city surrender Sheba—before besieging it, as required in the Law of Moses (Deut 20:10–12).

Then the woman moved on to note that she was peaceful and faithful—not a rebel against the crown (20:19). However, Joab was not treating her that way.

---

[26] See figure 9, "The Rebellions of Absalom (2 Samuel 15–19) and Sheba (2 Samuel 20)," at the end of the commentary on 17:1–29.

[27] Joab's action of besieging Abel-beth-maacah indicates that his initial goal was to extirpate Sheba and his followers from the land—even if that involved the loss of innocent lives in Abel. Had Joab originally wanted only to kill Sheba, he would have first sought to negotiate, not commenced building a siege ramp and battering the city's wall. His words in 20:20–21 appear simply to be a face-saving public denial when confronted by the accusation of the wise woman (20:19).

[28] Branch, "Women Who Win with Words," 307.

He was trying to destroy her and her city, "a mother in Israel." While it has been debated whether the woman's reference to "a mother in Israel" was to the city or to herself, it is probably best to understand it as a double entendre. Joab was attacking Israelite motherhood, the very means through which God grants his sacred gift of life. Motherhood was represented by the woman and also by the city. Note that the only other use of the phrase "a mother in Israel" in the OT was applied to a woman—Deborah (Judg 5:7). However, a walled city was considered the mother of its outlying villages, which were called its "daughters" (e.g., בָּנוֹת in Josh 15:47; Judg 1:27; 2 Chr 13:19). The villages were economically dependent on the larger city, and its walls also provided the people who lived in the villages a place of refuge from invading armies.

Finally, the woman noted that Joab's action would "swallow up Yahweh's inheritance" (20:19). Thus, she implied that Joab's actions were hostile not simply to Abel but also to Yahweh. The use of the word "inheritance" (נַחֲלָה) takes the reader back to 20:1, where Sheba claimed that the northern tribes had "no inheritance" (נַחֲלָה) in Jesse's son. If Joab were to destroy the city, he would prove Sheba to be correct.

Joab was cornered by her logic and quickly denied any intention of swallowing or destroying (20:20). Instead, he claimed that his only target was Sheba and that he would be content to vanquish him alone (20:21). Joab included Sheba's crime—"he rebelled against King David"—to make sure that the citizens of Abel understood that Sheba was guilty of treason and that Absalom was no longer a contender for the throne.

The account quickly draws to a close once the woman promised Sheba's head to Joab. The woman's wisdom was as convincing to the people of Abel as it was to Joab, and Sheba was decapitated (20:22). Joab sounded the end of the conflict on the ram's horn, the army dispersed, and Joab returned to David.[29]

David's Officials (20:23–26)

The list of David's officials is the second in the book. For the first, see the commentary on 8:15–18, including figure 7, which compares the two lists. The list here, however, appears to derive from the latter part of David's reign. It is placed in this chapter to demonstrate that Joab had regained his position as commander of the army despite David's attempts to demote him (19:14 [ET 19:13]; 20:6). In addition, unlike the previous list of officials, this list appears to be organized into three groups: commanders of the army (20:23), government administrators (20:24–25a), and priests (20:25b–26).

There are three changes from the earlier list. First is the inclusion of an official in charge of "the forced labor," Adoram (20:24). This position probably became necessary late in David's reign as he began to make preparations for the construction of the temple (972–969 BC; see 1 Chr 22:2–29:25, especially 1 Chr 22:2–5). Adoram probably was a fairly young man when he was

---

[29] See the textual notes on 20:22.

appointed, since he served in this position throughout Solomon's forty-year reign (1 Ki 4:6; 5:28 [ET 5:14]).[30] Late in Solomon's reign, when Adoram was much older, he was probably replaced for a while by Jeroboam (1 Ki 11:28). However, with Jeroboam's exile to Egypt, Adoram may have been brought back into service. Early in Rehoboam's reign Adoram was again the official in charge of forced labor when he was brutally murdered (1 Ki 12:18).

The second change is the elimination of David's sons from administrative positions in the palace (see the commentary on 8:18). After the outrageous behavior of his son Amnon (13:1–22) and the acts of murder and rebellion by his son Absalom (13:23–18:18), it may have been thought best to remove the princes from day-to-day administration in the kingdom.

The final change is the addition of Ira the Jairite as a priest of David (20:26). Once again, this may have been due to David's preparations for building the temple. Ira probably served alongside the high priests Zadok and Abiathar (20:25) and was in charge of the details of implementing David's orders concerning the priests and Levites (1 Chronicles 23–26).

---

[30] His name is give as Adoniram (אֲדֹנִירָם) in 1 Ki 4:6; 5:28 (ET 5:14).

2 Samuel 21:1–24:25

David the Faithful Warrior and King

David Avenges Saul's Killing of the Gibeonites

Translation

21 ¹For three years during the days of David there was a famine year after year, so David consulted Yahweh. Yahweh said, "[It is] because of Saul and because of the house of bloodshed, since he killed the Gibeonites."

²The king called the Gibeonites and spoke to them. (The Gibeonites are not [descended] from the Israelites. Rather, they are from a remnant of the Amorites. The Israelites had sworn an oath to them. However, Saul sought to strike them down in his zeal for the Israelites and Judah.) ³David said to the Gibeonites, "What can I do for you? With what can I make atonement so that you will bless Yahweh's inheritance?"

⁴The Gibeonites said to him, "For us it is not a matter of silver and gold with Saul and his house. In addition, we are not allowed to kill a man in Israel."

He said, "Whatever you say I will do for you."

⁵They said to the king, "The man who annihilated us and plotted against us, that we should be destroyed so as not to have a place within all the borders of Israel— ⁶let seven men from his descendants be given to us, and we will hang them [their dead bodies] before Yahweh in Gibeah of Saul, Yahweh's chosen [king]."

The king said, "I will give [them to you]."

⁷However, the king had compassion on Mephibosheth the son of Jonathan, Saul's son, because of Yahweh's oath between them, between David and Saul's son Jonathan. ⁸The king took the two sons of Aiah's daughter Rizpah whom she had borne to Saul—Armoni and Mephibosheth—as well as the five sons of Saul's daughter Merab whom she had borne to Adriel the son of Barzillai the Meholathite. ⁹He handed them over to the Gibeonites, and they hung them [their dead bodies] on the hill before Yahweh. The seven of them died together. They were killed in the first days of the harvest, at the beginning of the barley harvest.

¹⁰Aiah's daughter Rizpah took sackcloth and spread it out for herself on the rock from the beginning of the harvest until it rained from the sky on them. She did not allow a bird of the sky to rest on them by day nor a wild animal by night. ¹¹When David was told what Rizpah, Aiah's daughter and Saul's concubine, did, ¹²David went and took the bones of Saul and the bones of his son Jonathan from the citizens of Jabesh-gilead. (They had stolen them from the public square of Beth-shan, where the Philistines had hung them on the day the Philistines had struck Saul down at Gilboa.) ¹³He brought up the bones of Saul and the bones of his son Jonathan. They collected the bones of those who had been hung ¹⁴and interred the bones of Saul and his son Jonathan in the territory of Benjamin in Zela in the

tomb of his father, Kish. They did all that the king commanded. After this, God responded to the plea for the land.

Textual Notes

21:1 וַיְבַקֵּשׁ דָּוִד אֶת־פְּנֵי יְהוָה—"So David consulted Yahweh" is literally "and David sought Yahweh's face." This idiom, the Piel (D) of בָּקַשׁ, "seek," with the direct object פָּנִים, "face," refers to people seeking Yahweh's face in repentance and faith in Hos 5:15; Pss 24:6; 27:8; Ps 105:4 ‖ 1 Chr 16:11; 2 Chr 7:14 (cf. Zech 8:21–22). The idiom is also used for kings seeking to consult Solomon for his God-given wisdom (2 Chr 9:23; cf. Prov 29:26).

אֶל־שָׁאוּל וְאֶל־בֵּית הַדָּמִים—"Because of Saul and because of the house of blood-shed." The book of Samuel often uses the preposition אֶל in place of the preposition עַל (see the first textual note on 2 Sam 2:9 and the second textual note on 2 Sam 3:29). Twice here אֶל has the causal nuance "because of," which is more commonly expressed with עַל (as in the next clause, עַל־אֲשֶׁר־הֵמִית, "because/since he killed").

21:2 וְהַגִּבְעֹנִים לֹא מִבְּנֵי יִשְׂרָאֵל—"The Gibeonites are not [descended] from the Israelites." This could also mean "the Gibeonites are not [descended] from the sons of Israel," that is, not from any of the twelve sons of Jacob. The use of לֹא, rather than אֵין, in a nominal clause is emphatic (Joüon, § 160 b).

מִיֶּתֶר—"From a remnant of." For the noun יֶתֶר, "the rest, remnant, what remains," see the second textual note on 8:4.

נִשְׁבְּעוּ—"They had sworn an oath." The Niphal (N) of שָׁבַע referred to the swearing of the oath to the Gibeonites in Josh 9:15, 18, 19, 20.

לְהַכֹּתָם בְּקַנֹּאתוֹ—"To strike them down in his zeal." These two verbs are infinitive constructs. The first is the Hiphil (H) of נָכָה with a third masculine plural object suffix and the preposition לְ, indicating purpose. The second is the Piel (D) of קָנָא, "be jeal-ous" (a verb that is denominative from the noun קִנְאָה, "zeal") with the preposition בְּ and a third masculine singular subjective suffix. The infinitive's ending את- is formed as if from a third-*he* root (קנה) instead of a third-*aleph* root (קנא); see GKC, § 74 h.

21:3 אֲכַפֵּר וּבָרְכוּ—"Can I make atonement so that you will bless?" The Piel (D) of כָּפַר is frequent in Leviticus and Numbers as the liturgical technical term for making atone-ment by offering a vicarious sacrifice at the tabernacle (e.g., Lev 1:4; 4:20, 26, 31, 35). See also its Hithpael (HtD) in 1 Sam 3:14. The Piel masculine plural imperative (with the conjunction *waw*) וּבָרְכוּ expresses purpose, "so that you will bless" (GKC, § 110 i; Joüon, §§ 116 g; 161 m). David desires the Gibeonites to pronounce an oral benedic-tion that calls upon Yahweh to bless his people. For the Piel (D) of בָּרַךְ, see the textual note on 2 Sam 6:11–12, as well as the first textual note on 1 Sam 2:20 and the third tex-tual note on 1 Sam 9:13.[1]

21:4 לָנוּ—"For us" is the reading of the Qere and the LXX (ἡμῖν). The Kethib is לִי, "for me."

---

[1] Steinmann, *1 Samuel*, 90, 179.

וְאֵין־לָנוּ אִישׁ לְהָמִית—Literally "it does not exist for us to kill a man." The Hiphil (H) infinitive construct of מוּת with the preposition לְ has the sense of permission, thus "we are not allowed" (see Waltke-O'Connor, § 36.2.3f, including example 38).

מַה־אַתֶּם אֹמְרִים אֶעֱשֶׂה לָכֶם:—Literally "what are you saying I should do for you?" The imperfect אֶעֱשֶׂה is subordinate to the participle אֹמְרִים (GKC, § 120 c).

21:5 הָאִישׁ אֲשֶׁר כִּלָּנוּ—"The man who annihilated us." כִּלָּנוּ is the Piel (D) third masculine singular perfect of כָּלָה with a first common plural pronominal suffix. In the Qal (G), כָּלָה means "come to an end" or "perish," and its Piel (D) has the causative meaning "destroy, annihilate" (BDB, Piel, 2 c).

וַאֲשֶׁר דִּמָּה־לָנוּ—"And who plotted against us." In the Piel (D), the verb דָּמָה I usually means "to liken" or "to think," but here it has the nuance "to devise" or "to plot" evil (see BDB, Piel, 2, and *DCH*, Piel, 2 a). The preposition לְ has the sense of disadvantage, "against" (see BDB, 5 h (*b*) (γ)).

נִשְׁמַדְנוּ—"That we should be destroyed." In context this verb begins a purpose clause. It is the Niphal (N) first common plural perfect of שָׁמַד.

מֵהִתְיַצֵּב—"So as not to have a place." This is the Hithpael (HtD) infinitive construct of יָצַב. This verb, which occurs only in the Hithpael, usually means "take one's stand" (cf. 18:30; 23:12), but it can have the nuance "have a place" (see BDB, Hithpael, a). When the preposition מִן is prefixed to an infinitive construct, it often indicates a negative result, "so as not to" (BDB, 7 b (*a*)).

21:6 יֻתַּן־לָנוּ—"Let … be given to us." This verb is the Qere. It is the Qal passive (Gp) third masculine singular jussive of נָתַן, "give." The Kethib is יִנָּתֵן, the Niphal (N) third masculine singular jussive. 4QSam^a reads ונתתם, probably to be vocalized וּנְתַתֶּם, "and you [plural] will give," a Qal (G) second masculine plural perfect with *waw* consecutive.

וְהוֹקַעֲנוּם—"And we will hang them [their dead bodies]." This is the Hiphil (H) first common plural perfect of יָקַע with *waw* consecutive and a third masculine plural pronominal suffix. In the Qal (G), יָקַע means "to be dislocated" or "alienated." Although the meaning of its Hiphil is not certain, it probably refers to hanging the dead body of a person after he is executed. Its Hiphil recurs in the same sense in 21:9 (וַיֹּקִיעֵם), a third masculine plural preterite [imperfect with *waw* consecutive] with a third masculine plural suffix) and in a similar context in Num 25:4 (וְהוֹקַע אוֹתָם לַיהוָה), and its Hophal (Hp) masculine plural participle (with the article) הַמּוּקָעִים in 2 Sam 21:13 has the corresponding passive meaning, "those who had been hung." This is not to be confused with the modern practice of executing a person by hanging with a rope around the neck. Ancient practice in the OT era was to hang or impale the body after execution.[2] This was a precursor of the Roman practice of execution by crucifixion.[3]

בְּחִיר יְהוָה—"Yahweh's chosen [king]." This is the only instance in the book of Samuel of the noun בָּחִיר, "chosen one," but it is used elsewhere for, e.g., the Suffering Servant (Is 42:1), Yahweh's chosen people (Is 65:9, 15), David (Ps 89:4 [ET 89:3]), and

---

[2] See תָּלָה in Gen 40:19; Deut 21:22–23; Josh 8:29; 10:26; Esth 2:23; 5:14; 6:4; 7:9–10; 8:7; 9:13, 14, 25 (cf. Ezra 6:11).

[3] See Hengel, *Crucifixion*.

Moses (Ps 106:23). It is derived from the verb בָּחַר, "to choose," which was used for the choosing of Saul as the first king by Yahweh (1 Sam 10:24) and by Israel (1 Sam 12:13; cf. 1 Sam 8:18). Later it referred to Yahweh's choosing of David as king (2 Sam 6:21).

21:7 וַיַּחְמֹל—For חָמַל, "to have pity, compassion," see the third textual note on 12:4.

שְׁבֻעַת יְהוָה—"Yahweh's oath." David and Jonathan had sworn an oath that bound them together in the covenant love of Yahweh. See 1 Sam 18:3; 20:8, 16–17, 42; 23:18.

אֲשֶׁר בֵּינֹתָם בֵּין דָּוִד וּבֵין יְהוֹנָתָן בֶּן־שָׁאוּל׃—Literally "which (was) between them, between David and between Jonathan, Saul's son." בֵּינֹתָם is a feminine plural form of the preposition בֵּין, "between," with a third masculine plural suffix. When this feminine plural form is used with a suffix, it has an inclusive sense (see Waltke-O'Connor, § 11.2.6a and d, including example 18).

21:8 מִיכַל—"Michal" is the reading of Codex Leningradensis, most other Masoretic manuscripts, and most LXX manuscripts (Μιχολ). מֵ(י)רַב, "Merab," is the reading of two Masoretic manuscripts, followed by some LXX manuscripts, the Syriac, and the Targum. The MT (with מִיכַל) is probably the result of an inadvertent scribal substitution of the more common phrase מִיכַל בַּת־שָׁאוּל, "Michal the daughter of Saul" (1 Sam 18:20; 2 Sam 3:13; 6:16, 20, 23; 1 Chr 15:29) for מֵ(י)רַב בַּת־שָׁאוּל, "Merab the daughter of Saul," which occurs elsewhere only in 1 Sam 18:19. In addition, there are two other reasons to favor "Merab" as the correct reading: Michal was childless (2 Sam 6:23), and Adriel was Merab's husband (1 Sam 18:19).

21:9 וַיִּפְּלוּ שְׁבַעְתָּם יָחַד—"The seven of them died together" is literally "and the seven of them fell together." The Qere and the sole reading in a number of Masoretic manuscripts, שְׁבַעְתָּם, is the number שִׁבְעָה with a third masculine plural suffix, which is supported by the LXX (οἱ ἑπτὰ αὐτοί). The Kethib is the dual form שְׁבַעְתַּיִם, meaning "sevenfold" or "seven times."

וְהֵמָּה הֻמָתוּ—"(And) they were killed." The verb הֻמָתוּ is the Hophal (Hp) third common plural perfect of מוּת. The form of the third masculine plural pronoun (with the conjunction *waw*) is וְהֵמָּה according to the Qere and a number of Masoretic manuscripts. The Kethib is the synonymous וְהֵם.

בִּתְחִלַּת קְצִיר שְׂעֹרִים׃—Literally "at the beginning of the harvest of barley." In this construct chain, the preposition בְּ, "at," is included in the Qere, בִּתְחִלַּת, which is the sole reading in many Masoretic manuscripts and is supported by the LXX (ἐν ἀρχῇ). The preposition is absent in the Kethib, תְחִלַּת, so its construct chain is an accusative of time (GKC, § 118 i).

21:10 הַשַּׂק—The donning of שַׂק, "sackcloth," is part of the ritual for mourning the dead here, as also in, e.g., 3:31.

וַתַּטֵּהוּ—"And she spread it out." The Hiphil (H) of נָטָה, "to stretch out," here refers to spreading out a cloth on a rock. Cf. the textual note on 16:22.

עַד נִתַּךְ־מַיִם עֲלֵיהֶם מִן־הַשָּׁמָיִם—Literally "until water was poured on them from the sky." The verb נִתַּךְ is the Niphal (N) third masculine singular perfect of נָתַךְ. Its Niphal refers to the pouring of rain in Ex 9:33.

חַיַּת הַשָּׂדֶה—"A wild animal" is literally "an animal of the field." This refers to carnivorous animals, as does חַיַּת הָאָרֶץ in 1 Sam 17:46.

21:11 וַיֻּגַּד לְדָוִד אֵת אֲשֶׁר־עָשְׂתָה רִצְפָּה—Literally "and it was told to David what Rizpah did." The Hophal (Hp) of נגד is used impersonally; see the first textual note on 19:2 (ET 19:1). Here, the passive verb is construed with a direct object (... אֵת). For the construction, see GKC, § 121 a; Joüon, § 128 b. It is best translated with the indirect object as the subject of the passive verb.

פִּלֶגֶשׁ שָׁאוּל:—"Saul's concubine." For the status of wives and concubines, see the commentary on 5:13.

21:12 אֲשֶׁר גְּנָבוּ אֹתָם—Literally "which they stole them." The relative pronoun אֲשֶׁר refers back to "Saul" and "Jonathan," that is, their bodies, not just their bones. The valiant residents of Jabesh-gilead had retrieved the bodies of Saul and his slain sons after their corpses had been affixed to the wall of Beth-shan (1 Sam 31:11–12). For the verb גָּנַב, "steal," see the third textual note on 15:6. The pronominal suffix on אֹתָם, "them," is third masculine plural (whereas עַצְמוֹת, "the bones of," the plural construct form of noun עֶצֶם, is feminine). Hebrew relative clauses often include such a resumptive pronoun. It is not translated since English considers it to be redundant. Cf. the resumptive adverb in the next textual note.

אֲשֶׁר תְּלָאוּם שָׁמָּה—Literally "which they hung them there." For hanging, see the commentary on 1 Sam 31:11–13,[4] including footnote 13 (cf. the commentary on 2 Sam 18:9–10). The verb for "hang" here (תָּלָא or תָּלָה) is the same one (תָּלָה) used in, e.g., Gen 40:19, 22; Deut 21:22–23; Josh 8:29; 10:26; 2 Sam 4:12; 18:10. As in the previous textual note, the relative pronoun אֲשֶׁר refers to the bodies of Saul and Jonathan. The Qere and the sole reading in a number of Masoretic manuscripts is תְּלָאוּם, the Qal (G) third common plural perfect of תָּלָא with a third masculine plural pronominal suffix. The verb תָּלָא is a by-form of תָּלָה.[5] Alternatively, תְּלָאוּם could be explained as a form of תָּלָה, since third-*he* verbs are often patterned after third-*aleph* verbs (GKC, § 75 rr). The Kethib is תְּלוּם, the same form, but clearly from תָּלָה. According to the Qere, שָׁמָּה, the resumptive adverb שָׁם, "there," has a locative *he*, whereas the Kethib lacks one.

21:13 וַיַּעַל—"He brought up." This form of עָלָה (the third masculine singular preterite [imperfect with *waw* consecutive]) could be either Qal (G) or Hiphil (H). Since the verb has direct objects (אֶת־ ... וְאֶת־), it must be the Hiphil.

וַיַּאַסְפוּ—This is the Qal (G) third masculine plural preterite (imperfect with *waw* consecutive) of אָסַף, "to gather." See the first textual note on 11:27.

הַמּוּקָעִים:—"Those who had been hung." The definite article functions as a relative pronoun. This is the Hophal (Hp) masculine plural participle of יָקַע. See the second textual note on 21:6.

21:14 עַצְמוֹת־שָׁאוּל וִיהוֹנָתָן־בְּנוֹ—One Hebrew noun (עַצְמוֹת, "the bones of") can be in construct with two or more genitives (שָׁאוּל, "Saul," and וִיהוֹנָתָן־בְּנוֹ, "and Jonathan his son"). See Joüon, § 129 b. See also 1 Sam 15:9, 15.

---

[4] Steinmann, *1 Samuel*, 570–71.

[5] See the second textual note on 4:12; the sixth textual note on 18:9; and the textual note on 18:10.

וַיֵּעָתֵר אֱלֹהִים לָאָרֶץ—"God responded to the plea for the land." The same clause recurs in 24:25 but with יְהוָה, "Yahweh," in place of אֱלֹהִים, "God." The verb is the Niphal (N) third masculine singular preterite (imperfect with *waw* consecutive) of עָתַר. Its Qal (G) means "to pray" to God, while its Niphal means that God is "supplicated," that is, he graciously answers prayers and entreaties. The preposition לְ has the sense of advantage, "for" the benefit or sake of (see BDB, 5 h (*b*) and (*c*)).

Commentary

The Form and Content of 2 Samuel 21–24

The last major section of 2 Samuel has six major segments of varying length. It has been generally recognized that these segments have been arranged chiastically by the author:[6]

A A famine is sent because King Saul broke Israel's oath to the Gibeonites (21:1–14)
  B David's heroic soldiers kill the Philistine giants (21:15–22)
   C David's song of deliverance (22:1–51)
   C' David's last words (23:1–7)
  B' David's heroic soldiers (23:8–39)
A' A plague is sent because of David's selfish census (24:1–25)

Segments A and A' both describe a sin by one of Israel's kings that leads to God's judgment against all Israel. The judgment is rescinded in each case when David takes action and pleads with God for relief (21:14; 24:25).[7] Segments B and B' both highlight David's soldiers and their skill in serving king and country. Segments C and C' are both divinely inspired poems written by David, the anointed one,[8] as a prophet. Together this collection of miscellaneous events and persons from David's reign underscores important aspects of David as the king of Israel through whom Yahweh brings good to his people: In A and A' David intercedes for Israel. In B and B' David's skillfully assembled corps of competent warriors brings victory for God's redeemed. In C and C' David emphasizes God as the source of salvation, blessing, and every success.[9]

---

[6] McCarter, *II Samuel*, 18–19; Anderson, *2 Samuel*, 248; Baldwin, *1 and 2 Samuel*, 282–83; Bergen, *1, 2 Samuel*, 442.

[7] See the second textual note on 21:14.

[8] For מָשַׁח, "to anoint," with King David as its object, see the second textual note on 5:3 and the third textual note on 12:7. It is used for Samuel anointing David in 1 Sam 16:3, 12, 13; for the men of Judah anointing him in 2 Sam 2:4, 7; for Israel anointing him in 2 Sam 5:3, 17; and for Yahweh anointing him in 2 Sam 12:7. See also the cognate noun מָשִׁיחַ, "anointed one," literally "messiah," in the commentary on the messianic prophecies in 1 Sam 2:10 and 1 Sam 2:35 (Steinmann, *1 Samuel*, 80–81, 105–6). See further "The Promise to David (2 Samuel 7)" and "David and the Messianic Promise" in "Christ in Samuel" in the introduction (Steinmann, *1 Samuel*, 23–24, 25–26) and the excursus "הָאָדָם as 'the Man' in 2 Samuel 7:19 and 1 Chronicles 17:17" following the commentary on 2 Sam 7:1–29.

[9] See "Prosperity and Success Come Only from God" in "Other Theological Themes in Samuel" in the introduction (Steinmann, *1 Samuel*, 29).

The Gibeonites Avenged (21:1–14)

Sometime between 997 BC and 980 BC[10]

The chapter begins with a new chronological notice (21:1) that also serves to separate this final section of 2 Samuel (chapters 21–24) from the previous one (9:1–20:26). From 9:1 to 20:22 the material is arranged in chronological order,[11] with 20:23–26 serving as an appendix. The chronological information in 21:1 takes the reader back in time to some unspecified three-year period during David's reign. The author emphasizes that the famine was continuous ("year after year") during that time. Famines from lack of adequate rain were not uncommon in ancient Palestine. However, when the famine stretched on for three years, David concluded that Yahweh had allowed it for a particular reason. We are not told of the method he used for seeking Yahweh's face.[12] He may have sought Yahweh directly through prayer or by consulting one of Yahweh's prophets or priests. Elsewhere in the book of Samuel, Yahweh often spoke to David through a prophet (Nathan in 2 Sam 7:2–17; 12:1–14, 24–25; Gad in 1 Sam 22:5; 2 Sam 24:11–18). God also answered David through the high priest, who consulted Yahweh by means of the Urim and Thummim, although the usual phraseology in those passages is that David had first "inquired" (שָׁאַל) of Yahweh, and that verb is not used here.[13] The trustworthiness of the means through which God speaks to his people is a matter of life and death. In this case, people may have been dying because of the famine, and David's response to Yahweh's answer involved the execution of seven men (21:5–6, 8–9). Therefore it was of the utmost importance that David be certain that the answer was in fact a word from Yahweh. It could not be merely a conclusion based on human reasoning or emotions (whether of David or of his men). All of God's people—especially leaders—must base their decisions and actions on the clear, objective, external Word of God, which is his living voice, and not on their own subjective inferences or feelings about what they think God might want them to do.

The message to David was that God had been enforcing the oath that Israel had taken concerning the Gibeonites (Josh 9:3–27), an oath that had been violated by Saul (2 Sam 21:1–2). The book of Samuel does not record Saul's aggression against the Gibeonites, though it may have been the reason some fled from Beeroth to Gittaim (2 Sam 4:3). It is noteworthy that the author says that Saul attacked the Gibeonites out of his "zeal" for Israel (21:2).[14] Much of

---

[10] See the discussion of this event in "The Chronology of David's Reign" in the commentary on 5:1–5.

[11] The one exception to this chronological order is the narrative of Solomon's birth in 994 BC (12:24–25), which the author inserted into his description of the events of 997 BC (11:1–12:23, 26–31).

[12] See the first textual note on 21:1. The method of divine communication is not altogether clear in many of the other passages cited there.

[13] See the excursus "The Urim and Thummim" in Steinmann, *1 Samuel*, 272–75. For passages in which David "inquired" (שָׁאַל) of "Yahweh," see 1 Sam 23:2, 4; 30:8; 2 Sam 2:1; 5:19, 23.

[14] See the fourth textual note on 21:2.

1 Samuel records Saul's misguided zeal. Unlike David here, Saul often acted impetuously without consulting Yahweh, and from the start of his reign he defied the Word of God.[15] Here Saul supposed that his zeal was for God's people, but it was not zeal for God himself since it was not in accord with God's Word. Had his zeal been proper, he would have respected the oath taken in the days of Joshua and recorded in that eponymous biblical book (Josh 9:3–27).

Interestingly, David is not reported as having been told by Yahweh *how* to lift the famine from the land. Instead, David called the Gibeonites and allowed them to choose what action would be sufficient to "make atonement" for Saul's sin against them (21:3). The Gibeonite reply to David was elliptical (21:4). They said that it was not a matter of the payment of a fine. Then they noted that they were not allowed to execute anyone for the crime committed against them. This was an indirect way of asking David for capital punishment as atonement for Saul's misdeed. (In Jesus' day, his Jewish opponents cited the same prohibition as part of their demand that Jesus be executed [Jn 18:31].) David agreed to their proposal in principle. This led to their specific request. They asked for seven of Saul's descendants and the right to display their executed bodies in Gibeah (21:5–6). The number "seven" was probably symbolic and intended to represent the entire house of Saul. The public hanging of their dead bodies was intended to warn others in Israel so that they could see the consequences of breaking an oath to Yahweh, even if it were not an oath concerning fellow Israelites. In the case of the Gibeonites, the oath was a promise to allow those contrite Canaanites to live in the land. The Gibeonites asked that the bodies be hung "before Yahweh" in Gibeah (21:6), Saul's city (see 1 Sam 10:26). The display before God was intended to demonstrate both that they believed the wrong done to them had been avenged by God and that they now prayed for Yahweh to bless Israel since atonement had been made for the sin against them (see 21:3).

The author once again notes David's faithfulness to his oath to Jonathan (1 Sam 18:3; 20:8, 16–17, 42; 23:18) in mentioning that he spared Jonathan's son Mephibosheth (2 Sam 21:7; see also 9:1–13). David instead took the two sons of Saul's concubine Rizpah (21:8; cf. 3:7). Ironically, one of them was also named Mephibosheth.[16] David also took the five sons of Merab, Saul's

---

[15] Saul failed to carry out the mandate given him when he was anointed king to eradicate the Philistine garrison in Gibeah (1 Sam 10:7). See the commentary on 1 Sam 10:7–8 and figure 16, "Saul's Faltering Accession," in "Samuel Anoints Saul (9:26–10:8)" in the commentary on 1 Sam 9:26–10:16, as well as the beginning of the commentary on 1 Sam 10:17–27a (Steinmann, *1 Samuel*, 196–98, 203). Saul failed to trust Yahweh, and so he and his troops were terrified of the Philistines (1 Sam 13:6–7, 12; 17:11; 28:5). Yahweh "rejected" Saul because the apostate king had "rejected" Yahweh's Word (מָאַס, 1 Sam 15:23, 26; 16:1). The book of Samuel records only two instances in which Saul "asked" Yahweh (שָׁאַל), and both times God gave him no answer but was silent (1 Sam 14:37; 28:6).

[16] This once again is probably a bowdlerization of the name Merib-baal. Some names of members of Saul's family were most likely purposely bowdlerized to avoid any royal association with the pagan god Baal: Mephibosheth ("from the mouth of shame," 2 Sam 4:4; 9:6, 10, 11, 12, 13; 16:1, 4; 19:25, 26, 31 [ET 19:24, 25, 30]; 21:7, 8) instead of Merib-baal ("he contends with Baal," 1 Chr 8:34; 9:40) and Ish-bosheth ("man of shame," 2 Sam 2:8, 10, 12, 15; 3:8,

elder daughter, who was married to Adriel (1 Sam 18:19). Here we are told that Adriel's father was Barzillai the Meholathite. That is, he was from Abel-meholah in the Transjordan (Judg 7:22; 1 Ki 4:12), the city that would later be home to Elisha (1 Ki 19:16). This identification distinguishes this Barzillai from Barzillai the Gileadite, who had supported David.[17] The Gibeonites hung the bodies of the seven executed men (2 Sam 21:9) as they had said they would (21:6). The men were killed together "at the beginning of the barley harvest" in what we would identify as the month of April (21:9).

Rizpah's act of guarding the bodies to ward off predation by birds and other animals shows signs of both mourning (sackcloth) and respect for the dead by preserving the dignity of the corpses (21:10). Throughout the OT, bodies exposed to beasts were considered disgraced.[18] A person who was hung was cursed by God and was to be buried by nightfall (Deut 21:22–23; see also Josh 8:29; 10:26–27).[19] Rizpah's devotion to the dead in this matter is emphasized in her staying on guard until the famine, which had obviously been a result of drought, was broken by rain. It is unlikely that the rain was the normal early rain at the beginning of the wet season in fall, some six months after the execution. It is more likely that God showed that he had was now willing to lift his judgment against Israel by sending a rare spring rain during the harvest (cf. Prov 26:1).

David's reaction to Rizpah's devotion was to gather the bones of Saul and Jonathan and inter them with the bones of the executed men (21:11–14). The author reminds the reader that the bones of Saul and Jonathan were with the citizens of Jabesh-gilead and relates how they came into their possession (21:12; cf. 1 Sam 31:11–13). The ancestral tomb of Saul's family was that of the former king's father, Kish (2 Sam 21:14). It was in Zela, a city in the territory given to Benjamin (Josh 18:28).

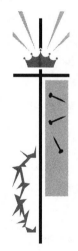

Following David's action, God graciously responded to Israel's prayers and ended the famine. Thus, the normal cycle of winter rains and spring and summer harvests resumed. Atonement had been made, and so Yahweh's inheritance was blessed (21:3). In the NT era, the people of God do not seek any such revenge against their persecutors, but instead pray for their salvation (Mt 5:44; Lk 6:28; 23:34). The crucifixion or "hanging"[20] of Jesus Christ on the cross is the one all-sufficient sacrifice that has made full atonement for the sins of the world. His death and resurrection grant all in Christ every blessing and the inheritance of eternal life.

14, 15; 4:5, 8, 12; see also 2 Sam 3:7), instead of Eshbaal ("man of the master/Baal," 1 Chr 8:33; 9:39). See further the second textual note on 2:8.

[17]   2 Sam 17:27; 19:32–35, 40 (ET 19:31–34, 39); 1 Ki 2:7; Ezra 2:61; Neh 7:63.

[18]   1 Sam 17:44, 46; 1 Ki 14:11; 16:4; 21:24; Jer 16:4; Ezek 39:4, 17–20; Ps 79:2; Rev 19:17–21.

[19]   See the commentary on 1 Sam 31:11–13, including footnote 13 (Steinmann, *1 Samuel*, 570–71; cf. the commentary on 2 Sam 18:9–10).

[20]   The verb κρεμάννυμι, "hang," is used in reference to the crucifixion of Christ in Acts 5:30; 10:39; Gal 3:13. Compare the verbs in the second textual note on 2 Sam 21:6 and the second textual note on 21:12.

2 Samuel 21:15–22
David Defeats the Philistine Giants

Translation

21 **15There was war again between the Philistines and Israel. David and his servants went down and fought the Philistines, and David became exhausted. 16Now Ishbi-benob, who was among the descendants of the Rephaim—his spear weighed three hundred shekels of bronze, and he was outfitted with new weapons. He intended to kill David. 17However, Zeruiah's son Abishai helped him. He struck the Philistine and killed him. At that time David's men took an oath to him: "You should not go out to war again with us. You should not extinguish Israel's lamp."**

18After this there was war again in Gob with the Philistines. At that time, Sibbecai the Hushathite struck down Saph, who was among the descendants of the Rephaim.

19There was war again in Gob with the Philistines, and Jair's son Elhanan struck down Lahmi the brother of Goliath the Gittite. (The shaft of his spear was like a weaver's beam.)

20There was war again in Gath. There was a tall man with six fingers on each hand and six toes on each foot, totaling twenty-four. He was also descended from the Rephaim. 21He mocked Israel, and Jonathan, the son of David's brother Shimei, struck him down.

22These four were descended from the Rephaim in Gath. They fell by the hand of David and his servants.

Textual Notes

21:15 וַתְּהִי־עֹוד מִלְחָמָה—Literally "and a war was/happened again." The same clause (sometimes with the article on מִלְחָמָה) recurs in 21:18 and begins 21:19 and 21:20. The feminine noun מִלְחָמָה, "war," is the subject of the feminine verb וַתְּהִי. The noun is derived from the verb לָחַם, whose Niphal (N) appears later in the verse (וַיִּלָּחֲמוּ) and means "to fight" a war.

לַפְּלִשְׁתִּים אֶת־יִשְׂרָאֵל—Literally "for/by the Philistines with Israel." Here אֶת is the preposition "with." See also אֶת־פְּלִשְׁתִּים, "with Philistines," later in 21:15 and עִם־פְּלִשְׁתִּים, "with Philistines," in 21:18, 19.

וַיָּעַף דָּוִד:—For the Qal (G) verb עִיף, "be(come) exhausted," see the third textual note on 16:2. The verb עִיף occurs five times in the OT, four times with this form, וַיָּעַף (cf. Joüon, § 80 k).

21:16 וְיִשְׁבִּי—"Now Ishbi-" is the reading of the Qere and the sole reading in many Masoretic manuscripts. It is supported by the LXX (Ιεσβι). The Kethib is וישבו, probably to be vocalized as וְיִשְׁבּוּ, "and Ishbo-."

בִּילִידֵי הָרָפָה—"Among the descendants of the Rephaim" is literally "among the descendants of the Rapha." The noun יָלִיד is derived from the verb יָלַד, "to bear [a child]," and denotes a "descendant." (Cf. the Qal passive [Gp] perfects of יֻלַּד in the fourth textual note on 21:20 and the textual note on 21:22.) The name רָפָה, "Rapha," is always used with the article (הָרָפָה, "the Rapha") and refers to the ancestor of the people called (הָ)רְפָאִים, "(the) Rephaim."[1] The construct phrase here with the plural of the noun יָלִיד and the prefixed preposition בְּ recurs in 21:18 but with the noun spelled defectively (בִּילִדֵי הָרָפָה). The parallel to 2 Sam 21:18 in 1 Chr 20:4 reads מִילִדֵי הָרְפָאִים, "among the descendants of the Rephaim."[2] Note also the name of the ancestor with the article (הָרָפָה) in 2 Sam 21:20 and the alternate spelling of his name with the article (הָרָפָא) in the parallel in 1 Chr 20:6 (and also in 1 Chr 20:8). Apparently the homonyms רָפָה and רָפָא are alternate phonetic ways to spell this name.

וּמִשְׁקַל קֵינוֹ—Literally "and the weight of his spear." This is the only OT occurrence of the noun קַיִן. Since antiquity it has been understood to mean "spear," as translated by the LXX (τοῦ δόρατος αὐτοῦ).

שְׁלֹשׁ מֵאוֹת מִשְׁקָל נְחֹשֶׁת—Literally "three hundred weight of bronze." Most likely the construct form of the noun מִשְׁקָל, "weight," should be read as the unit of weight שֶׁקֶל, "shekel." Apparently מִשְׁקָל here is a repetition of the word in the preceding phrase (see the prior textual note). Cf. the LXX: τριακοσίων σίκλων ὁλκὴ χαλκοῦ, "(the) weight of three hundred shekels of bronze."

וְהוּא חָגוּר חֲדָשָׁה—"And he was outfitted with new weapons" is literally "and he was wearing (something) new." For חָגוּר, the Qal passive (Gp) participle of חָגַר, see the second textual note on 6:14. This passive participle (like other verbs for "wearing" and "putting on") usually takes an accusative noun denoting what is worn (Joüon, § 121 o). The accusative here is the feminine adjective חֲדָשָׁה, "new," which does not modify any noun, so the translation understands it as a collective substantive, "new weapons." The LXX translated it as κορύνην, "a mace, club."

וַיֹּאמֶר—"He intended." This verb, which normally means "and he said," here records internal conversation or thought.

21:17 לֹא־תֵצֵא עוֹד אִתָּנוּ לַמִּלְחָמָה—Literally "you shall not go out again with us to the war." In the book of Samuel, the Qal (G) of יָצָא often refers to "going out" to battle. See the first textual note on 1 Sam 18:6[3] and the first textual note on 2 Sam 2:12.

וְלֹא תְכַבֶּה אֶת־נֵר יִשְׂרָאֵל׃—"You should not extinguish the lamp of Israel." The verb is the Piel (D) of כָּבָה, "to extinguish," which was used in a similar metaphor of extinguishing a burning "ember" (גַּחֶלֶת), that is, a woman's last son, in 2 Sam 14:7. Here its direct object is the noun נֵר, "lamp." That noun was the subject of the Qal (G) of כָּבָה in 1 Sam 3:3: "before God's lamp had gone out." In 2 Sam 22:29 David will acclaim Yahweh to be נֵירִי, "my lamp." The noun נֵר is used for God's Word in Ps 119:105 and his Davidic Messiah in Ps 132:17. See also the spelling נִיר in reference to the "lamp" of David in 1 Ki 11:36; 15:4; 2 Ki 8:19 ‖ 2 Chr 21:7. Jesus will twice declare, "I am the light of the world" (Jn 8:12; 9:5). See further the commentary.

---

[1] See "Rephaim" also in Gen 14:5; 15:20; Deut 2:11, 20 (twice); 3:11, 13; Josh 12:4; 13:12; 15:8; 17:15; 18:16; 2 Sam 5:18, 22; 23:13; Is 17:5; 1 Chr 11:15; 14:9.

[2] There is no parallel to 2 Sam 21:16 in 1 Chronicles 20 (or elsewhere).

[3] Steinmann, *1 Samuel*, 350.

21:18 וַיְהִי֙ אַחֲרֵי־כֵ֔ן—Literally "and it came to pass after this." The author frequently opens a new episode in the narrative with this Hebrew clause. See the commentary on 2:1.

בְּגֹ֑וב—"In Gob." This prepositional phrase recurs in 21:19. The parallel to 2 Sam 21:18 in 1 Chr 20:4 reads בְּגֶ֑זֶר, "in Gezer." (The parallel to 2 Sam 21:19 in 1 Chr 20:5 lacks any place-name.) Since "Gob" is never mentioned elsewhere, "Gezer" may well be the original reading. If so, בְּגֹוב in 21:18, 19 may be the result of a graphic confusion between *zayin* and *waw* and between *resh* and *bet*. Moreover, "Gezer" lay near Philistia.[4] LXX 2 Sam 21:18 reads ἐν Γεθ, "in Gath," which is displaced from 21:20, while LXX 2 Sam 21:19 has ἐν Γοβ, "in Gob."

אָ֤ז הִכָּה—Literally "then he struck down." For the use of the temporal adverb אָז with a perfect verb, see Joüon, § 113 i.

סַ֖ף—"Saph." The parallel in 1 Chr 20:4 reads סִפַּ֑י, "Sippai." However, LXX 1 Chr 20:4 reads Σαφου (which might reflect a Hebrew reading סָפוּ).

21:19 וַיַּ֣ךְ אֶלְחָנָ֣ן בֶּן־יַעְרֵי֩ אֹרְגִ֨ים בֵּ֤ית הַלַּחְמִי֙ אֵ֖ת גָּלְיָ֔ת—The MT literally states "Elhanan the son of Jaare-oregim the Bethlehemite struck down Goliath."[5] The reading in the parallel verse 1 Chr 20:5 is as follows:

וַיַּ֗ךְ אֶלְחָנָן֙ בֶּן־יָעִ֔יר אֶת־לַחְמִי֙ אֲחִ֣י גָּלְיָ֔ת

And Elhanan the son of Jair[6] struck down Lahmi the brother of Goliath.

The reading in 1 Chr 20:5 is to be preferred and is the basis for this commentary's translation of 2 Sam 21:19.[7] The reading in 2 Sam 21:19 appears corrupt for the following reasons:

---

[4] See 2 Sam 5:25; see also Josh 10:33; 12:12; 16:3, 10; 21:21; Judg 1:29; 1 Ki 9:15, 16, 17; 1 Chr 6:52 (ET 6:67); 7:28; 14:16; 20:4.

[5] Josephus appears to follow this reading in 21:19 by referring to Ἐφὰν ὁ συγγενὴς αὐτου, "Ephan, his [i.e., David's] kinsman" (*Antiquities*, 7.302). Josephus omits Elhanan's patronymic but apparently assumes that because Elhanan's father was from Bethlehem (per MT 2 Sam 21:19), he must have been related to David.

[6] In 1 Chr 20:5 the Qere is יָעִ֔יר, "Jair," while the Kethib יעור probably would be vocalized as יָעוּר, "Jaur."

[7] Fouts, "Who Really Killed Goliath?" 19–23, believes that the text in 1 Chr 20:5 is also corrupt. He proposes that the original text of both 2 Sam 21:19 and 1 Chr 20:5 might have read as follows (p. 23; the original reading has been given in Hebrew letters rather than Fouts' transliteration):

וַיַּ֗ךְ אֶלְחָנָן֙ בֶּן־(דּוֹדוֹ) בֵּ֣ית הַלַּחְמִ֗י אֶת־(?) אֲחִ֣י גָּלְיָ֣ת הַגִּתִּ֔י

And Elhanan the son of (Dodo) the Bethlehemite slew (?) the brother of Goliath the Gittite. (Cf. 2 Sam 23:24 ‖ 1 Chr 11:26; Fouts proposes that the name of Goliath's brother, where the question mark appears after the direct object marker, אֶת־, has been lost)

While this is an intriguing suggestion, Fouts fails to offer credible evidence or explanations for a number of his changes, including these with respect to 1 Chr 20:5:

- How did the name he presumes was original, דּוֹדוֹ, "Dodo," become יָעִ֔יר, "Jair" (the Qere in 1 Chr 20:5) or something similar in all ancient traditions?
- How did בֵּ֣ית, "Beth-," which he argues was in the original text, drop out when "Bethlehem" was so widely used in the OT and would have been well-known to every scribe?

1. The construct phrase יַעְרֵי אֹרְגִים seems dubious as a personal name, "Jaare-oregim." It would mean either "forests of weavers" or "honeycombs of weavers." (For both possible meanings of יַעַר, see the textual note on 1 Sam 14:25.[8])

2. The last word of the construct phrase יַעְרֵי אֹרְגִים is in form the Qal (G) masculine plural participle אֹרְגִים, oregim, "weavers." That word is also the last word in both 2 Sam 21:19 and 1 Chr 20:5 (in the phrase כִּמְנוֹר אֹרְגִים, literally "like a beam of weavers"). The word's appearance earlier in 2 Sam 21:19 (in the construct phrase יַעְרֵי אֹרְגִים) is apparently the result of the duplication of the verse's last word.[9]

3. The more frequent בֵּית הַלַּחְמִי, "the Bethlehemite" (1 Sam 16:1, 18; 17:58),[10] seems to have been substituted here in 2 Sam 21:19 for the less common אֶת־לַחְמִי, "[direct object marker] Lahmi," which occurs only in 1 Chr 20:5.[11]

4. David killed Goliath (1 Samuel 17). The statement in 2 Sam 21:19 that Elhanan killed Goliath would contradict that earlier chapter in the book of Samuel.[12]

5. The changes that were apparently made earlier in the verse (see points 2 and 3) required the change from אֲחִי גָּלְיָת, "the brother of Goliath" (1 Chr 20:5) to אֵת גָּלְיָת, "[direct object marker] Goliath" (2 Sam 21:19), since it would make no sense for Elhanan's father to be the brother of Goliath. In fact, a later scribe copying the text (after the changes in points 2 and 3 had occurred) may have noticed this and

---

- How did the direct object marker (אֶת־ is the third word in the words אֲחִי [?] אֶת בֵּית הַלַּחְמִי proposed by Fouts) get displaced to an earlier position in the text (it is the first of the three words אֶת־לַחְמִי אֲחִי in 1 Chr 20:5)?

[8] Steinmann, 1 Samuel, 260.

[9] Keil, The Books of Samuel, 465; Ackroyd, The Second Book of Samuel, 202–3.

[10] Note also the very common place-name בֵּית לֶחֶם (in pause בֵּית לָחֶם), "Bethlehem" (Gen 35:19; 48:7; Josh 19:15; Judg 12:8, 10; 17:7, 8, 9; 19:1, 2, 18; 1 Sam 16:4; 17:12, 15; 20:6, 28; 2 Sam 2:32; 23:14, 15, 16, 24; Jer 41:17; Micah 5:1 [ET 5:2]; Ruth 1:1, 2, 19, 22; 2:4; 4:11; Ezra 2:21; Neh 7:26; 1 Chr 2:51, 54; 4:4; 11:16, 17, 18, 26; 2 Chr 11:6).

[11] Keil, The Books of Samuel, 466. Note, however, that the name appears to have the gentilic ending י-, which is unusual for a personal name.

[12] Other options are less convincing. They include the following:

- There were two Gittites by the name of Goliath, one in 1 Samuel 17 and the other in 2 Sam 21:19 ‖ 1 Chr 20:5. Both of them had a spear whose shaft was "like a weaver's beam" (1 Sam 17:7; 2 Sam 21:19 ‖ 1 Chr 20:5).

- "Goliath" was a title, not a name, and therefore could have applied to more than one individual (Hertzberg, I and II Samuel, 387).

- "Elhanan" is an alternate name for "David," and "Jaare-oregim" was either David's mother's name or a scribal alteration of the name "Jesse" (Honeyman, "The Evidence for Regnal Names among the Hebrews," 23–24; Pákozdy, "'Elḥânân—der frühere Name Davids"; Baldwin, 1 and 2 Samuel, 286). Note that in 2 Sam 21:17 David's men took an oath that David would no longer go out to war with the army. 2 Sam 21:19 is clearly placed after the event in 21:15–17 and also subsequent to 21:18. Since David did not accompany the army, he therefore cannot be identified with Elhanan.

- To explain the contradiction between 2 Sam 21:19 and 1 Chr 20:5, scholars often argue that the Chronicler's version, which states that Elhanan killed Goliath's brother rather than Goliath himself, is simply an attempt to harmonize the account in 2 Sam 21:19 with 1 Samuel 17 (Smith, The Books of Samuel, 377). However, this view ignores the obvious difficulties in MT 2 Sam 21:19 (e.g., the name Jaare-oregim).

See also the discussion in Bergen, 1, 2 Samuel, 449–50.

assumed that אֲחִי was a mistake for אֵת and sought to correct the text by substituting אֵת, which he assumed was the correct word.[13]

21:20 אִישׁ מָדוֹן—This construct phrase with the Qere מָדוֹן means "a man of strife," that is, "a quarrelsome man." See similar construct phrases with the noun מָדוֹן in the plural in Prov 21:19; 25:24; 26:21; 27:15. The phrase with the Kethib מִדְיָן means "a man of Midian." The translation follows the reading in the parallel verse 1 Chr 20:6, אִישׁ מִדָּה, "a man of stature," that is, "a tall man." The same construct phrase is in 1 Chr 11:23.

וְאֶצְבְּעֹת יָדָיו וְאֶצְבְּעֹת רַגְלָיו שֵׁשׁ וָשֵׁשׁ עֶשְׂרִים וְאַרְבַּע מִסְפָּר—"With six fingers on each hand and six toes on each foot, totaling twenty-four" is literally "and the digits of his hands and the digits of his feet were six and six, twenty-four (in) number." The repetition שֵׁשׁ וָשֵׁשׁ, "six and six," is distributive, "six each."[14] The noun מִסְפָּר, "number," is an accusative of limitation (Joüon, § 127 b).

וְגַם־הוּא יֻלַּד לְהָרָפָה:—"He was also descended from the Rephaim" is literally "and also he was born to the Rapha." When the preposition לְ is prefixed to a word with the definite article, usually the ה is elided and its vowel appears under the preposition, but in לְהָרָפָה, the ה is not elided (GKC, § 35 n). For הָרָפָה, "the Rapha," see the second textual note on 21:16, which also has the noun יְלִיד, "a descendant," which is cognate to the verb יֻלַּד here. That verb, "he was descended," is a Qal passive (Gp) third masculine singular perfect of יָלַד, "to bear [a child]." It recurs in the plural in 21:22. By the time Hebrew became a written language, the Qal passive (Gp) stem ceased to be used for most verbs except for participles, which remained common (e.g., חָגוּר in 21:16; see the fifth textual note on 21:16). For many verbs, the Niphal (N) took over the function of the Qal passive (Gp); see Joüon, § 58 d. Qal passive (Gp) perfect forms are often indistinguishable from Pual (Dp) forms, as is the case here. See *IBH*, § 38 D; Joüon, § 58 a.[15]

21:21 וַיְחָרֵף—"He mocked." This is the Piel (D) third masculine singular preterite (imperfect with *waw* consecutive) of חָרַף, "revile, defy." This verb, usually used in the Piel (D), denotes taunting and shaming (*HALOT*, s.v. חרף II). It referred to Goliath's mockery of Israel and Yahweh in 1 Sam 17:10, 25, 26, 36, 45. It recurs in 2 Sam 23:9.

שִׁמְעָה—This Qere is "Shimeah." The translation follows the Kethib, שִׁמְעִי, "Shimei," which is supported by the LXX (Σεμεϊ) and occurs forty-three other times in the OT. The Qere harmonizes this text with 2 Sam 13:3, 32, where David's brother is called "Shimeah." This form of his name also dissociates him from the שִׁמְעִי, "Shimei,"

---

[13] Keil, *The Books of Samuel*, 466.

[14] Waltke-O'Connor, § 7.2.3b, n. 6.

[15] Qal passive (Gp) imperfect forms may be indistinguishable from Hophal (Hp) forms. There are twenty-two verbal roots that have active Qal passives in the OT (not including verbal roots that exhibit only Qal passive participles). Older lexica such as BDB parsed יֻלַּד as a Pual (Dp) perfect. Qal passive (Gp) verb forms also consternated older grammars, such as GKC, § 121 b.

who cursed David.[16] David's brother is called שַׁמָּה, "Shammah," in 1 Sam 16:9; 17:13.[17] In 1 Chr 20:7, the parallel to 2 Sam 21:21, he is called שִׁמְעָא, "Shimea."

21:22 יֻלְּדוּ לְהָרָפָה—"They were descended from the Rephaim" is literally "they were born to the Rapha." The verb יֻלְּדוּ is the Qal passive (Gp) third common plural perfect of יָלַד. See the third textual note on 21:20.

Commentary

Sometime between 997 BC and 980 BC[18]

Parallel: 2 Sam 21:18–22 ‖ 1 Chr 20:4–8

For the place of this passage in the structure of 2 Samuel 21–24, see "The Form and Content of 2 Samuel 21–24" in the commentary on 21:1–14. This section contains four short accounts about the exploits of David's soldiers, all involving the slaying of one of the Rephaim. Each incident is introduced similarly:

וַתְּהִי־עוֹד מִלְחָמָה לַפְּלִשְׁתִּים אֶת־יִשְׂרָאֵל

There was war again between the Philistines and Israel. (21:15)

וַיְהִי אַחֲרֵי־כֵן וַתְּהִי־עוֹד הַמִּלְחָמָה בְּגוֹב עִם־פְּלִשְׁתִּים

After this there was war again in Gob with the Philistines. (21:18)

וַתְּהִי־עוֹד הַמִּלְחָמָה בְּגוֹב עִם־פְּלִשְׁתִּים

There was war again in Gob with the Philistines. (21:19)

וַתְּהִי־עוֹד מִלְחָמָה בְּגַת

There was war again in Gath. (21:20)

All four accounts have this clause: literally "and war happened again" (וַתְּהִי־עוֹד מִלְחָמָה/הַמִּלְחָמָה).[19] The first three mention "the Philistines" as Israel's opponents. The last does not, but the same opponents are implicit: it is the only one to mention a Philistine city, "Gath" (21:20).[20] Three of the four mention the place of the battle, the first being the only exception. The second contains an additional chronological note at the beginning: וַיְהִי אַחֲרֵי־כֵן, "after this" (21:18). This note emphasizes that the final three confrontations took place after the army's oath that David would no longer accompany them in battle (21:17).

The first battle involved David, who fought alongside his troops (21:15). In ancient warfare commanders did not simply direct the troops from a distance but

---

[16] 2 Sam 16:5, 7, 13; 19:17, 19, 22, 24 (ET 19:16, 18, 21, 23); 1 Ki 2:8, 36, 38, 39, 40, 41, 42, 44.

[17] See שַׁמָּה, "Shammah," also in Gen 36:13, 17; 2 Sam 23:25, 33; 1 Chr 1:37. See also the variant name שַׁמָּא, "Shamma," in 2 Sam 23:11; 1 Chr 7:37.

[18] See "The Chronology of David's Reign" in the commentary on 5:1–5.

[19] See the first textual note on 21:15.

[20] The Philistine pentapolis consisted of Gaza, Ashdod, Ashkelon, Gath, and Ekron. These five cities are listed in Josh 13:3 and 1 Sam 6:17.

were commonly involved in combat. We are told that David became fatigued. Perhaps this was a combination of his more advanced age—he was no longer the young David who led Saul's troops against the Philistines[21]—and the Philistines' targeting of David as the key person to slay. We are told that Ishbi-benob attacked David, intending to kill him (21:16). The author emphasizes this Philistine's weapons, especially his bronze spear, which weighed three hundred shekels or about seven and a half pounds (three and a half kilograms). This was a heavy weapon, but it still weighed only half as much as Goliath's iron spear (1 Sam 17:7). Yet this time David needed help, and Abishai provided it (2 Sam 21:17).

This apparently was too much of a risk for David's troops to tolerate, and their oath reinforced their determination that the king was not to lead his troops into battle any longer (21:17; see the similar statement with the same two words לֹא־תֵצֵא, "you should/shall not go out," in 18:3). They mentioned that David's death would be the extinguishing of "Israel's lamp" (21:17). This is a reference to David as the bearer of the messianic promise. The "lamp" of David[22] would continue to be Israel's hope until Christ, the light of the world, would be born to provide Israel's eternal "light" (Jn 1:7–9; 8:12; 9:5; 12:46) and to be the "lamp" of the new Jerusalem (λύχνος, Rev 21:23; cf. 2 Pet 1:19).

The next skirmish took place at Gob, or more likely Gezer (see the second textual note on 21:18). Sibbecai, who killed Saph, was from Hushah.[23] This town was about four miles (six kilometers) west of Bethlehem. Its modern name is Ḥusan. Sibbecai was among David's thirty elite soldiers (1 Chr 11:29; see the textual note on 2 Sam 23:27).

The third confrontation with the Philistines was also at Gob, where Elhanan struck down Goliath's brother Lahmi (21:19). In the grammar of this verse, the simile that the shaft of his spear was "like a weaver's beam" (כִּמְנוֹר אֹרְגִים) could describe the spear of Goliath, as it does in 1 Sam 17:7, for "Goliath" is the closest antecedent of the pronoun in "his spear" (חֲנִיתוֹ, 2 Sam 21:19). It could also describe the spear of Goliath's brother Lahmi. Scholars have debated the point of the comparison, which the author does not provide. The simile could refer to the large diameter or length of the shaft,[24] which might be estimated at perhaps two inches thick and six feet long, but that is speculative. Another possibility is that the comparison refers to the construction of the spear. Based on evidence from Greece and Egypt for spears equipped with a thong and ring for throwing, Yadin has proposed that a spear with these accessories would appear similar to the equipment used with a weaver's beam.[25]

---

[21] That David was still a "youth" (נַעַר) is noted four times in his contest with Goliath (1 Sam 17:33, 42, 55, 58). See also 1 Sam 18:2, 5–7, 13–30; 19:8.

[22] See the second textual note on 21:17.

[23] A man called Hushah is mentioned in 1 Chr 4:4. The town may have been named after him.

[24] Krinetzki, "Ein Beitrag zur Stilanalyse der Goliathperikope," 191.

[25] Yadin, "Goliath's Javelin and the מְנוֹר אֹרְגִים." See also Steinmann, *1 Samuel*, 336–38.

The final clash took place in Gath (21:20). At this point it appears as if David's forces had taken the fight to the Philistines. The unnamed man from the Rephaim is remarkable for his physical abnormality—he had twenty-four digits instead of the usual twenty. This is a rare condition, medically attested also in modern times, called polydactyly or polydactylism.[26] We are told that like Goliath, he mocked Israel (see the first textual note on 21:21). The "Jonathan" who killed him was also from David's family. Like Abishai, this Jonathan was one of David's nephews. Apparently Jonathan was the brother of Jonadab (13:3).

The author summarizes the slayings of these four Rephaim as coming at the hand of David and his servants (21:22). David, however, did not actually kill any of them, and after the encounter with Ishbi-benob, he was not present with the army (21:17). Yet David receives credit not only because the acts were done under his authority as king but also because they demonstrated his skill in recruiting soldiers capable of defending Israel even against the most formidable of foes. In addition, it appears as if the author has purposely connected the killing of three of these men with David's slaying of Goliath:

Philistine	Weight of Spear	Shaft of Spear	Mocked Israel	Among the Rephaim
Goliath	1 Sam 17:7	1 Sam 17:7	1 Sam 17:10, 25, 26, 36, 45	2 Sam 17:19 (implied)
Ishbi-benob	2 Sam 21:16			2 Sam 21:16
Saph				2 Sam 2:18
Lahmi		2 Sam 21:19		2 Sam 21:22 (implied)
Unnamed			2 Sam 21:21	2 Sam 21:20

This yields another reason why David is explicitly connected to the deaths of these four Gittites: his slaying of Goliath served as the prototype for Israel's later victories over the Philistines, including these. As Yahweh was with David and delivered him from Goliath,[27] so Yahweh was with David's troops to grant them continued victory over Israel's enemies. This also points to David's greater Son, Jesus Christ.[28] His unblemished life of obedience, atoning death, and glorious resurrection gained the victory over our deadly enemies—sin, death, and

---

[26] See Barnett, "Six Fingers in Art and Archaeology," and Barnett, "Six Fingers and Toes."

[27] See the commentary on 1 Samuel 17 (Steinmann, *1 Samuel*, 335–43).

[28] See the commentary on 2 Samuel 7, as well as "Christ in Samuel" in the introduction (Steinmann, *1 Samuel*, 23–26).

Satan (Mt 4:1–11; 1 Cor 15:1–28; Heb 2:6–18). His triumph over them becomes ours as well. The triune God equips Christians with his Holy Spirit in their fight against these foes.[29]

---

[29] Mt 28:18–20; Acts 1:8; Rom 6:1–13; 1 Cor 15:54–58; Eph 6:10–17; 1 Thess 5:8.

2 Samuel 22:1–51
David's Song of Deliverance

Translation

22 ¹David spoke the words of this song to Yahweh on the day Yahweh delivered him from the grasp of all of his enemies and from the grasp of Saul. ²He said:

"Yahweh is my rock, my stronghold, and my deliverer, ³my God, my rock:
I take refuge in him.
My shield and the horn of my salvation, my citadel, my refuge:
my Savior, you save me from violence.

⁴"He is praiseworthy.
I call on Yahweh, and I am saved from my enemies.
⁵For the breaking waves of death engulfed me;
the floods of destruction terrified me.
⁶The ropes of Sheol surrounded me;
the snares of death confronted me.
⁷When I am in trouble, I call on Yahweh,
        to my God I call.
He heard my voice from his temple,
        and my shout was in his ears.

⁸"The earth shook and quaked;
the foundations of the heavens trembled;
they shook, because he was angry.
⁹Smoke rose from his nose;
fire from his mouth consumed;
coals burned from it.
¹⁰He stretched out the heavens and came down,
        a dark cloud beneath his feet.
¹¹He rode on a cherub and flew
        and soared on the wings of the wind.
¹²He placed darkness as a booth surrounding him,
        a collection of water, thick clouds.
¹³From the brightness before him fiery coals burned.
¹⁴Yahweh thundered from heaven;
the Most High made his voice [heard].
¹⁵He sent forth arrows and scattered them,
        lightning, and he routed them.
¹⁶The channels of the sea appeared;
        the foundations of the world were uncovered by Yahweh's rebuke,
        at the blast of the breath of his nose.

¹⁷"He sent from on high; he took me;
  he drew me out of many waters.
¹⁸He delivered me from my strong enemy,
    from those who hate me,
    because they were stronger than I.
¹⁹They confronted me on the day of my calamity,
    but Yahweh was my support.
²⁰He brought me out to a spacious place;
he rescued me because he delighted in me.

²¹"Yahweh has repaid me according to my righteousness;
according to the purity of my hands he has rewarded me.
²²For I have kept Yahweh's ways,
    and I did not act wickedly against my God.
²³For all his ordinances were before me,
and his statutes—I did not turn away from them.
²⁴I was blameless to him,
and I kept myself from my wrongdoing.
²⁵Yahweh rewarded me according to my righteousness,
    according to my purity in his sight.

²⁶"With a faithful person, you show yourself to be faithful.
With a blameless man, you show yourself to be blameless.
²⁷With the pure, you show yourself to be pure.
With the crooked, you show yourself to be shrewd.
²⁸You save a lowly people,
and your eyes are on the haughty—you humble [them].

²⁹"For you are my lamp, Yahweh,
and Yahweh illuminates my darkness.
³⁰For with you I can rush a troop,
and with my God I can leap over a wall.

³¹"He is the God whose way is blameless.
The Word of Yahweh is pure.
He is a shield for all who take refuge in him.
³²For who is God other than Yahweh?
And who is a rock other than our God?

³³"He is the God who clothes me with strength,
    and he makes my way blameless.
³⁴He makes my feet like a deer,
    and he makes me stand on the heights.
³⁵He trains my hands for war,
    and my arms can bend a bronze bow.

³⁶You gave me the shield of your salvation,
> and your help has made me great.

³⁷You widen my steps beneath me,
> and my ankles do not waver.

³⁸I pursue my enemies and destroy them,
> and I do not turn back until I finish them off.

³⁹I crush them, and they will not arise,
> and they fall beneath my feet.

⁴⁰You have clothed me with strength for battle.
You make those who arise against me bow beneath me.

⁴¹My enemies—you have made them flee from me;
> those who hate me—I annihilate them.

⁴²They cry out, but there is no one to save them;
> [they cry out] to Yahweh, but he does not answer them.

⁴³I pulverize them like dust on the surface of the road;
I trample them like mud in the streets.

⁴⁴"You have delivered me from arguments among my people.
You kept me as head of nations.
A people that I have not known serve me.

⁴⁵Foreigners are subservient in my presence.
As soon as their ears hear, they are obedient to me.

⁴⁶Foreigners become discouraged,
> and they came trembling from their fortifications.

⁴⁷"Yahweh lives, and may my rock be blessed!
May the God of the rock of my salvation be exalted!

⁴⁸He is the God who gives me vengeance and brings down peoples beneath me.

⁴⁹[He is the one] who leads me away from my enemies.
And you lift me up from those who rise against me.
You deliver me from violent men.

⁵⁰Therefore, I will praise you, Yahweh, among the nations,
> and I will make music for your name.

⁵¹He gives great victories to his king.
He shows faithfulness to his anointed one,
> to David and to his offspring forever."

Textual Notes

22:1 בְּיוֹם֩ הִצִּ֨יל יְהוָ֤ה אֹתוֹ֙—"On the day (when) Yahweh delivered him." The verb הִצִּיל is the Hiphil (H) of נָצַל, "save, deliver, rescue," probably the infinitive construct rather than the perfect.[1] Hiphil forms of this verb refer to Yahweh's saving action also

---

[1] The preformative of the Hiphil infinitive construct usually has *patach*, -הַ, rather than *hireq*, -הִ. Joüon, § 54 c, note 3, considers it "rather plausible" that the form here could be the perfect because of its use in an asyndetic (without אֲשֶׁר) relative clause.

415

in 22:18, 49. See the textual note on 1 Sam 10:18–19[2] and the second textual note on 2 Sam 14:16.

אֹיְבָיו—"His enemies." The participle of אָיַב, "be hostile to, at enmity with" (cf. the cognate noun אֵיבָה, "enmity," in Gen 3:15), is used as a substantive, "enemy," again in 22:4, 18, 38, 41, 49.

22:2–51 A note concerning line indentation in the translation of this poem: In general, the lines of the poem that are complete thoughts are aligned on the left. If a line completes or continues the thought of the previous line or lines, it is indented.

22:2 סַלְעִי—"My rock." The segholate noun סֶלַע denotes a rocky "crag" or "cliff" that affords safety (see 1 Sam 23:28; also, e.g., 1 Sam 13:6; 23:25). It is a close synonym of צוּר, which is also translated as "rock"; see the first textual note on 22:3. This poem contains many other terms that semantically overlap with each other to a greater or lesser degree.

וּמְצֻדָתִי—"(And) my stronghold." The noun מְצוּדָה refers to a literal military "stronghold" occupied by David offensively in 5:7, 9 and defensively in 5:17; 23:14. For synonyms in this poem, see the fifth and sixth textual notes on 22:3; the first textual note on 22:33; and the fourth textual note on 22:46.

וּמְפַלְטִי־לִי:—Literally "and my deliverer for me." וּמְפַלְטִי is the Piel (D) masculine singular participle of פָּלַט with the conjunction *waw* and a first common singular pronominal suffix. It is rare for a suffixed form to be followed by the preposition לְ with the same suffix (Joüon, § 146 f). The verb פָּלַט is usually used in the Piel, meaning "to deliver/bring [someone] into security" or "to enable [someone] to escape." It is a synonym of the Hiphil (H) of נָצַל (see the first textual note on 22:1) and the Hiphil of יָשַׁע (see the seventh textual note on 22:3), but it is much less common and is confined to poetry. Its Piel second masculine singular preterite (imperfect with *waw* consecutive) is used with a first common singular pronominal suffix in 22:44: וַתְּפַלְּטֵנִי, "(and) you have delivered me." Here the preposition לְ (in the sense of advantage) with the same suffix, לִי, may appear to be pleonastic and is omitted in Ps 18:3 (ET 18:2), but the identical combination appears in Ps 144:2 (וּמְפַלְטִי לִי).

22:3 אֱלֹהֵי צוּרִי—The construct phrase in the MT literally reads "the God of my rock," which affirms both that Yahweh is David's God and that he is his rock. The noun צוּר, "rock, cliff," recurs in 2 Sam 22:32, 47 and is a common metaphor for God as the refuge of those who trust in him (1 Sam 2:2; 2 Sam 23:3). The translation "my God, my rock," assumes a repointing to אֱלֹהַי צוּרִי to match אֵלִי צוּרִי in Ps 18:3 (ET 18:2).

אֶחֱסֶה־בּוֹ—"I take refuge in him." The verb חָסָה is always used in the Qal (G) and usually in poetry. It signifies faith and trust. Its Qal masculine plural participle is used with the definite article and the same prepositional phrase בּוֹ in 22:31: הַחֹסִים בּוֹ, "(the ones) who take refuge in him." The Psalms, including some by David, frequently use the cognate noun מַחְסֶה for God as a "refuge."[3]

---

[2] Steinmann, *1 Samuel*, 200–201.

[3] E.g., Pss 14:6; 46:2 (ET 46:1); 61:4 (ET 61:3); 62:8–9 (ET 62:7–8).

מָגִנִּי—"My shield." The noun מָגֵן refers to a soldier's "shield" as a military defense against attack in 1:21. It is used metaphorically for God here and again in 22:31 and for his salvation in 22:36.

וְקֶרֶן יִשְׁעִי—"And the horn of my salvation." This construct phrase affirms both that Yahweh is David's "horn" and that he is the source of his "salvation." The noun קֶרֶן is another word that is used in the book of Samuel both literally and figuratively. In 1 Sam 16:1, 13, it denotes the "horn" Samuel employed as a flask for the oil used to anoint David as king. Since the horns of a bull or ox were lethal weapons (see Ex 21:28–32; Deut 33:17; cf. 1 Ki 22:11), a "horn" also represents potent strength. In 1 Sam 2:10 "the horn of his Anointed One" is a messianic reference; see the commentary there, as well as Hannah's use of the noun in 1 Sam 2:1. The second noun here, יֵשַׁע, which recurs in 22:36, 47, is derived from the verb יָשַׁע, "to save" (see the seventh textual note on 22:3) and is translated as "salvation." A cognate noun for "salvation," יְשׁוּעָה, appears in 22:51. See also תְּשׁוּעָה in the first textual note on 19:3 (ET 19:2).

מִשְׂגַּבִּי—"My citadel." The noun מִשְׂגָּב is derived from the verb שָׂגַב, "be high, exalted." It can denote a literal fortification (e.g., Is 25:12; Jer 48:1) but is more frequently a metaphor for God, as often in the Psalms (e.g., Ps 46:8, 12 [ET 46:7, 11]), including, not surprisingly, psalms by David (e.g., Pss 9:10 [ET 9:9]; 18:3 [ET 18:2]). It is used together with צוּר (see the first textual note on 22:3) as a synonym here and in Pss 18:3 (ET 18:2); 62:3, 7 (ET 62:2, 6); 94:22. It is also used together with the noun מָנוֹס, "refuge," here (see the next textual note) and in Ps 59:17 (ET 59:16). For other terms in this poem that are at least partial synonyms of מִשְׂגָּב, see the second textual note on 22:2; the first textual note on 22:33; and the fourth textual note on 22:46.

וּמְנוּסִי—"(And) my refuge." The noun מָנוֹס, "refuge," is derived from the verb נוּס, "flee" (e.g., 19:4, 9 [ET 19:3, 8]; 23:11; 24:13), and suggests a place of escape when fleeing persecution, as is reinforced by the noun חָמָס, "violence," in the next line. This word and the three words in the next line (see the next textual note) are omitted in Ps 18:3 (ET 18:2). For synonyms of מָנוֹס, see the previous textual note.

מֹשִׁעִי מֵחָמָס תֹּשִׁעֵנִי—"My Savior, you save me from violence." Here the noun with the preposition מֵחָמָס, "from violence," is used abstractly for being saved from violent actions, but the phrase מֵאִישׁ חֲמָסִים, literally "from a man of violences," in 22:49, refers to rescue from the people who perpetrate those actions (see the fourth textual note on 22:49). The Hiphil (H) of יָשַׁע, "save," is used twice here: the first is the masculine singular participle (used as a substantive) with a first common singular suffix, מֹשִׁעִי, and the second is the second masculine singular imperfect with a first common singular suffix, תֹּשִׁעֵנִי, which recurs without a suffix in 22:28, תּוֹשִׁיעַ. This verb was used in the Torah of Moses for the exodus redemption (Ex 14:30 [cf. Ex 2:17]; Deut 20:4; see the textual note on 1 Sam 10:18–19 and the third textual note on 1 Sam 23:2[4]). For the use of this verb with God as subject, see the fourth textual note on 2 Sam 8:6. It is used with Yahweh as its subject in, e.g., 1 Sam 14:23; 2 Sam 3:18; 8:6, 14. For its Niphal (N), see the second textual note on 2 Sam 22:4. For cognate nouns, see the fourth textual note on 22:3.

---

4   Steinmann, *1 Samuel*, 200–201, 435.

22:4 מְהֻלָּל אֶקְרָא יְהוָה—"He is praiseworthy. I call on Yahweh." The first word is the Pual (Dp) participle of הָלַל, which is usually used in the Piel (D) with the active meaning "to praise."[5] This participle stands by itself syntactically and so is translated as a separate sentence. (Most English versions translate it as a modifier of יְהוָה.) Here and twice in 22:7 the imperfect אֶקְרָא has a timeless sense: David called upon Yahweh often in the past, continues to do so now, and will again in future troubles, including death itself. Here and in the first line of 22:7, אֶקְרָא takes יהוה as its direct object, which could mean "I call, 'Yahweh,'" but is translated as "I call on Yahweh," in harmony with the prepositional phrase in the second line of 22:7, וְאֶל־אֱלֹהַי אֶקְרָא, "(and) *to* my God I call."

אִוָּשֵׁעַ:—"I am saved." This is a Niphal (N) first common singular imperfect of יָשַׁע, whose meaning is the passive of the Hiphil (H) stem (see the seventh textual note on 22:3; Waltke-O'Connor, § 23.6.3a, including examples 2a and 2b). This imperfect too has a timeless sense. As Yahweh saved David in the past, David continues to be saved now and for eternity.

22:5 כִּי אֲפָפֻנִי מִשְׁבְּרֵי־מָוֶת—"For the breaking waves of death engulfed me." The verb in this clause and the two verbs in 22:6 are perfects and so are translated in the past tense. The noun מִשְׁבָּר is derived from the verb שָׁבַר, "break," and so can be rendered as a "breaking wave" or "breaker" (see also, e.g., Jonah 2:4 [ET 2:3]; Pss 42:8 [ET 42:7]; 93:4). Instead of its plural, as here, Ps 18:5 (ET 18:4) reads אֲפָפוּנִי חֶבְלֵי־מָוֶת, "the ropes of death engulfed/wrapped around me," perhaps influenced by "ropes" in 2 Sam 22:6 ‖ Ps 18:6 (ET 18:5; see the first textual note on 2 Sam 22:6).

בְּלִיַּעַל—For this noun, "destruction," see the third textual note on 16:7.

יְבַעֲתֻנִי:—"They terrified me." This is the Piel (D) third masculine plural imperfect of בָּעַת, "to terrify," with a first common singular object suffix. This verb occurs mostly in the Piel. It was used in 1 Sam 16:14–15 for an evil spirit "terrifying" Saul; see the second textual note on 1 Sam 16:14.[6] In this poetic context with three perfect verbs in 22:5a and 22:6 (see the first textual note on 22:5), this imperfect is also translated in the past tense. The imperfect aspect in Hebrew denotes an action that is not in a completed state. Here David's terror lasted for some time, and an imperfect verb makes the enduring effect on David in past time more vivid.

22:6 חֶבְלֵי שְׁאוֹל—"The ropes of Sheol." Note that "Sheol" (שְׁאוֹל) and "Saul" (שָׁאוּל) have the same consonants. "Sheol" here may allude to "Saul," who was named in 22:1 as one from whom David had been delivered by Yahweh. For שְׁאוֹל, see the fourth textual note and the commentary on 1 Sam 2:6,[7] where Hannah, in her song, declares that Yahweh brings people down to "Sheol" but is also able to raise them up again.

סַבֻּנִי—"They surrounded me." This is the Qal (G) perfect of סָבַב with a first common singular object suffix. Ps 18:6 (ET 18:5) has the synonymous form spelled fully, סְבָבוּנִי. Similarly, compare אֲפָפֻנִי in 2 Sam 22:5 with אֲפָפוּנִי in Ps 18:5 (ET 18:4).

---

[5] The Piel of הָלַל occurs seventy-five times in the Psalms, including its imperative in "praise Yah(weh)," that is, "hallelujah" (e.g., Pss 106:1; 111:1; 112:1; 113:1).

[6] Steinmann, *1 Samuel*, 314.

[7] Steinmann, *1 Samuel*, 72–73, 79.

22:7 בַּצַּר־לִי—"When I am in trouble" is literally "when distress is to me." The noun צַר II, "trouble, adversity, anguish," has the article and the preposition בְּ in a temporal sense. בַּצַּר is often used with the preposition לְ with a suffix in this construction (see צַר II in BDB and *DCH*).

אֶקְרָא ... אֶקְרָא—"I call ... I call." See the first textual note on 22:4. In place of the second verb, Ps 18:7 (ET 18:6) reads אֲשַׁוֵּעַ, "I shout," perhaps under the influence of the noun discussed in the next textual note.

וְשַׁוְעָתִי בְּאָזְנָיו—"And my shout was in his ears." The feminine noun שַׁוְעָה (also in 1 Sam 5:12) is derived from the verb שָׁוַע, which is used only in the Piel (D) and means "to cry for help." Ps 18:7 (ET 18:6) has the longer reading וְשַׁוְעָתִי לְפָנָיו ׀ תָּבוֹא בְאָזְנָיו, "and my shout before him came into his ears."

22:8 וַיִּתְגָּעַשׁ וַתִּרְעַשׁ הָאָרֶץ ... וַיִּתְגָּעֲשׁוּ—"The earth shook and quaked; ... they shook." The feminine noun אֶרֶץ, "earth," is the subject of the first two verbs. The first verb, which is the Qere, is the Hithpael (HtD) third masculine singular preterite (imperfect with *waw* consecutive) of גָּעַשׁ, "to shake back and forth, to and fro," whose plural is the third verb. The Kethib of the first verb is וַתִּגְעַשׁ, the Qal (G) of the same verb "to shake, quake," and it also is the reading in Ps 18:8 (ET 18:7). While גָּעַשׁ occurs ten times in the OT and with אֶרֶץ as its subject only here and in Ps 18:8 (ET 18:7), the second verb is the Qal of the more common synonym רָעַשׁ, which appears twenty-nine times in the OT, usually with אֶרֶץ as its subject.

מוֹסְדוֹת הַשָּׁמַיִם—"The foundations of the heavens." This is the only passage in the OT in which the feminine noun מוֹסָדָה is in construct with the "heavens." In three of its five OT occurrences, it is in construct with a term for the "earth" (either אֶרֶץ or the poetic synonym תֵּבֵל): see Is 40:21 and מֹסְדוֹת תֵּבֵל in 2 Sam 22:16 ‖ Ps 18:16 (ET 18:15). The reading in Ps 18:8 (ET 18:7) has the masculine noun מוֹסָד in construct: וּמוֹסְדֵי הָרִים, "and the foundations of the mountains" (as in Deut 32:22). The construct phrase מוֹסְדֵי־אֶרֶץ, "the foundations of the earth," appears in Is 24:18; Jer 31:37; Micah 6:2; Ps 82:5; Prov 8:29. מוֹסָד is never used in construct with "heavens."

יִרְגָּזוּ—"They trembled." Compare 1 Sam 14:15, where אֶרֶץ was the subject of the Qal (G) of רָגַז (as also in Joel 2:10; Amos 8:8; Ps 77:19 [ET 77:18]; Prov 30:21; cf. Hab 3:7).

חָרָה לוֹ:—"He was angry." For this construction, see the second textual note on 1 Sam 20:7[8] and the first textual note on 2 Sam 3:8.

22:9 גֶּחָלִים בָּעֲרוּ—"Coals burned." See the similar clause in 22:13: גַּחֲלֵי־אֵשׁ, literally "coals of fire burned." The masculine segholate noun גַּחַל, "a coal," is cognate to the feminine noun גַּחֶלֶת, "coal, ember," in 2 Sam 14:7. The plural of גַּחַל is the subject of the verb בָּעַר, "to burn" (intransitive), in 2 Sam 22:9, 13; Ezek 1:13; Ps 18:9 (ET 18:8).

מִמֶּנּוּ:—"From it." The translation assumes that the antecedent of the third masculine singular pronominal suffix is the preceding masculine noun פֶּה, "mouth" (מִפִּיו), but it could be "Yahweh" back in 22:7.

---

[8] Steinmann, *1 Samuel*, 390.

22:10 וַיֵּט שָׁמַיִם וַיֵּרַד—"He stretched out the heavens and came down." Except in the parallel Ps 18:10 (ET 18:9), elsewhere in the OT, the Qal (G) of נָטָה with the object noun שָׁמַיִם refers to God "stretching out the heavens" as his act of creation.[9] When David prays in Psalm 144 for Yahweh to "stretch aside the heavens and come down" to intervene for salvation, he uses the Hiphil (H) of נָטָה (Ps 144:5). David's language relates to NT passages in which the "heavens" are "opened" for God to accomplish salvation in Jesus Christ.[10]

וַעֲרָפֶל תַּחַת רַגְלָיו:—"A dark cloud beneath his feet." Cf. Mt 24:30; 26:64, where Jesus predicts his return "coming on the clouds of heaven."

22:11 וַיִּרְכַּב עַל־כְּרוּב—"He rode on a cherub." Yahweh is often depicted as "seated" or "enthroned" on the cherubim that overshadowed the mercy seat of the ark of the covenant, housed in the tabernacle and then in the temple. See the second textual note and the commentary on 1 Sam 4:4[11] and the fourth textual note and the commentary on 2 Sam 6:2. Here, however, the language is cosmic and depicts Yahweh flying from heaven to earth on his angelic chariot.

וַיֵּעֹף—"And he flew." This is the Qal (G) preterite (imperfect with *waw* consecutive) of עוּף, which is the verbal root of the noun עוֹף, "bird," often used in the construct phrase עוֹף הַשָּׁמַיִם, "bird(s) of the heavens" (e.g., 1 Sam 17:44, 46; 2 Sam 21:10).

וַיֵּרָא עַל־כַּנְפֵי־רוּחַ:—Codex Leningradensis and some other Masoretic manuscripts read וַיֵּרָא, "and he *appeared* on the wings of wind," a Niphal (N) preterite (imperfect with *waw* consecutive) of רָאָה, "to see." This is also the verb in Ps 18:11 (ET 18:10) according to some Masoretic manuscripts. (Its plural, וַיֵּרָאוּ, begins 2 Sam 22:16 ‖ Ps 18:16 [ET 18:15].) However, the verb וַיֵּדֶא, "and he *soared* on the wings of wind," is the verb in 2 Sam 22:11 according to many other Masoretic manuscripts as well as Codex Leningradensis and others in Ps 18:11 (ET 18:10). It is the Qal (G) preterite (imperfect with *waw* consecutive) of דָּאָה, which occurs elsewhere in the OT only three times, always describing the "soaring" or "swooping" of an eagle (Deut 28:49; Jer 48:40; 49:22). If וַיֵּדֶא is the original reading, then וַיֵּרָא was the product of a graphic confusion of *resh* and *dalet* and resulted in the substitution of this more common verb for a less common one.

22:12 וַיָּשֶׁת חֹשֶׁךְ סְבִיבֹתָיו סֻכּוֹת—Literally "and he set darkness surrounding him as booths." Ps 18:12 (ET 18:11) includes an additional word: יָשֶׁת חֹשֶׁךְ ׀ סִתְרוֹ סְבִיבוֹתָיו סֻכָּתוֹ, "and he set darkness as his covering, surrounding him as his booth." The noun חֹשֶׁךְ recurs in 2 Sam 22:29 with a suffix, חָשְׁכִּי, "my darkness."

חַשְׁרַת־מַיִם—"A collection of water." This is the sole instance of the noun חַשְׁרָה, "collection," in the OT. Ps 18:12 (ET 18:11) reads the noun חֲשֵׁכָה, "darkness," in construct: חֶשְׁכַת־מַיִם, "darkness of waters" (i.e., "dark waters"), which is supported by LXX 2 Sam 22:12, σκότος ὑδάτων, and LXX Ps 17:12 (MT 18:12; ET 18:11), σκοτεινὸν

---

[9] Is 40:22; 42:5; 44:24; 45:12; 51:13; Jer 10:12; 51:15; Zech 12:1; Ps 104:2; Job 9:8.

[10] Mt 3:16; Lk 3:21; Jn 1:51; Acts 10:11; Rev 19:11; cf. Rev 4:1; 11:19; 15:5.

[11] Steinmann, *1 Samuel*, 120, 126–27.

ὕδωρ. The difference may be due to a graphic confusion of *resh* and *kaph*, perhaps under the influence of חֹשֶׁךְ earlier in the verse (see the prior textual note).

עָבֵי שְׁחָקִים:—"Thick clouds" is literally "clouds of clouds." These two plural words are synonyms but may denote two different kinds of clouds.

22:13 בָּעֲרוּ גַּחֲלֵי־אֵשׁ:—"Fiery coals burned." See the first textual note on 22:9. The construct phrase גַּחֲלֵי־אֵשׁ, "coals of fire," appears also in Lev 16:12; Ezek 1:13; 10:2; Ps 18:13, 14 (ET 18:12, 13). The longer reading in Ps 18:13 (ET 18:12) is עָבָיו עָבְרוּ בָּרָד וְגַחֲלֵי־אֵשׁ, "his clouds passed by (with) hail and fiery coals."

22:14 יַרְעֵם—The Hiphil (H) of רָעַם means "to thunder." Its imperfect (sometimes with *waw* consecutive) is used similarly for Yahweh thundering in 1 Sam 2:10; 7:10; Ps 18:14 (ET 18:13); Job 37:4, 5. All these verses have the jussive form (יַרְעֵם) instead of the regular imperfect form (which would be יַרְעִים). A jussive form can have the meaning of a regular imperfect (cf. Joüon, § 114 g (1)). Ps 18:14 (ET 18:13) adds at the end of the verse בָּרָד וְגַחֲלֵי־אֵשׁ, "hail and fiery coals," which repeats the three words at the end of Ps 18:13 (ET 18:12).

22:15 בָּרָק וַיְהֻם:—The verb in the previous line [וַיִּשְׁלַח] is implied here: "[he sent forth] lightning, and he routed them." In place of the singular noun here, בָּרָק, "lightning," Ps 18:15 (ET 18:14) reads the plural, וּבְרָקִים, "and lightning flashes." The Qere and the sole reading in many Masoretic manuscripts is וַיְהֻם, "and he routed." The Qal (G) of הָמַם is literally "to confuse, vex, cause panic." The Kethib is the same verb but with a third masculine plural suffix, וַיְהֻמֵּם, "and he routed them," which is also in Ps 18:15 (ET 18:14). The inclusion of the pronoun in the Kethib in 2 Sam 22:15 is supported by LXX 2 Sam 22:15, καὶ ἐξέστησεν αὐτούς, and LXX Ps 17:15 (MT 18:15; ET 18:14), καὶ συνετάραξεν αὐτούς.

22:16 וַיֵּרָאוּ אֲפִקֵי יָם—"The channels of the sea appeared." For the verb, see the third textual note on 22:11. The singular noun יָם, "sea," is the reading of the MT and is supported by the LXX (θαλάσσης). One Masoretic manuscript and Ps 18:16 (ET 18:15) read the plural noun מַיִם, "water."[12]

מֹסְדוֹת תֵּבֵל—"The foundations of the world." See the second textual note on 22:8.

בְּגַעֲרַת יְהוָה—"By Yahweh's rebuke." Ps 18:16 (ET 18:15) reads מִגַּעֲרָתְךָ יְהוָה, "by your rebuke, Yahweh."

מִנִּשְׁמַת רוּחַ אַפּוֹ:—"At the blast of the breath of his nose." The noun רוּחַ can denote "hard breathing through the nostrils in anger" in reference to God's anger (BDB, 1 d (1), citing 2 Sam 22:16 ‖ Ps 18:16 [ET 18:15]). In place of אַפּוֹ, "his nose," Ps 18:16 (ET 18:15) reads אַפֶּךָ, "your nose."

22:17 יַמְשֵׁנִי מִמַּיִם רַבִּים:—"He drew me out from many waters." The verb is the Hiphil (H) of מָשָׁה with a first common singular suffix, as also in the parallel Ps 18:17 (ET 18:16). The only other instance of מָשָׁה is its Qal (G) in Ex 2:10, where Pharaoh's

---

[12] Cross and Freedman, "A Royal Song of Thanksgiving," 26, including n. 41, read יָם, "sea," in Ps 18:16 (ET 18:15) and claim that the initial *mem* of מַיִם was displaced from the end of the previous word, where it was enclitic.

daughter gives Moses his name, מֹשֶׁה, on the basis of this verb, saying, מִן־הַמַּיִם מְשִׁיתִהוּ, "from the water I drew him out."

22:18   יַצִּילֵנִי מֵאֹיְבִי עָז—"He delivered me from my strong enemy." A repetition of the verb יַצִּילֵנִי is implied in the second line of this verse. For the Hiphil (H) of נָצַל, see the first textual note on 22:1. In prose an adjective normally agrees with the noun it modifies in gender, number, and definiteness, but such concord is often absent in poetry. The pronominal suffix on אֹיְבִי, "my enemy" (see the second textual note on 22:1), makes the participle definite, but its modifying adjective עַז (in pause, עָז), "strong," lacks the article.

מִשֹּׂנְאַי—"From those who hate me." Many Masoretic manuscripts and Ps 18:18 (ET 18:17) include the prefixed conjunction *waw*, וּמִשֹּׂנְאַי, "*and* from those who hate me." The Qal (G) masculine plural participle of שָׂנֵא, "to hate," has the first common singular pronominal suffix in an objective sense. See also the Piel (D) participle in the second textual note on 22:41.

22:19   מִשְׁעָן—This masculine noun, "support," is in the parallel Ps 18:19 (ET 18:18) and elsewhere in the OT only in Is 3:1 (twice). Its feminine cognate מִשְׁעֶנֶת denotes a "staff" or a "crutch" upon which a person leans for support (e.g., Ex 21:19; 2 Ki 18:21 ‖ Is 36:6; Zech 8:4).

22:20   וַיֹּצֵא לַמֶּרְחָב אֹתִי—"He brought me out to a spacious place." The Hebrew word order is unusual. Normally a suffixed direct object marker (אֹתִי) would immediately follow the verb (וַיֹּצֵא) and precede a prepositional phrase (לַמֶּרְחָב). Ps 18:20 (ET 18:19) has synonymous wording (וַיּוֹצִיאֵנִי לַמֶּרְחָב) but in normal word order since the first common singular object ("me") is expressed by a pronominal suffix on the verb, וַיּוֹצִיאֵנִי. A wide, broad, or spacious place (מֶרְחָב) is a place of relief and salvation (see also 22:37a), compared to a narrow or cramped place of distress (e.g., צַר in 1 Sam 2:32; 2 Sam 22:7; see the first textual note on 22:7).[13]

יְחַלְּצֵנִי—"He rescued me." The Piel (D) of חָלַץ is a synonym of other verbs for rescuing and delivering (e.g., the Hiphil [H] of נָצַל and יָשַׁע), but is relatively rare and mostly confined to the poetry of the Psalms (ten of its fourteen occurrences, e.g., Pss 6:5 [ET 6:4]; 18:20 [ET 18:19]; 34:8 [ET 34:7]).

22:21   יִגְמְלֵנִי—"Yahweh has repaid me." For the verb גָּמַל, "repay, requite," see the textual note on 19:37 (ET 19:36).

כְּצִדְקָתִי—"According to my righteousness." The identical form of the feminine noun צְדָקָה with the preposition כְּ and a first common singular suffix recurs in the first clause of 22:25. The parallel verses Ps 18:21 (ET 18:20) and Ps 18:25 (ET 18:24) have כְּצִדְקִי, the analogous form of the masculine noun צֶדֶק. Yahweh is the source of the "righteousness" he gives to his people through their faith in him. For צְדָקָה, "righteousness," see the textual note on 2 Sam 8:15. In 1 Sam 12:7 the noun refers to Yahweh's "righteous deeds" for the sake of his people, and in 2 Sam 8:15 David, as the anointed king, administers Yahweh's "righteousness" among God's people. See the noun also

---

[13]   See also the cognate verb צָרַר, "be confined, be in distress," in 1 Sam 13:6; 28:15; 30:6; 2 Sam 1:26; 13:2; 20:3; 24:14.

in 1 Sam 26:23, where David declares that Yahweh requites a person according to "his righteousness," and in 2 Sam 19:29 (ET 19:28). See also the forensic sense of the Hiphil (H) of צָדַק in 2 Sam 15:4.

כְּבֹר יָדַי—"According to the purity of my hands." The noun בֹּר, "purity," recurs in the second line of 22:25. It is derived from the verb בָּרַר, for which, see the first textual note on 22:27. The cognate adjective בַּר can refer to Yahweh's Word, which is "pure" and enlightening (Ps 19:9 [ET 19:8]), and to those made "pure" in heart (Pss 24:4; 73:1).

יָשִׁיב לִי—"He has rewarded me." For the Hiphil (H) of שׁוּב with a preposition (here לְ) and Yahweh as the subject, meaning that Yahweh "pays back" or "rewards" a person, see the first textual note on 16:8. The idiom recurs in the first clause of 22:25.

22:22 וְלֹא רָשַׁעְתִּי מֵאֱלֹהָי—"And I did not act wickedly against my God." The verb רָשַׁע is cognate to the adjective רָשָׁע, which refers to "wicked" persons in 1 Sam 2:9; 24:14 (ET 24:13); 2 Sam 4:11.

22:23 מִשְׁפָּטָיו—"His ordinances." This suffixed plural of מִשְׁפָּט is the Qere and the reading in Ps 18:23 (ET 18:22). The Kethib could be vocalized as a defective, or *ḥaser*, spelling of the same word, מִשְׁפָּטָו, or as the suffixed singular מִשְׁפָּטוֹ, "his ordinance." For the noun מִשְׁפָּט, meaning divine "justice" or an "ordinance," as in the Torah, see the textual note on 2 Sam 8:15.

לֹא־אָסוּר מִמֶּנָּה—"I did not turn away from them." The third feminine singular suffix on מִמֶּנָּה, literally "from it," serves as a collective for the suffixed feminine plural וְחֻקֹּתָיו, "and his statutes." Ps 18:23 (ET 18:22) reads the verb as Hiphil (H) and the suffix as first common singular: לֹא־אָסִיר מֶנִּי, "I did not remove [them] from me." Here in 2 Sam 22:23 one Masoretic manuscript reads the verb as Hiphil, and a few read the suffix as first common singular.

22:24 וָאֶהְיֶה—"I was." This is the usual form of the Qal (G) preterite (imperfect with *waw* consecutive) of הָיָה. Ps 18:24 (ET 18:23) has the apocopated form וָאֱהִי.

תָמִים—"Blameless." This adjective recurs in 22:26, 31, 33. It is derived from the verb תָּמַם, "be finished, complete." In Leviticus and Numbers the adjective commonly refers to an acceptable "unblemished" offering. It is also used for a person deemed righteous (e.g., Gen 6:9; 17:1; Ps 119:1; Prov 11:5). See also the cognate verb תָּמַם in the second textual note on 2 Sam 22:26.

לוֹ—"To him." In place of this suffixed preposition, Ps 18:24 (ET 18:23) has עִמּוֹ, "with him."

וָאֶשְׁתַּמְּרָה—"And I kept myself" is the Hithpael (HtD) preterite (imperfect with *waw* consecutive) with paragogic *he* (GKC, § 49 e) of שָׁמַר, "to keep, guard," with a metathesis of the prefixed ת and the initial sibilant שׁ.[14] It has a reflexive or middle meaning. Ps 18:24 (ET 18:23) reads וָאֶשְׁתַּמֵּר, without paragogic *he*. The only other OT instance of the Hithpael of שָׁמַר is in Micah 6:16.

22:25 וַיָּשֶׁב יְהוָה לִי—"Yahweh rewarded me." See the fourth textual note on 22:21.

כְּצִדְקָתִי—"According to my righteousness." See the second textual note on 22:21.

---

[14] See Waltke-O'Connor, § 26.1.1b, including example 14.

כְּבֹרִי—"According to my purity." Ps 18:25 (ET 18:24) reads כְּבֹר יָדַי, "according to the purity of my hands," which is the same reading as in 2 Sam 22:21 (see the third textual note on 22:21) and is supported here by LXX 2 Sam 22:25 and LXX Ps 17:25 (MT 18:25; ET 18:24): κατὰ τὴν καθαριότητα τῶν χειρῶν μου.

22:26 חָסִיד—"A faithful person." For this substantivized adjective, see the first textual note on 1 Sam 2:9.[15] For the cognate noun חֶסֶד, used in 2 Sam 22:51, see the second textual note on 9:3 and the first textual note on 16:17.

תִּתְחַסָּד ... תִּתַּמָּם—"You show yourself to be faithful. ... You show yourself to be blameless." Both verbs are Hithpael (HtD) second masculine singular imperfects, of חָסַד and תָּמַם, respectively. The second verb would be תִּתְתַּמָּם (if not in pause), but the preformative ת of the Hithpael assimilates to the following ת (-תָּתְ- becomes -תָּ-).[16] For these and certain other verbs the Hithpael is reflexive-declarative.[17] See also the two Hithpael verbs in 22:27.

גִּבּוֹר—This MT reading means "elite soldier" (see, e.g., 1 Sam 2:4; 17:51; 2 Sam 1:19, 21). The translation follows the reading with גֶּבֶר, "man," found in a few Masoretic manuscripts, which is supported by the construct form גְּבַר in Ps 18:26 (ET 18:25) and by ἀνδρός in LXX 2 Sam 22:26 and LXX Ps 17:26 (MT 18:26; ET 18:25).

22:27 עִם־נָבָר תִּתָּבָר—"With the pure, you show yourself to be pure." נָבָר is the Niphal (N) participle of בָּרַר, which could have a reflexive meaning, "purify oneself," or a passive meaning, "be purified." תִּתָּבָר is the Hithpael (HtD) second masculine singular imperfect of בָּרַר, which has a reflexive-declarative sense; see the second textual note on 22:26 and the third textual note on 22:27.

עִקֵּשׁ—"Crooked" or "twisted." In Proverbs this adjective describes sinful and perverted people and stands as an antonym of terms for believers such as "straight" and "upright."[18]

תִּתַּפָּל:—"You show yourself to be shrewd." This difficult verb form most likely should be parsed as the Hithpael (HtD) second masculine singular imperfect of תָּפַל, a verb that would occur only here and would mean "be shrewd." Other proposed definitions are inappropriate for a verb whose subject is "Yahweh" (22:25).[19] Ps 18:27 (ET 18:26) reads תִּתְפַּתָּל, the Hithpael of פָּתַל, "show yourself to be clever." The only other instances of פָּתַל are Niphal (N), meaning "wrestle" in Gen 30:8 and "be twisted" in Job 5:13 and Prov 8:8, where it is a synonym of עִקֵּשׁ (see the prior textual note). LXX 2 Sam 22:27 considers the verb to be a cognate of עִקֵּשׁ and translates the clause as καὶ μετὰ στρεβλοῦ στρεβλωθήσῃ, "and with the crooked you will be deemed crooked"

---

[15] Steinmann, *1 Samuel*, 74.

[16] See Waltke-O'Connor, § 26.1.1b, including example 25.

[17] *IBH*, § 42 A; Waltke-O'Connor, § 26.2f.

[18] See the textual note and the commentary on Prov 2:15 in Steinmann, *Proverbs*, 92–93, 95.

[19] *HALOT* (s.v. תפל I) tentatively defines this Hithpael (HtD) as "exhibit stupid behaviour," and *DCH* (s.v. תפל) defines it as "act stupidly." BDB (s.v. פָּתַל, Hithpael) calls the verb form here "impossible" and emends it to the verb תִּתְפַּתָּל, as in Ps 18:27 (ET 18:26). The KJV translation of 2 Sam 22:27, "thou wilt shew thyself unsavoury," apparently connects this verb to תָּפֵל, "tasteless," and תִּפְלָה, "tastelessness."

(*NETS*). LXX Ps 17:27 has καὶ μετὰ στρεβλοῦ διαστρέψεις, "and with the crooked you will pervert" (*NETS*).

22:28 וְאֶת־עַם עָנִי תּוֹשִׁיעַ—Literally "and a lowly people you save." For the verb תּוֹשִׁיעַ, see the seventh textual note on 22:3. Ps 18:28 (ET 18:27) reads כִּי־אַתָּה עַם־עָנִי תּוֹשִׁיעַ, literally "for you, a lowly people you save"; the first two words may have been copied from the start of the next verse (כִּי־אַתָּה begins both Ps 18:29 [ET 18:28] and 2 Sam 22:29). Some have proposed that the conjunction should be deleted from וְאֶת־ and that the remaining consonants את are a defective, or *ḥaser*, spelling of the pronoun אַתָּה.[20]

וְעֵינֶיךָ עַל־רָמִים תַּשְׁפִּיל—"And your eyes are on the haughty—you humble [them]." The Qal (G) masculine plural participle רָמִים is of רוּם, "be high, exalted," here connoting arrogance. Ps 18:28 (ET 18:27) reads וְעֵינַיִם רָמוֹת תַּשְׁפִּיל, literally "and haughty eyes you humble,"[21] with the Qal (G) feminine plural participle of רוּם modifying the feminine dual noun עֵינַיִם, "eyes."

22:29 כִּי־אַתָּה נֵירִי יְהוָה—"For you are my lamp, Yahweh." For the noun נֵר, "lamp," here written plene, or *maleʾ*, see the second textual note on 21:17. Ps 18:29 (ET 18:28) reads כִּי־אַתָּה תָּאִיר נֵרִי, "for you light my lamp." The Hiphil (H) of אוֹר, "to be light," can have the causative meaning "to light" a lamp, wood, or fire (BDB, Hiphil, 3).

וַיהוָה יַגִּיהַּ חָשְׁכִּי—"And Yahweh illuminates my darkness." The verb יַגִּיהַּ is the Hiphil (H) third masculine singular imperfect of נָגַהּ, whose Qal (G) means "to shine" (e.g., Is 9:1 [ET 9:2]). In place of וַיהוָה, "and Yahweh," Ps 18:29 (ET 18:28) reads יְהוָה אֱלֹהַי, "Yahweh my God."

22:30 בְכֵה—"With you." This is the preposition בְּ with a second masculine singular suffix written with final *he* as a vowel marker. Ps 18:30 (ET 18:29) has the usual form בְּךָ.

אָרוּץ—"I can rush." This is the Qal (G) first common singular imperfect of רוּץ, "to run" with the modal sense "can" (see Joüon, § 113 l). In Ps 18:30 (ET 18:29) it is spelled defectively: אָרֻץ. The verb רוּץ was used similarly for David running forward to attack Goliath (1 Sam 17:48, 51). Cf. other runners in military contexts in, e.g., 1 Sam 4:12; 8:11; 2 Sam 18:19–26.

גְּדוּד—"A troop." This noun is used with this military meaning elsewhere in Samuel (1 Sam 30:8, 15, 23; 2 Sam 3:22; 4:2). Some scholars have suggested that because it is parallel to the noun שׁוּר, "wall," at the end of the verse, this noun here means "wall" and is derived from the verb גָּדַד, "cut" (see *HALOT*, s.v. גְּדוּד I; *CDCH*, s.v. גְּדוּד III).

בֵּאלֹהַי—This reading in Codex Leningradensis is "with my God." Many Masoretic manuscripts read וּבֵאלֹהַי, with the prefixed conjunction *waw*, "and with my God," which is the reading in Ps 18:30 (ET 18:29) and which is supported by LXX 2 Sam 22:30 and LXX Ps 17:30 (MT 18:30; ET 18:29): καὶ ἐν τῷ θεῷ μου.

---

[20] Cross and Freedman, "A Royal Song of Thanksgiving," 28, including n. 62.

[21] Cross and Freedman, "A Royal Song of Thanksgiving," 28, , including n. 63, propose a conflation of the readings of 2 Sam 22:28 and Ps 18:28 (ET 18:27) that means "but the [plural] haughty-eyed though dost humble."

אֲדַלֶּג־שׁוּר׃—"I can leap over a wall." The Piel (D) of דָּלַג refers to men "leaping" like a deer or gazelle in Is 35:6; Song 2:8. The Hebrew noun שׁוּר denotes a "wall" also in Gen 49:22. In Aramaic it denotes the rebuilt city walls of Jerusalem in Ezra 4:12, 13, 16.

22:31 הָאֵל תָּמִים דַּרְכּוֹ—Literally "the God—blameless is his way." This is equivalent to "God's way is blameless/perfect" (see GKC, § 140 d). אֵל is one of a couple of nouns for "God" that is shorter than אֱלֹהִים (see also the first textual note on 22:32). It recurs with the article in 22:33, 48, without the article in 22:32, and is found elsewhere in the book of Samuel only in 1 Sam 2:3; 2 Sam 23:5. It is most common in the poetry of the Psalms and Job.

אִמְרַת יְהוָה צְרוּפָה—"The Word of Yahweh is pure." This is the only instance in Samuel of the feminine noun אִמְרָה, "word," derived from the verb אָמַר, "say," but elsewhere it often refers to the divine Word (e.g., Deut 33:9; Is 5:24; Pss 12:7 (ET 12:6); 119:11, 41). Here it is modified by the feminine singular Qal passive (Gp) participle of צָרַף, "to refine, purify."

לְכֹל הַחֹסִים בּוֹ׃—"For all who take refuge in him." See the second textual note on 22:3.

22:32 אֵל—"God." See the first textual note on 22:31. Ps 18:32 (ET 18:31) has אֱלוֹהַּ, another noun for "God" that is shorter than אֱלֹהִים and that is usually found in poetry, most often in Job.

מִבַּלְעֲדֵי יְהוָה ... מִבַּלְעֲדֵי אֱלֹהֵינוּ׃—"Other than Yahweh … other than our God." These are the only two instances in Samuel of מִבַּלְעֲדֵי, which is a combination of the prepositions מִן + בַּל + עֲדֵי (a poetic form of עַד). This combination is used by Isaiah in similar affirmations that Yahweh is the only God (Is 43:11; 44:6, 8; 45:6, 21). In place of its second instance here, Ps 18:32 (ET 18:31) reads זוּלָתִי, "except" our God.

22:33 הָאֵל מָעוּזִּי חָיִל—The MT reads "(he is) the God (who is) my stronghold (in) strength." The noun חָיִל is epexegetical to מָעוּזִּי, and so מָעוּזִּי חָיִל could be translated as "my strong fortress" (GKC, § 131 r). This is the only instance in Samuel of the noun מָעוֹז, "stronghold," which is cognate to the noun עֹז, "strength" (e.g., 6:14), and the adjective עַז, "strong" (see the first textual note on 22:18).[22] The noun חָיִל, "strength," recurs in 22:40, and elsewhere in Samuel it can refer to an "army" or be part of a designation for a brave or elite soldier.[23] In place of the suffixed noun מָעוּזִּי in the MT, Ps 18:33 (ET 18:32) has הַמְאַזְּרֵנִי, the Piel (D) masculine singular participle of אָזַר, meaning "to clothe, gird, equip," with the article and a first common singular suffix, and 4QSamᵃ has מאזרני, the same suffixed participle without the article. For this Piel verb, see also the first textual note on 2 Sam 22:40. The translation "he is the God who clothes me with strength" follows those readings.

וַיַּתֵּר תָּמִים דַּרְכִּי׃—The verb וַיַּתֵּר is the Hiphil (H) third masculine singular preterite (imperfect with *waw* consecutive) of one of several homographic verbs נָתַר. The Hiphil of one נָתַר means "to make [someone] spring up" (see BDB, s.v. נָתַר I; *DCH*,

---

22 For synonyms of מָעוֹז, see the second textual note on 22:2; the fifth and sixth textual notes on 22:3; and the fourth textual note on 22:46.

23 See, e.g., 1 Sam 10:26; 14:52; 16:18; 17:20; 2 Sam 2:7; 8:9; 11:16; 24:2, 4.

s.v. נתר II). The Hiphil of another נָתַר means "to unfasten, set free" (see BDB, s.v. נָתַר II; *DCH*, s.v. נתר I). The translation "and he *makes* my way" follows the reading וַיִּתֵּן in Ps 18:33 (ET 18:32). If that was the original reading, the form in the MT is proba-bly the result of a graphic confusion of final *nun* and *resh*. The Qere of the object noun is דַּרְכִּי, "my way," which is the sole reading in many Masoretic manuscripts as well as the reading in Ps 18:33 (ET 18:32). It is also supported by LXX 2 Sam 22:33 and LXX Ps 17:33 (MT 18:33; ET 18:32): τὴν ὁδόν μου. The Kethib is דַּרְכּוֹ, "his way."

22:34 מְשַׁוֶּה רַגְלַי כָּאַיָּלוֹת—The verb מְשַׁוֶּה is the Piel (D) masculine singular partici-ple of שָׁוָה, but as in the prior textual note, the verb could be one of several homographs. One שָׁוָה means "to be like, resemble" in the Qal (G), and so its Piel (D) here results in the translation "he makes my feet like deer" (see *DCH*, s.v. שׁוה I, Piel 1 a; cf. BDB, s.v. שָׁוָה I). The sense could be filled out as "he makes my feet be like the feet of deer." Another שָׁוָה in the Piel means "to set, place" (see BDB, s.v. שָׁוָה II; cf. *DCH*, s.v. שׁוה II), which would result in a similar meaning. In either case, a similar idea is in 22:30b. The Qere of the object noun is רַגְלַי, "my feet," as in Ps 18:34 (ET 18:33), which is sup-ported by LXX 2 Sam 22:34 and LXX Ps 17:34 (MT 18:34; ET 18:33): τοὺς πόδας μου. The Kethib is רַגְלָיו, "his feet."

וְעַל בָּמוֹתַי יַעֲמִדֵנִי:—Literally "and upon my heights he makes me stand." The plu-ral of בָּמָה, "high place," has a first common singular suffix, בָּמוֹתַי, as in Ps 18:34 (ET 18:33; בָּמֹתַי). The translation "on the heights" presupposes the noun without a suffix, בָּמוֹת, which is supported by LXX 2 Sam 22:34, ἐπὶ τὰ ὕψη, as well as LXX Ps 17:34 (MT 18:34; ET 18:33), ἐπὶ τὰ ὑψηλά. Most English versions follow the LXX.[24] If בָּמוֹת was the original reading, the *yod* in the MT is probably a dittograph of the first letter of the next word, יַעֲמִדֵנִי (the Hiphil [H] third masculine singular imperfect of עָמַד with a first common singular suffix).

22:35 וְנִחַת קֶשֶׁת־נְחוּשָׁה זְרֹעֹתָי:—The verb וְנִחַת is the Piel (D) third masculine singu-lar perfect of נָחַת, meaning "bend, stretch a bow" (*DCH*, s.v. נחת I, Piel, 1; similarly, BDB, s.v. נָחַת, Piel), with *waw* consecutive. Its subject is the feminine plural with a suf-fix זְרֹעֹתָי, "my arms." Hebrew commonly employs a third masculine singular verb when it precedes its subject, even if the subject differs in gender and number (GKC, § 145 o). The verb in Ps 18:35 (ET 18:34) is וְנִחֲתָה, the Piel third feminine singular perfect with *waw* consecutive, which agrees with its subject, זְרוֹעֹתָי, in gender but not in number.

22:36 יִשְׁעֶךָ—"Your salvation." See the fourth textual note on 22:3.

וַעֲנֹתְךָ תַּרְבֵּנִי:—The first verb, וַעֲנֹתְךָ, is the Qal (G) infinitive construct of one of the homographic verbs עָנָה with the conjunction *waw* and a second masculine singu-lar suffix. Probably it represents עָנָה I, "to answer," although it could be עָנָה III, "to be bowed down, low" (cf. REB: "you stoop down to make me great"). The second verb, תַּרְבֵּנִי, is the Hiphil (H) imperfect of רָבָה with a first common singular suffix, meaning "make me great." It could be either third feminine singular or second masculine singular. Since the MT has no feminine noun to serve as its subject, it must be second mascu-line singular, and the preceding infinitive serves as an adverbial accusative, "by your

---

[24] HCSB, ESV, GW, NIV, NRSV.

answering you make me great." The translation follows the reading ועזרתך in 4QSamᵃ, which is to be vocalized as וְעֶזְרָתְךָ, "and your help." With this reading the feminine noun עֶזְרָה is the subject of תַּרְבֵּנִי, which is then to be parsed as third feminine singular: "and your help has made me great." While the noun עֶזְרָה is otherwise absent from Samuel, it is common in the Psalms as a term for God's saving "help" for which the psalmist prays.[25] Ps 18:36 (ET 18:35) has an additional clause before the final clause of the verse, and its final clause substitutes the feminine noun עֲנָוָה with the conjunction *waw* and a suffix, וְעַנְוָתְךָ, "and your humility," for וַעֲנֹתְךָ, the first word in the final clause of 2 Sam 22:36: וִימִינְךָ תִּסְעָדֵנִי וַעֲנֹתְךָ תַּרְבֵּנִי, "and your right hand supports me, and your humility makes me great." Some English translations follow that reading of the final clause also in 2 Sam 22:36 and translate וְעַנְוָתְךָ as "and your gentleness" (e.g., ESV; similarly, NKJV).

22:37   תַּרְחִיב צַעֲדִי תַחְתֵּנִי—"You widen my steps beneath me." The idea is that God grants David a broad and secure path through life, as opposed to a narrow and hazardous path. In the OT generally a broad place is associated with salvation; see the first textual note on 22:20. 4QSamᵃ omits תַחְתֵּנִי. This suffixed preposition in pause, תַּחְתֵּנִי, "beneath me," has the form of the first common singular suffix that is normally attached to a verb (GKC, § 103 d; Joüon, § 103 e, including note 1), and the same form (תַּחְתֵּנִי) recurs in pause in 22:40, 48. These three are the only instances in the OT where תַּחַת has that suffix. The nine other times in the OT where the preposition תַּחַת has the first common singular suffix, the form of the suffix indicates that תַּחַת is regarded as plural: תַּחְתַּי, or in pause, תַּחְתָּי, as in Ps 18:37, 40, 48 (ET 18:36, 39, 47).

וְלֹא מָעֲדוּ קַרְסֻלָּי:—"And my ankles do not waver." The uncommon verb מָעַד means "to slip, slide, totter." The noun קַרְסֹל is one of the few Hebrew quadriliterals. It appears in the OT only here and in the parallel Ps 18:37 (ET 18:36).

22:38   אֶרְדְּפָה אֹיְבַי וָאַשְׁמִידֵם—"I pursue my enemies and destroy them." The first verb is the Qal (G) singular cohortative of רָדַף (cf. GKC, § 108 e; "pseudo-cohortative," Waltke-O'Connor, § 34.5.3b, including note 28). The second is the Hiphil (H) first common singular preterite (imperfect with *waw* consecutive) of שָׁמַד. In Ps 18:38 (ET 18:37), the form of the first verb is the first common singular imperfect, and the second verb is the Hiphil (H) of נָשַׂג: אֶרְדּוֹף אוֹיְבַי וְאַשִּׂיגֵם, "I pursue my enemies and overtake them."

עַד־כַּלּוֹתָם:—This temporal clause is literally "until finishing off them." The verb כַּלּוֹתָם is the Piel (D) infinitive construct of כָּלָה with a third masculine plural object suffix. Another form of this Piel verb begins MT 22:39; see the next textual note.

22:39   וָאֲכַלֵּם וָאֶמְחָצֵם וְלֹא יְקוּמוּן—The MT reads "and I finish them off, and I crush them, and they will not arise." The translation omits the first word and the conjunction on the second word, following the reading in 4QSamᵃ (אמחצם ולוא יקומון) and Ps 18:39 (ET 18:38), which is supported by LXX 2 Sam 22:39. If יְקוּמוּן is considered an imperfect of capability, it could be translated as "they *cannot* arise."[26] The reading in

---

[25]   E.g., Pss 22:20 (ET 22:19); 27:9; 38:23 (ET 38:22); 40:14, 18 (ET 40:13, 17).

[26]   See Waltke-O'Connor, § 31.4c, including example 5.

Ps 18:39 (ET 18:38) is אֶמְחָצֵם וְלֹא־יֻכְלוּ קוּם, "I will crush them, and they will not be able to arise."

22:40 וַתַּזְרֵנִי חַיִל לַמִּלְחָמָה—"You have clothed me with strength for battle." The verb וַתַּזְרֵנִי is the Piel (D) second masculine singular preterite (imperfect with *waw* consecutive) of אָזַר, meaning "to clothe, equip," with a first common singular suffix. In this form the *aleph* is elided (GKC, § 68 k). The full form, וַתְּאַזְּרֵנִי, is in Ps 18:40 (ET 18:39) and is the reading here in 4QSamᵃ (תאזרנ[י]). See the similar wordings in the first textual note on 2 Sam 22:33 and in 1 Sam 2:4.

קָמָי—"Those who arise against me." The participle of קוּם can be used with a pronominal suffix and without a prepositional phrase to refer to enemies who "arise" with hostile purpose against the person(s) denoted by the suffix, as again in 22:49 (וּמִקָּמַי); see also Ex 15:7; 32:25; Deut 33:11; Pss 44:6 (ET 44:5); 74:23; Lam 3:62. This meaning is more apparent when the participle is used in a fuller context with a prepositional phrase; see the third textual note on 2 Sam 18:31, as well as, e.g., Deut 28:7.

22:41 וְאֹיְבַי תַּתָּה לִּי עֹרֶף—Literally "and my enemies—you have placed to me (the back of their) neck." This and the next line both begin with a designation of David's foes as a *casus pendens* (GKC, § 116 w), as shown in the translation. The verb תַּתָּה is the Qal (G) second masculine singular perfect of נָתַן with an assimilation of both *nun* consonants and with the fuller spelling of the suffix, תָּה-, in place of the usual תָּ- (see the second textual note on 2:26 and GKC, § 44 g; Joüon, § 42 f). Ps 18:41 (ET 18:40) has the synonymous form נָתַתָּה, in which, as usual, the first *nun* is not assimilated. This idiom most likely means that the enemies turn the backs of their necks toward David as they flee. See Ex 23:27; see also Josh 7:12; Jer 2:27; 32:33; 2 Chr 29:6. It is less likely that this idiom refers to the victor grasping the necks of the defeated enemies (as in Gen 49:8) or stepping on their necks as they lie on the ground (as in Josh 10:24).

מְשַׂנְאַי וָאַצְמִיתֵם:—Literally "my haters—and I annihilate them." The Piel (D) participle מְשַׂנְאַי is a *casus pendens* (GKC, § 116 w). This participle of שָׂנֵא, "to hate," is used as a noun and may be more forceful than the suffixed Qal (G) participle שֹׂנְאִי discussed in the second textual note on 22:18. The Hiphil (H) of צָמַת, "destroy, annihilate," occurs ten times in the OT, always in poetry and mostly in the Psalms. Here the conjunction is on that second verb, not on the first. In Ps 18:41 (ET 18:40), the conjunction is on the first verb, but not the second: וּמְשַׂנְאַי אַצְמִיתֵם, "and my enemies—I annihilate them." 4QSamᵃ apparently lacks the conjunction: [משנאי] אצמיתם[ם].

The preterite (imperfect with *waw* consecutive) וָאַצְמִיתֵם, "(and) I annihilate them," indicates the logical consequence of God's previous action of making David's enemies flee (see Waltke-O'Connor, § 33.2.1d). David used a different construction in the previous verse to convey the same concept: a preterite (imperfect with *waw* consecutive) verb indicating past action ("you have clothed me") was followed by an imperfect verb ("you make [those who arise against me] bow") that indicates a general situation whose time is unspecified, that is, it most likely happened in the past, it may also be happening now, and it may be repeated in the future. Such a verb is best represented in English by the present tense. That David was able to use two distinct strategies to convey these similar sequences in adjacent verses testifies to his skill as a poet and rhetorician.

22:42 יִשְׁעוּ—This is the Qal (G) third masculine plural imperfect of שָׁעָה, "to look, gaze," which in context would have to signify looking about for help or deliverance. The translation follows the reading יְשַׁוְּעוּ, "they cry for help," in Ps 18:42 (ET 18:41), which is the Piel (D) imperfect of שָׁוַע (see the cognate noun in the third textual note on 22:7). That Hebrew reading here is presupposed by LXX 2 Sam 22:42 (βοήσονται). Apparently the MT verb יִשְׁעוּ suffered from haplography of the medial *waw*.

וְאֵין מֹשִׁיעַ—Literally "and there is no savior." The verb is the Hiphil (H) masculine singular participle of יָשַׁע (see the seventh textual note on 22:3). The plene, or *maleʾ*, spelling מוֹשִׁיעַ is in Ps 18:42 (ET 18:41).

אֶל־יְהוָה—"To Yahweh." Ps 18:42 (ET 18:41) has the equivalent עַל־יְהוָה.

עָנָם:—This is the Qal (G) third masculine singular perfect of עָנָה, "answer," with a third masculine plural object suffix. Cf. the second textual note on 22:36.

22:43 וְאֶשְׁחָקֵם—"I pulverize them." The rare verb שָׁחַק appears elsewhere in the OT only in the parallel verse Ps 18:43 (ET 18:42) and in Ex 30:36; Job 14:19, always in the Qal (G).

כַּעֲפַר־אָרֶץ—The MT reads "like dust of (the) earth." The translation "on the surface of the road" follows the reading of 4QSamᵃ (עַל] פני ארח), to be vocalized as עַל פְּנֵי־אֹרַח). Since it matches the parallel prepositional phrase in the next line, כְּטִיט־חוּצוֹת, "like mud of the streets," it is probably the original reading. The reading in the MT is probably the result of an inadvertent substitution of a more familiar phrase.[27] This may have been prompted by the visual similarity of the words אֹרַח and אָרֶץ. Ps 18:43 (ET 18:42) reads כַּעֲפָר עַל־פְּנֵי־רוּחַ, "like dust on the face of the wind," which probably arose from an accidental haplography of the *aleph* on אֹרַח.

אֲדִקֵּם אֶרְקָעֵם:—Codex Leningradensis reads two first common singular imperfect verbs, each with a third masculine plural object suffix: the Hiphil (H) of דָּקַק and the Qal (G) of רָקַע, respectively: "I crush them; I trample them." (For רָקַע meaning "trample" underfoot, see Ezek 6:11; 25:6.) The first verb, אֲדִקֵּם, is supported by LXX 2 Sam 22:43, which has only one verb: ἐλέπτυνα αὐτούς. But many other Masoretic manuscripts replace the verb's *daleth* with *resh* and read אֲרִקֵּם, the Hiphil (H) of רִיק, which would mean "I empty them." In Ps 18:43 (ET 18:42), the plene, or *maleʾ*, spelling of that verb, אֲרִיקֵם, is the reading in Codex Leningradensis, but many other Masoretic manuscripts read אֲדִקֵּם, as here in 2 Sam 22:43. In Ps 18:43 (ET 18:42), most Masoretic manuscripts, including Codex Leningradensis, have only the first verb (אֲרִיקֵם or אֲדִקֵּם), but two manuscripts include both of the verbs as here in 2 Sam 22:43 according to Codex Leningradensis. In 2 Sam 22:43 a few Masoretic manuscripts and 4QSamᵃ (ארקעם) have only the second verb.

22:44 וַתְּפַלְּטֵנִי—"You have delivered me." See the third textual note on 22:2.

מֵרִיבֵי עַמִּי—"From arguments among my people." The first noun is the plural of רִיב, which can denote "strife" or a "dispute, quarrel" or a legal accusation. In place of the suffixed noun עַמִּי, "my people," Ps 18:44 (ET 18:43) reads עָם, "people." Some

---

[27] See כַּעֲפַר הָאָרֶץ, "like the dust of the earth," in Gen 13:16; 28:14; 2 Chr 1:9; עֲפַר הָאָרֶץ, "the dust of the earth," in Ex 8:12, 13 (ET 8:16, 17); Is 40:12; and עֲפַר־אֶרֶץ, "dust of (the) earth," in Amos 2:7; Job 14:19.

propose that עַמִּי is a shortened form of the plural, עַמִּים, "peoples," without a suffix (see GKC, § 87 f; cf. עַמִּים in 22:48).

תִּשְׁמְרֵנִי—"You kept me." Ps 18:44 (ET 18:43) reads תְּשִׂימֵנִי, "you appointed me."

עַם לֹא־יָדַעְתִּי—The negated verb forms an asyndetic relative clause, "a people *that* I have not known" (see Joüon, § 158 c). This could be phrased more fully with the relative pronoun אֲשֶׁר and a retrospective pronoun, i.e., עַם אֲשֶׁר לֹא־יְדַעְתִּיו (cf. Deut 34:10).

יַעַבְדֻנִי:—"They serve me." This is a defective, or *ḥaser*, spelling of the Qal (G) third masculine plural imperfect of עָבַד with a first common singular suffix. Ps 18:44 (ET 18:43) has the full spelling: יַעַבְדוּנִי.

22:45 The order of the lines is reversed in Ps 18:45 (ET 18:44) and also probably in 4QSamᵃ, which begins the verse with לשמ, though the rest of the verse is missing.

בְּנֵי נֵכָר—Literally "sons of a foreigner," this construct phrase, with בֵּן in the singular or the plural, is a designation for non-Israelites (e.g., Ex 12:43; Is 60:10; Ps 144:7; Neh 9:2). The same construct phrase also begins the next verse (2 Sam 22:46).

יִתְכַּחֲשׁוּ־לִי—Literally "they are subservient to me." This verb is the Hithpael (HtD) imperfect of כָּחַשׁ. The Hithpael of this verb has a reflexive-declarative meaning, "show oneself to be compliant."[28] This stem of כָּחַשׁ appears only here. For it BDB gives "shall come cringing to me." Ps 18:45 (ET 18:44) has יְכַחֲשׁוּ, the Piel imperfect of כָּחַשׁ, with the same meaning.

לִשְׁמוֹעַ אֹזֶן יִשָּׁמְעוּ לִי:—Literally "to hearing of an ear they are obedient to me." לִשְׁמוֹעַ is the Qal (G) infinitive construct (with לְ) of שָׁמַע, whose Qal means "to hear." Ps 18:45 (ET 18:44) substitutes a noun (with לְ): לְשֵׁמַע, "to a hearing." יִשָּׁמְעוּ is the Niphal (N) third masculine plural imperfect of the same verb, and in this stem it can mean "be heard," "be obeyed," or "be obedient" (see BDB, Niphal, 1, 3).

22:46 בְּנֵי נֵכָר—See the second textual note on 22:45.

יִבֹּלוּ—"They become discouraged." This is the Qal (G) third masculine plural imperfect of נָבֵל, "to sink, droop" from exhaustion or, here, from "discouragement" (BDB, Qal, 1).

וְיַחְגְּרוּ—This is the Qal (G) third masculine plural imperfect of חָגַר, "to wear, gird on [oneself]," which makes little sense with the following prepositional phrase (see the next textual note). 4QSamᵃ reads לא יחגרו, "they do not wear," which is also difficult to understand in context. The reading of Ps 18:46 (ET 18:45) is וְיַחְרְגוּ, the Qal imperfect of חָרַג, "to quake, tremble." This root occurs only here in the OT, but its meaning is supported by an Arabic cognate, and "they came trembling" fits the context well. If it is the original reading, the MT displays an accidental metathesis of the *gimel* and *resh*.

מִמִּסְגְּרוֹתָם:—"From their fortifications." The feminine noun מִסְגֶּרֶת is derived from the verb סָגַר, "shut up, enclose," and denotes a fortified stronghold here and in Ps 18:46 (ET 18:45); Micah 7:17. For synonyms, see the second textual note on 2 Sam 22:2; the fifth and sixth textual notes on 22:3; and the first textual note on 22:33.

---

[28] See *IBH*, § 42 A; Waltke-O'Connor, § 26.2f.

22:47 חַי־יְהוָה—"(As) Yahweh lives." For this oath formula appealing to Yahweh, see the first textual note on 2 Sam 2:27; see also the second textual note on 1 Sam 14:45.[29]

וּבָרוּךְ צוּרִי—"And may my rock be blessed!" For the use of the Qal passive (Gp) participle בָּרוּךְ, "blessed," to laud God, see the third textual note on 18:28. The noun צוּר, "rock," appears twice in this verse as a metaphor for God; see the first textual note on 22:3.

וְיָרֻם—"May he be exalted!" is a Qal (G) third masculine singular jussive of רוּם (with a conjunctive *waw*) spelled defectively. Ps 18:47 (ET 18:46) uses the full spelling: וְיָרוּם.

אֱלֹהֵי צוּר יִשְׁעִי:—"The God of the rock of my salvation." A number of Masoretic manuscripts and Ps 18:47 (ET 18:46) omit צוּר, "rock." For יִשְׁעִי, see the fourth textual note on 2 Sam 22:3.

22:48 הָאֵל—For "the God," see the first textual note on 22:31.

נְקָמֹת—For this feminine plural noun, literally "vengeances," see the first textual note on 4:8.

וּמֹרִיד—"And (who) brings down." מֹרִיד is the Hiphil (H) masculine singular participle of יָרַד, "go down." Hannah's Song used the identical Hiphil (H) participle to describe Yahweh's ability to bring people down to Sheol (1 Sam 2:6; cf. the third textual note on 2 Sam 22:49). Ps 18:48 (ET 18:47) reads וַיַּדְבֵּר, "and he subdues," a Hiphil (H) preterite (imperfect with *waw* consecutive) of one of the homographic verbs דָּבַר (*HALOT*, s.v. דבר I; *CDCH*, s.v. דבר II).

22:49 וּמוֹצִיאִי מֵאֹיְבָי—Literally "and bringing out me from my enemies." Both participles (the Hiphil [H] of יָצָא and the Qal [G] of אָיַב) have a first common singular suffix referring to David. Ps 18:49 (ET 18:48) reads מְפַלְטִי מֵאֹיְבָי, "who delivers me from my enemies." Its first participle is the Piel (D) of פָּלַט with a first common singular suffix; the same suffixed participle (there with the conjunction) is discussed in the third textual note on 22:2.

וּמִקָּמַי—"And from those who rise against me." For this participle of קוּם, see the second textual note on 22:40. Ps 18:49 (ET 18:48) reads אַף מִן־קָמַי, "also from those who rise against me."

תְּרוֹמְמֵנִי—"You lift me up." This is the Polel (D) second masculine singular imperfect of רוּם. Hannah's Song used its Polel participle, מְרוֹמֵם, to extol Yahweh as the one who lifts up the lowly (1 Sam 2:7) after noting his ability to raise the dead (1 Sam 2:6; cf. the third textual note on 2 Sam 22:48).

מֵאִישׁ חֲמָסִים—Literally "from a man of violences," this is translated as "from violent men" because אִישׁ is used collectively here. The noun חָמָס denotes the "violence" of persecution also in 22:3 (see the seventh textual note on 22:3). Its plural here is an intensive plural. The identical construct phrase (מֵאִישׁ חֲמָסִים) is in Ps 140:2, 5 (ET 140:1, 4). The construct phrase with the singular, אִישׁ חָמָס, is in the parallel verse Ps 18:49 (ET 18:48) as well as Ps 140:12 (ET 140:11); Prov 3:31; 16:29.

---

[29] Steinmann, *1 Samuel*, 265.

תַּצִּילֵנִי:—"You deliver me." For the Hiphil (H) of נצל, see the first textual note on 22:1.

22:50 אוֹדְךָ—"I will praise you." This is the Hiphil (H) first common singular imperfect of יָדָה with a second masculine singular object suffix. This is the sole use of יָדָה in the book of Samuel, but its Hiphil is common in the Psalms. See the same form as here, אוֹדְךָ, also in Ps 18:50 (ET 18:49) and in other psalms by David, e.g., Pss 30:13 (ET 30:12); 35:18; 52:11 (ET 52:9); 57:10 (ET 57:9), and also אוֹדֶה in, e.g., Pss 7:18 (ET 7:17); 9:2 (ET 9:1); 32:5.

יְהוָה בַּגּוֹיִם—"Yahweh, among the nations." Ps 18:50 (ET 18:49) has the reverse word order, בַּגּוֹיִם ׀ יְהוָה, "among the nations, Yahweh."

אֲזַמֵּר:—"I will make music." This is the Piel (D) of זָמַר, another verb that appears only here in the book of Samuel but is common in the Psalms,[30] including those by David. See אֲזַמֵּר (the first common singular imperfect) or אֲזַמְּרָה (the singular cohortative, as in Ps 18:50 [ET 18:49]) in, e.g., Pss 7:18 (ET 7:17); 9:3 (ET 9:2); 27:6; 57:8, 10 (ET 57:7, 9); 59:18 (ET 59:17).

22:51 מִגְדּוֹל יְשׁוּעוֹת מַלְכּוֹ—This reading with the Qere מִגְדּוֹל could mean that Yahweh is "a tower of salvations of/for his king." For nouns for "salvation" that are cognate to יְשׁוּעָה here, see the fourth textual note on 22:3. מִגְדּוֹל here is defined as "tower" by BDB (s.v. מִגְדּוֹל) and *DCH* (s.v. מִגְדּוֹל I) and is so translated by some English versions.[31] However, this would be the only instance where "tower" is spelled מִגְדּוֹל rather than מִגְדָּל.[32] "Tower" (מִגְדּוֹל) would be yet another metaphor for Yahweh as a stronghold or fortress.[33] מִגְדּוֹל is also the spelling of the place-name Migdol.[34] The translation "he gives great victories to his king" follows the Kethib, which has the Hiphil (H) masculine singular participle מַגְדִּיל in place of the noun מִגְדּוֹל. This Kethib is supported by LXX 2 Sam 22:51 and LXX Ps 17:51 (MT 18:51; ET 18:50): μεγαλύνων. This participle is also the Qere (מַגְדִּיל) in MT Ps 18:51 (ET 18:50); the Kethib מגדל could be vocalized as a defective, or *haser*, spelling of the same participle, מַגְדִּל.

וְעֹשֶׂה־חֶסֶד לִמְשִׁיחוֹ—For the noun חֶסֶד as God's "faithfulness," see the second textual note on 9:3 and the first textual note on 16:17. For cognate terms, see the first and second textual notes on 22:26. The noun מָשִׁיחַ, "anointed one," is translated by the LXX as χριστός, "christ," here and regularly elsewhere. For its messianic significance, see the commentary on 1 Sam 2:10 and 1 Sam 2:35.[35] It designates David also in 2 Sam 19:22 (ET 19:21); 23:1. It is derived from the verb מָשַׁח, "to anoint" (see the second textual note on 5:3 and the third textual note on 12:7). This verb refers to the anointing of David in 1 Sam 16:3, 12, 13; 2 Sam 2:4, 7; 5:3, 17; 12:7.

---

[30] See also the first textual note on 22:50.

[31] E.g., HCSB, NRSV.

[32] E.g., Gen 11:4, 5; Judg 8:9, 17; 9:51, 52; 2 Ki 9:17; 17:9; 18:8.

[33] See also the second textual note on 22:2; the fifth and sixth textual notes on 22:3; and the first textual note on 22:33.

[34] See "Migdol" in Ex 14:2; Num 33:7; Jer 44:1; 46:14; Ezek 29:10; 30:6.

[35] Steinmann, *1 Samuel*, 80–81, 105–6.

וּלְזַרְעוֹ עַד־עוֹלָם:—The noun זֶרַע, "seed, offspring," refers to David's offspring in 1 Sam 20:42 and in 2 Sam 7:12 in the messianic prophecy of 2 Samuel 7, which also features the prepositional phrase עַד־עוֹלָם, "forever" (7:13, 16, 24–26; cf. לְעוֹלָם twice in 7:29).

Commentary

975 BC (?)[36]

Parallel: 2 Samuel 22 ‖ Psalm 18

For the place of this passage in the structure of 2 Samuel 21–24, see "The Form and Content of 2 Samuel 21–24" in the commentary on 21:1–14. This song of David is also found in the book of Psalms as Psalm 18. The textual notes discuss differences in the texts of these two records of David's victory song. Some of these differences may be due to errors in transmission. However, it is also possible that the version in the Psalter had been slightly revised by David before it was given to the director of the choirs (see לַמְנַצֵּחַ in the superscription of Psalm 18) and that some of the differences are due to his editing.

This song also contains echoes of Hannah's song at the beginning of the book of Samuel (1 Sam 2:1–10):

2 Samuel 22:1–51	1 Samuel 2:1–10
Yahweh is a "rock" (צוּר): 2 Sam 22:3, 32, 47	Yahweh is a "rock" (צוּר): 1 Sam 2:2
Yahweh is a "horn" of salvation: 2 Sam 22:3	Yahweh lifts up the "horn" of his Anointed One: 1 Sam 2:10
David is rescued from "the ropes of Sheol": 2 Sam 22:4–6	Yahweh brings down to Sheol and back up: 1 Sam 2:6
Yahweh thunders from heaven: 2 Sam 22:14	Yahweh thunders in heaven: 1 Sam 2:10
Yahweh uncovers the world's foundations: 2 Sam 22:16	The foundations of the earth are Yahweh's: 1 Sam 2:8
Yahweh widens David's steps: 2 Sam 22:37	Yahweh guards the steps of his faithful: 1 Sam 2:9
Yahweh clothes David with strength: 2 Sam 22:40	Yahweh arms the weak with strength: 1 Sam 2:4
	Yahweh gives strength to his messianic King: 1 Sam 2:10

These echoes serve to bind the long book of Samuel together and foreground the theme of God's gracious salvation through his royal Anointed One (1 Sam 2:10; 2 Sam 22:51; cf. 2 Sam 22:3). The author of Samuel does not often

---

[36] See "The Chronology of David's Reign" in the commentary on 5:1–5.

tell the reader how God is involved in the events he relates. However, these two songs alert readers that in everything that happens in this book, God is the one who rescues his faithful people and grants blessings to Israel.

Introduction: The Occasion for David's Song (22:1)

We are told that this song originated when Yahweh delivered David "from the grasp of all of his enemies" (22:1). This would seem to place it somewhere in the later part of David's reign, perhaps after Sheba's rebellion.[37] "From the grasp of Saul" is appended as a separate prepositional phrase. Saul is the only one named, and he is not called an "enemy." This is a reminder that although Saul had sought to kill David, David had always treated Saul with respect as Yahweh's "anointed,"[38] even to the point of twice sparing his life (1 Samuel 24 and 26).

David's Relationship to Yahweh (22:2–3)

The song begins with David's description of his relationship to Yahweh. Five descriptions of God[39] are followed by a statement: "I take refuge in him" (22:2–3a). David then adds another six descriptions,[40] again followed by a statement (22:3b): "you save me from violence."

Some of these descriptions are reminiscent of David's time on the run from Saul: "rock" (סֶלַע, 2 Sam 22:2; see 1 Sam 23:25–28; see also 1 Sam 13:6); "stronghold" (מְצוּדָה, 2 Sam 22:2; see 1 Sam 22:4–5; 24:23 [ET 24:22]; see also 2 Sam 5:7, 9, 17; 23:14); "rock" (צוּר, 2 Sam 22:3; see 1 Sam 24:3 [ET 24:2]; see also 2 Sam 22:32, 47; 23:3). God as "my deliverer" (מְפַלְטִי, 2 Sam 22:2) may refer to the success in overcoming Sheba's challenge to David's throne (see the commentary on 22:44, which has the same verb). Yahweh as "the horn of [David's] salvation" (22:3) is a messianic reference (cf. also 22:51) near the end of the book of Samuel that ties back to the beginning of the book (1 Sam 2:10; cf. 1 Sam 2:1, 35).[41]

David's Praises Yahweh for Saving His Life (22:4–7)

David prefaces the next section of his poem with the statement that Yahweh is praiseworthy (22:4). This statement is illustrated by what Yahweh did for David: he heard when David called. David's call (אֶקְרָא יְהוָה, "I call on Yahweh," 22:4, 7) and Yahweh's response ("he heard," 22:7) frame this section. David

---

[37] See the commentary on 22:44. For Sheba's rebellion, see 2 Samuel 20.

[38] See 1 Sam 24:7, 11 (ET 24:6, 10); 26:9, 11, 16, 23; 2 Sam 1:14, 16.

[39] "Yahweh is my rock, my stronghold, and my deliverer, my God, my rock." See the three textual notes on 22:2 and the first textual note on 22:3, which has a phrase that serves as a double description.

[40] "My shield and the horn of my salvation, my citadel, my refuge: my Savior." See the third, fourth, fifth, sixth, and seventh textual notes on 22:3. "The horn of my salvation" is counted as a double description; see the fourth textual note on 22:3.

[41] See also the fourth textual note on 22:3.

paints a dire picture of his plight from which Yahweh rescued him. He was close to death (22:5–6), yet God listened and saved him (cf. Ps 116:3). God heard David "from his temple" (2 Sam 22:7). This is a reference to Yahweh's heavenly temple (Ps 11:4) and prepares for the next section of David's song, where God comes forth from heaven to rescue Israel's king. Ultimately, salvation will come from the new temple, Jesus Christ, who will be razed and then raised on the third day (Mt 12:6; Mk 14:58; 15:29; Jn 2:18–22; Rev 21:22).

Yahweh in His Anger Comes to Defend David (22:8–16)

Yahweh's reaction to David's plea caused tremors in heaven and earth from Yahweh's holy anger against those who would attack his anointed one (22:8). The phrase "the foundations of the heavens" is unique in the OT (see the second textual note on 22:8). The cosmic quaking of creation before God is a common OT poetic motif.[42] David then depicts Yahweh's holy anger and judgment with metaphors of fire (22:9, 13), again common in the OT.[43]

Yahweh is next depicted as accompanied by phenomena in the sky (22:10–13). He is said to have "stretched out the heavens" as he came down to earth (22:10) riding on a cherub and the wings of the wind (22:11). Stretching out the heavens is a depiction of Yahweh found elsewhere (Is 40:22; Pss 104:2; 144:5). Cherubim are often associated with Yahweh's presence (Ex 25:20; 1 Ki 6:23–28; Ezek 10:1–22; Ps 99:1), and he is said to ride on clouds (cf. 2 Sam 22:12) and the wings of the wind in Ps 104:3 (see also Is 19:1).

Yahweh controls the storm from his position in the sky (2 Sam 22:14–16). Scholars often claim that this is similar to the way Baal, the storm god in Canaanite myths, is depicted.[44] However, unlike Baal, Yahweh is not simply a god of storms and rain. David, in effect, is depicting Yahweh as greater than Baal—he not only controls the storms, but he also controls the very foundations of the heavens and the earth (22:8, 16). Again, thunder (22:14) is frequently associated with God and his power.[45] Lightning (22:15) is also said to be his weapon—his arrow—in other OT passages.[46]

God's action causes both sea and land to reveal their lowermost places: the sea its channels and the world its foundations (22:16). Though the Hebrew phrase "the foundations of the world" (מֹסְדוֹת תֵּבֵל) is unique to this song, the similar expression "the foundations of the earth" (מוֹסְדֵי־אָרֶץ) is found elsewhere.[47]

---

[42] Judg 5:4–5; Is 5:25; 24:18–23; 63:19b (ET 64:1); Pss 68:9 (ET 68:8); 77:19 (ET 77:18; cf. Rev 11:13, 19; 16:18; 20:11).

[43] Deut 4:24; Is 30:27; 65:5; 66:15; Ezek 21:36 (ET 21:31); 22:31; Ps 144:5 (cf. 2 Pet 3:7–12; Rev 20:14–15).

[44] E.g., McCarter, *II Samuel*, 467; Anderson, *2 Samuel*, 263; Bergen, *1, 2 Samuel*, 455.

[45] 1 Sam 7:9–10; Pss 77:19 (ET 77:18); 104:7; Job 37:4; cf. Ex 19:16; Jer 10:13; 51:16; Ps 68:34 (ET 68:33).

[46] Hab 3:11; Zech 9:14; Ps 144:6; cf. Ex 19:16; Pss 77:19 (ET 77:18); 97:4; Job 37:4.

[47] Is 24:18; Jer 31:37; Micah 6:2; Ps 82:5; Prov 8:29.

This impressive portrayal of Yahweh in action shows him to be master of heaven and earth. Moreover, he uses his mastery to defend his people. All of this stems from the triune God as both Creator and Redeemer. Thus, in David's song, as in the rest of Scripture, there exists a close connection between its teaching on the creation and its fall and its teaching that God uses means within his creation to save his people. This connection is made even more vivid when God takes on human flesh in Christ (Jn 1:14; cf. Col 1:19; 2:9). The one through and by whom all things were created (Jn 1:3; 1 Cor 8:6) took on the form of his creatures in order to save them from their sins. Although the incarnate Christ humbled himself to appear in human form as a servant (Phil 2:6–8), as God he still retained power over wind and storm (Mk 4:36–41). Now risen and exalted, he wields all authority in heaven and on earth (Mt 28:18).

Yahweh Rescues David from His Enemies (22:17–20)

David moves to Yahweh saving him from his enemies. David takes no credit here. He was in water that he could not navigate and from which Yahweh plucked him (22:17; cf. 22:5). His enemies were stronger than he (22:18), but Yahweh was his support (22:19). David earlier had been in trouble; he was literally confined in a narrow or tight space (בַּצַּר־לִי, 22:7). Now, however, Yahweh rescues him and brings him out to a wide, spacious place (לְמֶרְחָב, 22:20). Yahweh did this not because David deserved it, but because of his delight in David for the sake of the Son of David, with whom he was well-pleased (Mt 1:1; 3:17; 12:18; 17:5; 2 Pet 1:17).

Yahweh's Reason for Rescuing David (22:21–25)

The next section of the song is well-defined by similar statements at the beginning and the end: "Yahweh has repaid me according to my righteousness; according to the purity of my hands he has rewarded me. … Yahweh rewarded me according to my righteousness, according to my purity in his sight" (22:21, 25). Here David claims not to have acted wickedly but to have kept God's statutes (22:22–23). He was blameless and did no wrong (22:24). These statements might appear to say that David had earned God's favor and that is why God delighted in him. Yet the reader of the book of Samuel knows better: David had sinned by committing adultery and murder (11:1–27). He was not blameless (24:10, 17). However, David is not referring to his intrinsic righteousness here. He is instead describing his righteousness as he appears before God. After he confessed his sins, the prophet absolved him; he was forgiven (12:13; see also 24:18–25). Thus, he was declared righteous not by his own righteousness but by a righteousness he received by grace alone and through faith alone—the righteousness of Christ (Rom 5:21; Phil 1:9–11; 3:8–9). David's trust in God's promise of forgiveness grasped this righteousness, and God credited this righteousness as David's own.[48] Thus, David could claim to have kept God's statutes, and indeed David is depicted throughout the book of Samuel as striving to keep God's Law. Though he did this imperfectly and often fell into sin, he was confident that God had clothed him in righteousness to cover his sinful failings.[49]

How Yahweh Deals with the Faithful and the Unbelieving (22:26–28)

In order to further develop the concept of what it means to be righteous in God's sight, David explicates the difference between God's relationship to the people he has endowed with faith versus those who do not know Yahweh. David first notes that God reveals himself as faithful, blameless, and pure to those who have received these gifts from Yahweh through faith (22:26–27a). However, God displays something altogether different to those who are crooked: they see only his "shrewd" way of dealing with sinners (22:27b). Thus, God saves the lowly who do not trust in their own righteousness, but he humbles those who are haughty—those whose confidence is in their own achievements (22:28).

What Yahweh Enables David to Do (22:29–30)

As a consequence of his previous statements, David once again notes that it was God who enabled him to overcome his enemies. Without God, David, like all humans, was impotent and in darkness. However, God illuminated him (22:29). This statement looks forward in faith to the Messiah (see Jn 8:12; 12:46; Eph 5:8; 1 Pet 2:9). Thus, with God's help, David was able to be a miraculously successful warrior-king (22:30).

Yahweh's Holy and Unique Nature (22:31–32)

Yahweh was able to make David blameless and pure because these are intrinsic qualities of Yahweh and his Word (22:31). Yahweh's self-revelation in his Word inspired David to trust in him as a shield and refuge (cf. 22:2–3). David adds that Yahweh is unique: he alone is God. There is no other trustworthy rock (22:32; cf. 22:2–3).

Yahweh Equips David to Be a Warrior (22:33–43)

David next describes God's outfitting him as a warrior. It is interesting that at the beginning of this description he notes again that God made his way blameless (22:33)—that his service as a warrior was not contrary to God's Law but was a vocation Yahweh had ordained (1 Sam 8:19–22). This section first depicts the various skills God gave to David (2 Sam 22:34–37). Perhaps the most perplexing is the ability to bend a bronze bow (22:35). Using a bow made

---

[48] See Rom 4:5–8. See also Gen 15:6; Pss 23:3; 24:5; 31:2 (ET 31:1); 35:24; 51:16 (ET 51:14); 71:2.

[49] See Psalm 51 (especially Ps 51:9 [ET 51:7]); Gal 3:26–29; Col 3:10.

of bronze as a weapon would require superhuman strength. For this reason Pinker proposed that the noun נְחוּשָׁה, "bronze," ought instead to be understood as an adjective meaning "snake-like," derived from the noun נָחָשׁ, "snake."[50] According to this theory such a bow was a double-curved bow—very difficult but not impossible to bend. However, David's point is that even impossible feats are made possible by God (Mk 9:23; 10:27).

David then describes his victory over his enemies—total victory granted by God (22:38–43). They also cry out, as David did (22:7), but not in faith, so Yahweh does not answer. They are crushed under his feet.[51]

Yahweh Equips David to Be King (22:44–46)

David then notes that Yahweh had also freed him from disputes among his people (22:44). This is probably a reference to the arguments between Judah and the other tribes over David's return to the throne (19:41–44 [ET 19:40–43]). These arguments led to Sheba's rebellion (20:1–22). Yet God retained David as king and even set him over foreign nations (22:44–46). They were subservient to him and to Israel, echoing the words of Moses (Deut 33:29).

Praise for Yahweh (22:47–51)

David's closing praise for Yahweh begins by picking up his opening theme of God as "rock" and "Savior" (22:47; see 22:2–3). Then he summarizes what God has done:

1. He subjugated "peoples" (עַמִּים) to David (22:48).
2. He delivered David from violent insurrections (22:49)—perhaps another reference to Sheba (2 Samuel 20) as well as Absalom (2 Samuel 15–18).

David's response to these is to praise God in music among the nations over whom Yahweh has set him (22:50).

David's final worshipful acclamation speaks of the victories Yahweh grants—not simply to King David himself but also to "his offspring forever" (וּלְזַרְעוֹ עַד־עוֹלָם, 22:51). This is a reference to the promised Messiah from David's line (see 7:12–16).[52] The victories of David, therefore, were only a foretaste of the eternal victories that the Messiah would win for all of God's people of all times (Psalm 110; see also Pss 16:8–11; 22:20–32 [ET 22:19–31]; 23:6).[53]

---

[50] Pinker, "On the Meaning of קשת נחושה."

[51] See Gen 3:15; Num 24:17; Rom 16:20; see also in these psalms by David: Pss 17:13; 110:5–6; 143:12.

[52] See also the excursus "הָאָדָם as 'the Man' in 2 Samuel 7:19 and 1 Chronicles 17:17" following the commentary on 7:1–29.

[53] See Baldwin, *1 and 2 Samuel*, 290, who also understands 22:51 as messianic. Many scholars recognize Ps 110:1 as the OT verse that has the most quotations and allusions in the NT (e.g., Mt 22:44; 26:64; Mk 12:36; 14:62; Lk 20:42–43; 22:69; Acts 2:34–35; Rom 8:34; 1 Cor 15:25; Eph 1:20; Col 3:1; Heb 1:3, 13; 8:1; 10:12).

David's Last Words

Translation

23 ¹These are the last words of David:

"The oracle of Jesse's son David,

and the oracle of the man raised on high,

the anointed one of the God of Jacob,

the sweet singer of the songs of Israel:

²Yahweh's Spirit spoke by me,

and his Word was on my tongue.

³The God of Israel said;

the Rock of Israel spoke to me:

'The one who rules over mankind is righteous when he rules [with] the fear of God,

⁴and he is like the light of the morning when the sun dawns,

[like] a morning [with] no clouds,

better than the brightness from rain [that makes] vegetation [sprout] from the land.'

⁵Indeed, is not my house like this with God?

Indeed, he has established an eternal covenant for me,

arranged in every way and secured.

Indeed, my entire salvation and every desire—won't he certainly make it blossom?

⁶However, good-for-nothing persons are like a thorn that is thrown away— all of them.

Indeed, one cannot handle them.

⁷Moreover, a man should touch them only with iron or a shaft of a spear.

They will be completely destroyed by fire."

Textual Notes

23:1–7 For the line indentation of the poem's translation, see the textual note on 22:2–51.

23:1 וּנְאֻם ... נְאֻם—"Oracle ... oracle." This noun was used twice also in the prophecy by the unnamed "man of God" (1 Sam 2:27) in 1 Sam 2:30. The vast majority of its three hundred and seventy-six occurrences in the OT are in the prophets. The term casts David's last words as a prophecy and suggests that David was a prophet (cf. the prophesying of his predecessor Saul in 1 Sam 10:10–13; 19:23–24). See further the commentary.

הֻקַם עָל—"(Who was) raised on high." The verb is the Hophal (Hp) third masculine singular perfect of קוּם. In a few OT passages עַל (in pause עָל) is used as a substantive, "height" (BDB, s.v. עַל, I), and it is so used here as an adverbial accusative, "on high" (see Joüon, § 103 a). The common preposition עַל, "upon," may be derived from this noun (Waltke-O'Connor, § 11.2.13a). 4QSamᵃ reads הקים אל, to be pointed as הֵקִים אֵל, "the man (whom) *God raised.*"

מְשִׁיחַ אֱלֹהֵי יַעֲקֹב—This construct chain means "the anointed one of the God of Jacob." For the noun מָשִׁיחַ in reference to David, see the second textual note on 22:51. It refers to David also in 19:22 (ET 19:21). See also its use in the messianic prophecies of 1 Sam 2:10 and 1 Sam 2:35.

וּנְעִים זְמִרוֹת יִשְׂרָאֵל׃—"The sweet singer of the songs of Israel." English versions commonly condense these words to "(and) the sweet psalmist of Israel" (KJV, ESV, NASB; cf. REB: "and the singer of Israel's psalms"). The first word in this construct chain could be the adjective נָעִים I, "pleasant, delightful," which is common and is derived from the verb נָעֵם I, "be pleasant." More likely, however, it is the homographic adjective נָעִים II, "musical, sweet sounding," used as a substantive, "sweet sounding one, singer" (so *DCH*, s.v. נָעִים II; similarly, BDB, s.v. נָעִים II, under the root נעם II). This adjective appears elsewhere in the OT only in Ps 81:3 (ET 81:2). It is derived from a root נעם that does not occur in the OT but that has cognates in Arabic, Syriac, and postbiblical Hebrew. The second word in the construct chain here, זְמִרוֹת, is the plural construct form of the masculine noun זָמִיר I, "song," which occurs six times in the OT, including twice in the Psalter (Pss 95:2; 119:54). It is derived from the verb זָמַר I, used only in the Piel (D), "to make music." This verb is common in the Psalms, including those by David. Psalmists often use it in the first person singular to promise, "I will make music" to Yahweh, as David did in 2 Sam 22:50. See also, e.g., Pss 7:18 (ET 7:17); 9:3 (ET 9:2); 27:6; 57:8, 10 (ET 57:7, 9); 59:18 (ET 59:17).

23:2 רוּחַ יְהוָה דִּבֶּר־בִּי וּמִלָּתוֹ עַל־לְשׁוֹנִי׃—The feminine noun רוּחַ, "Spirit," in the construct phrase "the Spirit of Yahweh" is the grammatical subject of the verb דִּבֶּר, "spoke," but the form of the verb is masculine (third singular), not feminine. Likewise, the most natural grammatical antecedent of the masculine (third singular) pronoun on וּמִלָּתוֹ, "and *his* Word," is רוּחַ, "Spirit." Perhaps these two masculine forms are the result of the close association of "Spirit" with (masculine) "Yahweh." In Scripture the triune God is generally construed as masculine, and so the Spirit may be construed as masculine because he is the third person of the Trinity. Likewise in the NT when the neuter Greek noun τὸ πνεῦμα refers to the Holy Spirit, it sometimes is construed as masculine.[1]

23:3 אֱלֹהֵי יִשְׂרָאֵל—"The God of Israel." 4QSamᵃ reads אלוהי יעקב, "the God of Jacob," as in 23:1.

לִי דִּבֶּר צוּר יִשְׂרָאֵל—The prepositional phrase לִי is placed first for emphasis, literally "to me spoke the Rock of Israel." For the noun צוּר, "rock, cliff," as a metaphor for God, see the first textual note on 22:3 and the commentary on 22:2–3.

מוֹשֵׁל בָּאָדָם צַדִּיק מוֹשֵׁל יִרְאַת אֱלֹהִים׃—According to the Masoretic system of accentuation, when two adjacent words both have *zaqeph* (בָּאָדָם צַדִּיק), the first one (-֔, *zaqeph qatan*) functions as a stronger disjunctive than the second (-֕, *zaqeph gadol*). Therefore the first two words form a participial clause as a *casus pendens* (GKC,

---

[1] Jn 14:26; 15:26; 16:13–14; Eph 1:13–14.

§ 116 w). In the main clause, צַדִּיק is a predicate adjective,[2] and the following מוֹשֵׁל is its subject: literally "the one ruling over mankind—righteous is the one ruling [with] the fear of God." Many Masoretic manuscripts include the preposition בְּ in the phrase בְּיִרְאַת אֱלֹהִים, "*with* the fear of God," which is attested in the Syriac and the Targum and is supported by the Lucianic version of the LXX, two Old Latin manuscripts, and the Vulgate. The construct phrase here, יִרְאַת אֱלֹהִים, "the fear of God," occurs elsewhere only in Gen 20:11; Neh 5:15 (cf. "in the fear of our God," Neh 5:9). It pertains especially to general revelation, the natural knowledge of God that is evident in creation and that is to govern all human authorities (see further the commentary). The related phrase יִרְאַת יְהוָה, "the fear of Yahweh," is more common, occurring twenty-one times.[3] Since it contains the personal covenant name of the God who saved Israel, it is more closely associated with the special revelation of God's will (as in Scripture and by Christ), both condemning Law and the saving Gospel of the Messiah. The Davidic Messiah reigns over God's kingdom and the entire world with "the fear of Yahweh" (Is 11:2, 3). Among God's people "the fear of Yahweh" is inculcated by divine wisdom (e.g., Ps 111:10; Prov 1:7; 2:5; 14:27).

23:4 וּכְאוֹר—"And (he is) like (the) light." The conjunction is omitted in 4QSam[a] (כאור), as well as the Syriac, the Lucianic version of the LXX, two Old Latin manuscripts, and the Vulgate.

יִזְרַח־שָׁמֶשׁ—The verb זָרַח, "rise" (eighteen times in the OT), usually has the noun שֶׁמֶשׁ, "sun," as its subject. When the noun precedes the verb, the verb form is feminine (2 Ki 3:22; Nah 3:17). When the verb precedes, it can be either masculine (as here; also Gen 32:32 [ET 32:31]; Eccl 1:5) or feminine (Ex 22:2 [ET 22:3]; Mal 3:20 [ET 4:2]; Ps 104:22).

בֹּקֶר לֹא עָבוֹת—The negative לֹא followed by a noun can form a negative clause that modifies another noun: "*a morning* when there are *not clouds*, i.e. *a cloudless morning*" (GKC, § 152 u; see also Joüon, § 160 o). Usually the plural of the noun עָב, "cloud," is masculine in form (עָבִים). The feminine plural form here, עָבוֹת, occurs also in Ps 77:18 (ET 77:17) and seems to be reserved for high poetic style (Joüon, § 90 e).

מִנֹּגַהּ—"Better than the brightness." The preposition מִן prefixed to the noun נֹגַהּ, "brightness" (cf. the verb נָגַהּ in 22:29), is understood to be used comparatively here.

23:5–6 כִּי ... כִּי ... כִּי ... כִּי ... כִּי—This conjunction is understood to be asseverative, "indeed" or "certainly," five times in these two verses (see *HALOT*, s.v. כִּי II, A 1).

23:5 לֹא־כֵן—Some translations take this as a negative statement, "is not so" (NKJV). Most, however, interpret it as a question expecting a positive answer, "is it not so?" and the final clause of the verse, כִּי־לֹא יַצְמִיחַ, is to be interpreted in the same way, "won't he certainly make it blossom?" Neither the phrase here nor the final clause of the verse has an explicit marker of a question, but Hebrew questions are often unmarked; see

---

[2] Cf. KJV, NKJV. Some other English versions append the adjective צַדִּיק to the participial clause and translate it adverbially, e.g., "he who rules over men righteously" (NASB; similarly, ESV).

[3] Is 11:2, 3; 33:6; Pss 19:10 (ET 19:9); 34:12 (ET 34:11); 111:10; Prov 1:7, 29; 2:5; 8:13; 9:10; 10:27; 14:26, 27; 15:16, 33; 16:6; 19:23; 22:4; 23:17; 2 Chr 19:9 (cf. Prov 31:30).

Joüon, § 161 a, and the first textual note on 1 Sam 11:12.[4] The second word here, כֵּן, is most likely the adverb "so, thus" or "this way" (see *HALOT*, s.v. כֵּן II), which can follow an asseverative כִּי (see BDB, s.v. כֵּן I, 2 c (*d*)).[5] Some interpret כֵּן to be the adjective "right, correct."[6]

עִם־אֵל—"With God." For אֵל, "God," see the first textual note on 22:31.

בְּרִית עוֹלָם—Literally "a covenant of eternity," this construct phrase has an adjectival genitive, thus "eternal covenant." For בְּרִית, "covenant," see the first textual note on 5:3. Here in 23:5 David refers to Yahweh's messianic promise to his house (2 Samuel 7).

עֲרוּכָה בַכֹּל וּשְׁמֻרָה—"Arranged in every way and secured." The two Qal passive (Gp) participles function adjectivally and are feminine to match the feminine gender of בְּרִית, "covenant." Elsewhere in Samuel the active Qal (G) of עָרַךְ refers to "arranging" troops for battle (see the first textual note on 1 Sam 4:2[7] and the first textual note on 2 Sam 10:8). In the Qal passive stem, it means "be arranged, be ordered, be made ready" or "be prepared" (see *DCH*, s.v. ערך I, Qal, 7 a, b, c), and Yahweh is the implied agent of the passive here.

When Yahweh is the subject of the verb שָׁמַר, it can mean "keep, preserve, protect" (see 22:44) and can refer to God maintaining his covenant[8] (see BDB, Qal, 4 a, b). The Qal passive here has the corresponding passive meaning, implying that Yahweh is the one who guarantees his covenant by his own oath, maintains it, and preserves it for eternity.

כָל־יִשְׁעִי—"My entire salvation." For the noun יֶשַׁע, "salvation," see the fourth textual note on 8:6 and also the fourth and seventh textual notes on 22:3.

כִּי־לֹא יַצְמִיחַ—"Won't he certainly make it blossom?" For the understanding of this statement as a question, see the first textual note on 23:5. The verb is the Hiphil (H) third masculine singular imperfect of צָמַח, "sprout, grow." See the fifth textual note on 10:5.

23:6 וּבְלִיַּעַל כְּקוֹץ מֻנָד כֻּלָּהַם—The sentence structure is literally "and good-for-nothing(s)—like a thorn thrown away (are) all of them." See GKC, § 143 a. For the compound noun בְּלִיַּעַל, "good-for-nothing (one)," see the third textual note on 16:7. In 1 Sam 2:12; 10:27; 2 Sam 22:5 (cf. 1 Sam 30:22), a plural word is in construct with this word, and the construct phrase is the subject or implied subject of a plural verb. Here the word must be intended as a plural because of the plural pronouns on prepositions (כֻּלָּהַם, "all of them," 23:6; בָּהֶם, "[on] them," 23:7) and plural verbs (יִקָּחוּ, literally "they will [not] be taken," 23:6; יִשָּׂרְפוּ, literally "they will be burned," 23:7) that refer back to it.

כְּקוֹץ—The noun קוֹץ, "thorn," was in the divine curse uttered after the creation fell into sin (Gen 3:18). See also, e.g., Is 32:13; 33:12; Hos 10:8.

---

4 Steinmann, *1 Samuel*, 211.

5 כֵּן I is listed in alphabetical order rather than under a root.

6 E.g., Anderson, *2 Samuel*, 266–67; HCSB; NET. For this adjective, see BDB, s.v. כֵּן II, under the root כון I, and *HALOT*, s.v. כֵּן I.

7 Steinmann, *1 Samuel*, 119.

8 E.g., Deut 7:9, 12; 1 Ki 8:23; Ps 89:29 (ET 89:28); Dan 9:4; Neh 1:5; 9:32; 2 Chr 6:14.

מֻנָּד—"Thrown away." This is the Hophal (Hp) masculine singular participle of נָדַד, "flee, wander."

כֻּלָּהַם—"All of them." This unique spelling is a pausal form of כֹּל with a third masculine plural suffix (GKC, § 91 f; Joüon, § 94 h). The usual spelling is כֻּלָּם. This refers to all "good-for-nothing (persons)."

לֹא בְיָד יֻקָּחוּ:—Literally "in a hand they will not (or cannot) be taken." The verb is the Niphal (N) third masculine plural imperfect of לָקַח. Its implied subject must be the same people to which the third masculine plural pronoun on the preceding כֻּלָּהַם refers (see the prior textual note).

23:7 וְאִישׁ יִגַּע בָּהֶם—"Moreover, a man should touch them." The Qal (G) of נָגַע, "touch," often takes the preposition בְּ prefixed to what is touched. See also, e.g., 14:10.

יִמָּלֵא בַרְזֶל וְעֵץ חֲנִית—The verb יִמָּלֵא is the Niphal (N) third masculine singular imperfect of מָלֵא: literally "it will be filled." In this context it must mean that the hand of a man who touches the good-for-nothing persons "should be filled" with a weapon, that is, he must arm himself with an implement of "iron" (בַרְזֶל) or with "wood of a spear" (וְעֵץ חֲנִית), that is the wooden shaft of a spear. See BDB, s.v. מָלֵא, Niphal, 1, which points to the use of the Piel (D) of מָלֵא with the meaning "fill the hand," that is, "to grasp" something (2 Ki 9:24; cf. Lev 9:17). Most English versions follow this line of interpretation. The translation "should touch them *only with*" assumes that יִמָּלֵא should be read as אִם־לֹא, which is implied by the Lucianic version of the LXX (ἐὰν μή) and two Old Latin manuscripts.[9]

וּבָאֵשׁ שָׂרוֹף יִשָּׂרְפוּ—"They will be completely destroyed by fire" is literally "and with the fire they will be thoroughly burned." The infinitive absolute emphasizes the action and can be translated by an adverb, "completely" or "thoroughly." שָׂרוֹף is the Qal (G) infinitive absolute of שָׂרַף, "to burn," and יִשָּׂרְפוּ is its Niphal (N) third masculine plural imperfect. When the infinitive absolute of a verb is used together with a finite form of the same verb, usually the infinitive absolute is in the same stem, but a Qal infinitive absolute can be used with other stems (GKC, § 113 w; Joüon, § 123 p; Waltke-O'Connor, § 35.2.1d). The verb שָׂרַף is regularly used with the noun אֵשׁ, "fire," with the definite article and the prefixed preposition בְּ in an instrumental sense, בָּאֵשׁ, "with fire" (also, e.g., 1 Sam 30:1, 3, 14).

בַּשָּׁבֶת:—If this word is the preposition בְּ with the definite article prefixed to the common noun שָׁבֶת, "place, seat" (from יָשַׁב), then this prepositional phrase means "on the spot" (*DCH*, s.v. שָׁבֶת I, 1 c) or "in (their) place" (see, e.g., KJV, NASB). Alternatively, שָׁבֶת could be the rare noun "cessation" (from שָׁבַת), in which case the prepositional phrase could mean "completely" or "to extermination." The LXX reading αἰσχύνη αὐτῶν, "in/by their shame," apparently read בַּשָּׁבֶת as a form of the noun בֹּשֶׁת, "shame."

---

[9] Olmo Lete, "David's Farewell Oracle," 423, also favors this reading.

Commentary

c. 969 BC[10]

For the place of this passage in the structure of 2 Samuel 21–24, see "The Form and Content of 2 Samuel 21–24" in the commentary on 21:1–14. This short poem is described as "the last words of David" (23:1). This probably means that these were David's last public words to Israel, a distillation of the divine wisdom he had learned in his life and forty-year reign, not necessarily that they were the last things he ever said. The poem itself is fairly difficult Hebrew and has given rise to quite a few studies that have attempted to explain various features of the text.[11]

The first two lines of the poem call it an "oracle" (נְאֻם, 23:1). This word is often used to describe a prophetic utterance, and David here is claiming to speak as God's prophet. Note the similarity of these lines to Num 24:3, 16. David uses four descriptors for himself. As Jesse's son he was not born to royalty, but as the next two lines say, he was raised by God to this high position, anointed to be king. In this capacity he was a preliminary fulfillment of Hannah's words in 1 Sam 2:10. However, David was not the definitive anointed one, and his words look forward to the ultimate fulfillment of Hannah's words in Christ (cf. 2 Sam 23:5).[12] Finally, David calls himself "the sweet singer of the songs of Israel" (23:1). Although the author has not depicted King David as singing or composing songs apart from this one and the immediately preceding one (22:1–51), he introduced readers to David as a musician who skillfully played the lyre (1 Sam 16:14–23; cf. 1 Sam 18:10; 19:9), and the superscriptions of seventy-three psalms ascribe their composition to David.

The king further reinforces his position as a prophet by claiming that Yahweh's Spirit inspired his words (23:2–3a). Compare Ps 45:2 (ET 45:1) and similar declarations of inspiration by the Suffering Servant in Is 50:4; 61:1. In his victory song (2 Samuel 22), David called God "my rock" (צוּרִי, 22:3, 47) and "the rock of my salvation" (צוּר יִשְׁעִי, 22:47). Now he calls Yahweh "the Rock of Israel" (צוּר יִשְׂרָאֵל, 23:3).

The message David conveys from God has three main parts. The first is about a godly ruler (23:3b–4). Such a person rules justly in righteousness, that is, he rules in "the fear of God" (יִרְאַת אֱלֹהִים, 23:3b).[13] This Hebrew phrase

---

[10] See "The Chronology of David's Reign" in the commentary on 5:1–5.

[11] E.g., Freedman, "II Samuel 23:4"; Mettinger, "The Last Words of David"; Naéh, "A New Suggestion Regarding 2 Samuel xxiii 7"; Olmo Lete, "David's Farewell Oracle"; Rendsburg, "The Northern Origin of 'the Last Words of David'"; Rendsburg, "Additional Notes on 'the Last Words of David'"; Richardson, "The Last Words of David"; see also the various commentaries.

[12] See "Christ in Samuel" in the introduction (Steinmann, *1 Samuel*, 23–26); the commentary on 1 Sam 2:10, 35 (Steinmann, *1 Samuel*, 80–81, 105–6); the beginning of the commentary on 2 Sam 6:1–23; the commentary on 2 Sam 7:1–29; and the excursus "הָאָדָם as 'the Man' in 2 Samuel 7:19 and 1 Chronicles 17:17" following the commentary on 7:1–29.

[13] See the third textual note on 23:3.

occurs only two other times in the OT (Gen 20:11; Neh 5:15). In both of those verses it is connected to the ethics of human government. In Gen 20:11 Abraham expressed his fear of losing his life to the Canaanites because he perceived that there was no "fear of God" among them. He would be killed, he thought, with impunity. In Neh 5:15 Nehemiah explained why he refrained from placing oppressive taxes on his fellow Judeans. His motivation was "the fear of God." Thus, this phrase is used to denote a ruler's or government's respect for God— among the community of believers (Neh 5:15) and also among unbelievers (Gen 20:11), who should at least know the natural law, that is, the divine order God has built into the creation. Even secular governments are accountable to God's Law, and their laws should reflect the second table of the Decalogue (Ex 20:12–17; Deut 5:16–21). Rulers are to implement government that respects the command to love one's neighbor as oneself.[14]

Godly government under the Rock of Israel is characterized by three comparisons involving illumination (23:4): like the morning light at sunrise, like a morning on a cloudless day, and better than brightness from rain. The final comparison is expanded by noting the rain's life-giving effect on the creation— it enables vegetation to sprout and flourish. Likewise, the reign of the Messiah by Word and Spirit (cf. 23:1–3) allows God's people to grow and prosper under his blessing like plants thrive given sunlight and rain (Is 55:3–11; 61:11; Ps 65:10–11 [ET 65:9–10]).

David opens the second part of his prophecy with the statement that in God's sight his house is like what he has described (2 Sam 23:5). David is not claiming that his government was perfect and always followed God's Word. His adultery with Bathsheba and his murder of Uriah (11:1–27) violated the Fifth and Sixth Commandments (Ex 20:13–14; Deut 5:17–18), showing that he did not always rule justly. However, David here is looking forward to the ultimate ruler and government that will come from his house: the Messiah.[15] God had given that pledge to David in "an eternal covenant" (2 Sam 23:5; see 2 Samuel 7), as promised to his ancestor Abraham.[16] That covenant was arranged and assured by God, so David could confidently assert that his house was the government that God envisioned in his holy Word. Moreover, David was certain that this government would come to fruition—it would blossom, although in him it was only the bud. However, it would eventually lead to the full flower in the Messiah.

The third and final part of God's oracle through David concerns wicked men, those without respect for God's messianic king or Word. Like thorns, they cause injury and cannot be handled safely (2 Sam 23:6). Instead, human rulers need to use the power of weapons of iron and the spear (Paul will later call it

---

[14] Lev 19:18; Mt 19:19; 22:39; Mk 12:31, 33; Lk 10:27; Rom 13:9–10; Gal 5:14; James 2:8.

[15] See, e.g., Is 7:13–14; 9:5–6 (ET 9:6–7); 11:1–16; 16:5; 22:22; 37:35; 55:3; 61:1–11; 65:17–25.

[16] See "eternal covenant" in Gen 17:7, 13, 19; Is 55:3; 61:8; Jer 32:40; 50:5; 1 Chr 16:17; Ezek 16:60; 37:26; Ps 105:10; see also Gen 9:16.

"the sword" [Rom 13:4]) and mete out punishment to curb violent human ways and establish effective government among recalcitrant sinners in this world (2 Sam 23:7). In the final judgment when Christ comes again, such unbelievers will be burned in unquenchable fire[17] and will not inhabit the new heavens and new earth, which will be the habitation of believers in the eternal kingdom of the Christ.[18]

---

[17] Mt 3:12; 7:19; 13:40; 25:41; Lk 3:9, 17; 16:22–24; Jn 15:6; 2 Thess 1:8; Rev 20:15; 21:8.

[18] Is 65:17–25; 66:22; 1 Cor 6:9–11; Gal 5:19–21; Eph 5:5; 2 Pet 3:13; Revelation 21–22.

David's Elite Troops

Translation

23 [8]These are the names of David's elite soldiers:

Eshbaal the son of Hachmoni, the chief of the Three. He wielded his spear against eight hundred men whom he pierced at one time.

[9]After him was Eleazar the son of Dodo the Ahohite. He was among the three elite soldiers with David when they defied the Philistines when they assembled there for battle. When the men of Israel retreated, [10]he arose and struck down the Philistines until his hand was exhausted and his hand stuck to his sword. Yahweh gained an impressive victory that day. The troops returned, (following) after him, but only to plunder [the bodies].

[11]After him was Shammah the son of Agee, a Hararite. The Philistines had assembled at Lehi where there was a plot of land full of lentils. When the troops fled from the Philistines, [12]he took his stand in the middle of the plot, defended it, and struck down the Philistines. Yahweh gained an impressive victory.

[13]Three of the thirty chief soldiers came at harvest time to David at the cave of Adullam while a detachment of Philistines was camping in the Valley of Rephaim. ([14]At that time David was in the stronghold, and a Philistine garrison was then at Bethlehem.) [15]David had a desire and said, "I wish someone would give me water to drink from the well in Bethlehem that is at the gate." [16]The three elite soldiers broke through the Philistine camp and drew water from the well in Bethlehem that is at the gate. They carried [it] and brought [it] back to David, but he would not drink it. He poured it out to Yahweh. [17]He said, "I would never do such a thing, O Yahweh! This is the blood of the men who went at the risk of their lives." So he was not willing to drink [it].

The three elite soldiers did these things.

[18]Now Abishai the brother of Joab the son of Zeruiah was chief of the Thirty. He wielded his spear against three hundred men, whom he pierced. He gained a reputation among the Three. [19]Was he not more honored than the Three? He became their commander, but he did not join the Three.

[20]Benaiah the son of Jehoiada was the son of a capable man of many deeds from Kabzeel. He struck down two [sons] of Ariel of Moab. He went down into a cistern and struck down a lion on the day that it snowed. [21]He struck down an Egyptian man, a handsome man. A spear was in the hand of the Egyptian. He [Benaiah] went down to him with a club, grabbed the spear from the Egyptian's hand, and killed him with his own spear. [22]Benaiah the son of Jehoiada did these things, and he gained a reputation among the three elite soldiers. [23]He was more honored than the Thirty, but he was not one of the Three. David put him in charge of his bodyguard.

²⁴Asah-el the brother of Joab was among the Thirty.

Elhanan the son of Dodo [from] Bethlehem;

²⁵Shammah the Harodite;

Elika the Harodite;

²⁶Helez the Paltite;

Ira the son of Ikkesh, the Tekoite;

²⁷Abiezer the Anathothite;

Sibbecai the Hushite;

²⁸Zalmon the Ahohite;

Maharai the Netophathite;

²⁹Heled the son of Baanah, the Netophathite;

Ittai the son of Ribai from Gibeah of the Benjaminites;

³⁰Benaiah the Pirathonite;

Hurai from the brooks of Gaash;

³¹Abi-albon the Arbathite;

Azmaveth the Baharumite;

³²Eliahba the Shaalbonite;

the sons of Jashen;

Jonathan [the son of] ³³Shammah the Hararite;

Ahiam the son of Sharar the Ararite;

³⁴Eliphelet the son of Ahasbai, the son of the Maacathite;

Eliam the son of Ahithophel the Gilonite;

³⁵Hezrai the Carmelite;

Paari the Arbite;

³⁶Igal the son of Nathan from Zobah;

Bani the Gadite;

³⁷Zelek the Ammonite;

Naharai the Beerothite, the armor bearer of Joab the son of Zeruiah;

³⁸Ira the Ithrite;

Gareb the Ithrite;

³⁹Uriah the Hittite.

Total: thirty-seven.

Textual Notes

23:8 אֵלֶּה שְׁמוֹת הַגִּבֹּרִים אֲשֶׁר לְדָוִד—Literally "these are the names of the warriors who belonged to David." This construction has a two-word construct phrase (שְׁמוֹת הַגִּבֹּרִים) and a relative (אֲשֶׁר) clause with לְ in the sense of possession. See also Song 1:1. It is used instead of a three-word construct chain (שְׁמוֹת־גִּבֹּרֵי־דָוִד), which would have implied that David had no other warriors besides the ones named here. In this passage גִּבֹּרִים is translated as "elite soldiers" (2 Sam 23:8, 9, 16, 17, 22) since it refers to David's most elite commandos. גִּבּוֹר means "elite soldier" also in, e.g., 1 Sam 2:4; 17:51; 2 Sam 1:19, 21.

יֹשֵׁב בַּשֶּׁבֶת—This name in the MT is "Josheb-bashebeth." The translation follows the name in the Lucianic version of the LXX, Ιεσβααλ, "Eshbaal," which would

449

be יֶשְׁבַּעַל in Hebrew. LXX 1 Chr 11:11 reads Ιεσεβααλ, perhaps corresponding to "Eshbaal." Here the LXX reads Ιεβοσθε, "Ish-bosheth." The parallel in MT 1 Chr 11:11 reads יָשָׁבְעָם, "Jashobeam." It appears as if the original name here was "Eshbaal," but it was purposely bowdlerized to "Ish-bosheth" (e.g., LXX 2 Sam 23:8), as was done also for Saul's son (see the second textual note on 2:8). The MT then seems to be a further scribal corruption of "Ish-bosheth." In 1 Chr 11:11 it appears as if the final *lamed* on "Eshbaal" was mistakenly replaced with a *mem*.

תַּחְכְּמֹנִי—The MT reads "Tahcemoni" and is probably the result of a graphic confusion of -ת in place of בן. The translation follows the reading in 1 Chr 11:11, בֶּן־חַכְמוֹנִי, "the son of Hachmoni." This name occurs also in 1 Chr 27:32. LXX 2 Sam 23:8 reads ὁ Χαναναῖος, "the Canaanite."

רֹאשׁ הַשָּׁלִשִׁי—"The chief of the Three." The noun רֹאשׁ, literally "head," means "chief" also in 23:13, 18. The word הַשָּׁלִשִׁי is difficult (the marginal Masoretic note ל marks it as unique). Many Masoretic manuscripts spell the second noun fully as הַשָּׁלִישִׁי, which is equally difficult. One explanation is that this word is the noun שָׁלִישׁ, "officer" (as in, e.g., 2 Ki 7:2, 17, 19; see BDB, s.v. שָׁלִישׁ III; *DCH*, s.v. שָׁלִישׁ III), and that its ending, ־ִי, is a defective spelling of the masculine plural ending ־ִים (GKC, § 87 f), in which case this construct phrase would mean "the chief of the officers." Some English versions translate it as "chief of the captains" (e.g., NASB; similarly, KJV, NKJV). In the parallel verse 1 Chr 11:11, the Qere is הַשָּׁלִישִׁים, "the officers," and the Kethib is הַשָּׁלוֹשִׁים, "the Thirty."

If the word here had a *shewa* under the first *shin* (-הַשְּׁ) instead of a *qamets* (-הַשָּׁ), thus either הַשְּׁלִשִׁי or הַשְּׁלִישִׁי, it would be the ordinal number with the article: "the third." LXX 2 Sam 23:8 apparently understood its unvocalized Hebrew *Vorlage* to have that word and translated the phrase as ἄρχων τοῦ τρίτου, "(the) leader of the third."

The translation follows the reading of the Lucianic version of the LXX, which has the cardinal number with the article: τῶν τριῶν, "of the Three," which would be הַשְּׁלֹשָׁה in Hebrew. Some English versions have "chief of the three" (e.g., ESV, REB). That reading is consistent with other phrases in this chapter that refer to "the Three": בַּשְּׁלֹשָׁה (הַ)גִּבֹּרִים, "among the three elite soldiers," in 23:9, 22; בַּשְּׁלֹשָׁה, "among the Three," in 23:18; הַשְּׁלֹשָׁה, "the Three," in 23:19 (twice), 23; and שְׁלֹשֶׁת הַגִּבֹּרִים, "the three elite soldiers," in 23:16, 17 (see the first textual note on 23:16). For "the Thirty" (הַשְּׁלֹשִׁים), see the first textual note on 23:13.

הוּא עֲדִינוֹ הָעֶצְנִי—Whether one reads the Qere הָעֶצְנִי or the Kethib הָעֶצְנוֹ, MT 2 Sam 23:8 is rather incomprehensible. The translation and most English versions follow the reading in 1 Chr 11:11: הוּא־עוֹרֵר אֶת־חֲנִיתוֹ, "he wielded his spear," which is also in 2 Sam 23:18. The verb עוֹרֵר is the Polel (D) third masculine singular perfect of עוּר, "arouse, awake." In the Polel it means "set in motion" or "wield, brandish" (BDB, s.v. עוּר I, Polel). See the noun חֲנִית, "spear," in 2 Sam 23:7, 18, 21; see it also in, e.g., 1 Sam 17:7, 45, 47; 2 Sam 1:6.

עַל־שְׁמֹנֶה מֵאוֹת חָלָל—Literally "against eight hundred pierced (men)." 1 Chr 11:11 reads שְׁלֹשׁ־מֵאוֹת, "three hundred," which is the number of men pierced by Abishai in the analogous phrase in 23:18 (see the third textual note on 23:18). The singular adjective חָלָל, "pierced, slain," is derived from the verb חָלַל, "to pierce" (see the second textual note on 1:19). Its singular is used here as a class noun (Waltke-O'Connor, § 7.2.2b, example 6) or collective, as also in 1:19, 25. It is translated as a relative clause, "whom he pierced," here and also in 23:18.

בְּפַעַם אֶחָת:—"At one time." The segholate noun פַּעַם, "an instance, time," is usually construed as feminine, as in 1 Sam 26:8, where it is modified by the feminine numeral אַחַת, "one." Here the Qere, אֶחָת, which is the sole reading in some Masoretic manuscripts, is a pausal form of that feminine numeral, while the Kethib, אֶחָד, is the masculine form.

23:9 וְאַחֲרָיו—"After him." This Qere is the normal spelling of the preposition אַחַר with a third masculine singular pronominal suffix (and the article). The Kethib, וְאַחֲרוֹ, is the only instance where the preposition has the form of the suffix that would go on a singular noun.

דּוֹדוֹ—"Dodo" is the Qere and the reading in 1 Chr 11:12. The Kethib is דּוֹדִי, "Dodi." 1QSam omits "the son of Dodo."

בֶּן־אֲחֹחִי—"The son of an Ahohite" is the reading in 2 Sam 23:9 and 1QSam (בן אחוחי). The translation "the Ahohite" follows the reading הָאֲחוֹחִי in 1 Chr 11:12.

The man's full designation as found in 1 Chr 11:12 and presumed to be the original reading here in 2 Sam 23:9 is אֶלְעָזָר בֶּן־דּוֹדוֹ הָאֲחוֹחִי. The construction consists of a man's name, followed by "the son of" and his father's name, followed by a gentilic adjective (usually with the article). In such a construction, found several times in this listing of David's thirty elite soldiers, it is syntactically possible that the gentilic refers to the son, here "Eleazar the son of Dodo, the Ahohite," and it is also possible that it refers to the father, here "Eleazar the son of Dodo the Ahohite." Sometimes the context gives an indication. For example, "Ahithophel the Gilonite" (23:34) is likely the same "Ahithophel the Gilonite" mentioned in 15:12. Sometimes, as in this verse, there is nothing contextually to indicate which man's name the gentilic is meant to modify, although in most cases a man and his father would have been from the same place and thus both could be described with the same gentilic.

בִּשְׁלֹשָׁה הַגִּבֹּרִים—"(He was) among the three elite soldiers." See the discussion in the fourth textual note on 23:8. The article is present in the Qere, הַגִּבֹּרִים, whereas it is absent in the Kethib, גִּבֹּרִים.

עִם־דָּוִד—Instead of just "with David," 1 Chr 11:13 has the longer reading הוּא־הָיָה עִם־דָּוִיד בַּפַּס דַּמִּים, "he was with David in Pas-dammim." See the commentary.

בְּחָרְפָם—"When they defied." This is the Piel (D) infinitive construct of חָרַף, "mock, revile, defy," with the preposition בְּ and a third masculine plural suffix serving as the subject. See the first textual note on 21:21.

נֶאֶסְפוּ־שָׁם לַמִּלְחָמָה—"(When) they assembled there for battle." For the Niphal (N) of אָסַף (as well as its active Qal [G]) for troops gathering together for battle, see the first textual note on 6:1. Its Niphal recurs in the same sense in 23:11.

וַיַּעֲלוּ אִישׁ יִשְׂרָאֵל:—"When the men of Israel retreated." The Qal (G) of עָלָה can mean "go up" to attack in battle (see BDB, Qal, 2 c), but it can also have the opposite meaning, "withdraw, retreat" (BDB, 1 e), as here.

23:10 יָגְעָה יָדוֹ—"His hand was exhausted." The verb יָגַע means "be exhausted, weary from exertion." The subject of its Qal (G) third feminine singular perfect here is the feminine noun יָד, "hand," with a third masculine singular suffix. See the first textual note on 17:2 for the adjective that is cognate to the verb. Cf. also the idiom for exhaustion with יָד, "hand," in the second textual note on 17:2.

וַיַּעַשׂ יְהוָה תְּשׁוּעָה גְדוֹלָה—Literally "and Yahweh did a great salvation." This clause recurs in 23:12 and was used also in 1 Sam 19:5. Similar, but without the adjective גְּדוֹלָה, is the clause in 1 Sam 11:13. For the feminine noun תְּשׁוּעָה, "salvation" or "victory," see the first textual note on 19:3 (ET 19:2). Cf. also the fourth and seventh textual notes on 22:3. Although translated as "victory" in this military context, this divine act was part of the history of God saving his people. Their ultimate salvific victory comes in Jesus Christ (1 Cor 15:54–57; 1 Jn 5:4).

וְהָעָם יָשֻׁבוּ אַחֲרָיו אַךְ־לְפַשֵּׁט:—"(And) the troops returned, (following) after him, but only to plunder [the bodies]." In military contexts the noun with the article הָעָם, "the people," often denotes "the troops," as again in 23:11 (see the first textual note on 1 Sam 4:3[1] and the second textual note on 2 Sam 1:4). The imperfect יָשֻׁבוּ has an incipient nuance and refers to limited action: the troops (slowly) returned, but not to join Eleazar in fighting the enemy; their timidity limited their action to stripping the spoils off of the corpses of those Eleazar had already killed (see Waltke-O'Connor, § 31.2c, including example 9). The preposition אַחַר with a suffix is used in the pregnant sense of "(following) after" (see the second textual note on 1 Sam 12:14[2] and the first textual note on 2 Sam 20:2). The infinitive construct (with the preposition לְ) לְפַשֵּׁט is the Piel (D) of פָּשַׁט, meaning "to strip off, remove [clothing, etc.]."

23:11 שַׁמָּא בֶן־אָגֵא הָרָרִי—"Shammah the son of Agee, a Hararite." For this construction with a patronymic followed by a gentilic, see the third textual note on 23:9. For "Shammah," see the textual note on 23:32c–33a. For the meaning of "Hararite," see the commentary.

לַחַיָּה—This Hebrew text is difficult. The MT can be explained without emendation in one of two ways. First, the noun חַיָּה I, "wild animal(s)," is common in the OT, and the singular can be a collective. This text could be a prepositional phrase with the preposition לְ and the noun חַיָּה I used as a place-name, as the LXX understood it: εἰς Θηρία, "at Wild Animals." Second, the noun חַיָּה here could be a homograph that, with the preposition לְ, means "into a company, band, community" (see HCSB, NIV), since חַיָּה appears to be used with that meaning in 23:13 (see the third textual note on 23:13). But that meaning seems less likely here because the following clause refers to a place: וַתְּהִי־שָׁם חֶלְקַת הַשָּׂדֶה מְלֵאָה עֲדָשִׁים, literally "and there was there a portion of the field filled (with) lentils." Since the adverb שָׁם, "there," often refers to a previously mentioned place, it is likely that לַחַיָּה here refers to a place. In keeping with that understanding but in preference to the first option, the translation reflects a third option: it follows the suggestion of BDB (s.v. לְחִי II) and *HALOT* (s.v. לְחִי II) that the text should be repointed

---

[1] Steinmann, *1 Samuel*, 120.

[2] Steinmann, *1 Samuel*, 220.

to לֶחְיָה, "at Lehi" (the place-name לֶחִי, "Lehi,"[3] with a directional *he*). Some English versions understand the text in this way (ESV, GW, NET, NRSV).

חֶלְקַת הַשָּׂדֶה֙ מְלֵאָה עֲדָשִׁים—Literally "a portion of the field filled (with) lentils." The feminine noun חֶלְקָה in construct, חֶלְקַת, is indefinite despite being in construct with the definite noun הַשָּׂדֶה֙ (see Joüon, § 139 b). This indefinite noun, חֶלְקַת, "a portion," is modified by the indefinite feminine form מְלֵאָה. It could be the feminine form of the adjective מָלֵא, "full," or the Qal (G) feminine singular participle of מָלֵא, "be full," which often describes the earth or land and takes an accusative of material (see BDB, Qal, 1 a, b). Here the accusative is the plural of the noun עֲדָשָׁה, "lentil," a noun that occurs elsewhere only in Gen 25:34; 2 Sam 17:28; Ezek 4:9.

וְהָעָם נָס—"When the troops fled." When a singular collective noun such as עַם is the subject, the verb can be singular (as here, the Qal [G] of נוּס) or plural, as in the parallel in 1 Chr 11:13 (וְהָעָם נָסוּ) and also in 2 Sam 23:10 (וְהָעָם יָשֻׁבוּ). See Joüon, § 150 e.

23:12 וַיִּתְיַצֵּב—"He took his stand." The verb יָצַב occurs only in the Hithpael (HtD) and usually means "take one's stand" (BDB; cf. 18:13, 30; 21:5).

וַיַּצִּילֶהָ—Literally "and he saved it." In context this is translated as "(and he) defended it." The Hiphil (H) of נָצַל, "save, deliver, rescue," usually refers to Yahweh's saving action, which he carries out here through Shammah. See the textual note on 1 Sam 10:18–19[4] and the second textual note on 2 Sam 14:16.

וַיַּעַשׂ יְהוָה תְּשׁוּעָה גְדוֹלָה:—See the second textual note on 23:10.

23:13 וַיֵּרְדוּ שְׁלֹשָׁה מֵהַשְּׁלֹשִׁים רֹאשׁ—"Three from the thirty chief soldiers came down." For the first number, the Qere, שְׁלֹשָׁה, "three," is the sole reading in many Masoretic manuscripts. It is supported by the LXX (τρεῖς) and is the reading in the parallel verse 1 Chr 11:15. The Kethib of the first number is שְׁלֹשִׁים, "thirty," but "thirty from the thirty" would mean that all of the chief soldiers came down. The second number is "the Thirty" (הַשְּׁלֹשִׁים), who are mentioned again in 23:18, 23, 24 (see the first textual note on 23:18 for the reading there). The singular noun רֹאשׁ, "head, chief," is placed after מֵהַשְּׁלֹשִׁים, "from the Thirty," as a class noun (cf. Waltke-O'Connor, § 7.2.2b) indicating that all of "the Thirty" were "chief soldiers." See the discussion of רֹאשׁ in the fourth textual note on 23:8.

מְעָרַת עֲדֻלָּם—"The cave of Adullam." This was David's hiding place in 1 Sam 22:1. וְחַיַּת פְּלִשְׁתִּים חֹנָה—"While a detachment of Philistines was camping." If וְחַיַּת (a feminine noun חַיָּה with the conjunction *waw* and in construct) is the correct reading here, this noun occurs only here and perhaps in Ps 68:11 (ET 68:10). BDB defines it as "community" (s.v. חַיָּה II), whereas *DCH* gives "troop, band" (s.v חַיָּה III). (Cf. מַצָּב in the second textual note on 23:14.) The meaning "detachment" is conjectural and based on the LXX's τάγμα, "division, group." 1 Chr 11:15 reads וּמַחֲנֵה פְלִשְׁתִּים חֹנָה, "and an encampment of Philistines was camping," with the noun מַחֲנֶה (as in 23:16), which is derived from the verb חָנָה, "encamp." In both 2 Sam 23:13 and 1 Chr 11:15, the third

---

word in this clause is the Qal (G) feminine singular participle of that verb: חֹנָה, "was camping."

23:14 בַּמְּצוּדָה—For the noun מְצוּדָה, "stronghold," see the second textual note on 22:2 and the commentary on 22:2–3.

וּמַצַּב פְּלִשְׁתִּים—As here, the noun מַצָּב referred to a "garrison" of Philistines in 1 Sam 13:23; 14:1, 4, 6, 11, 15.

23:15 וַיִּתְאַוֶּה—"He had a desire." The verb אָוָה I is used in the Piel (D) and (as here) the Hithpael (HtD), meaning "to desire, long for," and often refers to a desire for food (1 Sam 2:16) or drink.

מִי יַשְׁקֵנִי מַיִם—Literally "who will give me water to drink?" A wish can be expressed by an exclamatory question with an imperfect verb (Joüon, § 163 d; Waltke-O'Connor, § 18.2f, including example 33). See the fourth textual note on 19:1 (ET 18:33). יַשְׁקֵנִי is the Hiphil (H) third masculine singular imperfect of שָׁקָה with a first common singular object suffix. The Qal (G) of שָׁתָה means "to drink" (water, etc.), as in 23:16–17. For the causative meaning "to give [someone] [something] to drink," the Hiphil (H) of שָׁקָה is used (as also in 1 Sam 30:11). שָׁתָה is never used in the Hiphil (H), and שָׁקָה is never used in the Qal (G).

מִבְּאר בֵּית־לֶחֶם—"From the well of Bethlehem." The identical construct chain recurs in 23:16, and the noun בְּאר is also used in 23:20. בְּאר is an alternate spelling of the noun בּוֹר (or, spelled defectively, בֹּר), "well." A number of Masoretic manuscripts, the Qere in some manuscripts, and 1 Chr 11:17 have one of those spellings. Cf. the synonym בְּאר, "well, cistern," in 2 Sam 17:18, 19, 21.

בַּשָּׁעַר:—"At the gate." This is a pausal form of בַּשַּׁעַר (as in 23:16), the segholate noun שַׁעַר with the preposition בְּ and the article.

23:16 שְׁלֹשֶׁת הַגִּבֹּרִים—"The three elite soldiers." Here and in 23:17 the numeral שְׁלֹשָׁה, "three," is in construct with the plural noun with the article הַגִּבֹּרִים, "the elite soldiers." The phrase does not have a partitive sense, "three *of* the elite soldiers." Rather, it means "the triad of the elite soldiers" or "the three elite soldiers." This construction is common when the things numbered are regarded as forming a single group and also when they have the article (here on הַגִּבֹּרִים). See Joüon, § 142 d. For הַגִּבֹּרִים, see the first textual note on 23:8. For "three," see the fourth textual note on 23:8.

וַיִּשְׂאוּ וַיָּבִאוּ—"They carried [it] and brought [it] back." The first verb is the Qal (G) of נָשָׂא, and the second is the Hiphil (H) of בּוֹא.

וְלֹא אָבָה לִשְׁתּוֹתָם—Literally "and he was not willing to drink them." The identical clause recurs in 23:17. For the Qal (G) verb אָבָה, "be willing," with an infinitive construct with the preposition לְ as a complement to specify the action the person is (or is not) willing to do, see the first textual note on 13:14. לִשְׁתּוֹתָם is the Qal infinitive construct of שָׁתָה, "drink" (see the second textual note on 23:15), with לְ and a third masculine plural object suffix that refers back to the masculine plural noun מַיִם, "water," earlier in the verse.

וַיַּסֵּךְ אֹתָם—Literally "and he poured out them." The verb is the Hiphil (H) third masculine singular preterite (imperfect with *waw* consecutive) of נָסַךְ. Its Hiphil denotes pouring out a libation as an offering to God (e.g., Gen 35:14; Num 28:7; see also its

Hophal [Hp] in Ex 25:29; 37:16). אֹתָם is the direct object marker אֵת with a third masculine plural suffix that refers back to מַיִם, "water," earlier in the verse.

23:17 חָלִילָה לִּי יְהוָה—Literally "it is a profanity to me, O Yahweh." See the second textual note on 1 Sam 2:30.[5]

מֵעֲשֹׂתִי זֹאת—Literally "from my doing this," this means "I will not do this." When the preposition מִן is prefixed to an infinitive construct, it can have the force of a negation, "so that not" (BDB, s.v. מִן, 7 b (a)). עֲשֹׂתִי is the Qal (G) infinitive construct of עָשָׂה, "to do," with a first common singular suffix that serves as its subject.

הֲדַם הָאֲנָשִׁים—Literally "(is this not) the blood of the men?" The interrogative *he* prefixed to the noun דָּם (in construct) expects an affirmative answer (cf. the first textual note on 23:19). Therefore it is translated as an affirmation: "this is the blood of the men." A verb must be supplied (cf. GKC, § 167 a).

הַהֹלְכִים בְּנַפְשׁוֹתָם—"Who went at the risk of their lives." A definite article on a participle (הַהֹלְכִים) can have the force of a relative pronoun, "who." The preposition בְּ on נַפְשׁוֹתָם has the sense of price or cost (see BDB, s.v. בְּ I, III 3 a; cf. Waltke-O'Connor, § 11.2.5d, including n. 29). See the first textual note on 18:13.

שְׁלֹשֶׁת הַגִּבֹּרִים:—"The three elite soldiers." See the first textual note on 23:16.

23:18 רֹאשׁ הַשְּׁלֹשָׁה—This reading with the Qere הַשְּׁלֹשָׁה, literally "the head of the Three," is the reading one might have expected in 23:8 (see the fourth textual note on 23:8). The Qere is the sole reading in most Masoretic manuscripts and is supported by the LXX (ἐν τοῖς τρισίν) and the Vulgate (*de tribus*). The Kethib has the ordinal numeral with the article הַשְּׁלִשִׁי, "the third." For both the Qere and the Kethib, see the discussion in the fourth textual note on 23:8. The translation "the Thirty" follows the reading הַשְּׁלֹשִׁים in two Masoretic manuscripts and ܬܠܬܝܢ in the Syriac Peshitta. For הַשְּׁלֹשִׁים, "the Thirty," see the first textual note on 23:13; the phrase occurs also in 23:23, 24.

וְהוּא עוֹרֵר אֶת־חֲנִיתוֹ—See the discussion of this reading in the fifth textual note on 23:8.

עַל־שְׁלֹשׁ מֵאוֹת חָלָל—"Against three hundred men, whom he pierced." See the discussion of this construction in the sixth textual note on 23:8, which describes a feat by Eshbaal.

וְלוֹ־שֵׁם בַּשְּׁלֹשָׁה:—Literally "and to him (belonged) a name among the Three." This nominal sentence recurs at the end of 23:22 with הַגִּבֹּרִים, "the elite soldiers," appended. The noun שֵׁם, "name," can refer to a famous reputation of a person (7:9; 8:13) or to God's renown (7:23). For "the Three," see the fourth textual note on 23:8.

23:19 מִן־הַשְּׁלֹשָׁה הֲכִי נִכְבָּד—"Was he not more honored than the Three?" The interrogative *he* on הֲכִי, "is it that?" frames a rhetorical question that expects an affirmative answer (cf. the third textual note on 23:17). The preposition מִן is used comparatively, "more than" (cf. מִנֹּגַהּ, "better than the brightness," in the fourth textual note on 23:4). The meaning of נִכְבָּד, the Niphal (N) masculine singular participle of כָּבֵד, is the passive of the meaning of its Piel (D), "to honor," for which, see the first textual note on 10:3. 1 Chr 11:21 reads מִן־הַשְּׁלוֹשָׁה בַשְּׁנַיִם נִכְבָּד, "he was honored twice more than the

---

5 Steinmann, *1 Samuel*, 100.

Three." A similar clause, but with the plural of the number and without הֲכִי, forms a statement at the beginning of 23:23: מִן־הַשְּׁלֹשִׁים נִכְבָּד, "he [Benaiah] was more honored than the Thirty."

וְעַד־הַשְּׁלֹשָׁה לֹא־בָא:—Literally "and as far as the Three he did not come." The preposition עַד is used with an abstract goal: "he did not attain *to* (the level of the elite force) The Three" (Waltke-O'Connor, § 11.2.12d, example 8).

23:20 בֶּן־אִישׁ־חַיִל—"The son of a capable man." This construct chain with the Qere חַיִל is sole the reading in 1 Chr 11:22. The construct phrase אִישׁ־חַיִל, literally "a man of valor" (or its plural equivalent, אַנְשֵׁי־חַיִל) often signifies outstanding competence and bravery.[6] See אַנְשֵׁי־חַיִל, "the best soldiers," in the second textual note on 11:16. The reading here with the Kethib חַי is בֶּן־אִישׁ־חַי, "(the) son of a living man," which seems to be missing the final consonant, ל, on the last word.

רַב־פְּעָלִים—The adjective רַב is in construct with the plural of the noun פֹּעַל, literally "many of deeds," meaning that Jehoiada (the "capable man" and the nearest antecedent) had accomplished many deeds.

שְׁנֵי אֲרִאֵל מוֹאָב—"Two [?] of Ariel of Moab" is the reading of the MT here and in 1 Chr 11:22. LXX 2 Sam 23:20 reads τοὺς δύο υἱοὺς Αριηλ τοῦ Μωαβ, "the two *sons* of Ariel of Moab," which would correspond to a four-word Hebrew construct chain, שְׁנֵי בְּנֵי אֲרִאֵל מוֹאָב. The LXX may represent a more original text, and בְּנֵי may have been omitted accidentally by homoioteleuton (it has the same ending as שְׁנֵי). "Ariel" appears to be a proper name meaning "lion of God" (אֲרִי־אֵל written defectively as אֲרִאֵל). See the next textual note.

הָאֲרִי—This Qere, literally "the lion," is also the reading in 1 Chr 11:22. The Kethib is the synonymous longer spelling of the noun with the article, הָאַרְיֵה, "the lion." Hebrew typically uses an article with nouns that are specific in the mind of the narrator, whereas English would use an indefinite article. See also the third textual note on 23:21. See Joüon, § 137 o; the first textual note on 15:13; the fourth textual note on 17:9; and the second textual note on 17:17.

בְּיוֹם הַשָּׁלֶג:—This construct phrase is literally "on the day of the snow." This must have been a rare and memorable meteorological event. Cf. "the earthquake" as a historical reference point in Amos 1:1.

23:21 וְהוּא־הִכָּה אֶת־אִישׁ מִצְרִי—"He struck down an Egyptian man." The marker of the definite direct object, אֵת, can be used with an object that is grammatically indefinite but has a certain logical determination in the mind of the author (Joüon, § 125 h).

אִישׁ מַרְאֶה—This construct phrase, with the Qere אִישׁ, literally means "a man of appearance." The noun מַרְאֶה is used in phrases that describe a man as handsome in 1 Sam 17:42 (cf. 1 Sam 16:7) and a woman as beautiful in 2 Sam 11:2; 14:27. The Kethib is the relative pronoun אֲשֶׁר: אֲשֶׁר מַרְאֶה, "who was (handsome in) appearance." 1 Chr 11:23 reads אִישׁ מִדָּה ׀ חָמֵשׁ בָּאַמָּה, "a tall man, five cubits."

---

[6] See, e.g., Gen 47:6; Ex 18:21, 25; Judg 3:29; 20:44, 46; 1 Sam 31:12; 2 Sam 11:16; 24:9; 1 Ki 1:42; Nah 2:4 (ET 2:3); Ps 76:6 (ET 76:5); Neh 11:6; 1 Chr 10:12; 26:8.

בַּשֵּׁבֶט—Literally "with the club." The Hebrew definite article can be used with an object when it is used for a certain purpose or goal (Joüon, § 137 m).

וַיִּגְזֹל—"He grabbed." This is the only instance of the verb גָּזַל, "tear away, seize, rob" (BDB), in the book of Samuel, but it is common elsewhere in the OT.

23:22 וְלוֹ־שֵׁם בִּשְׁלֹשָׁה הַגִּבֹּרִים:—See the fourth textual note on 23:18.

23:23 מִן־הַשְּׁלֹשִׁים נִכְבָּד—See the first textual note on 23:19. Here the number is plural, הַשְּׁלֹשִׁים, "the Thirty." For this larger group of elite commandos, see the first textual note on 23:13. They are mentioned again in 23:24.

וְאֶל־הַשְּׁלֹשָׁה לֹא־בָא—See the second textual note on 23:19. Here the preposition אֶל replaces the preposition עַד there.

וַיְשִׂמֵהוּ דָוִד אֶל־מִשְׁמַעְתּוֹ:—"David put him in charge of his bodyguard" is literally "and David set him to/over his bodyguard." In place of the preposition אֶל, which usually means "to," 1 Chr 11:25 reads עַל, "over." Samuel is one of the OT books in which אֶל is often used with the sense of עַל (BDB, s.v. אֶל, note 2; see the first textual note on 2:9 and the second textual note on 3:29). The feminine segholate noun מִשְׁמַעַת, "bodyguard," was also in 1 Sam 22:14.

23:24 בַּשְּׁלֹשִׁים—"Among the Thirty." For this group, see the first textual note on 23:13.

בֵּית לָחֶם:—"[From] Bethlehem." 1 Chr 11:26 reads מִבֵּית לָחֶם, "from Bethlehem."

23:25 שַׁמָּה—"Shammah." 1 Chr 11:27 reads שַׁמּוֹת, "Shammoth."

אֱלִיקָא הַחֲרֹדִי:—"Elika the Harodite" is omitted in 1 Chr 11:27.

23:26 חֶלֶץ הַפַּלְטִי—"Helez the Paltite." The gentilic adjective הַפַּלְטִי, "the Paltite," indicates that this man was from Beth-pelet in the south of Judah (Josh 15:27). The parallel verse 1 Chr 11:27 calls him חֶלֶץ הַפְּלוֹנִי, "Helez the Pelonite." Apparently he is mentioned again in 1 Chr 27:10 as the one in charge of the division of David's army for the seventh month; there he is called חֶלֶץ הַפְּלוֹנִי מִן־בְּנֵי אֶפְרַיִם, "Helez the Pelonite from the descendants of Ephraim." While Helez was descended from Ephraim, he probably made his home in Beth-pelet in Judah. The designation "Pelonite" is probably a corruption of "Paltite" since there is no known person or place called "Pelon."

עִירָא בֶן־עִקֵּשׁ הַתְּקוֹעִי:—"Ira the son of Ikkesh, the Tekoite." For this construction with a patronymic followed by a gentilic, see the third textual note on 23:9. The gentilic adjective here associates a person with the place-name "Tekoa" (תְּקוֹעַ, 14:2). The feminine form of this adjective, תְּקֹעִית, was in 14:4, 9.

23:27 מְבֻנַּי הַחֻשָׁתִי:—This reading in the MT is "Mebunnai the Hushathite." The translation "Sibbecai the Hushathite" follows the reading סִבְּכַי הַחֻשָׁתִי in 1 Chr 11:29. If that is the original reading, then 2 Sam 23:27 has suffered from a double graphic confusion: *mem* for *samek* and *nun* for *kaph*. The translation in LXX 2 Sam 23:27 ἐκ τῶν υἱῶν τοῦ Ασωθίτου, "from the sons of the Hushathite," supports MT 2 Sam 23:27 but vocalized the first word (which would have been unpointed in its *Vorlage*) as מִבְּנֵי, "from the sons of."

23:28 צַלְמוֹן הָאֲחֹחִי—"Zalmon the Ahohite." In place of this name, 1 Chr 11:29 reads עִילַי הָאֲחוֹחִי, "Ilai the Ahohite."

23:29 חֵלֶב—This reading in Codex Leningradensis is "Heleb." The translation "Heled" follows the reading חֵלֶד in many Masoretic manuscripts and 1 Chr 11:30. Zech 6:10 and 1 Chr 27:15 have a similar name: חֶלְדָּי, "Heldai."

בֶּן־בַּעֲנָה הַנְּטֹפָתִי—"The son of Baanah, the Netophathite." For this construction with a patronymic followed by a gentilic, see the third textual note on 23:9.

23:30 הִדַּי—This reading, "Hiddai," is a unique name. The translation "Hurai" follows the reading חוּרַי in 1 Chr 11:32. It is also supported by Ουρι in LXX 2 Sam 23:30 and 1 Chr 11:32. The exact name חוּרַי, "Hurai," occurs only in 1 Chr 11:32, but variations of it occur frequently in the OT.[7] If it is original, then הִדַּי in 2 Sam 23:30 is the result of a double graphic confusion of *he* in place of *chet* and *daleth* in place of *resh*.

23:31 אֲבִי־עַלְבוֹן—"Abi-albon" is a unique name. 1 Chr 11:32 reads אֲבִיאֵל, "Abiel," a name known elsewhere (1 Sam 9:1; 14:51) and supported by Αβιηλ in LXX 2 Sam 23:31 and 1 Chr 11:32.

עַזְמָוֶת—"Azmaveth." This name is a compound of עַז, "strong," and מָוֶת, "death."[8] This name could be a reference to God as stronger than death (cf. 1 Cor 15:22–26), or perhaps it describes this elite soldier as strong enough to serve faithfully even in the face of death. Cf. עַזָּה כַמָּוֶת אַהֲבָה, "love is as strong as death" (Song 8:6).

הַבַּרְחֻמִי:—This reading is "the Barhumite." The translation "the Baharumite" follows the reading הַבַּחֲרוּמִי in 1 Chr 11:33, which indicates he was from the Benjaminite town of Bahurim.[9] If that is the original reading, then 2 Sam 23:31 suffered corruption caused by a metathesis of *chet* and *resh*.

23:32b בְּנֵי יָשֵׁן—"The sons of Jashen." 1 Chr 11:34 reads בְּנֵי הָשֵׁם הַגִּזוֹנִי, "the sons of Hashem the Gizonite." Neither the author of Samuel nor the Chronicler provides the number and names of these sons. Most likely two sons are intended. See the third textual note on 23:39.

23:32c–33a יְהוֹנָתָן: שַׁמָּה הַהֲרָרִי—"Jonathan [the son of] Shammah the Hararite." The translation assumes that the original reading included the noun in construct בֶּן־, "the son of," based on the Lucianic version of the LXX[10] and 1 Chr 11:34, which reads יוֹנָתָן בֶּן־שָׁגֵה הַהֲרָרִי, "Jonathan the son of Shagee the Hararite." Many English versions also assume that בֶּן־ should be restored.[11] Apparently "Shammah" (spelled שַׁמָּא in 2 Sam 23:11 and שַׁמָּה in 23:33) was the father of "Jonathan" (יְהוֹנָתָן, 23:32), and Shammah's father was "Agee" (אָגֵא, 23:11). It seems that in 1 Chr 11:34 the name of Shammah's father, "Agee" (אָגֵא, 23:11), intruded on his name, "Shammah" (שַׁמָּא or שַׁמָּה), resulting in the corrupt combination שָׁגֵה, "Shagee" (i.e., *Sh*ammah plus A*gee*, 1 Chr 11:34).

---

[7] See חוּר, "Hur," in Ex 17:10, 12; 24:14; 31:2; 35:30; 38:22; Num 31:8; Josh 13:21; Neh 3:9; 1 Chr 2:19, 20, 50; 4:1, 4; 2 Chr 1:5; בֶּן־חוּר, "Ben-hur," in 1 Ki 4:8; חוּרִי, "Huri," in 1 Chr 5:14; and חוֹרִי, "Hori," in Gen 36:22; Num 13:5; 1 Chr 1:39.

[8] Cf. the noun צַלְמָוֶת, "shadow of death, gloom, deep darkness" (*DCH*), in, e.g., Is 9:1 (ET 9:2); Pss 23:4; 107:10, 14; Job 38:17.

[9] 2 Sam 3:16; 16:5; 17:18; 19:17 (ET 19:16); 1 Ki 2:8.

[10] See McCarter, *II Samuel*, 493.

[11] E.g., HCSB, GW, NET, NIV, NRSV.

For the construction with a patronymic followed by a gentilic, see the third textual note on 23:9.

23:33b אֲחִיאָם בֶּן־שָׁרָר הָאֲרָרִי—"Ahiam the son of Sharar the Ararite." 1 Chr 11:35 reads אֲחִיאָם בֶּן־שָׂכָר הַהֲרָרִי, "Ahiam the son of Sacar the Hararite." It is impossible to decide which patronymic is the likely original. Regarding the gentilic adjective for Sharar/Sacar, the form in 23:33, הָאֲרָרִי, "the Ararite," is probably secondary, and the original is likely הַהֲרָרִי, "the Hararite," in 1 Chr 11:35, because הַהֲרָרִי, "the Hararite," described Shammah earlier in 23:33 and the anarthrous הֲרָרִי, "a Hararite," designated Shammah in 23:11. For the construction with a patronymic followed by a gentilic, see the third textual note on 23:9.

23:34 אֱלִיפֶלֶט בֶּן־אֲחַסְבַּי בֶּן־הַמַּעֲכָתִי—"Eliphelet the son of Ahasbai, the son of the Maacathite." 1 Chr 11:35 reads אֱלִיפַל בֶּן־אוּר, "Eliphal the son of Ur."

אֱלִיעָם בֶּן־אֲחִיתֹפֶל הַגִּלֹנִי׃—"Eliam the son of Ahithophel the Gilonite." The gentilic adjective "the Gilonite" most likely identifies "Ahithophel" as the same "Ahithophel the Gilonite" (15:12) who served as Absalom's astute counselor (2 Samuel 15–17; see 16:23) before his advice was changed to foolishness (15:31; 17:14) and he hanged himself (17:23). Surprisingly, this counselor who plotted against David seems to have had a son who was one of David's Thirty. For the construction with a patronymic followed by a gentilic, see the third textual note on 23:9.

23:35–36 At this point there is a divergence with the parallel in 1 Chr 11:36–38:

2 Samuel 23:35–36	1 Chronicles 11:36–38
חֶצְרַי הַכַּרְמְלִי, *Hezrai the Carmelite*	חֵפֶר הַמְּכֵרָתִי, Hepher the Mecherathite
פַּעֲרַי הָאַרְבִּי, Paari the Arbite	אֲחִיָּה הַפְּלֹנִי, Ahijah the Pelonite
יִגְאָל בֶּן־נָתָן מִצֹּבָה, Igal the son of Nathan from Zobah	חֶצְרוֹ הַכַּרְמְלִי, *Hezro the Carmelite*
בָּנִי הַגָּדִי, Bani the Gadite	נַעֲרַי בֶּן־אֶזְבָּי, Naarai the son of Ezbai
	יוֹאֵל אֲחִי נָתָן, Joel the brother of Nathan
	מִבְחָר בֶּן־הַגְרִי, Mibhar the son of Hagri

23:35 חֶצְרַי—This Qere is "Hezrai," whereas the Kethib is חֶצְרוֹ, "Hezro," as in 1 Chr 11:37.

23:37 נֹשֵׂא כְּלֵי יוֹאָב—This reading, with the Qere נֹשֵׂא, is also the reading in 1 Chr 11:39. The Qal (G) masculine singular participle of נָשָׂא, "carry," in construct with the plural of the noun כְּלִי, "equipment," denotes the military position of "armor bearer." See the second textual note on 1 Sam 14:1.[12] Thus, the construct chain here means

---

[12] Steinmann, *1 Samuel*, 247. The phrase refers to Jonathan's armor bearer in 1 Sam 14:1, 6, 7, 12, 13, 14, 17. It refers to Saul's armor bearer in 1 Sam 31:4, 5, 6. In 1 Sam 16:21 David became Saul's armor bearer.

"the armor bearer of Joab." Joab had ten armor bearers according to 2 Sam 18:15. That may explain why the Kethib here, נֹשְׂאֵי, is the plural participle in construct, resulting in נֹשְׂאֵי כְּלֵי יוֹאָב, "Joab's armor bearers." See also the third textual note on 11:3, which observes that 4QSamᵃ includes an interpretive gloss, [נ]ושא כלי יואב, that identifies Uriah the Hittite as "Joab's armor [b]earer." The close proximity of the Kethib in 23:37b, which refers to "Joab's armor bearers" (in the plural), to the reference to "Uriah the Hittite" in 23:39 may have led some scribes to conclude that Uriah was one of them.

23:39 אוּרִיָּה הַחִתִּי—The list ends at this point with "Uriah the Hittite." He is the same faithful soldier named in 2 Samuel 11, where David committed adultery with his wife, Bathsheba, and then had him killed; see the commentary on 11:1–27.

After "Uriah the Hittite" (1 Chr 11:41a), 1 Chr 11:41b–47 contains the names of sixteen more elite soldiers.

כֹּל—Here this noun is used absolutely (without the article and not in construct with a following genitive) in the sense of the numerical "sum" or "total" (see *DCH*, s.v. כֹּל I, 1; BDB, s.v. כֹּל, 2 a).

שְׁלֹשִׁים וְשִׁבְעָה:—"Thirty-seven." "The Three" (23:8)[13] are the first three names given, Eshbaal, Eleazar, and Shammah (23:8–12), with annotations of their heroics in 23:13–17. Then Abishai and Benaiah are named in 23:18–23. A total of thirty are named in 23:24–39 (not counting the names of their fathers). In addition, 23:32b refers to "the sons of Jashen" without giving their number. If that phrase refers to two "sons of Jashen" then the total in 23:8–39 is "thirty seven" (23:39):

- Five are named in 23:8–23.
- Thirty are named in 23:24–39.
- Two unnamed "sons of Jashen" are mentioned in 23:32b.

Commentary

1002–969 BC[14]

Parallel: 2 Sam 23:8–39 ‖ 1 Chr 11:10–41a

For the place of this passage in the structure of 2 Samuel 21–24, see "The Form and Content of 2 Samuel 21–24" in the commentary on 21:1–14. This section highlights the elite corps of soldiers assembled by David, beginning with his time at "the cave of Adullam" (2 Sam 23:13), when he was hiding from Saul (1 Sam 22:1). Since the list includes Asah-el (2 Sam 23:24), who was killed by Abner in 2:18–23, the corps itself most probably dates to the earliest part of David's reign when he was king of Judah only (see 2:1–7; he was anointed king of Israel in 5:3). The exploits of the thirty-seven men listed here demonstrate God's salvific blessing on Israel through the faithful soldiers of the anointed messianic king, David.[15] They delivered Israel from those who had oppressed them, especially the Philistines (23:9–17). David had "thirty chief soldiers"

---

[13] The Three are referenced also in 23:13, 16, 17, 18, 19, 22, 23.

[14] See "The Chronology of David's Reign" in the commentary on 5:1–5.

[15] See "Christ in Samuel" in the introduction (Steinmann, *1 Samuel*, 23–26); the commentary on 1 Sam 2:10, 35 (Steinmann, *1 Samuel*, 80–81, 105–6); the beginning of the commentary

(23:13; see also 23:23, 24), but the list gives a "total" of "thirty-seven" (23:39). The discrepancy in these numbers is not a mistake. Instead, it is to be explained by the fact that, over the course of time, some of the Thirty died in battle and were replaced. The author narrates the deaths of two: Asah-el (23:24; see 2:23) and Uriah (23:39; see 11:17). It is likely that others were also killed or left David's service and that the list includes the names of five who took their places.

Eshbaal, the Chief of the Three (23:8)

The leader of the most elite of David's soldiers was Eshbaal. His father was Hachmoni, which means that Eshbaal was the brother of Jehiel, who served as attendant for David's sons (1 Chr 27:32). Eshbaal's feat of killing eight hundred in one battle, far surpassing Abishai's three hundred (23:18), marked him as the logical choice for the head of the Three.

Eleazar, One of the Three (23:9–10)

Eleazar was the son of Dodo the Ahohite (23:9). Dodo may be the same person as Dodai the Ahohite, who was in charge of the division of David's army for the second month (1 Chr 27:4). Eleazar was from the tribe of Benjamin; he traced his lineage back to Benjamin's son Bela and his son Ahoah (1 Chr 8:1, 3–4). Although the author of Samuel does not state where Eleazar joined David and the other two of the Three to defy the Philistines, the parallel verse 1 Chr 11:13 says that it was at a place called Pas-dammim. This was probably the same as Ephes-dammim, where David slew Goliath (1 Sam 17:1). Therefore, the account of Eleazar's heroic stand when the rest of the troops in his contingent fled is probably a reference to the battle that followed David's victory over the Philistine giant (1 Samuel 17), an "impressive victory" of salvation gained by "Yahweh" (see the second textual note on 2 Sam 23:10; see also 1 Sam 17:45–47).

Shammah, One of the Three (23:11–12)

The third of the Three was Shammah. He is identified by his father's name and as a "Hararite" (הָרָרִי, 23:11). This gentilic probably denotes someone who lived in "the hill country" (הָהָר) of Judah.[16] Shammah appears to have been the father of Jonathan, who was among the Thirty (see the textual note on 23:32c–33a; for "the Thirty," see the first textual note on 23:13). This battle with the Philistines at Lehi, which was also the place where Samson had slain many Philistines (Judg 15:9–19), is not mentioned elsewhere. It probably took place when David was serving as commander of Saul's troops (1 Sam 18:5).

---

on 2 Sam 6:1–23; the commentary on 2 Sam 7:1–29; and the excursus "הָאָדָם as 'the Man' in 2 Samuel 7:19 and 1 Chronicles 17:17" following the commentary on 7:1–29.

[16] See הָהָר, "the hill country," and הַר יְהוּדָה, "the hill country of Judah," in, e.g., Josh 11:21.

The Three Bring Water to David (23:13–17)

The final account of the Three relates that they were among the first to gather to David following his flight from Saul's court (2 Sam 23:13; cf. 1 Sam 22:1). The Philistines were in the Valley of Rephaim. The exact location of this valley is unknown. However, many identify its probable site with modern el-Baqʻa, southwest of Jerusalem. The northern extremity of this valley approaches the Hinnom Valley on the south end of Jerusalem (cf. 2 Sam 5:18, 22). The incursion of the Philistines deep into Judean territory at Bethlehem (2 Sam 23:14) illustrates the extent to which Saul's apostasy[17] and his mad persecution of David (1 Samuel 19–30), the former commander of his army (1 Sam 18:5), allowed Israel's enemies to once again oppress God's people. David was at the cave of Adullam (1 Sam 22:1).[18] Adullam was about sixteen miles (twenty-six kilometers) southwest of Jerusalem.

David's remark about wanting to drink water from the well at the gate of Bethlehem (2 Sam 23:15) was probably a nostalgic yearning for his hometown (see 1 Sam 16:1–13), which the Philistines were now occupying. It was unlikely that David and his men had no water, since securing a reliable water supply would have been one of the first tasks of a seasoned soldier and commander. However, the Three showed their commitment to David by penetrating Philistine lines and retrieving some water from the well (2 Sam 23:16).[19] David's refusal to drink it demonstrated his respect for their courage and commitment. The water represented their life's blood, which they had risked (23:17). Therefore, David poured it out as a sacrifice to Yahweh (23:16), who alone was worthy to receive such a costly commodity.[20] The final notice that "the three elite soldiers did these things" (23:17) not only serves to close out the narratives about these soldiers but also identifies these three as the most elite among "the Thirty."[21]

---

[17] Yahweh rejected Saul because Saul had rejected Yahweh's Word (1 Sam 15:22–29; 16:1, 14). As soon as Saul was chosen to be king, his apostasy became evident. He failed to carry out the mandate implied in 1 Sam 10:7 to eradicate the Philistine garrison in Gibeah. See the commentary on 1 Sam 10:7–8 and figure 16, "Saul's Faltering Accession," in "Samuel Anoints Saul (9:26–10:8)" in the commentary on 1 Sam 9:26–10:16, as well as the beginning of the commentary on 1 Sam 10:17–27a (Steinmann, *1 Samuel*, 196–98, 203). The failure to trust in Yahweh caused Saul and his troops to be terrified of the Philistines (1 Sam 13:7, 12; 17:11; 28:5).

[18] Note, however, that the "stronghold" mentioned in 2 Sam 23:14; 1 Chr 11:16 was near Adullam and was not the same stronghold as the one mentioned in 1 Sam 22:4–5, which was in Moab. See the commentary on 1 Sam 22:4–5 (Steinmann, *1 Samuel*, 422).

[19] Compare the desire for living water by a Samaritan woman at a well (Jn 4:13–15).

[20] The lifeblood of Christ was poured out (cf. Is 53:12) as the precious commodity that purchased our salvation (1 Pet 1:18–19; cf. Acts 3:6). In the Sacrament of the Altar we drink his blood, poured out for the forgiveness of sins (Mt 26:28; Mk 14:24; Lk 22:20).

[21] For "the Thirty," see the first textual note on 23:13.

Abishai, Joab's Brother (23:18–19)

We are told that Joab's brother Abishai was chief of "the Thirty" (see the first textual note on 23:18). As the son of David's sister Zeruiah (2 Sam 2:18; 1 Chr 2:13–16), Abishai was from Bethlehem, David's hometown (1 Sam 16:1–13). Not only was Abishai intrepid in battle; he also achieved a reputation as a warrior that rivaled that of the Three. As the commander of "the Thirty" (23:18) and thus also of "the Three" (23:19), he was more honored than they but not numbered among them (23:19).

Benaiah (23:20–23)

Benaiah hailed from Kabzeel (2 Sam 23:20) in the extreme south of Judah near Edom (Josh 15:21). Under Solomon Benaiah replaced Joab as commander of the army (1 Ki 2:35). During David's reign Benaiah was in charge of the division of the army for the third month and exercised this authority through his son Ammizabad (1 Chr 27:5–6). The author connects Benaiah's two heroic deeds via a play on words: he struck down two sons of "Ariel" (אֲרִאֵל), whose name means "lion of God," and he also struck down a "lion" (אֲרִי) on a snowy day.[22] That the author refers to this day as "*the* day that it snowed"[23] emphasizes a specific day in history and also the fact that snow was so rare in Israel that a snowy day was memorable.

Benaiah's slaying of an Egyptian was another impressive feat. He disarmed the man and killed him with his own weapon (23:21). This coup is even more impressive when information from 1 Chr 11:23 is included: the Egyptian was five cubits tall, about seven and a half feet or 229 centimeters, comparable to Goliath (see the third textual note on 1 Sam 17:4[24]). As with Abishai, because of Benaiah's celebrated adroitness "he gained a reputation among the three (elite soldiers)" (וְלוֹ־שֵׁם בִּשְׁלֹשָׁה in 23:22, as in 23:18). David rewarded him by promoting him to be the commanding officer of "his bodyguard" (23:23), which consisted of the Cherethites and Pelethites (see 8:18; 20:23).

The Rest of the Thirty (23:24–39)

The rest of the Thirty are simply listed without their accomplishments. There are thirty-one entries in the list as reconstructed in the translation above. Names are provided for thirty, and one of the entries ("the sons of Jashen," 23:32b) probably refers to two unnamed individuals, resulting in a total of thirty-two persons in these verses (see the third textual note on 23:39, as well as the textual notes on 23:32b and 23:32c–33a).

---

[22] See the third and fourth textual notes on 23:20.

[23] See the fifth textual note on 23:20.

[24] Steinmann, *1 Samuel*, 326–27.

Joab's brother Asah-el[25] was part of the Thirty (2 Sam 23:24). He was one of David's nephews, one of the three sons of David's sister Zeruiah (2 Sam 2:18; 1 Chr 2:13–16). Thus, he was from Bethlehem, David's hometown (1 Sam 16:1–13). He was in charge of the division of the army for the fourth month, and after his death at the hands of Abner (2 Sam 2:23), he was succeed by his son Zebadiah (1 Chr 27:7).

Elhanan was one of David's fellow Bethlehemites (2 Sam 23:24). His killing of one of the Rephaim among the Philistines is related in 21:19 (see also 21:22).

Shammah and Elika were from Harod (2 Sam 23:25), probably a village after which the spring of Harod (Judg 7:1) was named. It was near Jezreel in Judah.

Helez was from Beth-pelet (2 Sam 23:26) in the south of Judah (Josh 15:27). He was in charge of the division of the army for the seventh month (1 Chr 27:10; see the first textual note on 2 Sam 23:26).

Ikkesh's son Ira was from Tekoa in Judah (2 Sam 23:26), which would later be the home of the prophet Amos (Amos 1:1). He was in charge of the division of the army for the sixth month (1 Chr 27:9).

Abiezer was from Anathoth (2 Sam 23:27), a Levitical town within the borders of Benjamin (Josh 21:18). It lay some three miles (five kilometers) northeast of Jerusalem. Anathoth was the town where the high priest Abiathar lived after he was deposed by Solomon (1 Ki 2:26). Later it would be the home of Jeremiah (Jer 1:1). Abiezer was in charge of the division of the army for the ninth month (1 Chr 27:12).

Sibbecai was from Hushah (2 Sam 23:27), probably a Judahite city that was about four miles (six kilometers) west of Bethlehem. Its modern name is Ḥusan. His killing of one of the Rephaim among the Philistines is related in 2 Sam 21:18. He was in charge of David's military division for the eighth month (1 Chr 27:11).

Zalmon, like Eleazar (2 Sam 23:9–10), was an Ahohite from the tribe of Benjamin (2 Sam 23:28).

Maharai and Heled were from Netophath (2 Sam 23:28–29), a town that lay near Bethlehem in Judah (cf. Ezra 2:22; Neh 7:26). Maharai was in charge of the division of the army for the tenth month (1 Chr 27:13). Heled, who is called Heldai in 1 Chr 27:15, was in charge of the division of the army for the twelfth month.

Ittai was from Saul's hometown of Gibeah (2 Sam 23:29; cf. 1 Sam 10:26).

The Benaiah mentioned in 2 Sam 23:30 (cf. 23:20–23) was from Pirathon in the territory of Ephraim. It had been the home of the judge Abdon (Judg 12:15). Benaiah was in charge of the division of the army for the eleventh month (1 Chr 27:14).

---

[25] 2 Sam 23:24; see also 2 Sam 2:30; 3:27; 23:24; 1 Chr 2:16; 11:26; 27:7. His name is also spelled Asahel: 2 Sam 2:18, 19, 20, 21, 22, 23, 32; 3:30.

Hurai was from the brooks at the base of Mount Gaash (2 Sam 23:30) south of Timnath-serah/Timnath-heres in the territory of Ephraim (Josh 24:30; Judg 2:9).

Abi-albon was an Arbathite (2 Sam 23:31), which probably indicates that he was from Beth-arabah in Judah (Josh 15:6, 61), since most of David's elite soldiers were from Judah. Less likely, he may have been from the city by the same name in Benjamin (Josh 18:22).

Azmaveth was from Bahurim in the territory of Benjamin (see the third textual note on 23:31).

Eliahba was from Shaalbin (2 Sam 23:32), also called Shaalbim (Judg 1:35; 1 Ki 4:9). Shaalbin lay in the territory originally allotted to the tribe of Dan (Josh 19:40–42), but the Danites failed to dislodge the Amorites who lived there (Judg 1:34–35). The city apparently became part of the territory of Ephraim (cf. 1 Ki 4:8–9) after that tribe pressed its Amorite inhabitants into forced labor (Judg 1:35).

"The Thirty" must have included two "sons of Jashen" (2 Sam 23:32), since two would bring the total number of men in the list to "thirty-seven" (see the third textual note on 23:39).

Jonathan was the son of Shammah, one of the Three (see the textual note on 23:32c–33a; cf. 23:11–12). Like his father, he would have been from the hill country of Judah (see the commentary on 23:11).

Ahiam was also from the hill country of Judah (see the textual note on 23:33b and the commentary on 23:11).

Eliphelet was from the Maacathite clan of Judah (2 Sam 23:34; cf. 1 Chr 4:19).[26]

Eliam was from the Judean town of Giloh (2 Sam 23:34; cf. Josh 15:51; 2 Sam 15:12). He probably was the father of Bathsheba (cf. 2 Sam 11:3).

Hezrai was from Carmel (2 Sam 23:35), probably the Judean city by that name.[27] It was situated eight miles (thirteen kilometers) southeast of Hebron.

Paari was probably from the city of Arab in Judah (2 Sam 23:35; cf. Josh 15:52).

Igal was from Zobah (2 Sam 23:36), the Aramean kingdom defeated by David (8:3). He is the first non-Israelite listed among the Thirty and the only Aramean. The other men in the list who are identified as non-Israelites are Zelek the Ammonite (23:37), Ira and Gareb the Ithrites (23:38), and Uriah the Hittite (23:39). That David recruited them to be members of the Thirty and that they were prepared to lay down their lives for the sake of Yahweh's people and the king whom Yahweh had anointed (12:7) implies that these men had become

---

[26] Less likely, Eliphelet could have been from the Aramean kingdom of Maacah (e.g., 2 Sam 10:6, 8). However, his name, "Eliphelet" (אֱלִיפָלֶט), which means "God of deliverance," and especially his position in the list among other Israelites and before those who were definitely non-Israelite (see the commentary on 23:36) seem to indicate that he was an Israelite.

[27] Josh 15:55; 1 Sam 15:12; 25:2, 5, 7, 40; see also 1 Sam 27:3; 30:5; 2 Sam 2:2; 3:3; 1 Chr 3:1.

worshipers of Yahweh, the God of Israel and the only true God. They served in the army of "Yahweh of armies."[28] The actions and words of Uriah the Hittite in 11:8–13 demonstrate his exemplary faith.[29]

We know nothing about Bani except that he was an Israelite from the tribe of Gad (2 Sam 23:36).

Zelek is the second non-Israelite among the Thirty and the only Ammonite (2 Sam 23:37).

Naharai was from Beeroth (2 Sam 23:37), a city in Benjamin (Josh 9:17; 18:25; 2 Sam 4:2).

Ira and Gareb were Ithrites (2 Sam 23:28), probably one of the clans of the Hivites who occupied Kiriath-jearim before it became part of the territory of Judah (1 Chr 2:53).[30] Thus, they were descendants of Canaanite peoples.

Uriah the Hittite (2 Sam 23:39) was most likely descended from the sons of Heth[31] and thus was ethnically a member of the peoples of Canaan.[32] However, his name, meaning "my light is Yahweh," implies that he, and perhaps his parents and other ancestors before him, had been converted to the worship of Yahweh.[33] He is the last of the five non-Israelites in the Thirty.[34] It is interesting to note that the terse list in 23:24–39 begins with Asah-el, one of David's soldiers who died in battle (2:23; 3:30), and ends with the only other one of David's soldiers known to have died in battle.[35]

The "total" of "thirty-seven" given at the end of the list (23:39) includes all the names beginning with Eshbaal (23:8) and ending with Uriah (23:39). The number is accurate and implies that there were two "sons of Jashen" (23:32) among the Thirty.[36] At least nineteen of the thirty-seven were from David's tribe of Judah, and there were at least five who were not ethnically Israelites but had been grafted into the Israel of God by faith.[37] See figure 10.

---

[28] E.g., 2 Sam 6:2; 7:26–27. See the fourth textual note on 1 Sam 1:3 (Steinmann, *1 Samuel*, 44) and the second textual note on 2 Sam 5:10, which refers to "Yahweh, the God of armies."

[29] See the commentary on 2 Samuel 11, as well as the commentary on 23:39, which names Uriah.

[30] The Gibeonites were the original inhabitants of Kiriath-jearim, and they were Hivites (see Joshua 9, especially Josh 9:7, 17).

[31] Heth was the second son of Canaan (Gen 10:15; 1 Chr 1:13).

[32] See the commentary on 2 Sam 11:3, as well as the second textual note on 1 Sam 26:6 (Steinmann, *1 Samuel*, 492–93).

[33] Again, see the commentary on 11:3.

[34] For the others, see the commentary on 23:36.

[35] For the sordid account of how David committed adultery with Uriah's wife, Bathsheba, and then had Uriah killed in battle, see 2 Samuel 11. See also the accusation by Nathan the prophet in 12:9–10.

[36] Some commentators unjustifiably claim that the total is inaccurate (e.g., Ackroyd, *The Second Book of Samuel*, 226) or that the total can be achieved only by assuming that Joab was implicitly included among the Thirty (Baldwin, *1 and 2 Samuel*, 294; Hertzberg, *I and II Samuel*, 408). For a defense of the number's accuracy, see the third textual note on 23:39.

[37] See the commentary on 23:36.

Figure 10

The Ethnic Origins of David's Elite Soldiers Known as "the Thirty"

Nineteen from Judah

Shammah (23:11–12)	Hill country of Judah	Maharai (23:28)	Netophah
Abishai (23:18–19)	Bethlehem	Heled (23:29)	Netophah
Benaiah (23:20–23)	Kabzeel	Abi-albon (23:31)	Beth-arabah
Asah-el (23:24)	Bethlehem	Jonathan (23:32–33)	Hill country of Judah
Elhanan (23:24)	Bethlehem	Ahiam (23:33)	Hill country of Judah
Shammah (23:25)	Harod	Eliphelet (23:34)	From the Maacathite
Elika (23:25)	Harod		clan of Judah
Helez (23:26)	Beth-pelet	Eliam (23:34)	Giloh
Ira (23:26)	Tekoa	Hezrai (23:35)	Carmel
Sibbecai (23:27)	Hushah	Paari (23:35)	Arab

Five from Benjamin

Eleazar (23:9–10)	Descendant of Ahoah	Azmaveth (23:31)	Bahurim
Zalmon (23:28)	Descendant of Ahoah	Naharai (23:37)	Beeroth
Ittai (23:29)	Gibeah		

Three from Ephraim

Beniah (23:30)	Pirathon	Eliahba (23:32)	Shaalbin
Hurai (23:30)	Near Mount Gaash		

One from Levi

Abiezer (23:27)   Anathoth

One from Gad

Bani (23:36)

Three Whose Origins Cannot Be Determined

Eshbaal (23:8)
The two sons of Jashen (23:32)

Five Non-Israelites

Igal (23:36)	Zobah	Gareb (23:38)	A Hivite from
Zelek (23:37)	Ammon		Kiriath-jearim
Ira (23:38)	A Hivite from	Uriah (23:39)	A Hittite
	Kiriath-jearim		

David's Census Leads to Repentance and a Place to Build the Temple

Translation

24 [1]Once again the wrath of Yahweh burned against Israel. He incited David against them, saying, "Go, number Israel and Judah." [2]The king said to Joab, the commander of the army, who was with him, "Go through all the tribes of Israel from Dan to Beersheba, and register the troops so that I can know the number of the troops."

[3]Joab said to the king, "May Yahweh your God multiply the troops a hundred times over while the eyes of the king are looking. But why does my lord the king wish to do this thing?"

[4]However, the king's word overruled Joab and the commanders of the army, so Joab and the commanders of the army went out from the king's presence to register the troops of Israel. [5]They crossed the Jordan River and camped south of the city of Aroer, which is in the midst of the valley. [They went to] Gad and to Jazer. [6]They came to Gilead and to the land of Tahtim-hodshi. Then they came to Dan-jaan and around to Sidon. [7]They came to the fortress of Tyre and all the cities of the Hivites and the Canaanites. Then they went out to the Negev of Judah at Beersheba. [8]When they had gone through the entire land, they came to Jerusalem at the end of nine months and twenty days. [9]Joab gave the number of the registration of the troops to the king. Israel was eight hundred thousand men capable of using a sword, and the men of Judah were five hundred thousand men.

[10]David's conscience bothered him after he had counted the troops. David said to Yahweh, "I have committed a terrible sin. Now, Yahweh, please take away your servant's guilt, for I have acted very foolishly."

[11]When David got up in the morning, the Word of Yahweh had come to the prophet Gad, David's seer: [12]"Go and speak to David, 'Thus says Yahweh: "I offer you three options. Choose one of them, and I will do it to you."'"

[13]So Gad went to David and told him. He said to him, "Should seven years of famine come to you in your land? Or [should there come] three months when you flee before your enemies as they pursue you? Or should there be three days of a plague in your land? Now consider [this], and decide what answer I should take back to the one who sent me."

[14]David said to Gad, "I'm in a very tight spot. Let us fall into Yahweh's hand, because his compassion is abundant. Do not let me fall into the hand of man." [15]So Yahweh imposed a plague on Israel from the morning until the appointed time, and from Dan to Beersheba seventy thousand men from the people died.

[16]The Angel stretched out his hand toward Jerusalem to destroy it, but Yahweh relented concerning the devastation. He said to the Angel who was destroying the people, "[It is] great [enough]! Now withdraw your hand." The Angel of Yahweh was at the threshing floor of Araunah the Jebusite. David looked up and saw the Angel of Yahweh standing between the earth and the heavens, and his drawn sword in his hand was stretched over Jerusalem. The elders fell upon their faces, having clothed themselves with sackcloth.

[17]David said to Yahweh when he saw the Angel who was striking down the people, "I sinned and I committed a crime. But these sheep—what have they done? Let your hand be on me and my father's household."

[18]So Gad came to David that day and said to him, "Go up. Set up an altar to Yahweh on the threshing floor of Araunah the Jebusite." [19]So David went up according to Gad's word, just as Yahweh had commanded.

[20]Araunah looked down and saw the king and four of his sons with him, having clothed themselves with sackcloth. Araunah was threshing wheat. David came to Araunah, and he saw the king and his servants coming over to him. Having clothed themselves with sackcloth, they were coming to him. Araunah went out and bowed with his face on the ground to the king. [21]Araunah said, "Why has my lord the king come to his servant?"

David said, "To buy the threshing floor from you in order to build an altar to Yahweh. Then the plague on the people will be halted."

[22]Araunah said to David, "May my lord the king take and offer up whatever is good in his eyes. See the oxen for the burnt offering and the threshing sledges and the yokes of the oxen for wood." [23]Araunah gave everything to the king. Araunah said to the king, "May Yahweh your God be pleased with you."

[24]The king said to Araunah, "No. I will most certainly buy [it] from you for a [fair] price. I will not offer burnt offerings to Yahweh my God that cost nothing." So David took the threshing floor and the oxen for fifty shekels of silver. [25]David built an altar there to Yahweh and offered up burnt offerings and peace offerings. Yahweh responded to the plea for the land, and the plague was halted from Israel.

Textual Notes

24:1 וַיֹּסֶף אַף־יְהוָה לַחֲרוֹת בְּיִשְׂרָאֵל—"Once again the wrath of Yahweh burned against Israel." The first verb is the Hiphil (H) third masculine singular preterite (imperfect with *waw* consecutive) of יָסַף, "do again; multiply." (For the meaning "multiply," see the first textual note on 24:3.) Hiphil forms of this verb commonly take an infinitive construct as a verbal complement, as also in, e.g., 2 Sam 2:22; 5:22. For this construction, see the first textual note on 1 Sam 3:6[1] and Joüon, §§ 102 g, 124 c, 177 b. The infinitive construct here, לַחֲרוֹת, is the Qal (G) of חָרָה, "burn," with the preposition לְ. For the idiom with the noun אַף, "anger," as the subject of the verb חָרָה, "burn," see the first textual note on 2 Sam 6:7, where too it is Yahweh's anger that burns. Here in 24:1 "once again"

---

[1] Steinmann, *1 Samuel*, 110.

refers back to 21:1–14 as the previous time when Yahweh displayed his anger. See the commentary.

וַיָּסֶת—"He incited" is a Hiphil (H) third masculine singular preterite (imperfect with *waw* consecutive) of סוּת, "incite, lure." Yahweh was the subject of the Hiphil (H) of this verb also in 1 Sam 26:19 (a hypothetical conditional).

לֵךְ מְנֵה—"Go, number." These are Qal (G) masculine singular imperatives. The first is of הָלַךְ, which often signifies preliminary or preparatory action for carrying out the second verb, which denotes the main action. The second imperative here is of מָנָה, "to number." It is used for David's action of numbering the troops in 1 Chr 21:1, 17; 27:24 and for the king of Aram counting troops in 1 Ki 20:25. In some passages מָנָה is used for saying that God's people cannot be numbered because they are so numerous on account of God's blessing (Qal [G] and/or Niphal [N] in Gen 13:16; Num 23:10; 1 Ki 3:8).

24:2 שַׂר־הַחַיִל—"The commander of the army." See the corresponding construct phrase with the plural, שָׂרֵי הֶחָיִל, "the commanders of the army," in 24:4. Elsewhere in Samuel חַיִל can refer to an "army" (e.g., 1 Sam 10:26; 17:20; 2 Sam 8:9). It can also be part of a designation for a brave or elite soldier; see the third textual note on 24:9.

שׁוּט—"Go through." This is the Qal (G) masculine singular imperative of שׁוּט I. In the Qal this verb means to "travel about" (see Job 1:7; 2:2). After this command is carried out, the Qal third masculine plural preterite (imperfect with *waw* consecutive) וַיָּשֻׁטוּ will be used in 24:8, "when they had gone through."

וּפִקְדוּ—"And register." In military contexts the Qal (G) of פָּקַד can mean "to count" or "number" troops. Here it refers to registering their numbers. The Qal imperative פִּקְדוּ is plural, indicating that Joab is to enlist subordinate army commanders to help him do this; see 24:4, which uses the Qal infinitive construct (with לְ) לִפְקֹד to denote their purpose "to register." For פָּקַד, see further the first textual note on 2 Sam 18:1, as well as the textual note on 1 Sam 14:17.[2]

הָעָם ... הָעָם—In military contexts the noun with the article הָעָם, "the people," often denotes "the troops"; see the first textual note on 1 Sam 4:3[3] and the second textual note on 2 Sam 1:4. Its meaning here and in 24:3, 4, 9, 10, as clarified by "men capable of using a sword" in 24:9, makes these men potential troops. That is, they are able-bodied men who could be conscripted if needed. However, they are not troops in the modern sense that they were serving in a standing army. However, הָעָם has the more general meaning "the people" in 24:15, 21, as does עַם with the article in the prepositional phrase בָּעָם in 24:16, 17.

וְיָדַעְתִּי—"So that I can know." After the preceding imperatives (שׁוּט ... וּפִקְדוּ), this perfect with *waw* consecutive indicates purpose (Joüon, § 119 m; see also Joüon, § 119 i, note 2).

24:3 וְיוֹסֵף יְהוָה אֱלֹהֶיךָ אֶל־הָעָם—"May Yahweh your God multiply the troops." The verb יוֹסֵף is the Hiphil (H) third masculine singular jussive of יָסַף with a conjunctive

---

[2] Steinmann, *1 Samuel*, 250.

[3] Steinmann, *1 Samuel*, 120.

waw, expressing the volitive nuance of a desire or prayer (see Joüon, §§ 114 h; 177 l). The regular form of the imperfect would be יוֹסִיף. Here the verb takes the preposition אֶל with its direct object, הָעָם, "the troops."

וְכָהֵם ׀ כָהֵם מֵאָה פְעָמִים—"A hundred times over" is literally "like these and like these a hundred times." The repetition of the preposition כְּ with a third masculine plural suffix and the plural of the noun פַּעַם, a "time" (see the seventh textual note on 23:8), has a multiplicative meaning (GKC, § 134 r; Waltke-O'Connor, § 15.4a, including example 11).

וְעֵינֵי אֲדֹנִי־הַמֶּלֶךְ רֹאוֹת—Literally "and the eyes of my lord the king are seeing." This is translated as a temporal clause ("while …"). The dual construct form (עֵינֵי) of the (usually) feminine noun עַיִן, "eye," is the subject of רֹאוֹת, the Qal (G) feminine plural participle of רָאָה, "see, watch."

לָמָּה חָפֵץ—"Why does he wish?" The Qal (G) masculine singular חָפֵץ could be either the third masculine singular perfect or the participle of חָפֵץ, "to delight in, desire." See the same form in 1 Sam 2:25; 18:22; 19:1; 2 Sam 20:11, 20.

24:4 וַיֶּחֱזַק דְּבַר־הַמֶּלֶךְ אֶל־יוֹאָב וְעַל שָׂרֵי הֶחָיִל—"However, the king's word overruled Joab and the commanders of the army." The Qal (G) of חָזַק, "be strong," with the prepositions אֶל … עַל could also be rendered as "prevailed against." Samuel is one of the OT books in which the preposition אֶל is often used in place of the preposition עַל (see the first textual note on 2:9 and the second textual note on 3:29). Here both prepositions have an adversative sense. This is the only verse in the OT that has this construction with the Qal of חָזַק and the preposition אֶל. Other verses have such a construction with חָזַק and the preposition עַל. See Mal 3:13; see also Gen 47:20; Ex 12:33; Dan 11:5; 2 Chr 8:3; 27:5.

לִפְקֹד—"To register." See the third textual note on 24:2.

אֶת־הָעָם אֶת־יִשְׂרָאֵל:—"The troops of Israel." These two direct objects of the infinitive construct (with לְ) לִפְקֹד are in apposition, literally "to register the troops, (to register) Israel." The appositional second noun serves as a modifier of the first: "to register the Israelite troops" or "to register Israel's troops."

24:5 וַיַּעַבְרוּ אֶת־הַיַּרְדֵּן—"They crossed the Jordan River." This clause with the Qal (G) third masculine plural preterite (imperfect with *waw* consecutive) of עָבַר was also in 2:29; 17:22.

וַיַּחֲנוּ—"And they camped." The book of Samuel often uses the Qal (G) of חָנָה for establishing/living in a military encampment. See the second textual note on 1 Sam 11:1;[4] see also, e.g., 1 Sam 28:4; 2 Sam 11:11; 12:28.

יְמִין הָעִיר—"South of the city" is literally "right of the city." Directions are often given assuming one is facing east. That places the south on one's right side. See יָמִין, "right," meaning "south," also in 1 Sam 23:19, 24.

הַגָּד וְאֶל־יַעְזֵר:—Literally "the Gad and to Jazer." A verb of motion must be implied here. The translation supplies "they went to." Cf. וַיָּבֹאוּ, "and/then they came (to)," which occurs at the beginning of both the first clause and the second clause of 24:6.

---

[4] Steinmann, *1 Samuel*, 208–9.

24:6 וְאֶל־אֶרֶץ תַּחְתִּים חָדְשִׁי—"And to the land of Tahtim-hodshi" refers to an otherwise unattested place. On the basis of the Lucianic version of the LXX (εἰς γῆν Χεττιειμ Καδης), some reconstruct this as וְאֶל־אֶרֶץ הַחִתִּים קָדֵשָׁה, "and to the land of the Hittites, to Kadesh."[5] However Kadesh (Kedesh) in Naphtali (Tell Qades near Lake Huleh) would be too far south and Kadesh on the Orontes River is too far north. Others would emend the text to וְאֶל־אֶרֶץ תַּחַת חֶרְמוֹן, "and to the region below [Mount] Hermon" (cf. Josh 11:3 as well as Josh 11:17; 13:5).[6] This is an attractive solution, but it lacks any support from the ancient versions.

יַּעַן—"Jaan" is an otherwise unknown place-name. Perhaps this spelling is a variation of עִיּוֹן, "Iyyon/Ijon," in the territory of Naphtali (1 Ki 15:20; 2 Ki 15:29; 2 Chr 16:4).

24:7 מִבְצַר־צֹר—"The fortress of Tyre." This construct phrase with the noun מִבְצָר, "fortress" (1 Sam 6:18), is also in Josh 19:29. Instead of referring only to one fortress within the city, it designates Tyre itself as a fortified city.

24:8 וַיָּשֻׁטוּ בְּכָל־הָאָרֶץ—"When they had gone through the entire land." For the verb וַיָּשֻׁטוּ, see the second textual note on 24:2.

24:9 אֶת־מִסְפַּר מִפְקַד־הָעָם—"The number of the registration of the troops." The construct phrase מִסְפַּר הָעָם, "the number of the troops," was in 24:2. The noun מִסְפָּר is derived from the verb סָפַר, "to count, number" (see the second textual note on 24:10). The construct chain here includes מִפְקַד, the construct form of the noun מִפְקָד, "registration," which is derived from the verb פָּקַד, "register" (see the third textual note on 24:2). The noun מִפְקָד occurs elsewhere in the OT only in the parallel verse 1 Chr 21:5 and in Ezek 43:21 ("appointed place"); Neh 3:31; 2 Chr 31:13.

וַתְּהִי יִשְׂרָאֵל—"Israel was." Here יִשְׂרָאֵל is used as the name of the people or land. It is construed as the feminine subject of the third feminine singular verb וַתְּהִי (Joüon, § 150 e; Waltke-O'Connor, § 6.4.1d). Later in the verse a different construction is used for Judah: the construct phrase אִישׁ יְהוּדָה, "the men of Judah," is the subject of a nominal sentence expressing their number.

אִישׁ־חַיִל שֹׁלֵף חֶרֶב—"Men capable of using a sword" is literally "a man of strength, drawing a sword." For the construct phrase אִישׁ־חַיִל, see the first textual notes on 1 Sam 31:12[7] and 2 Sam 23:20. Here the singular אִישׁ is used as a collective, "men." The noun חַיִל, "strength," can also be used in other designations of elite soldiers (e.g., 1 Sam 14:52; 16:18; 2 Sam 2:7; 11:16). The verb שֹׁלֵף is the Qal (G) masculine singular participle of שָׁלַף, "to draw," used twenty-five times in the OT, always in the Qal or the Qal passive (Gp) and almost always with the feminine noun חֶרֶב, "sword." The participial

---

5   See HCSB, ESV, NRSV. See also the discussions in McCarter, *II Samuel*, 504–5, and Anderson, *2 Samuel*, 281. There are problems with this reconstruction due to the fact that the Lucianic manuscripts vary at this point. See further the discussion in Skehan, "Joab's Census: How Far North?" 42–43.

6   Skehan, "Joab's Census: How Far North?" 45; McCarter, *II Samuel*, 502, 504–5; Anderson, *2 Samuel*, 280–81. Skehan, 45, n. 20, traces the origin of this emendation to Ewald in his *Geschichte des Volkes Israel*. See Heinrich Ewald, *Geschichte des Volkes Israel* (Göttingen: Dieterich, 1845), 2/1:627, including n. 2.

7   Steinmann, *1 Samuel*, 568.

clause שֹׁלֵף חֶרֶב, "(a man) drawing a sword," is a designation for an able-bodied soldier that appears nine times in the OT (see also, e.g., Judg 8:10; 20:2, 15, 17; 2 Ki 3:26), always in a collective sense, and once with a plural participle (שֹׁלְפֵי חֶרֶב, Judg 20:25).

24:10 וַיֵּךְ לֵב־דָּוִד אֹתוֹ—"David's conscience bothered him" is literally "and the heart of David struck him." The identical Hebrew clause denoted David's remorse after he cut off a piece of Saul's robe (1 Sam 24:6 [ET 24:5]). This phraseology (the noun לֵב as the subject of the Hiphil [H] of נָכָה) appears nowhere else in the OT. It is absent from the parallel account in 1 Chr 21:5–7, which has וַיַּךְ אֶת־יִשְׂרָאֵל, "and he [God] struck Israel (1 Chr 21:7).

סָפַר אֶת־הָעָם—"He had counted the troops." The Qal (G) of סָפַר means "to count, number." The cognate noun מִסְפָּר, "number" (24:2, 9), is derived from it.

חָטָאתִי מְאֹד אֲשֶׁר עָשִׂיתִי—"I have committed a terrible sin" is literally "I sinned greatly which I did," i.e., "I sinned greatly by what I did." See the verb חָטָאתִי, "I sinned," in the textual note on 19:21 (ET 19:20), where, however, it was spoken by Shimei. Saul also used it twice in confessions to Samuel (1 Sam 15:24, 30) and in his confession to David in 1 Sam 26:21. The identical verb, חָטָאתִי, is the first verb in David's double confession in 2 Sam 24:17 (see the first textual note on 24:17). David also used it in his simple confession of adultery and murder in 12:13: חָטָאתִי לַיהוָה (see the first textual note on 12:13). The corporate confessions of Israel in 1 Sam 7:6; 12:10 used the corresponding plural חָטָאנוּ. Contrast David's declaration that he had not sinned against Saul (וְלֹא־חָטָאתִי לָךְ, 1 Sam 24:12 [ET 24:11]).

הַעֲבֶר־נָא אֶת־עֲוֹן עַבְדְּךָ—"Please take away your servant's guilt." The verb הַעֲבֶר is the Hiphil (H) masculine singular imperative of עָבַר. It is unusual for a person to direct an imperative to God; this is a forceful plea (cf. Joüon, § 114 m). The Hiphil (H) of עָבַר can mean "cause to pass away, take away" and can refer to God pardoning guilt (BDB, Hiphil, 4). The prophet Nathan used the Hiphil perfect of עָבַר in this sense in his absolution of David in 12:13. The noun עָוֹן can refer to a person's "guilt" (BDB, 2) and/or to the divine "punishment" for it (BDB, s.v. עָוֹן, 3, under the root עוה II). Here David likely prays for Yahweh both to remove his guilt and to refrain from punishing him because of it.

כִּי נִסְכַּלְתִּי מְאֹד:—"For I have acted very foolishly." The Niphal (N) of סָכַל can refer to committing a sin as a foolish action. See the first textual note on 1 Sam 13:13,[8] where Samuel uses the verb to denote apostate Saul's transgression of Yahweh's commandment. In 1 Sam 26:21 Saul employs the Hiphil of סָכַל in his confession to David. See also its Piel (D) in the third textual note on 2 Sam 15:31.

24:11 וּדְבַר־יְהוָה הָיָה אֶל־גָּד—Literally "and the Word of Yahweh was to Gad." For this formula of divine revelation, see the textual note on 2 Sam 7:4. For the revelatory, theophanic, Christological "Word of Yahweh," see the third textual note on 1 Sam 3:1.[9]

הַנָּבִיא חֹזֵה דָוִד—"The prophet, the seer of David." In 1 Sam 9:9 the author informed us that at the time when the book of Samuel was written the noun נָבִיא had become the

---

8 Steinmann, *1 Samuel*, 235.

9 Steinmann, *1 Samuel*, 109.

usual designation of a "prophet," whereas earlier the common term was the participle רֹאֶה, "seer." The second term here is a synonym of the earlier term in 1 Sam 9:9. חֹזֵה is the construct form of חֹזֶה, the Qal (G) masculine singular participle of חָזָה, "to see." This is the only instance of חָזָה in Samuel; see, however, the discussion of the cognate noun חִזָּיוֹן, "a (prophetic) vision," in the second textual note on 2 Sam 7:17.

24:12 הָלוֹךְ וְדִבַּרְתָּ—"Go and speak." Both of these verbs are used with imperatival force, although neither is an imperative in form. The first is the Qal infinitive absolute of הָלַךְ. For its imperatival sense, see Joüon, § 123 u; Waltke-O'Connor, § 35.5.1a, including example 4. The second is the Piel (D) second masculine singular perfect of דָּבַר with *waw* consecutive.

כֹּה אָמַר יְהוָה—"Thus says Yahweh." This prophetic formula introduces divine speech; see the second textual note on 7:5.

שָׁלֹשׁ אָנֹכִי נוֹטֵל עָלֶיךָ—Literally "three (things) I am imposing on you." The verb נוֹטֵל is the Qal (G) masculine singular participle of the rare verb נָטַל, which can take the preposition עַל and mean "lay upon, impose upon," as here and in Lam 3:28.[10] In this context it is translated as "offer" (so *DCH*, s.v. נטל, Qal, 2) because David can decide which one of the three will be imposed upon him.

בְּחַר־לְךָ אַחַת־מֵהֶם—Literally "choose for yourself one from them." David is to decide which punishment God the Judge will inflict on him and his people. Ironically, the verb בָּחַר, "choose," was used earlier for Yahweh's gracious choice of David to be the anointed ruler over his people (2 Sam 6:21; cf. 2 Sam 16:18; it is also implied in 1 Sam 16:8–10, where Samuel declares that Yahweh "has not chosen" David's brothers). The sense of the suffixed preposition מִן is partitive.

וְאֶעֱשֶׂה־לָּךְ:—"And I will do it to you." The preposition לְ here has the sense of disadvantage: "to you" means "to your harm" or "against you" (see BDB, 5 h (*b*) (γ); *DCH*, 18), rather than advantage, "for your benefit" (see BDB, 5 h (*b*) (α); *DCH*, 7). See also the next textual note.

24:13 הֲתָבוֹא לְךָ שֶׁבַע שָׁנִים ׀ רָעָב ׀ בְּאַרְצֶךָ—Literally "should there come to you seven years, famine, in your land?" The verb הֲתָבוֹא is the Qal (G) third feminine singular imperfect of בּוֹא, "come," prefixed with an interrogative *he*. The verb agrees in gender and number with the first word of its subject, the feminine singular noun שֶׁבַע, "seven" (cf. Joüon, § 150 g). Here in the phrase שֶׁבַע שָׁנִים, "seven years," and in the following phrase שְׁלֹשָׁה חֳדָשִׁים, "three months," the numeral is in the absolute state and precedes the noun that it numbers (contrast שְׁלֹשֶׁת יָמִים, "three days," later in the verse; see the third textual note on 24:13). Here the noun רָעָב, "famine," is in apposition to שֶׁבַע שָׁנִים, "seven years" (Waltke-O'Connor, § 12.1e). As in the prior textual note, the preposition לְ again has the sense of disadvantage, and "to you" emphasizes that David is the culprit who caused the whole land to suffer. Yahweh calls it "your land" (in the phrase

---

[10] Besides 2 Sam 24:12 and Lam 3:28 the only other instance of the Qal in the OT is in Is 40:15, where it may mean "lift up" or "weigh."

בְּאַרְצֶךָ, as also in the third option) because, as the anointed king, David was responsible for its welfare. Cf. Gen 3:17–19, where Adam's sin brought a curse upon the entire creation.

The MT reading שֶׁבַע שָׁנִים, "seven years," is supported by Josephus.[11] The parallel in 1 Chr 21:12 reads שָׁלוֹשׁ שָׁנִים, "three years," which is supported by τρία ἔτη in both LXX 2 Sam 24:13 and LXX 1 Chr 21:12. A number of English versions follow LXX 2 Sam 24:13 and MT/LXX 1 Chr 21:12.[12] This would make each one of the triad of options in 2 Sam 24:13 contain the number "three": "three years … three months … three days," as in 1 Chr 21:12. The symmetry makes it a tempting reading. However, the harder reading in MT 2 Sam 24:13 is most likely the correct original, and 1 Chr 21:12 (as well as LXX 2 Sam 24:13) may have been altered to create the triply parallel "three."

אִם־שְׁלֹשָׁה חֳדָשִׁים נֻסְךָ לִפְנֵי־צָרֶיךָ וְהוּא רֹדְפֶךָ—"Or [should there come] three months when you flee before your enemies as they pursue you?" The hypothetical particle אִם, "if," introduces the second option and also the third. It functions like the English conjunction "or." The Qal (G) infinitive construct נֻסְךָ, from נוּס, "to flee," has a second masculine singular suffix that serves as its subject, and it is translated as a temporal clause: "when you flee." This suffix recurs on two other words in this question (צָרֶיךָ … רֹדְפֶךָ), and it is singular, so it highlights David's culpability. The first suffixed word is the plural of the noun צַר III, "enemy" (from the verb צָרַר II, "show hostility toward"). This is the only occurrence of this noun in Samuel (it is a synonym of the noun אֹיֵב, "enemy," which occurs thirty-seven times in Samuel). The use of צַר here may be reflected in David's response with the verb צָרַר I (see the first textual note on 24:14). The plural צָרֶיךָ, "your enemies," is treated as a grammatically singular group and is the antecedent of the third masculine singular personal pronoun in וְהוּא, which, in turn, is the subject of the Qal masculine singular suffixed participle רֹדְפֶךָ: literally "and he is pursuing you [singular]."

וְאִם־הֱיוֹת שְׁלֹשֶׁת יָמִים דֶּבֶר בְּאַרְצֶךָ—"Or should there be three days, a plague, in your land?" The verb in this third option, הֱיוֹת, is the Qal (G) infinitive construct of הָיָה. In context it is translated modally: "should … be." Unlike in the preceding two options (see the first textual note on 24:13), here the construct form of the number (שְׁלֹשֶׁת) is bound to the noun numbered (יָמִים); see Joüon, § 142 d. The noun דֶּבֶר, "pestilence, plague," is in apposition to שְׁלֹשֶׁת יָמִים, "three days" (see the first textual note on 24:13). This noun, which recurs in 24:15, denoted one of the ten plagues God inflicted on Egypt (Ex 9:3; see also Ex 9:15). It is also the punishment in one of the divine curses upon Israel when it would become unfaithful (Deut 28:21). This word is common in the prophets Jeremiah and Ezekiel as an impending divine judgment associated with Judah's fall and exile to Babylon.[13] Cf. the synonym מַגֵּפָה in the second textual note on 24:21.

עַתָּה דַּע וּרְאֵה—"Now consider, and decide." The two Qal (G) masculine singular imperatives (of יָדַע and רָאָה, respectively) are literally "know and see."

---

[11] Josephus, *Antiquities*, 7.321.

[12] HCSB, ESV, NIV, NRSV.

[13] E.g., Jer 21:6–9; 29:17–18; 32:36; 38:2; Ezek 5:12, 17; 6:11–12; 7:15.

מָה־אָשִׁיב שֹׁלְחִי דָּבָר׃—Here the interrogative pronoun מָה, "what?" is followed (after two intervening words) by a noun with which it is in apposition, דָּבָר, literally "word," translated as "answer." In such a construction, the pronoun functions like an adjective: "what answer" (BDB, s.v. מָה, 1 a (*a*); see also Joüon, § 144 d). The phrase "what answer" is the direct object of the imperative "decide" (see the previous textual note), and it is modified by אָשִׁיב שֹׁלְחִי, "I should take back to the one who sent me." The participle with an objective suffix שֹׁלְחִי, "the one who sent me," refers to Yahweh. The verb שָׁלַח often refers to God "sending" (and sometimes not "sending") a prophet.[14] Jesus frequently speaks of himself as the Son whom God the Father "sent."[15]

24:14 צַר־לִי מְאֹד—"I'm in a very tight spot" is literally "it is very tight to me." The verb צַר is the Qal (G) third masculine singular perfect of צָרַר I, "be tight, cramped, narrow." Saul used the identical wording for himself in 1 Sam 28:15. See צָרַר with לְ also in 1 Sam 13:6; 30:6; 2 Sam 1:26; 13:2; 22:7.

נִפְּלָה—"Let us fall." This is the Qal (G) plural cohortative of נָפַל. The root letter *nun* has been assimilated and is marked by *daghesh* (-פּ-). Compare its singular cohortative in the fifth textual note on 24:14. Cf. Joüon, § 114 c; Waltke-O'Connor, § 34.5.1a, including example 7.

בְיַד־יְהוָה ... וּבְיַד־אָדָם—"Into the hand of Yahweh … but [not] into the hand of man." This phraseology contrasts Yahweh, who is abundantly compassionate (see the next textual note), with mankind, who, by implication, lacks compassion.

רַבִּים רַחֲמָיו—"His compassion is abundant" is literally "many are his mercies." The noun רַחֲמִים, "compassion," is an intensive plural, and this word is always used in the plural. While this is its only appearance in the book of Samuel, it commonly refers to Yahweh's compassion in the Prophets (e.g., Is 54:7; 63:7; Zech 1:16) and the Psalms, including psalms by David (e.g., Pss 25:6; 40:12 [ET 40:11]; 51:3 [ET 51:1]). The Qere here, רַחֲמָיו, is the word's plene, or *male'*, spelling, while the Kethib, רַחֲמָו, is a defective, or *ḥaser*, spelling.

אַל־אֶפֹּלָה׃—"Do not let me fall." The verb אֶפֹּלָה is the Qal (G) singular cohortative of נָפַל. The adverb אַל is used to negate cohortatives (Joüon, § 160 f). Compare the plural cohortative of נָפַל in the second textual note on 24:14.

24:15 עֵת מוֹעֵד—"(The) appointed time." This unique construct phrase is literally "(the) time of (the) appointed time." Other verses include both of the nouns עֵת, "time," and מוֹעֵד, "appointed time, season," but in separate syntactical constructions.[16] For the meaning of the phrase here, see further the commentary.

שֶׁבַע שִׁבְעִים אֶלֶף אִישׁ׃—This reading in the MT is literally "seven seventy thousand men." If the numbers are added together, this would be "seventy-seven thousand," or if שֶׁבַע is intended as a multiplier (cf. Joüon, § 142 q), then this number would be 7 x 70,000 = 490,000 men. However, the MT reading may involve a transcription error where the letters שבע ("seven") were accidentally duplicated before שבעים ("seventy").

---

[14] Ex 3:12–15; Judg 6:8; Is 6:8; 61:1; Jer 7:25; 14:14–15; 25:4; Ezek 2:3–4; 3:5–6.

[15] See ἀποστέλλω, in, e.g., Mt 10:40; 21:37; Lk 4:18; Jn 3:17, 34; 5:36; 6:57.

[16] Gen 18:14; 2 Ki 4:16–17; Jer 8:7; Hos 2:11 (ET 2:9); Ps 102:14 (ET 102:13); Dan 11:35.

LXX 2 Sam 24:15 reads ἑβδομήκοντα χιλιάδες ἀνδρῶν, "seventy thousand men." The reading in the parallel verse 1 Chr 21:14 is שִׁבְעִים אֶלֶף אִישׁ, "seventy thousand men," which is supported by LXX 1 Chr 21:14 and Josephus.[17] Elsewhere in the OT "seventy-seven" is written with the higher number denoting tens first ("seventy") and the lower number denoting the single digit ("seven") second and with the conjunction: שִׁבְעִים וְשִׁבְעָה, "seventy and seven" (Judg 8:14; Ezra 8:35). If seventy-seven thousand were intentional, one would expect it to be written with the conjunction. Compare the number here (שֶׁבַע שִׁבְעִים אֶלֶף) to the following numbers:

- שְׁנַיִם וְעֶשְׂרִים אֶלֶף, "twenty-two thousand" (Num 3:39; Judg 20:21)
- שְׁלֹשָׁה וְעֶשְׂרִים אֶלֶף, "twenty-three thousand" (Num 26:62)
- אַרְבָּעָה וְעֶשְׂרִים אֶלֶף, "twenty-four thousand" (Num 25:9)
- שְׁנַיִם וּשְׁלֹשִׁים אֶלֶף, "thirty-two thousand" (Num 31:35; 1 Chr 19:7)
- שִׁשָּׁה וּשְׁלֹשִׁים אֶלֶף, "thirty-six thousand" (Num 31:38, 44)

For these reasons most English versions follow the reading "seventy thousand" in LXX 2 Sam 24:15 and MT/LXX 1 Chr 21:14.[18]

24:16a לְשַׁחֲתָהּ—"To destroy it." This Piel (D) infinitive construct of שָׁחַת with the preposition לְ and a third feminine singular object suffix denotes purpose. For the verb שָׁחַת, meaning "to destroy" or "kill" in either the Piel (D) stem (as here) or the Hiphil (H) stem (as in the fourth textual note on 24:16a), see the fourth textual note on 11:1. The feminine suffix refers back to יְרוּשָׁלַםִ, "Jerusalem"; in Hebrew, cities are grammatically feminine.

וַיִּנָּחֶם יְהוָה—"But Yahweh relented." When the verb נָחַם in the Niphal (N) has a human subject, it can mean "to repent" of a sin, but with God as its subject, it means "to relent." See the second textual note on 10:2.

הָרָעָה—"The devastation." For the noun רָעָה ("evil") in the sense of "disaster" or "calamity" as divine punishment, see the fifth textual note on 17:14.

לַמַּלְאָךְ הַמַּשְׁחִית—"To the Angel who was destroying." The same clause is in the parallel verse 1 Chr 21:15. The Hiphil (H) masculine plural participle of שָׁחַת refers to angels "destroying" Sodom in Gen 19:13. In the Chronicler's account, the third option offered to David for punishment (cf. 2 Sam 24:13) included "the Angel of Yahweh" as the one "destroying" (מַשְׁחִית) for three days (1 Chr 21:12). The participle מַשְׁחִית refers to Yahweh himself in Gen 6:13; 19:14; Jer 51:25; Ezek 9:8.

רַב—"[It is] great [enough]!" The adjective רַב, "great, many," is used as an exclamation, as also in Gen 45:28; 1 Ki 19:4; and the parallel verse 1 Chr 21:15 (BDB, s.v. רַב I, 1 f).

הֶרֶף יָדֶךָ—"Withdraw your hand." The verb הֶרֶף is the Hiphil (H) masculine singular imperative of רָפָה. In the Qal (G), this verb can have the intransitive meaning that hands "relax" or "drop." Its Hiphil (H) is transitive, literally "to make [one's hand] drop" (see BDB, Hiphil, 1).

---

[17] Josephus, *Antiquities*, 7.326.

[18] HCSB, ESV, GW, NET, NIV, NRSV.

וּמַלְאַךְ יְהוָה הָיָה—"The Angel of Yahweh was." Instead of הָיָה, "he was," 4QSam^a (עומד) and the parallel in 1 Chr 21:15 (עֹמֵד) have the Qal (G) masculine singular participle of עָמַד, meaning that the Angel "was standing."

גֹּרֶן—"The threshing floor of." This noun, here in construct with the following name (see the next textual note), recurs in 24:18, 21, 24. See also 1 Sam 23:1; 2 Sam 6:6. For an explanation of the threshing process, see the commentary.

הָאֲרַוְנָה הַיְבֻסִי:—"Araunah the Jebusite." The first word is the Qere, "Araunah" with the article. The Kethib is הָאוֹרְנָה, "Ornah" with the article. 1 Chr 21:15 reads אָרְנָן, "Ornan," without an article. Compare the second textual note on 24:18.

24:16b   For the rest of the verse, the translation follows the text preserved in 4QSam^a, which indicates that the end of 2 Sam 24:16 was omitted by homoioarchton. The omitted text appears in a similar form as 1 Chr 21:16, which has no parallel in MT 2 Sam 24:16–17. The scribe's eye must have skipped from וי at the beginning of the omitted text (וישא) to וי at the beginning of 2 Sam 24:17 (וַיֹּאמֶר).[19] Josephus also includes the details of this text in his recounting of the events.[20] The following comparison first gives the relevant portions of MT 2 Sam 24:16–17, then those of 2 Sam 24:16–17 in 4QSam^a, and finally those of MT 1 Chr 21:15–17:

... וּמַלְאַךְ יְהוָה הָיָה עִם־גֹּרֶן הָאֲרַוְנָה הַיְבֻסִי: [17]וַיֹּאמֶר דָּוִד ... [16]

[16]... The Angel of Yahweh was at the threshing floor of Araunah the Jebusite. [17]David said ... (MT 2 Sam 24:16–17)

[16]... ומלאך י]הוה עומד עמן גרן ארן[נא הינ[ב]וסי וישא [דו]יד את עיניו
וירא את מלאך יהוה עומד בינ[ן] הארץ ובין הנ[ש]מני[ם וחרנ]בנו שלופה
בידו נטוא[נ]ה על ירושלים ויפלו הזקנים ע[נ]ל [פנ]יהם מתכנסים ב[שקים
[17]ונ[ין]אמר דויד ...

[16]... The Angel of Ya]hweh was standing at [the threshing floor of Ar]na the Je[b]usite. [Dav]id lifted up [his eyes and saw the Angel of Yahweh standing between] the earth and the [hea]v[en]s, and his swor[d] was drawn in his hand, stretch[ed over Jerusalem. The elders fell up]on their [faces,] having clo[thed themselves with] sackcloth. [17]David said ... (2 Sam 24:16–17 in 4QSam^a)

... [15]וּמַלְאַךְ יְהוָה עֹמֵד עִם־גֹּרֶן אָרְנָן הַיְבוּסִי: [16]וַיִּשָּׂא דָוִיד אֶת־עֵינָיו וַיַּרְא
אֶת־מַלְאַךְ יְהוָה עֹמֵד בֵּין הָאָרֶץ וּבֵין הַשָּׁמַיִם וְחַרְבּוֹ שְׁלוּפָה בְּיָדוֹ נְטוּיָה
עַל־יְרוּשָׁלָ͏ִם וַיִּפֹּל דָּוִיד וְהַזְּקֵנִים מְכֻסִּים בַּשַּׂקִּים עַל־פְּנֵיהֶם: [17]וַיֹּאמֶר דָּוִיד ...

[15]... The Angel of Yahweh was standing at the threshing floor of Ornan the Jebusite. [16]David lifted up his eyes and saw the Angel of Yahweh standing between the earth and the heavens, and his sword was drawn in his hand, stretched out over Jerusalem. David and the elders, clothed with sackcloth, fell upon their faces. [17]David said ... (MT 1 Chr 21:15–17)

---

[19]   See the discussion in Ulrich, *The Qumran Text of Samuel and Josephus*, 156–57.

[20]   Josephus, *Antiquities*, 7.327.

24:17 הִנֵּה אָנֹכִי חָטָאתִי וְאָנֹכִי הֶעֱוֵיתִי—Literally "look, I, I sinned and I, I commit-ted iniquity." The redundant pronoun אָנֹכִי in each clause is emphatic (Joüon, § 146 a). David takes full responsibility for the disaster. The Qal (G) perfect חָטָאתִי, "I sinned," was also in David's confessions in 12:13; 24:10; see the third textual note on 24:10. For the Hiphil (H) of עָוָה, which means "commit iniquity," see the second textual note on 7:14. Shimei uses both of these verbs (חָטָא and עָוָה) in his confession to David in 19:20–21 (ET 19:19–20).

וְאֵלֶּה הַצֹּאן—"But these sheep." The pronoun אֵלֶּה forms an explicit antithesis (*IBH*, § 24 B). The innocence of the sheep contrasts with David's guilt.

24:18 עֲלֵה הָקֵם—These are masculine singular imperatives. The first is the Qal (G) of עָלָה, "go up," and the second is the Hiphil (H) of קוּם, meaning "to set up" or "to con-struct." In the messianic promise of 2 Samuel 7, the Hiphil (H) of קוּם was not used for the construction of the temple but did refer to Yahweh "raising up" David's seed (2 Sam 7:12; see also 7:25). It will refer to Solomon "erecting" the pillars of the temple (1 Ki 7:21) and to Yahweh "fulfilling" his promises to David (1 Ki 2:4; 6:12; 9:5), including his promise that David's son would build the temple (1 Ki 8:20).

אֲרַוְנָה—This Qere reads "Araunah." The Kethib is אֲרַנְיָה, "Aranyah." 1 Chr 21:18 reads אָרְנָן, "Ornan." Compare the ninth textual note on 24:16a.

24:20 From 4QSam[a] it appears as if both MT 2 Sam 24:20 and its parallel in MT 1 Chr 21:20 have suffered from parablepsis.[21] Josephus' telling of the story includes that Araunah bowed to the king, which is in 4QSam[a] and MT 2 Sam 24:20, but not in MT 1 Chr 21:20. Josephus also incudes that Araunah was threshing wheat, which is in 4QSam[a] and MT 1 Chr 21:20 but not in MT 2 Sam 24:20.[22] This indicates that the MT is defective in both cases. The following first gives MT 2 Sam 24:20, then 2 Sam 24:20 in 4QSam[a] with an explanation of how it differs, and finally MT 1 Chr 21:20 with an explanation of its differences. Textual notes on some of the vocabulary is provided below these quotations.

וַיַּשְׁקֵף אֲרַוְנָה וַיַּרְא אֶת־הַמֶּלֶךְ וְאֶת־עֲבָדָיו עֹבְרִים עָלָיו
וַיֵּצֵא אֲרַוְנָה וַיִּשְׁתַּחוּ לַמֶּלֶךְ אַפָּיו אָרְצָה׃

Araunah looked down and saw the king and his servants coming over to him. Araunah went out and bowed to the king with his face to the ground. (MT 2 Sam 24:20)

וישקף] ארנא וירא את המלך דויד ואת ארבעת בניו עמו מתחבאים] בשקים
וארנא דש חטים] ויבא דויד עד ארנא] וירא א̇ת המלך ועבדיו עברים אליו
מתכ]סים בשקים בא]ים אליו ויצא ארנא וישתחו לדוינ̇ד על אפיו ארצה]

[Arna] looked down [and saw *King David and four of his sons with him, hav-ing hidden/clothed themselves*] **with sackcloth.** *Arna was threshing wheat.* **[David came to Arna,] and he saw** [the king and his servants coming over to him, having cover]ed themselves with sackcloth and com[ing to him.

---

[21] See the discussion in Ulrich, *The Qumran Text of Samuel and Josephus*, 157–59.

[22] Josephus, *Antiquities*, 7.330.

Arna went out and bowed] to Davi[d with his face to the ground]. (2 Sam 24:20 in 4QSamᵃ; words or equivalent expressions that it includes but that are absent from MT 2 Sam 24:20 are in *italic*; words absent from MT 1 Chr 21:20 are in **bold**; words absent from both MT 2 Sam 24:20 and MT 1 Chr 21:20 are in ***bold italic***)

The first text that is absent in MT 2 Sam 24:20 apparently was omitted due to homoioarchton from "King David and" (אֶת הַמֶּלֶךְ דָּוִיד וְ) to the following "the king and" (אֶ[ת] הַמֶּלֶךְ וְ). The second text that is absent in MT 2 Sam 24:20 apparently was omitted due to homoioarchton from "to him" (אֵלָיו) to "to him" (אֵלָיו).

וַיָּשָׁב אָרְנָן וַיַּרְא אֶת־הַמַּלְאָךְ וְאַרְבַּעַת בָּנָיו עִמּוֹ מִתְחַבְּאִים וְאָרְנָן דָּשׁ חִטִּים:

Ornan returned and saw the Angel and four of his sons with him, having hidden/clothed themselves. Ornan was threshing wheat. (MT 1 Chr 21:20)

A striking incongruity in MT 1 Chr 21:20 is that it refers to "the Angel," that is, "the Angel of Yahweh" (מַלְאַךְ יְהוָה, 1 Chr 21:18), "*and four of his sons*." The attribution of these "sons" to "the Angel," rather than to David, is an indication that the text has been corrupted. The first text that apparently was omitted from MT 1 Chr 21:20 is due to homoioteleuton from the *mem* at the end of "having hidden/clothed themselves" (מִתְחַבְּאִים) to the *mem* at the end of "with sackcloth" (בשקים in 4QSamᵃ). The second text apparently was omitted due to homoioarchton from "and he came" (ויבא in 4QSamᵃ) to the same word at the beginning of MT 1 Chr 21:21 (וַיָּבֹא, "and he came").

וַיַּשְׁקֵף—"He looked down." The Hiphil (H) of שָׁקַף often refers to "looking down" from a higher elevation to a lower one. See the second textual note on 6:16.

מִתְחַבְּאִים—"Having hidden/clothed themselves." This word is absent from MT 2 Sam 24:20 but is present in 1 Chr 21:20 and is also attested in 4QSamᵃ in 2 Sam 24:20. It is the Hithpael (HtD) masculine plural participle of חָבָא, "hide." Elsewhere in Samuel this verb occurs in the Niphal (N) stem (1 Sam 10:22; 19:2; 2 Sam 17:9) and in the Hithpael (1 Sam 13:6; 14:11, 22; 23:23), both with the reflexive meaning "hide oneself." The context here would require it to mean "clothe oneself," as confirmed by the Hithpael (HtD) participle of כָּסָה later in 4QSamᵃ, to be vocalized מִתְכַּסִּים, "having covered themselves," a participle that occurs with that meaning in 2 Ki 19:2 ‖ Is 37:2.

וַיִּשְׁתַּחוּ לַמֶּלֶךְ אַפָּיו אָרְצָה:—Literally "and he bowed to the king [with] his face to the ground." For similar clauses, see the second textual note on 18:28. The verb וַיִּשְׁתַּחוּ is the Hishtaphel of חָוָה, "to bow down, worship"; see the third textual note on 1 Sam 1:3.[23] For the form here, וַיִּשְׁתַּחוּ, see the second textual note on 1 Sam 1:28.[24]

24:21 לִקְנוֹת ... לִבְנוֹת—"To buy ... to build." Each of these two Qal (G) infinitive constructs with the preposition לְ expresses purpose. The first is of קָנָה, "purchase," which recurs three times in 24:24, where David fulfills this purpose. The second is of בָּנָה, "build," which referred to building an altar also in 1 Sam 7:17; 14:35. It denoted

---

[23] Steinmann, *1 Samuel*, 44.

[24] Steinmann, *1 Samuel*, 62.

the building of a house for or by Yahweh in 2 Sam 7:5, 7, 13, 27. This verb is reused for David's fulfillment in 24:25.

וְתֵעָצַר הַמַּגֵּפָה מֵעַל הָעָם:—Literally "and the plague will be restrained from upon the people." The same vocabulary will describe the fulfillment in 24:25, but with the preterite (imperfect with *waw* consecutive) and with "Israel" in place of "the people." The verb וְתֵעָצַר is the Niphal (N) third feminine singular imperfect of עָצַר, whose Qal (G) means "hold back, restrain" (1 Sam 9:17). Its Niphal refers to the halting of a plague also in Num 17:13, 15 (ET 16:48, 50); 25:8; Ps 106:30; 1 Chr 21:22. The verb is feminine to match its feminine subject, הַמַּגֵּפָה, "the plague." This noun is a synonym of דֶּבֶר (see the third textual note on 24:13). It is derived from the verb נָגַף, "to strike, smite" (e.g., 1 Sam 4:2–3; 2 Sam 10:15, 19). The noun מַגֵּפָה referred to a "plague" also in 1 Sam 6:4 and to a "slaughter" in 1 Sam 4:17; 2 Sam 17:9; 18:7.

24:22 יִקַּח וְיַעַל—Literally "may he take and may he offer up." These two third masculine singular verbs are jussives. The first is the Qal (G) of לָקַח. The second is of עָלָה. The form יַעַל could be the Qal jussive, which would mean "go up," but the context indicates that it is the Hiphil (H) jussive, "offer up" a sacrifice. The cognate noun עֹלָה, "a burnt offering," appears later in this verse. See also the cognate accusative constructions in 24:24, 25 (see further the fourth textual note on 24:24). See Leviticus 1 for the liturgical sacrifice of burnt offerings.

בְּעֵינָיו—This Qere is the suffixed dual, "in his eyes." The Kethib is בְּעֵינוֹ, a defective, or *ḥaser*, spelling of the same word. For this Qere/Kethib, see also the second textual note on 19:19 (ET 19:18).

וְהַמֹּרִגִּים—"And the threshing sledges." This is the plural of the noun מוֹרַג with the article. Instead of this form with -רִגּ-, one would expect -רָגּ- (see GKC, § 93 pp).

וּכְלֵי הַבָּקָר—"And the yokes of the oxen" is literally "and the implements of the oxen." The noun כְּלִי can denote a variety of different vessels or implements. See, e.g., 1 Sam 8:12; 10:22; 14:1; 2 Sam 8:10.

24:23 הַכֹּל נָתַן אֲרַוְנָה הַמֶּלֶךְ לַמֶּלֶךְ—The MT literally reads "the whole Araunah gave the king to the king." It could mean "King Araunah gives everything to the king," spoken as if Araunah was the last Jebusite king of Jerusalem.[25] It could also be interpreted as if the quotation from 24:22 continues with Araunah speaking in the third person, using הַמֶּלֶךְ as a vocative: "Araunah gives everything, O king, to the king" (see Joüon, § 112 f; Waltke-O'Connor, § 30.5.1d, including example 28).[26] A few Masoretic manuscripts omit הַמֶּלֶךְ and have only לַמֶּלֶךְ, "to the king." That reading is also supported by the LXX and two Old Latin manuscripts. The word הַמֶּלֶךְ in the MT is probably the result of accidental duplication.

יְהוָה אֱלֹהֶיךָ יִרְצֶךָ:—"May Yahweh your God be pleased with you." The verb יִרְצֶךָ is the Qal (G) jussive of רָצָה, "be gracious, favorable," with a second masculine singular

---

[25] This has occasionally been advocated (e.g., Ahlström, "Der Prophet Nathan und der Tempelbau," 117–18). However, the evidence for it is slim and unconvincing.

[26] Similarly, HCSB. When הַמֶּלֶךְ is a vocative it can be translated as "Your Majesty." See the third textual note on 1 Sam 26:17 (Steinmann, *1 Samuel*, 496) and the fourth textual note on 2 Sam 14:4.

suffix. With God as the subject, its Qal can refer to his gracious acceptance of a worshiper who sacrifices an offering (e.g., Jer 14:10, 12; Ezek 20:40, 41; Hos 8:13). In Leviticus its Niphal (N) indicates that a vicarious sacrifice has been accepted for atonement and God forgives the sinner (e.g., Lev 1:4; 22:27; negated in Lev 7:18; 19:7; 22:23, 25); see also Is 40:2. Its Qal indicates that God is pleased with his Suffering Servant (Is 42:1). David uses it to call upon God to be pleased to deliver him (Ps 40:14 [ET 40:13]; see also, e.g., Pss 44:4 [ET 44:3]; 51:18 [ET 51:16]; 147:10–11; 149:4).

24:24 לֹא כִּי־קָנוֹ אֶקְנֶה—"No. I will most certainly buy [it]." The form קָנוֹ (see GKC, § 75 n) is the Qal (G) infinitive absolute of קָנָה, "purchase, buy," used to strengthen the affirmation that David will buy it and not receive it gratis (Joüon, § 123 e, i). The synonymous form קָנֹה is the reading in many Masoretic manuscripts. אֶקְנֶה is the first common singular imperfect of קָנָה. (For its infinitive construct, see the first textual note on 24:21.) The infinitive absolute can be used to emphasize an opposition or contrasting action, to do something else "instead of" or "rather than" the alternative (see GKC, § 113 p; Joüon, § 123 i).

מֵאוֹתְךָ—Literally "from with you." This word appears to be a form of the direct object marker (-אוֹת) but probably is an unusual form of the preposition אֵת, "with," with a prefixed preposition מִן and a second masculine singular suffix. Many Masoretic manuscripts have the usual form of the preposition, מֵאִתְּךָ. The LXX reads παρὰ σοῦ.

בִּמְחִיר—"For a [fair] price." The preposition בְּ can be used in the sense of price or cost (BDB, s.v. בְּ I, III 3). Here it is prefixed to the noun מְחִיר, "price" (see, e.g., 1 Ki 10:28; 21:2).

וְלֹא אַעֲלֶה לַיהוָה אֱלֹהַי עֹלוֹת—"I will not offer burnt offerings to Yahweh my God." In form אַעֲלֶה could be either the Qal (G) or the Hiphil (H) first common singular imperfect. The context requires the Hiphil (H), which is often used with the cognate noun עֹלָה, "sacrifice, burnt offering," as its direct object, as here and in the next verse (see also, e.g., Gen 8:20; 22:2; 1 Sam 6:14–15; 7:9–10; 2 Sam 6:17–18).

חִנָּם—"That cost nothing" is literally "gratuitously" or "gratis." This word is one of the few true adverbs in Hebrew. It is derived from the verb חָנַן, "be gracious," and has the adverbial ending ◌ָם. It has a similar sense, denoting a transaction at no cost, in, e.g., Gen 29:15; Ex 21:2, 11. It has the theological sense "by grace alone" in Job 1:9 (cf. Is 52:3, 5).

בְּכֶסֶף שְׁקָלִים חֲמִשִּׁים:—"For fifty shekels of silver." Again the preposition בְּ has the sense of price or cost (BDB, s.v. בְּ I, III 3; see also the third textual note on 24:24). "Fifty shekels" is about twenty ounces. That amount is confirmed by Josephus.[27] 1 Chr 21:25 reads שִׁקְלֵי זָהָב מִשְׁקָל שֵׁשׁ מֵאוֹת, literally "shekels of gold, a weight of six hundred," that is, "six hundred shekels of gold." That would have been about fifteen pounds (6.8 kilograms) of gold, an exorbitant price. The figure of six hundred gold shekels was perhaps displaced from 2 Chr 9:15 ǁ 1 Ki 10:16, which gives this as the weight of gold used by Solomon to make decorative shields for his palace.

24:25 וַיִּבֶן—"He built." For בָּנָה, see the first textual note on 24:21.

---

[27] Josephus, *Antiquities*, 7.332.

וַיַּעַל עֹלוֹת—"And he offered up burnt offerings." For this cognate accusative construction, see the fourth textual note on 24:24.

וּשְׁלָמִים—"And peace offerings." See Leviticus 3 for the liturgical legislation.

וַיֵּעָתֵר יְהוָה לָאָרֶץ—"Yahweh responded to the plea for the land." This means that Yahweh was graciously disposed and favorably answered prayer. See the second textual note on 21:14.

וַתֵּעָצַר הַמַּגֵּפָה מֵעַל יִשְׂרָאֵל:—"And the plague was halted from Israel." See the second textual note on 24:21.

Commentary

972 BC[28]

Parallel: 2 Sam 24:1–25 ‖ 1 Chr 21:1–27 (see also 1 Chr 21:28–22:1)

For the place of this passage in the structure of 2 Samuel 21–24, see "The Form and Content of 2 Samuel 21–24" in the commentary on 21:1–14. This final chapter of the book of Samuel does not bring David's reign to a close—that will be handled in the opening portion of the book of Kings (1 Ki 1:1–2:11). Instead, this chapter ties together two themes that were introduced earlier in the book: David's desire to build a temple for Yahweh (7:1–17) and David's double sin of adultery with Bathsheba and murder of her husband, Uriah (2 Samuel 11). At the beginning of this chapter we read of God's anger burning against Israel (24:1). This anger was the result of Israel's attempt to place a king on the throne whom Yahweh had not chosen—Absalom (see the commentary on 24:1). The chapter ends with David acquiring a place to build the temple (24:18–25; see 1 Chr 22:1). Thus, the chain of disastrous consequences initiated by David's sin (2 Samuel 11) was permanently ended, and the first step was taken to fulfill David's desire for Yahweh to have a house in Jerusalem, a house where the sacrifices stipulated by God would be offered for the forgiveness of sins and life everlasting.[29]

David Orders a Census of Israel (24:1–3)

The chapter begins with Yahweh's anger "once again" directed at Israel (24:1). "Once again" refers back to 21:1–14, where Yahweh's anger over Saul's sin had brought a famine on the land. At that time seven sons of Saul were given over to death to appease the divine anger, and God again became favorable to the land (21:14). This time, the reason for Yahweh's anger is not stated. Some believe it simply is unknown.[30] Others offer a variety of reasons. For instance, one proposal is that God was angry because David was preparing to impose forced labor on Israel.[31] However, considering that Solomon later used forced labor without consequence during his reign (1 Ki 5:27–32 [ET 5:13–18]), that

---

[28] See "The Chronology of David's Reign" in the commentary on 5:1–5.

[29] See Pss 16:11; 23:4–6; 27:4; cf. 1 Ki 8:15–20, 30, 34, 36.

[30] E.g., McCarter, *II Samuel*, 508.

[31] Bakon, "David's Sin: Counting the People."

is not likely. Josephus believed it was the result of David not collecting the half-shekel poll tax that was to accompany any census (Ex 30:12–13).[32] This would explain the plague *after the census*, but not God's initial wrath. Instead, the author, who does not often explain the reasons for the events he relates, expects his readers to make the connection. Earlier he had quoted Israel as saying that *they*—not God—had anointed Absalom king (2 Sam 19:11 [ET 19:10]). This was a clear violation of the Law of Moses, where Israel was to appoint only a king whom God had chosen (Deut 17:14–15).[33] The rise of Absalom as a challenger to his father, David, was a result of David's sin (compare 2 Sam 12:11–12 with 16:21–22). Thus, David himself was as culpable as Israel in provoking God's wrath.

One indication that it was Israel's sin of making Absalom king that aroused Yahweh's wrath is found in the Chronicler's reason for David taking the census. He does not say that it was "Yahweh" who "incited David" (2 Sam 24:1) but rather that "Satan stood against Israel and incited David" (1 Chr 21:1). The Chronicler does not record David's sin (2 Samuel 11) or its consequences. Thus, he does not mention that Israel had made Absalom king and that they participated in his rebellion against David. Therefore, the Chronicler apparently reasoned that he should not mention Yahweh's anger at Israel at this point (1 Chr 21:1) because he had not provided his readers with the historical background material that justified this divine wrath. Instead, he simply noted the means by which Yahweh accomplished his will—by using Satan.[34] This shift indicates that the Chronicler most likely understood the reason for Yahweh's wrath to be Israel's sin of supporting Absalom's insurrection, but because of his compositional strategy he depicted Satan as the instigator of David's sin in ordering the census.

David's command to Joab was to take a census so that he could know how many the troops numbered (24:2). To that end, David's order was for Joab to count the troops throughout the entire nation of Israel, from Dan in the north to Beersheba in the south (cf. 1 Sam 3:20; 2 Sam 17:11).

Taking the census was not simply for the purpose of satisfying David's curiosity or to stroke his ego. After David had regained his throne in Jerusalem (19:10–44 [ET 19:9–43]), he understandably would have been nervous about his enemies attacking him or about rebellion among nations he had subdued. These enemies may have perceived weakness in David's position following Israel's civil strife. David was motivated by a desire to have a ready source of draftees should there be trouble. In fact, the entire chapter implies that this census was primarily for military purposes: The census was conducted by Joab and the commanders of the army (24:4). The reported numbers were of men who

---

[32] Josephus, *Antiquities*, 7.318.

[33] God had chosen Saul to be the first king (1 Samuel 8–12) and then David to be his successor (1 Sam 16:1–13; 2 Sam 5:1–5).

[34] Gard, "The Chronicler's David," 239.

were able to render military service (24:9). The second of the three possible punishments for David's sin was three months of being routed by his enemies (24:13). The longer text of 24:16 depicts the Angel of Yahweh using a "sword" to bring the plague (see the textual note on 24:16b).

Joab once again sounded a counterpoint to David and was the voice of reason (24:3). Sensing that David's motivation was to determine whether he could gain the victory over his enemies by the sheer number of soldiers he could muster, Joab expressed the prayer that Yahweh would multiply the nation a hundredfold while David was still king. After all, victory does not come from the size of one's army but from Yahweh. This truth is reiterated throughout the book of Samuel[35] and notably by David himself in his finer moments.[36]

Joab Takes the Census (24:4–9)

David overruled Joab, who apparently was joined in his opinion of the inadvisability of the census by the army's officers (24:4). The account of the order in which the census was taken (24:5–8) shows that Joab proceeded in a counterclockwise manner around Israel's outer border. Presumably while doing this he also recorded the Israelite troops in the interior. He started at Aroer in the Arnon River Valley (24:5), the southernmost city in Israel east of the Jordan (Deut 2:36; Josh 13:9, 16). He then moved north to Gad and the city of Jazer.[37] Then Joab went further north to Gilead before turning west on Israel's northern border in the territory of the tribes of Dan and Naphtali (24:6; see the textual notes). The "fortress of Tyre" (24:7) probably refers to the mainland portion of that Phoenician city, which lay on the northern border of Asher (Josh 19:29). He then moved south along the Mediterranean coast, which is probably where he passed through the cities of the Hivites (Shechem [Gen 34:2]; Gibeon [Josh 9:3–7]; the Lebanon coast [Judg 3:3]) and Canaanites (2 Sam 24:7). Finally, he turned east toward Beersheba along the southern border of Judah. He and the other commanders returned to Judah nine months and twenty days later (24:8). Since ancient Israel followed a soli-lunar calendar with months that alternated between twenty-nine and thirty days, the census took two hundred eighty-five or two hundred eighty-six days.[38]

Joab's report to David gave round numbers for the totals (24:9): eight hundred thousand (800,000) for Israel and five hundred thousand (500,000) for Judah, for a total of one million three hundred thousand (1,300,000).[39] The

---

[35] E.g., 1 Sam 7:3; 10:18; 14:6, 12, 23; 2 Sam 3:18; 22:1.

[36] E.g., 1 Sam 17:37, 45–47; 26:24; 2 Sam 4:9; 7:23; 22:3–4, 18, 20, 44, 49.

[37] See Jazer also in Num 21:32; 32:1, 3, 35; Josh 13:25; 21:39; Is 16:8, 9; Jer 48:32; 1 Chr 6:66 (ET 6:81); 26:31.

[38] On the Israelite calendar, see the discussion in Steinmann, *From Abraham to Paul*, 12–15.

[39] 1 Chr 21:5 reports the numbers of men who could wield the sword as one million one hundred thousand (1,100,000) in Israel and four hundred and seventy thousand (470,000) in Judah, resulting in a sum total of one million five hundred and seventy thousand (1,570,000). Josephus (*Antiquities*, 7.320) states them as nine hundred thousand (900,000) and four hundred

Chronicler noted that, despite David's orders, Joab did not include Benjamin and Levi in the census (1 Chr 21:6).

David's Confession and the Punishment of Israel (24:10–15)

After the census was completed David's conscience convicted him (24:10) because of his anthropocentric motive for ordering the census (see the commentary on 24:2). He confessed his sin and asked to be forgiven. This contrasts with 11:1–12:13, where David did not admit his guilt until after a prophet had cornered and convicted him by means of a divine revelation. Here David behaves in a manner befitting every believer.[40] God sent Gad, the prophet who served as David's personal seer, with a message (24:11–12).[41] We might ask why Yahweh did not simply instruct Gad to announce that David was forgiven and say nothing more. However, the situation resembles the one in 12:10–14, where David confessed his sin and the prophet Nathan announced Yahweh's forgiveness but also declared that temporal consequences of David's sin would ensue.[42] Here too Yahweh's prophetic spokesman declared that David's sin would have a dire consequence, but this time David was given a choice of what it would be. The three options that the prophet presented to David were progressively shorter in length while increasingly more severe in intensity (24:13).

David's reply did not choose among the three, but simply eliminated the second one—he did not want to fall into the hands of men (24:14). Previously David had dealt with a famine sent by Yahweh as punishment (21:1–14), and he was prepared to undergo such a chastisement again. However, this time God chose the plague, perhaps because plague was associated with an improper census procedure in Ex 30:12–13. There it was the result of failing to collect the half-shekel poll tax, but 2 Samuel 24 gives no indication that Joab did not collect this tax.[43] Perhaps Yahweh's choice of the plague also served to distinguish this punishment on Israel from the famine that had resulted from Saul's sin (21:1).

---

thousand (400,000), respectively, for a total of one million three hundred thousand (1,300,000). The numbers in these three texts are similar in order of magnitude, and the totals in 2 Sam 24:9 and Josephus are the same (1,300,000). However, each of the texts is somewhat different than the other two. Unless all of them are simply to be taken as approximate or rounded, at least two of these three texts have suffered from some kind of corruption in the process of transmission. Numbers are among the most easily miscopied items in any text.

[40] When Christians gather for worship, they confess their sins and receive God's forgiveness through the absolution. They can also seek private confession and absolution from the pastor at any time. In this life believers never are able to "progress" to the point where they do not sin and have no need for regular confession and absolution. If they imagine that they have stopped sinning they deceive themselves (1 Jn 1:8–9). See the apostle Paul's description of his own life in Romans 7 and the excursus "Who Is the 'I' in Romans 7:14–25? Christian or Non-Christian?" in Middendorf, *Romans 1–8*, 584–97.

[41] Gad had given David advice before he became king (1 Sam 22:5).

[42] See the commentary on 12:1–15.

[43] Contrary to Josephus, *Antiquities*, 7.318; McCarter, *II Samuel*, 514; Hertzberg, *I and II Samuel*, 411–12.

We are told that the plague started in the morning and lasted until "the appointed time" (עֵת מוֹעֵד, see the first textual note on 24:15). This is probably a reference to the appointed time for the evening sacrifice.[44] Note that David would offer sacrifices at the conclusion of this time, when the plague would cease (24:25). Just as David's census covered Dan to Beersheba, so Yahweh's plague also encompassed the same territory. In that area seventy thousand men died (see the second textual note on 24:15).

Yahweh Accepts David's Sacrifice (24:16–25)

For the first time the author introduces the agent of God's judgment—an Angel whom he later in the verse calls "the Angel of Yahweh" (24:16). We are told that the Angel was about to strike Jerusalem when Yahweh relented and ordered the Angel to stop. The Angel apparently had approached the city from the north, and we are told that he was at Araunah's threshing floor. Araunah is called "the Jebusite," one of the ancient Canaanite inhabitants of Jerusalem (5:6–8).

The threshing floor was an outdoor area where grain was threshed. That is, this is where the barley or wheat was collected and the unwanted parts of the plant were discarded. This was accomplished by first separating the grain from the stalks by running a sledge over the harvest. Then the grain and the chaff (the crushed pieces of the stalks) were thrown up into the air with threshing forks. The lighter chaff tended to blow downwind while the heavier grain fell more directly downward.[45] After repeated use of the threshing forks, the grain could be gathered into a granary and the chaff could be burned (Mt 3:12; Lk 3:17). To take advantage of the wind, threshing floors tended to be on windswept elevated ground.

David saw the Angel of Yahweh above the threshing floor with "his drawn sword in his hand," ready to strike (24:16).[46] Jerusalem's elders also saw him and fell down in a posture of worship, acknowledging the Angel to be God.[47] They had already shown their repentance by donning sackcloth. The author of Samuel records that Yahweh spoke to the Angel (24:16), suggesting that the Angel was a person distinct from Yahweh, but the author also connects them by calling the Angel "the Angel of Yahweh." Then in 24:17, when relating that David saw the Angel and spoke, the author writes: "David said to Yahweh." This could mean that David was speaking to Yahweh in the person of the Angel. In 24:16 the hand of the Angel was extended to strike Jerusalem, but in 24:17

---

[44] Note the phrase, עֵת מִנְחַת־עֶרֶב, "(the) time of (the) evening sacrifice," in Dan 9:21. Note also מִנְחַת־עֶרֶב in Ps 141:2 and מִנְחַת הָעֶרֶב in 2 Ki 16:15; Ezra 9:4, 5.

[45] See Jer 13:24; Hos 13:3; Pss 1:4; 35:5; 83:14 (ET 83:13); Job 21:18; Dan 2:35.

[46] Regarding the text with "his sword," see the textual note on 24:16b.

[47] Contrast the created angel who refused to be worshiped in Rev 22:8–9. In Rev 1:17 John fell prostrate at the feet of Jesus, who accepted this act of worship and raised him up. Similarly, Ezekiel fell prostrate before the glory of Yahweh and was raised up by the Spirit (Ezek 1:28–2:2; 3:23–24; 43:3–5).

David asked for Yahweh's hand ("your hand") to be against him and his house instead; David equated the Angel's hand with Yahweh's hand. In 24:17 David confessed his sin in the presence of the Angel and prayed, apparently to the Angel (just as he had confessed and prayed to Yahweh in 24:10), for the punishment to be diverted from the people and toward him. As is often the case in the OT, the Angel of Yahweh was not simply one of God's heavenly messengers but was, in fact, God himself.[48] He was reminiscent of the divine man who identified himself as "the commander of Yahweh's army," who also had "his drawn sword in his hand," ready to strike down the Canaanites, and Joshua worshiped him (Josh 5:13–15). That the Angel of Yahweh brandished a sword is not unlike NT portraits of Jesus Christ in which he too wields a sword.[49]

Since antiquity Christians have recognized that the Angel of Yahweh in the OT was not a created angel, but an appearance of the preincarnate Christ, the coeternal and uncreated Son of God, the second person of the Trinity. The dialogue in 24:16 can be understood as God the Father speaking to his Son; the three persons of the Trinity are distinct yet coequal.[50] Augustine, for instance, in commenting on Exodus 3, wrote:

> But when Moses was sent to lead the children of Israel out of Egypt, it is written that the Lord appeared to him thus: "Now Moses kept the flock of Jethro his father-in-law, the priest of Midian: and he led the flock to the back side of the desert, and came to the mountain of God, even to Horeb. And the Angel of the Lord appeared unto him in a flame of fire, out of the midst of a bush; and he looked, and, behold, the bush burned with fire, and the bush was not consumed. And Moses said, I will now turn aside, and see this great sight, why the bush is not burnt. And when the Lord saw that he turned aside to see, God called unto him out of the midst of the bush, and said, I am the God of thy father, the God of Abraham, the God of Isaac, and the God of Jacob" [Ex 3:1–4a, 6a]. He is here also first called the Angel of the Lord, and then God. Was an angel, then, the God of Abraham, and the God of Isaac, and the God of Jacob? Therefore He may be rightly understood to be the Saviour Himself, of whom the apostle says, "Whose are the fathers, and of whom as concerning the flesh Christ came, who is over all, God blessed for ever" [Rom 9:5].[51]

In the episode here in 2 Samuel, however, the Angel did not communicate directly with David. Instead Gad was again sent to David to instruct him what to do, indicating that God had accepted David's plea (24:18). The author is careful

---

[48] For examples, see Gen 16:7–14, where Hagar interacts with the Angel of Yahweh as God and recognizes him as divine; Gen 22:11–18, where the Angel of Yahweh makes statements to Abraham that demonstrate that Yahweh himself is talking in the person of the Angel; Judg 2:1–5, where the Angel of Yahweh claims to be the God who brought the Israelites out of Egypt and made a covenant with them; and Judg 13:1–23, where Manoah comes to recognize that the Angel of Yahweh is God.

[49] See Rev 19:11–21 with "sword" in 19:15, 21. See also Rev 1:16; 2:12, 16 and cf. Mt 10:34; Eph 6:17; Heb 4:12.

[50] See the Athanasian Creed, verses 4–6, 13–16, 24–25 (*LSB* 319–20).

[51] Augustine, *On the Holy Trinity*, 2.13 (*NPNF*[1] 3:48). For a recent scholarly treatment, see Gieschen, *Angelomorphic Christology*. See also Steinmann, *Daniel*, 497–507.

to note that David followed Yahweh's command to build an altar on Araunah's threshing floor (24:19). David's obedience in faith is emphasized by the only use of the clause כַּאֲשֶׁר צִוָּה יְהוָה, "just as Yahweh had commanded," in the book of Samuel (24:19). This clause frequently appears elsewhere in OT affirmations that a believer did exactly what Yahweh had mandated.[52]

As David came up to the threshing floor, Araunah looked down and saw him, four of his sons, and his servants coming up to him clothed with sackcloth (see the first textual note on 24:20). Araunah was threshing wheat, indicating that it was late spring or early summer at the end of the harvest.

What ensues in David's conversation with Araunah is a negotiation to buy the threshing floor (24:21–24) that is similar to Abraham's negotiation with the Hittites to purchase the field and cave at Machpelah (Gen 23:3–20).[53] In both arbitrations the owner offers to give the property gratis, but the acquirer refuses and insists on paying the full price for it. Abraham made it clear that he sought permanent ownership because he wanted the property for a cemetery. David's initial proposal might have been perceived as a request to use the property temporarily for a one-time sacrifice. In any case, Araunah offered to give the field as well as animals and firewood to David for free (2 Sam 24:22–23). In his response David tactfully countered that a sacrifice of goods obtained at no cost would not be a sacrifice worthy of Yahweh (24:24). David understood from the Angel's action and Gad's words that Yahweh had chosen the threshing floor as the place where he was to be worshiped in perpetuity (Ps 78:68–69; 1 Chr 22:1). Therefore, it was imperative that David purchase it for the worship of Yahweh as a permanent possession.

David paid fifty shekels of silver (about twenty ounces or 567 grams) for the land (see the sixth textual note on 24:24). This was the price indicated by the Law of Moses as a fair value for a large field to be consecrated to God (Lev 27:16). Since David was not purchasing a large field, but only a threshing floor along with the oxen and yokes, he paid a generous surplus for the property he acquired from Araunah.

The book closes with David's sacrifices on the threshing floor and Yahweh's response of grace by ending the plague (24:25). Thus, the sequence of events that began with David's adultery (2 Samuel 11) is brought to a close, and the book ends on a forward-looking note. The place for a magnificent house for

---

[52] Sixty other OT verses have same clause that is in 2 Sam 24:19, כַּאֲשֶׁר צִוָּה יהוה, "just as Yahweh had commanded." Most (fifty-three) of them are in Exodus–Deuteronomy, and they usually refer to Moses, Aaron, and/or the people conforming to the divine Word; see, e.g., Ex 7:6, 10, 20; Lev 8:4, 9, 13, 17, 21, 29; Num 1:19; 2:33; Deut 1:19; 5:32; Josh 10:40; Jer 13:5. Nine other verses have the similar clause כְּכֹל אֲשֶׁר צִוָּה יהוה, "according to all that Yahweh had commanded" (Ex 39:32, 42; 40:16; Num 1:54; 2:34; 8:20; 9:5; 30:1 [ET 29:40]; Deut 1:3). A total of a hundred and twenty-two OT verses have צִוָּה יהוה, "Yahweh (had) commanded," and ninety-eight of them are in Exodus–Deuteronomy.

[53] Orel, "The Deal of Machpelah"; McDonough, " 'And David Was Old, Advanced in Years.' "

Yahweh that David had desired had now been chosen by God and acquired by David.

The messianic promises of the book of Samuel were in the process of fulfillment. The temple would be the divinely ordained place where sacrifices for sin would be offered to appease God's anger. In the fullness of time, on Golgotha, in the vicinity of the temple, the Son of David would offer himself as the perfect, all-sufficient sacrifice that takes away the sin of the world. By his atoning death and victorious resurrection, Jesus Christ would enact the promise to David that Yahweh himself would build an everlasting house and establish the kingdom without end (2 Samuel 7).[54]

---

[54] See the commentary on 2 Sam 7:1–29 and the excursus that follows it, "הָאָדָם as 'the Man' in 2 Samuel 7:19 and 1 Chronicles 17:17." See also "Christ in Samuel" in the introduction (Steinmann, *1 Samuel*, 23–26); the commentary on 1 Sam 2:10 and 1 Sam 2:35 (Steinmann, *1 Samuel*, 80–81, 105–6); and the beginning of the commentary on 2 Sam 6:1–23.

Index of Subjects

Index of Passages